The NALCO
Water Handbook

OTHER McGRAW-HILL HANDBOOKS OF INTEREST

American Institute of Physics · American Institute of Physics Handbook
American Water Works Association · Water Quality and Treatment
Baumeister · Marks' Standard Handbook for Mechanical Engineers
Brater and King · Handbook of Hydraulics
Burington · Handbook of Mathematical Tables and Formulas
Burington and May · Handbook of Probability and Statistics with Tables
Chow · Handbook of Applied Hydrology
Condon and Odishaw · Handbook of Physics
Crocker and King · Piping Handbook
Davis and Sorensen · Handbook of Applied Hydraulics
Dean · Lange's Handbook of Chemistry
Fink and Beaty · Standard Handbook for Electrical Engineers
Flugge · Handbook of Engineering Mechanics
Foster · Handbook of Municipal Administration and Engineering
Hicks · Standard Handbook of Engineering Calculations
Ireson · Reliability Handbook
Juan · Quality Control Handbook
Karassik, Krutzsch, Fraser, and Messina · Pump Handbook
La Londe and Janes · Concrete Engineering Handbook
Lewis · Management Handbook for Plant Engineers
Lewis and Marron · Facilities and Plant Engineering Handbook
Machol · System Engineering Handbook
Maynard · Handbook of Business Administration
Maynard · Industrial Engineering Handbook
Merritt · Building Construction Handbook
Merritt · Standard Handbook for Civil Engineers
Morrow · Maintenance Engineering Handbook
Perry · Engineering Manual
Raznjevic · Handbook of Thermodynamic Tables and Charts
Rothbart · Mechanical Design and Systems Handbook
Smeaton · Switchgear and Control Handbook
Streeter · Handbook of Fluid Dynamics
Stubbs · Handbook of Heavy Construction
Truxal · Control Engineers' Handbook
Tuma · Engineering Mathematics Handbook
Tuma · Handbook of Physical Calculations
Tuma · Technology Mathematics Handbook
Urquhart · Civil Engineering Handbook

The NALCO
Water Handbook

Nalco Chemical Company

FRANK N. KEMMER *Editor-in-chief*

JOHN McCALLION *Associate editor*

McGRAW-HILL BOOK COMPANY
New York St. Louis San Francisco Auckland Bogotá
Düsseldorf Johannesburg London Madrid
Mexico Montreal New Delhi Panama
Paris São Paulo Singapore
Sydney Tokyo Toronto

Library of Congress Cataloging in Publication Data

Nalco Chemical Company.
  The NALCO water handbook.

  Includes index.
  1. Water—Handbooks, manuals, etc.
I. Kemmer, Frank N.   II.   Title.
QD169.W3N34   1979   546'.22   78-25825

34567890   KPKP   86543210

*The editors for this book were Harold B. Crawford and Joseph Williams,
the designer was Naomi Auerbach, and the production supervisor
was Teresa F. Leaden. It was set in Baskerville by
Monotype Composition, Inc.*

Printed and bound by The Kingsport Press.

Contents

v

SECTION 3   Uses of Water

SECTION 4   Specialized Water Treatment Technologies

Glossary follows Chapter 43
Appendix follows Glossary
Index follows Appendix

Preface

This handbook has been prepared as a reference for the many professionals who from time to time need information on water as it relates to their own specialized activities. They may be in such diverse occupations as plant manager, architect, utilities superintendent, city engineer, legislator, or environmental administrator. The book may also serve as a textbook or reference for those pursuing careers in water or the environmental sciences.

There are four sections to this handbook. The first is an introduction to the nature of water, dealing with the fundamentals of chemistry, biology, and water analysis. The second section explores the unit operations of water conditioning. Next is an overview of important industrial and municipal uses of water, including recycle and disposal. The fourth section includes chapters on the major water treatment technologies, such as treatment for cooling, steam generation, and oil recovery. The first section has been published separately as a soft-cover book titled, *WATER: The Universal Solvent.*

It is impossible for me to acknowledge all the ideas of many friends and authors whose experiences, added to my own during the forty years of my career in this field, may appear in this book. But fortunately I am able to acknowledge my associates at Nalco who contributed individual chapters in their specialized fields to this handbook. These include: P. A. Barker, J. A. Beardsley, J. M. Bouwens, G. A. Casedy, R. J. Christensen, J. L. Cole, L. J. Domzalski, R. P. Dudley, C. R. Hoefs, J. C. Jennings, K. E. Katnik, E. F.

Klen, G. F. McIntyre, D. G. Morse, K. Odland, M. T. Perin, J. E. Phelan, D. T. Reed, R. S. Robertson, and R. F. Tuka. Many others too numerous to mention have made valuable suggestions, and others have added to early drafts of the manuscript, including M. L. Beardsley, J. C. Grier, J. J. Hickey, M. L. Palmer, and R. W. Youngs.

During the months of gestation of this handbook, the assiduous attention of John McCallion to innumerable editorial details and Beverly Newmeller to preparation of the manuscript and illustrations were indispensable in ensuring a safe delivery.

Frank N. Kemmer

The NALCO
Water Handbook

Chapter 1

The Water Molecule

Three-quarters of the surface of the earth is covered with water. While this is an impressive statistic, it is pale beside the spectacular photographs that have come to us from outer space. They reveal a beautiful blue planet bathed in water, partly hidden by a veil of vapor.

Life came into being in this water. As living things became more complex and specialized, they left the sea for the land, taking water with them as the major part of their bodies. On the planet Earth, water is life.

A philosopher observed that the proper study of mankind is man; the water chemist paraphrases this: "The proper study of water is the water molecule." The formula for water—H_2O—by itself tells us only its composition and molecular weight. It does nothing to explain the remarkable properties that result from its unique molecular arrangement (see Figure 1.1). Two hydrogen atoms are located 105° apart, adjacent to the oxygen atom, so that the molecule is asymmetrical, positively charged on the hydrogen side, and negatively charged on the oxygen side. For this reason, water is said to be dipolar. This causes the molecules to agglomerate, the hydrogen of one molecule attracting the oxygen of a neighboring molecule. The linking of molecules resulting from this attractive force is called "hydrogen bonding."

One of the consequences of hydrogen bonding is that molecules of H_2O cannot leave the surface of a body of water as readily as they would be able to without this inter-molecular attraction. The energy required to rupture the hydrogen bond and liberate a molecule of H_2O to form vapor is much greater than for other common chemical compounds. Because of this, the water vapor—steam—has a high energy content and is an effective medium for transferring energy in industrial plant operations, buildings, and homes.

Water also releases more heat upon freezing than do other compounds. Furthermore, for each incremental change in temperature, water absorbs or releases

Figure 1.1   The joining of di-atomic hydrogen and oxygen molecules to produce water molecules of a polar nature.

more heat than many substances (heat capacity), so it is an effective heat transfer medium.

The freezing of water is unusual compared to other liquids. Hydrogen bonding produces a crystal arrangement that causes ice to expand beyond its original liquid volume, so that its density is less than that of the liquid, and the ice floats. If this were not the case, lakes would freeze from the bottom up, and life as we know it could not exist.

Table 1.1 compares the boiling point and other heat properties of water with similar molecules, such as hydrogen sulfide, and with dissimilar compounds that are liquid at room temperature.

TABLE 1.1   Thermal Properties of Water and Similar Compounds

Substance	Specific heat	Freezing point, °C	Boiling point, °C	Latent heat of evaporation, cal/gram
H_2O	1.00	0	100	540
H_2S		−83	−62	132
Methanol	0.57	−98	65	263
Ethanol	0.54	−117	79	204
Benzene	0.39	6	80	94

HIGH SURFACE TENSION

In addition to its unusual heat properties, water has physical properties quite different from other liquids. Its high surface tension is easily demonstrated by the experiment of "floating" a needle on the surface of water in a glass (Figure 1.2). This high surface tension, due to hydrogen bonding, also causes water to rise in a capillary tube (Figure 1.3). This capillarity is partly responsible for the system of circulation developed by living plants through their roots and tissue systems.

Figure 1.2 A steel needle, with a density about seven times that of water, can be made to float because of water's high surface tension.

Water is often called the universal solvent. Water molecules in contact with a crystal orient themselves to neutralize the attractive forces between the ions in the crystal structure. The liberated ions are then hydrated by these water molecules as shown in Figure 1.4, preventing them from recombining and recrystalizing. This solvency and hydration effect is shown quantitatively by water's relatively high dielectric constant.

Water ionizes so very slightly, producing only 10^{-7} moles of hydrogen and 10^{-7} moles of hydroxyl ions per liter, that it is an insulator—it cannot conduct electrical current. As salts or other ionizing materials dissolve in water, electrical conductivity develops. The conductivity of naturally-occurring waters provides a measure of their dissolved mineral content (Figure 1.5).

Figure 1.3 A meniscus forms (left) when hydrogen atoms reach upward to wet oxide surfaces at the water line in a glass tube. The drawing at the right shows how "hydrogen bonding" of water to a thin glass tube causes the water in the tube to rise above the level of the surrounding water.

(Water Molecule)

Figure 1.4 The orientation of water molecules tends to keep ions from recombining and thus precipitating from solution. This accounts for water's capabilities as a solvent.

Another important phenomenon occurring in water solutions related to dissolved matter (solutes) rather than to water (solvent) is osmotic pressure. If two aqueous solutions are separated by a membrane, water will pass from the more dilute into the more concentrated one. This important process controls the performance of all living cells. It explains the effectiveness of food preservation by salting; the salt creates a strong solution, disrupting the cells of organisms that might cause food spoilage, as the water inside their bodies leaves in an attempt to dilute the external salt solution. In specially designed membrane cells, the osmotic flow of water across the membrane can be reversed by applying a sufficiently high pressure to the more concentrated solution. This process of "reverse osmosis" is a practical one for desalination of water.

Viscosity is a final property of water affecting its treatment and use. It is a measure of internal friction—the friction of one layer of molecules moving across another. As water temperature rises, this internal friction decreases. Because of the temperature effect, dissolved salts and gases can diffuse more rapidly through warmer water; chemical treatment is hastened, and the physical

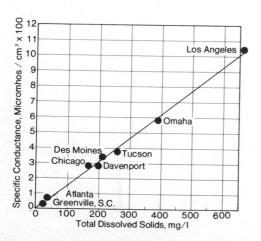

Figure 1.5 Dissolved solids content of water can be estimated from its specific conductance.

Figure 1.6 Surface tension and viscosity both decrease as water is heated.

processes of sedimentation and degasification proceed faster. The effect of temperature on viscosity is shown in Figure 1.6.

SUGGESTED READING

Boys, C. V.: *Soap Bubbles*. Doubleday & Company, 1959.
Buswell, A. M., and Rodebush, W. H.: "Water." *Scientific American*. p. 76, April, 1956.
Carson, Rachel: *The Sea Around Us*. Oxford University Press, 1951.
Day, John A., and Davis, Kenneth S.: *Water: The Mirror of Science*. Doubleday & Company, 1961.
King, Thompson: *Water, Miracle of Nature*, The Macmillan Company, 1953.
Leopold, Luna B., and Davis, Kenneth S.: *Water*. Life Science Library. Time, Incorporated, 1974.

Chapter 2

Water Sources and Uses

Water has moved in ceaseless migration across the face of the Earth since earliest time. Well-established currents such as the Gulf Stream and the Humboldt Current continuously circulate in the seas, regulating the Earth's climate and providing sustenance for the fisheries on which much of the world's population relies. Where stopped by land barricades, the sea, refusing to be held back completely, releases its water vapor to condense and fall somewhere inland as rain to attack the land barrier. This continual evaporation and condensation is the hydrologic cycle.

TABLE 2.1   Water Balance in the United States
[Figures in billion gallons per day (bgd)]*

Precipitation	4250
Evaporation and transpiration	3000
Runoff	1250
Withdrawal	310
Irrigation	142
Industry†	142
Municipal	26
Consumed‡	90
Returned to streams	220

SOURCE: National Academy of Sciences— National Research Council Publ. 1000-B, 1962.

* bgd × 44 = m³/sec.

† Principally utility cooling water (approximately 100 bgd).

‡ Principally irrigation loss to ground and evaporation.

Over the United States mainland, rainfall averages approximately 4250×10^9 gallons a day (1.6×10^{10} m³/day). Of this, about two-thirds returns to the atmosphere through evaporation directly from the surface of lakes and rivers and transpiration from plant foliage. This leaves approximately 1250×10^9 gallons a day (0.46×10^{10} m³/day) to flow across or through the earth to return to the sea (Table 2.1).

Abundant supplies of water attracted the American colonists to settlements along rivers. Their waterfalls became the principal sources of power for early industry.

Along the Eastern seaboard, river waters were of excellent quality, ideal for textile and paper manufacture. As the frontiers moved inland, settlers found that the salinity of the streams became higher, particularly where long rivers flowed over relatively soluble rock formations. Figure 2.1 compares the chemical properties of some of the major rivers in the United States. Table 2.2 shows how water quality, using Colorado River data, is influenced from the headwaters to the discharge to the sea. The quality of such rivers is affected by rainfall, the

Identification of Analyses Tabulated Below:

A. Delaware at Morrisville, PA   D. Ohio at Steubenville, Ohio

B. Edisto at Charleston, SC   E. Tennessee at Decatur, AL

C. Chattahoochee at Atlanta, GA   F. Mississippi at St. Louis, MO

Constituent	As	A	B	C	D	E	F
Calcium	CaCO₃	35	17	9	57	58	125
Magnesium	"	19	3	4	30	20	57
Sodium	"	4	10	5	14	18	66
Total Electrolyte	CaCO₃	58	30	18	101	96	248
Bicarbonate	CaCO₃	10	19	12	13	55	128
Carbonate	"	0	0	0	0	0	0
Hydroxyl	"	0	0	0	0	0	0
Sulfate	"	35	2	2	79	15	93
Chloride	"	10	8	3	8	21	23
Nitrate	"	3	1	1	1	4	4
Fluoride	"	NR	NR	0	TR	1	NR
M Alk.	CaCO₃	10	19	12	13	55	128
P Alk.	"	0	0	0	0	0	0
Carbon Dioxide	"	1	20	2	15	10	3
pH		7.1	6.1	6.9	6.4	7.0	7.9
Silica	SiO₂	4.7	5	10	5.6	5.6	13
Iron	Fe	0.1	0.2	0.1	TR	0.1	NR
Turbidity		NR	NR	26	88	50	NR
TDS		84	46	33	143	113	326
Color		7	54	4	2	30	19

pH in pH units; color in APHA units; all others in mg/l

Figure 2.1 Selected river analyses.

Identification of Analyses Tabulated Below:

G. Missouri at Great Falls, MT

H. Missouri at Kansas City

I. Neches at Evadale, TX

J. Colorado as delivered to Los Angeles, CA

K. Columbia at Wenatchee, WA

L. Sacramento at Sacramento, CA

Constituent	As	G	H	I	J	K	L
Calcium	CaCO₃	100	152	17	198	50	12
Magnesium	"	49	70	16	105	16	8
Sodium	"	47	86	23	220	25	5
Total Electrolyte	CaCO₃	196	308	56	523	91	25
Bicarbonate	CaCO₃	140	158	17	113	60	20
Carbonate	"	0	TR	0	7	0	0
Hydroxyl	"	0	0	0	0	0	0
Sulfate	"	36	120	13	302	22	2
Chloride	"	16	27	25	100	2	2
Nitrate	"	2	3	1	Nil	1	1
Fluoride	"	2	NR	0	1	TR	0
M Alk.	CaCO₃	140	158	17	120	60	20
P Alk.	"	0	TR	0	4	0	0
Carbon Dioxide	"	TR	NR	4	0	4	2
pH		8.4	8.3	6.7	8.4	7.7	7.2
Silica	SiO₂	19	12	16	8	9.6	9.2
Iron	Fe	TR	NR	0.6	Nil	TR	0
Turbidity		150	2000	35	NR	3	36
TDS		234	365	96	661	100	36
Color		NR	NR	60	NR	NR	15
pH in pH units; color in APHA units; all others in mg/l							

Figure 2.1 Selected river analyses (continued).

geological nature of the watershed, conditions of evaporation, and by seasonal changes in stream flow.

EFFECTS OF RAINFALL

The sudden dilution of a river by heavy rainfall can be a disruptive factor in a water treatment plant. The location of a river water intake should be carefully chosen with this problem in mind. In the operation of a treatment plant, it is common practice to adjust the chemical dosages according to effluent water quality. However, there are many water supplies so variable that it is necessary to base changes in chemical treatment on raw water characteristics rather than on finished water quality. This imposes a hardship on the treatment plant operators, requiring their constant attention to analysis and control.

Tides create another important influence on surface water quality in that they slow, or actually reverse, normal river flow. This is particularly pronounced during periods of low rainfall. The change in water quality between high and

TABLE 2.2 Colorado River—1964–1965*

Location	Total dissolved solids, mg/l	Total hardness, mg/l as CaCO$_3$	pH
Hot Sulfur Springs, CO	92	56	7.4
Glenwood Springs, CO	292	159	7.6
Cameo, CO	380	181	7.7
Cisco, UT	530	276	7.7
Lees Ferry, AZ	609	300	7.6
Grand Canyon, AZ	655	307	7.8
Parker Dam, AZ-CA—3/15/65	753	360	7.8

* USGS Water Supply Paper, 1965.

low tide sometimes justifies the installation of raw water supply reservoirs to receive water at low tide when the river flows unimpeded and quality is at its best. Plants so equipped stop pumping at high tide when saline bay waters move upstream into the upper channel. An example of the effect of tides and seasonal runoff is given in Table 2.3, showing the enormous variations in the Delaware River near Wilmington, Delaware.

LOW TEMPERATURES HINDER TREATMENT

Another characteristic of surface waters is seasonal temperature changes. This complicates treatment, particularly affecting the coagulation process in the winter. Low temperatures also create problems with air-binding of filters due to the increased solubility of gases and higher water viscosity. This causes pressure drop through the filter beds to increase, releasing gas and disrupting flow.

Another effect of temperature change occurs in water-cooled systems of industrial plants where heat exchange equipment is usually designed for the least favorable condition—the higher summer temperatures of surface waters. In winter when the temperature is low,. the flow must often be restricted to prevent overcooling. Lower water velocities may allow silting in heat transfer equipment, which can lead to corrosion and to pressure loss when higher cooling rates are needed.

Because rivers are warmer in the summer, designers take this into account in most water-dependent systems. But a complication arises in that many waste waters contain heat from plant processes, and this added heat compounds the natural rise of the summer, sometimes producing an effluent warm enough to create an unhealthy condition for aquatic life. Pollution discharges not only add to the heat load of the river, but they usually also add to the oxygen demand and may have a pronounced influence on the oxygen content of the river water.

ALGAE AFFECTS O$_2$ LEVELS

When pollutants are biodegradable, bacterial activity in the stream increases with pollution load, tending to reduce the dissolved oxygen level in the stream, but there are offsetting factors. The principal one is the presence of algae in the stream; algae will produce oxygen by photosynthesis in daylight—often causing supersaturation on bright, sunny days—with a falloff at night as the process is restricted. This diurnal cycle affects not only dissolved oxygen, but also carbon dioxide, and thus pH. This can have a strong influence on the coagulation of a water supply in municipal and industrial water treatment plants.

It is unusual to find high levels of dissolved iron in surface waters, except where the water supply is highly colored and has a relatively low pH. In this case, the iron usually is complexed by the organic matter causing the color. An exception to this would be where there is acid mine drainage into the river; in this case, the iron is introduced into the water in the reduced (ferrous) condition and a lack of dissolved oxygen prevents its oxidation to the less soluble ferric state.

When a river is dammed, the water quality may be considerably different from that of the flowing stream. The impoundment behind the dam then takes on the characteristics of a lake. In deep impoundments, it is common to find stratification, with oxygen depletion in the bottom, stagnant zone, and development of significant levels of iron and manganese in the bottom water, even though the surface remains free of these heavy metals.

From flowing streams and rivers, water may diffuse into underground aquifers when the surrounding water table is low; or, water may feed into the river from

TABLE 2.3   Delaware River at Memorial Bridge near Wilmington, Delaware*
Specific Conductivity, micromhos/cm at 25°C October 1969–September 1970, showing variations for day with maximum and day with minimum reading

Date	Maximum	Minimum	Mean
October 16	6880	2660	4420
October 7	6220	1400	3540
November 2	8820	3500	5650
November 26	2460	420	1370
December 9	6940	1100	3610
December 27	240	100	145
January 23	5440	960	2580
January 17	2700	100	1470
February 27	980	180	493
February 24	560	100	235
March 21	3240	200	1450
March 27	1700	100	
April 23	1240	220	289
April 5	120	100	105
May 24	4520	920	
May 12	870	170	613
June 22	3900	200	1110
June 1	1740	180	905
July 20	6380	860	2930
July 7	2500	100	1380
August 19	8920	1900	5030
August 2	4060	560	2060
September 20	8300	3500	5630
September 1	5940	1740	3820

* USGS Water Supply Paper 2151.

these aquifers when the water table is high. This, too, influences chemical composition, particularly iron and manganese in certain streams.

In the impoundment of major rivers, such as the Columbia, the Colorado and those in the Tennessee Valley system, the mineral content of the lakes behind the dams is similar to that in the river, as would be expected. On the other hand, natural or artificial impoundment of streams in smaller watershed areas of abundant rainfall produces water supplies of very low mineral content. This accounts for the excellent quality of such municipal waters as Greenville, South Carolina, New York City, and Boston, as shown by Figure 2.2.

WHERE RIVER MEETS OCEAN

The quality of water in estuaries where rivers meet the sea is unpredictable, depending on river flow, tidal conditions, the size of the basin or bay, and the presence or absence of land formations that restrict the flow to the sea. In large basins, such as Albemarle Sound on the East Coast, the water, although saline,

Identification of Analyses Tabulated Below:

A. Greenville, SC   D. Frederick, MD

B. New York City (Catskill)   E. Little Rock, AR

C. Boston   F. Colorado Springs, CO

Constituent	As	A	B	C	D	E	F
Calcium	CaCO₃	3	12	10	2	6	15
Magnesium	''	2	7	3	1	4	4
Sodium	''	4	4	1	6	1	11
Total Electrolyte	CaCO₃	9	23	14	9	11	30
Bicarbonate	CaCO₃	6	8	5	4	8	15
Carbonate	''	0	0	0	0	0	0
Hydroxyl	''	0	0	0	0	0	0
Sulfate	''	2	11	6	3	0	4
Chloride	''	1	4	3	2	3	4
Nitrate	''	0	0	0	0	0	1
Fluoride	"	0	0	0	0	0	6
M Alk.	CaCO₃	6	8	5	4	8	15
P Alk.	''	0	0	0	0	0	0
Carbon Dioxide	"	6	2	5	8	2	2
pH		6.2	6.9	6.3	6.1	7.1	7.4
Silica	SiO₂	7.8	2.5	0.9	3.0	3.5	8.4
Iron	Fe	0	0	0.1	0	NR	0.4
Manganese	Mn	0	0	0	0	NR	0.0
Turbidity		NR	2	1	1	10	NR
TDS		17	34	33	12	25	33
Color		6	1	7	3	35	NR
pH in pH units; color in APHA units; all others in mg/l							

Figure 2.2 Impoundments in watersheds supplied principally by precipitation.

is of relatively uniform composition because of mixing of the shallow water by wind; but in smaller bays the quality will change with the tides and the flow of the river. It is one of the miracles of nature that aquatic life adapts to these changes and flourishes in such tidal areas.

Many of the major rivers of the world finally reach the ocean through deltas, which have some of the characteristics of an estuary. In many instances, the flow of these rivers is so great that the dilution of the ocean can be measured for miles out to sea. Some plants have used the brackish waters of tidal basins as cooling tower makeup, since the water is low enough in dissolved solids to be concentrated by evaporation without severe scaling problems just as fresh waters are. The use of brackish water for this purpose permits installation of much smaller pipelines than would be needed if once-through cooling were practiced. One example is a chemical plant on the island of Trinidad, which is able to use water from the bay side of the island as cooling tower makeup. This water is diluted enough by the immense flow of the Orinoco River so that its salinity is lower than typical ocean water permitting it to concentrate by evaporation without causing scale problems.

Out at sea, where surface waters have become part of the circulation system, the composition of the ocean water is remarkably uniform, as shown in Table 2.4. There are, of course, local changes in salinity as mentioned earlier caused by upwelling of subsurface waters into the ocean, the flow of mighty rivers into the sea, or the melting of glaciers and the polar ice caps. Even though it isn't usable by land animals, sea water is a valuable source of water for industry and is widely used for cooling.

LAKES AS RESERVOIRS

Lakes are a major source of fresh water. They are of particular significance in North America, where Canada and the United States share, in the Great Lakes Basin, what is usually considered to be the largest fresh water supply in the world. In the Soviet Union, a single body of water, Lake Baikal in Siberia, con-

TABLE 2.4 Composition of Ocean Waters
(U.S. Naval Oceanographic Office, 1966)

Location	Temperature, °C	Salinity, parts per thousand
North Atlantic		
Central water	4–17	35.1–36.2
Bottom water	1–3	34.8–34.9
South Atlantic		
Central water	5–16	34.3–35.6
Bottom water	0–2	34.5–34.9
Mediterranean	6–10	35.3–36.4
Red Sea	9	35.5
Indian Ocean, central water	6–15	34.5–35.4
North Pacific		
Eastern	10–16	34.0–34.6
Western	7–16	34.1–34.6
Sub-arctic	2–10	33.5–34.4
South Pacific		
Eastern	9–16	34.3–35.1
Western	7–16	34.5–35.5
Sub-antarctic	3–7	34.1–34.6

tains about the same volume of fresh water as the entire Great Lakes system, 5500 cubic miles (2.3×10^4 km³). Lake Baikal is about 5000 ft (1525 m) deep with a surface area of about 11,000 square miles (2.8×10^6 ha), compared to 95,000 square miles for the Great Lakes. Together, the Great Lakes and Lake Baikal contain 40% of the world's presently available fresh water.

Of the Great Lakes, Lake Superior is the largest, with a total area of about 32,000 square miles and a maximum depth of approximately 1300 feet. It is also "the different lake" with a significantly lower dissolved solids content than the other Great Lakes due to differences in geologic formations of the lake bed and to temperature (Figure 2.3). The analyses of Lake Michigan and Lake Erie are also shown in Figure 2.3. Even though these two lakes are different in configuration, area, and depth, their chemical compositions are similar. This concentration of mineral matter is maintained fairly uniformly until the water of the Great Lakes is finally discharged from Lake Ontario into the St. Lawrence River.

The composition of lake water changes seasonally and sometimes even daily with weather conditions. Although the major dissolved mineral constituents

Identification of Analyses Tabulated Below:							
A. Lake Superior at Duluth				D. Seneca Lake, Geneva, New York			
B. Lake Michigan at Chicago				E. Lake Coeur d'Alene, Idaho			
C. Lake Erie at Erie, PA				F. Clear Lake, West Palm Beach, FL			
Constituent	As	A	B	C	D	E	F
Calcium	CaCO₃	35	80	90	100	18	68
Magnesium	''	9	41	33	41	10	11
Sodium	''	6	19	20	135	2	23
Total Electrolyte	CaCO₃	50	140	143	276	30	102
Bicarbonate	CaCO₃	42	113	91	97	19	50
Carbonate	''	0	0	0	0	0	0
Hydroxyl	''	0	0	0	0	0	0
Sulfate	''	1	18	25	35	10	12
Chloride	''	5	9	27	142	1	40
Nitrate	''	2	NR	Nil	2	Nil	NR
Fluoride	"	TR	TR	TR	TR	TR	1
M Alk.	CaCO₃	42	113	91	97	19	50
P Alk.	''	0	TR	0	0	0	0
Carbon Dioxide	"	4	Nil	5	5	4	2
pH		7.4	8.2	7.5	7.6	7.0	7.7
Silica	SiO₂	3.3	2.3	1.2	1.9	10	2.2
Iron	Fe	0.2	0.1	TR	TR	NR	0.6
Turbidity		1	12	Nil	NR	7	18
TDS		54	171	172	323	58	173
Color		1	3	2	1	NR	25
pH in pH units; color in APHA units; all others in mg/l							

Figure 2.3 Selected lake analyses.

Figure 2.4 In summer, lake water temperature drops with increasing depth. *(Adapted from "The Microscopy of Drinking Water," by Whipple and Fair.)*

may not be greatly affected by seasons and weather, such factors as dissolved oxygen, temperature, suspended solids, turbidity, and carbon dioxide will change because of biological activity. Another factor that creates change is the seasonal turnover that occurs in most lakes in the United States during the spring and fall.

An excellent classification of lakes is given in "The Microscopy of Drinking Water" by Whipple and Fair. Using as their basis for categorizing lakes the nature of the thermocline (temperature barriers) at different times of the year, they have defined three types of lakes: polar, temperate, and tropical, with those in the United States being chiefly in the second category.

SEASONAL TURNOVER

In temperate lakes over 200 ft (60 m) deep (first order), the bottom water is at the temperature of maximum density, 39.2°F (4°C), year round. After the ice cover thaws in spring, the surface water gradually warms from 32°F to 39.2°F (0 to 4°C), within which temperature range its density increases; vertical circulation commences as the surface reaches the bottom water temperature. After this "spring turnover," the surface rises above 39.2°F and its density decreases as it continues to warm through the summer. The temperature gradient in the summer is illustrated by Figure 2.4.

The fall and winter cooling again reduces the surface temperature to its maximum density, and the "fall turnover" occurs.

During the period of summer stagnation, vertical circulation is induced by wind, but this force is not strong enough to cause mixing of the bottom water, the hypolimnion. The circulation pattern induced by wind is illustrated in Figure 2.5.

A similar turnover occurs in lakes of the second order, in the approximate range of 25–200 feet deep. In the second order lake, the bottom temperature changes measurably, but is never far from that of maximum density. Figure 2.6 illustrates surface and bottom temperatures of a 60-foot-deep lake, with turnover occurring at the points where the temperature curves cross.

In lakes of less than about 25 feet deep (third order), vertical circulation is induced almost exclusively by wind action rather than density differences, so there is little difference between surface and bottom temperatures.

An understanding of these characteristics of lakes is necessary to properly locate water intakes and discharges. It aids in anticipating the changes in water

Figure 2.5 Wind-induced lake water circulation. *(Adapted from "The Microscopy of Drinking Water," by Whipple and Fair.)*

treatment needed to meet changes in composition caused by turnover and wind-induced circulation.

Another characteristic of lake waters, usually seasonal and related to biological activity, is taste and odor. Except where these may be introduced by waste water discharges, they are usually attributed to organic matter such as essential oils produced by the algae growth.

SUBSURFACE WATER

Underground reservoirs constitute a major source of fresh water. In terms of storage capacity, underground aquifers worldwide contain over 90% of the total fresh water available for man's use (Figure 2.7). Much of this is too deep to be exploited economically. In the United States, where the Great Lakes contain such a large volume of fresh water, the proportion of surface water to ground water is much higher; but even here, it is estimated that at least 50% of total available fresh water storage is in underground aquifers.

Over 60 bgd (2600 m³/sec) of water is withdrawn from wells for irrigation of the United States mainland (Figure 2.8). This well water usage is about the same as the total water used by municipalities throughout the United States. Over 80% of the municipalities in the United States depend on well water, although less than 30% of the total volume of water treated for municipal use is from this source. The largest well field in the U.S. supplies 72 MGD to the city of Tacoma (Figure 2.9).

Figure 2.6 Annual temperature variation of surface and bottom water in a 60-foot-deep lake. *(Adapted from "The Microscopy of Drinking Water," by Whipple and Fair.)*

Figure 2.7 More than 97% of the earth's water is in the oceans. All the rivers of the world contain only 0.02% of the world's total water. (There is some dispute among experts on the exact quantity of groundwater.) *(From "Water of the World," U.S. Dept. of the Interior/ Geological Survey.)*

WELL WATERS CONSTANT

Underground water usually moves very slowly. Its flow is measured in feet per year compared to surface streams where velocities are in the feet-per-second range. Because of this, the composition of any one well is usually quite constant. Although shallow wells may vary seasonally in temperature, most wells are also constant in temperature, usually in the range of 50–60°F (10–16°C). Since the water has passed through miles of porous rock formation, it is invariably clear if the well has been properly developed to keep fine sand from entering the casing.

Since the composition is related to the chemistry of the geological formations through which the water has passed, waters from wells drilled into different strata have different characteristics. Some aquifers are so large that they may cover several states in total area, and wells drilled into that particular aquifer produce water of similar composition. For that reason, with good geological information it is possible to make some generalizations about the composition of well waters in different parts of the United States. Selected analyses are shown in Figure 2.10.

Figure 2.8 The rate of withdrawal of groundwater for irrigation in the U.S. has increased rapidly since 1950. (*With permission from "The Johnson Drillers Journal," July–August 1979.*)

Figure 2.9 Groundwater availability in the United States. Supplies are relatively scarce in the western third of the country, but plentiful in the East and Middle West. (*From* Chemical Week *by special permission. Copyright 1977 by McGraw-Hill, Inc.*)

Identification of Analyses Tabulated Below:

A. Manhattan, Kansas   D. Phoenix, Arizona

B. Amarillo, Texas, Well No. 1   E. Norman, Oklahoma

C. Baytown, Texas, Well No. 1   F. Richland, Washington

Constituent	As	A	B	C	D	E	F
Calcium	$CaCO_3$	282	145	25	192	5	125
Magnesium	''	86	255	14	230	3	65
Sodium	''	65	84	593	319	462	38
Total Electrolyte	$CaCO_3$	433	484	632	741	470	228
Bicarbonate	$CaCO_3$	352	366	384	220	295	169
Carbonate	''	0	0	0	0	57	0
Hydroxyl	''	0	0	0	0	0	0
Sulfate	''	54	86	Nil	128	98	45
Chloride	''	25	24	245	312	18	13
Nitrate	''	1	3	0	79	1	1
Fluoride	''	1	5	3	2	1	Nil
M Alk.	$CaCO_3$	352	366	384	220	352	169
P Alk.	''	0	0	0	0	29	0
Carbon Dioxide	''	35	20	20	5	0	8
pH		7.3	7.6	7.6	7.9	9.1	7.7
Silica	SiO_2	31	61	26	27	9.7	55
Iron	Fe	6.9	Nil	0.3	Nil	Nil	Nil
Manganese	Mn	1.4	NR	0	NR	NR	0
Turbidity							
TDS		488	530	733	887	550	307
Color		2	NR	10	3	5	5

pH in pH units; color in APHA units; all others in mg/l

Figure 2.10   Selected well waters.

CO₂ AND MINERALS

As water filters through the ground, soil organisms consume dissolved oxygen and produce carbon dioxide, one of the principal corrosive agents in dissolving the minerals from geological structures. It is common to find iron and manganese in waters that are devoid of oxygen if they have been in contact with iron-bearing minerals. Shallow wells containing oxygen are generally free of iron.

Extensive records on the composition of well waters are available from the U.S. Geological Survey and also from most state agencies regulating the use of water as a natural resource. Most well drillers also have records of subsurface supplies, including both chemical composition and water yield.

The water produced with oil, called connate water or oil-field brine, is unique and creates unusual problems in handling and treatment for reuse or disposal. It is usually more concentrated than sea water, often exceeding 100,000 mg/l in total salinity; this and the reduction in temperature and pressure as the brine travels upward from great depths cause difficult problems of scale and corrosion control. Several analyses are shown by Table 2.5.

Identification of Analyses Tabulated Below:						
G. Camden, NJ, Well No. 1				J. Ft. Lauderdale, FL		
H. Camden, NJ, Well No. 7				K. Bastrop, LA		
I. Camden, NJ, Well No. 9N				L. Dallas, TX, Well No. 39		

Constituent	As	G	H	I	J	K	L
Calcium	$CaCO_3$	60	18	42	230	4	15
Magnesium	"	38	19	41	8	2	9
Sodium	"	42	28	31	22	616	838
Total Electrolyte	$CaCO_3$	140	65	114	260	622	862
Bicarbonate	$CaCO_3$	50	1	91	235	356	452
Carbonate	"	0	0	0	0	0	TR
Hydroxyl	"	0	0	0	0	0	0
Sulfate	"	38	42	12	TR	2	270
Chloride	"	50	18	10	25	262	134
Nitrate	"	1	4	1	NR	1	1
Fluoride	"	1	0	0	NR	1	5
M Alk.	$CaCO_3$	50	1	91	235	356	452
P Alk.	"	0	0	0	0	0	TR
Carbon Dioxide	"	80	80	30	10	5	Nil
pH		6.0	4.6	6.8	7.7	8.0	8.2
Silica	SiO_2	13	6.1	3.9	22	11	22
Iron	Fe	1.2	TR	21	1.6	TR	TR
Manganese	Mn	0.3	TR	5.6	NR	NR	0
Turbidity							
TDS		181	103	118	314	697	1040
Color		3	2	3	59	35	0
pH in pH units; color in APHA units; all others in mg/l						

Figure 2.10 Selected well waters (continued).

In many areas of the country, particularly the West and Southwest, under-ground water is being mined. This has resulted in net loss of water, which has steadily reduced the level of the water table and has contributed to land sub-sidence. In some areas, such as Long Island, heavy withdrawal has resulted in

TABLE 2.5 Examples of Connate Water

Constituent	A	B	C	D
Calcium, mg/l Ca	8,300	2,630	1,500	630
Magnesium, mg/l Mg	260	690	500	40
Sodium, mg/l Na	56,250	16,800	9,150	5,640
Bicarbonate, mg/l HCO_3	50	315	1,000	500
Sulfate, mg/l SO_4	180	2,880	2,000	120
Chloride, mg/l Cl	98,300	30,500	17,800	8,350
TDS, mg/l	166,652	54,072	32,329	15,417

GROUP ⟶

PERIOD	I A	II A	III A	IV A	V A	VI A	VII A	0
1	1.01 +1 −1 **H** 1							He
2	6.94 +1 **Li** 3	9.01 +2 **Be** 4	10.81 +3 **B** 5	12.01 +2 +4 −4 **C** 6	14.01 +1 −1 +2 −2 +3 −3 +4 +5 **N** 7	16.00 −2 **O** 8	19.00 −1 **F** 9	Ne
3	23.00 +1 **Na** 11	24.31 +2 **Mg** 12	26.98 +3 **Al** 13	28.09 +2 +4 −4 **Si** 14	30.97 +3 +5 −3 **P** 15	32.06 +4 +6 −2 **S** 16	35.45 +1 +5 +7 −1 **Cl** 17	Ar
4	39.10 +1 **K** 19	40.08 +2 **Ca** 20	Ga	Ge	74.92 +3 +5 −3 **As** 33	78.96 +4 +6 −2 **Se** 34	79.90 +1 +5 −1 **Br** 35	Kr
5	Rb	87.62 +2 **Sr** 38	In	118.69 +2 +4 **Sn** 50	121.75 +3 +5 −3 **Sb** 51	Te	126.90 +1 +5 +7 −1 **I** 53	Xe
6	Cs	137.34 +2 **Ba** 56	Tl	207.19 +2 +4 **Pb** 82	Bi			

(TRANSITION ELEMENTS — label between II A and III A columns)

TRANSITION ELEMENTS

	I B	II B	III B	IV B	V B	VI B	VII B	VIII B		
4				47.90 +2 +3 +4 **Ti** 22	50.94 +2 +3 +4 +5 **V** 23	52.00 +2 +3 +6 **Cr** 24	54.94 +2 +4 +7 **Mn** 25	58.85 +2 +3 **Fe** 26	50.93 +2 +3 **Co** 27	58.71 +2 +3 **Ni** 28
4	63.55 +1 +2 **Cu** 29	65.37 +2 **Zn** 30				Mo				
5	107.87 +1 **Ag** 47	112.40 +2 **Co** 48								
6	Au	200.59 +1 +2 **Hg** 80								

Figure 3.1 Periodic chart of elements. The elements of interest to the water chemist are in boldface; rare elements are omitted. Atomic weights are shown in the upper left corners; atomic numbers below in boldface. Valences are shown to the right of the chemical symbol. The symbols are identified throughout the text.

not in his time been discovered. A modern version of his periodic chart, modified to accent the elements of particular interest to water chemists, is reproduced in Figure 3.1.

At one time the atomic weights developed by chemists differed from those developed by nuclear physicists. Those arrived at by the chemists had been based on a system of logic which assigned to oxygen an atomic weight of 16 as a starting point. Oxygen combines with some metals and other elements in more than one proportion: for example, there are two oxides of carbon, CO_2 and CO. From this kind of information and the measured weights of the materials found in chemical reactions, using the assumption of oxygen having an atomic weight of 16 made it possible to calculate the atomic weight of other elements.

The physicist uses the mass of the proton in the nucleus as unity. Scientists have discovered that there are several varieties of many of the elements, called isotopes, attributed to differences in the nucleus. An isotope of an element is an atom having the same structure as the element—the same electrons orbiting the nucleus, and the same protons in the nucleus, but having more or fewer neutrons. For example, isotopes of hydrogen are deuterium, having one neutron in addition to the proton in the nucleus, and tritium, having two neutrons in addition to the proton. These have weights of 2 and 3 relative to hydrogen at one. This basically accounts for the differences in numbers arrived at by the physicist and the chemist, since the latter was working with elements found in nature, and therefore, containing the element itself plus its naturally-occurring isotopes.

Chapter 3
Basic Chemistry

Comparing the atom to the solar system is useful in developing an understanding of basic chemical principles. The sun is likened to the nucleus of the atom and the planets to the electrons moving in orbits about the nucleus. The physicist, who would probably find the analogy simplistic, is concerned mostly with activity within the nucleus, whereas the chemist deals principally with the activity of the planetary electrons. Chemical reactions between atoms or molecules involve only these electrons; there are no changes in the nuclei.

The nucleus is made up of protons, having a positive electrical charge, and neutrons, without any charge. The positive charges in the nucleus are balanced by the negatively charged electrons orbiting it. Since the mass of an electron is less than 0.02% of the mass of a proton, for practical purposes the weight of the atom may be considered to be entirely in the nucleus.

Atoms are identified by name, atomic number, and atomic weight. The atomic number is the number of electrons in orbit about the nucleus, and, therefore, the number of protons in the nucleus. The weight of the atom is the sum of the protons and neutrons in the nucleus. The names and symbols are of historical interest. Some are ancient history; the symbol for lead is Pb from the Latin *plumbum,* from which is derived the word "plumber;" others are recent, such as fermium, atomic number 100, named for Enrico Fermi.

PERIODIC CHART OF ELEMENTS

Over 100 years ago, studying the elements known at that time, the Russian chemist Mendeleev tabulated the atomic weights of different elements in increasing order, and observed a repetition, or periodicity of certain significant physical properties of these elements. He constructed from this a periodic chart of sufficient accuracy to enable him to predict the properties of elements which had

TABLE 2.6   Annual Water Use by Types of Industry
(1972 census of manufactures estimated for 1973)

Industry	Water usage, bgd		
	Gross*	Intake	Discharge
Primary metal manufacture	24.2	13.5	13.1
Chemicals and allied products	30.4	11.4	10.7
Paper and allied products	22.3	6.6	6.3
Petroleum and coal products	32.0	3.5	3.2
Food	4.3	2.2	2.0
Transportation equipment	5.4	0.7	0.6
Machinery	4.1	0.8	0.7
Textile mill products	1.2	0.5	0.4
All industries	130	41.0	38.5

* The difference between gross usage and intake represents the success in conserving water by in-plant reuse.

intrusion of sea water inland. Here, underground injection is being practiced to provide an intermediate barrier to hold back the salt water from the fresh water wells. Injection water of this kind must be free of pollution, since the pollution of an underground aquifer can be very serious, so much time being required to displace the pollutant once it has gotten into the aquifer.

Table 2.1 lists the distribution of the water resources of the United States, and the rates of withdrawal and consumption. That portion of this fresh water used by industry, not including utility cooling water, is shown in Table 2.6. Most of this water is drawn from the Great Lakes and the river systems shown in Figure 2.11.

SUGGESTED READING

Nordell, Eskel: *Water Treatment for Industrial and Other Uses.* Reinhold, 1961.
Penman, H. L.: "The Water Cycle." *Scientific American,* p. 149, September, 1970.
Todd, David K., ed.: *The Water Encyclopedia.* Water Information Center, Port Washington, N. Y., 1970.
U.S. Department of Commerce: "Water Use in Manufacturing." *1972 Census of Manufactures.* MC 72(SR)4.
U.S. Geological Survey: "The Industrial Utility of Public Water Supplies in the United States." Paper 1299 and 1300, 1952.
Whipple, George C.: *The Microscopy of Drinking Water,* 4th ed. rev. Fair, G. M., and Whipple, M. C., 1933. John Wiley & Sons.

Figure 2.11 Major rivers of the United States. Map shows that surface water is much more abundant in the eastern states. (*From Chemical Week by special permission. Copyright 1977 by McGraw-Hill, Inc.*)

All rivers with flows exceeding 100 cfs.
Numbers are in 1000 cfs units for streamflows over 400 cfs.

The isotope most familiar to the layman is probably U^{235}, which is found in natural uranium (atomic weight 238.03). U^{235} is fissionable, and became well-known as the basic material used in the first atomic bomb. Because U^{235} and U^{238} behave identically in chemical reactions, they must be separated by extremely sophisticated physical processes based on their very small difference in atomic weight, 235 versus 238.

FROM ATOMS TO MOLECULES

Atoms can combine to form molecules. The molecules may be as simple as the association of two hydrogen atoms to form molecular hydrogen, H_2. Molecules made up of a number of different atoms are called compounds. These vary from the simple union of sodium and chlorine to form sodium chloride, $NaCl$, having a molecular weight of 58.5 (the sum of the sodium atomic weight and the chlorine atomic weight) to extremely elaborate combinations of carbon, hydrogen, nitrogen, and phosphorus found in such structures as the DNA (deoxyribonucleic acid) molecule, the fundamental unit in all cells, which carries the genetic code. DNA has a molecular weight in the thousands. In water treatment, man-made molecules having molecular weights on the order of 5 million are used to coagulate suspended solids in water.

The atom is defined as the smallest unit of matter retaining the characteristics of an element; a molecule is the smallest unit of matter retaining the properties of a compound.

Since the weights of atoms and molecules are relative, and because the units themselves are unimaginably small, the chemist works with units he identifies as moles. A mole is an arbitrary unit weighing in grams the same as the weight of the material arrived at by adding the atomic weights of its constituents. For example, calcium carbonate ($CaCO_3$), a compound familiar to water chemists, has a molecular weight of 100, so a mole of calcium carbonate weighs 100 grams.

This is also called the gram-molecular weight. A mole of any material contains exactly the same number of molecules as a mole of any other material. This is Avogadro's Number, 6.02×10^{23}. When dealing with gases, a mole of any gas, containing 6.02×10^{23} molecules, always occupies 22.4 liters at 0°Celsius and 760 mm total pressure.

IMPURITIES IN WATER

Practically speaking, no chemical is pure, whether naturally occurring or man-made. Most industrial chemicals have a level of impurity usually measured in percentage, or parts per hundred. The water chemist seldom deals with water sources having percentage levels of impurity, except for sea water (about 3% dissolved mineral impurities), connate waters (produced with some crude oils, sometimes containing 20–30% dissolved salts), brackish waters, and certain industrial waste waters. Since the water chemist is usually working with fresh water, he measures the impurity level in parts per million (ppm), 10,000 ppm equaling 1%; a sample of water from Lake Michigan, containing about 150 ppm, has an impurity level of only 0.015%. Since a liter of distilled water weighs 1000 g or 1,000,000 mg, it is apparent that 1 mg of impurity in a liter represents 1 ppm. However, a liter of seawater weighs about 1032 g, so 1 mg of impurity in seawater is less than 1 ppm. Because the density of the water may be quite high, the use of mg/l is more precise than ppm, although for practical purposes, they are identical when dealing with fresh water. This book will use mg/l, the preferred notation.

Anything in water that is not H_2O is a contaminant or impurity. All water is impure, and it is the principal job of the water chemist to define these impurities, set specifications for each impurity acceptable for the intended use of the water after treatment, and devise economical treatment methods to reach the quality limits that have been set. It is important to recognize that the terms impurity, contamination, and pollution are subjective ones. In this book, a contaminant is considered a pollutant when its concentration reaches a level that may be harmful either to aquatic life or to the public health if the water is for potable purposes. Dissolved impurities in water are broadly classified as inorganic salts—dissolved from minerals in the geological formations containing the water source, and organic matter—related to aquatic life and vegetative cover of the watershed. In most fresh waters, dissolved matter is largely inorganic.

To the water chemist, the molecular weight of a mineral is usually of less use in calculations than its equivalent weight, because most minerals dissolved in water are ionized. To understand the definition and usage of equivalent weight, the behavior of ionic solutions —called electrolytes—should be examined.

ELECTROLYTES

Water is known as the universal solvent. When it dissolves a mineral, new materials are produced from the atoms released by the mineral. These are fundamental particles called ions. The breakup of a chemical compound by dissolution in water forms cations, which are positively charged, and anions, which are negatively charged. Generally, an increase in water temperature causes an increase in the solubility of most salts. Important and notable exceptions are $CaCO_3$, $CaSO_4$, $MgCO_3$, and $Mg(OH)_2$, all of which become less soluble as the temperature increases.

There are a number of ways in which this phenomenon of ionization can be demonstrated. The simplest is an experiment in which an electric light is connected to an electrical circuit having two separated poles inserted in a beaker of water (Figure 3.2). Salt is added to the water in small increments, and gradually the light brightens, the intensity being proportional to the amount of salt added. In pure water the circuit is open; current begins to flow only after sodium and chloride ions from the salt are present to transport electrons through the solution. If crystals of sugar are added to the water instead of salt, nothing happens; salt is an electrolyte and sugar is not.

It was observed many years ago that impurities in water lower its freezing point. Upon careful investigation it was discovered that one mole/liter of a non-

Figure 3.2 Pure water is nonconductive, but addition of an ionizing salt allows current to pass.

electrolyte such as sugar or alcohol dissolved in water lowers the freezing point by 1.86°C. It was found that one mole/liter of sodium chloride lowered the freezing point by almost twice the value found for sugar and alcohol, and one mole/liter of sodium sulfate produced almost three times this depression. This is due to the production of two ions, sodium and chloride, from one molecule of sodium chloride salt, and three ions, two sodiums and one sulfate, from one molecule of sodium sulfate (Na_2SO_4).

IONS AND ELECTRIC CURRENT

When sodium chloride dissolves in water to produce sodium and chloride ions, the sodium loses the single electron in its outer orbit to the chloride ion. The sodium, having lost a negative charge, becomes positively charged by one unit, and the chloride, having retained the electron, becomes negatively charged by one unit. If two electrodes are immersed in the solution of sodium chloride and direct current is applied, sodium will move toward the negatively charged electrode (which is called a cathode), and the chloride ion will move to the positively charged electrode (called the anode). It is because of this direction of movement that the positive sodium ion is called a cation and the negative chloride ion an anion.

Those elements shown in columns 1A and 1B of the Periodic Chart become cations with a charge of +1 when dissolved in water. Similarly, the elements in columns 2A and 2B become cations with a charge of +2. On the opposite side of the Periodic Table, elements in column 6A become anions with a charge of −2, and those in column 7A become anions with a charge of −1. These charges are called the valences of the ions; the common ions in water are mono-, di-, or trivalent. (See "Signs and Conventions in Electrochemistry," in the Appendix.)

Ions made up of several different atoms are called radicals. Common radicals in water chemistry include ammonium, NH_4^{+1}, a cation; and nitrate, NO_3^{-1}, sulfate, SO_4^{-2}, and phosphate, PO_4^{-3}, which are anions.

Elements that form cations in aqueous solution may be broadly classified as alkali metals (e.g., sodium, potassium), alkaline earth metals (e.g., magnesium, calcium), and heavy metals (e.g., iron, manganese).

In their elemental form, each of these can displace hydrogen from aqueous solutions. Sodium and potassium are so active that they will react with water itself to liberate hydrogen:

$$2 \ Na + 2 \ H_2O \rightarrow (2) \ H_2 \uparrow + 2 \ NaOH \tag{1}$$

Magnesium will not react with cold water, but it will react with acid, which is a solution of the hydrogen ion:

$$Mg + 2 \ HCl \rightarrow H_2 \uparrow + MgCl_2 \tag{2}$$

ELECTROMOTIVE SERIES

These cations can be classified, then, according to their reactivity in an order known as the electromotive series, shown in Table 3.1. Not only will the more reactive metals displace hydrogen from solution, but they will even displace metals below them in the series. For example, if a strip of iron is placed in a solution of copper sulfate, the copper will plate out on the strip as the iron goes into solution:

$$Fe + CuSO_4 \rightarrow Cu + FeSO_4 \tag{3}$$

In comparing reactions (1) and (2), to produce one molecule of hydrogen requires two atoms of sodium but only one atom of magnesium, because the sodium has a charge +1, while the magnesium ion has a charge of +2. This provides one basis for the concept of equivalent weight: The equivalent weight of a cation is that weight which will displace 1.0 gram of hydrogen from aqueous solution. In most reactions, equivalent weight is the molecular weight of a substance divided by its valence.

TABLE 3.1   Electromotive Series of Elements

Element	Half-cell reaction	Voltage, E°
Potassium	$K^+ + e \rightarrow K$	−2.93
Calcium	$Ca^{++} + 2e \rightarrow Ca$	−2.87
Sodium	$Na^+ + e \rightarrow Na$	−2.71
Magnesium	$Mg^{++} + 2e \rightarrow Mg$	−2.37
Aluminum	$Al^{+++} + 3e \rightarrow Al$	−1.66
Zinc	$Zn^{++} + 2e \rightarrow Zn$	−0.76
Iron	$Fe^{++} + 2e \rightarrow Fe$	−0.44
Nickel	$Ni^{++} + 2e \rightarrow Ni$	−0.25
Tin	$Sn^{++} + 2e \rightarrow Sn$	−0.14
Lead	$Pb^{++} + 2e \rightarrow Pb$	−0.13
Hydrogen	$2H^+ + 2e \rightarrow H_2$	−0.00
Copper	$Cu^{++} + 2e \rightarrow Cu$	0.34
Mercury	$Hg_2^{++} + 2e \rightarrow 2Hg$	0.79
Silver	$Ag^+ + e \rightarrow Ag$	0.80
Gold	$Au^{+++} + 3e \rightarrow Au$	1.50

* The voltage is that developed by an electrode of the element immersed in a molal solution (one mole dissolved in 1000 g of water) of its ions shown in the half-cell reaction.

When direct current is passed through an aqueous solution of an electrolyte (the process of electrolysis), a unit of electricity called the Faraday, equal to 96,500 coulombs (ampere-seconds), causes one equivalent of cations to react at the cathode and one equivalent of anions at the anode. In the electrolysis of HCl:

$$2 \, HCl \rightarrow H_2 \uparrow + Cl_2 \uparrow \qquad (4)$$

In this reaction, one Faraday releases 1.0 g of hydrogen gas at the cathode and 35.45 g of chlorine gas at the anode. The molecular weights and equivalent weights of some common electrolytes are shown in Table 3.2 (see also Chapter 4).

TABLE 3.2   Weights of Some Common Compounds Used in Water Treatment

Common name	Formula	Mol. wt.*	Equiv. wt.
Table salt	$NaCl$	58.5	58.5
Caustic soda	$NaOH$	40	40
Salt cake	Na_2SO_4	142	71
Soda ash	Na_2CO_3	106	53
Limestone	$CaCO_3$	100	50
Quicklime	CaO	56	28
Slaked lime	$Ca(OH)_2$	74	37
Gypsum	$CaSO_4 \cdot 2H_2O$	172.2	86.1
Muriatic acid	HCl	36.5	36.5
Sulfuric acid	H_2SO_4	98	49
Aqua ammonia	NH_4OH	35	35

* Also called formula weight.

COLLOIDAL SYSTEMS

Some types of matter can be dispersed in water even though not truly soluble. This dispersion is accomplished by breaking down the material into an extremely small size, at the upper end of the size range for ions and molecules. Particles of this size are called colloids.

The surface of almost all matter—glass, steel, plastic—has a residue of electrical charges. This can lead to the development of high surface voltage, as demonstrated on a small scale by the discharge of a spark of static electricity on a cold, dry day, and on a large scale by lightning. As matter is reduced in size, the ratio of surface charge to mass increases exponentially. Assume that a cube of sand measuring 1.0 millimeter on each side is reduced to colloidal size of 100 millimicrons (1 millimicron = 10^{-6} millimeter), this would produce 10^{12} colloidal particles with a total surface 10,000 times larger than the original grain with a correspondingly larger surface charge.

It is this high surface charge, which is negative for silica (sand) in the example given, which causes colloidal particles to repel one another, thus maintaining the stability of the dispersion.

OXIDATION AND REDUCTION

The Periodic Chart shows that a number of elements have more than one valence. This is of great importance to the water chemist; an example is iron, whose oxide is quite soluble in water when its valence is +2 and almost completely insoluble when its valence is +3. If the valence of a material becomes more positive or less negative, it is said to be oxidized. Reduction occurs when valence becomes more negative or less positive—for example, in the change of iron +3 to iron +2, the iron is said to have been reduced. Another example of this is the chromate radical, CrO_4^{-2}, in which chromium has a valence of +6; when this is reduced, the chromium is changed in valence to +3.

In this example, an effective corrosion inhibitor, chromate, becomes a heavy metal cation with no useful properties, and it precipitates as $Cr(OH)_3$ to produce suspended matter.

Certain water treatment chemicals, such as chlorine gas, are effective because they are strong oxidizers. When chlorine is present in its elemental form, it has zero valence. If the chlorine attacks carbon in its elemental state, the carbon changes from zero valence to +4 and forms CO_2 gas, and the chlorine is reduced from zero valence state to the chloride anion, Cl^{-1}. In reactions of this kind, one material is oxidized and the other is reduced, with a net change of zero in the electrical balance of the system, since there are as many positive charges produced as negative charges.

SOLVENT ACTION OF WATER

The solvent action of water varies from one mineral to another. Table 3.3 shows the solubility of some common compounds in water.

Like minerals, gases and organic matter are soluble in water. Henry's Law states that the amount of gas dissolved in water is directly proportional to the pressure of the gas above the water surface. In any gas system the pressure percent equals volume percent equals mole percent.

$$\frac{P_g}{P_t} = \frac{V_g}{V_t} = \frac{M_g}{M_t}$$

The atmosphere is approximately 20% oxygen and 80% nitrogen. At atmos-

TABLE 3.3   Solubility of Some Inorganic Compounds in Water at 20°C

Cation	Compound (solid phase in parenthesis)	Solubility, wt %
H^+	HCl	41.9
	HNO_3	*
	H_2SO_4	*
Na^+	NaCl	26.5
	$NaOH(\cdot 1H_2O)$	52.1
	$NaNO_3$	46.7
	$Na_2CO_3(\cdot 10H_2O)$	17.7
	$Na_2SO_4(\cdot 10H_2O)$	16.2
	$Na_3PO_4(\cdot 12H_2O)$	9.1
K^+	KCl	25.4
	$KOH(\cdot 2H_2O)$	52.8
	KNO_3	24.0
	$K_2CO_3(\cdot 2H_2O)$	53.5
Mg^{+2}	$MgCl_2(\cdot 6H_2O)$	35.3
	$Mg(OH)_2$	Nil
	$MgCO_3$	Nil
	$MgSO_4(\cdot 7H_2O)$	26.2
Ca^{+2}	$CaCl_2(\cdot 6H_2O)$	42.7
	$Ca(OH)_2$	0.17
	$CaCO_3$	Nil
	$CaSO_4(\cdot 2H_2O)$	0.20
	$Ca_3(PO_4)_2$	Nil
Fe^{+2}	$FeCl_2(\cdot 4H_2O)$	40.8
	$Fe(OH)_2$	Nil
Fe^{+3}	$FeCl_3$	47.9
	$Fe(OH)_3$	Nil

* Infinitely soluble.

pheric pressure of 760 mm of mercury, then, the partial pressure of oxygen is 152 mm and the partial pressure of nitrogen is 608 mm. At these partial pressures, the approximate concentration of oxygen in water is about 10 mg/l and nitrogen is about 15 mg/l. Even though four times as many nitrogen molecules are bombarding the water as oxygen molecules, less than twice as many go into solution. If the total gas pressure at the water surface would double, so would the concentration of oxygen and nitrogen in the water solution. Unlike most mineral salts, which become more soluble at higher temperatures, gases decrease in solubility as the temperature rises.

ORGANIC CHEMICALS

Organic matter is a broad category that includes both natural and synthetic molecules containing carbon, and usually hydrogen. All living matter is made up of organic molecules. At one time, organic chemistry was considered to involve those carbon-containing compounds produced by living things. But most organic materials can now be made synthetically, so their relation to living things is not a necessary condition, although it is still true, of course, that life processes are involved with organic chemicals. Organics can be extremely soluble in water—as is the case with alcohol and sugar, or may be quite insoluble—as most plastics are. Even when dissolved in water at less than 1 mg/l, certain organic compounds may still cause serious physiological effects. Modern technology makes it possible to analyze such toxic organic materials as pesticides at concentrations in the part per billion (ppb) range. To put this in perspective, analyzing 1 ppb (one microgram of contaminant per liter of water) is comparable to seeing a bottle cap on the Earth's equator from an orbiting satellite.

Just as elements combine to form radicals in inorganic chemistry, so do elements combine with carbon to form functional groups with their own individual properties. The major kinds of organic functional groups and compounds of importance to the water chemist are listed in Table 3.4.

TABLE 3.4   A Summary of Important Organic Groups and Compounds

---

1. Compounds of C and H

   CH_4: methane; $CH_3—$: the methyl group

   $H_3C—CH_3$: ethane; $CH_3—CH_2—$: the ethyl group

   $H_3C—CH_2—CH_3$: propane; $CH_3—CH_2—CH_2—$: the propyl group

   $H_3C—CH_2—CH_2—CH_3$: butane, a straight chain compound, since the carbons are linear (joined in a single line).

$$CH_3$$
$$\backslash$$
   $CH_3—CH_3—CH_3$: isobutane, a branched chain compound having the same empirical formula as butane; an isomer of butane

   $CH_3—CH_2—CH_2—CH_2—CH_2—CH_3$: hexane, another saturated compound in the straight chain series. The straight chain and branched chain isomers are called aliphatic compounds.

   $H_2C=CH_2$: ethylene; an unsaturated compound, so-called because additional H could be added. The suffix "ene" and the double bond (=) in the structural formula denote unsaturation.

   $HC≡CH$: acetylene; a compound having an even greater degree of unsaturation, indicated by a triple bond (≡).

   cyclohexane, a cyclic compound, since the carbon chain forms a closed configuration.

   benzene, an unsaturated cyclic compound, also called aromatic. The structural formula is often shown as a simple hexagon.

NOTE: Formulas may be simplified by a number of shorthand notations, e.g., hexane, $CH_3(CH_2)_4CH_3$

2. Functional Groups Containing C and O

   (a) $—\overset{\overset{\textstyle O}{\|}}{C}—$: a carbonyl group present in Ketones, acids, and aldehydes

   Example: $CH_3—\overset{\overset{\textstyle O}{\|}}{C}—CH_2CH_3$ is methyl ethyl ketone

   (b) $—\overset{|}{\underset{|}{C}}—O—\overset{|}{\underset{|}{C}}—$: an ether

   Example: $CH_3—O—CH_2CH_3$ is methyl ethyl ether

   General example: $R—O—R'$, where R and R' are alkyl groups such as methyl and ethyl; or aryl groups, such as phenyl or benzyl.

3. Functional Groups Containing C, H, and O

TABLE 3.4   A Summary of Important Organic Groups and Compounds   (Continued)

(a) $\overset{\displaystyle O}{\overset{\|}{-C}}$—OH: an acid; also written—COOH, called the carboxyl group
Example: CH_3—CH_2—COOH is propionic acid

(b) $-\overset{|}{\underset{|}{C}}$—OH: an alcohol. —OH is a hydroxyl group, often identified by the suffix,
"ol"
Example 1: CH_3—OH is methyl alcohol, or methanol
Example 2: $CH_3CH_2CH_2OH$ n-propyl alcohol (or propanol) where "n" means normal, or straight chain.
$CH_3CHOHCH_3$ isopropyl alcohol where "iso" means isomer, or a compound having the same molecular weight as the normal compound but a different structure

Example 3:   is phenol, a cyclic alcohol. A simplified formula is C_6H_5OH

General Example: R—OH, where R is an alkyl group such as methyl, ethyl, etc.

NOTE: 1. The alcohol is analogous to a base in inorganic chemistry. It reacts with organic acids to form esters such as stearyl glyceride (fat), the reaction product of the alcohol glycerine with a long-chain acid, stearic acid.

2. Alcohols also react with caustic to produce alcoholates, such as CH_3—CH_2—ONa, sodium ethylate.

(c) $\overset{\displaystyle O}{\overset{\|}{-C}}$—H: an aldehyde
Example: CH_3—CH_2—CH_2—CHO butyraldehyde
General example: R—CHO

4. Functional Groups Containing C, H, and N
R, R′, and R″ represent alkyl (straight chain) and aryl (cyclic) organic groups such as methyl, ethyl, phenyl, etc.
R—NH_2: a primary amine, a basic material similar to ammonia (NH_3)
R—NH—R′: a secondary amine
$R-\overset{\displaystyle R'}{\underset{}{\overset{|}{N}}}-R''$: a tertiary amine

$\left[R-\overset{\displaystyle R'}{\underset{\displaystyle R''}{\overset{|}{\underset{|}{N}}}}-R'''\right]^{+}$—$OH^-$: a quaternary amine, a strong organic base

NOTE: being basic, amines react with inorganic acids to form amine salts and with organic acids to form amides:

$$R—NH_2 + HCl \rightarrow R—NH_2 \cdot HCl$$
$$R—NH_2 + R'COOH \rightarrow R—NH—CO—R' + H_2O$$

5. Polymers
Polymers are large molecules constructed of aggregations of individual units called monomers.
Example 1: $CH_2{=}CH_2$, ethylene monomer. These units join to form ethylene polymer:
—CH_2—CH_2—CH_2—CH_2—CH_2—CH_2 etc.

TABLE 3.4   A Summary of Important Organic Groups and Compounds (Continued)

This polymerized ethylene is called polyethylene. It is a homopolymer, because all units are the same.

Example 2: acrylamide monomer: $CH_2\!=\!CH\!-\!CONH_2$

The building unit is [$CH_2\!=\!CH$]

$$O\!=\!C\!-\!NH_2$$

which joins others to form polyacrylamide:

$-CH_2-CH---CH_2-CH---CH_2-CH-$

$O\!=\!C\!-\!NH_2 \quad O\!=\!C\!-\!N\ H_2 \quad O\!=\!C\!-\!NH_2$

This is also a homopolymer because all units are the same.

Example 3: Two different monomers may be polymerized, forming a copolymer. For example, acrylamide can be copolymerized with acrylic acid ($CH_2\!=\!CH\!-\!COOH$):

$-CH_2-CH---CH_2-CH-$

$O\!=\!C\!-\!NH_2 \qquad O\!=\!C\!-\!OH$

This is called a polyacrylate. It is an anionic polymer, since the acrylate unit is anionic in nature, with the H^+ ion being an exchangeable cation.

A great variety of monomers can be copolymerized in this fashion. By selecting monomers carefully, and combining them in the right proportions, molecular weight and strength of anionic or cationic charge in the final polymer can be controlled.

PREDICTING SOLUBILITIES

There are a few rules of thumb to use in determining the solubility of any chemical compound—inorganic or organic—in water: the salts of sodium, potassium and ammonium are highly soluble; mineral acids (H_2SO_4, HCl) are soluble; with the exception of certain heavy metal cations (Pb, Ag), most halides (Cl, Br, I) are soluble, except for fluoride; most carbonates, hydroxides, and phosphates are only slightly soluble, with the exception of those associated with Na^+, K^+, and NH_4^+. A simplified solubility chart is given in Table 3.5. Solubility data are determined only by laboratory investigation. For those materials that are very slightly soluble, which this text arbitrarily defines as being less than 2000 mg/l (the approximate solubility of $CaSO_4$), the Solubility Product is a useful tool.

The Solubility Product makes it possible to calculate the residual solubility of a chemical after chemical treatment to remove it from water by precipitation. According to the Solubility Product concept, the concentration of cations multiplied by the concentration of anions gives a product which is a constant at a given temperature. For calcium carbonate, a simple example, this expression would be:

$$[Ca^{+2}] \times [CO_3^{-2}] = K_S$$

In this example, the concentration of both the calcium and the carbonate is given in moles/liter (or moles·liter^{-1}). The Solubility Product in this case is expressed in moles^2·liters^{-2}. In a reaction where more than a single cation and anion are formed, the expression is more involved, as with magnesium hydroxide·

$$Mg(OH)_2 \leftrightharpoons Mg^{+2} + 2\ OH^- \tag{5}$$

$$K_S = [Mg^{+2}] \times [OH^-]^2$$

in which case the units are moles^3·liters^{-3}.

TABLE 3.5   Simplified Solubility Chart

Anion → ↓ Cation	F^-	Cl^-	Br^-	I^-	HCO_3^-	OH^-	NO_3^-	CO_3^{-2}	SO_4^{-2}	S^{-2}	CrO_4^{-2}	PO_4^{-3}
Na^+	S	S	S	S	S	S	S	S	S	S	S	S
K^+	S	S	S	S	S	S	S	S	S	S	S	S
NH_4^+	S	S	S	S	S	S	S	S	S	S	S	S
H^+	S	S	S	S	CO_2	H_2O	S	CO_2	S	H_2S	S	S
Ca^{+2}	I	S	S	S	SS	VSS	S	I	VSS	X	S	I
Mg^{+2}	VSS	S	S	S	S	I	S	VSS	S	X	S	I
Ba^{+2}	VSS	S	S	S	VSS	S	S	VSS	I	X	I	I
Sr^{+2}	VSS	S	S	S	VSS	SS	S	I	VSS	X	VSS	I
Zn^{+2}	S	S	S	S	VSS	I	S	I	S	I	VSS	I
Fe^{+2}	SS	S	S	S	SS	VSS	S	VSS	S	I	X	I
Fe^{+3}	SS	S	S	S	I	I	S	I	S	X	X	I
Al^{+3}	S	S	S	S	X	I	S	X	S	X	X	I
Ag^{+1}	I	I	I	I	I	I	S	VSS	S	I	I	I
Pb^{+2}	VSS	S	SS	VSS	I	VSS	S	I	I	I	I	I
Hg^{+1}	I	I	I	I	I	I	S	S	VSS	I	VSS	I
Hg^{+2}	SS	S	S	I	I	I	S	I	VSS	I	SS	I
Cu^{+2}	SS	S	S	VSS	I	I	S	I	S	I	I	I

S—Soluble, over 5000 mg/l
SS—Slightly soluble, 2000–5000 mg/l
VSS—Very slightly soluble, 20–2000 mg/l
I—Insoluble, less than 20 mg/l
X—Not a compound

In the case of $CaCO_3$, this mathematical expression is the equation for a hyperbola. The solubility of calcium carbonate is found at that point where the calcium equals the carbonate concentrations on the curve (Figure 3.3.) It will be seen, then, that to reduce the solubility of calcium in water, the introduction of extra carbonate ions—for example, by adding sodium carbonate—will reduce the calcium ions. Solubility Products of significance in water chemistry are shown in Table 3.6.

FOREIGN IONS INTERFERE

The precipitation of most inorganic solids from water is so affected by the formation of ion-pairs and complexes that the Solubility Product is of limited

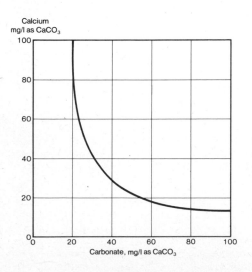

Calcium
mg/l as $CaCO_3$

Carbonate, mg/l as $CaCO_3$

Figure 3.3 Plot of calcium ions versus carbonate ions in saturated $CaCO_3$ solutions forms a hyperbola.

TABLE 3.6   Solubility Products at 25°C of Typical Hydroxides and Carbonates

Reaction	Solubility product, K_{sp}*
$Fe(OH)_2 \leftrightarrows Fe^{+2} + 2OH^-$	1×10^{-14}
$Fe(OH)_3 \leftrightarrows Fe^{+3} + 3OH^-$	2×10^{-39}
$Al(OH)_3 + 3H^+ \leftrightarrows Al^{+3} + 3H_2O$	1×10^{-9}
$ZnO + 2H \leftrightarrows Zn^{+2} + H_2O$	6.7×10^{-12}
$Mn(OH)_2 \leftrightarrows Mn^{+2} + 2OH^-$	1.6×10^{-13}
$Ca(OH)_2 \leftrightarrows Ca^{+2} + 2OH^-$	3.7×10^{-6}
$CaCO_3 \leftrightarrows Ca^{+2} + CO_3^{-2}$	5×10^{-9}
$Mg(OH)_2 \leftrightarrows Mg^{+2} + 2OH^-$	1×10^{-11}
$MgCO_3 \rightleftharpoons Mg^{+2} + CO_3^{-2}$	1×10^{-5}

From "Aquatic Chemistry," Stumm & Morgan.
* From concentrations in moles/liter.

value in predicting actual treatment results. Because of the great variety of ions in most water systems, it is seldom that a pure precipitate, such as $CaCO_3$, is formed. The inclusion of foreign ions in the precipitate and the formation of a variety of ion-pairs in the solution, in effect, increase the solubility of $CaCO_3$.

Even if pure $CaCO_3$ precipitates, it may form two kinds of crystals, calcite (the more stable) and aragonite, which have different solubilities.

Just as the water molecule can form chains (Chapter 1), so can ions associate themselves with one another. For example, calcium may be present in water as Ca^{+2}, or it may exist as $Ca(HCO_3)^+$, or $Ca(OH)^+$. Magnesium may be present, also, in a variety of ionic forms: e.g., Mg^{+2} and $MgHCO_3^+$.

The water molecule itself may take part in these reactions, usually associating with heavy metal cations in a ratio of 4:1 or 6:1. For example, iron in water may be present as $Fe(H_2O)_6^{+3}$ as well as Fe^{+3}.

In the presence of ammonia, copper is complexed, so that in addition to the presence of copper ions, Cu^{+2}, there is also present a whole family of cuprammonium complexes from $CuNH_3^{+2}$ to $Cu(NH_3)_5^{+2}$.

The presence of such ion-pairs in solution increases the solubility of the precipitated salt. Equally as complicated is the nature of the precipitate. In the softening of water with lime, the following reactions are usually expected:

$$Ca(HCO_3)_2 + Ca(OH)_2 \rightarrow 2CaCO_3\downarrow + 2H_2O \qquad (6)$$
$$Mg(HCO_3)_2 + 2Ca(OH)_2 \rightarrow Mg(OH)_2\downarrow + 2CaCO_3\downarrow + 2H_2O \qquad (7)$$

In reaction (6), the calcium may be precipitated with trace amounts of other cations, such as strontium, producing a crystalline form more soluble than calcite. The solubility of $CaCO_3$ determined for freshly precipitated material produced by reacting Na_2CO_3 with $CaSO_4$, for example, is higher than that obtained when calcite is ground and stirred into distilled water. The same effect is observed with almost all slightly soluble materials. The solubility of the precipitate may be expected to diminish with time and approach that of the pure solid as it ages and dehydrates.

In reaction (7), depending on temperature and pH, the magnesium may precipitate as a mixture of brucite [$Mg(OH)_2$], magnesite ($MgCO_3$), nesque-1 honite ($MgCO_3 \cdot 3H_2O$), or hydromagnesite [$Mg_4(CO_3)_3(OH)_2 \cdot 3H_2O$]. Each of these compounds has its own solubility.

OTHER ANOMALIES

Another factor affecting solubility is the presence of organic matter dissolved in water. It has been amply demonstrated that the residual calcium from lime softening of sewage at ambient temperatures is 2–3 times the solubility in fresh

Calcium in Solution
mg/l as CaCO₃

NaCl in solution, mg/l as CaCO₃

Figure 3.4 Calcium sulfate (gypsum) solubility increases with increasing sodium chloride.

water, presumably due to organic complexes. If the same sewage is heated over about 150°F (66°C), the reactions with lime are about the same as obtained with fresh water. Inexplicably, the same effect is not observed with magnesium precipitation.

One example of complex effects on precipitation is found in the coagulation of water with alum $[Al_2(SO_4)_3 \cdot 14H_2O]$, where the following reaction would be expected:

$$Al_2(SO_4)_3 + 6H_2O \rightarrow 2Al(OH)_3\downarrow + 3H_2SO_4 \qquad (8)$$

However, analysis of the precipitated floc will show the presence of sulfate in the solids, indicating that some SO_4^{-2} anions have replaced OH^{-1} anions in the lattice of the precipitate.

A final factor affecting solubility of these slightly soluble compounds is the so-called "ionic strength" of the aqueous solution. The higher the concentration of foreign ions not included in the precipitate, the more soluble is the precipitate. This means that $CaSO_4$, for example, is more soluble in sea water containing about 30,000 mg/l NaCl, and in oil field brines, containing up to 150,000 mg/l NaCl, than in fresh water containing 100 mg/l dissolved solids (see Figure 3.4).

The Solubility Product, then, is seen to be a useful concept when used qualitatively or developed empirically for a specific system, but of limited value when taken directly from a handbook. (In fact, such data from different handbooks frequently disagree.)

EQUILIBRIUM

Another concept closely related to the Solubility Product is the Equilibrium Constant, also called the Dissociation Constant.

Not all chemical reactions go to completion because the products of the reaction exert a restraining effect on the reactants. The chemist shows this by the following conventions:

$$2H_2 + O_2 \rightarrow 2H_2O\uparrow \qquad (9)$$

This reaction goes to completion—sometimes explosively. The yield arrow shows this reaction going in only one direction.

$$3Fe + 4H_2O \rightleftharpoons Fe_3O_4 + 4H_2\uparrow \qquad (10)$$

In this reaction, if the hydrogen generated in the process is continually removed, the reaction proceeds to the right; if the system is contained, however, an equilibrium is reached, in which case all four materials, Fe, H_2O, Fe_3O_4, and H_2, are found in the container; if extra hydrogen is then introduced into the system, the reaction will move to the left.

Such an equilibrium can be expressed mathematically. In the reaction

$$A + BC \rightleftharpoons AB + C \tag{11}$$

the equilibrium constant is given as

$$K = \frac{[AB] \times [C]}{[A] \times [BC]}$$

where the bracketed values are expressed in concentration units, usually moles per liter.

When the equilibrium is related to the ionization of an electrolyte in water, the degree of ionization can be calculated, as shown for the reactions in Table 3.7.

TABLE 3.7   Ionization of Electrolytes

Reaction	Degree of ionization*
$NaCl \rightleftharpoons Na^+ + Cl^-$	0.85
$Na_2CO_3 \rightleftharpoons 2Na^+ + CO_3^{-2}$	0.70
$HCl \rightleftharpoons H^+ + Cl^-$	0.92
$H_2CO_3 \rightleftharpoons H^+ + HCO_3^-$	0.0017
$NaOH \rightleftharpoons Na^+ + OH^-$	0.91
$NH_4OH \rightleftharpoons NH_4^+ + OH^-$	0.013

* In a 0.1 N solution at 18°C.

NOTE: From this tabulation is seen that some electrolytes are highly ionized, and are called strong salts, acids or bases; others are very slightly ionized, and are called weak electrolytes.

PRACTICAL VALUE OF EQUILIBRIUM CONSTANTS

Strong electrolytes, such as sodium chloride, completely ionize in fresh water, so that the Equilibrium Constant is of no value in calculations involving this particular salt. However, calculations involving weak electrolytes rely on the Equilibrium Constant to show the distribution of the reacting materials and products both in their ionic and non-ionized forms. This provides data useful in selecting chemical processes for removal of various contaminants from water. For example, the equilibrium constants for gases that ionize in water, such as hydrogen sulfide and ammonia, make it possible to calculate the optimum pH values for removal of these materials from water in their gaseous form. Typical dissociation constants are shown in Table 3.8.

SOLID REACTANTS

There are two distinctive mechanisms by which materials dissolved in water react with solids; these are adsorption and ion exchange.

Adsorption is the adhesion of a layer of molecules or colloidal particles to the surfaces of a solid, which is usually porous. The gas mask is a common illustration of the use of this process. The mask contains a cannister of adsorbent material, usually activated carbon, capable of removing and storing hazardous or

TABLE 3.8   Dissociation Constants of Weak Acids and Bases

Calcium hydroxide	$Ca(OH)_2$	3.74×10^{-3}
Phosphoric acid	H_3PO_4	7.5×10^{-3}
Lead hydroxide	$Pb(OH)_2$	9.6×10^{-4}
Ammonium hydroxide	NH_4OH	1.8×10^{-5}
Acetic acid	CH_3COOH	1.8×10^{-5}
Carbonic acid	H_2CO_3	4.3×10^{-7}
Hypochlorous acid	$HClO$	3.5×10^{-8}
Boric acid	H_3BO_3	5.8×10^{-10}

toxic gases so that the person wearing the mask can safely breathe even though in a contaminated atmosphere. In water systems, a similar activated carbon removes organic molecules which cause taste and odor problems.

Another example of the process is the adsorption of SiO_2, a negatively charged colloid, on freshly precipitated $Mg(OH)_2$.

The amount of adsorbent required for effective removal cannot be determined from a chemical equation. However, for any given system experimental data are easily plotted on a semi-log graph, producing a straight line—the Freudlich Isotherm, Figure 3.5.

Ion exchange is the process of removing unwanted ions from a solution in an equivalent exchange for preferred ions supplied by a solid having a special structure to do this. The solid, an ion exchange material—also called a zeolite—must be recharged periodically with the preferred ions. In this regeneration, the accumulated unwanted ions are flushed to waste.

The removal of calcium ions (hardness) by sodium zeolite, a common process, is shown by the reaction:

$$Ca^{+2} + Na_2X \rightarrow CaX + 2Na^+ \tag{12}$$

the letter X representing the cation exchange solid.

Figure 3.5 Freundlich isotherms showing adsorption effectiveness of (left) $Mg(OH)_2$ toward SiO_2 and (right) activated carbon toward organics (COD).

Many clays have ion exchange properties. This is an important aspect of soil chemistry and plant nutrition. One of these clays, clinoptilolite, is used to remove ammonia from waste water. However, most ion exchangers are synthetic organic materials formulated for specific applications.

CHELATION

A final concept of great importance to water chemistry is the process of chelation. A chelating agent is a molecule—usually organic—which is soluble in water and can undergo reactions with metal ions to hold them in solution. So chelation is analogous to ion exchange, with the difference being the solubility of the exchange material: in chelation, the exchange material is very soluble in water as a large molecule; in ion exchange, the exchange material is insoluble in water and is a large solid particle.

The chemical equation for chelation is similar to that for ion exchange. For example, a common chelant is the sodium salt of ethylene diamine tetraacetic acid (EDTA). Added to water, this chelant reacts with calcium ions to keep them in solution, preventing the formation of $CaCO_3$ scale:

$$Ca^{+2} + Na_4EDTA \rightarrow CaNa_2EDTA + 2Na^+ \tag{13}$$

NOTE: The above is an oversimplification of a complex field of chemistry—coordination chemistry. The organic portion of the EDTA compound forms bonds (ligands) with the central cation (Ca^{+2} or Mg^{+2}) other than ionic bonds, so the reaction shown is only part of the chelation process.

There are a number of natural organic materials in water which have chelating ability, such as humic acid and lignin. Because of their chelating abilities, some organic materials interfere with certain water softening processes.

Somewhat related to chelation is the process of sequestration, also called "threshold treatment." A variety of phosphate compounds called polyphosphates are used in this process to prevent formation of iron, manganese and $CaCO_3$ deposits. Condensed phosphates are produced by dehydration of one or more orthophosphate (PO_4^{-3}) compounds. If monosodium phosphate is used, the condensed product is sodium metaphosphate:

$$NaH_2PO_4 - H_2O = NaPO_3$$

With disodium phosphate, sodium pyrophosphate is formed:

$$2Na_2HPO_4 - H_2O = Na_4P_2O_7$$

The kinds of condensed phosphates formed can be varied by using different mixtures of orthophosphates. The condensed phosphates form chains containing the P—O—P group, as shown below for tripolyphosphate:

Proper selection of raw materials can produce long chains, called polyphosphates, which have strong electrostatic charges and which resist hydration (reversion) to the original orthophosphate form. The noncrystalline (glassy) phosphates with an $Na_2O : P_2O_5$ ratio of about 1.0 or slightly over are most stable and useful for threshold treatment. The most commonly used product is called hexametaphosphate $(NaPO_3)_6$.

Water containing a high concentration of calcium that is in a condition to precipitate, treated with only 0.5 mg/l of polyphosphate, can be kept from depositing $CaCO_3$ scale. The amount of polyphosphate required for effective scale control is far less than that required for softening on a stoichiometric basis, hence the name "threshold treatment." Polyphosphates can also hold Fe and Mn in solution (sequestration) in an environment where they would otherwise precipitate, e.g., in the presence of oxygen or chlorine at a pH over 8.

Other properties of polyphosphates are useful in water treatment. When $CaCO_3$ precipitates in the presence of polyphosphates, the usual calcite crystal form is distorted, and the scale structure is weak. Because they are strongly charged, polyphosphates adsorb on silt particles, and help to keep them from settling because the individual particles repel one another.

The value of polyphosphates is destroyed if they revert to orthophosphate. Solutions of glassy polyphosphates remain stable for months, but in the water system they may be reverted by low pH, high temperature, and the presence of the oxides of certain heavy metals, including iron.

SUGGESTED READING

Degering, E. F., Ed., et al.: *Organic Chemistry*. College Outline Series. Barnes & Noble, 1955.

Gelender, M., and Geffner, S. L.: *Review Text in Chemistry*. Amsco School Publications, 1964.

Moore, F. J., and Hall, W. T.: *A History of Chemistry*. McGraw-Hill, 1931.

Nalco Chemical Company: *The Chemistry of Industrial Water Treatment*. 1967.

Chapter **4**

Water Chemistry and Interpretation of Water Analyses

The common denominator of the majority of water problems is hardness. Hardness is one of the folk terms inherited from the past with origins in household use of water for washing. It was found that some waters were hard to use in doing the family laundry. More soap was needed to produce suds in these waters—so much so that many houses had a rain barrel or a cistern to collect soft rain water for washing. Indeed, this relation between hardness and suds was so fundamental that the chemist devised a standard solution of soap, which was used for many years to determine the hardness of water. Thus, tradition defines hardness as the soap-consuming capacity of water. For practical purposes, it is the calcium and magnesium content of water, although heavy metals such as iron and manganese also consume soap.

Hardness, then, is the solution in water of both calcium and magnesium as cations, independent of the nature of the anions present. It has usually been expressed in terms of calcium carbonate, $CaCO_3$. This is a fortuitous choice because the molecular weight of $CaCO_3$ is 100 and its equivalent weight is 50, providing a convenient unit of exchange for expressing all ions in water, rather than showing each with its own equivalent weight. This is comparable to having the dollar as a convenient unit of exchange in international currency rather than dealing in a mixture of marks, pounds, pesos and francs.

The water analyses used for illustration in this book are based on the calcium carbonate equivalent concept, a widely used, but not universal, form for reporting a water analysis. There are several other forms also used in the United States: (1) most analyses of the U.S. Geological Survey and other Government agencies report ions as they actually exist, usually in ppm or mg/l; (2) some chemists report ionic constituents in equivalents per million, arrived at by taking the concentration of each ion in ppm as shown in the typical USGS report, and dividing this by equivalent weight.

TABLE 4.1   Comparison of Water Analysis Report Methods—
Mississippi River at Vicksburg

Component	mg/l*	epm†	mg/l as CaCO₃‡
Calcium	46	2.30	115
Magnesium	14	1.15	57
Sodium	32	1.39	75§
Potassium	2.7	0.07	NR
Total cations	NR	4.91	247
Bicarbonate	154	2.52	126
Sulfate	67	1.40	70
Chloride	34	0.96	48
Nitrate	3.6	0.06	3
Total anions	NR	4.94	247
Total Hardness	172		
Dissolved Solids	304		
Conductance (μmhos)	483		
pH¶	7.5		
Silica (as SiO₂)	8.3		
Iron (as Fe)	0.03		
Maganese (as Mn)	0.0		
Color¶	15		

NR = Not reported.
* USGS method (Water Supply Paper 1299), originally in ppm.
† Equivalents per million; in the above example, for calcium, epm = 46/20 (equivalent weight) = 2.30.
‡ CaCO₃ equivalent form, mg/l as CaCO₃.
§ By difference.
¶ pH in pH units, color in APHA units.

Table 4.1 compares these three methods of reporting a water analysis. In column two, the sum of all the anions determined by analysis is 4.94. This slightly exceeds the total cations as determined by analysis, 4.91. Since the water must be electrically neutral, the sum of the cations should equal the sum of the anions; but it is not unusual to find a modest discrepancy, usually because some minor constituents—perhaps ammonia (a cation) in this case—haven't been reported, or because of limitations of individual ion tests.

In the ionic method of reporting results, silica, iron, and manganese are not commonly reported in ionic form. These materials are usually colloidal. Strictly speaking, in a deep well water devoid of oxygen, iron and manganese are soluble in the reduced forms (Fe^{+2} and Mn^{+2}) and should be reported as cations if their concentrations are a significant portion of the total. Silica may be an anion at concentrations over 50 mg/l.

The common convention in using the $CaCO_3$ equivalent form is to overlook the analysis of sodium and potassium and to report these ions together as sodium, determined as the difference between the sum of the total anions and the hardness of the water. This maintains the electrical neutrality of the system. (If ammonia is determined, it should be reported as the cation, and the sodium content determined by the difference reduced accordingly.)

A convenient method for converting one analytical form to another is shown in Table 4.2. In this book, concentrations will normally be expressed in mg/l.

TABLE 4.2 Calcium Carbonate (CaCO₃) Equivalent of Common Substances

	Formula	Molecular weight	Equivalent weight	Substance to CaCO$_3$ equivalent (multiply by)	CaCO$_3$ equivalent to substance (multiply by)
Compounds					
Aluminum sulfate (anhydrous)	Al$_2$(SO$_4$)$_3$	342.1	57.0	0.88	1.14
Aluminum sulfate (hydrated)	Al$_2$(SO$_4$)$_3 \cdot$14H$_2$O*	600.0	100.0	0.5	2.0
Aluminum hydroxide	Al(OH)$_3$	78.0	26.0	1.92	0.52
Aluminum oxide (Alumina)	Al$_2$O$_3$	101.9	17.0	2.94	0.34
Sodium aluminate	Na$_2$Al$_2$O$_4$	163.9	27.3	1.83	0.55
Barium sulfate	BaSO$_4$	233.4	116.7	0.43	2.33
Calcium bicarbonate	Ca(HCO$_3$)$_2$	162.1	81.1	0.62	1.62
Calcium carbonate	CaCO$_3$	100.1	50.0	1.00	1.00
Calcium chloride	CaCl$_2$	111.0	55.5	0.90	1.11
Calcium hydroxide	Ca(OH)$_2$	74.1	37.1	1.35	0.74
Calcium oxide	CaO	56.1	28.0	1.79	0.56
Calcium sulfate (anhydrous)	CaSO$_4$	136.1	68.1	0.74	1.36
Calcium sulfate (gypsum)	CaSO$_4 \cdot$2H$_2$O	172.2	86.1	0.58	1.72
Calcium phosphate	Ca$_3$(PO$_4$)$_2$	310.3	51.7	0.97	1.03
Ferric sulfate	Fe$_2$(SO$_4$)$_3$	399.9	66.7	0.75	1.33
Ferrous sulfate (anhydrous)	FeSO$_4$	151.9	76.0	0.66	1.52
Magnesium oxide	MgO	40.3	20.2	2.48	0.40
Magnesium bicarbonate	Mg(HCO$_3$)$_2$	146.3	73.2	0.68	1.46
Magnesium carbonate	MgCO$_3$	84.3	42.2	1.19	0.84
Magnesium chloride	MgCl$_2$	95.2	47.6	1.05	0.95
Magnesium hydroxide	Mg(OH)$_2$	58.3	29.2	1.71	0.58
Magnesium phosphate	Mg$_3$(PO$_4$)$_2$	262.9	43.8	1.14	0.88
Magnesium sulfate (anhydrous)	MgSO$_4$	120.4	60.2	0.83	1.20
Magnesium sulfate (Epsom Salts)	MgSO$_4 \cdot$7H$_2$O	246.5	123.3	0.41	2.47
Manganese chloride	MnCl$_2$	125.8	62.9	0.80	1.26
Manganese hydroxide	Mn(OH)$_2$	89.0	44.4	1.13	0.89
Potassium iodide	KI	166.0	166.0	0.30	3.32
Silver chloride	AgCl	143.3	143.3	0.35	2.87
Silver nitrate	AgNO$_3$	169.9	169.9	0.29	3.40
Silica	SiO$_2$	60.1	30.0	1.67	0.60
Sodium bicarbonate	NaHCO$_3$	84.0	84.0	0.60	1.68
Sodium carbonate	Na$_2$CO$_3$	106.0	53.0	0.94	1.06
Sodium chloride	NaCl	58.5	58.5	0.85	1.17
Sodium hydroxide	NaOH	40.0	40.0	1.25	0.80
Sodium nitrate	NaNO$_3$	85.0	85.0	0.59	1.70
Tri-sodium phos.	Na$_3$PO$_4 \cdot$12H$_2$O	380.2	126.7	0.40	2.53
Tri-sodium phos. (anhydrous)	Na$_3$PO$_4$	164.0	54.7	0.91	1.09
Disodium phos.	Na$_2$HPO$_4 \cdot$12H$_2$O	358.2	119.4	0.42	2.39
Disodium phos. (anhydrous)	Na$_2$HPO$_4$	142.0	47.3	1.06	0.95
Monosodium phos.	NaH$_2$PO$_4 \cdot$H$_2$O	138.1	46.0	1.09	0.92
Monosodium phos. (anhydrous)	NaH$_2$PO$_4$	120.0	40.0	1.25	0.80
Sodium metaphosphate	NaPO$_3$	102.0	34.0	1.47	0.68
Sodium sulfate	Na$_2$SO$_4$	142.1	71.0	0.70	1.42
Sodium sulfite	Na$_2$SO$_2$	126.1	63.0	0.79	1.26
Positive Ions					
Aluminum	Al^{+3}	27.0	9.0	5.56	0.18
Ammonium	NH$_4{}^+$	18.0	18.0	2.78	0.36

TABLE 4.2   Calcium Carbonate (CaCO₃) Equivalent of Common Substances   *(Continued)*

	Formula	Molecular weight	Equivalent weight	Substance to $CaCO_3$ equivalent (multiply by)	$CaCO_3$ equivalent to substance (multiply by)
Barium	Ba^{+2}	137.4	68.7	0.73	1.37
Calcium	Ca^{+2}	40.1	20.0	2.50	0.40
Copper	Cu^{+2}	63.6	31.8	1.57	0.64
Hydrogen	H^+	1.0	1.0	50.0	0.02
Ferric iron	Fe^{+3}	55.8	18.6	2.69	0.37
Ferrous iron	Fe^{+2}	55.8	27.9	1.79	0.56
Magnesium	Mg^{+2}	24.3	12.2	4.10	0.24
Manganese	Mn^{+2}	54.9	27.5	1.82	0.55
Potassium	K^+	39.1	39.1	1.28	0.78
Sodium	Na^+	23.0	23.0	2.18	0.46
Strontium	Sr^{+2}	87.6	43.8	1.14	0.88
Zinc	Zn^{+2}	65.4	32.7	1.53	0.65
Negative Ions					
Bicarbonate	HCO_3^-	61.0	61.0	0.82	1.22
Carbonate	CO_3^{-2}	60.0	30.0	1.67	0.60
Chloride	Cl^-	35.5	35.5	1.41	0.71
Chromate	CrO_4^{-2}	116.0	58.0	0.86	1.16
Fluoride	F^-	19.0	19.0	2.63	0.38
Iodide	I^-	126.9	126.9	0.39	2.54
Hydroxyl	OH^-	17.0	17.0	2.94	0.34
Nitrate	NO_3^-	62.0	62.0	0.81	1.24
Phosphate (tribasic)	PO_4^{-3}	95.0	31.7	1.58	0.63
Phosphate (dibasic)	HPO_4^{-2}	96.0	48.0	1.04	0.96
Phosphate (monobasic)	$H_2PO_4^-$	97.0	97.0	0.52	1.94
Sulfate	SO_4^{-2}	96.1	48.0	1.04	0.96
Bisulfate	HSO_4^-	97.1	97.1	0.52	1.94
Sulfite	SO_3^{-2}	80.1	40.0	1.25	0.80
Bisulfite	HSO_3^-	81.1	81.1	0.62	1.62
Sulfide	S^{-2}	32.1	16.0	3.13	0.32

* Empirical formula of commercial alum.

WASTE WATER ANALYSES

Waste waters usually contain a number of ions that may not be shown in this illustration. Composition depends on the kind of plant operations through which the water has passed before becoming waste. For example, heavy metals such as zinc and copper may be present in the waste from plating operations; chromate may be present as an anion in the blowdown from evaporative cooling systems: fluoride may be present as an anion or an anionic complex in waste water from glass manufacturing.

Probably the most fundamental concept in the approach to understanding water chemistry is the acidity-alkalinity relationship. The first step in grasping this is an understanding of the dissociation of the water molecule itself into hydrogen ions and hydroxyl ions, according to equation:

$$H_2O \rightleftharpoons H^+ + OH^- \tag{1}$$
$$K = [H^+] \times [OH^-] = 10^{-14}$$

(For the sake of simplicity, this book will use the hydrogen ion, H^+, while recognizing that it actually exists in a hydrated form, the hydronium ion—H_3O^+.)

The pH Notation

Since the dissociation constant is so very small, 10^{-14}, at neutrality where there are the same number of hydrogen and hydroxyl ions there are only 10^{-7} moles per liter of each. This is equal to only 10^{-4} millimoles per liter, corresponding to an actual concentration of only 0.0001 mg/l H^+ ion, equivalent to 0.005 mg/l as $CaCO_3$. Because we are dealing with such small numbers in the dissociation of water into its ions, it is more convenient to substitute an expression involving the power of 10. This expression is defined as pH, in which the relationship is:

$$pH = \log \frac{1}{[H^+]} = -\log [H^+]$$

The dissociation constant, K, changes with temperature, and this must be taken into account in interpreting data involving H^+ and OH^- ions. For example, many water treatment operations are carried out at high temperatures, and samples from the system are usually cooled prior to analysis. The H^+ and OH^- concentrations measured on the cooled sample, even though different from those in the hot system, are usually used for control purposes. But a physical chemist needing to know the conditions prevailing in the hot system must use the dissociation constant for the temperature in that system.

The hydrogen ion concentration can be measured with a pH meter. It can also be titrated (see glossary) when the concentration becomes large enough to be detectable by chemical analysis. Since pH is a logarithmic function, the hydrogen ion concentration increases by a factor of 10 for each unit of pH reduction.

When the pH drops below approximately 5, the hydrogen ion begins to reach mg/l levels, concentrated enough to be determined by titration, using the correct organic dye indicator. The chemical indicator originally selected by the water chemist for this purpose was methyl orange, changing color at pH 4.2–4.4. The color change of this indicator was so subtle—orange on the alkaline side to salmon pink on the acid side—that researchers looked for a substitute to give a more pronounced color change. The one they developed produces a blue color on the alkaline side and red on the acid side, with gray at the endpoint. Even though this special indicator has replaced methyl orange, the water chemist still defines alkalinity as methyl orange alkalinity ("M" alkalinity) which exists above the approximate pH range of 4.2–4.4. "M" *acidity* is strong mineral acidity which exists below this pH range. An approximate relationship between pH value and mineral acidity is shown in Table 4.3.

The measure of pH, then, by a pH meter (or by a suitable colorimetric comparator) can be very valuable in determining the hydrogen and hydroxyl ion concentrations in the pH range above 4.2–4.4. It can also be used below this pH in the absence of reagents for performing an actual acidity titration.

USE OF METER FOR [OH⁻]

Because the dissociation constant of water is approximately 10^{-14}, and pH has been defined as $-\log [H^+]$, the hydroxyl ion concentration can also be determined by a pH meter since the following relationships hold:

$$pOH = 14 - pH$$
$$pOH = \log \frac{1}{[OH^-]}$$

TABLE 4.3   Mineral Acidity* vs. pH

H^+, mg/l as $CaCO_3$	pH
2–3	4.3
4–5	4.0
6–7	3.9
8–9	3.8
10–11	3.7
12–13	3.6
14–16	3.5
17–20	3.4
21–25	3.3
26–30	3.2
31–40	3.1
41–50	3.0

* Mineral acidity is the presence of H^+ ion in mg/l concentrations.

As the pH of a water is increased and exceeds about 9.6–9.8, a measurable concentration of hydroxyl ions begins to appear. The hydroxyl alkalinity (caustic or OH alkalinity) can be determined either by using a pH meter (or the equivalent in a colorimetric comparator) or by titration. The relationship between hydroxyl alkalinity and pH is shown in Table 4.4.

An understanding of these concepts is necessary to put these acidity-alkalinity relationships into perspective. To the theoretical chemist, a pH of 7 is considered neutral; to the water chemist, a pH of 7 in itself means very little. He must also know how much total alkalinity and how much free or combined CO_2 may be present. For the water chemist, then, the dividing point between acidity and alkalinity is not pH 7.0, but rather the "M" alkalinity endpoint, corresponding to a pH of approximately 4.4.

The water chemist is also concerned with "P" alkalinity (phenolphthalein alkalinity) which exists when the pH is over a range of 8.2–8.4, corresponding to the change in phenolphthalein indicator from a colorless condition below 8.2 to pink or red above 8.4. In most natural water supplies, the pH is less than 8.2, so there is no "P" alkalinity. Very few natural waters have a pH below about 5.0, so it is seldom that strong mineral acids are found in fresh water. The pH range between the "M" endpoint and the "P" endpoint defines the alkaline

TABLE 4.4   Caustic Alkalinity vs. pH

OH, mg/l as $CaCO_3$	pH
2–3	9.7
4–5	10.0
6–7	10.1
8–9	10.2
10–11	10.3
12–13	10.4
14–16	10.5
17–20	10.6
21–25	10.7
26–30	10.8
31–40	10.9
41–50	11.0

range where bicarbonate alkalinity exists and weak acids may be present, the most prominent of which is carbonic acid—carbon dioxide in solution.

THE IMPORTANCE OF CO$_2$

The atmosphere is a mixture of gases containing about 79% N_2 and 21% O_2 by volume. However, it also includes 0.04% CO_2, extremely important to the balance of life on the planet. Carbon dioxide is produced by the combustion of fuel. Even before man's activities made a significant contribution to the CO_2 content of the atmosphere, the respiration of animal life—which is also a fuel consuming process—introduced CO_2 into the air. Plants containing chlorophyll utilize carbon dioxide in building cellular material such as carbohydrates. This reaction is called photosynthesis because photons of energy from the sun are needed for the reaction.

$$6CO_2 + 6H_2O \xrightarrow{\text{chlorophyll}} (CH_2O)_6 + 6O_2 \tag{2}$$
$$\text{or} \quad C_6H_{12}O_6 \text{ (glucose)} + 6O_2$$

The chlorophyll catalyzes the reaction between water and CO_2. Since the solubility of CO_2 in water is less than 2000 mg/l at ambient air temperatures in a CO_2-saturated atmosphere, at the normal atmospheric level of 0.04% CO_2 less than 1 mg/l CO_2 dissolves in rain water. However, once the rain water penetrates the mantle of soil, it is exposed to CO_2 gas levels a hundredfold greater than in the atmosphere, created by the respiration of soil organisms as they convert organic food into its products of combustion. Well waters, then, which have percolated through this CO_2-rich zone may contain from ten to several hundred mg/l dissolved CO_2.

When CO_2 dissolves in water, it reacts with water to form carbonic acid, which dissociates into the hydrogen ion and the bicarbonate ion according to the reaction:

$$CO_2 + H_2O \;\rightleftharpoons\; H_2CO_3 \;\rightleftharpoons\; H^+ + HCO_3^- \tag{3}$$

If distilled water is completely saturated with CO_2, approximately 1600 mg/l dissolve in the water, and the pH is decreased to approximately 4. The equivalent amount of a strong acid like H_2SO_4 would decrease the pH to about 2.5, illustrating the weak character of carbonic acid.

THE SOURCE OF ALKALINITY

The alkalinity of most natural water supplies is caused by dissolved bicarbonate (HCO_3^-) salts. The following equations show how water containing CO_2 from the atmosphere and from respiration of soil organisms dissolves magnesium and calcium from a common mineral, dolomite ($CaCO_3 \cdot MgCO_3$) to produce hardness and alkalinity in ground water:

$$H_2O + CO_2 + MgCO_3 \;\rightarrow\; Mg(HCO_3)_2 \;\rightleftharpoons\; Mg^{+2} + 2(HCO_3^-) \tag{4}$$
$$H_2O + CO_2 + CaCO_3 \;\rightarrow\; Ca(HCO_3)_2 \;\rightleftharpoons\; Ca^{+2} + 2(HCO_3^-) \tag{5}$$

In the pH range of 4.4–8.2, there remains a balance between excess CO_2 and bicarbonate ions which is measured by pH value as shown in Figure 4.1.

This shows that a water containing 1 mg/l CO_2 and 10 mg/l alkalinity has the same pH as one containing 10 mg/l CO_2 and 100 mg/l alkalinity. In the first case, the addition of 1 mg/l CO_2 would produce a large change in pH, whereas in the second case, the same 1 mg/l CO_2 addition would not produce a noticeable

Figure 4.1 Approximate relationship of carbon dioxide, alkalinity, and pH value.

change. The alkalinity moderates or "buffers" the pH change, and alkalinity is known as a buffer.

Water attacks and dissolves many other minerals from the lithosphere in addition to dolomite. Figure 4.2 shows the distribution of the elements in the Earth's crust. The three most prominent are present in the form of oxides, SiO_2, Al_2O_3 and Fe_2O_3, which are only very slightly soluble in water. The next most common elements, calcium, sodium, potassium, and magnesium, are seen to be the most prominent cations present in most fresh water supplies, as illustrated by the several water analyses included in this and earlier chapters.

$CO_3^=/HCO_3^-$ DISTRIBUTION

Most natural waters contain bicarbonate alkalinity and are at a pH less than about 8.2–8.4. Above this pH, CO_2 ceases to exist in measurable quantities, and the carbonate ion begins to make itself known. The equilibrium reaction is as follows:

$$HCO_3^- \quad \rightleftharpoons \quad CO_3^{-2} + H^+ \tag{6}$$

Figure 4.2 Distribution of elements in the earth's crust.

Figure 4.3 Variation of the carbonate/bicarbonate ion distribution with pH.

Many lime-treated waters have a pH above the phenolphthalein endpoint—that is, they contain "P" alkalinity. In the range of pH 8.2–9.6, the bicarbonate and carbonate ions exist together in the absence of measurable carbon dioxide or hydroxyl ions. The distribution between the carbonate and bicarbonate ions can be determined approximately by the relationships shown in Figure 4.3. They can also be calculated after measuring "P" and "M" alkalinities according to the following equations.

$$CO_3 = 2 \times P$$
$$HCO_3 = M - CO_3 = M - 2P$$

The distribution of all forms of CO_2-related ions is shown by Figure 4.4. In this figure, free CO_2 is CO_2 gas; HCO_3^- is referred to as halfbound CO_2, and $CO_3^=$ as bound CO_2.

Figure 4.4 Effect of changing pH on distribution of different CO_2 related ions in solution.

a = $CO_3^=$, or bound CO_2
b = HCO_3^-, or half-bound CO_2
c = H_2CO_3, or CO_2 gas

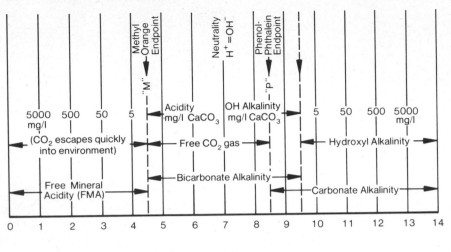

Figure 4.5 Acidity and various types of alkalinity and their pH ranges.

As the pH increases above 9.6, the hydroxyl alkalinity becomes measurable. Its concentration can be determined by pH meter, as shown in Table 4.4, or the distribution between carbonate and hydroxyl can be calculated as follows:

$$CO_3 = 2(M - P)$$
$$OH^- = 2P - M$$
$$HCO_3^- = O$$

These are very useful approximations for interpreting most water analyses. The various regimes of acidity and alkalinity are illustrated by Figure 4.5.

Figure 4.6 Neutralization of alkaline water with H_2SO_4 (assume 50 mg/l "M" alkalinity).

Calcium
mg/l as CaCO₃

Cold Water
@ 50-70°F (10 -21°C)

Hot Water @220°F (104°C)

Carbonate, mg/l as CaCO₃

Figure 4.7 CaCO₃ solubility in hot and cold systems—empirical data based on 60–90 minutes reaction time and settling time.

INTERFERING IONS

These approximations are subject to some interferences, especially in contaminated waters. Common interferences are ammonia, and alkaline anions other than carbonate and bicarbonate, such as sulfide, phosphate, and borate.

These P and M relationships have a long history of use in water treatment. Most plant data relating to results of lime softening, for example, are based on these convenient calculations. They trace their history to titration curves of Na_2CO_3 and NaOH added to water and neutralized with acid, Figure 4.6.

These relationships are not consistent, however, with the theoretical distribution between HCO_3^{-1} and CO_3^{-2} based on dissociation constants. The theoretical distribution between these ions, Figure 4.4, indicates that at a pH as high as 10.3, for example, where OH^- alkalinity is about 10 mg/l as $CaCO_3$, there are equal quantities of HCO_3^{-1} and CO_3^{-2} present.

Although inconsistent with this physical chemistry theory, in dealing with results of lime softening where pH exceeds 10 and alkalinity is less than 50 mg/l, this book uses the P and M relationships as a convenience and because so much field data have been developed from them. This practice tends to overstate carbonate alkalinity because it indicates no HCO_3^{-1} alkalinity exists in the presence of OH^{-1}. For example, at M = 50 mg/l and P = 25 mg/l, CO_3^{-2} = 50 mg/l at pH 9.8 (Figure 4.3); however, Figure 4.4 shows CO_3^{-2} to be only 25% of total alkalinity, or 12.5 mg/l at pH 9.8. This accounts for part of the discrepancy observed between theoretical $CaCO_3$ solubility and that actually achieved in practice by lime softening where the results are interpreted from the P and M relationships.

Examination of these acidity-alkalinity relationships in water reveals that the solubility of minerals such as calcium carbonate and magnesium hydroxide is more complicated to predict than the solubility product concept suggests. For example, in the case of calcium precipitating from water as calcium carbonate, it is now apparent that there are numerous equilibrium reactions occurring in the water, affecting the interpretation of simple chemical data. For that reason, water chemists usually rely on empirical data based on reported plant experiences to estimate results of a precipitation reaction.

Figure 4.7 shows data generally used for predicting calcium carbonate solubility, specifically related to precipitation in a lime-softening operation. The

Figure 4.8 Cold lime softening of sewage (upper two curves) compared to noncontaminated water.

difference in results between hot process (above approximately 212°F (100°C) and cold process (river water temperatures) is considerably beyond what would be predicted by simple solubility data which show a decrease of only about 2 mg/l solubility at the higher temperature. The empirical temperature effect must be caused by other factors such as rate of reaction (which, as a rule of thumb, doubles for each 18°F (10°C) temperature increase), the nature of the crystalline or amorphous precipitate, and the possible effect of coagulating organic materials at higher temperature.

As an example of this, in cold lime softening of municipal sewage, residual calcium carbonate is invariably higher than when the same process is used in the treatment of fresh water. This is illustrated in Figure 4.8. If, however, the sewage is heated above approximately 160°F (71°C), then results approach those achieved in fresh water.

EFFECTS OF IMPURITIES

If magnesium is precipitated with calcium carbonate, the residual calcium in solution may be increased. The inclusion of other impurities, such as strontium, has also been shown to increase the solubility of calcium carbonate. It would seem, then, that empirical data from a variety of plants should be used cautiously in estimating what to expect in a given situation; if the calculation involves lime treatment of an unknown water supply and the contamination levels are not fully defined, there is no substitute for an actual bench test to determine the response of that water to lime treatment.

Magnesium solubility is as difficult to predict with accuracy as calcium solubility, and for the same general reasons. The solubility of magnesium hydroxide is reported to be in the range of 30–40 mg/l at 77°F (25°C). Because of the difference in solubility product relationships,

$$K_{Ca} = [Ca^{+2}] \times [CO_3^{-2}] \qquad K_{Mg} = [Mg^{+2}] \times [OH^-]^2$$

magnesium concentration is affected more by changes in hydroxyl concentration than calcium is by changes in carbonate concentration. Any increase in carbonate produces a corresponding decrease in calcium, but an increase in hydroxyl concentration affects the magnesium concentration in a squared relationship. Thus a doubling of OH^- will cause Mg^{+2} to drop to one-fourth its original value.

When water is softened with lime—in the pH range of 9.5–10.5—magnesium precipitates as the hydroxide and the precipitate is positively charged. In the same pH range, $CaCO_3$ precipitate is negatively charged. Furthermore, silica in the system is usually present as a strong, negatively-charged colloid. Sodium aluminate may be introduced in the system as a strong anionic complex. All of this may account for the co-precipitation of magnesium with calcium, the strong adsorption of silica on $Mg(OH)_2$ precipitate, and the low residual magnesium often achieved by the treatment of water with sodium aluminate in addition to lime.

In conventional softening operations, then, it is usual to show that lime treatment of fresh water produces a $CaCO_3$ solubility of approximately 35 mg/l cold and 25 mg/l hot, and a residual magnesium hydroxide solubility of approximately 35 mg/l cold and 2–3 mg/l hot.

Calcium carbonate and magnesium hydroxide are precipitated in the lime softening operation; however, these can also precipitate from the unstable water—that is, a water containing these materials in a supersaturated condition—if anything is done to the system to upset the equilibrium. This could be an increase in temperature, a decrease in pressure, turbulence, or contact with surfaces which seed the chemical precipitation. The most common product of instability of fresh water is $CaCO_3$; in sea water the usual precipitate is $Mg(OH)_2$ or one of its complex carbonate hydroxide salts.

THE MARBLE TEST

A water can be be evaluated for its $CaCO_3$ stability by testing or by theoretical calculation from known data. The Marble Test, although infrequently used for control purposes, is a valuable test to illustrate the principles of calcium carbonate stability. If an unstable water is supersaturated, then the addition of finely-powdered marble ($CaCO_3$) to a sample of the water should cause calcium carbonate to precipitate and coat the marble. The effect is measured by a reduction in both the hardness and alkalinity of the water, measured after the suspension has settled and the water has been filtered. There is also a decrease in pH of the marble-contacted water, which is said to have a positive saturation index.

On the other hand, if the water sample is undersaturated with respect to $CaCO_3$—that is, if it is an aggressive, corrosive water—then some of the fine marble added to the sample dissolves, increasing the hardness, alkalinity and pH. This water is said to have a negative saturation index.

Working with the $CaCO_3$ equilibrium values, incorporating the dissociation factors for carbonic acid, bicarbonate and carbonate, and based on the theoretical solubility of $CaCO_3$ at different temperatures, as affected by water salinity, Langelier developed a method for predicting the saturation pH (called pH_s) of any water. If the actual pH of the water is below the calculated level (pH_s), the water has a negative Langelier Index and will dissolve $CaCO_3$. This is generally also interpreted to indicate that the water may be corrosive to steel if oxygen is present. If the measured pH exceeds pH_s, the Langelier Index is positive, and being supersaturated with $CaCO_3$, the water is likely to form scale. The greater the deviation of actual pH from pH_s, the more pronounced is the instability. The saturation pH_s and the Langelier Index can be determined from a water analysis by reference to Figure 4.9.

$$\text{Langelier Index} = pH - pH_s$$

Ca Hardness, mg/l as CaCO₃ · · · · · · · · · · pH Value at Saturation (pHₛ)

EXAMPLE:
Raw Water Calcium	= 240 mg/l
Alkalinity	= 190 mg/l
pH	= 6.8
Temperature	= 70°F
From Chart: pHₛ	= 7.3
Langelier Index	= 6.8 − 7.3 = −0.5

Figure 4.9 Determination of pH_s and Langelier Index from hardness, alkalinity, and temperature.

THE RYZNAR INDEX

Based on studies of reported conditions of scaling and corrosion in a variety of municipal systems, Ryznar modified the Langelier Index to more reliably predict the likelihood of scale forming or corrosion occurring, based on pH and pH_s, using his Stability Index.

$$\text{Stability Index (SI)} = 2pH_s - pH$$

In using this index, a water is considered to be corrosive when the Stability Index exceeds approximately 6.0 and to be scale-forming when the index is less than 6.0.

The Langelier Index has been modified by Stiff and Davis for oil field brines, where the high salinity affects ionic strength and influences $CaCO_3$ solubility. This Index is:

$$\text{SDI} = pH - pCa - pAlk - K$$

where pH is used as measured,

$$pCa = \log 1/[Ca]$$
$$pAlk = \log 1/[Alk]$$
$$K = \text{constant based on total ionic strength and temperature}$$

TABLE 4.5   Calculation of Total Ionic Strength

1. Calculate all ions in mg/l as $CaCO_3$.
2. Multiply monovalent ions by 1×10^{-5}, and divalent ions by 2×10^{-5}.
3. Add the sum of factored ions to determine total ionic strength, μ
   (all ions in mg/l as $CaCO_3$) Example:

Ca	900	$\times (2 \times 10^{-5}) =$	1800×10^{-5}
Mg	1200	$\times (2 \times 10^{-5}) =$	2400×10^{-5}
Na	18,500	$\times (1 \times 10^{-5}) =$	$18,500 \times 10^{-5}$
TE	20,600 (total electrolytes)		
HCO_3	500	$\times (1 \times 10^{-5}) =$	500×10^{-5}
SO_4	800	$\times (2 \times 10^{-5}) =$	1600×10^{-5}
Cl	19,300	$\times (1 \times 10^{-5}) =$	$19,300 \times 10^{-5}$

Ionic strength, $\mu = 44,100 \times 10^{-5} = 0.44$

Ionic strength of the solution is calculated as in Table 4.5; K is then calculated from temperature using Figure 4.10; pCa and pAlk are obtained by reference to Figure 4.11.

Such data developed for oil field brine may become useful in wastewater applications such as treatment of open recirculating cooling water systems for zero discharge. Similar indexes have been developed for other commonly-occurring minerals depositing in distribution systems and heat exchangers. Notable among these indexes are those for calcium phosphate and magnesium hydroxide. These are of much more limited value to the water chemist than the Langelier Index or the Ryznar Index, chiefly because of the variety of complexes which form and the different solubility values for each of the complexes involved in the system.

The effect of ionic strength is very pronounced in the illustration of $CaSO_4$ solubility in a concentrating recirculating cooling water, shown in Figure 4.12. The predicted solubility of Ca with increasing SO_4 concentration is shown by curve A; actually, the Ca concentration reaches a minimum of about 900 mg/l as $CaCO_3$ which is maintained even at SO_4 concentrations in excess of 25,000 mg/l.

Figure 4.10   Ionic strength vs. Stiff-Davis Index constant at different temperatures.

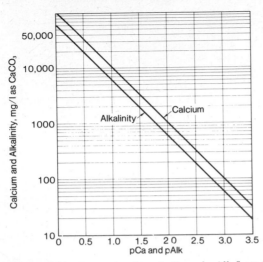

Figure 4.11   Determination of pCa and pAlk from concentrations.

DISSOLVED GASES

Further consideration of the Langelier Index provides instruction on the nature and effects of gases dissolved in water. Carbon dioxide, for example, dissolves to form carbonic acid, which ionizes to produce H^+ and HCO_3^- ions. Other ionizing gases include sulfur dioxide, hydrogen sulfide, and hydrocyanic acid, which form weak acids when dissolved in water. Because of this effect, the addition of a strong acid to water containing these gases will force the equilibrium to the left, essentially eliminating the ionized portion so that all of the gas is in molecular form and free to escape from the water as gas molecules. For example, with CO_2:

$$CO_2 + H_2O \rightleftharpoons H_2CO_8 \rightleftharpoons H^+ + HCO_3 \tag{7}$$

The addition of H^+ ions by addition of H_2SO_4 would force the reaction to the left.

Figure 4.12 Effect of ionic strength solubility of $CaSO_4$ in a recirculating cooling water.

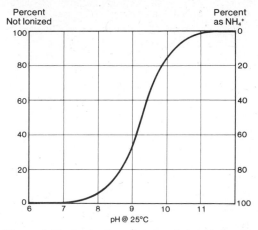

Figure 4.13 Ionization of ammonia in solution as a function of pH.

On the other end of the scale is ammonia, which dissolves and ionizes to form a weak base according to the equation:

$$NH_3 + H_2O \rightleftharpoons NH_4OH \rightleftharpoons NH_4^+ + OH^- \tag{8}$$

As opposed to acidic gases, which are converted to the molecular form by the addition of a strong acid, in this case the addition of a strong alkali, such as sodium hydroxide, will force the reaction to the left and produce molecular ammonia which is then free to escape as a gas molecule (Figure 4.13).

There are other gases that dissolve in water, but do not ionize. Among these are oxygen, nitrogen and methane. The most prominent of these in its effect on water systems is oxygen. If a water has a negative Langelier Index (a positive Stability Index) it is considered aggressive and corrosion is expected. This corrosion, however, is usually caused by dissolved oxygen which is free to attack the bare metal surface when it is wetted by a water which cannot form a protective calcium carbonate film or scale. An example of this is condensate in a steam plant: in a tight system free of oxygen, plain carbon steel piping is successfully used to handle this condensate without undue corrosion problems; if oxygen finds its way into the system through valve or pump leaks, the condensate becomes extremely aggressive and corrosion occurs, unless the metal can be protected by a film-forming corrosion inhibitor.

MINERALS AND CONDUCTANCE

An important consideration in water chemistry is electrical conductivity. The higher the mineral content of the water, the higher its conductivity. This has several important consequences. First, the higher the conductivity, the more freely can electrical current flow through the water, and the more rapid is the corrosion rate if other conditions favor corrosion. Second, the higher the conductivity, the less completely ionized are the minerals dissolved in the water as the ions are packed more closely together and collide more frequently. This decreases the activity coefficient, or freedom, increasing the solubility of $CaCO_3$ and other slightly soluble materials. As a result, $CaCO_3$ is more soluble in sea water than in fresh water under equal conditions of pH, alkalinity, and temperature, as explained in the earlier discussion of the Stiff-Davis Stability Index.

Figure 4.14 Volumetric determination of settleable solids in Imhoff cones.

There are many factors involved in the corrosion process, of which pH, conductivity, temperature, and dissolved oxygen are usually foremost. Other important factors in the corrosion mechanism include the presence of dissimilar metals in the system, with the more anodic becoming corroded, and dissimilarities in the metallurgical structure of a single metal in the system. An example of this is zinc in brass, whereby one portion of the metal surface, the zinc crystals, become anodic relative to an adjoining cathodic portion, the copper.

All of these corrosion mechanisms may be magnified by the presence of suspended matter, particularly if velocities are low and the material deposits to form a concentration cell, or the velocities are exceedingly high and a combination of erosion and corrosion magnifies the individual effects of each to produce a very rapid rate of attack.

SOLID MATTER

Solid matter occurs in most waters as suspended solids and colloidal matter. The concentration of suspended solids is determined by filtration, the collected solids on the filter membrane being dried and weighed. Those suspended solids which are large and heavy are called settleable solids, and these may be determined volumetrically in a settling cone as a simple control test (Figure 4.14), or weighed. The solids remaining with supernatant water above the settled matter are fine, and are called turbidity.

Turbidity in water is measured by the effect of the fine suspended particles on a light beam (Figure 4.15). Light-interference analytical methods are classified as nephelometric, and one system of turbidity measurement uses *nephelometric turbidity units* (NTU). The original nephelometric method used a standardized candle, providing results in Jackson Turbidity Units (JTU), named for the man who developed the standard candle. Turbidity standards prepared with formazin for comparator tube determinations have given rise to a third turbidity unit, the FTU.

The JTU is measured with a transmitted light beam, while the NTU is measured by light scattering, so there is no comparison between the two units that applies to all waters. In the case of turbidity standards prepared from 325 mesh diatomaceous earth, a reading of 100 NTU is equivalent to about 40 JTU.

Colloidal matter in water is sometimes beneficial and sometimes harmful. Beneficial colloids are those that provide a dispersant effect by acting as protective colloids. In a suspension of clay or silt in water, the smallest particles usually carry a negative charge. If these negative charges are neutralized, the particles are coagulated; however, if additional negative charges are introduced into the system deliberately, sedimentation may be prevented. Sodium silicate probably works in this way; so too do some kinds of organic materials in water, such as lignins and tannins which occur in highly-colored water sources. Silica in itself can be troublesome, forming a very hard scale when it deposits on heat transfer surfaces. So adsorbents are used for the removal of these colloidal materials from water when they exceed acceptable concentration limits. Many of the heavy metals are present in colloidal form and are removed from water by coagulation, filtration, adsorption, or a combination of these.

MANY ORGANICS SOLUBLE

While tannin and lignin are generally present as colloidal suspensions in water, many organic compounds are actually soluble in water. There is an astounding variety of organic compounds in water, put there both by nature and man. It is unusual for a water analysis to show all of this organic matter broken down by individual molecular constituents, because of the great variety. If the analyst should know what may be present (for example, alkyl-benzyl sulfonate detergent, ABS) he can find it; but in the absence of this kind of information he must rely on a battery of non-specific tests. Those tests shown in Table 4.6 are evidence of carbonaceous materials, but cannot distinguish between them. They are reasonably simple, inexpensive control methods. Interpretation is usually difficult; it is not at all unusual to find an increase in one test, such as BOD, with a concurrent decrease in another test, such as TOC.

Figure 4.16 shows the diversity of change in color, TOC, and BOD in the Hackensack River. Variations in color, LOI and COD for the Hudson River are shown in Figure 4.17. Finally, Table 4.7 shows an increase in BOD with a decrease in COD along the Connecticut River at progressive downstream sampling stations.

A great deal of experience is required, involving collection of considerable data for analysis, to decide on the significant tests for organic matter for a given water treatment control application. Some help can be gained in recognizing that the COD test itself involves a powerful oxidizing agent, chromic acid; therefore, the test is comparable to combustion of the organic matter in an

Figure 4.15 Turbidity in this water scatters Tyndall beam as it passes through cell.

TABLE 4.6   Organic Matter in Water, Nonspecific Tests

Test	Description
BOD	**Biochemical oxygen demand.** Measures the ability of common bacteria to digest organic matter, usually in a 5-day incubation at 20°C, by analyzing depletion of oxygen. This measures biodegradable organic matter. Expressed as O_2.
CCE	**Carbon-chloroform extract.** Organics adsorbed on an activated carbon cartridge are extracted from the carbon by chloroform. The extract is weighed or further analyzed.
CAE	**Carbon-alcohol extract.** Organics adsorbed on an activated carbon cartridge are extracted from the carbon by ethyl-alcohol. (This is performed after the chloroform extraction of the same column.)
COD	**Chemical oxygen demand.** Measures the ability of hot chromic acid solution to oxidize organic matter. This analyzes both biodegradable and non-biodegradable (refractory) organic matter. Expressed as O_2.
Color	**Color.** This is a rough measure of tannin, lignin and other humic matter in surface waters and certain wastes, such as kraft pulping wastes. Reported in APHA units, related to platinum standard.
IDOD	**Immediate dissolved oxygen demand.** Measures the presence of strong reducing matter in wastes which would have an immediate effect in reducing the oxygen level of receiving streams. Determined by measuring reduction in oxygen 15 minutes after dilution of sample with an O_2-saturated water. Expressed as O_2.
LOI	**Loss on ignition.** In this determination, the water sample is first evaporated to dryness, then weighed. The solids are then heated to a dull red heat and reweighed. The difference in the two weights is loss on ignition. The firing step burns off organic matter, but it also affects mineral composition, as in the breakdown of carbonates to oxides, so the loss is not all organic.
O_2 Consumed	**Oxygen consumed from permanganate.** Measures the susceptibility of organic matter in sample to oxidation by $KMnO_4$. Not as strongly oxidizing as chromic acid. Preceded the COD test and still a useful control test. Reported as O_2.
Solvent Extractables	**Extractables.** Measures the organic matter directly extractable from water, usually using hexane, although CCl_4 and $CHCl_3$ are also used.
TOC	**Total organic carbon.** Measures the CO_2 produced from organics when a water sample is atomized into a combustion chamber. The CO_2 equivalent to the alkalinity may be removed first, or this equivalent may be subtracted from the total CO_2 to determine organic carbon. Reported as C.

TABLE 4.7   Connecticut River Organic Matter
(USGS Paper 2151)

Station	COD	BOD	Other
Wilder, Vt. (9/1/70)	19	0.8	Color—32
Northfield (9/1/70)	15	1.4	Color—12
Thompsonville (9/1/70)	9	2.8	LOI—19

Figure 4.16 Variation of color, TOC, and BOD in the Hackensack River.

aqueous medium. On this basis, some theoretical relationships between the several organic indexes can be drawn, as shown in Table 4.8.

Finding a specific organic molecular species in water usually requires sophisticated procedures and equipment and is generally too expensive to be justified as a routine control; it may be done only for specific purposes where toxic materials may be suspected and the analysis is essential for environmental control purposes. Even in this case, the analysis is usually performed on a daily composite, hourly grab sample or other scheduled samples, since continuous analysis is seldom practical.

Figure 4.17 Variation of color, LOI, and COD in the Hudson River.

TABLE 4.8   Organic Matter in Water—Theoretical Relationships of Several Indicators

1. Total Organic Carbon (TOC), as Carbon (C)

    (A) If present as a carbohydrate, $(CH_2O)_n$
        TOC × 2.5 = organic matter

    (b) If present as a biomass,*
        TOC × 2.8 = organic matter

2. Chemical Oxygen Demand (COD) as O_2†

    (a) If present as carbohydrate, $(CH_2O)_n$
        COD = 2.67 × TOC as O_2

    (b) If present as biomass,
        COD = 3.6 × TOC, as O_2

    (c) If present as hydrocarbon, $(-CH_2-)_{n'}$
        COD = 3.4 × TOC, as O_2

3. Biochemical Oxygen Demand $(BOD)_5$, as O_2

    (a) If present as carbohydrate or biomass, BOD is approximately 0.7–0.8 × COD.

    (b) Other organic materials show lower ratios of BOD/COD as follows:

Compound	BOD	COD	Ratio*
Ethyl alcohol	1.0–1.5	2.1	0.5–0.7
Butyric acid	0.9	1.8	0.5
Acetaldehyde	1.3	1.8	0.7
Acetone	0.5–1.0	2.2	0.3–0.5
Ethyl ether	0.03	2.6	0.01
Diethanolamine	0.1	2.1	0.05
Gasoline	0.08	3.5	0.02
Benzene	0.0	3.1	0.00

   * This ratio is a rough measure of the ability of bacteria to digest the organic matter present (biodegradability).

4. Total Organic Nitrogen, as N:

    (a) If present in biomass, N × 16 = organic matter

   * For algal biomass, a relationship of $C_{106}H_{263}O_{110}N_{16}P$ has been suggested; for bacterial matter, the relationship $C_{60}H_{87}O_{23}N_{12}P$ has been used. These correspond to a C:H:O relationship of 1:2.5:1 and 1:1.45:0.4 respectively compared to 1:2:1 for carbohydrates.

   † The ratio of COD/TOC varies considerably from sample to sample, even on a common waste stream from a single plant. Figure 4.18 plots COD and TOC on a chemical plant waste. Although the plot shows an average ratio of 3.0, individual samples range from 2 to 5.

SUGGESTED READING

American Water Works Association: *Water Quality and Treatment*. McGraw-Hill, 1971.

Blanchard, D. C.: *From Raindrops to Volcanoes*. Anchor Books. Doubleday & Company, 1967.

Cowan, J. C., and Weintritt, D. G.: *Water-formed Scale Deposits*. Gulf Publishing Company, Houston, 1976.

Day, A. D., and Davis, K. S.: *Water, The Mirror of Science*. Anchor Books. Doubleday & Company, 1961.

Deevey, E. S., Jr.: "Mineral Cycles." *Scientific American*, p. 149, September, 1970.

Henderson, L. J.: *The Fitness of the Environment*. Beacon Press, 1958.

Nordell, Eskel: *Water Treatment for Industrial and Other Uses*. Reinhold, 1961.

Rapport, S., and Wright, H., et al., eds.: *The Crust of the Earth*. The New American Library, 1955.

Rubin, J., ed.: *Aqueous-Environmental Chemistry of Metals*. "Crystal Growth Kinetics of

Figure 4.18 Relationship between COD and TOC in chemical plant's waste.

Minerals Encountered in Water Treatment Processes," Nancollas, G. H., and Reddy, M. M., Ann Arbor Science Publishers, Inc., 1976.
Stumm, W., and Morgan, J. J.: *Aquatic Chemistry.* John Wiley & Sons, 1970.
Weber, W. J., Jr., et al.: *Physicochemical Processes for Water Quality Control.* John Wiley & Sons, 1972.

Chapter 5
Aquatic Biology

Scientists picture the primordial Earth as a planet washed by a hot sea and bathed in an atmosphere containing water vapor, ammonia, methane and hydrogen. Testing this theory, Stanley Miller at the University of Chicago duplicated these conditions in the laboratory. He distilled sea water in a special apparatus, passed the vapor with ammonia, methane and hydrogen through an electrical discharge at frequent intervals, and condensed the "rain" to return to the boiling sea water. Within a week the sea water had turned red. Analysis showed that it contained amino acids, which are the building blocks of protein substances.

Whether this is what really happened early in the Earth's history is not important; the experiment demonstrated that the basic ingredients of life could have been made in some such fashion, setting the stage for life to come into existence in the sea. The saline fluids in most living things may be an inheritance from such early beginnings.

There are both physical and chemical conditions that define a healthy environment for aquatic organisms. Among the physical conditions are temperature, pressure, osmotic pressure, light, and turbidity.

MODERATE TEMPERATURES PREFERRED

Although a few organisms can live in hot water, most prefer a moderate temperature. Because there are so many varieties of aquatic life, it is impossible to generalize about an optimum temperature for a healthy aquatic environment. Among bacteria, some prefer warm water, some cold, and others grow best at intermediate temperatures (Figure 5.1). The majority of aquatic organisms have become acclimated to the prevailing ranges of temperatures of surface waters and underground aquifers.

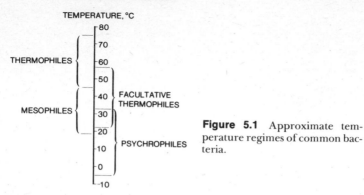

Figure 5.1 Approximate temperature regimes of common bacteria.

Fresh water fish populations are broadly classed as game fish and rough fish depending on preference for cold water or warm water, respectively. This is the extent to which generalizations can be made about water temperature without focusing on specific organisms.

The influence of pressure is also specific for different organisms. Pressure is determined by the water depth, but the preferred depth for an organism is not always directly related to pressure. It may be more closely related to the depth of sunlight penetration, temperature, dissolved oxygen content, and other factors indirectly influenced by depth.

Osmotic pressure is an important consideration because it affects the movement of water into or from the cell. Osmosis is the process by which water molecules move through a permeable membrane separating a weak solution from a strong solution in a direction to dilute the stronger solution. A cell that has reached equilibrium with sea water may rupture because of the inrush of water molecules if it is suddenly exposed to fresh water. Since osmotic pressure is influenced by solution concentration, the salinity of the aquatic environment is an important factor controlling the biota able to live in that environment. Solutions causing swelling of the cell are hypotonic; those producing shrinkage are hypertonic; and those in equilibrium with the cell fluid are isotonic.

Another important physical consideration is water turbidity. Suspended solids and turbidity have important consequences, including obstruction of sunlight, blanketing of the bottom causing a shift in the population of bottom organisms, and abrasion or clogging of gills and other organs of larger aquatic species.

THE ROLE OF CHEMISTRY

The chemical nature of the aquatic environment plays a major role in establishing and supporting the aquatic population; but just as the chemical conditions affect the biota, so too do the organisms affect their chemical environment.

The primary chemical consideration is food. A class of organisms called autotrophs, including algae and certain bacteria, are able to synthesize their own food from carbon dioxide and water. The more complex carbon-containing organic matter, such as polysaccharides, becomes food for other types of microorganisms. Some of these organic molecules are too large to pass through the cell membrane. Bacteria have developed a process for taking care of this problem: they produce enzymes which break down the large organic molecule into smaller components which can then be transported across the cell membrane and used as food (Figure 5.2). Larger organisms use algae and bacteria as their food supply, and in turn become the food for higher forms of life. This progression is known as the food chain.

Those organisms that feed on algae and other forms of plant life are herbivores; those which prey on protozoa and larger animals are carnivores. Some organisms serve a useful purpose in feeding on decaying matter; these are known as saprophytes.

SIX IMPORTANT ELEMENTS

In the process of metabolism, all cells must reproduce themselves and form new cellular matter. The most common elements required for biosynthesis in the order of their occurrence are C, H, O, N, and S. A sixth element, P, is of considerable importance also, especially as it is present in sewage and is considered a good nutrient for algae. It is also a major component of agricultural fertilizers, so it is present in storm runoff from farmland. There is usually an ample supply of C, H, O, and S in various forms in the water to encourage growth of aquatic life. In the deliberate culture of bacteria, such as in the biological digestion process for waste treatment, there may be insufficient N and P in the water for healthy growth. In that case, these elements are added to produce the ratio represented by the empirical formulas sometimes used to represent some of the major constituents in protoplasm, $C_{106}H_{263}O_{110}N_{16}P$ in the case of algae and $C_{60}H_{87}O_{23}N_{12}P$ for aerobic bacteria. In addition to these major nutrients, there are countless minor nutrients, some of which are generally required by almost all organisms, and some of which are specific for certain organisms. One example is magnesium: it is required by all organisms for cell growth; but it also has a specific use in the chlorophyll molecule which is required by plant life; a second is iron which is generally needed in small amounts by all cells, but is specifically needed for the hemoglobin found in the blood stream of animals. Aquatic organisms concentrate different minerals in different organs of their bodies. For example, the respiratory system of the sea cucumber contains a high concentration of vanadium; the distinctive flavor of scallops is due to the presence of copper in its hemocyanin, analogous to the iron in hemoglobin.

Low pH in water has a primary effect on aquatic organisms because it inhibits enzymatic activity. Some bacteria can live in acid conditions, as illustrated by the bacterial activity responsible for the acidity in coal mine drainage. Other organisms prefer alkaline conditions and can exist at fairly high pH levels; algae faced with the need to obtain CO_2 will break down bicarbonate to carbonate, in the absence of CO_2 gas, often producing a pH above 9. However, most organisms seem most comfortable in a pH range of about 6.5–8.5.

The pH of the aquatic environment may have secondary, indirect effects. For example, if ammonia is present, pH determines the ratio of the ionized

Figure 5.2 The exact mechanism by which enzymes break down large molecules is uncertain, but it is believed to be related to a matching of molecular shapes.

portion to the portion present as a gas. Since nonionized ammonia may be toxic to certain aquatic organisms, pH can have an indirect influence on the health of the aquatic population.

SOME NEED OXYGEN, OTHERS DON'T

Oxygen influences both microscopic life and larger life forms. The bacteria that require oxygen, and that produce CO_2 as a by-product, are known as aerobic organisms. Those which can live without oxygen are called anaerobes. Some, called facultative organisms, can adapt to either situation. In a deep lake, the oxygen at the surface will support aerobic organisms, and the bottom layers devoid of oxygen may support a population of anaerobic bacteria. The action of anaerobic bacteria is called fermentation, and the by-products are carbon dioxide, methane, hydrogen, ammonia, and hydrogen sulfide. In swamps, where the continual accumulation of dying vegetation leads to fermentation of the bottom, organic-rich layers, the production of methane may be sufficient to produce the phenomenon known as swamp fire.

In most surface water, there is a symbiotic relationship between oxygen-producing algae and oxygen-utilizing bacteria occurring together in slime masses, although individual colonies of each of these microbes also thrive separately. The amount of oxygen produced by the algae is directly affected by sunlight, so the oxygen content of most surface waters increases during the day and falls off at night.

The oxygen content of surface waters has a strong influence on the species of fish in the aquatic population. Trout and other game fish usually require high oxygen levels and prefer lower temperatures; rough fish, such as carp and catfish, can survive at oxygen levels as low as 2 mg/l and can also tolerate warmer water.

Although the presence of algae may be beneficial in the production of dissolved oxygen, too much produces blooms which are extremely troublesome and can lead to eutrophication (slow death) of the body of water (Figure 5.3).

Figure 5.3 Algae bloom occurs when phosphorus, nitrogen, and nutrients are abundant. Bacteria feeding on the algae multiply rapidly, producing debris that speeds up the eutrophication process.

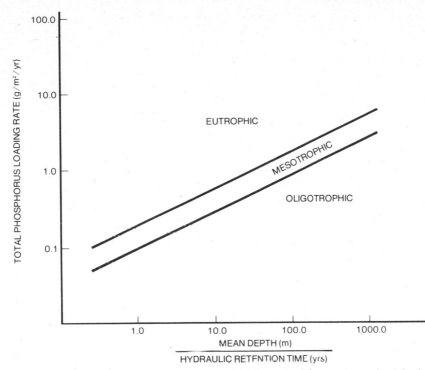

Figure 5.4 How phosphorus affects eutrophication of a lake, as determined by its geometry. [(*From National Water Quality Inventory, EPA 440/9-75-014.)*]

When algae have reached the end of their growing season, they die and provide a rich source of organic material for bacteria. With an ample food supply, the bacteria may initially grow at an exponential rate, consuming dissolved oxygen in the process. The process slows down as food is consumed and waste products accumulate. Even large bodies of water, e.g., Lake Erie, may become completely devoid of dissolved oxygen in certain areas where this process has occurred. Since the growth of the algae that starts the process of eutrophication is dependent on nitrogen and phosphorus as fertilizers, the concentration of these nutrients entering the body of water has a strong influence on the rate of eutrophication. A relationship between the input of nutrients and the geometry of the lake has been hypothesized (Figure 5.4). Even those waters classed as oligotrophic (abundant in oxygen, deficient in plant nutrients) are destined to become filled with debris eventually, even though the rate of organic production is very low. The largest lake in the world, Lake Baikal in Siberia, located on a geologic fault, has a water depth of about 5000 feet (1525 m); beneath this is an accumulation of another 20,000 feet (6000 m) of sediment.

A final chemical factor influencing the aquatic biota is toxic matter in a variety of forms. Many toxic materials are produced by nature; for example, there are many toxic varieties of algae. Other toxic materials may be present because of municipal sewage or industrial waste discharges. Some elements that are required in trace amounts for healthy aquatic growth are toxic at higher concentrations.

The aquatic organisms of concern to both water users and naturalists are (a) microorganisms, which are visible only under the microscope; (b) macroorganisms, which are visible to the unaided eye, but generally rather small; and (c) higher life forms.

MICROBIAL ANALYSES

In considering the various fields of aquatic biology, it is found that there are two principal kinds of analyses used to identify microorganisms: the first is that used by the municipal water treatment plants for control purposes to assure that the finished water is free of pathogenic organisms. Coliform bacteria are used as indicator organisms in this test. Although these are not pathogenic, they are found in the intestinal tract of all warm-blooded animals, so their presence is a warning that pathogenic organisms may also be present. A more positive indication of a health hazard is the further identification of some of these as fecal coliform bacteria. The effluent is tested at a frequency specified by law and must meet minimum counts for coliform organisms on a statistically significant number of samples. These records are submitted to the control agency, usually at the state level. In addition to determining coliform organisms, the municipal plant may on its own initiative analyze for specific organisms based on its past operating experience with biologically-related problems. For example, the spring turnover in a lake may introduce filter-clogging organisms at the water intake: a regular evaluation for the organisms which experience has found in the past to cause filter problems is a helpful control measure. Later in the year, certain algal blooms may produce tastes or odors in the finished water, and analysis for these specific algae can forewarn the plant of the time when activated carbon may be needed for taste or odor control (Table 5.1).

TABLE 5.1   Odors Produced by Algae

Species	Moderate	Abundant
Anabaena	Grassy, Nasturtium	Septic
Asterionella	Geranium, spicy	Fishy
Dinobryon	Violet	Fishy
Melosira	Geranium	Musty
Oscillatoria	Grassy	Musty
Stephanodiscus	Geranium	Fishy
Synura	Cucumber	Fishy
Tabellaria	Geranium	Fishy
Volvox	Fishy	Fishy

MICROBES IN INDUSTRY

Microbiological analyses conducted to pinpoint problems in industrial water systems, the second type of analysis, are considerably more complex. Figures 5.5 to 5.8 show such analyses for a river, a recirculating cooling water system, a paper mill system and a waste plant discharge.

In this type of analysis, although total count is a very significant number, by itself it means little unless samples collected at regularly scheduled times from the same location are analyzed and compared for the levels of populations and the species (organisms) normally encountered. The particular analyses shown break down the microbiological life into three categories: bacteria, fungi, and algae. In each category, the specific organisms sought are those that experience has shown to be the most troublesome in industrial systems.

At the head of the list are slime-forming aerobic bacteria. The most common of these is *Pseudomonas*. When organisms other than those shown on the

REPORT OF
MICROBIOLOGICAL ANALYSIS

NALCO

Company ▬▬▬▬▬▬	Analysis No. 018047
	Sampling Date 04/21/77
Address ▬▬▬▬▬▬	Date Rec'd by NALCO 04/25/77

Sample Marked   RIVER WATER

Physical Appearance

CLEAR LIQUID

(All counts express quantity of organisms per ML of sample)

BACTERIA

AEROBIC SLIME FORMING
Non-Sporeforming

Flavobacterium	NEG IN 1/10
Mucoids (S)	NEG IN 1/10
Aerobacter	NEG IN 1/10
Pseudomonas	2,500

Sporeforming

B. subtilis
B. cereus
B. megatherium
B. mycoides

ANAEROBIC CORROSIVE

Desulfovibrio	20
Clostridia	

IRON DEPOSITING

Sphaerotilus	NONE
Gallionella	

OTHER BACTERIA   NONE

TOTAL COUNT   5,000

REMARKS:

FUNGI

MOLDS

Aspergillus	1
Penicillium	
Trichoderma	
Alternaria	
FUSARIUM	3

YEASTS

Torula	NONE
Monilia	
Saccharomyces	
Rhodotorula	

ALGAE

BLUE GREEN	NONE
Oscillatoria	
GREEN	NONE
Chlorococcus	
DIATOMS	NONE

OTHER ORGANISMS

NONE

Ronald Christensen
Head, Microbiological Laboratory

NALCO CHEMICAL COMPANY
6216 W. 66TH PLACE □ CHICAGO, ILLINOIS 60638

Figure 5.5   Microbial analysis of a river water.

standard analytical form are found, these are noted in the appropriate location. For example, *E. coli* found are reported as aerobic, nonsporeforming bacteria; the sulfur-producing bacteria, *Beggiatoa,* is reported under the column for "Other Bacteria" when it is identified. Organisms other than bacteria, fungi, and algae include the protozoa and rotifiers that are often found grazing on the floc containing the other microorganisms. Actinomyces are sometimes identified by special techniques, as these can contribute significantly to tastes and odors in finished water.

When a wastewater is analyzed, it is sometimes necessary to determine fecal coliform and fecal streptococci to establish the need for final disinfection. If

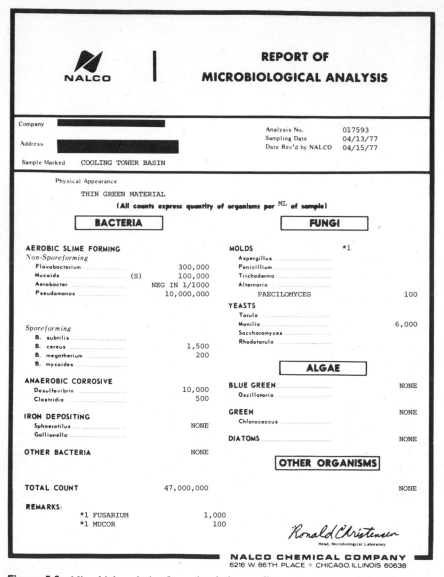

Figure 5.6   Microbial analysis of a recirculating cooling water.

the sample is taken from a stream below a wastewater discharge, a common variety of bacteria called *Sphaerotilus* is often found. This is usually classed as an iron-depositing bacteria, but iron is not needed for its growth.

If a bioassay is being made of a stream to assess its health, a census must be made of many larger organisms. Macroorganisms—visible to the unaided eye—include a variety of worms, crustacea and larvae. A healthy stream contains a large number of species with relatively low populations. These provide food for the higher forms of life, such as fish, crawfish, and shrimp.

THREE LIVING ZONES

Three well-defined habitats must be examined in making a complete bioassay of a stream or lake: the littoral area just off the shoreline; the limnetic zone, or open water beyond the shore; and the benthic zone at the bottom. There is an endless variety of organisms indigenous to each of these zones, and a periodic evaluation of their populations is needed to assess the health of the lake and the effect of municipal or industrial discharges.

NALCO

REPORT OF
MICROBIOLOGICAL ANALYSIS

Company

Address

Sample Marked   PAPER MACHINE HEADBOX

Analysis No.	017531
Sampling Date	04/13/77
Date Rec'd by NALCO	04/15/77

Physical Appearance

THICK STOCK

(All counts express quantity of organisms per ℠ of sample)

BACTERIA

AEROBIC SLIME FORMING
Non-Sporeforming
Flavobacterium .... NEG IN 1/1000
Mucoids .... (S)   NEG IN 1/1000
Aerobacter   6,000
Pseudomonas 29,000,000

Sporeforming
B. subtilis .... NEG IN 1/100
B. cereus
B. megatherium
B. mycoides

ANAEROBIC CORROSIVE
Desulfovibrio   3,000
Clostridia .... NEG IN 1/100

IRON DEPOSITING
Sphaerotilus
Gallionella

OTHER BACTERIA
    *FACULTATIVE   200

TOTAL COUNT   59,000,000

FUNGI

MOLDS   *1
Aspergillus   200
Penicillium
Trichoderma
Alternaria
    FUSARIUM   200

YEASTS
Torula   100
Monilia   4,000
Saccharomyces
Rhodotorula

ALGAE

BLUE GREEN
Oscillatoria

GREEN
Chlorococcus

DIATOMS

OTHER ORGANISMS

REMARKS:
    *1 PAECILOMYCES   100

*EITHER AEROBIC OR ANAEROBIC IN ORIGINAL SAMPLE

Ronald Christensen
Head, Microbiological Laboratory

NALCO CHEMICAL COMPANY
6216 W. 66TH PLACE □ CHICAGO, ILLINOIS 60638

Figure 5.7   Microbial analysis of a liquid sample from a paper machine headbox.

NALCO

REPORT OF

MICROBIOLOGICAL ANALYSIS

Company

Address

Analysis No.	112906
Sampling Date	05/20/70
Date Rec'd by NALCO	05/21/70

Sample Marked   WASTE TREATMENT PLANT EFFLUENT - PAPER MILL

Physical Appearance

COLORLESS LIQUID WITH FLOC

(All counts express quantity of organisms per ML of sample)

BACTERIA

AEROBIC SLIME FORMING
Non-Sporeforming

Flavobacterium	NEG IN 1/1000
Mucoids	NEG IN 1/1000
Aerobacter	1,150
Pseudomonas	11,600
E. COLI	150

Sporeforming

B. subtilis	
B. cereus	
B. megatherium	
B. mycoides	2

ANAEROBIC CORROSIVE

Desulfovibrio	40
Clostridia	

IRON DEPOSITING

Sphaerotilus	NONE
Gallionella	

OTHER BACTERIA

	NONE

TOTAL COUNT 650,000

REMARKS:

FUNGI

MOLDS

Aspergillus	5
Penicillium	
Trichoderma	
Alternaria	
FUSARIUM	5

YEASTS

Torula	
Monilia	
Saccharomyces	30
Rhodotorula	

ALGAE

BLUE GREEN	NONE
Oscillatoria	

GREEN	
Chlorococcus	NONE
DIATOMS	NONE

OTHER ORGANISMS

PROTOZOA	FEW

Ronald Christensen
Head, Microbiological Laboratory

NALCO CHEMICAL COMPANY
6216 W. 66TH PLACE □ CHICAGO, ILLINOIS 60638

Figure 5.8   Microbial analysis of a waste treatment plant discharge.

If such discharges have not been properly treated, the receiving body of water becomes polluted. In fact, by definition, pollution refers to contaminants that degrade the body of water, either wiping out desirable populations or hastening eutrophication. The mere presence of contaminants, which exist in all waters, does not constitute pollution.

Of the indicators of pollution, certainly dissolved oxygen level is the foremost. A reduction of dissolved oxygen is always apparent in a receiving stream immediately below a wastewater discharge. Figure 5.9 shows the oxygen content at each sampling location along a stream. The data are typical of the effect of a wastewater discharge on a receiving stream. If the stream is severely pol-

Figure 5.9 Hypothetical oxygen sag curve, showing the concentration of dissolved oxygen and degradable waste (measured as BOD) at various sampling stations along a river with two points of waste discharge.

luted, oxygen may disappear entirely. There will be a zone of degradation below the point of discharge where the water may become septic and foul odors develop. Depending on the type of exposure of the stream to the atmosphere—that is, whether the stream is turbulent or limpid—oxygen will be redissolved in the water, and the stream will rapidly or slowly recover.

Correlating closely to the oxygen sag curve is the change in stream biota below the point of discharge: the number of species of organisms drops precipitately, and the population of undesirable organisms, such as sludge worms, increases rapidly. Farther down stream as the river begins to recover, species of desirable organisms begin to reappear, as shown by Figure 5.10.

CHEMICAL INDICATORS

Certain chemical tests, too, correlate with the oxygen sag curve, as shown by Figure 5.11. The BOD values shown are a measure of food for bacteria (Chapter 4). When food is introduced, bacteria begin to multiply rapidly at an exponential rate, resulting in the reduction of dissolved oxygen in the water. As food

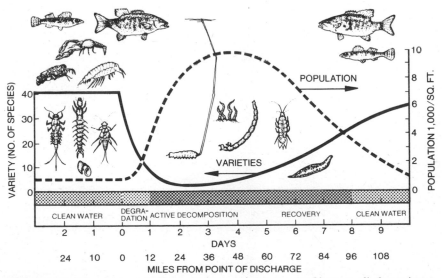

Figure 5.10 Changes in population of macro-organisms caused by waste discharge into a clean stream. *(From "Biological Field Investigative Data for Water Pollution Surveys," by W. M. Ingram, K. M. Mackenthum, and A. F. Bartsch.)*

Figure 5.11 The oxygen sag curve may be followed by a variety of analyses showing effects of biological activity.

is consumed, as indicated by a reduction in BOD, the bacterial populations die off and become food for protozoa, which in turn die off and become food for rotifers and crustaceans, as shown by Figure 5.12. This marks the return of the stream to a healthy condition.

Because pollution of a stream is quickly shown by these effects on the biota, periodic bioassays of a river above and below the point of wastewater discharge to determine variety and density of aquatic species is a practical means of monitoring the performance of a waste treatment plant. Other bioassay methods are being developed that rely on the reactions of fish exposed to an effluent stream, usually at a controlled dilution rate. It is quite possible that a waste treatment plant may perform within the specifications of the effluent guidelines established by Federal regulations, and yet the effluent may be damaging

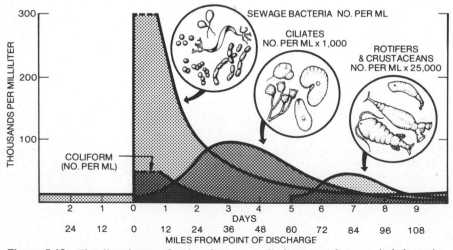

Figure 5.12 The disturbance of a river by a waste discharge produces an imbalance in the population distribution. The types of species found indicate the condition of the stream at each sampling point. *(From Ingram, Mackenthum, and Bartsch.)*

to the stream because of the presence of toxic materials for which there may be no analysis. For that reason, biological studies to evaluate the suitability of an effluent for mixing into the receiving stream are valuable.

It is seen, then, that gross pollution of a stream has severe biological implications, but that a well-treated effluent may have little or no effect on the receiving stream, depending to a large extent on the ability of the stream to recover through the natural process of reaeration.

BACTERIA CAN HELP

In most municipal sewage plants, microbiology can be applied as a beneficial science for the destruction of pollutants in wastewater. In such a process, the wastewater is collected and held under controlled conditions, similar to a balanced aquarium, and bacteria are introduced with the proper application of nutrients to break down and digest the organic wastes. Under such controlled conditions, the final discharge does not impose an excessive oxygen demand on the receiving stream.

While bacteria can be beneficial in the purification of wastewater, when they are uncontrolled in industrial water systems, microbiological organisms produce an endless variety of problems. Aside from diseases such as typhoid and dysentery, which are common threats from exposure to waters that have not been disinfected, the potential for equipment damage and product damage due to microbiological activity is great. Slime masses are often part of deposits found in water distribution systems and water-using equipment. Corrosion is often accelerated because of biological activity; this is particularly true where deposits form and anaerobic bacteria are shielded from the flowing water stream by these deposits, permitting them to corrode steel piping by the H_2S produced through their metabolism. However, proper identification of the organisms entering a system and found in deposits enables the water engineer to develop a chemical program for controlling these problems by application of biocides or dispersants, or a combination of both.

SUGGESTED READING

Cairns, J., and Dickson, K. L., eds.: *Biological Methods for Assessment of Water Quality.* "Use of Aquatic Invertebrates in the Assessment of Water Quality," Gaufin, A. R. STP 528. Ameican Society for Testing Materials, 1973.

Edmonson, W. T., Ed., et al.: *Fresh Water Biology.* John Wiley & Sons, 1959.

Ingram, W. M., Mackenthun, K. M., and Bartsch, A. F.: *Biological Field Investigative Data for Water Pollution Surveys.* U. S. Department of Interior, U. S. Government Printing Office, 1966.

Mackenthun, K. M., and Ingram, W. M.: *Biological Associated Problems in Fresh Water Environments.* U. S. Department of Interior. U. S. Government Printing Office, 1967.

Mowat, Anne: "Measurement of Metal Toxicity by BOD." *Journal Water Pollution Control Federation,* p 853, May, 1976.

Palmer, C. M., and Tarzwell, C. M.: "Algae of Importance in Water Supplies." *Public Works,* p 107, June 1955.

Whipple, George C.: *The Microscopy of Drinking Water,* 4th ed. rev. Fair, G. M., and Whipple, M. C., 1933. John Wiley & Sons.

Chapter 6
Water Contaminants: Occurrence and Treatment

The introduction of contaminants into water supplies has been shown to be related to rainfall, the geological nature of the watershed or underground aquifer, and the activities of nature and the human population. Water contaminants to be examined in more detail fall in two categories: dissolved matter (Table 6.1) and non-soluble constituents (Table 6.2). Dissolved gases are included in discussions of the biological cycles affecting water quality.

As shown in Table 6.1, soluble materials in water are arbitrarily assigned to five classifications, the first four of which are based on concentration levels, with the last covering those materials usually transient because continuing reactions in the aquatic environment change their concentrations.

Many materials are transient because of biological activity. The change in CO_2 and O_2 content with sunlight is one example. Equilibrium between NH_3, N_2, NO_2^{-1} and NO_3^{-1} is another, discussed later in this chapter as part of the nitrogen cycle. (See Class 2, Secondary Constituents.)

There are also longer term processes by which Nature cycles matter through living organisms, which in turn modify the environment and leave their records in the rocks. This chapter examines the sources of contaminants in water, many of which are minerals created by living things. Perhaps the best known are the chalk cliffs of Dover and the coral atolls of the Pacific, both composed of $CaCO_3$.

Discussing these atolls in his essay on formation of mineral deposits, C. C. Furnace says, "To the casual observer, it would seem that the polyp has built these great masses of land out of nothing; but, of course, it cannot do that any more than man can. It has taken calcium compounds from very dilute solutions of sea water and built up a shell of calcium compounds to protect itself. In this process of following its preordained metabolic rite, it has concentrated calcium by several thousandfold in the form of an insoluble compound. In-

TABLE 6.1   Soluble Material in Water Supplies

Class 1	Primary constituents—generally over 5 mg/l		
	Bicarbonate	Magnesium	Sodium
	Calcium	Organic matter	Sulfate
	Chloride	Silica	Total dissolved solids
Class 2	Secondary constituents—Generally over 0.1 mg/l		
	Ammonia	Iron	Potassium
	Borate	Nitrate	Strontium
	Fluoride		
Class 3	Tertiary constituents—generally over 0.01 mg/l		
	Aluminum	Copper	Phosphate
	Arsenic	Lead	Zinc
	Barium	Lithium	
	Bromide	Manganese	
Class 4	Trace constituents—generally less than 0.01 mg/l		
	Antimony	Cobalt	Tin
	Cadmium	Mercury	Titanium
	Chromium	Nickel	

Class 5	Transient constituents
	Acidity-Alkalinity
	Biological Cycles
	Carbon Cycle Constituents
	Organic $C/CH_4/CO/CO_2/(CH_2O)_n/C$-Tissue
	Oxygen Cycle
	O_2/CO_2
	Nitrogen Cycle Constituents
	Organic $N/NH_3/NO_2^{-1}/NO_3^{-1}/N^0/$Amino Acids
	Sulfur Cycle Constituents
	Organic $S/HS^{-1}/SO_3^{-2}/SO_4^{-2}/S^0$
	Redox Reactions
	Oxidizing Materials
	From the natural environment—O_2, S
	Treatment residues—Cl_2, CrO_4^{-2}
	Reducing Materials
	From the natural environment—
	Organics, Fe^{+2}, Mn^{+2}, HS^{-1}
	Treatment Residues—
	Organics, Fe^{+2}, SO_2, SO_3^{-2}
	Radionuclides

significant as the coral polyp may appear, it is one of the most important creatures in changing the character of the earth's surface."

Many other natural cycles have been operating over countless geologic ages to produce deposits of sulfur, iron, manganese, silica, and phosphate, to name only a few. In the village of Batsto, New Jersey, the early American colonists set up the first blast furnace in the New World. Their source of iron ore was "bog iron"—pure iron oxide precipitated from artesian water by iron-depositing bacteria.

So the presence of many of the mineral constituents in water supplies may simply represent the return to the aquatic environment of a loan made by the earth to living organisms long ago.

As an aid to appreciating the solubilities of the constituents being examined, and thus the limitations of their occurrence in natural water supplies and the residuals which may be reached in precipitation processes, Figures 6.1, 6.2 and 6.6 present solubility characteristics in appropriate locations in the text.

TABLE 6.2 Nonsoluble Constituents
in Water Supplies

Class 1	**Solids**
	Floating
	Settleable
	Suspended

Class 2	**Microbial organisms**
	Algae
	Bacteria
	Fungi
	Viruses

CLASS 1—PRIMARY CONSTITUENTS

This includes dissolved solids generally exceeding 5 mg/l, and often several orders of magnitude above this level.

Bicarbonate (HCO_3^-—Molecular Weight 61)

The bicarbonate ion is the principal alkaline constituent of almost all water supplies. It is generally found in the range of 5–500 mg/l, as $CaCO_3$. Its introduction into the water by the dissolving action of bacterially produced CO_2 on carbonate-containing minerals has been explained elsewhere. Normal activities of the human population also introduce alkaline materials into water, evidenced by a typical increase of alkalinity of sewage plant effluent of 100–150 mg/l above the alkalinity of the municipal water supply. Much of this is due to the alkalinity of industrial and domestic detergents.

Alkalinity in drinking water supplies seldom exceeds 300 mg/l. The control of alkalinity is important in many industrial applications because of its significance in the calcium carbonate Stability Index. Alkalinity control is important in both concentrated boiler water and cooling water in evaporative cooling systems. Makeup for these systems must often be treated for alkalinity reduction either by lime softening or direct acid addition. Alkalinity is objectionable in certain other industries, such as the beverage industry, where it neutralizes the acidity of fruit flavors, and in textile operations, where it interferes with acid dyeing.

Calcium (Ca^{+2}—Atomic Weight 40; Group IIA, Alkaline Earth Metal, Figs. 6.1 and 6.6)

Calcium is the major component of hardness in water and usually is in the range of 5–500 mg/l, as $CaCO_3$, (2–200 mg/l as Ca). It is present in many minerals, principally limestone and gypsum. Limestone deposits are often the residue of the fossils of tiny aquatic organisms, such as polyps, that have taken calcium from the sea water in which they lived, and used it for their skeletons. This is but one of many cycles in nature whereby some component of the environment is continually withdrawn by living things and eventually returned directly or indirectly.

Calcium removed from water in softening operations is later returned to the environment, often to the watershed, by way of a precipitate or a brine which is the by-product of the softening reaction. Calcium is a major factor in determining Stability Index. Calcium reduction is often required in treating cooling tower makeup. Complete removal is required for many industrial operations, particularly for boiler makeup, textile finishing operations, and cleaning and rinsing in metal finishing operations.

Calcium hardness can be reduced to a level of 35 mg/l as $CaCO_3$ by cold lime-soda softening, and to less than 25 mg/l by hot lime-soda softening. It is reduced to less than 1 mg/l by cation exchange methods.

Figure 6.1   Theoretical solubilities of carbonate compounds in a water system closed to an external CO_2 environment at 25°C. (*From "Aquatic Chemistry," by W. Stumm and J. J. Morgan.*)

Chloride (Cl⁻—Atomic Weight 35.5; Group VIIA, Halide)

Since almost all chloride salts are highly soluble in water, chloride is common in fresh water supplies, ranging from 10 to 100 mg/l. Sea water contains over 30,000 mg/l as NaCl, and certain underground brine wells may actually be saturated, approximately 25% NaCl. Many geological formations were once sedimentary rocks in the sea, so it is not surprising that they contain residues of chlorides that are continually leaching into fresh water sources. The chloride content of sewage is typically 20–50 mg/l above the concentration of the municipal water supply, accounting in part for the gradual increase in salinity of rivers as they proceed from the headwaters to the sea.

Anion exchange is the only chemical process capable of removing chlorides from water; however, physical processes such as evaporation and reverse osmosis can separate a feedwater into two streams, one with a reduced chloride and the other with an increased chloride content.

The recommended upper limit for chloride in drinking waters is 250 mg/l, based entirely on taste, not on any known physiological hazards.

Magnesium (Mg^{+2}—Atomic Weight 12.1; Group IIA, Alkaline Earth Metal, Figs. 6.1 and 6.2)

The magnesium hardness of a water is usually about one-third of the total hardness, the remaining two-thirds being calcium hardness. Magnesium

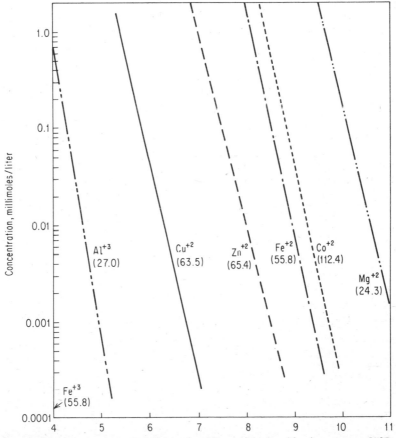

Figure 6.2 Theoretical solubilities of oxides and hydroxides in water at 25°C. *(From "Aquatic Chemistry," by W. Stumm and J. J. Morgan.)*

typically ranges from 10–50 mg/l (about 40–200 mg/l as $CaCO_3$). In sea water, magnesium concentration is about 5 times that of calcium on an equivalent basis. The production of magnesium hydroxide from sea water is the starting point in the manufacture of magnesium. Magnesium is a prominent component of many minerals, including dolomite, magnesite, and numerous varieties of clay.

Since magnesium carbonate is appreciably more soluble than calcium carbonate, it is seldom a major component in scale. However, it must be removed along with calcium where soft water is required for boiler makeup or for process applications. It may be removed by lime softening to a residual of 30–50 mg/l as $CaCO_3$ cold, or 1–2 mg/l as $CaCO_3$ hot. It is also reduced by ion exchange to less than 1 mg/l as $CaCO_3$.

Organic Matter (Carbon, C^{+4}—Atomic Weight 12; Group IVA, Nonmetal)

Since organic material makes up a significant part of the soil and because it is used by aquatic organisms to build their bodies and produce food, it is inevitable that water-soluble organic products of metabolism should be present in all water supplies. There is not much information available on specific organic compounds in most water sources.

Many waters have a yellowish or tea color due to decayed vegetation leached from the watershed by runoff. These organic materials are broadly classified as humic substances, further categorized as humic acid (a water-soluble compound), fulvic acid (alkali soluble material) and humin (high-molecular weight, water insoluble matter). These organic compounds are molecules having many functional groups containing oxygen and hydrogen atoms in various proportions, so that when organic matter is reported as carbon, as it is in the TOC determination, it is probable that the molecular weight of these humic organic molecules is 2.0–2.5 times greater than the value reported as carbon. A survey of 80 municipal supplies of the United States showed an average total organic carbon content in the finished water of 2.2 mg/l, as C, so the organic matter was probably on the order of 5 mg/l.

There are a variety of indexes for measuring the gross organic content of water, and there is generally no correlation between them. The organic matter at a sampling station on the Mississippi River as determined by these indexes is shown in Figure 6.3. Because some of the functional groups in humic compounds have ion exchange properties, they tend to chelate heavy metals. In spite of this, there is no correlation whatever between the color of a water and its total heavy metal concentration.

Some organic materials are truly soluble, but much of it—certainly the humic matter—is present in colloidal form and can generally be removed by coagulation. Alum coagulation at a pH of 5.5–6.0 typically reduces color to less than 5 APHA units. Organic matter such as is found in domestic sewage often inhibits calcium carbonate precipitation. If the natural color exceeds about 50, it must be partially removed for lime softening to occur. Organic matter may be removed by activated carbon treatment, widely practiced in municipal treatment plants when organic matter causes objectionable tastes or odors in the finished water. Generally these tastes and odors are produced by algae, each species having its characteristic odor or taste just as with land plants. Also like land plants, algae produce organic compounds which may be toxic if enough is ingested by fish or animals.

Certain organic materials in water polluted by agricultural runoff (such as pesticide residues) or by industrial wastes in concentrations far below 1 mg/l still exert a significant effect on the biota of the receiving stream. Even when the

Figure 6.3   Organic matter in the Mississippi River at Cape Girardeau, 1969–70. *(From USGS Water Supply Paper 2156.)*

effect is not dramatic, as with fish kill, it may have long-term consequences, such as affecting reproduction or disrupting the food chain.

Organic matter is objectionable in municipal water chiefly for aesthetic reasons. It can be troublesome in industrial supplies by interfering with treatment processes. It is a major factor in the fouling of anion exchange resins, degrading effluent quality of demineralized water and requiring early replacement of resin.

Sodium (Na⁺—Atomic Weight 23; Group IA, Alkali Metal)

All sodium salts are highly soluble in water, although certain complexes in minerals are not. The high chloride content of brines and sea water is usually associated with the sodium ion. In fresh waters, its range is usually 10–100 mg/l (about 20–200 mg/l as $CaCO_3$). Sodium is present in certain types of clay and feldspar. There is an increase of sodium in municipal sewage of 40–70 mg/l in excess of the municipal water supply. Its concentration is not limited by Federal Drinking Water Standards, so persons on low sodium diets may require special sources of potable water. The only chemical process for removing sodium is cation exchange in the hydrogen cycle. Evaporation and reverse osmosis also reduce sodium, producing a product stream low in sodium and a spent brine high in sodium.

Silica (SiO₂—Molecular Weight 60; Oxide of Silicon, Group IV, Nonmetal)

Silica is present in almost all minerals, and is found in fresh water in a range of 1–100 mg/l. The skeletons of diatoms are pure silica, so the silica content of surface waters may be affected by seasonal diatom blooms. Silica is considered to be colloidal because its reaction with adsorbents like MgO and $Fe(OH)_3$ show characteristics similar to typical colloids. At high concentrations—over 50 mg/l—the adsorption isotherms (Chapter 3) no longer apply, and it appears that chemical precipitation occurs instead. There is probably an equilibrium between the silica in colloidal form and the bisilicate ($HSiO_3^-$) anion. Because of this complexity, it is difficult to predict the conditions under which silica can be kept in solution as water concentrates during evaporation.

Silica is objectionable at high concentration in cooling tower makeup because of this uncertainty about its solubility limits.

It is objectionable in boiler feedwater makeup not only because it may form a scale in the boiler itself, but also because it volatilizes at high temperatures and redeposits on turbine blades. Treatment processes that remove silica are: adsorption on magnesium precipitates in the lime softening operation; adsorption on ferric hydroxide in coagulation processes using iron salts; and anion exchange in the demineralization process.

Sulfate (SO_4^{-2}—Molecular Weight 96; Oxide of Sulfur, Group VIA, Nonmetal)

Sulfate dissolves in water from certain minerals, especially gypsum, or appears from the oxidation of sulfide minerals. Its typical range is 5–200 mg/l. The suggested upper limit in potable water is 250 mg/l, based on taste and its potential cathartic effect. Because calcium sulfate is relatively insoluble—less than 2000 mg/l—sulfate may be objectionable in concentrating water high in calcium, as in an evaporative system. High sulfate levels may be reduced measurably by massive lime or lime-aluminate treatment, or in rare cases by precipitation with barium carbonate. It may also be reduced by anion exchange. In the coagulation of water with alum, sulfate is introduced at a rate of 1 mg/l SO_4 for each 2 mg/l alum added, while an equivalent amount of alkalinity is neutralized.

Total Dissolved Solids

Since this is the sum of all materials dissolved in the water, it has many mineral sources. Its usual range is 25–5000 mg/l. The suggested limit for public water supplies, based on potability, is 500 mg/l. The principal effect of dissolved solids on industrial processes is to limit the extent to which a water can be concentrated before it must be discarded. High concentrations affect the taste of beverages. The related electrical conductivity tends to accelerate corrosion processes. A reduction in dissolved solids is achieved by a reduction in the individual components.

CLASS 2—SECONDARY CONSTITUENTS

These are generally present in concentrations greater than 0.1 mg/l and occasionally in the range of 1–10 mg/l.

Ammonia (NH_3—Molecular Weight 17, usually Expressed as N; (Nitrogen), Atomic Weight 14, Group VA, Nonmetal)

Ammonia gas is extremely soluble in water, reacting with water to produce ammonium hydroxide. Since this ionizes in water to form $NH_4^+ + OH^-$, at high pH, free ammonia gas is present in a non-ionized form. At the pH of most water supplies, ammonia is completely ionized.

$$NH_3 + H_2O \rightleftharpoons NH_4OH \rightleftharpoons NH_4^+ + OH^- \tag{1}$$

(The addition of excess OH^- drives the reaction to the left.)

Ammonia is one of the transient constituents in water as it is part of the nitrogen cycle and is influenced by biological activity. As is seen in the illustration of the nitrogen cycle, Figure 6.4, ammonia is the natural product of decay of organic nitrogen compounds. These compounds first originate as plant protein matter, which may be transformed into animal protein. The return of this protein material to the environment through death of the organism or through waste elimination produces the organic nitrogen compounds in the environment which then decay to produce ammonia.

Because this biological process also occurs in sewage treatment plants, ammonia is a common constituent of municipal sewage plant effluent, in which its usual concentration is 10–20 mg/1. It also finds its way into surface supplies from the agricultural runoff in areas where ammonia is applied to land as a fertilizer. Animal feed lots also contribute ammonia, which may run off into surface streams or find its way into underground aquifers.

The effect of sewage plant effluent on the ammonia content of a receiving stream is shown in Figure 6.5. Ammonia is oxidized by bacterial action first to nitrite and then to nitrate, so the concentration is continually being affected by the input from decay of organic nitrogen compounds and by the output, which is the uptake by bacteria to convert ammonia to nitrate.

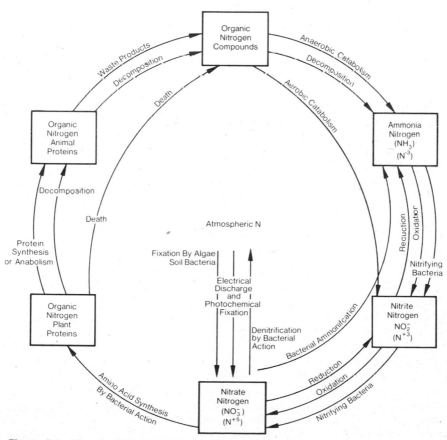

Figure 6.4   The nitrogen cycle.

Figure 6.5 The effect of sewage plant discharge on the Trinity River below Dallas, Texas, 1969–70. *(From USGS Water Supply Paper 2157.)*

The typical concentration range in most surface supplies is from 0.1 to 1.0 mg/l, expressed as N. It is not usually present in well waters, having been converted to nitrate by soil bacteria. Certain industrial discharges, such as coke plant wastes, are high in ammonia and account for the ammonia content of some surface waters.

The concentration of ammonia is not restricted by drinking water standards. Ammonia is corrosive to copper alloys, so it is of concern in cooling systems and in boiler feedwater.

Ammonia is often deliberately added as the nitrogen source for biological waste treatment systems. This is because the bacteria require nitrogen to produce protein substances (Figure 6.4), so the nitrogen is usually applied at the ratio of one part of nitrogen per 20 parts of food, measured as BOD.

Ammonia can be removed by degasification, by cation exchange on the hydrogen cycle, and by adsorption by certain clays, such as clinoptilolite. It is also reduced in concentration by biological activity, as noted above.

Borate [B(OH)₄, Compound of Boron, Atomic Weight 10.8; Group IIIA, Nonmetal]

Most of the world's boron is contained in sea water, at 5 mg/1 B. Pure supplies of sodium borate occur in arid regions where inland seas have evaporated to dryness, especially in volcanic areas. Boron is frequently present in fresh water supplies from these same geological areas.

It is present in water as non-ionized boric acid, $B(OH)_3$. At high pH, (over 10), most of it is present as the borate anion, B $(OH)_4^-$. It has little known significance in water chemistry. Its concentration is not limited in municipal waters by potable water standards. It can be damaging to citrus crops if present in irrigation water, if the irrigation methods tend to concentrate the material in the soil. Although boron is in the same group on the Periodic Chart as aluminum, it behaves more like silica in aqueous systems; it can be removed by anion exchange and by adsorption.

Fluoride (F^+—Atomic Weight 19; Group VIIA, Halide)

Fluoride is a common constituent of many minerals, including apatite and mica. It is common practice to add fluoride to municipal water to provide a residual of 1.5–2.5 mg/1, which is beneficial for the control of dental caries. Concentrations above approximately 5 mg/1 are detrimental, however, usually causing mottled, brittle tooth structure. Because of this, the concentration is limited by drinking water standards. High concentrations are present in waste waters from glass manufacture, steel manufacture, and foundry operations. Lime precipitation can reduce this to 10–20 mg/1. Fluoride is also reduced by anion exchange and by adsorption on calcium phosphate and magnesium hydroxide. Fluoride forms a number of complexes, so residuals in fluoride wastes should be analyzed chemically and not by the use of a fluoride electrode.

Iron (Fe^{+2} and Fe^{+3}—Atomic Weight 55.9; Group VIII, Transition Element, Figures 6.1, 6.2, and 6.6)

Iron is found in many igneous rocks and in clay minerals. In the absence of oxygen, iron is quite soluble in the reduced state. (As seen in the analysis of well waters containing iron.) When oxidized in a pH range of 7–8.5, iron is almost completely insoluble, and the concentration can be readily reduced to less than 0.3 mg/1, the maximum set by drinking water standards. Because iron is so insoluble when oxidized completely, the actual residual iron after treatment is determined by how well the colloidal iron has been coagulated and filtered from the water.

Because iron is a product of corrosion in steel piping systems, often the iron found in water from a distribution system is from this source and does not represent iron left from the treatment process in the water treatment plant.

Nitrate [NO_3^-—Molecular Weight, 62, Usually Expressed as N (Nitrogen), Atomic Weight 14; Group VA, Nonmetal]

Nitrate, like ammonia, comes into water via the nitrogen cycle, rather than through dissolving minerals. Its concentration is limited by drinking water standards to 45 mg/l for physiological reasons. There are no reported uses of water where nitrate is a restrictive factor. There is an increase of total nitrogen in sewage plant effluent in the range of 20–40 mg/l as N above the level in the water supply. A great deal of this is ammonia, but some is nitrate. The only chemical process that removes nitrate is anion exchange; nitrate can be converted to nitrogen in a biological system by the action of the nitrifying bacteria. The nitrate content of well water is usually appreciably higher than surface water.

Potassium (K^+—Atomic Weight 39.1; Group IA, Alkaline Metal)

Potassium is closely related to sodium—so much so that it is seldom analyzed as a separate constituent in water analysis. Its occurrence is less widespread in nature, and for that reason it is found at lower concentrations than sodium.

It has no significance in public water supplies or in water used for industrial purposes. As with sodium it can be removed chemically only by cation exchange, or by physical processes such as evaporation and reverse osmosis.

Strontium (Sr^{+2}—Atomic Weight 87.6; Group IIA, Alkaline Earth Metal, Figure 6.1)

Strontium is in the same family as calcium and magnesium. Although its solubility in the presence of bicarbonate is significant (about half that of calcium) its occurrence is usually restricted to geological formations where lead ores occur, so its concentration in water is typically quite low. It is completely removed by any process used for calcium removal. If not removed by softening, in a scaling water it will be a contributor to the scale problem.

CLASS 3—TERTIARY CONSTITUENTS

This group includes materials generally found at concentrations exceeding 0.01 mg/l.

Aluminum (Al^{+3}—Atomic Weight 27; Group IIIA, Metal)

Although aluminum constitutes a high percentage of the Earth's crust as a common component of a wide variety of minerals and clays, its solubility in water is so low that it is seldom a cause for concern either in municipal supplies or industrial water systems. However, in industrial systems, the carryover of alum floc from a clarifier may cause deposit problems, particularly in cooling systems where phosphate may be applied as a stabilizing treatment. Aluminum found in treated water systems is usually there because of colloidal residues (alumina, Al_2O_3) from the coagulation of the water if alum or aluminate is used as the coagulant. If the residuals are objectionable, they can be removed by improved filtration practices.

As shown by the solubility curves (Figure 6.6) aluminum is amphoteric, being present as Al^{+3} or lower valence hydroxyl forms at low pH and the aluminate anion at higher pH's. As might be expected from this amphoteric nature, alumina particles are positively charged at low pH and negatively charged at high pH, as indicated by Figure 6.7. The effectiveness of alum in precipitating negatively charged colloids, such as clay particles from water, is more likely related to the charge on the precipitated alumina than the charge on the aluminum ion itself, since the aluminum ion is not soluble in the typical coagulation pH range of 5–7. Its strong negative charge at pH 10.0–10.5 helps explain the effectiveness of sodium aluminate in precipitating magnesium hardness, which is positively charged at this pH.

Arsenic (As—Atomic Weight 74.9; Group VA, Nonmetal)

The solubility of arsenic in water is so low that its presence is usually an indicator of either mining or metallurgical operations in the watershed or runoff from agricultural areas where arsenical materials have been used as industrial poisons. If in colloidal form, it would be removed by conventional water treatment processes. Federal regulations limit the content in public water supplies to a maximum of 0.1 mg/l total arsenic. If the material is present in organic form, it may be removed by oxidation of the organic material and subsequent coagulation, or by an adsorption process.

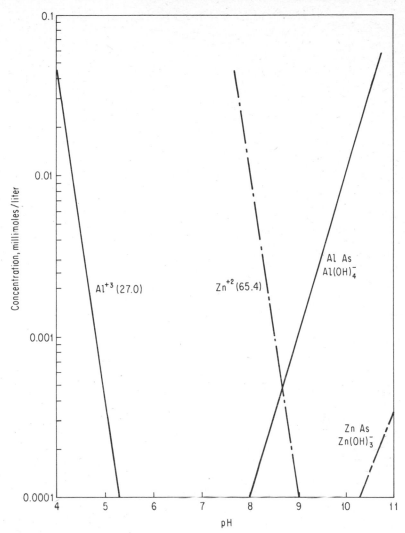

Figure 6.6 Theoretical solubilities of oxides and hydroxides in water at 25°C, showing amphoteric nature of aluminum and zinc. *(From "Aquatic Chemistry," by W. Stumm and J. J. Morgan.)*

Barium (Ba⁺²—Atomic Weight 137.3; Group IIA, Alkaline Earth Metal)

In natural waters containing bicarbonate and sulfate, the solubility of barium is less than 0.1 mg/l, and it is seldom found at concentrations exceeding 0.05 mg/l. Removal to low residuals can be expected in conventional lime treatment processes. There are instances of barium being added to water for the specific purpose of sulfate reduction. The reaction is hindered because the barium reagent itself is so insoluble that considerable time is needed for the reactions to occur; furthermore, sulfate deposition on the surface of the barium reagent makes the process inefficient. Barium is limited in drinking water to a maximum concentration of 1 mg/l.

Figure 6.7   Variation of particle charge with the nature of the particle and pH. *(From "Aquatic Chemistry," by W. Stumm and J. J. Morgan.)*

Bromide (Br⁻—Atomic Weight 79.9; Group VIIA, Halide)

Bromine is found in sea water at about 65 mg/l as the bromide ion; some connate waters produced with oil contain several hundred mg/l and are the source of commercial bromine. Over 0.05 mg/l in fresh water may indicate the presence of industrial wastes, possibly from the use of bromo-organo compounds as biocides or pesticides.

Copper (Cu⁺²—Atomic Weight 63.5; Group IB Metal)

Copper may be present in water from contact with copper-bearing minerals or mineral wastes from copper production. It is more likely, however, that the copper found in water will be a product of corrosion of copper or copper alloy piping or fittings, or may have been added deliberately to a water supply reservoir for algae control, as copper sulfate. When copper sulfate is added for algae control, because its solubility is limited, organic chelating materials may be added to the copper sulfate formulation to keep the copper from precipitating and, therefore, maintain its effectiveness. Drinking water regulations limit the municipal water supply concentration to 1 mg/l maximum. At higher concentrations, the water has an astringent taste. If a water supply is corrosive to copper, the first drawing or tapping of the supply from piping which has been idle overnight may contain relatively high concentrations, and ingestion of this water may cause immediate vomiting. In industrial supplies, the presence of copper can be objectionable as it is corrosive to aluminum. Copper is essential to certain aquatic organisms, being present in hemocyanin in shellfish, the equivalent of hemoglobin in humans.

Lead (Pb⁺²—Atomic Weight 207.2; Group IV, Metal)

The presence of lead in fresh water usually indicates contamination from metallurgical wastes or from lead-containing industrial poisons, such as lead arsenate. However, lead may also appear in water as a result of corrosion of lead-bearing alloys, such as solder. Being amphoteric, lead is attacked in the presence of caustic alkalinity.

The limitation on lead in drinking water has been established as 0.05 mg/l, which should be readily achieved with good filtration practice. In waste waters where lead may be complexed with organic matter, it may be solubilized, and oxidation of the organic may be required for complete lead removal.

Lithium (Li⁺—Atomic Weight 6.9; Group IA Alkali Metal)

This alkaline earth element is rare in nature and seldom analyzed in water. There are no records of experience indicating that this material is of concern either in industrial or municipal water supplies. Its salts have a wide variety of uses, but the industrial consumption is so low that it is not likely to be a significant factor in the waste waters from industries using these products.

Manganese (Mn⁺², Mn⁺⁴—Atomic Weight 54.9; Group VIIB, Metal)

Manganese is present in many soils and sediments as well as in metamorphic rocks. In water free of oxygen, it is readily dissolved in the manganous (Mn^{+2}) state and may be found in deep well waters at concentrations as high as 2–3 mg/l. It is also found with iron in acid mine drainage. Waste waters from metallurgical and mining operations frequently contain manganese.

It is an elusive material to deal with because of the great variety of complexes it can form depending on the oxidation state, pH, bicarbonate-carbonate-OH equilibria, and the presence of other materials, particularly iron.

It is limited to 0.05 mg/l maximum by drinking water regulations, because higher concentrations cause manganese deposits and staining of plumbing fixtures and clothing. However, concentrations even less than this can cause similar effects, as it may accumulate in the distribution system as a deposit, to be released in higher concentrations later, if the environment should change, such as by change in pH, CO_2 content, oxidation potential, or alkalinity.

In industrial systems it is as objectionable as iron, particularly in textile manufacture or the manufacture of bleached pulp, since small amounts of deposited manganese can slough off to cause stained products which must be rejected. Reduction to levels as low as 0.01 mg/l are required for certain textile finishing operations.

In the oxidized state, manganese is quite insoluble, and can be lowered in concentration, even in an alum coagulation process by super chlorination with adequate filtration, even at a pH as low as 6.5. However, the conventional process for removal of manganese by itself is oxidation plus elevation of the pH to approximately 9–9.5, with retention of approximately 30 minutes in a reaction vessel before filtration. Filters that have gained a coating of manganese oxides can work very effectively, but may slough manganese if the aquatic environment is radically changed. Manganese is also precipitated by the continuous application of potassium permanganate ahead of a manganese form of zeolite.

Organic materials can chelate manganese much as they chelate iron, so destruction of the organic matter is often a necessary part of the manganese removal process.

Because manganese accumulates in sediments, it is common to find high levels of manganese in deep water where none may be apparent at the surface. This should be studied in designing the proper intake structure for a plant water supply. An example of this is illustrated in Figure 6.8, showing the manganese concentrations in a lake at various times of the year and at different depths in the lake.

Phosphate (PO₄⁻³, Molecular Weight 95; Compound of Phosphorus P—Atomic Weight 31)

Phosphorus is found in many common minerals such as apatite, in the form of phosphate (PO_4^{-3}—equivalent weight 31.7). Since phosphate compounds are widely used in fertilizers and detergents, it is common to find phosphate in silt from agricultural runoff, with fairly high concentrations being found in municipal waste water, usually in the range 15–30 mg/l as PO_4 (about 5–10 mg/l P). Since phosphate is commonly blamed as the primary cause of excessive algal growths, which lead to eutrophication of lakes and streams, a reduction of phosphate is being brought about by legislation restricting the amount of phosphate in detergents and also requiring treatment of municipal sewage for phosphate removal.

Phosphate may be present in water as HPO_4^{-2} and $H_2PO_4^-$ as well as the higher pH form, PO_4^{-3}. The distribution as affected by pH is shown in Figure 6.9.

Phosphate can be reduced to very low levels by treatment with alum, sodium aluminate, or ferric chloride, with a formation of insoluble aluminum phosphate and iron phosphate. It can also be precipitated with lime at a pH over 10 to produce residuals less than 2–3 mg/l in the form of hydroxyapatite; in a hot process system, the residuals would be less than 0.5 mg/l.

Figure 6.8 Manganese concentration in the top and bottom layers of a lake, as affected by seasonal changes. *(From "Chemistry of Manganese in Lake Mendota, Wisconsin," Environmental Science and Technology, December 1968.)*

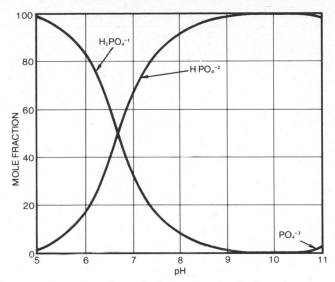

Figure 6.9 The effect of pH on the distribution of various phosphate species.

These phosphate precipitates are often colloidal, and filtration is required to achieve the low residuals specified.

Zinc (Zn⁺²—Atomic Weight 63.4; Group IIB, Metal)

Zinc is a Group IIB metal, behaving quite like calcium in solution, although of considerably lower solubility in natural waters with a neutral pH and having bicarbonate alkalinity. (See Figure 6.6 for its solubility characteristics.) Zinc is seldom found at concentrations over 1 mg/l, with a typical concentration being approximately 0.05 mg/l. Because it tends to have an astringent taste, its concentration in public water supplies is limited to 5 mg/l maximum.

Zinc may be present in water because of waste discharges from mining, metallurgical, or metal finishing operations. It may also appear because of corrosion of galvanized steel piping. It is often included in proprietary corrosion inhibitors where its effect on steel piping is similar to that of galvanizing.

Zinc would be removed in lime softening operations to residuals well below 0.1 mg/l. It can also be removed by cation exchange on either the sodium or the hydrogen cycle.

CLASS 4—TRACE CONSTITUENTS

Materials in this group (Table 6.3) are generally found at concentrations less than 0.01 mg/l.

CLASS 5—TRANSIENT CONSTITUENTS

This class includes constituents which change in concentration or activity not by dilution, dissolution, or precipitation, but rather by changes in the aquatic environment which disturb the equilibrium. These changes may come about from biological activity, oxidation-reduction potential, or radioactive decay.

TABLE 6.3—Class 4—Trace Constituents

Constituent	Occurrence*	Behavior†
Antimony (Sb, Group VA, At. Wt. 74.9)	Leaching of metallurgical slags; colloidal hydrous oxides	Insoluble in aqueous systems containing $HCO_3/CO_3/OH$. Filterable.
Cadmium (Cd, Group IIB, At. Wt. 112.4)	Plating wastes; limited solubility as Cd^{+2}. Note: Restricted in potable water supplies to 0.01 mg/l maximum.	Behaves as Ca and Zn (see Figure 6.6). Can be precipitated as carbonate or removed by cation exchange.
Chromium (Cr, Group VIB, At. Wt. 52)	Plating wastes, cooling tower blowdown. Soluble as $CrO_4^{-2}(Cr^{+6})$; insoluble as Cr^{+3}. Note: Restricted in potable water supplies to 0.05 mg/l maximum as Cr.	As CrO_4^{+2}, oxidizing agent. Can be reduced by SO_2 to Cr^{+3} or removed by anion exchange. As Cr^{+3}, colloidal hydrous oxide at neutral pH, filterable.
Cobalt (Co, Group VIII, At. Wt. 59)	Present in copper and nickel bearing ore tailings; ceramic wastes.	Behaves as iron.
Cyanide (CN⁻, Eq. Wt. 26)	Wastes from plating shops, coke plants, blast furnaces, petroleum refining. Note: Restricted in potable water supplies to 0.2 mg/l maximum.	Behaves as Cl^-, No_3^-, highly soluble. Can be oxidized with Cl_2 to CNO^- and $N_2 + CO_2$. Reduced in activated sludge biodigestion. Removable by anion exchange. Forms complexes with Cd, Fe.
Mercury (Hg, Group IIB, At. Wt. 200.6)	Wastes from electrolytic NaOH production, leaching of coal ash. Note: Restricted in potable water supplies to 0.002 mg/l maximum.	May be methylated by bacterial activity and taken up by the aquatic food chain. Removed by closing plant loop or by reduction and filtration.
Nickel (Ni, Group VIII, At. Wt. 58.7)	Plating wastes; electric furnace slag or dust; ore tailings.	Ni^{+2} behaves as iron, Fe^{+2}. Seldom present as Ni^{+3}. Precipitates as hydroxide and basic carbonate. Sulfide precipitates are insoluble. Removable by cation exchange.
Tin (Sn, Group IVA, At. Wt. 118.7)	Tinplate waste.	Converted to hydrous oxide colloid at neutral pH or in HCO_3/CO_3 environment.
Titanium (Ti, Group IVB, At. Wt. 47.9)	Ilmenite in well formation.	Colloidal TiO_2. Removed by filtration.

* Most constituents in Class 4 are introduced by industrial waste discharges, and are more generally found in surface than in well waters.

† Removal processes for metals may be hindered by the presence of chelating materials, e.g. citrate, EDTA, etc.

Acidity-Alkalinity

The typical domain of almost all natural waters is characterized by a pH range of 6–8, the presence of bicarbonate alkalinity, and some CO_2 dissolved in the water. All waters tend to reach this equilibrium: it is the end result of the chemical reactions that cause the weathering of rocks and of the oxidation-reduction reactions which are mediated by aquatic organisms. Because of this, the few exceptional streams that contain free mineral acidity usually dissipate this condition by accelerated weathering of the alkaline components of the rocks they contact. Likewise, when the pH exceeds 8 and carbonate alkalinity begins to appear, this is brought into balance by reaction with carbon dioxide from the atmosphere or from respiration of aquatic life.

Uncontrolled discharge of industrial wastes could wipe out this natural buffering effect of equilibrium between the aquatic environment, the atmosphere, and the lithosphere.

Since legislation now prohibits such discharge, the only circumstances that can cause waters to fall outside the natural conditions are accidental spills of large volumes of strong chemicals, seepage of acid mine drainage into a stream, or acid rain from air pollution. The mine seepage may not be controllable because of inability to locate the source or the point of entry into the stream.

Carbon Cycle Constituents Carbon. C—Atomic Weight 12.0; Group IVA, Nonmetal, see Figure 6.10)

Carbon is one of the primary elements of living matter, as shown by the generalized formula for biomass. It has been hypothesized that Earth's primitive environment contained carbon in the form of methane plus ammonia, water, and hydrogen gases. Methane is one of the carbon compounds present in the carbon cycle (Figure 6.10), produced by fermentation of larger organic molecules. Carbon dioxide and bicarbonate-carbonate alkalinity are also prominent in the cycle.

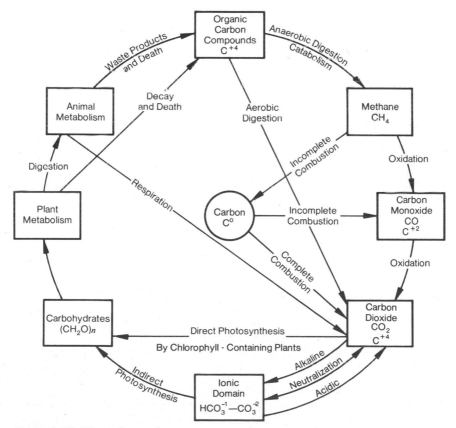

Figure 6.10   The carbon cycle.

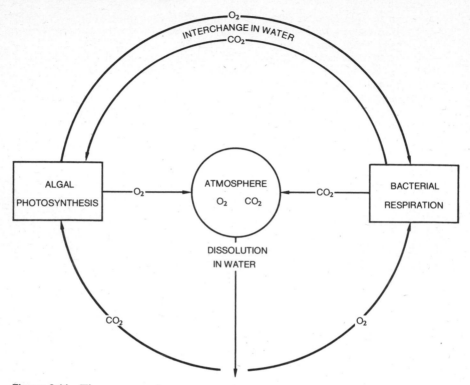

Figure 6.11   The oxygen cycle.

These reactions are proceeding in the aquatic environment in the carbon cycle, Figure 6.10.

Methane, a major component of natural gas, is produced by anaerobic decomposition of organic chemical compounds. Methane is given off by anaerobic decomposition of organic sediments in marsh gases, and the concentration may become so high that the swamp gas may ignite. It is more common to find methane in well waters in areas where natural gas is produced than in surface waters.

Oxygen Cycle Constituents

The most common carbon-containing gas is carbon dioxide, discussed in earlier chapters. The carbon dioxide content of surface waters is greatly influenced by bacterial and algal symbiotic existence, illustrated by the oxygen cycle, Figure 6.11. During bright sunlight, the photosynthetic reactions proceed so rapidly that the water may actually become super-saturated with oxygen, beyond the capacity of the bacteria to utilize. If algae require more carbon dioxide than is available from bacterial respiration, they assimilate carbon dioxide from the bicarbonate alkalinity, producing a trace of carbonate alkalinity. For that reason, carbon dioxide and oxygen are variable in most surface supplies, as affected by sunlight and the photosynthetic process (Figure 6.12).

The plant tissue built up by photosynthesis is eventually metabolized by larger aquatic organisms that produce organic compounds and discharge them in their wastes. Organic compounds are also produced by the death and decay of the

Figure 6.12 Diurnal variation of oxygen and carbon dioxide in a surface water.

aquatic plants and fish life. Organic matter thus produced becomes food for bacteria and is returned to the cycle as methane by anaerobes and as carbon dioxide by aerobic bacteria.

Deep well water often contains over 25 mg/l CO_2, and may be saturated with this gas at the hydrostatic pressure and temperature in the water table. A drop in pressure as water flows across the well screen may cause the CO_2 to come out of solution, disrupting the equilibrium and depositing $CaCO_3$ scale.

The theoretical solubility of oxygen exposed to the atmosphere is dependent on the temperature (Figure 6.13). Excess oxygen concentration is due to photosynthesis, and a deficiency is usually caused by bacterial activity or reducing agents.

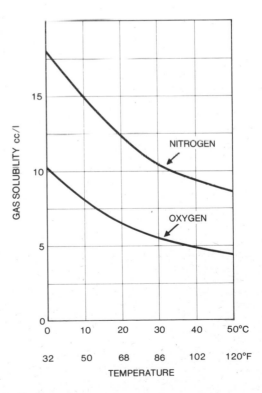

Figure 6.13 Solubilities of oxygen and nitrogen in water at various temperatures.

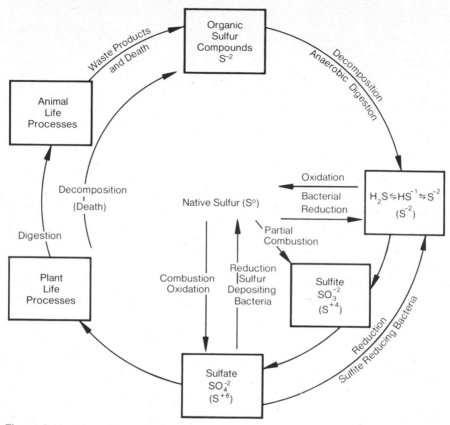

Figure 6.14 The sulfur cycle.

Nitrogen Cycle Constituents (Figure 6.4)

Constituents of the nitrogen cycle have been discussed earlier. As was true with the carbon cycle, the nitrogen cycle is involved with life in the aquatic environment.

Sulfur Cycle (Figure 6.14)

Because sulfur is in the same family as oxygen, there are many compounds where sulfur replaces oxygen in a compound with similar properties. For example, ethanol (CH_3CH_2OH) and ethyl mercaptan (CH_3CH_2SH) are analogous compounds with only the sulfur and oxygen atoms interchanged.

Certain bacteria can metabolize the sulfur atom in hydrogen sulfide, just as algae and other plants can metabolize oxygen from water in photosynthesis to produce free oxygen and carbohydrate. The byproduct of the bacterial process of splitting H_2S is free sulfur. The corresponding chemical equations are:

$$CO_2 + 2\ H_2O \xrightarrow[\text{photosynthesis}]{\text{Algal}} CH_2O + O_2 + H_2O \tag{2}$$

$$CO_2 + 2\ H_2S \xrightarrow[\text{action}]{\text{Bacterial}} CH_2O + 2\ S + H_2O \tag{3}$$

Hydrogen sulfide, which is present in some deep well waters and some stagnant surface waters, is generally produced by the anaerobic decomposition of organic compounds containing sulfur or by sulfate-reducing bacteria capable of converting sulfate to sulfide.[1]

All of these biological processes that occur in nature can be put to work under controlled conditions by the water specialist, to digest and eliminate undesirable organic wastes or their byproducts.

Oxidation-Reduction Potential

Some materials in water are transient because they tend to oxidize or reduce other constituents, either through biological activity, as illustrated by the several biological cycles, or directly. The presence of these materials has already been considered in the text covering the biological cycles and the constituents taking part in these cycles.

The only significant oxidizing materials encountered in the natural environment that can participate in chemical reactions without needing a biological route are oxygen, which is prevalent in surface supplies, and sulfur, which is encountered by subsurface waters in contact with native sulfur, a special situation. There are numerous oxidizing materials that can appear as residues in treated wastewaters—among these are free chlorine and chromate.

The common reducing materials are organic material, ferrous iron, Fe^{+2}, manganese, Mn^{+2}, and bisulfide, HS^-, from the natural environment; reducing materials which may be added as treatment byproducts or waste residues include a wide variety of organic matter, ferrous iron from such operations as steel pickling, and sulfite, present in certain kinds of pulp mill wastes.

Radionuclides

Water itself is not radioactive, but may contain elements that are. These enter the water cycle as wastes from nuclear power plants, fallout from nuclear blasts, or the byproducts of metallurgical processing of radioactive materials. In very rare cases, well waters may contain radionuclides —common radioactive elements and their isotopes—as natural contaminants.

The water chemist normally deals with concentrations at part per million (mg/l) levels. One mole of any substance represents its molecular weight, so that the concentration of one mole per liter as calcium carbonate represents 100 grams per liter as $CaCO_3$. Since a mole contains 6×10^{23} molecules, 100 grams per liter contains this number of molecules, and 100 milligrams per liter (100 mg/l) contains 6×10^{20} molecules. Even at the very low concentration level of only one part per billion (0.001 mg/l), then, there are still 6×10^{15} molecules as calcium carbonate in a liter of water. Concentrations of radioactive substances at this level would be extremely dangerous.

In chemical change, one element reacts with another in a process involving the electrons surrounding the nucleus, with the nucleus remaining unchanged. Energy may be given off or may be absorbed in the form of heat. With nuclear reactions, on the other hand, only the nucleus is affected, and the products of

[1] In each of these cycles involving biological activity, the changes occurring in surface water are much more pronounced than those occurring in deep well waters. The surface supplies are constantly inoculated by microbes from the air and from the soil and supplied with solar energy. On the other hand, well water usually represents a dead-end in the cycle, with the water generally having a long residence time in the aquifer, with the likelihood that most organisms have been filtered by the porous formation so that all of the microbes may have been removed from the strata at the well screen. Because of this, it is common to find that the consituents of the carbon cycle, particularly CO_2, those of the nitrogen cycle, particularly NO_3^-, and those of the sulfur cycle, particularly SO_4^{-2} and HS^-, are relatively constant in well waters. For the same reason, the concentrations of CO_2, NO_3^-, and HS^-, are generally higher in deep well water than in surface supplies.

reaction may include nuclear particles (such as protons, neutrons, or electrons) and energy, including heat and electromagnetic radiation. The typical by-products of nuclear reactions, then, are alpha particles, electrons, and electromagnetic radiations. The general characteristics of these emanations are shown in Table 6.4.

TABLE 6.4   Types of Radiation

Alpha	Helium nuclei, charge +2, mass 4.	Can penetrate air, but is stopped by solids.
Beta	Electrons charge −1, mass 0.	About 1000 times more penetrating than alpha radiation. Can penetrate 2–3 mm into solids.
Gamma	Similar to X-rays	Can penetrate air or solids about ten times deeper than beta radiation.

Some nuclear reactions are extremely rapid, occurring in a split second, but others may require 1000 years. Because these reactions may never go to completion, the life of a material participating in a nuclear reaction (called a radio-nuclide) is expressed as the time required for one-half its energy to be dissipated, its half-life. Each nuclear disintegration can be measured by the particles given off. The unit of measurement is the curie, defined as 3.7×10^{10} disintegrations per second. The levels of radioactive disintegration of concern to the water technologist are so far below this, that they are expressed as micromicrocuries, or picocuries (pCi), a pCi being equal to 2.2 disintegrations per minute.

A variety of radionuclides may be found in waters leaving a nuclear power plant. The government license to operate such a plant specifies the particular radionuclides which must be identified individually. This requires sophisticated and painstaking analytical techniques. In municipal supplies, it is not required that individual species be identified because the radiation levels are so low, but an analysis is required for alpha radiation, which is assumed to be contributed by Ra^{226}, beta radiation (assumed to be contributed by strontium, Sr^{90}) and gross beta activity. Table 6.5 shows the relative relationship between occupational levels and potable water levels and also relates the radiation intensity to the concentration of Ra^{226} or Sr^{90} in the water. It is obvious that the concentration levels are far below those considered significant when dealing with non-radioactive contaminants in water supplies.

TABLE 6.5   Radionuclide Contamination in Water

	Ra^{226}	Sr^{90}
Occupational levels (body exposure)		
pCi/1	4×10^1	8×10^2
ppb	4×10^{-5}	4×10^{-6}
Potable levels (ingestion)		
pCi/1	3	10^1
ppb	3×10^{-6}	5×10^{-8}

The heavier radionuclides are generally insoluble and may be removed by coagulation and filtration; the soluble constituents may be removed by ion exchange. These processes become quite complicated when the radionuclides are present in very low concentrations and the treatment process may first have to react with more common contamination, such as calcium and magnesium, at concentrations far above those of the radionuclides before the radionuclides are reduced to acceptable levels.

SUGGESTED READING

Davies, S. N., and DeWiest, R. C. M.: *Hydrogeology.* John Wiley & Sons, 1966.

Faust, S. J., and Hunter, J. V.: *Organic Compounds in the Aquatic Environment,* Marcel Dekker, Inc., 1961.

McKee, J. E., and Wolf, H. W.: *Water Quality Criteria.* State Water Quality Control Board, Resources Agency of California, 1963.

Nordell, Eskel: *Water Treatment for Industrial and Other Uses.* Reinhold, 1961.

Rubin, J., Ed.: *Aqueous-Environmental Chemistry of Metals.* "Sources and Distribution of Trace Metals in Aquatic Environments," Williams, S. L., et al. Ann Arbor Science Publishers, Inc., 1976.

Stumm, W., and Morgan, J. J.: *Aquatic Chemistry.* John Wiley & Sons, 1970.

Todd, Dand K.: *The Water Encyclopedia.* Port Washington, N. Y., Water Information Center, 1970.

U.S. Environmental Protection Agency: *National Water Quality Inventory,* Report to Congress. EPA-440/9-75-014, 1975.

U.S. Environmental Protection Agency: *Quality Criteria for Water.* EPA-440/9-76-023, 1976.

U.S. Environmental Protection Agency: *Recommended Uniform Effluent Concentration.* U.S. Government Printing Office, 1973.

Chapter 7
Water Gauging, Sampling, and Analysis

Knowing the rate of flow of water and the concentrations of substances it carries is necessary to the solution of many problems in water supply, utilization and ultimate disposal. Development of such information requires:

a. Measurement, or gauging, of water flow rates.

b. Collection of representative samples of the water

c. Examination and analysis of the samples

For purposes of establishing user charges, as well as operating treatment facilities and proportioning treatment chemicals, most plants meter incoming water supplies. The total flow as well as the flow to individual processing areas within a plant may be measured.

After collection and treatment, water is usually distributed through completely filled mains and pipes under the pressure (head) produced at the intake. The rate of flow, then, depends principally upon the difference in pressure existing between the inlet and outlet, and the size of the pipe. The pressure difference establishes the velocity of water flowing through the line. The rate of flow equals the cross-sectional area of the pipe multiplied by the velocity of the water movement through it, or

$$Q = AV$$

where Q = volume of flow past a given point per unit of time

A = cross-sectional area of the pipe or conduit

V = velocity of fluid travel in terms of distance per unit of time

Some water meters, called displacement meters, measure flow by responding to the volume of water throughput. A familiar example is the disc type meter widely used in homes and buildings. In this design, the displacement of the disc, usually by a rotary motion, is directly proportional to the volume of water passing

Figure 7.1 The turbine meter is widely used in industrial plants to measure the consumption of municipal water, where measurement of flow rate is not essential. (*Courtesy Neptune International Corporation.*)

through the meter body. The disc rotation drives a gear train actuating a totalizer comparable to the mileage indicator in an automobile. Another displacement meter is the turbine type flow transmitter (Figure 7.1), in which water causes a multi-blade rotor to spin at a velocity proportional to flow rate.

USING PRESSURE CHANGES

A different method, that measures flow indirectly, responds to pressure differential manifestations of water velocity. Because water is incompressible, the quantity passing one point in a full conduit in a unit of time is exactly the same as that passing any other point, regardless of line size restrictions or changes occurring along the conduit. Since the volumetric flow is constant, the velocity must increase where flow passes through a restriction. The pressure at the restriction decreases in proportion to such velocity increase. This relationship is the basis for operation of widely-used differential pressure type measuring devices where the restriction is a thin plate orifice, flow nozzle, or venturi tube. Such devices are carefully designed to be installed in the path of flow to create a velocity increase and a corresponding pressure decrease which can be accurately measured. The formula for calculating flow through the thin-plate orifice is:

	English		**Metric**
	$Q = 11.782d^2f\sqrt{H}$	$=$	$0.0125d^2f\sqrt{H}$
where Q =	gpm		m³/min
d =	orifice diam., inches		cm
H =	head loss, feet of H$_2$O		m

$f = 1$, unless d is more than 50% of pipe diameter D.

The factor f is calculated as follows:

$$f = \sqrt{\frac{1}{1 - (d/D)^4}}$$

Figure 7.2 shows an enclosed orifice installation and the correct location of the pipe taps for measuring head loss. Flow through an orifice based on head loss can be determined from the graph in Figure 7.3.

With the enclosed orifice, either a mercury manometer type meter body or a diaphragm type differential converter (Figure 7.4) is connected by means of suitable pipe taps to measure the differential pressure.

Thin plate orifices are the least expensive, easiest to install, and the most widely used of the differential pressure type devices for flow measurement. But an undesirable feature, as illustrated in Figure 7.5, is that they produce a relatively high permanent pressure loss. The venturi tube (Figure 7.6) is designed to reduce this loss to a negligible level. Venturi tubes offer the additional advantages of freedom from accumulation of entrapped solids. But, they are expensive compared to other devices. Flow nozzles fall between venturi tubes and thin plate orifices in both cost and permanent head loss.

Another differential pressure type flow measuring device, providing inexpensive and accurate measurement of relatively small rates of flow for clean water, is the rotameter, Figure 7.7. Transparent rotameter tubes have a tapered inner bore increasing in diameter from bottom to top of the tube. A metal bob in the tube comes to an equilibrium position at a point where the annular flow around it produces just the velocity and pressure difference needed to support its weight. The bob position alongside the calibrated graduations on the rotameter tube directly indicates rate of flow.

Some supply water metering methods do not require the installation of inline primary devices. For example, there is always a frictional loss of pressure proportional to water velocity across any pipe fitting in a line flowing full under pressure. Pipe elbows can be calibrated, though with considerably less accuracy than orifice plates or venturis, for use with flow measuring devices.

For very large supply lines, where the installation of permanent inline primary devices might be impractical or costly, pitot tubes (Figure 7.8) are useful for gauging flows. These are inserted into the line through special pressure fittings and positioned to measure the velocity head of the flowing water. The velocity head is the difference between the total head, sensed by the probe aperture facing upstream, and the static head in the line. Because velocities in a pipe are usually greater at the center of the pipe than along the walls, flow calcula-

Figure 7.2 Typical arrangement for installation of an orifice to meter flow rate as well as volume.

Figure 7.3   Flow through orifice plates based on differential head.

tions are based on the average of ten velocities measured at specific locations as the pitot traverses the diameter of the pipe. This average velocity multiplied by the cross-sectional area of the pipe produces the volumetric flow.

Methods Not Related to Pressure Drop

A supply water metering method not requiring the installation of inline primary devices is the magnetic flow meter (Figure 7.9). Offering no obstruction to flow, magnetic meter bodies are not subject to fouling by sediment as are differential pressure type primary devices. The principle of operation is based on Faraday's Law of Induction: a conductor moving through a magnetic field produces a voltage proportional to the velocity of the conductor. The water flowing through the pipe is the conductor, and an electrically energized coil produces the magnetic field. The induced voltage, proportional to velocity of flow, is measured by electrodes in contact with the water and transmitted to a meter that converts the signal to flow readout, taking into account the pipe diameter as a constant in initial calibration of the meter.

Another technique, applicable to occasional flow measurement in laterals not equipped with meters, is the measurement of the velocity of an additive injected into the line. The injected additive may cause a measurable increase in

Figure 7.4 Differential pressure cell used to convert head loss across a metering element into a signal to activate a recording and integrating device. *(Courtesy The Foxboro Company.)*

conductivity, such as by sodium chloride addition, or an increase in color, such as by dye injection. The salt or dye is injected in a slug into the line upstream, and the travel of the salt or dye cloud is carefully timed between downstream sampling points a known distance apart. The conductivity chart example shown in Figure 7.10 illustrates the measurement of passage time between the recorded median conductivity values of a dissolved salt slug flowing past two sampling points. For dye injection, similar charts can be obtained through the use of commercially available recording fluorometers.

Where none of the preceding methods can be used, it may be possible to approximate supply water flow on the basis of line pressure readings and pump curves, draw-down from a supply tank, or by electrical amperage draw of the supply pump motor. Amperage readings can be converted to approximate flow discharge values from the pump curve normally supplied by the manufacturer. Newer plants provide permanent facilities for measuring wastewater flow as well as water supply. Many older plants lack such devices. In either case, wastewater flow is often quite different from raw water supply in that it may be collected in open sewers or flumes instead of closed piping.

ORIFICE METER

Figure 7.5 Comparison of differential head to permanent head loss for flow through an orifice.

FLOW

D = MAXIMUM PRESSURE DIFFERENTIAL
P = PERMANENT PRESSURE LOSS.

VENTURI TUBE

UPSTREAM PRESSURE

P

D

H₁   H₂

FLOW

D = MAXIMUM PRESSURE DIFFERENTIAL
P = PERMANENT PRESSURE LOSS.
FLOW IS PROPORTIONAL TO SQUARE ROOT OF
PRESSURE DIFFERENTIAL H₁ MINUS H₂

Figure 7.6 Differential head and permanent head loss for flow through a venturi tube.

Measuring Wastewater Flows

Measuring these flows of wastewater often challenges the ingenuity of the expert. The stream may flow through subterranean sewers difficult of access. A careful survey of the sewerage system may reveal junction boxes and manholes where some type of measuring device may be installed. Wherever sewers, pipelines and trenches are accessible, accurate measurement of flow is possible. Some of the devices and procedures used are listed in Table 7.1.

Weirs are used frequently because of their simplicity and relative ease of use in wastewater flow measurement.

Figure 7.7 Typical rotameter used to indicate rate of flow. An output signal can be provided for remote indication and recording. *(Courtesy Fischer & Porter Co.)*

Figure 7.8 Pitot tube installation, showing connections for differential head measurement. *(Courtesy The Foxboro Company.)*

Commonly used weirs are either the rectangular or V-notch type. Rectangular weirs are applicable for flows of 100–4000 gpm (0.4–15.1 m³/min). V-notch weirs are more accurate at lower flows and are widely used for measurements in the 20–400 gpm range (0.08–15.1 m³/min).

Flow is proportional to the head of water above the lowest point of the weir opening, as shown in Figure 7.11. Head may be measured manually with a gauge or automatically by float mechanisms. Typical design of a weir box is shown in Figure 7.12.

In the use of weirs for wastewater flow measurement, care must be taken to avoid the accumulation of solids in the bottom of the box behind the weir.

Parshall flumes are used for measurement of flows in ditches and open channels where only very small head drops are available. These provide good accuracy over wide flow ranges. Under normal freeflow conditions, for example, a Parshall flume with 9″ throat width will accurately measure flows ranging from 45–2800 gpm (0.17–10.6 m³/min). A further advantage is that this flume design offers no traps for debris to settle.

Figure 7.9 The magnetic meter provides for unobstructed flow, offering advantages in metering sludges. *(Courtesy The Foxboro Company.)*

Figure 7.10 The conductivity method of flow measurement requires care in slugging and measuring chemical concentrations. This provides only a single measurement for each application, but is useful in establishing flow data in inaccessible sewers.

Figure 7.13 illustrates typical Parshall flume design. Prefabricated flume liners can be purchased in almost any required size. The liner can simply be used as the inside form for a concrete structure, with the liner left permanently in place. For temporary use, wood construction may be employed.

Flow is proportional to the head (depth) of water in the converging section of the flume, measured two-thirds of the length of the converging section upstream of the throat. Flow versus head measurement, for a 9″ throat width flume, is shown in Figure 7.14.

There are a number of other flume designs including easily installed prefabricated fiberglass fumes such as illustrated in Figure 7.15.

For automatic measurement of head at flumes and weirs of most varieties and sizes, relatively inexpensive instruments with suitable charts and flow totalizers are readily available. Typical float actuated instruments are pictured in Figure 7.16.

For measurement of flows in larger channels, receiving streams, and rivers, a useful procedure for approximating flows is to calculate the average cross-sectional area of the stream over a selected segment of known length; then to drop a suitable float into the water upstream of the selected test segment, and measure the time required for the float to travel the known length of the test segment.

To minimize the effects of wind, the float should be almost submerged. For such surface floats, if nothing is known of velocity distribution from top to bottom of the stream, mean velocity is usually assumed to be 0.8 times the surface velocity. Therefore, flow may be calculated as follows:

Flow (cfs) = 0.8 Float Velocity (ft/sec) × Stream Cross Section (sq ft)
Flow (m³/sec) = 0.8 × m/sec × m²

TABLE 7.1   Methods of Wastewater Flow Measurement

A. **For open channels**
   1. Weirs
   2. Flumes
   3. Float timing

B. **For discharge from open-end pipes**
   1. Discharge Timing Method
   2. Pipe Cap Orifice Method
   3. Coordinate Measurement
   4. California Pipe Method

C. **Indirect methods**
   1. Chemical Concentration
   2. Temperature Measurement

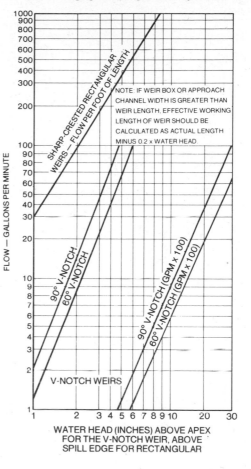

Figure 7.11 Flow charts for weirs based on water level measurements. The plot for the rectangular weir can be used to estimate the flow over a dam or over the uniform spilling edge of a clarifier.

Open Pipe Discharges

For open pipe discharge the simplest method is the discharge timing method. This is adaptable to small flows usually under 30 gpm (0.1 m³/min) where it is possible to catch the discharge in a container of known capacity. The container is put under the waste discharge and the filling is timed. This is repeated at least three times.

For larger volumes of free flow from vertical pipes into open sumps, another simple flow measurement technique is the use of a drilled and beveled pipe cap orifice, Figure 7.17.

Flow is a function of the pressure differential across the orifice. Since the flow discharges to atmosphere, flow for this device is simply proportional to the square root of the gauge pressure measured. The flow chart previously given for thin plate orifices can be used (Figure 7.3).

The coordinate measurement method is used to estimate flow of waste from the end of a horizontal pipe, where it is possible to observe all or part of the free-fall discharge. No devices or equipment installations are needed with this technique. Figure 7.18 illustrates coordinate measurement and flow calculation.

The California pipe method is a relatively accurate measurement which utilizes open-end discharge from a horizontal pipe segment having a length

Figure 7.12 Construction of a weir box.

equivalent to six pipe diameters. For example, a four-inch-diameter pipe used for this method should be at least 24 inches long. Figure 7.19 illustrates this method of flow measurement. Figure 7.20 plots flow versus measured water depth and pipe diameter.

The chemical concentration technique, which is applicable to either open or closed sewer systems, employs fixed rate injection of a suitable chemical into the flowing stream and testing downstream for the resultant concentration of that chemical. Flow may then be approximated as follows:

$$Q = \frac{2000\,I}{C_1 - C_2}$$

where Q = flow, gpm ($\times$ 3.785 = 1/min)

    I = chemical injected, lb/hr ($\times$ 0.454 = kg/hr)

    C_1 = upstream concentration of chemical

         (same chemical as I), mg/l

    C_2 = downstream concentration of chemical, mg/l

  2000 = conversion factor

The chemical selected for injection must be readily soluble in the flowing stream, should be compatible and non-reactive with other ions in stream, and should be easy to analyze with reasonable accuracy. Care should be taken to allow adequate mixing and distribution of the chemical in the stream ahead of point of downstream sampling.

Start with a chemical injection rate calculated to give a 100 mg/l analysis increase for the estimated flow. Using common salt, for example, approximately 5 lb/hr injection per 100 gpm flow would be required for 100 mg/l increase in NaCl reading.

ESTIMATING INDIVIDUAL FLOWS

There is a simple method used for measuring the flows in tributary streams when the flow in the combined sewer is known.

A common variable, such as conductivity or temperature, of all streams is

Figure 7.13   Construction of a Parshall flume.

Figure in chart:

PARSHALL FLUME
9-INCH THROAT WIDTH

BASIS: GPM = 1795.2 WH$^{1.522W^{.026}}$
WHERE: H = UPSTREAM HEAD (FEET)
W = THROAT WIDTH (FEET)

FLOW — GALLONS PER MINUTE

WATER HEAD (INCHES) MEASURED IN FLUME
CONVERGING SECTION ⅔ DISTANT UPSTREAM
OF THROAT INLET

Figure 7.14 Flow chart for a Parshall flume.

measured. The flow rates in the tributaries may then be calculated as a ratio of the tributary conductivities or temperatures from the following equations. The ratio then does not carry any unit label.

$$Q_t = Q_1 + Q_2$$
$$Q_t \lambda_t = Q_1 \lambda_1 + Q_2 \lambda_2$$
$$\text{or } Q_t T_t = Q_1 T_1 + Q_2 T_2$$

Figure 7.15 Installation of a prefabricated flume. *(Courtesy of F. B. Leopold Co.)*

Figure 7.16 Typical level measuring devices for weirs and flumes. *(Courtesy Leopold F. Stevens Instruments, Inc.)*

where Q_f = total flow rate
Q_1 = first tributary flow rate
Q_2 = second tributary flow rate
λ = conductivity
T = temperature

Substituting and solving for the ratio of Q_1 to Q_2,

$$\frac{Q_1}{Q_2} = \frac{\lambda_f - \lambda_2}{\lambda_1 - \lambda_f} \quad \text{or} \quad \frac{(T_1 - T_2)}{(T_1 - T_T)}$$

For example:

Main stream flow (Q_f) = 498 gpm (1.89 m³/min)
Main stream conductivity (λ_f) = 1120 μmho
Tributary 1 conductivity (λ_1) = 1500 μmho
Tributary 2 conductivity (λ_2) = 340 μmho

$$\frac{Q_1}{Q_2} = \frac{1120 - 340}{1500 - 1120} = 2.05$$

Figure 7.17 Simple open orifice cap measurement of flow to a sewer or open receiver.

$$FLOW\,(GPM) = 1800\,\frac{X\,(S)}{\sqrt{Y}}$$

WHERE:
X = DISTANCE IN FEET
Y = DISTANCE IN FEET
S = CROSS SECTIONAL AREA, IN SQUARE
    FEET, OF THE PIPE OR PORTION OF
    THE PIPE FILLED BY THE STREAM.

Figure 7.18 Measurements needed to measure flow by the coordinate method.

The flow of tributary 1 is calculated as follows:

$$Q_1 = \frac{Q_1}{Q_1 + Q_2} \times Q_t$$

if $Q_2 = x$, then $Q_1 = 2.05x$ and

$$\frac{Q_1}{Q_1 + Q_2} = \frac{2.05x}{2.05x + x} = \frac{2.05}{3.05}$$

$$Q_1 = \frac{2.05}{3.05} \times 498 = 335 \text{ gpm } (1.27 \text{ m}^3/\text{min})$$

$$Q_2 = 498 - 335 = 163 \text{ gpm } (0.62 \text{ m}^3/\text{min})$$

SAMPLING

The success of an entire water project may depend on the collection of a representative sample. In most water supply systems, this is rarely a problem. The composition of the supply water is seldom subject to either continuous or sudden, instantaneous variation. Even a surface water diluted by a spring downpour will usually change gradually enough so that the water treatment plant operator

AT LEAST 6 × D

(IN INCHES)

Figure 7.19 Measurements needed for the California pipe method.

Figure 7.20 Flow chart for California pipe method.

can cope with it. He must be aware of past climatological history and must schedule sampling based on the weatherman's predictions of rainfall.

Some supplies fluctuate because the town or plant draws on several wells of different composition, and these wells may cut in and out depending on demand. Here, too, it is usually possible to anticipate when the changeover in wells may occur, so that sampling can be scheduled accordingly.

SUSPENDED SOLIDS

With these relatively constant quality water streams, the presence of suspended solids may be one of the factors requiring special care in sampling. In the distribution pipe, suspended solids have a tendency to travel along the pipe wall, so that a sample pipe with its opening in the wall of the distribution pipe may trap more suspended solids than would be representative of the water flowing through the pipe. So, where suspended solids content is important, as in industrial condensate systems, the sampling line should protrude into the flow of the stream. A similar situation develops in open distribution flumes if floating matter is present. Flushing of lines and rinsing of containers with sample are always necessary to help assure drawing a representative sample once the correct provisions have been made for the sampling line.

Sampling wastewater correctly in an industrial complex often requires ingenuity. First, something must be known about the sewer system to select the best sample location. For example, if the sewer pipe is not completely filled, there may be three strata in the flowing water: the upper contains floating matter, the center may be free of floating matter and sediment, and the lower contains solids that have settled in spite of the velocity through the pipe. Truly representative sampling could conceivably require turbulent mixing upstream of the sampling location. Usually a compromise is made because mixing may be impossible: the person doing the sampling must decide what data are the most significant for plant control purposes.

ASSESS VARIABILITY FIRST

A first step in deciding on a sampling schedule is to determine an instrumental profile of the stream to be sampled. One procedure is to install automatic recording conductivity, pH, and temperature instruments at the point to be sampled— to operate over at least a 24-hour period. If the results show wide fluctuations, then the frequency of these fluctuations can be used as a guide for sampling intervals. There may be some periodicity in the readings, indicating a repetitive operation within the plant; if so, this should be investigated. If the readings remain relatively steady, samples can be widely spaced.

In the absence of continuous recording of conductivity, pH and temperature, manual samples should be taken following a checkerboard schedule, illustrated by Table 7.2. With this program, which requires data on water flow rate, samples are obtained every hour for a full operating day.

Each sample should be checked for conductivity and appearance. Those found to vary widely from the norm should be checked for pH and temperature. A measured volume of each sample should then be taken in proportion to flow rate past the point of sampling at the time of sampling. If a number of sewers flow into a main sewer, then the checkerboard schedule shows the measured volume of each sample to be taken in proportion to the flow to make an hourly plant composite. A more complete analysis is then made on the composite. Following this procedure for the whole day, a graph of analytical data plotted against time of sampling provides a clue for checking plant records to see which plant operations may have caused the deviations from normal conductivity, pH or temperature. Table 7.2 shows a checkerboard sampling program with five sampling points on tributary sewers leading to a common collection main. For such a program to be successful, the flow rate through each lateral must be known either by measurement or by reliable estimate.

AUTOMATIC SAMPLERS

A variety of samplers are available, the choice depending on the water source to be sampled. Samplers for surface waters can obtain samples from whatever depth may be desired. A complete program for surface waters would include sampling at a number of elevations from surface to bottom (Figure 7.21).

Wastewater samplers have special characteristics depending on the nature of the waste. Some of these devices, such as that illustrated in Figure 7.22, are designed for placement in a calibrated flume, such as a Parshall flume: the sampler is shaped so that the volume delivered on each cycle to a sample container is proportional to the flow.

Other samplers, such as those illustrated in Figure 7.23, operate on a timed sequence, and the identification of each sample must then be referred to a flowmeter chart so that a flow-proportional composite can be prepared from the individual samples.

Electrical, mechanical, and pneumatic samplers are available. Great care must be taken in the selection of the proper instrument for sampling based on knowledge of the operating conditions within the plant and the nature of the wastewater being sampled. There is certainly nothing more frustrating to a water survey team than to set up a sampling device and to return 24 hours later to

TABLE 7.2 Checkerboard Sampling
(Note: 1 ml of sample collected for each gpm of stream flow)

Time	Station						Composite (hourly plant,* ml)
	1	2	3	4	5	Total	
	Flow rate at time of sampling, gpm						
9 A.M.	15	105	70	0	180	370	370
10	2	90	55	75	175	397	397
11	8	90	100	60	175	433	433
12 noon	6	90	150	0	205	445	445
1 P.M.	10	95	45	10	160	320	320
2	10	10⁵	45	25	175	360	360
3	1	100	50	35	170	356	356
4	5	110	150	30	165	460	460
5	6	160	160	10	170	446	446
6	10	105	105	50	200	460	460
7	15	110	110	55	210	480	480
8	2	90	90	70	190	442	442
9	3	75	75	70	195	428	428
10	8	60	60	15	170	343	343
11	10	105	105	30	160	405	405
12 midnight	12	120	120	40	165	437	437
Average	7.7	96	93	36	179	417	417
Daily composite,† ml	123	1535	1390	575	2865	6582	6582‡

* Hourly plant composites (H-Series, or Horizontal) are taken by withdrawing from each bottle a volume proportional to flow at the time of sampling (for example, 1 ml/gpm) and combining. Each individual sample is examined for odor and color and checked for pH, TDS, or both. The composite may then be analyzed for other constituents, for example, oil. If the composite is too small, use 2 ml/gpm or more to make a larger composite.

† Daily composite at each sample station by the same technique. These may be more extensively analyzed for BOD, COD, mineral components, special toxicants (for example, cyanide from a refinery overhead), etc.

‡ The hourly composites may be combined as a daily total plant composite using the residue after tests have been run and combining on a proportional basis. For example, if only 100 ml has been used for analysis, measure out ½ of original volume of each hourly composite, combine, and use as total plant composite for one day.

find the sample container empty because the device has failed through lack of power or by clogging of the water channels or ports.

Once the sample has been taken, the person responsible should make certain observations and measurements before sending it to the laboratory. These observations should include appearance (color, haziness, turbidity, presence of floc, oil on surface), odor, and measurements that are valid only on a fresh sample (temperature, dissolved oxygen, and pH).

There are many reference books on water analysis procedures, some of which include simplified control tests as well as standard, or referee, methods.

Table 7.3 lists typical methods of analysis used for control purposes and in field studies. Most control laboratories in municipal and industrial plants are equipped to conduct these analyses. In doing survey work or in providing

Figure 7.21 This sampler used for surface water studies is tripped to close at predetermined depth.

technical service, most water specialists have miniaturized analytical equipment so that most of the tests shown in Table 7.3 can be conducted using portable test kits (Figure 7.24). Examples of the success that has been achieved in miniaturizing equipment for portability are the spectrophotometer, shown in Figure 7.25, and the membrane technique for bacteriological counts shown in Figure 7.26.

Figure 7.22 A sampler used to obtain flow-proportioned samples from a flume. *(Courtesy Lakeside Equipment Corporation.)*

Figure 7.23   A programmed sampler obtaining intermittent sewage samples.

The list in Table 7.3 does not include specialized test equipment such as corrosion meters, corrosion coupons, steam quality meters, and pH, conductivity, and temperature recorders.

Many of these analytical control procedures are modifications of standard methods acceptable to regulatory agencies. When a sample is taken for record purposes, standard methods must be used, and the sample is usually sent to a

Figure 7.24   One type of portable laboratory used for field and plant surveys and for monitoring services.

Figure 7.25 A miniature spectrophotometer used for a wide variety of analyses in the laboratory or in field studies. (*Courtesy Bausch & Lomb.*)

water laboratory fully equipped to follow these procedures. Figure 7.27 shows the application of special equipment available for analysis of water and water-formed deposits in such a laboratory.

Chemical analysts continually face new challenges in analyzing water supplies and waste discharges. Not only is there a growing need to measure a broader spectrum of water constituents, but also lower concentrations are being measured. To meet the need for rapid, accurate identification of water impurities, instrumental techniques are becoming more important.

Many techniques for analyzing the inorganic constituents in water and wastewater are well established and have been commonly used for many years. However, technological advances in analytical chemistry are continually creating new and more sensitive techniques and instruments for measuring these inorganic constituents. These advances, coupled with the deep concern over the health effects of certain of these inorganic materials at very low concentrations in drinking water and foods that necessarily come in contact with water, result in a constantly changing state-of-the-art in analytical chemistry.

Recently, emphasis on identifying and measuring organic constituents in water has been increasing. Because of physiological concerns, the volume of activity in organic analysis of water continues to grow. Although advances are being made, knowledge in this area is limited. Recent advances in gas and liquid chromatography and the availability of a computerized mass spectrometer-coupled gas chromatograph should lead to improved techniques.

Figure 7.26 Microbes are collected and cultured by pretreated elements which are not easily incubated. The sampler has a fine grid printed on it to facilitate counting of colonies. (*Courtesy Millipore Corporation.*)

TABLE 7.3 Analytical Control Methods

Type	Common tests
1. Volumetric (Titration)	Alkalinity, hardness, chloride, sulfite, chelate, zinc, COD
2. Spectrophotometric	Phosphate, iron, manganese, chromate, silica, nitrate, sulfate
3. Instrumental	Conductivity, ion selective electrode (F, CN), O_2, turbidity
4. Extraction	Oil, specific organics, filming inhibitors
5. Incubation	Plate counts, membrane filters, BOD

Brief descriptions of some of the instruments used for water analysis along with types of impurities and concentration ranges for each are given below. This section has been divided into inorganic and organic analysis instrumentation groupings depending on the principal use of each instrument. However, most instruments have some applications in both organic and inorganic analysis.

INORGANIC ANALYSIS

Atomic Absorption Spectroscopy (Figure 7.28)

Atomic absorption is a technique for measuring specific metals in both aqueous and nonaqueous systems. Although atomic absorption is widely used in other types of analytical problems, it is uniquely suited to analyze water because of the sensitivities available and the wide diversity of cations and metallic constituents it can detect.

The operation of the instrument is simple and rapid. About 68 different elements can be determined with varying degrees of sensitivity in the mg/l range and below. Results are accurate to within 5% of true values. The technique is relatively interference-free compared to wet chemical procedures and it is much faster. The use of this technique has continued to grow as the need for measuring heavy metals in various waste streams has become more important.

Figure 7.27 A display of the various devices and techniques commonly used for water analysis.

Figure 7.28 Simplified diagram of atomic absorption spectrophotometer.

Typical analyses performed by atomic absorption spectrophotometers include:

a. Raw water—trace metals and hardness
b. Brines and salts—heavy metals and other trace impurities
c. Plant effluents—pollutants such as Cr, Sn, Mn, Pb, and Hg
d. Treated water—hardness (to 0.1 ppm), Fe, and Cu

Optical Emission Spectrography (Figure 7.29)

The optical emission spectrograph is similar in principle to the atomic absorption spectroscope. It is a tool for qualitative and quantitative elemental analysis of solids, liquids, or gaseous materials. It has been used for many years for measuring low or trace level element concentrations in various matrices in manufacturing control and research applications. It has been used extensively for quality control analyses of metals in the steel, aluminum, and other metal industries. Improvements in instrument design and availability of analytical techniques for solution analysis by optical emission make this technique useful in the analysis of water samples.

Concentration steps are often required to provide the sensitivity needed for

Figure 7.29 Optical emission spectrograph.

Figure 7.30 Ion selective electrode with output measuring device.

water analyses. This technique, nevertheless, provides the simplest and most rapid method for a complete qualitative analysis of aqueous solutions. Standardization of concentration methods and establishment of basic analytical techniques make it possible to obtain both a qualitative and quantitative picture of the elements accurate to within 10% of true values.

The optical emission spectrograph used in conjunction with atomic absorption provides a high degree of flexibility in monitoring water or wastewater for a complete qualitative and quantitative picture of the many constituents that are important in treatment control.

Ion Selective Electrodes (Figure 7.30)

A variety of ion selective electrodes have proved valuable in water analysis through the direct potentiometric measurement of specific ions in aqueous systems. They can also be used as endpoint detectors for potentiometric titrations. These electrodes respond only to ionic materials, so to use them, sample preparation is sometimes necessary. The cyanide electrode, for example, requires distillation of the sample to break down complex metal cyanides that are not detectable with the electrode.

Electrodes specific for anions are especially useful since previous chemical procedures for analyzing anions were tedious. Electrodes are available for such anions as sulfide, fluoride, cyanide, and nitrate. These make it possible to monitor specific anions continuously in a water system, as is commonly done with pH instrumentation.

The ion selective electrodes work like pH electrodes, depending on a potential developed across a thin membrane by the difference in the concentrations of the ion to be measured on each side of the ionically conducting thin layer. The concentration within the electrode is fixed and the potential varies with the concentration of ions in the sample.

X-ray Fluorescence and Diffraction
(Figures 7.31, 7.32)

X-ray fluorescence has been used extensively for the analysis of water-formed deposits and corrosion products from various industrial systems. When the fluorescence technique is supplemented by several chemical methods of analysis, it is possible to obtain complete identification of these deposits. In wastewater analyses, the fluorescence method is used to characterize particulate matter filtered from the sample.

X-ray diffraction is used to identify crystalline materials in water-formed

VARIABLE
POSITION
CRYSTAL

X-RAY TUBE

θ

SAMPLE

SOLLER SLIT

PROTECTIVE
BOX

2θ

COUNTER-PRODUCES OUTPUT FOR EACH
ANGULAR POSITION (θ) OF CRYSTAL

Figure 7.31   X-ray fluorescence.

deposits. Based on the elemental analysis obtained by fluorescence techniques, one of several crystalline structures may exist, and identifying the structure may provide a clue to the mechanism of deposit formation. X-ray diffraction has limited usefulness in identifying organic materials.

In X-ray fluorescence, the sample, irradiated with high intensity X-rays, fluoresces to produce the X-ray line spectra of the elements present in the sample. The spectra are dispersed within the instrument to allow readout of these lines correlated to a particular analysis program. In X-ray diffraction, the crystalline material acts as a three-dimensional grating for the X-rays. The diffracted X-rays produce a pattern formed by the various sets of parallel planes which define the crystal lattice.

Flame Emission

Flame emission spectroscopy provides a sensitive, rapid method of analysis for the alkali metals in water. The method is less sensitive and more prone to interferences than atomic absorption spectroscopy, but it takes only about half the time.

DIFFRACTOMETER
CIRCLE

SAMPLE MOUNTED
ON TURNTABLE

θ

2θ

θ

0

SCANNING DEVICE
MEASURES OUTPUT AT
EACH ANGULAR POSITION

Figure 7.32   Diagram of X-ray diffraction instrument.

Visible and Ultraviolet Spectrophotometry

These techniques, especially using the visible region of the spectrum, continue in wide use today after many years of service. They are invaluable tools for measuring many inorganic constituents in water. They also have some applications in organic analyses, primarily in the ultraviolet region.

Microscopic Techniques

The analyst uses various microscopic techniques to characterize particulate material in water. These particulates must first be separated by filtration or other means. Light microscopy has been a much used tool for making particulate identification. Modern microscopes routinely provide magnification of 2000X. An experienced microscopist can often identify the chemical composition of particulate material by simple microscopic observation. He may add certain reagents to the specimen under observation to verify the presence of certain elements.

Recent improvements in electron microscopy have advanced the use of microscopic techniques in water chemistry. Both the transmission electron microscope and the scanning electron microscope are used in water analyses.

Transmission Electron Microscope (TEM)
(Figure 7.33)

Transmission electron microscopy (TEM) is used for the direct observation of small particulates stable in a high vacuum. Form and structure (morphology) can be established for rigid surfaces such as ceramics, metals, plastics, fibers and other organic and inorganic solids separated from water. The magnification range of the TEM is 220X to 1,000,000X with a resolution of two Angstrom units (2 Å).

Scanning Electron Microscopy (SEM)

The scanning electron microscope can be used for morphological characterization of particulates such as clays, spores, pollen, and bottom sediment. Particle size determination in the range of 0.05 to 100 microns can be made. The magnification range is from 20X to 200,000X with a resolution of 100 Å. This tech-

Figure 7.33 A view of the components of a transmission electron microscope.

Figure 7.34   Diatoms and silt observed by the scanning electron microscope at 1000X magnification.

nique has been used extensively for characterizing very small particulates in water (Figure 7.34).

Both the SEM and the TEM can be equipped with X-ray detectors to determine the elements present in the portion of the specimen in the beam of the microscope (Figure 7.35). In some cases it is even possible to obtain a quantitative analysis of the sample.

Miscellaneous Instrumental and Wet Chemical Analyses

There continues to be a great need for the "wet chemistry" methods of water analysis. In many cases they are the only ones acceptable to regulatory agencies. Chemical oxygen demand (COD), biochemical oxygen demand (BOD), and microorganism counts are examples. Although improved wet techniques have been developed, the methods are still tedious and time-consuming.

Many of the anions in water are analyzed by classical chemical methods because faster, more economical techniques are not yet available. In many cases, automated devices have been developed to facilitate these "wet chemistry" procedures (Figure 7.36).

Many instrumental techniques require chemical pretreatment of the sample to solubilize the constituent to be analyzed; to concentrate or dilute to the range of the instrument; or to handle chemical or instrumental interferences.

Total Carbon Analyzer (Figure 7.37)

The total carbon analyzer is used for the quantitative determination of carbonaceous material in aqueous media. The instrument accepts only a very small sample (approximately 20 microliters), so it is necessary that the carbon-containing materials be either dissolved or dispersed homogeneously. The instrument can be operated over several concentration ranges, such as 0–100 or 0–1000 mg/l. The sensitivity and accuracy are approximately 1–2% of the range covered, providing a capability to measure 1–2 mg/l of total carbon.

Most carbon analyzers measure both organic and inorganic carbon. To analyze only the organic carbon, it is necessary to remove the carbonate before injecting the sample into the instrument. Where chemical or biochemical oxygen demand tests (COD or BOD) are necessary to monitor organic pollutants, it may be possible to establish a correlation between total organic carbon (TOC) analysis and the COD or BOD values. The carbon analyzer requires 5–10 minutes per sample including pretreatment time. With the COD or BOD tests, considerably more operator time is required and results are not available for 3–4 hours in the case of the COD test, and 5 days for the BOD test.

Figure 7.35 Observation of particulates in a wastewater sample by SEM, with simultaneous analysis of individual particles 1 and 2, identified as a precipitate containing calcium, sulfur, and aluminum; and a diatom.

Figure 7.36   An automatic device for wet analysis of a battery of samples. *(Courtesy Technicon Instruments Corporation.)*

ORGANIC ANALYSIS

Infrared Spectroscopy (Figure 7.38)

Infrared spectroscopy (IR) is used to detect the presence of most organic functional groups, such as -COOH, -CHO, -CH$_3$, and -OH. Essentially all forms of organic materials that can be separated from water, wastewater, and water-formed deposits can be characterized by this method after appropriate sample

Figure 7.37   Total carbon analyzer in use for determining organic matter in water.

Figure 7.38 The infrared analyzer differentiates the functional groups on organic molecules extracted from water.

preparation. This technique is qualitative, since the separated fraction is usually a mixture. The sensitivity for various organic functional groups varies greatly but for ideal cases is as low as a few percent of the fraction analyzed. Detailed characterization of complex mixtures requires information from other types of analyses and chemical separations, such as elemental data and thin layer chromatopography.

An example of an IR spectrum is shown in Figure 7.39. The information shown led to the selection of additional analytical tools to more fully identify the organic materials present. The identification of fatty bisamide and polyethylene glycol ester pinpointed the production areas where process pollution was occurring.

IR is typically used on solvent extracts and, therefore, gives information on the least polar, nonvolatile components of a sample. New procedures are being developed for more effective separation of additional types of organic materials to be characterized by IR.

Nuclear Magnetic Resonance (Figure 7.40)

The IR spectrum provides a fingerprint by which to compare organic matter in a water sample to patterns of known compounds. The nuclear magnetic resonance (NMR) spectroscope supplements the IR analysis by differentiating structural elements in the organic molecules, using radio frequency energy.

Liquid Chromatography (Figure 7.41)

Liquid chromatography (LC) is a technique used for the separation and determination of a specific material in a liquid sample.

A fixed volume of sample is injected at the head of a separative column packed with a bed of adsorbent material. A mobile liquid is then forced through the column to cause the components to be differentiated into separate bands in the bed. A detector at the effluent of the separative column then analyzes these bands (analytes) as they leave the column. Several different types of separation columns using different mechanisms of analyte retention, and different mobile

Figure 7.39   The IR spectrum of an extract of a chemical plant wastewater used to detect the source of organic pollution.

Figure 7.40 Schematic diagram of NMR analyzer.

liquids can be selected depending on the particular separation objective. Many types of detectors have been used; the most widely used sensitive detector is the ultraviolet spectrophotometer.

Gas Chromatography

Gas chromatography (GC) is used for the determination of volatile materials in water samples. Some of these can be measured directly; others may require separation or special preparation. Where the analyte is not sufficiently volatile it may be extracted from water and then treated with chemical reagents to convert it into a volatile compound.

To fractionate a sample, it is vaporized and swept by a stream of inert carrier gas into the chromatographic column. The components separate into bands as the carrier gas passes through the column packing. The separated components are measured at the end of the column by various types of detectors. Examples of materials analyzed by the GC technique include pesticides and chlorinated solvents.

Figure 7.41 Diagram illustrating the principles of liquid chromatography.

Figure 7.42 Simplified diagram of a gas chromatograph.

The mass spectrometer is one of the detectors used with GC for the identification of the structures of compounds. Gases are ideal samples for the mass spectrometer (MS). The MS operates by bombarding gaseous molecules with energetic electrically charged particles. The energy transferred to the gas molecules fragments them into smaller charged particles in a reproducible manner. The mass and relative abundances of these charged fragments is determined by a scanning instrument which produces the mass spectrum related to the analyte.

SUGGESTED READING

APHA, AWWA, and WPCF: *Standard Methods for the Examination of Water and Wastewater.* 1971.

American Society for Testing and Materials: *Annual Book of ASTM Standards,* Part 23: "Water and Atmospheric Analyses." 1973.

Envirex Inc.: *Handbook for Sampling and Sample Preservation of Water and Wastewater,* September 1976. U.S. Department of Commerce, National Technical Information Service, PB-259 946.

McCrone, W. C., and Delly, J. S.: *The Particle Atlas,* 2nd edition, Ann Arbor Science Publishers, Inc., 1973.

U.S. Department of the Interior, Bureau of Reclamation: *Water Measurement Manual.* U.S. Government Printing Office, 1967.

Chapter 8
Coagulation and Flocculation

The processes of coagulation and flocculation are employed to separate suspended solids from water whenever their natural subsidence rates are too slow to provide effective clarification. Water clarification, lime softening, sludge thickening and dewatering depend on correct application of the theories of coagulation and flocculation for their success.

Taking surface water clarification as an example, turbid raw water contains suspended matter—both settleable solids, particles large enough to settle quiescently, and dispersed solids, particles which will not readily settle. A significant portion of these non-settleable solids may be colloidal. Each particle is stabilized by negative electrical charges on its surface, causing it to repel neighboring particles, just as magnetic poles repel each other. Since this prevents these charged particles from colliding to form larger masses, called flocs, they do not settle. Coagulation is the destabilization of these colloids by neutralizing the forces that keep them apart. This is generally accomplished by adding chemical coagulants and applying mixing energy. Aluminum salts, iron salts, or polyelectrolytes are the chemicals usually used.

Figure 8.1 illustrates how these chemicals reduce the electrical charges on colloidal surfaces, allowing the colloidal particles to agglomerate into flocs. These initially small flocs join, creating larger, settleable agglomerates. The destabilization step is coagulation (charge neutralization); the floc-building stage is flocculation.

The terms coagulation and flocculation are often used interchangeably; however, when seen as two different mechanisms they can provide a better understanding of clarification and dewatering.

Figure 8.1 *(a) Coagulation:* The addition of a coagulant neutralizes charges, collapsing the "cloud" surrounding the colloids so they can agglomerate. *(b) Flocculation:* The bridging of the flocculant chemical between agglomerated colloidal particles forms large settleable flocs.

COAGULATION

Colloidal species encountered in raw water and wastewater include clay, silica, iron and other heavy metals, color and organic solids, such as the debris of dead organisms. Colloids may also be produced in precipitation processes such as lime softening. Oil in wastewater is frequently colloidal.

Among the wide variety of colloidal materials in water, there is a broad distribution of particle sizes. Table 8.1 shows how particle size affects the tendency of particles to settle in quiet water. Colloids always require coagulation to achieve an effective size and settling rate; but even larger particles, which are not truly colloidal and would settle if given enough time, may require coagulation to form larger, faster settling floc.

When insufficient settling time is available in a treatment plant to remove suspended solids, coagulation and flocculation may cause them to grow in size

TABLE 8.1   Sedimentation of Small Particles of Silica of 2.65 Sp. Gr.

Typical	mm	Micron	Surface area (total)	Settling time, 1 m fall
Gravel	10.	10,000	3.14 cm²	1 sec
Coarse sand	1.	1,000	31.4 cm²	10 sec
Fine sand	0.1	100	314 cm²	125 sec
Silt	0.01	10	0.314 m²	108 min
Bacteria	0.001	1	3.14 m²	180 hr
Colloidal matter	0.0001	0.1	31.4 m²	755 days

NOTE: Particles larger than 100 microns are visible to the naked eye and are considered to be settleable solids. In the range of 10–100 microns, they are considered to be turbidity. Below 10 microns they are considered colloidal. Particles larger than 0.1 micron are visible by light microscope; below 0.1 micron, the electron microscope is used for detection.

and settle rapidly enough to overcome the physical limitation of the plant design.

Colloids are categorized as hydrophobic (water hating) or hydrophilic (water loving). Hydrophobic colloids do not react with water; most natural clays are hydrophobic. Hydrophilic colloids react with water; the organics causing color are hydrophilic. Of importance in water treatment, the hydrophilic colloids may chemically react with the coagulant used in the treatment process. So hydrophilic colloids require more coagulant than hydrophobic, which do not chemically react with the coagulant. For example, removal of color from a water having an APHA color of 50 requires higher coagulant dosages than removal of 50 JTU turbidity.

COLLOIDAL FORCES

Several theories have been advanced to describe the colloidal particle and the forces surrounding it. For practical purposes the determination of the nature and strength of the particle charge is all that is needed to define the colloidal system. The particle charge strength, illustrated as the layer surrounding the colloid in Figure 8.1, affects how closely colloids can approach.

Zeta potential is a measurement of this force. For colloids in natural water sources in a pH range of 5-8, the zeta potential is generally -14 to -30 millivolts; the more negative the number, the stronger the particle charge. As the zeta potential diminishes, the particles can approach one another more closely, increasing the likelihood of collision. In a conventional clarification system at a pH of 6–8, coagulants provide the positive charges to reduce the negative zeta potential. Coagulation usually occurs at a zeta potential which is still slightly negative, so complete charge neutralization is not usually required. If too much coagulant is added, the particle surface will become positively charged (a positive zeta potential), and the particle will be redispersed.

Coagulants may be required in high pH water treatment systems, such as in lime softening. Calcium carbonate particles also carry a negative charge, and cationic coagulants may be useful in reducing residual colloidal hardness. Magnesium hydroxide, on the other hand, carries a positive charge until the pH exceeds 11; so in lime or lime-soda softening processes where both $CaCO_3$ and $Mg(OH)_2$ precipitate, the oppositely charged particles coprecipitate. This coprecipitation in past geologic periods produced the mineral dolomite, $CaCO_3 \cdot MgCO_3$. The coagulation and flocculation of materials other than silt and color which are the common targets of a water clarification program are discussed in the chapter on precipitation processes.

Zeta potential is determined indirectly from data obtained in observing particle motion under a microscope. Figure 8.2 shows a typical instrument employed for this determination. Zeta potential measurements have been used successfully to control plant coagulant dosages. However, for selecting the best coagulant, zeta potential readings alone are not reliable. Observation of results in a jar test remain the best method of coagulant selection.

Mixing is required to supplement coagulant addition to destroy stability in the colloidal system. For particles to agglomerate they must collide, and mixing promotes collision. Brownian movement, the random motion imparted to small particles by bombardment by individual water molecules, is always present as a natural mixing force. However, additional mixing energy is almost always required. High intensity mixing which distributes the coagulant and promotes rapid collisions is most effective. The frequency and number of particle collisions are also important in coagulation. In a low turbidity water, the addition of solids such as clay or the recycle of previously settled solids may be required to increase the number of particle collisions.

Figure 8.2 The "Zeta-Reader," an instrument for continuously observing the mobility of particles in water and measuring zeta potential. *(Courtesy of Komline-Sanderson Engineering Corporation.)*

FLOCCULATION

The floc formed by the agglomeration of several colloids may not be large enough to settle or dewater at the desired rate. A flocculant gathers together floc particles in a net, bridging from one surface to another and binding the individual particles into large agglomerates as shown in Figure 8.3. Alum, iron salts, and high molecular weight polymers are common flocculants. Flocculation is promoted by slow mixing, which brings the flocs gently together; too high a mixing velocity tears them apart, and they seldom reform to their optimum size and strength. Flocculation not only increases the size of floc particles, but it also affects the physical nature of the floc. Sludges and slurries, when flocculated, dewater at faster rates on sand beds and in mechanical dewatering equipment because of the less gelatinous structure of the floc.

COAGULATION AND FLOCCULATION CHEMICALS

Historically, metal coagulants (alum and iron salts) have been most widely used in water clarification. These products function both as coagulants and flocculants. When added to water, they form positively charged species in the typical pH range for clarification, about 6–7. This hydrolysis reaction produces insoluble gelatinous aluminum or ferric hydroxide. Even if there are no suspended solids in the water initially, the metal coagulants form flocs which enmesh the destabilized colloids. However, the voluminous sludges produced by the addition of metal coagulants create disposal problems because they are usually difficult to dewater. This is why alum and iron salts are not often used to improve efficiency of centrifuges, filter presses, and other dewatering devices.

Metal coagulants are particularly sensitive to pH and alkalinity. If pH is not in the proper range, clarification is poor, and iron or aluminum may be solubilized and cause problems to the water user. The lower the coagulant dosage, the more

Figure 8.3 Photomicrographs illustrating the coagulation process. Left, turbid river water, showing fine dispersion of tiny solid particles. Right, same water treated with coagulant. Particles are "collected" in the floc. (130X)

sensitive the floc is to pH changes (Figure 8.4). Table 8.2 lists some important properties of common coagulants.

The introduction of activated silica in the 1940's significantly improved the performance of alum and iron salts as coagulants and flocculants in water clarification. The subsequent development of a variety of organic polymers called

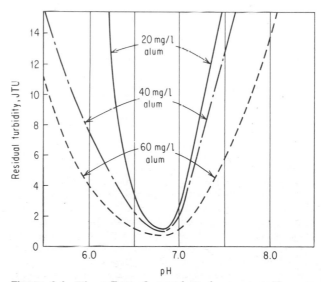

Figure 8.4 The effect of coagulant dosage on pH range limitations. The optimum pH remains almost constant, but the pH range becomes less restrictive as coagulant dosage increases.

TABLE 8.2   Properties of Common Coagulants

Common name	Formula	Equiv. weight	pH at 1%	Availability
Alum	$Al_2(SO_4)_3 \cdot 14H_2O$	100	3.4	Lump—17% Al_2O_3
				Liquid—8.5% Al_2O_3
Lime	$Ca(OH)_2$	40	12	Lump—as CaO
				Powder—93–95%
				Slurry—15–20%
Ferric chloride	$FeCl_3 \cdot 6H_2O$	91	3–4	Lump—20% Fe
				Liquid—20% Fe
Ferric sulfate	$Fe_2(SO_4)_2 \cdot 3H_2O$	51.5	3–4	Granular—18.5% Fe
Copperas	$FeSO_4 \cdot 7H_2O$	139	3–4	Granular—20% Fe
Sodium aluminate	$Na_2Al_2O_4$	100	11–12	Flake—46% Al_2O_3
				Liquid—2.6% Al_2O_3

polyelectrolytes in the next decade was an even more spectacular contribution to water treatment technology.

Polyelectrolytes are large water-soluble organic molecules made up of small building blocks called monomers, repeated in a long chain. They usually incorporate in their structures ion exchange sites which give the molecule an ionic charge. Those having a positive charge are cationic, and those with a negative charge are anionic. These molecules react with colloidal material in the water by neutralizing charge or by bridging (tying together) individual particles to form a visible, insoluble precipitate or floc.

TAILORING POLYELECTROLYTES

The performance of these materials can be modified to suit the nature of the colloidal matter to be removed from the water. These modifications include variations in molecular weight and ion exchange capacity. These materials can also be produced without an ionic charge; these are called nonionic polymers. Although they are not, strictly speaking, polyelectrolytes, nonionic polymers exhibit many of the same flocculating properties in solution, and are generally considered as part of the general polyelectrolyte family of compounds.

Although most polyelectrolytes are synthetic organic materials, nature also produces an endless variety of such materials. Some of these are chemically processed to improve performance and are commercially available.

The cationic polyelectrolytes are either polyamines or quaternary amines. In water, a polyamine hydrolyzes as follows:

$$\begin{array}{c} R \\ \diagdown \\ \diagup \\ R \end{array} NH + H_2O \rightarrow \begin{array}{c} R \\ \diagdown \\ \diagup \\ R' \end{array} NH \cdot H^+ + OH^-$$

Because of the hydrolysis to yield OH^-, at high pH, the reaction is forced to the left, and the polymer becomes nonionic. This is illustrated by Figure 8.5, which shows loss in exchange capacity for a specific polyamine as pH increases.

In contrast, the quaternary polymers are but slightly affected by pH, remaining positively charged over a broad pH range (Figure 8.5).

The anionic polymers incorporate a carboxyl group (—COOH) in their structure. These ionize in the following manner:

$$R\text{–}COOH \leftrightharpoons R\text{–}COO^- + H^+$$

The hydrogen ion forces the reaction to the left, so anionics become nonionic at low pH.

The ionic nature of polyelectrolytes is only one factor determining the performance of these materials as coagulants and flocculants. Other factors, such as the polar nature of non-ionic bonds in the molecule, molecular size, and molecular geometry, also play a large part and may in some cases overshadow the effects of charge and charge density. Hence, high molecular weight nonionic polymers are effective flocculants in many systems because of their ability to attract and hold colloidal particles at polar sites on the molecule. Furthermore, because of their molecular size, they can bridge together many small particles.

So, as a general rule, cationics are designed to work at lower pH values, anionics at higher. Nonionics and quaternaries are only slightly influenced by pH. The general rule should not be interpreted to mean that anionic polymers do not work at low pH value; it simply means they are no longer ionic. They may produce good results in flocculating solids at low pH simply because of their nonionic bonds. The same applies to cationics; even though they are not charged at high pH, they may act as effective coagulants because of their polar groups.

Organic polymers overcome many of the problems inherent in the use of alum or iron salts. These polymers are long chain organic molecules made up of small building blocks, called monomers, repeated along the chain. Depending on the selection of monomers and processing methods, a wide variety of polymers can be made of various configurations and molecular weights. Molecular weight is proportional to polymer chain length; the wide selection of structures and molecular weights makes it possible to design a polymer specifically for a given coagulation or flocculation problem, but this is seldom practical for economic reasons.

Organic polymers used in water treatment are of two major types, coagulants and flocculants. Coagulants are positively charged molecules of relatively low molecular weight. Although they exhibit some tendency for bridging, they are not particularly effective flocculants. Flocculant polymers have much higher molecular weights, providing long bridges between small flocs to enhance particle growth. Flocculants are either cationic, anionic, or nonionic. The flocculant that works best in any system can be determined only through laboratory screening and in-plant testing. Polymer flocculants, unlike coagulants, are not selected for neutralization. Table 8.3 lists some characteristics of commonly used organic coagulants and flocculants used in water treatment.

Unlike inorganic salts, polymers do not produce voluminous, gelatinous floc. In applications where additional solids improve results, inorganic coagulants or

Figure 8.5 Generalized plot showing loss of cationic strength for tertiary polyamines as pH increases, and relative pH independence of quaternary amine coagulants.

TABLE 8.3 Some Characteristics of Organic Polymers

Class	Mol. wt. ranges	Form and availability

1. Cationic coagulants
    Polyamines
    Polyquaternaries
    PolyDADMAC
    Epi-DMA
	Below
	100,000
		All are available as aqueous solutions

2. Cationic flocculants
    Copolymers of:
    Acrylamide and DMAEM
    Acrylamide and DADMAC
    Mannich amines
	Over
	1,000,000
		Powders or emulsions

3. Nonionic flocculants Polyacrylamides	Over 1,000,000	Powders or emulsions

4. Anionic flocculants
    Polyacrylates
    Copolymers of acrylamide
    and acrylate
	Over
	1,000,000
		Powders or emulsions

NOTE: DADMAC: diallyl-dimethyl ammonium chloride
Epi: epichlorhydrin
DMA: dimethylamine
DMAEM: dimethyl-aminoethyl-methacrylate

clay may be required to supplement the use of polymers. Polymers do not affect pH, nor is their performance as sensitive to the pH of the treated water as metal coagulants.

ACTIVATED SILICA

Some inorganic compounds can be polymerized in water to form inorganic polymer flocculants. Activated silica (sometimes identified as $^-SiO_2^-$) is an example. When sodium silicate, which contains alkali, is diluted to 1.5–2.0% and then partially neutralized (usually with chlorine or sodium bicarbonate), the silica becomes colloidal and then begins to slowly polymerize. After aging for 15–30 minutes, the solution is diluted to about 0.5–1.0% SiO_2 arresting further polymerization, producing activated silica. Although this preparation procedure is complicated, this is a very effective flocculant for such applications as assisting alum treatment for color removal and improving the softening of organic-containing waters, such as some of the colored well waters in Florida.

APPLICATIONS OF COAGULATION
AND FLOCCULATION

A sample of turbid water in a graduated cylinder separates into two layers, the settleable and the colloidal solids (Figure 8.6). In raw water clarification a coagulant is almost always used since the colloidal haze must be removed to produce the low turbidity demanded by most water-using processes. In wastewater clarification, a coagulant is required only where the suspended solids create a problem in meeting effluent guidelines; here a flocculant may be required to speed the settling rate.

Two types of laboratory tests are used to select the best chemical and approximate dosage level required for clarification: (1) the jar test, and (2) the cylinder

Figure 8.6   The solid particles in the left cone are a conglomeration of materials of various particle sizes, identified as suspended solids. After settling for 30 minutes, two fractions are obtained (right cone): settleable solids, expressed as ml/l and turbidity, expressed in nephelometric units.

test. The jar test is used when the stream to be clarified has less than approximately 5000 mg/l suspended solids. Raw water clarification, settling of biological solids, and most primary waste streams are in this category. The cylinder test is used for heavy slurry streams where suspended solids exceed approximately 5000 mg/l. Coal and mineral processing wastes and the sludge resulting from a primary clarification are examples of heavy slurries.

The jar test simulates the types of mixing and settling conditions found in a clarification plant. The laboratory unit for running these tests (Figure 8.7) allows up to six individual tests to be run simultaneously. The jar tester has a variable speed motor that allows control of the mixing energy in the jars.

Figure 8.7   This type of gang-stirrer is widely used for jar testing both as a research tool and a plant control device.

Figure 8.8 (*a*) The coagulant is measured into a sample of turbid water with a high degree of mixing. (*b*) After coagulant addition, particle growth occurs because of charge neutralization. Additional coagulant or a high molecular flocculant may then be added. (*c*) After flocculation, at a very low stirring speed—10–15 rpm, for example—the sample is examined after an established time period. Note the fine, pinpoint floc which has escaped entrapment by the larger floc. (*d*) The supernatant is examined and tested after 5–10 minutes settling time, and the nature and volume of the floc may be recorded. In some cases, the floc is reclaimed for use in the next series of jar tests.

Clarification results are sensitive to chemical dosage, mixing energy, and length of mixing. Figure 8.8 shows a typical sequence in jar testing where a colloidal haze is removed. The coagulant is added with high energy to disperse it in the water and promote increased frequency of collisions. The duration may be short, less than one minute. A polymer flocculant, if required, is added during the last few seconds of the rapid mix. In the slow mix period which follows, floc building proceeds until the floc becomes so big that shear forces finally overcome the bridging forces, breaking the floc apart. This limits the size of the floc. After slow mixing for an optimum period of time, found only by repeated tests (usually 5–20 minutes), the jars are allowed to settle for 5–10 minutes.

Jars with different chemicals or the same chemical at different dosages are run side by side and the results compared. Floc settling rate, final clarity or suspended solids, and volume of sludge produced (if measurable) are contrasted between jars. Although clarity can be judged by the eye, the more accurate standard measurement is made with a turbidimeter (Figure 8.9). Other quality tests such as pH, BOD, color, COD, and soluble metals, are run on the settled water to establish performance standards.

The cylinder test, designed to indicate how fast the suspended solids will settle, employs a 500 ml stoppered graduated cylinder, stopwatch, and labware for dosing the chemical being evaluated. The slurry sample is placed in the cylinder, chemical is added, and the cylinder gently inverted several times. Mixing is much less severe than in the jar test because solids are present at much higher levels, so that frequent collisions can occur at the lower mixing energy. After mixing, the cylinder is set upright, and the interface between the water and the settling solids observed. Time and solids level are recorded, and the data are plotted on a graph. As in the jar test, a number of analytical tests can be run on the clear water; however, rapid settling rate is usually the goal. By running coagulants and flocculants at different dosages and comparing settling rates, the most effective products are selected. Figure 8.10 illustrates the results of cylinder tests conducted on a coal slurry.

Figure 8.9 Turbidimeter used for continuously monitoring a raw water stream to assist in the control of coagulant dosage. *(Courtesy of Hach Chemical Company.)*

Figure 8.10 Cylinder tests on a coal slurry. After chemical treatment, the 500-ml cylinder is inverted several times to mix and induce flocculation, and the drop in solids interface is measured at fixed time intervals, as shown above.

PLANT DESIGN

The flowsheet of a surface water clarification plant shows how the principles of coagulation and flocculation apply to actual plant design. Generally, the lower the suspended solids in the process stream, or the higher the required effluent clarity, the more critical is mixing to the final results. Surface water is relatively low in suspended solids and removal to a low concentration of residual solids is usually required. For this reason many water plants are designed with flash mixing and flocculation mixing. The jar test protocol of rapid and slow mixing, which works best for raw water clarification, is duplicated on the plant scale. Flash mixing is accomplished in several ways: in-line hydraulic mixing (Figure 8.11), and high-speed mixing in a small mixing basin (Figure 8.12). The coagulant is added at or before the flash mix.

Flocculation mixing occurs in gently stirred compartments. Two common flocculator designs are the horizontal reel (Figure 8.13) and the turbine mixer (Figure 8.14). Variable speed motors may be provided to allow variation in mixing energy. Some plants employ hydraulic flocculation mixing, but this has limited use because its effectiveness falls off at reduced flows.

Figure 8.11   High energy in-line mixer used for optimizing the effectiveness of polymer coagulants in water treatment systems. *(Courtesy of Mixing Equipment Company.)*

Figure 8.12   Flash mixers are designed to disperse chemicals throughout the water instantaneously, prior to flocculation. *(Courtesy of FMC Corporation.)*

Figure 8.13   Reel-type paddle flocculator in a municipal water treatment plant. *(Courtesy of Envirex, a Rexnord Company.)*

Figure 8.14   Turbine-type flocculators installed in a large water treatment plant. *(Courtesy of Envirex, a Rexnord Company.)*

Silt or color removal in raw water is done using two basic treatment schemes: conventional clarification, or direct filtration. The most common plant operation is conventional: rapid mix, slow mix, sedimentation and filtration (Figure 8.15). Historically, alum has been most widely used, because the optimum pH is often below 6.0. It is fed at the head of the plant, sometimes in conjunction with alkali for pH control. Iron salts are seldom used. Because alum floc is light, a polymer flocculant is usually required to reduce the carryover of floc from the settling basin to the filters.

Polymer coagulants often are used to either replace or reduce inorganic salts. The polymer coagulant is added at the flash mix. In some water, alum can be replaced only if clay is fed to add enough to the raw water to insure high collision frequency and to add weight to the floc. An alternate method is to return sludge from the bottom of the settling basin to the rapid mix.

When the color or turbidity is very low in the raw water, direct filtration is often practiced in water clarification plants. In a direct filtration plant, water passes through flash mixing, sometimes a flocculator, and then directly to the filters (Figure 8.16). There are so few solids in the water that the filters do not plug excessively. A polymer is used as the primary coagulant in this process, since inorganic salts add solids which could clog the filter.

Wastewater streams usually have higher solids than raw water and the required suspended solids removal may not be as stringent. Generally, for wastewater clarification, hydraulic mixing has been widely used in the past; but newer plants are being designed with mechanical mixing similar to raw water clarification plants to improve removal of suspended solids.

Figure 8.15 Conventional design water treatment plant showing reel-type flocculation units, rectangular sedimentation basins in parallel, with common wall construction, and sludge collection flights. Final filtration is not shown. *(Courtesy of FMC Corporation.)*

Figure 8.16   Flow sheet showing direct filtration preceded by flash mix and flocculation for preparation of water for a small municipality. *(Courtesy of Neptune Microfloc, Inc.)*

SUGGESTED READING

American Water Works Association: *Water Quality and Treatment*, McGraw-Hill, New York, 1971.

Leviel, Roger (ed.), et al.: *Water Treatment Handbook*, Infilco-Degremont, Inc., Taylor & Carlisle, New York, distributors.

Nordell, Eskel: *Water Treatment for Industrial and Other Uses*, Reinhold, New York, 1961.

Vold, M. J., and Vold, R. D.: *Colloid Chemistry: The Science of Large Molecules, Small Particles, and Surfaces*, Reinhold, New York, 1964.

Chapter 9
Solids/Liquids Separation

Solids/liquids separation in water treatment includes the processes for removal of suspended solids from water by sedimentation, straining, flotation and filtration; it also includes solids thickening and dewatering by gravity, sedimentation, flotation, centrifugation, and filtration. Suspended solids are defined as those captured by filtration through a glass wool mat or a 0.45 micron filter membrane. Those solids passing through are considered to be colloidal or dissolved. Selection of the specific process or combined processes for removal of suspended solids from water depends on the character of the solids, their concentration, and the required filtrate clarity. For example, very large and heavy solids can be removed by a simple bar screen or strainer. Fine solids may require both sedimentation and filtration, usually aided by chemical treatment. The approximate relationship of particle size to the S/L separation devices used in water treatment is shown by Figure 9.1.

Straining includes such conventional devices as bar screens (Figure 9.2), traveling trash screens, and microstrainers. In some plants, instead of using screens, a device called a comminutor grinds the solids so they will settle and not interfere with the sedimentation equipment.

MICROSTRAINING

In some applications, microstraining can be used instead of granular media filtration for solids reduction. Microstraining has been used for many years for algae removal in England and is used as a tertiary polishing step in some wastewater treatment plants in the United States.

A typical microstraining system is shown in Figure 9.3. The unit consists of a motor driven rotating drum mounted horizontally in a rectangular pit or vat. The rigid drum support structure has either a stainless steel or plastic (poly-

Figure 9.1 Approximate operating regions of solids/liquids separation devices in treating water.

ester) woven screen covering fastened to it. Mesh size is normally in the 15–60 micron range. Sometimes a pleated configuration is used to increase surface area.

Feed passes from the inside to the outside of the drum depositing solids on the inner surface. Water jets on top of the screen dislodge collected solids into a waste hopper. Where biological growth is a problem, the units may be equipped with UV lights. The peripheral drum speed is usually adjustable. Filtration rates are in the 10–30 gpm/ft² range. Pressure drop through the screen is 3–6″ H_2O while head loss through the complete system is in the 12–18″ H_2O range. Microstrainer effluent is used to backwash and for solids removal. If grease, algae, or slime are present, hot water wash and industrial cleaners may be required at regular intervals to dislodge these materials.

SEDIMENTATION

Sedimentation is the removal of suspended solids from water by gravitational settling. Flotation is also a gravity separation but is treated as a separate process. To produce sedimentation, the velocity of the water must be reduced to a point where solids will settle by gravity if the detention time in the sedimentation vessel is great enough. The effect of overflow rate on settling is shown in Figure 9.4.

The settling rate of particles is affected by their size, shape and density as well as by the liquid they are settling through. As a particle settles, it accelerates until the frictional drag of its surface against the liquid equals the weight of the particle in the suspending fluid. The relationship governing particle settling is given by the following equation:

Figure 9.2 Bar screen with automatic cleaning mechanism. *(Courtesy of Envirex, a Rexnord Company.)*

$$F \propto g \frac{(S_1 - S_2)}{V}$$

where F = impelling force
g = gravitational constant
V = volume of the particle
S_1 = density of the particle
S_2 = density of the fluid

HINDERED SETTLING

When particles settle through a liquid in free fall, the liquid displaced by the particles moves upward and the space between the particles is so large that the counterflow of water does not interpose friction. When the particles approach the bottom of the vessel and begin to form a liquid/solid interface, their free-fall velocity is arrested. The collected solids, or sludge, now slowly compact in a process known as hindered settling. In hindered settling, the particles are spaced so closely that the friction produced by the velocity of the water being displaced interferes with particle movement. Figure 9.5 illustrates the change from free fall to hindered settling. As sedimentation continues, the particles reach a previously established dense sludge layer; settling then becomes even slower due to the apparent increase in density in the liquid through which the particles are settling (Figure 9.6).

Figure 9.3   Microstrainer used for removal of fine suspended solids from storm water or wastewater. *(Courtesy of Cochrane Division, the Crane Company.)*

Settling rate is also affected by water temperature. Raising the temperature from 32 to 85°F (0 to 29°C) doubles the settling rate for a given discrete particle because both the density and viscosity of the water are reduced.

In clarification, the major objective of the sedimentation is a clear effluent water rather than a dense underflow sludge. Clarification is used for raw water preparation and for wastewater treatment. Many process applications also use clarification, e.g., separation of fines from coal preparation tailings.

GRAVITY CLARIFIER DESIGN

There are three major types of gravity clarifiers; plain sedimentation, solids contact units, and inclined plane settlers. There are several designs of plain sedimentation basins (clarifiers): center feed (the most common), rectangular, and peripheral feed. The center feed clarifier has four distinct sections, each with its own function (Figure 9.7).

The inlet section provides a smooth transition from the high velocities of the influent pipe to the low uniform velocity required in the settling zone. This

Figure 9.4 Percent removal vs. overflow rate based on settling velocity data for a specific system.

velocity change must be carefully controlled to avoid turbulence, short-circuiting, and carryover.

The quiescent settling zone must be large enough to reduce the net upward flow of water to a velocity below the subsidence rate of the solids. The outlet zone provides a transition from the low velocity of the settling zone to the relatively high overflow velocities.

The fourth section, the sludge zone, must effectively settle, compact, and collect solids and remove this sludge from the clarifier without disturbing the sedimentation zone above. The bottom of a circular clarifier is normally sloped 5 to 8 degrees to the center of the unit where sludge is collected in a hopper for removal. Usually, mechanically driven sludge scrapers plow or rake the sludge down the sloping bottom to the sludge hopper. Some of the collected sludge may be returned to the feedwell for seeding, if chemical treatment is applied.

The rectangular basin is somewhat like a section taken through a center feed clarifier with the inlet at one end, and the outlet at the other. A typical rectangular clarifier has a length to width ratio of approximately 4 to 1. Sludge removal in rectangular sedimentation tanks is normally accomplished by a dual purpose flight system. The flights first skim the surface for removal of floating matter and then travel along the bottom to convey the sludge to a discharge hopper.

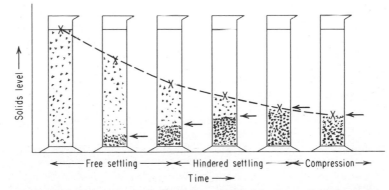

Figure 9.5 The steps in settling of particulates in water: Particles at first fall freely through the water. As they come closer together, their rate of sedimentation is restricted, and settled sludge volume increases. In the final stages, compaction or compression becomes very slow.

(a)   (b)

Figure 9.6 (*a*) Hindered settling is reached as particulates become so close to each other that the passages between them restrict the ability of water to escape from the sludge. (*b*) Compaction occurs naturally, but slowly, by gravity and by dehydration of the particulates; it is aided by gently moving the sludge to develop crevices behind the moving pickets or scraper blades for water release.

However, the surface skimming is not a common feature, being used almost exclusively for wastewater rather than raw water treatment. This flight system must move slowly to avoid turbulence, which could interfere with settling. An advantage of this type of clarifier is that common walls can be used between multiple units to reduce construction costs (Figure 9.8).

The peripheral feed (rim feed) clarifier (Figure 9.9) attempts to use the entire volume of the circular clarifier basin for sedimentation. Water enters the lower section at the periphery at extremely low velocities providing immediate sedimentation of large particles. The velocity accelerates toward the center, then drops as the flow is reversed and redirected to a peripheral overflow weir. Since the flow pattern depends entirely on hydraulics, this type of clarifier is sensitive to temperature changes and load fluctuations. Recirculation of sludge is very difficult in the peripheral feed design.

A second major category of clarifier is the solids contact unit, available in two basic types; the slurry recirculation clarifier and the sludge blanket clarifier (Figures 9.10 and 9.11). Both of these combine chemical mixing, flocculation and clarification in a single unit. In the mixing zone of a solids contact clarifier, the solids concentration may be as much as 100 times that of the simple clarifier. This high solids level greatly increases the rate of chemical destabilization reactions and particle growth. Because of these features, the solids contact units are usually used in lime softening. In the slurry recirculation unit, the high floc volume is maintained by recirculation from the flocculation zone to the clarification zone. In the blanket type clarifier, the floc solids are maintained in a fluidized blanket through which the water must flow. Because of the increased solids in a solids contact unit, clarifier size may be reduced. The even distribution of the inlet flow and the vertical flow pattern of this type clarifier provided better performance than standard horizontal flow clarifiers. In passing through the sludge blanket, the larger floc settles to the bottom by gravity and the remaining fine floc is removed by straining and adsorption.

Variable speed mixers are used to control flocculation and solids concentration in the reaction zone. The solids concentration in the reaction zone is maintained by bleeding solids out of the system to balance those coming in with the raw water and the solids produced by chemical reaction. Sludge removal can be accomplished either by a sludge blow off pipe as in Figure 9.12, or by a conventional rake and pump system as in Figure 9.13. Balancing the solids budget—solids input versus output—is the most difficult aspect of controlling a sludge blanket unit.

Figure 9.7 Simple centerfeed clarifier with scum skimmer and sludge scraper. *(Courtesy of Envirotech.)*

CONTROL OF FLOW PATTERN

Two major problems with gravity clarifiers are short-circuiting and random eddy currents. These are related in that both can be induced by changes in flow, inlet composition, temperature, and specific gravity. They are both aggravated by localized sludge deposits, which block the normal flow pattern.

It is quite obvious that in the conventional circular clarifier, water must be relatively stagnant in a significant proportion of the total volume in detention. Notably, there is no flow in the annular space below the peripheral overflow launder. The actual detention can be determined by measuring effluent chloride

Figure 9.8 Side-by-side rectangular clarifiers with common wall, each with a traveling bridge sludge collector. *(Courtesy of Walker Process Division, Chicago Bridge & Iron Company.)*

concentrations or conductivity at timed intervals after injecting a measured slug of salt into the feed. The results of this should be discussed with the equipment designer if short-circuiting is suspected.

Eddy currents are usually readily observed, showing up as an apparent boiling of the sludge. Often these disturbances can be traced to weather conditions, such as high winds or bright sunlight which either heats the sludge unevenly or encourages algal production of O_2.

Floc separators have been a solution to these problems in many gravity clarifiers. These units, made up in modules for installation in a variety of clarifier designs, add just enough frictional resistance to flow to even out the hydraulic pattern and eliminate the problems of short-circuiting and eddy currents. Figure 9.14 shows a typical installation of floc barriers in a sludge-blanket type clarifier. Figure 9.15 shows the design of one kind of floc barrier module.

Figure 9.9 Peripheral feed clarifier with sludge pipe and scum removal device. *(Courtesy of Envirex, a Rexnord Company.)*

Rapid mixing and recirculation

Slow mixing and floc formation

Chemical introduction

Treated water effluent

Clarified water

Clear water separation

Raw water influent

Sludge recirculation

Sludge removal

Sedimentation

Figure 9.10 Slurry recirculation design clarifier. *(Courtesy of Ecodyne Corporation.)*

EFFLUENT COLLECTOR FLUME

AGITATOR

CHEMICAL FEED INLETS

INFLUENT

SKIMMING SLOT

EFFLUENT

SLUDGE BLOW OFF LINE

SAMPLE CONNS.

SWING SAMPLE INDICATOR

SLUDGE CONCENTRATOR

AGITATOR ARM

MIXING ZONE

BAFFLES

PRECIPITATOR DRAIN

Figure 9.11 Sludge blanket clarifier providing increasing area for the water rising in the outer annulus, resulting in reducing velocity to match sludge settling rate. *(Courtesy of The Permutit Company.)*

Figure 9.12 Sludge collection pipe (arrow) for periodic removal of sludge to a collection hopper. *(Courtesy of Envirex, a Rexnord Company.)*

In most gravity clarifiers, the mean water depth through which sludge particles must fall is on the order of five feet or more. The time required for the sludge to fall this distance is a critical factor in limiting the clarifier capacity. Two similar modifications to the standard design of gravity clarifiers reduce the distance of fall from feet to inches, increasing the effective rise rate and radically reducing space requirements for clarification. These are the tube settler and the lamellae separator, classified as inclined plane settlers.

The so-called tube-settler may in fact be a series of inclined tubes, somewhat like a heat exchanger bundle connected at the inlet to a flocculation chamber

Figure 9.13 Circular sludge collectors, with rakes designed for corner cleaning. *(Courtesy of FMC Corporation.)*

EFFLUENT COLLECTOR (G)

DETENTION ZONE (B)

REACTION ZONE (A)

SETTLING ZONE (C)

SLUDGE RECIRCULATING IMPELLER (D)

INCLINED PLANE (E) SEPARATED

SLUDGE REMOVAL SUMP (F)

SLUDGE SCRAPER ARM

SLUDGE BLOWDOWN LINE

Figure 9.14 Installation of floc separator modules in a sludge blanket clarifier. *(Courtesy of Ecodyne Corporation.)*

and at the outlet to a clear well (Figure 9.16). The angle of inclination is varied to suit the required duty. It is affected by the concentration and nature of the solids, and by the ensuing processes of water filtration and sludge thickening. The tube-settler may also be a vessel packed with floc separators or with parallel inclined plates.

Figure 9.15 Plastic module of inclined plates simulating inclined tubes. These modules help equalize water distribution. *(Courtesy of Neptune Microfloc, Inc.)*

The lamellae separator (Figure 9.17) is more intricate, but the same principle applies in that the sludge particles have a very short settling distance, and the accumulated sludge is induced to flocculate and concentrate as it rolls down the inclined surface. These units are ideally suited for localized treatment of individual waste streams in cramped locations. An example is the installation of lamellae separators for treating chemical plant wastes (Figure 9.18).

A final example of a gravity clarifier, which is a modification of the plain sedimentation unit, is the rectangular drag tank (Figure 9.19). This is designed for removal of dense solids, such as granulated slag from a foundry cupola. As the solids are dragged from the vessel by flights moving up the beach, water drains off, producing a relatively dry mass. Fragile solids are broken down by the movement of the flights up the beach, so the drag tank is limited in the type of solids that can be separated. The detention is usually short, and overflow clarity rather poor, even when chemicals are used for coagulation and flocculation. However, the drag tank can be modified, such as by providing an hour or so of detention and preflocculating the feed, to deliver clear water, as in handling scale pit solids in a steel mill (Figure 9.20).

ESSENTIALLY HORIZONTAL TUBE SETTLER

STEEPLY INCLINED TUBE SETTLER

Figure 9.16 The basic tube settler configurations used with flocculation and filtration. *(Courtesy of Neptune Microfloc, Inc.)*

FLOW DISTRIBUTION ORIFICES

DISCHARGE FLUMES

OVERFLOW BOX

FEED BOX

FLOCCULATION TANK

OVERFLOW
(EFFLUENT)

FLASH MIX
TANK

COAGULANT
AID

FEED
(INFLUENT)

LAMELLA
PLATES

VIBRATOR
PACK

SLUDGE HOPPER
(REMOVABLE)

UNDERFLOW
(SLUDGE)

Figure 9.17 Closely spaced inclined plates (lamella) multiply the available settling surface in a small volume and reduce installation space. *(Courtesy of Parkson Corporation.)*

FLOTATION CLARIFICATION

Solids can also be removed from water using an air-flotation clarifier such as
the one shown in Figure 9.21. In this unit, light solids are floated to the surface
by air bubbles and skimmed off while heavier solids are settled and removed in
the normal fashion.

Air flotation has been used for many years in the mining industry for concentrating mineral ores, and in the paper industry for treating white water for
fiber recovery and water clarification. The use of dissolved air flotation has
broadened to include treatment of oily waste from refineries, petrochemical
plants, steel rolling mills, automotive plants, and railroad terminals. In these industries, the oil in the waste may coat solids particles, giving them a tendency to
float rather than settle. In these applications, the air flotation clarifier is often
preceded by an API separator for the removal of free oil (Figure 9.22).

Another important application of dissolved air flotation is food industry waste
treatment. Meat and seafood processing plants, canneries, and wineries have
significantly reduced BOD and suspended solids using air flotation equipment.

Figure 9.18 Installation of a lamella-type settler in
a chemical plant, clarifying wastewater. *(Courtesy of
Parkson Corporation.)*

In flotation clarification, the waste flow is usually pressurized and supersaturated with air. When the pressure is released, air comes out of solution,
forming micro-bubbles, which float the solids to the surface. In some cases,
instead of pressurizing the influent, a portion of the effluent is recycled through
an air-saturation tank to meet the feed stream, as discussed later.

In treating wastes containing solids which tend to float, air flotation may be so
effective that it may reduce clarification time to 15–20 minutes detention time,

Figure 9.19 Simple separator for settling and removal of gritty, non-hydrous
solids from wastewater. Some dewatering occurs on the incline above the water
line. *(Courtesy of FMC Corporation.)*

Figure 9.20 Steel mill scale pit, provided with oil skimmer and sludge collector. *(Courtesy of FMC Corporation.)*

compared to the several hours typical of gravity sedimentation. As with gravity clarifiers, it is often necessary to add coagulant or flocculant chemicals such as ferric chloride and alum to flotation units to aid in floc formation, using lime if needed for pH adjustment. Polyelectrolytes have been gaining acceptance for this application, and in almost all cases, they increase the efficiency of a

Figure 9.21 Typical horizontal air flotation unit.

Figure 9.22 Typical design of API separator. *(Courtesy of Envirex, Inc., a Rexnord Company.)*

flotation clarifier. Cylinder tests, pilot plant tests, or both are used to select the best chemical program.

THEORY

The amount of air that can be dissolved in water is determined by Henry's Law, which states that for nonionizing gases of low solubility, the volume dissolved in water varies with absolute pressure. At 75 psia (5 bars), for example, 5 times as much air can be dissolved in water as at atmospheric pressure. The quantity of gas that will theoretically be released from solution when pressure is reduced to atmospheric is:

$$G_R = G_A \left(\frac{P_A}{14.7} - 1 \right)$$

where G_R = gas released, mg/l

G_A = gas solubility at atmospheric pressure, mg/l (See Table 9.1.)

P_A = absolute pressure in saturation tank, psia

TABLE 9.1   Gas Solubility at Atmospheric Pressure in cc/l

Temperature	O_2	N_2	Air
0°C(32°F)	10.3	18.0	28.3
10°C(50°F)	8.0	15.0	23.0
20°C(68°F)	6.5	12.3	18.8
30°C(86°F)	5.5	10.5	16.0
40°C(104°F)	4.9	9.2	14.1
50°C(122°F)	4.5	8.5	13.0

The above must be corrected for the efficiency of gas absorption in the saturation vessel, which is influenced by mixing and detention time. The efficiency varies in the range of 40–60%, so the gas released would typically be about half of that determined by the above formula.

The air bubbles formed in a DAF unit normally carry a slight negative charge. Depending on the type of particulate matter and the degree of agglomeration of the solids, the air bubbles can attach themselves by any of the following mechanisms:

1. Simple adhesion of the air bubble to the solid surface. This can occur either through collision or by formation of the air bubble on the particle surface.

2. Trapping of air bubbles under sludge floc, such that the waste particle "takes a ride" to the surface. Sometimes referred to as "screening," this implies that there need be no real attachment of air bubbles to sludge particles to accomplish flotation.

3. Incorporation of air bubbles into floc structures. This is believed to be the most efficient mode of air usage because there is less chance of floc separation from the air bubble. This process is encouraged by the use of polyelectrolytes, which when applied correctly, will cause the flocculation of sludge particles at the sites where air bubbles are coming out of solution.

Since the net specific gravity of the air-solid or air-liquid particles is less than that of water, they rise to the surface. There, they consolidate to form a float, which can be removed by mechanical skimmers. The clear subnatant is withdrawn from the bottom of the unit. Figure 9.21 shows a cross section of a typical horizontal unit.

Usually the size of a flotation unit is selected on the basis of solids loading on the bottom, expressed as lb/hr/sq ft of floor area. Depending on the nature of the solids, the floor loading ranges from 0.5 to 5.0 lb/hr/sq ft (2.5–25 kg/hr/m²).

The hydraulic load and inlet solids concentration must be balanced to arrive at an acceptable floor loading. For instance, a unit designed to handle a floor loading of 2 lb/hr/sq ft can handle a hydraulic loading of 0.8 gpm/sq ft (0.33 m³/min/m²) at 0.5% solids (5000 mg/1) or 1.6 gpm/sq ft at 0.25% solids (2500 mg/l) with about equal efficiency. A lower flow rate should be maintained as a safety factor to allow for fluctuations in concentrations. A high effluent solids concentration may be the result of an overloaded unit; when this happens the unit feed should be closed and effluent recycled to allow the tank to clear. If this is a persistent problem, it may be possible to increase the amount of dissolved air by increasing the pressure or the flow rate of the pressurized stream. It may be necessary to decrease the unit feed stream to compensate for the overload situation. If the unit is shut down on a daily basis, clear water should be recycled routinely prior to shutdown to remove suspended and floated material.

TYPES OF FLOTATION SYSTEMS

There are three basic types of dissolved air flotation systems in use (Figure 9.23). In direct aeration, the entire waste stream is pressurized and aerated. In this case, the material to be separated must be able to withstand the shearing forces in the pressure pump and pressure release valve, or the floc must quickly re-form after the pressure is released. This method is often used when the waste contains oils (e.g., an API separator effluent).

In partial aeration, only a fraction of the waste stream is pressurized. This method reduces pumping costs when the solids load is light, but it is only applicable where low to moderate amounts of oil are present. The amount of pressurized flow is varied based on the required ratio of air to solids on a weight basis —normally in the range of 0.01 to 0.06.

Effluent recycle is recommended where fragile floc is formed. This floc would be destroyed by the intense mixing which occurs in the pressurization system. Gas is dissolved in the recycle stream. This stream is then combined with the feed stream at a point where the pressure is released. Mixing of these streams prior to entering the flotation zone results in intimate contact of the precipitated gas and suspended solids to effect efficient flotation. Effluent recirculation is required when light flocculent solids, such as biological or hydroxide sludges are to be thickened. Flotation areas must be large when effluent recirculation is employed, since hydraulic loading is based on both feed and recycle flows.

(a) Total aeration of raw waste

(b) Partial aeration of raw waste

(c) Aeration of recycle

Figure 9.23 Several operating schemes for air flotation clarification.

Flotation is also practiced by application of dispersed air into a vessel containing water with oily or solid particulates. Air is mechanically entrained and dispersed through the liquid as fine bubbles in contrast to release of dissolved gas from solution. The dispersed air flotation design is especially suitable for treating oily wastewater (Figure 9.24).

FILTRATION

Granular Media Filtration

Granular media filtration is generally applicable for removal of suspended solids in the 5-50 mg/l range where an effluent of less than 1 JTU is required. Sand filters have been used for many years as a final polishing step in municipal and industrial water plants where the clarifier effluent contains 5-20 mg/l of suspended solids. In areas where a very low turbidity raw water source is available, some plants use granular media filtration as the only treatment process for solids removal, particularly for industrial process water. Granular media filters are also being used to filter cooling water sidestreams to reduce suspended solids buildup where effluent clarity is not critical. Granular media filters may handle suspended solids up to 1000 mg/l and provide about 90% removal.

A number of mechanisms are involved in solids removal by filtration, some physical and others chemical. These filtration mechanisms include adsorption and straining.

Adsorption is dependent on the physical characteristics of the suspended solids and the filter media. It is a function of filter media grain size and such floc properties as size, shear strength, and adhesiveness. Adsorption is also affected by the chemical characteristics of the suspended solids, the water, and the filter media. The amount of surface exposed for adsorption is enormous—about 3000–5000 sq ft/cu ft of media. Straining, which occurs in all granular media filters, is the major factor controlling the length of filter runs. A major objective of good filter design is to minimize straining since it leads to rapid head loss. This occurs because straining causes cake formation on the surface of the filter bed (particularly on sand filters), with the deposited cake then acting as the filter media. The filter media in essence becomes finer as the cake forms, and head loss increases exponentially with time.

Of the several types of filtration media used to remove suspended solids, the most common is silica sand, but crushed anthracite is also widely used. When a single medium such as silica sand is used, it will classify in the filtration vessel according to size, the smallest particles rising to the top. When water flows downward through the sand, which is the traditional path, solids form a mat on the surface, and filtration typically occurs in the top few inches. The sand is cleaned by upward washing with water or with water and air (backwash), and this hydraulically classifies the bed, keeping the finest material on top. If the sand could be loaded into a filter with the larger grains at the top and the smaller at the bottom, this coarse to fine grading would allow in-depth penetration. The increased solids storage would allow longer filter runs. However, since backwashing fluidizes the bed, the washed sand would again return to a fine to coarse grading.

If a single medium bed is used, the only path to coarse to fine filtration is up flow. Water is applied into the bottom of the bed. Solids can penetrate the coarser grain medium, resulting in deeper bed filtration. Backwashing occurs in

Figure 9.24   Dispersed air flotation, typically used for clarification of oily waste. (*Courtesy of Wemco Division, Envirotech Corporation.*)

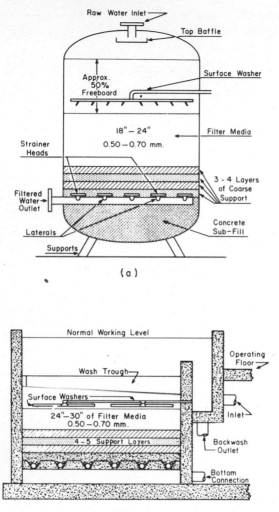

Figure 9.25 Schematic details of filtration units. (*a*) Pressure filter, vertical cylindrical design, fabricated of steel. Usually limited to 10′-0″ diameter. (*b*) Gravity filter, usually of concrete construction; used in larger municipal and industrial plants.

the same direction as the filtration. The bed is classified fine at the top to coarse at the bottom. Upflow filters operate at up to 5 gpm/sq ft.

Typical single medium filters operate downflow at 2 gpm/sq ft of bed area in potable water service, and up to 3 gpm/sq ft in industrial filtration. The filter bed is 24 to 30″ deep, supported on several courses of graded gravel (Figure 9.25*a* and *b*).

Silica sand normally has a grain size of 0.5 to 0.8 mm. Anthracite is usually about 0.7 mm. Smaller grains filter better, but filter runs are short. Larger grains allow longer filter runs, but if the flow is too high, hydraulic breakthrough will occur. A coarse filter media will produce acceptable effluent and reasonable filter runs if its depth is increased.

MULTI-MEDIA FILTER BEDS

A stacked media bed or two layers (dual media) is one answer to providing coarse to fine filtration in a downflow pattern. The two materials selected have different grain sizes and different specific gravities. Normally, ground anthracite is used in conjunction with silica sand. The anthracite grains with a specific gravity of 1.6 and a grain size of 1 mm settle slower than sand with a specific gravity of 2.65 and a grain size of 0.5 mm, so the coarse anthracite rests on top of the fine sand after backwashing. In a typical dual media bed, 20″ of anthracite is placed above 10″ of sand. The coarse anthracite allows deeper bed penetration and provides longer filter runs at higher filter rates. The finer sand polishes the effluent. Under normal conditions, this dual media can produce acceptable effluent at flow rates up to 5 gpm/sq ft of bed area.

Just as coarse-to-fine dual media is more effective than a single medium filter, further improvement can be gained by introducing a third, smaller, heavier media under the sand. Garnet with a specific gravity of 4.5 and a very fine grain size settling faster than the silica sand can be used as the bottom layer. A typical multi-media contains 18″ of 1.0–1.5 mm anthracite, 8″ of 0.5 mm silica sand, and 4″ of 0.2–0.4 mm garnet. This filter operates at higher flow rates and provides deeper penetration and longer filter runs than a single or dual media filter.

To design a filter for maximum performance, the first consideration is the desired quality of effluent. The selection of filter design required to produce an effluent of 0.1 JTU is different from that required to produce 1.0 JTU.

Flow rate through a filter is critical, since it limits the throughput and dictates the number of filters required. Generally, as flow rate increases, penetration into the filter increases. The flow rate is limited by the head available and the media size. As the media starts to load with solids, the net velocity at a given flow rate increases until shear forces tear the solids apart and they escape into the effluent. Most filters are designed to be backwashed before this breakthrough occurs at a point determined by head loss. Typically, single media filters are backwashed when the head loss reaches about 10 ft. In deep bed filtration, a terminal head loss of 15 to 20 ft is tolerable.

In a finer grain media, since solids removal is primarily accomplished in the first few inches, increasing bed depth is of little value except for improving hydraulic distribution. But in coarse filters where penetration is wanted, the coarser the media the deeper must be the bed for equivalent effluent quality.

Water temperature affects filter performance due to viscosity. At 32°F, water viscosity is 44% higher than at 72°F. Backwashing, on the other hand, improves with cold water, since increased viscosity more effectively scours the bed to remove solids. Floc formation is much slower at low temperatures so the filterability at a given plant may vary seasonally. In the summer, floc may stay on the surface, but penetrate deeply into the filter in the winter.

The best method of determining filter media selection for a chemical coagulation/flocculation program is by operation of a pilot test column. A typical column is shown in Figure 9.26. Chemicals can be fed directly to the column or into a separate flash mix tank ahead of the column. Various laboratory tests have been used to determine filterability, but none are as accurate as the pilot test column.

Septum Filters

Where suspended solids concentrations are very low, septum filtration can be used. These filters are often referred to as DE (diatomaceous earth) filters since this material is usually used as a filter precoat, although other filter aids can be used. The septum filter (Figure 9.27) relies on a thin layer of precoat applied as a slurry to a porous septum to produce a filtering surface to strain the suspended solids. In most cases water being filtered is pumped through the filter under pressure; in special designs where low head loss is possible the water may be

Figure 9.26   Pilot plant dual-media filter being evaluated
for wastewater filtration in a steel mill. *(Courtesy of Graver
Water Conditioning Division, Ecodyne Corporation.)*

pulled through using vacuum. As the filter becomes plugged, head loss increases
and the solids, including precoat, have to be removed by reversing the flow
through the unit. A new precoat is then applied and filtration is resumed. Usually in addition to the precoat, a body feed of filter aid is used. This body feed is
simply additional filter aid added to the influent to extend filter runs by continually providing a fresh filter surface. Because the filter aid has a different
shape (morphology) than the solids in the water, the heterogeneous mixture is
more permeable than the solids alone.

A relatively high ratio of filter aid to suspended solids is required to operate
septum filters making operating costs fairly high. Therefore, these units are not
as common as granular media filters in most industrial systems. DE filters are
often used for applications such as municipal swimming pools, and they are
excellent for removal of oil from industrial plant condensate.

Septum filters can be cleaned of accumulated solids by air-bumping, a procedure requiring little or no water and producing a thick slurry or cake of accumulated solids. This simplifies solids disposal, and reduces backwash water requirements. They can also be fitted into a relatively small space, compared to granular
media filters.

While diatomaceous earth—the fossil remains of diatoms, a type of algae
having a silica skeleton—is the commonly used filter aid (see Figure 9.28), mixtures of DE and asbestos are often used. At the high temperatures encountered
in filtration of oily condensate, silica dissolves from the DE filter cake, so Solka-

Floc®, a cellulosic product, is used to avoid this problem if the condensate is to be fed to a boiler.

THICKENING

Thickening is a solids/liquids separation method used to increase the solids content of a slurry prior to dewatering. Thickening normally follows a clarification process where the suspended solids have been separated from the liquid. In clarification, solids are normally in the 10–1000 mg/l range, while influent to a thickener is usually in the 0.5–10% range.

The purpose of thickening is to increase the solids of the underflow; in clarification, the purpose is to remove solids and produce a clear effluent. The clarity of water leaving a thickener is not as critical as the density of the underflow, since the effluent water normally is recycled back to the head of the plant. The thickened sludge must remain liquid to the extent that it can be pumped to subsequent dewatering operations. In municipal waste treatment plants, where digestion follows thickening, improved digestion and conservation of digester space is achieved through thickening.

In the clarifier, solids have separated from the water primarily by free-fall. The solids collected in the lower region have encountered the effects of hindered settling. In the thickener, there is no free-fall; the process of hindered settling controls the design and the final compaction of sludge.

Gravity thickening and flotation thickening are the two major methods.

Gravity Thickening

Gravity thickening is often used in municipal plants for primary sludges and in industrial plants for chemical sludges. A typical thickening operation in a steel mill will double the solids concentration. The gravity process works well when the specific gravity of the solids is much greater than that of the liquid.

A gravity thickener is constructed much like a clarifier: usually they are circu-

Figure 9.27 Cross-section of a typical septum-type filter designed for use of diatomite or similar filter aid in water filtration. *(Courtesy of Croll Reynolds Engineering Company.)*

Figure 9.28 Photomicrograph of diatomite filter aid, showing variety of sizes and shapes of particles used for water filtration. *(Courtesy of Johns-Manville.)*

lar with a side wall depth of approximately 10 feet and with the floor sloping toward the center (Figure 9.29). The floor angle is greater than in a clarifier, normally 8 to 10°. As in a clarifier, the sludge is moved to a well by a rake assembly and then pumped out by a positive displacement pump. In a gravity thickener, because the process of hindered settling controls solids compaction, the sludge rake arm has a dual purpose; besides raking the solids to the sludge well, the arm is constructed like a picket fence to gently muddle the slurry, dislodging interstitial water from the sludge and preventing bridging of the solids.

As the sludge blanket gets deeper, up to about 3 feet, the density of the solids increases, after which there is little advantage in increasing sludge depth. When thickening municipal sludges, close attention must be paid to the length of time sludge is in the thickener, since it can become septic and produce gas bubbles that may upset the system. This is particularly true with thickening biological secondary sludge. If septic sludge is encountered, chlorine may be added to the feed to the thickener. The SVR (sludge volume ratio), which is used to monitor sludge age, is the volume of sludge in the blanket divided by the daily volume of sludge pumped from the thickener. This gives the retention time, which is normally between 0.5 and 2 days.

Chemical Treatment

Chemicals may aid gravity thickening. Salts of iron and aluminum have little effect; in some cases they improve the overflow clarity, but do not provide increased loading. Polymer flocculants are effective aids to gravity thickening, forming larger, heavier floc particles, which settle faster and form a denser sludge. Depending on the system involved, these polymers can be cationic, nonionic or anionic in character. Effective dosages of polymers usually are in the range of 2 to 20 lb/ton of sludge solids on a dry solids basis. Two test methods are used to determine the best chemical program: these are a simple cylinder settling test and a stirred thickening test shown in Figure 9.30, where the stirrer rotates at only 0.1–1.0 rpm. The sludge is mixed with chemical, placed in the thickening apparatus, and stirred. Effectiveness of treatment is determined by measuring the density of sludge samples removed from the bottom of the beaker and comparing to the concentration of unthickened sludge. An alternate method is to measure the percentage of supernate in each sample of settled sludge representing untreated and treated conditions.

When polymer is used in gravity thickening, special attention should be given to the application point and to the dilution water rate. Since older gravity thickeners were not designed specifically to use polymers, feed taps are often not readily available. Suitable feed points would be either directly ahead of the thickener to the feed pump, or into the sludge feed line. Dilution water needs to be adjusted for optimum dispersion of the polymer into the sludge without defeating the goal of water removal.

Thickening by Flotation

An alternate to gravity thickening is flotation thickening. This is usually more effective than gravity thickening when the solids being thickened have a specific gravity near or less than that of the liquid from which they are being removed. Because of its high solids loading, a DAF (dissolved air flotation) thickener normally occupies ⅓ or less of the space required for a gravity thickener.

Flotation may be either dispersed air or dissolved air. In dispersed air flotation, bubbles larger than 100 microns are generated by mechanical shearing

Figure 9.29   Sludge thickener designed for thickening pulp mill waste sludge prior to dewatering. (*Courtesy of Passavant Corporation.*)

Picket thickener mechanism
operating at 0.1 to 1.0 rpm

Pickets

Ring stand

Two-liter graduated cylinder

Thickened sludge

Figure 9.30 Sludge thickening test apparatus. Note: Results are appreciably influenced by sludge depth, a greater depth hindering compaction rate. The test time varies from minutes to hours, and is best judged by the plot of sludge level vs. time to determine the time required to fall 1–2 inches. *(Courtesy of Eimco Division, Envirotech Corporation.)*

devices acting on air injected into the water in a flotation cell (Figure 9.24). In the dissolved air flotation process, discussed earlier as a clarification process, the slurry being thickened or a portion of the recycle flow is supersaturated with air under pressure. When the pressure is released, air is precipitated as small bubbles in the 10–100 micron size range. The air bubbles attach to the solids, increasing the buoyancy of the particles, and causing them to rise to the surface and concentrate.

Biological suspended solids are usually difficult to settle; however, with the addition of dissolved air bubbles and polymer, these particles have a tendency to float.

Flotation Aids   The DAF thickening process is often augmented by the addition of chemical aids. Chemicals that have been used include inorganics, such as ferric chloride and lime, and organic polyelectrolytes. Of the polyelectrolytes used, the most effective have been either moderate molecular weight polyamines or very high molecular weight flocculants. In most cases, cationic flocculants are used. They are particularly effective in flocculating biological solids. Introduction of the polymer into the line at a point where bubbles are precipitating and contacting the solids normally produces the best results.

Methods of evaluating flotation aids vary with the type of slurry being thickened. A standard cylinder settling test is often used to determine which polymers

Figure 9.31 Bench apparatus for air flotation studies. *(Courtesy of Infilco Degremont Incorporated.)*

will form stable floc. Floatability of a waste sludge can easily be determined using the apparatus shown in Figure 9.31. More sophisticated pilot plant test equipment such as is shown in Figure 9.32 can also be used to develop chemical programs. This equipment can closely duplicate the conditions found in actual DAF thickeners.

Figure 9.32 Pilot plant for evaluation of dissolved air flotation results on specific wastewater problems. *(Courtesy of Komline-Sanderson Engineering Corporation.)*

In summary, DAF can be an effective method of thickening materials that have a tendency to float. The use of DAF to concentrate sludge offers some advantages over gravity thickening. This is especially true in the case of concentration of activated biological sludge, which is troublesome to concentrate by gravity. Gravity thickening of waste activated sludge will seldom yield concentrated sludge of more than 2% solids. Dissolved air flotation of the same sludge will normally yield greater than 4% solids in the float. During the concentration operation, since air is used, the sludge will remain fresh and not become septic as it can if left in a gravity thickener.

CENTRIFUGATION

Solids concentration or thickening can also be accomplished by centrifugation. The three widely used types of centrifuges are basket, solid bowl, and disk-nozzle. The basket and solid bowl centrifuges are more commonly used in dewatering of sludges.

The disk-nozzle centrifuge (Figure 9.33), while primarily a liquid/liquid separation unit, can be used to thicken slurries for further dewatering. It is suitable for thickening a slurry with very fine uniform particle size since it creates greater centrifugal force than a solid bowl centrifuge.

Slurry is fed into the center of the machine at the top and then directed to an area on the outside of the disks (Figure 9.33a). The disks are stacked in the centrifuge so that they are 0.10–0.25" apart. The solids settle as the feed is forced through this narrow space. Since this distance is so narrow, particles do not have far to travel. The settled solids slide down the underside of the plates and out of the bowl wall where compaction takes place prior to discharge through nozzles in the periphery. The centrate passes under the sludge and is discharged from the center of the centrifuge. Since the disk-nozzle centrifuge has such close tolerances it is subject to frequent plugging when coarse solids are encountered. For this reason coarse solids are often screened from the fluid before it enters the centrifuge.

Figure 9.33 Schematic of several methods of operating a disk centrifuge: (a) basic scheme of operation; (b) with recycle of solids.

Figure 9.34 Cutaway showing typical details of a basket centrifuge used for dewatering of difficult sludges, and sludges that are highly abrasive. *(Courtesy of The De Laval Separator Company.)*

A basket centrifuge may also be used for slurry thickening. In a basket centrifuge (Figure 9.34) dewatering is a batch process. The slurry enters through a feed line from the top to a point near the bottom of the rotating drum. If the drum has solid (imperforate) walls, the centrate is collected by a skimmer or by simply overflowing a weir at the top of the bowl. The perforate bowl centrifuge has a drum with holes similar to that of an automatic washing machine. This type of centrifuge uses a filter medium placed on the inside of the drum, and water, under centrifugal force, passes through the cake and the medium to the outside of the drum from which it drains. After the machine is loaded, speed is increased to effect separation. After the centrate is removed, the centrifuge is slowed down for unloading. A knife or "plow" is then moved into the bowl to cut out the cake. This plow is hydraulically operated and is adjusted so as not to cut into the bowl wall.

Basket centrifuges are used where solids recovery and cake dryness are most important. Since perforate bowl machines can easily be equipped with wash sprays, they are often used where cakes need to be purified and washed as in the pharmaceutical industry.

DEWATERING

Dewatering is normally the final step in a solids/liquids separation. The goal is to produce a cake of such density and strength as to permit hauling to a final disposal site as a solid waste. It usually follows clarification and thickening operations. In waste treatment, the dewatering method is often dictated by the nature of the solids being dewatered and the final method of solids disposal. If sludge is being incinerated, as in the case of a raw or biological sewage sludge, it is necessary to extract as much water as possible to minimize the requirement for auxiliary fuel for incineration. If solids are being used in a land reclamation program or as landfill, it may not be necessary to dewater to such an extent.

Centrifugation

Centrifugation has long been used for dewatering as well as for thickening, discussed earlier. Selection of the proper centrifuge is important since design characteristics can be tailored to meet specific application needs. There are several inherent advantages in centrifugation that make it attractive for many dewatering applications. Among the important advantages are compact design, high throughput, and relative simplicity of operation. Auxiliary equipment is very simple.

Solid Bowl Centrifuge

The type of centrifuge normally used in dewatering applications as opposed to thickening is the solid bowl unit. These are widely used in municipal sewage plants, paper mills, steel mills, textile mills, and refineries. They are also used extensively in mining operations, such as processing coal and refuse. In more moderate climates, they can be installed and operated outdoors.

Principles of Operation   There are three solid bowl designs: conical, cylindrical, and conical-cylindrical. The conical bowl achieves maximum solids dryness, but at the expense of centrate clarity by employing a large beach area over a small centrate pool volume. In comparison, the cylindrical bowl has a deep centrate pool throughout its entire length and provides good centrate clarity, but relatively wet cake.

The conical-cylindrical design (Figure 9.35) is the most commonly used solid bowl centrifuge. It is flexible in its ability to shift the balance of cake dryness and centrate quality over a broad range by changing pool depth depending upon the desired performance criteria. The conical-cylindrical solid bowl centrifuge consists of a rotating unit comprising a bowl and a conveyor joining through a special system of gears which causes the bowl and conveyor to rotate in the same direction, but at slightly different speeds. Most solid bowl centrifuges operate at 1500–2500 rpm. The conveyor normally operates at 50–150 rpm lower. The conical section at one end of the bowl forms a dewatering beach over which the conveyor pushes the sludge to outlet ports. The clarified supernatant liquid is allowed to escape over weirs or is removed by a skimmer. If centrate and sludge cake leave the same end of the bowl, the centrifuge is called a concurrent type; if they leave the machine at opposite ends, the centrifuge is a countercurrent type.

The slurry to be dewatered enters the rotating bowl through a feed pipe extending into the hollow shaft of the rotating screw conveyor and is distributed through ports into a pool within the rotating bowl (Figure 9.36). The slurry pool forms a concentric ring of liquid on the inner wall of the bowl. The solids are settled by centrifugal forces to the peripheral surface of the rotating bowl. The depth of the bowl and its volume can be varied by adjustment of the overflow weir plates or a skimmer. The overflowing liquid is removed by pumping or by gravity. The helical rotating conveyor pushes the solids to the conical section where the solids are forced out of the water and free water drains from the solids back into the pool.

Figure 9.35 Cutaway view of a horizontal solid-bowl continuous centrifuge showing typical design features. *(Courtesy of Bird Machine Company, Inc.)*

Slurry feed pumps should be of the nonpulsating type. A progressing cavity pump is normally recommended, since it affords positive displacement without surging. Sludge feed and chemical feed pumps should be interlocked to stop automatically if the centrifuging or cake conveying operation is interrupted. A wash water system is normally included to provide a means of flushing the machine when it is to be shut down. This prevents the accumulation of solids that may cause vibrations because of imbalance. In general, those sludges that separate more readily and concentrate to the greatest thickness by plain sedimentation can be dewatered most efficiently by centrifuge.

Theory

The solid bowl centrifuge can be compared with a horizontal clarifier as illustrated in Figure 9.37. Both processes are applications of Stokes' Law:

$$V = \frac{2R^2(S_1 - S_2)g}{9\mu}$$

where V = settling velocity
R = particle radius
S_1 = specific gravity of particle
S_2 = specific gravity of liquid
g = acceleration due to gravity
μ = viscosity

The important difference between the processes of sedimentation and centrifugation is that centrifugation increases the g factor from 1.0 to 2000–3000. Another difference is this high gravitational force of the centrifuge reduces the required detention so that the particles have only to settle a very short distance—inches instead of feet.

Design Variables   There are several design variables to be considered when choosing a centrifuge for a specific dewatering application, the most important being bowl design, rotational speed, and conveyor (scroll) speed.

Bowl Design   As the bowl length increases, retention time increases, resulting in drier cake and clearer centrates. However, power requirements also increase,

Figure 9.36 Operation of a solid-bowl centrifuge. *(Courtesy of Sharples Division, Pennwalt Corporation.)*

(a)

(b)

Figure 9.37 A centrifuge has the same basic characteristics as a clarifier. It's a clarifier whose base is wrapped around a center line so it can be rotated to generate elevated G's. *(Courtesy of Sharples Division, Pennwalt Corporation.)*

since they are proportional to the volume contained in the centrifuge. As with bowl length, increasing the diameter of a centrifuge results in drier cakes and clearer filtrate at the same feed rate. Besides requiring higher power input, a larger diameter machine requires more critical balancing, since the center of gravity moves farther from the center.

Speed   As might be expected, higher bowl speeds produce drier cakes and clearer centrates, but also increase the wear on the machine. When centrifuging abrasive materials, low speed centrifuges are preferred. As the conveyor speed differential increases, machine throughput can increase, but at the expense of a wetter cake and dirtier centrate. While bowl speed and scroll speed differential are treated as a design variable, it is possible by changing pulleys and gear boxes to alter them on existing machines, so they are also an operating variable. On some newer machines the scroll speed differential can be varied while the centrifuge is operating.

Operational Variables   In operating a centrifuge for slurry dewatering, the following variables must be balanced to obtain the desired results:

1. *Sludge flow.* The sludge feed rate is one of the more important variables. The rate of sludge feed affects both clarity and cake dryness. As sludge flow increases, machine throughput increases, but at the expense of centrate clarity and cake dryness (Figure 9.38). Extremely high flows cause machine flooding. Very low flow rates produce extremely dry cakes causing increased wear of the conveyor scroll. Sludge should be pumped to the machine at the highest rate that will not cause the carryover of excessive fines in the centrate.

2. *Chemical conditioning.* Polyelectrolytes have been used with success to increase the recovery efficiency of centrifuges. They may also increase throughput and widen the spectrum of sludge characteristics that can be processed. The most active polymers are of high molecular weight, either anionic, nonionic, or cationic, depending on the sludge being dewatered. The degree of solids recovery and cake dryness can be regulated over a wide range depending on the amount of chemical used (Figure 9.39). The use of flocculation aids sometimes

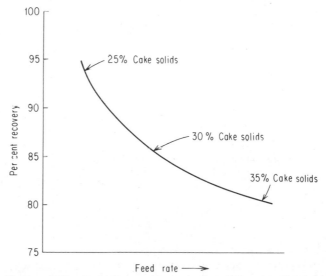

Figure 9.38 Typical centrifuge performance on digested primary sewage solids.

Figure 9.39 Effect of polyelectrolyte treatment on centrifuge performance.

produces wetter sludge because of the increased capture of fines. The variables that affect the efficiency of chemical conditioning are dosage, dilution, and chemical injection point. Cylinder settling tests should be run to select the proper polymer and its approximate dosage. Exact dosages can only be determined in the centrifuge. If a centrifuge has been designed with more than one polymer application point, all points should be evaluated. The purpose of an internal feed point is to add polymer to the pool after the heavy, easily settleable solids have been removed. However, it is sometimes advantageous to add polymer to the total sludge stream, thereby using the heavier solids to help in bridging and flocculating the finer ones. Since in either case conditioning time is relatively short, it is important to dilute polymer to a level that will provide good distribution into the sludge without overloading the machine with dilution water.

3. *Pool depth.* Pool depth determines pool volume and affects both clarification and cake dryness. Lowering the pool exposes more drainable deck area, increases the dewatering time, and produces a drier cake; conversely, increasing pool depth increases clarification by increasing detention time. However, just as in sedimentation, too deep a pool prevents a particle from reaching the sediment zone in time to avoid being discharged with the effluent. Theory indicates that the thinnest possible layer in the bowl or in a sedimentation basin gives maximum clarification. In practice, this is not true because of practical inefficiencies. Thin layers mean high linear liquid velocities and the resuspension of nonsettling fine materials. Also, at minimum pool depths the moving conveyor tends to redisperse solids as does turbulence in the feed zone. Consequently, it is normally found that a medium pool depth gives optimum performance. Increasing the pool depth beyond the optimum depth does not contribute to clarity as the retention time and the distance the particle must settle are both directly proportional to the pool depth. The shallower the pool in the centrifuge, the longer the drainage time for solids on the beach out of the pool and generally the drier the settled solids (Figure 9.40). Fine particles, however, compact to a limiting dryness at the bowl wall under the pool and capillary forces may prevent appreciable drainage of liquid from the interstices of the sludge on the beach. In this case, a

shallow pool is no advantage, and in fact a deep pool often improves conveying and removal of this type of sludge solids.

All conditions of operating variables should be evaluated to fine tune operating parameters for a given centrifuge application. Gradual changes should be made, allowing 10 to 15 minutes between changes.

System Evaluation   To determine whether a program is successful, some performance criteria must be established. The desired results, whether it be dry cake or clear centrate, will determine the weighting of the following criteria.

Recovery.   Centrifuge dewatering performance is normally stated in terms of recovery, expressed as the percentage of suspended solids in the sludge feed that ends up in the discharged sludge cake. Recovery is computed using the following equation:

$$\% \text{ Efficiency} = \frac{C_i - C_0}{C_i} \times 100$$

where C_i = feed solids concentration in, mg/l
C_0 = centrate solids concentration out, mg/l

Note that this formula is not corrected for dissolved solids, which must be taken into account when centrifuging a chemical process liquor, such as a 10% brine. Where the water slurry contains less than 500 mg/l and the feed solids exceed 2%, the above formula is adequate for most plant calculations.

Yield.   The amount of cake throughput expressed in dry pounds of solids per hour is the centrifuge yield. This is not an efficiency factor since the machine could conceivably have a high yield, but a poor centrate. Yield is determined by multiplying the pounds of wet cake per hour by the percent solids (on a dry basis) in the wet cake. For example, 2100 pounds of wet cake per hour at 30% solids is equal to 700 pounds solids per hour, dry basis.

Centrate Quality.   Centrate quality refers to the amount of suspended solids in the centrate and is directly related to recovery. Typically, solids found in the centrate are extremely fine. Since the centrate is normally settled and recycled through the system, running with a poor centrate will eventually build fines in the system and lower the recovery rate. Getting 100% recovery, on the other hand, is uneconomical and is not necessary to meet real plant needs.

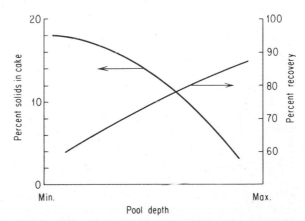

Figure 9.40 The effect of pool depth on centrifuge performance. The deeper pool limits the area available for cake dewatering, but increases detention.

Figure   9.41 Operating sequence of rotary-drum vacuum filter.

Cake Solids.   The desired degree of cake dryness will depend on final disposition of the solids. If solids are to be incinerated, low moisture is desired. As drier solids entail higher dewatering costs, higher scroll wear, and lower yield, cake solids should not be higher than realistically needed for final disposal.

Vacuum Filtration

Rotary vacuum filters have been used for many years by industry and municipalities to dewater waste sludges. They are also used in many process applications such as the pulping operations in paper mills. The mining industry also uses vacuum filters extensively in coal recovery and in ore processing. Solids content of the filter cake may vary considerably depending on the slurry being dewatered. Inorganic slurries may dewater to 70% solids, whereas a biological sludge may only dewater to a 20% solids level.

Principles of Operation   A rotary vacuum filter consists of a perforated cylindrical drum rotating in a vat containing the suspension to be dewatered. Vacuum is applied to the interior and solids/liquids separation is accomplished by drawing the liquid through a filter medium, leaving solids on the medium for separate collection. As the drum rotates, this medium provides a continuous filter going through the following sequence (Figure 9.41).

1. *Cake formation.* During this step, the drum is submerged in a vat containing slurry and vacuum is applied. The first solids that collect on the medium act as a filter for subsequent cake formation. For this reason, it is desirable that the cake be formed gradually.

2. *Liquid extraction or drying.* A vacuum is also applied during the liquid extraction or drying step. Water is drawn out of the filter cake through the filter media to the inside of the drum and from there into a filtrate receiver.

3. *Filter cake removal.* Removal of the filter cake from the drum can be accomplished by one of several methods discussed later.

4. *Media washing.* This final step in the cycle of vacuum filter operation can be accomplished on a continuous or intermittent basis. High pressure water sprays are normally used. These sprays dislodge the particles that could build up and clog the medium. It often becomes necessary to acid wash the filter media on a routine basis. This is particularly true when ferric chloride and lime are used as conditioning chemicals.

Types of Vacuum Filters   There are several variations of rotary vacuum filters. The drum filter (Figure 9.42) uses a "doctor blade" to scrape off the cake for discharge. It is sometimes supplemented by a pressure blowback in the discharge zone. Air pressure from the inside of the drum just ahead of the doctor blade loosens the cake for subsequent removal by the doctor blade. The filter medium never leaves the drum surface on this type filter. The filter medium may be either a stainless steel mesh or a synthetic or natural fiber fabric. The more common materials are nylon, polypropylene and polyethylene. These media come in a wide range of porosities to meet specific application needs. A filter medium should be selected with porosity small enough to obtain an acceptable filtrate, but large enough to avoid plugging. Consideration also should be given to the compatibility of the medium with the slurry being filtered.

A second type of vacuum filter is the belt filter (Figure 9.43) in which the filter medium is a continuous belt that leaves the drum surface and travels over a short radius discharge roll. This sharp change in curvature normally causes the sludge cake to fall from the media. In some cases, it is also necessary to use a doctor blade to insure maximum production. The advantage of this filter over a drum filter is that the media are washed on both sides.

The coil type filter (Figure 9.44) employs two layers of stainless steel coil springs arranged in a corduroy fashion around the drum. These layered springs act as the filter medium. On completion of the dewatering cycle the two layers of springs leave the drum and are separated from each other in such a manner that the filtered sludge cake is lifted off the lower layer of coil springs and discharged from the upper layer with the aid of a positioned tine bar. The two layers of springs are then washed separately by sprays and returned to the drum by grooved aligning rolls. Because of its positive filter cake release system, the coil filter is often selected for dewatering of sludges with poor release tendencies.

A fourth type of vacuum filter, the continuous disc filter (Figure 9.45) operates on the same general principle as other vacuum filters except that the filtering surface is on both sides of several discs mounted perpendicular to a rotating horizontal center shaft. Filtrate is collected from each disc and cake is removed by scrapers.

Auxiliary Equipment   There are a number of auxiliary devices required for operation of rotary filters. These include vacuum pump, vacuum receiver, filtrate pump, sludge pump, and chemical conditioning equipment

Normally each filter has its own vacuum pump. Vacuum pumps may be

Figure 9.42 Assembly of a typical rotary-drum vacuum filter. (*Courtesy of Dorr-Oliver, Inc.*)

Figure 9.43 Design features and operating sequence of rotary-drum belt-type vacuum filter. *(Courtesy of Envirex, a Rexnord Company.)*

either reciprocating positive displacement type, centrifugal or rotary positive types. Reciprocating pumps are the most efficient for high vacuum of 20-25″ of mercury. The required capacity for a vacuum pump is determined in part by the porosity of the filter medium. If the filter medium is changed to one more porous, this may result in the vacuum pump being undersized. In operation this condition may be evidenced by an inability of the vacuum system to prevent backflowing of filtrate as the drum turns out of the sludge in the vat. Of course, poor performance of the vacuum system can also result from normal wear or poor maintenance.

Each vacuum filter must be supplied with a vacuum receiver between the filter

Figure 9.44 Cross section of a coil filter. *(Courtesy of Komline-Sanderson Engineering Corporation.)*

Figure 9.45   Disk-type vacuum filter used for solids which form a thick cake. *(Courtesy of Dorr-Oliver Incorporated.)*

valve and the vacuum pump. The receiver acts as a separator of air and filtrate, as well as a reservoir for the filtrate pump suction.

Sludge feed pumps can be of the piston, diaphragm or progressing cavity type. They should be installed so that their capacity is constant at a given setting and should be interlocked to a level sensing device to stop at a predetermined high liquid level in the filter vat, and to automatically restart when the filter has caught up. A separate pump should be provided for each filter conditioning tank combination. Pumps should have stroke counters or some other flow totalizing device.

Chemical conditioning equipment includes chemical storage tanks, sludge conditioning tank and chemical preparation and feed systems. Sludge conditioning containers may be horizontal tanks, vertical tanks or horizontal rotating drums. The sludge should flow by gravity from the conditioning tank to the filter vat to minimize floc damage. To provide optimum sludge mixing and flocculation under varying conditions, sludge conditioning tanks should be provided with variable speed mixer drives, removable weirs and multiple points of chemical application. Rates of rotation of mixers generally should be adjustable between 10 and 60 rpm, depending on the design of the stirrers.

Operating Variables   There are several variables to be balanced to operate a vacuum filter efficiently. Since each sludge being filtered has its own dewatering characteristics, the variables must be tuned to give the desired results. Changes should be made in small increments and the system given at least ½ hour to react and reach a new equilibrium. If the filter vat is filled with improperly conditioned sludge, it is best to drain the pan and start over.

Sludge conditioning.   Polyelectrolytes, ferric chloride and lime are conditioning chemicals used to coagulate and flocculate solids in suspension. The larger floc particles filter more easily and have less tendency to blind the filters. With the use of iron and lime, deposits may accumulate on the filter medium and necessitate periodic acid cleaning. To properly coagulate and flocculate a sludge for vacuum filtration, controlled mixing is required. Conditioning tanks normally are sized to provide retention time of 30–60 seconds. With too little mixing, polymer will not be properly dispersed; too much mixing breaks the floc. The proper amount of mixing for a particular sludge must be determined empirically.

Vat agitation.   The conditioned sludge must be agitated in the filter pan to eliminate settling. Organic sludges without heavy solids usually require only intermittent agitation.

Vat level.   Conditioned sludge in the filter pan should be set at a level which, when coupled with drum cycle time, gives the desired cake thickness. Higher vat levels give thicker and somewhat wetter cakes than low levels if other variables are kept constant.

Cycle times.   The drum speed should be adjusted to give the desired cake thickness and moisture content. For most applications, a higher speed resulting in a thinner, drier cake (¼ to ½ inch) is better than a low speed producing thick (1 inch) cakes.

Vacuum.   Normally vacuum filters are run with as much vacuum as can be attained. Since usually only one vacuum pump is used per filter, it is necessary to balance vacuum between the cake forming and drying sections. Higher pickup vacuum will produce wetter cakes and greater sludge dewatering rates.

Filter media.   A variety of filter media is available, providing a selection of size and weave. The coarser media normally give drier cakes, but at the cost of fines escaping into the filtrate. Filter leaf tests can be used to determine the proper medium for a particular application (Figure 9.46).

Sludge density.   Thicker sludges will filter and release from the medium more easily than thin sludges. Fillers such as sawdust, diatomaceous earth, and fly ash are sometimes added to thicken thin sludges. Where sludges are incinerated, recycled ash fed to the thickener ahead of the filter may increase solids and improve performance.

Sludge particle size.   By achieving high recovery (capture) performance, the level of recycled fines accumulating in the plant can be minimized. If the level of fines in the plant becomes too high, filter blinding can occur. Fines can also upset other plant processes, such as clarification and BOD removal, by overloading their solids separation capacity.

System Evaluation   To determine whether a program is successful some per-

(a)

(b)

(c)

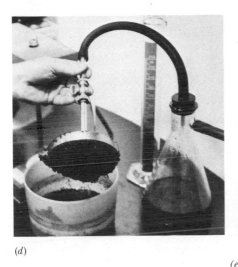

(d)

(e)

Figure 9.46 (a) Apparatus required for complete evaluation of vacuum filtration for sludge dewatering. (b) Chemical is added to the sludge with carefully controlled stirring to flocculate the sludge particles. (c) The test filter pad is submerged in the flocculated sludge for a measured time under a controlled vacuum with filtrate being collected. (d) The filter pad is removed from the pan with a motion simulating the withdrawal of the drum surface from the vat. (e) The vacuum is shut off after a measured time, during which the filtrate continues to flow into the collecting flask.

formance benchmarks must be established. Desired results, such as a dry cake, a clear filtrate, or high production can be determined by the following criteria:

1. *Filter yield.* The most common measure of filter performance is expressed as pounds of dry solids per square foot per hour. Typical filter loadings are 3–10 pounds per square foot per hour for a municipal plant, 8–10 pounds per square foot per hour for an industrial plant. Some industrial filters dewatering inor-

ganic sludges are rated in the 40–300 pounds per square foot per hour range. Filter yield measures only the rate of production in terms of dry solids equivalent, not filter efficiency.

2. *Filter efficiency.* Since the vacuum filter is a device used for separating cake solids from a thinner sludge, the actual efficiency of the process is determined by the percentage of feed solids recovered in the filter cake. This is calculated by the same formula as used for the centrifuge. Solids removal efficiencies in vacuum filters have ranged from what 85% for coarse mesh or coiled media to 99% with close weave, long nap media. Since recycled filtrate solids increase the load on the plant treatment unit, they should be kept to a minimum or balanced within cost effectiveness for overall plant operations.

3. *Filter cake quality.* Filter cake moisture content varies with the type of slurry handled and filter time in drum submersion. Good filter performance does not always mean producing the driest possible cake. Cake moisture should be adjusted to obtain only as dry a cake as is required for the intended end use. Anything more is inefficient and wasteful of filter capacity.

4. *Filtrate quality.* Suspended solids content is the most important indicator of filtrate quality. This depends on the filter medium (fine or coarse), the quality of filter feed slurry (percent fines), and the amount of vacuum. Generally, filtrate suspended solids should be kept as low as possible, especially when the filtrate is settled and returned to a thickener in advance of the filter. A high percentage of solids in the filtrate can result in a buildup of recirculating solids, interfering with thickener and filter operation. Overtreating to a water-clear filtrate is not necessary since a small amount of fines will not generally cause such upsets.

Vacuum filters lend themselves to a wide variety of dewatering operations. In most cases, thickening of the slurry prior to vacuum filtration will increase filter yield substantially. The Buchner funnel test is useful in evaluation and selection of a chemical program to aid vacuum filtration. The filter leaf test can also be a valuable tool in program selection, as well as in the actual media selection and determination of filter yields in a vacuum filter installation.

Plate-and-Frame Filter Presses

In addition to centrifuge and vacuum filter dewatering, sludges can also be dewatered by pressure filtration. One method of pressure filtration is the plate and frame press. The press consists of vertical plates held in a frame and pressed together between a fixed and a moving end (Figure 9.47). Each plate is fitted with a medium, normally woven monofilament polypropylene. Water passes through the cloth and out the press. The solids are collected on the surface of the cloth.

Slurry is fed to the press until the flow rate drops radically. Most presses operate at pressures of 100–250 psig. When filtrate flow stops, the pressure is relieved and the unit opened. Usually, presses are equipped with an automatic opening gear which separates the plates so that dry sludge cake can be discharged.

When the plates are separated the cake normally falls out. Presses are commonly installed above floor level so that a hopper can be placed under the press to collect dry cake. Because of the high pressures involved, plate and frame presses produce much drier cakes than either centrifuges or vacuum filters. However, plate and frame presses are not as widely used since they operate on a batch basis rather than continuously.

Chemical conditioning aids are normally used to shorten filter time and produce drier cakes. When it is available, fly ash may be used. It is not unusual to use as much as a ton of fly ash to dewater a ton of sludge. Polyelectrolytes can be

Figure 9.47 Solid cake dropping from filter press opened for discharge. *(Courtesy of Passavant Corporation.)*

used to replace part, and in many cases, all of the fly ash. Ferric chloride and lime have also been used to condition sludges prior to plate and frame presses.

Belt Filter Press

Another type of pressure filter is the belt pressure filter. A typical unit as shown in Figure 9.48 has three distinct dewatering zones. The draining zone, the press zone, and the shear zone. Since free drainage is essential to the operation of a belt press, it is necessary to first condition the sludge. Most belt presses are equipped with a conditioning tank in which polymers are mixed with the feed sludge. The conditioned sludge then flows to the draining zone where initial thickening takes place. The sludge then passes between two screens where pressure is applied and partial dewatering takes place. Finally, by increasing the pressure on the belts, shear is applied to the partially dewatered sludge.

Figure 9.48 Two of a variety of designs of belt presses for sludge dewatering. (*a*) The Andritz machine was adapted from a device used for pulp dewatering. *(Courtesy of Tait-Andritz.)*

(b)

(c)

Figure 9.48   (b) This design was developed for sewage plant sludges. *(Courtesy of Infilco Degremont, Inc.)*; (c) In this photo, conditioned sewage sludge is shown leaving the gravity drainage section and entering the pressure section of this belt filter press, where shear forces produce further dewatering. *(Courtesy of Ralph B. Carter Company.)*

The belt is normally a relatively coarse mesh stainless steel fabric. Since sludge is applied to the top of the media, sludge pickup is not a problem as with the vacuum filter. These units are particularly desirable when difficult to dewater sludges are encountered.

Drying Beds

Drying beds are often used to dewater waste sludges, where land is available and climatic conditions are favorable. In early designs, sand was used as the filtering medium. The typical sand bed has tile underdrains covered by 12″ of graded gravel, then topped with 6–9″ of 0.3 to 1.2 mm sand, with a uniformity coefficient less than 5.0 (Figure 9.49).

Under the right circumstances, the drying bed provides advantages over mechanical dewatering devices; such as low operating costs due to low energy requirements, little maintenance and minimal operator attention. They have the ability to handle variable sludges and to produce drier cakes than most mechanical devices. There are, however, limitations to their use, such as high land requirements and weather dependency. Since drying beds are outdoors, odor may be a problem if the sludge is high in organic matter.

For effective dewatering on drying beds, the sludge must have physical properties which allow drainage of contained water without blinding of the filtering medium. Water drainage should be rapid and relatively complete, reducing to a minimum the residue that must be evaporated. The sludge applied to the drying bed should be as thick as possible to reduce the required drying time. Chemicals that improve the release of free water have proven effective in speeding drainage and significantly reducing drying time.

Drying beds have been popular for dewatering municipal sewage sludges, including primary, aerobically or anaerobically digested, and mixtures of primary with biological sludges. Many other types of sludges are dewatered on drying beds, including water plant clarification sludges, softening sludges, and industrial sludges.

Drying bed designs generally fall into the following categories: impervious bottom beds, impervious bottom with drainage strips, sand beds, and sand beds with multiple cement tracks to provide complete mechanical unloading.

Figure 9.49 Conventional sand drying bed with tile underdrain system, shown here during construction.

Figure 9.50 Combination concrete and sand drying bed has full-width drive down ramp and concrete strips spaced to match tire widths. Unloading is fast and efficient with minimal sand losses. (Designed by Baxter & Woodman Engineers, Crystal Lake, Illinois.)

The simple impervious bottom beds and those with drainage strips are relatively easy to install and maintain, but they require longer drying times due to the reduced water drainage. Originally, sand beds were designed with clay tile as the underdrain system. The clay tile tended to break easily, ruling out the use of mechanical equipment for dry sludge removal. In addition, sludge removal with mechanical loaders has caused relatively high sand losses, which can be an important consideration if sand is scarce.

Some plants have been very successful with resilient plastic underdrain tile and ﬧecially designed buckets to skim off the dry sludge from the sand. A relatively ﹀w bed using alternating sand and cement strips throughout the entire bed, coupled with a drive-down ramp across the full width of the bed, allows a front endloader to make parallel passes when removing the dried sludge (Figure 9.50). The cement strips spaced at tire track distances prevent the bucket from digging into the sand media. This bed appears to offer the advantage of hard surface support along with open sand drainage The use of polymer will significantly increase the dewatering speed and therefore reduce the area required.

Where sand beds are already in place, polymer addition will allow more complete drying and reduce the volume of dried sludge to be hauled away. Surface loading rates can often be two or more times as great as on beds not using polymer dewatering chemicals.

Sludge application will largely depend on local plant needs and the type of bed used. Normally, sludges are applied from 6–10 inches deep, depending on local conditions and the amount of sludge available for drying. Addition of new sludge on top of partially dried sludge is not recommended. An exception to this may be thin digester supernate which is sent to the drying bed first in order to minimize its impact on the primary clarifier. In this case chemical must be used in order to prevent blinding of the drying bed by multiple sludge applications.

MISCELLANEOUS DEVICES

An entire volume could be devoted to the subject of solids/liquids separation devices. Only the most familiar have been discussed in this chapter. To illustrate how special problems can produce special solutions, four examples of specific solids/liquids separator designs are presented to conclude this chapter:

Cyclone Separators (Figure 9.51) Often difficulties are encountered from the presence of very fine sand in a well water. This may be caused by improper com-

Figure 9.51   Desanding cyclone often used on well waters carrying fine sand. (*Courtesy of Dorr-Oliver Incorporated.*)

pletion of the well or failure of the well screen. For some purposes, the fine sand may be an acceptable contaminant, but it may cause erosion or may plug filters and ion exchange beds. The hydraulic cyclone is a common solution to this problem, separating the sand from water by centrifugal force. These cyclones are also used extensively in the pulp/paper industry as pulp cleaners. The heavy silt, rust particles, or other debris is rather easily separated from lightweight pulp fibers by the centrifugal forces in the cyclones.

TABLE 9.2   Strainer Size versus Size of Particle Passing Through

Mesh size*	Particle size†		Category of solids
	Inches	Microns	
10	0.079	2000	↑
20	0.033	840	
30	0.023	590	Settleable
40	0.017	420	Solids,
60	0.012	250	Visible to
80	0.007	180	naked eye
100	0.006	150	↕
200	0.0027	70	Turbidity,
270	0.0020	50	visible through light
325	0.0016	40	microscope ↓

* Mesh is the number of openings per unit of length, which is inches in this case.
† The opening depends both on mesh and the size of wire forming the screen. In this case U.S. Standard Screen dimensions are given. Commercial screens may not match established screen standards. For example, if stainless steel wire is used, because it is stronger than most other materials the wire may be smaller and the opening correspondingly larger than standard screen dimensions.

(a)

(b)

Figure 9.52 (*a*) Cutaway showing internal details of an automatic backwash strainer. (*b*) Automatic backwash strainer in service on scale pit water in a steel mill, recirculating water for roll cooling. (*Courtesy of Ronninger-Petter Division, Dover Corporation.*)

Strainers (Figure 9.52)   An alternative to cyclone separators is often a mechanical device to strain particulates from water. These units may handle particles in the size range of 10–200 microns. They are used where smaller suspended solids would not harm the process (as in roll-cooling in a steel mill), but larger particles could clog piping, distributors, or spray nozzles. Many designs include motor drives for rotation of the sieve openings for cleaning on a programmed basis.

Tubular Cartridge Filters (Figure 9.53)   The distribution of clarified water through an extensive pipeline may result in the reintroduction of solids, such as scale or corrosion products, into the water so its quality is below acceptable stand-

Figure 9.53 Typical in-depth tubular filter elements. *(Courtesy of The Carborundum Company.)*

Figure 9.54 Inclined (side-hill) sieves, installed as trash screens in a municipal sewage plant handling a mixture of domestic and industrial wastes. *(Courtesy of C-E Bauer.)*

ards at the point of use. Tubular cartridge filter elements are often used for final polishing of process water for such critical operations as textile dyeing, where particulates, particularly rust, could damage the finished goods. Both expendable and cleanable elements are available.

Cross-flow Sieves (Figure 9.54)   This type of solids/liquid separator combines the techniques of screening with initial separation caused by a change in direction of fluid flow. The screening slots are at right angles to flow, and the incline angle of the screening device is selected to give complete drainage of water through the slots before the flow reaches the base of the incline. This device is used for separation of fibrous materials from water, producing a dewatered pulp and water which may be recycled or disposed of more readily free of the bulk of solids.

SUGGESTED READING

American Water Works Association: *Water Quality and Treatment,* McGraw-Hill, New York, 1971.
Fair, G. M., Geyer, J. C., and Okun, D. A.: *Elements of Water Supply and Wastewater Treatment,* John Wiley & Sons, New York, 1971.
Infilco-Degremont, Inc. *Water Treatment Handbook.* Roger Leviel, ed. Taylor & Carlisle, distributors. New York.
New York State Department of Health: "Manual of Instruction for Sewage Treatment Plant Operators," Health Education Service, Albany, undated.
Nordell, Eskel: *Water Treatment for Industrial and Other Uses,* Reinhold, New York, 1961.
Water Pollution Control Federation: WPCF Manual of Practice No. 8, "Sewage Treatment Plant Design," Washington, D.C., 1963.

Chapter **10**

Precipitation

Once water has been taken from its source, where it may have been in a state of equilibrium, it is often exposed to pumping, aeration, and heating, any of which may upset its stability and lead to corrosion or scaling. Whether a particular water will tend to corrode metal or form a $CaCO_3$ scale can be roughly predicted by its Stability Index, which can be calculated from the solubility product of calcium carbonate and the concentrations of certain ions in the water. The same principles used in predicting water stability apply to all precipitation processes.

The precipitation process makes use of the solubility product of a compound containing an ion or radical that is considered detrimental, and that should, therefore, be removed before the water is put to use. The reduction of calcium ion concentration by precipitation as calcium carbonate is one example of this.

Adsorption is a process with some similarities to precipitation. The choice of an adsorbent and the degree of removal that can be achieved may be only roughly determined; data for estimating purposes may be found in technical literature, and these are useful as a guide to bench evaluation of the selected process. An example of adsorption is removal of silica from water on magnesium hydroxide precipitate.

Temperature is an important factor in both precipitation and adsorption reactions. The solubility product is affected by temperature; knowing the solubility characteristics of the desired precipitate will influence the selection of treatment equipment. For example, if preheating water to a higher temperature produces improved results over those expected at ambient temperature, then heat exchangers may be justified. Temperature also influences the rates of all chemical reactions, and heating may make it possible to select smaller reaction or sedimentation vessels for the process.

One of the fundamental principles of precipitation is that the size of a precipitate increases if the chemical reaction is encouraged to occur on previously precipitated particles. If a small crystal and a large crystal of the same substance are placed in a saturated solution of the substance in a beaker, the small crystal will slowly disappear as the larger one grows; if a crystal of salt is introduced into a supersaturated, clear salt solution, it will grow as salt comes out of solution on the surface of the seed crystal in preference to forming individual crystal nuclei. Because of these reactions, most precipitation processes in water treatment are conducted by introducing precipitating chemicals into the water in the presence of previously precipitated sludge.

SOFTENING BY PRECIPITATION

Lime softening, the most widely used precipitation process, serves well to illustrate the importance of four key variables in precipitation: (1) solubility, (2) particle charge, (3) temperature, and (4) time. Lime softening is the reduction of hardness by the application of hydrated lime to water to precipitate $CaCO_3$, $Mg(OH)_2$, or both.

At first glance, it may appear paradoxical that lime, a compound of calcium, can be added to water to remove calcium; the explanation is that the hydroxyl radical is the reactive component of lime, converting CO_2 and HCO_3^- to CO_3^{-2}, causing $CaCO_3$ to precipitate, as shown by reactions (1), (2) and (3).

$$Ca(OH)_2 \rightleftharpoons Ca^{+2} + 2OH^- \tag{1}$$

$$Ca(OH)_2 + 2CO_2 \rightarrow Ca(HCO_3)_2 \tag{2}$$

or, in ionic form:

$$2OH^- + 2CO_2 \rightarrow 2HCO_3^-$$

$$Ca(OH)_2 + Ca(HCO_3)_2 \rightarrow 2CaCO_3 \downarrow + 2H_2O \tag{3}$$

in ionic form:

$$2OH^- + 2HCO_3^- \rightarrow 2CO_3^{-2} + 2H_2O$$

Other hydroxide compounds (NaOH, KOH) could also be used, but these cannot usually compete against the low cost of lime except in special circumstances where they may be available as by-products.

Most softening reactions are carried out at a pH of about 10. At this pH, $CaCO_3$ usually carries a negative, and $Mg(OH)_2$ a positive, charge. If these charges are not neutralized, colloidal hardness may resist flocculation and carry over into the effluent. Cationic coagulants may be needed when the bulk of the precipitate is negatively charged $CaCO_3$, as in partial lime softening. Sodium aluminate is frequently used as an anionic coagulant when low magnesium residuals [positively-charged $Mg(OH)_2$] are needed in complete lime softening. The coagulant may be supplemented by an anionic or a nonionic flocculant.

The water chemist distinguishes between cold process lime softening, usually carried out in the range of 40–90°F, and hot process, at 215–230°F. Results achievable at intermediate temperatures are often of interest. Obtaining data in the intermediate range may require bench testing, as very few plants have operated in this range. At about 120°F, silica removal, which is negligible in cold process softening, increases. At about 140–160°F, lime softening of sewage, which is rather incomplete cold, begins to approach hot process results. These phenomena illustrate the importance of laboratory testing under actual operating conditions to obtain reliable data before a plant is designed and built.

PARTIAL LIME SOFTENING

The most prevalent precipitation process in water treatment is the reduction of calcium hardness by its precipitation as $CaCO_3$. Since the alkalinity of most

Figure 10.1 The data used for estimating calcium carbonate residuals in conventional lime softening plants with 60–90 minutes detention.

waters is in the bicarbonate form, and because there is usually CO_2 present, the precipitation of calcium carbonate requires the conversion of CO_2 and bicarbonate to carbonate, as shown by reactions (1), (2) and (3).

As was pointed out previously, $CaCO_3$ precipitation is not as simple a reaction as it appears to be because of the formation of ion pairs and because of interferences, such as the stabilization of colloidal calcium carbonate preventing its precipitation in the normal reaction time. Because of this, the theoretical solubility curve is of limited value in predicting the actual results that might be achieved in a precipitation reaction such as partial lime softening. For estimating purposes, the solubility as shown by Figure 10.1 is commonly used in the water treatment industry. This assumes the solubility of calcium carbonate at ambient river water or well water temperatures to be about 35 mg/l as $CaCO_3$. (Obviously, if the water supply is already less than 35 mg/l in calcium hardness, lime softening for calcium reduction is of no value.) It also assumes about 60 minutes detention in the reaction tank.

In predicting the results of partial lime softening, there are two cases to be considered, one in which the calcium hardness of the raw water exceeds its alkalinity and the other in which the alkalinity exceeds the calcium hardness. Where the calcium exceeds the alkalinity (Figure 10.2), the results of treatment are calculated by establishing first that there has been no change in any anions except alkalinity, which is converted to 35 mg/l CO_3, as $CaCO_3$. In the cation portion of the analysis, the magnesium is shown as being reduced by about 10%. The sodium remains unchanged, and the calcium is then calculated by difference. Figure 10.2 shows an analysis of a raw water having a calcium hardness exceeding the alkalinity, with results after partial lime softening, following this method of calculation. The approximation of pH is taken from alkalinity relationships discussed in an earlier chapter.

Where the alkalinity exceeds the calcium (as shown in Figure 10.3), the cation section of the analysis is calculated first: the calcium is shown as 35 mg/l; the

Identification of Analyses Tabulated Below:

A. Raw water @ 60°F   D. _____

B. Estimated results   E. _____

C. _____   F. _____

Constituent	As	A	B	C	D	E	F
Calcium	CaCO₃	125	65				
Magnesium	"	65	60				
Sodium	"	20	20				
Total Electrolyte	CaCO₃	210	145				
Bicarbonate	CaCO₃	100	0				
Carbonate	"	0	35				
Hydroxyl	"	0	0				
Sulfate	"	60	60				
Chloride	"	50	50				
Nitrate	"						
M Alk.	CaCO₃	100	35				
P Alk.	"	0	18				
Carbon Dioxide		10	10				
pH		7.3	10.0				
Silica		10	10				
Iron	Fe	0.2	Nil				
Turbidity							
TDS		230	165				
Color							

Figure 10.2   Partial cold lime softening results where $Ca > M$ alkalinity in the raw water analysis.

magnesium is reduced by 10%, and the sodium is unchanged. In the anion section of the analysis, except for alkalinity, the remaining anions are unchanged. The total alkalinity is then calculated by difference. Of the total alkalinity, at least 35 mg/l must be present as carbonate. The balance may be bicarbonate, or as much of this may be converted to carbonate as wished, depending on the desired Stability Index and pH of the system. Figure 10.3 shows a raw water having an alkalinity in excess of calcium hardness and shows the results of treatment, with several examples of varying degrees of conversion of bicarbonate to carbonate.

With experience in using such calculations and in reviewing actual plant results, the water treatment engineer can improve accuracy in prediction of results of partial lime softening. For example, it is apparent that if the calcium is greatly in excess of alkalinity in the raw water, the shape of the solubility product curve is such that the carbonate would be lowered below 35 mg/l. Carbonate alkalinities as low as 20 mg/l have been observed in partial lime softening of well water at 55°F (13°C) having an excess calcium of more than 200 mg/l.

The reason for showing a magnesium reduction despite the fact that this may not be one of the goals of the treatment program is that it is impossible to instantaneously mix a slurry of lime into a large body of water; at the point of lime introduction the water is massively overtreated with lime, and it is inevitable that some magnesium will precipitate because of this. The 10% reduction is arbitrary and empirical, based on a ratio of Ca:Mg of 2:1; if this ratio is reduced, magnesium reduction increases.

$$Mg^{+2} + Ca(OH)_2 \rightarrow Mg(OH)_2 \downarrow + Ca^{+2} \tag{4}$$

In this process, the lime requirement is based on the CO_2, alkalinity converted to carbonate, and magnesium reduction. A simplified chart for determining lime requirement is shown in Figure 10.4.

Identification of Analyses Tabulated Below:

A. Raw water @ 60°F   D.

B. Estimated results with complete conversion to CO_3

C. Estimated results with partial conversion to CO_3

Constituent	As	A	B	C	D	E	F
Calcium	CaCO₃	100	35	35			
Magnesium	"	50	45	45			
Sodium	"	75	75	75			
Total Electrolyte	CaCO₃	225	155	155			
Bicarbonate	CaCO₃	125	0	20			
Carbonate	"	0	55	35			
Hydroxyl	"	0	0	0			
Sulfate	"	50	50	50			
Chloride	"	50	50	50			
Nitrate	"						
M Alk.	CaCO₃	125	55	55			
P Alk.	"	0	28	18			
Carbon Dioxide		0	0	0			
pH		8.3	10.0	9.8			
Silica		8	8	8			
Iron	Fe	0.3	Nil	Nil			
Turbidity							
TDS		255	185	185			
Color							

Figure 10.3 Partial cold lime softening results where M alkalinity > Ca in the raw water analysis.

Figure 10.4 Cold process lime softening.

COMPLETE LIME SOFTENING

Sometimes the residual calcium hardness after partial lime softening may still be higher than the municipality or industrial operation requires. If so, additional calcium reduction is achieved by adding soda ash. The reaction is as follows:

$$Ca^{+2} + Na_2CO_3 \rightarrow CaCO_3 \downarrow + 2Na^+ \tag{5}$$

As calcium is precipitated as $CaCO_3$, it is replaced by the sodium from the soda ash. Using the same example as shown earlier for partial lime softening, Figure 10.2, the further reduction of calcium hardness by soda ash addition in several stages is shown in Figure 10.5. The amount of soda ash required is simply calculated on the basis of the additional calcium hardness reduction wanted. This addition can continue until the calcium reaches a level of about 35 mg/l; beyond this, excess soda ash has only a partial, rather than a direct, effect in reducing calcium further. Figure 10.5 shows the results of excess soda ash addition on calcium hardness, alkalinity, and dissolved solids.

If reduction of magnesium is desired along with calcium reduction, additional lime must be added beyond that required for partial softening to react with all of the magnesium and to provide an excess hydroxide alkalinity. The procedure for estimating results again depends on which of two categories the water falls into: in the first, the total hardness exceeds total alkalinity, and in the second the reverse is true.

Where total hardness exceeds alkalinity, the anions are calculated first. There is no change in anions other than alkalinity. Since magnesium reduction is desired, an excess hydroxide alkalinity of 20 mg/l is usually selected. The carbonate alkalinity is shown as 35 mg/l, and there is no bicarbonate alkalinity. In the cation section, the sodium is unchanged and the magnesium is reduced to 20 mg/l. The calcium is then determined by the difference. If this calcium level is still higher than desired, soda ash is added to reduce it, and each increment of calcium reduction results in an incremental sodium increase.

The lime is again calculated as that required for CO_2, bicarbonate conversion, and magnesium reduction plus an excess of 20 mg/l. The soda ash dosage is calculated by the desired calcium reduction in a step-wise fashion. Figure 10.6 shows complete cold process lime soda softening of a well water where the hardness exceeds the alkalinity.

At one time, batch lime-soda softening was a common process in treating water for steam locomotives. Hardness levels considerably below those shown in Figure 10.6 were achieved because of the long detention time. Batch softeners are still in use in some steel mills today producing final hardness of less than 20 mg/l.

When the alkalinity exceeds the hardness, the cation section is calculated first, and soda ash is never used. The sodium is shown unchanged, the calcium is reduced to 35 mg/l, and the magnesium reduced to 20 mg/l. The anions other than alkalinity remain unchanged, the hydroxide alkalinity is shown as 20 mg/l, and the balance is carbonate. If this carbonate alkalinity is too high, it can be

Identification of Analyses Tabulated Below:

A. Raw water @ 60°F
D. "C" after an additional 30 mg/l soda ash*

B. Estimated results with lime
E.

C. "B" after addition of 30 mg/l soda ash*F.

Constituent	As	A	B	C	D	E	F
Calcium	$CaCO_3$	125	65	35	20		
Magnesium	"	65	60	60	60		
Sodium	"	20	20	50	80		
Total Electrolyte	$CaCO_3$	210	145	145	160		
Bicarbonate	$CaCO_3$	100	0	0	0		
Carbonate	"	0	35	35	50		
Hydroxyl	"	0	0	0	0		
Sulfate	"	60	60	60	60		
Chloride	"	50	50	50	50		
Nitrate	"						
M Alk.	$CaCO_3$	100	35	35	50		
P Alk.	"	0	18	18	25		
Carbon Dioxide		10	0	0	0		
pH		7.3	10	10	10		
Silica		10	10	10	10		
Iron	Fe	0.2	Nil	Nil	Nil		
Turbidity							
TDS		230	165	165	180		
Color							
*Expressed as $CaCO_3$	$\equiv$	32 mg/l Na_2CO_3					

Figure 10.5   Cold lime-soda softening for calcium reduction.

Identification of Analyses Tabulated Below:							

A. Raw well water @ 55°F   D. _____

B. After lime treatment   E. _____

C. After lime-soda treatment   F. _____

Constituent	As	A	B	C	D	E	F
Calcium	CaCO₃	175	110	20			
Magnesium	"	100	20	20			
Sodium	"	25	25	130			
Total Electrolyte	CaCO₃	300	155	170			
Bicarbonate	CaCO₃	200	0	0			
Carbonate	"	0	35	50			
Hydroxyl	"	0	20	20			
Sulfate	"	60	60	60			
Chloride	"	40	40	40			
Nitrate	"						
M Alk.	CaCO₃	200	55	70			
P Alk.	"	0	38	45			
Carbon Dioxide		20	0	0			
pH		7.3	10.6	10.6			
Silica		15	12	12			
Iron	Fe	0.5	Nil	Nil			
Turbidity							
TDS		350	205	220			
Color							

Figure 10.6 Complete cold lime-soda softening where raw water hardness exceeds alkalinity.

reduced by the addition of gypsum, $CaSO_4$, each increment of gypsum producing an equivalent reduction of alkalinity, according to the following reaction:

$$CO_3^{-2} + CaSO_4 \rightarrow CaCO_3 \downarrow + SO_4^{-2} \qquad (6)$$

In all of these cold process reactions, it is extremely important that previously precipitated sludge be returned to the reaction chamber for mixing with raw water and treatment chemicals. A typical design of a cold process lime softening precipitation unit is shown in Figure 10.7. Another design, shown in Figure 10.8, is a unit in which the reactions occur on a bed of calcium carbonate granules. This is more compact than the first design, but it requires sophisticated chemical feed equipment so that the chemical feed rate is instantaneously adjusted to changes in water flow rate, since there is no provision for recirculation within the reaction vessel itself.

Figure 10.7 Typical sludge-blanket-type cold process lime softener with high-rate sludge recirculation. *(Courtesy of Infilco Degremont Incorporated.)*

MORE COMPLETE SOFTENING AT HIGHER TEMPERATURES

Hot process softening is somewhat different in that the solubility of calcium and magnesium are both lower at elevated temperatures, and the rate of reaction is considerably increased. The $CaCO_3$ precipitates as calcite in the cold process and aragonite in the hot process. The precipitates settle much faster in hot water, whose density and viscosity are appreciably less than cold water's. There are two basic hot process systems, lime-soda and lime-zeolite.

The lime-soda process is similar to the cold process system, but the results are

Figure 10.8 Granular bed lime softener producing a concentrated, pellet-like sludge. *(Courtesy of The Permutit Company.)*

Identification of Analyses Tabulated Below:

A. Raw well water @ 55°F   D. _____

B. After treatment*   E. _____

C. _____   F. _____

Constituent	As	A	B	C	D	E	F
Calcium	CaCO₃	175	15				
Magnesium	"	100	2				
Sodium	"	25	133				
Total Electrolyte	CaCO₃	300	150				
Bicarbonate	CaCO₃	200	0				
Carbonate	"	0	40				
Hydroxyl	"	0	10				
Sulfate	"	60	60				
Chloride	"	40	40				
Nitrate	"						
M Alk.	CaCO₃	200	40				
P Alk.	"	0	25				
Carbon Dioxide		20	0				
pH		7.3	10.3				
Silica		15	1-2				
Iron	Fe	0.5	0				
Turbidity							
TDS		350	185				
Color							

* Not corrected for about 15% steam dilution

Figure 10.9   Hot process lime-soda softening at 220°F.

different, as shown in Figure 10.9. The amount of lime required is less because usually none is needed for CO_2 reaction, since most CO_2 is eliminated by heating the water and spraying it into the reaction vessel. Some high CO_2 well waters are difficult to degas, and may require excess lime for the residual CO_2. Silica is appreciably reduced by adsorption on the magnesium hydroxide precipitate, and the residual hydroxide alkalinity needed for magnesium precipitation is also considerably reduced.

There are two basic designs of hot process softeners applicable either to the lime-soda process or the lime-zeolite process. The first (Figure 10.10) is a sludge blanket design, particularly effective where silica reduction is important, but somewhat sensitive to load fluctuations. The second (Figure 10.11) is called a downflow design, and depends on a recirculation pump entirely for providing sludge contact; it is generally not quite as effective for silica reduction as the sludge blanket unit, but is less susceptible to upsets caused by load fluctutations.

With the lime-zeolite design, complete hardness removal is achieved and lower

DIRECT CONTACT
GAS CONCENTRATOR

VACUUM BREAKER

EXHAUST HEAD

WASH WATER
RETURN

VENT

MULTIPORT
RELIEF VALVE

REGULATING
VALVE

RAW WATER
INLET

STEAM INLET

CONN. FOR RECORDING
THERMOMETER

LEVEL CONTROL

CHEMICAL INLET

TREATED WATER
OUTLET

WASH WATER
OUTLET

DESLUDGING
VALVE

OVERFLOW TRAP

SAMPLING CONN'S.

OVERFLOW TO WASTE

TO WASTE

SLUDGE BLOW-OFF VALVE

Figure 10.10 Sludge blanket design of hot process softener with accessory equipment. *(Courtesy of Cochrane Division, the Crane Company.)*

alkalinity levels can be produced because soda ash is not required for reducing calcium hardness. Figure 10.12 shows the results of treating a water high in excess hardness. If the water has an alkalinity in excess of hardness, alkalinity reduction can be achieved either by acid feed ahead of the softener or by the addition of gypsum to the reaction zone. Figure 10.13 illustrates a complete lime-zeolite system.

Figure 10.11 Downflow design of hot process softener with control devices and provision for sludge recirculation. *(Courtesy of Cochrane Division, the Crane Company.)*

HEAVY METALS REMOVAL

Heavy metals are usually removed from water by precipitation, although ion exchange and adsorption are also used. Iron is a typical example of a heavy metal requiring removal, because it is a common constituent of well water and must be removed from potable supplies. It is also frequently found in wastewaters requiring treatment before discharge.

The hydroxides of heavy metals are usually insoluble, so lime is commonly used for precipitating them. However, sometimes the carbonates or sulfides are less soluble than the hydroxides, so precipitation in these forms must also be considered. There are probably situations where economics justify partial precipitation with lime to the solubility level of the hydroxide followed by a secondary treatment with sulfide for reduction to the specified limits (Figure 10.14). So, the choice of the reactant is the first consideration in the precipitation of heavy metals. Since solubility is affected by temperature, this becomes a second consideration.

A third important factor in precipitation of heavy metals is the valence state of the metal in the water. For example, ferrous iron is considerably more soluble than ferric iron. Because of this, treatment of the water with an oxidizing agent such as chlorine or potassium permanganate to convert ferrous iron to the ferric state is an essential part of the iron removal process. Another example is chromium, whose hexavalent form, chromate, CrO_4^{-2} ($Cr^{+6} + O_4^{-8}$), is con-

Identification of Analyses Tabulated Below:							
A. Raw well water @ 55°F			D.				
B. After lime treatment*			E.				
C. "B" after zeolite treatment*			F.				

Constituent	As	A	B	C	D	E	F
Calcium	CaCO₃	175	98	Nil			
Magnesium	''	100	2	Nil			
Sodium	''	25	25	125			
Total Electrolyte	CaCO₃	300	125	125			
Bicarbonate	CaCO₃	200	0	0			
Carbonate	''	0	15	15			
Hydroxyl	''	0	10	10			
Sulfate	''	60	60	60			
Chloride	''	40	40	40			
Nitrate	''						
M Alk.	CaCO₃	200	25	25			
P Alk.	''	0	18	18			
Carbon Dioxide		20	0	0			
pH		7.3	10.3	10.3			
Silica		15	1–2	1–2			
Iron	Fe	0.5	0	0			
Turbidity							
TDS		350	160	160			
Color							
* Not corrected for approximately 15% steam dilution							

Figure 10.12 Hot process lime-zeolite treatment at 220°F.

Figure 10.13 Line diagram of a typical hot lime–zeolite system. (*Courtesy of Cochrane Division, the Crane Company.*)

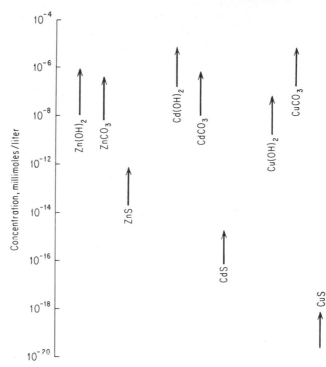

Figure 10.14   Comparison of sulfide solubilities of certain cations to their hydroxides and carbonates

solubaly more soluble than the trivalent form, Cr^{+3}. In this case, the chromate (in which Cr is present as Cr^{+6}) must be reduced, usually with SO_2 at a low pH, for removal of chromium (as Cr^{+3}) by a precipitation process.

A fourth aspect of the precipitation process is the zeta potential of the initial heavy metal colloidal precipitate. In many plants where heavy metals are being removed, one of the principal problems in reaching the desired effluent limits is the colloidal state of the precipitated materials—they have not been properly neutralized, coagulated, and flocculated.

A final aspect of heavy metals precipitation is the possible formation of complex ions, which are common when dealing with wastewaters containing ammonia, fluoride, or cyanide along with the heavy metals. For example, iron may be complexed as the ferrocyanide ion, which is rather soluble, and will remain in solution unless the complex can be broken by chemical treatment.

BENCH TESTING

Because of these important aspects in the precipitation of heavy metals, there is no way to predict the best solution of a specific problem without undergoing a series of bench tests to evaluate the alternatives available. The removal of iron from water is an interesting example of this.

In the precipitation of iron from water, the first step is the oxidation to the ferric condition, as illustrated by the following reaction:

$$2Fe^{+2} + Cl_2{}^0 \rightarrow 2Fe^{+3} + 2Cl^- \tag{7}$$

Figure 10.15 Schematic of iron removal filter plant. Closed pressure aerator may be used in place of the open tower shown. Where an overhead storage tank is used for tower or plant supply, this can be used to supply backwash water.

Sometimes air can be used successfully to oxidize iron, but most frequently chlorine or potassium permanganate is required. The chlorine may be applied as chlorine gas or as calcium hypochlorite. Unless there is past experience with a specific water supply, each of these oxidation reagents must be evaluated to select the best process.

The pH of the water must be adjusted to an optimum value, determined not only by the solubility of the precipitate, but also by its charge. It may be necessary to determine the zeta potential in selecting the optimum pH for treatment. There are distinctive differences in the chemical used for pH adjustment also. For example, lime is usually more effective than caustic soda at the same pH, and this may very well be attributed to the charge on the particles and charge neutralization.

Once the iron has been oxidized and precipitated, the volume of sludge produced must be examined to decide whether the treated water can then be clarified by direct filtration or will require treatment through a sedimentation tank prior to filtration. Generally where the iron is less than 5 mg/l, the oxidized water can be fed directly to a filter. This is usually a mixed media filter provided with air scour devices so that the bed can be kept clean.

A typical iron removal plant of this type used in municipal service is illustrated by Figure 10.15.

Manganese-treated zeolite is often used as the filtration medium in filters of this type. Where this is done, permanganate may be fed to the water ahead of these filters, and lime may be fed for pH correction as well. Those who have worked with this process claim that the oxides of manganese produced by this reaction are catalytic to the oxidation of iron within the filter bed. A permanganate-treated water supply using manganese zeolite as the filter medium is illustrated by Figure 10.16.

One of the complications of the iron removal process is the fact that many iron-bearing waters also contain sulfide. This adds to the demand for chlorine or other oxidizing agents.

SILICA REMOVAL

Although silica can be removed by adsorption on iron floc in the coagulation process, efficiency is low. For that reason, where silica removal is required, it is usually done in a hot or warm process system. The silica is adsorbed on magnesium hydroxide precipitate, which is either formed from the lime softening reaction or added by using dolomitic lime as the water softening reagent. Typically, the equipment used is similar to the hot process softeners shown in Figures 10.10 and 10.11. Since the process can be made to operate effectively at temperatures as low as 120°F, these systems can be modified to maintain this temperature within rather close limits, which is necessary to avoid thermal currents that would upset the sedimentation process.

The results anticipated by precipitation of magnesium hydroxide for adsorption of silica are shown by Figure 10.17.

MISCELLANEOUS PROCESSES

Using lime softening or iron removal type equipment, precipitation processes are often used to remove manganese from raw water supplies, phosphate from municipal sewage, fluorides from industrial wastes, and copper from metallurgical wastes. Each system is unique and requires bench testing to determine the best reagent for the process, optimum pH, proper temperature conditions, and the nature of the sludge expected, which will influence the selection of solids/liquid separation devices.

The test procedures usually involve a modification of the jar test where there may be provision for heating if high temperature is required for minimum solubility. In doing these tests, the residuals are usually determined both on the supernatant sample and also on a filtrate after the supernatant has passed through a 0.45 micron membrane filter. The volume of sludge produced is measured with an Imhoff cone to help establish the type of solids/liquids separation equipment required. If the jar test does not produce good results, more sophisticated equipment, such as a zeta meter, may be needed to more precisely determine the nature of the particle being removed.

In all of these processes, accurate and reliable chemical feeding is essential. The pH may be critical, so the chemicals used for pH control must be proportioned to the flow of water and be corrected by a signal showing deviations from the control pH setting.

Although there are instruments available for recording effluent hardness,

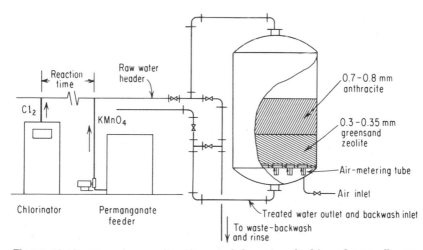

Figure 10.16 Manganese zeolite filter used for removal of iron from well water supplies.

Figure 10.17   Silica reduction in hot process softening.

where a precipitation process is selected for removal of heavy metals there may not be an instrument available for a direct measurement of the heavy metal after treatment. This imposes special limitations on the plant, often requiring that the treated effluent be held temporarily in an inspection basin. The operator analyzes the final discharge and the precipitator effluents, and if specifications are not met, he must correct the treatment before the plant effluent is discharged from the retention basin to a receiving stream or sewer.

SUGGESTED READING

American Water Works Association: *Water Quality and Treatment,* McGraw-Hill, New York, 1971.
Infilco-Degremont, Inc.: *Water Treatment Handbook,* Roger Leviel (ed.), Taylor & Carlisle, distributors, New York.
Nordell, Eskel: *Water Treatment for Industrial and Other Uses,* Reinhold, New York, 1961.
Rubin, J., ed.: Aqueous-Environmental Chemistry of Metals. "Crystal Growth Kinetics of Minerals Encountered in Water Treatment Processes," Nancollas, G. H., and Reddy, M. M. Ann Arbor Science Publishers, Inc., 1976.

Chapter 11
Emulsion Breaking

An emulsion is an intimate mixture of two liquid phases, such as oil and water, in which either phase may be dispersed in the other. In water chemistry, two types of emulsions are commonly found, oily waste water (oil emulsified in water or O/W emulsions) and waste oil emulsions (water emulsified in oil or W/O emulsions).

Oily waste and waste oil emulsions can usually be differentiated visually. O/W emulsion appears to be just oily, dirty water; a drop of the emulsion added to water disperses (Figure 11.1a). A W/O emulsion is usually thick and viscous; a drop of this emulsion added to water does not disperse (Figure 11.1b).

OIL-IN-WATER-EMULSIONS

An oily waste emulsion, in which oil is dispersed in the water phase, may contain any of various types of oil in a wide range of concentrations. These oils are defined as substances that can be extracted from water by hexane, carbon tetrachloride, chloroform or freon. In addition to oils, typical contaminants of these emulsions may be solids, silt, metal particles, emulsifiers, cleaners, soaps, solvents and other residues. The types of oils found in these emulsions will depend on the industry. They may be fats, lubricants, cutting fluids, heavy hydrocarbons such as tars, grease, crude oils, and diesel oils, and also light hydrocarbons including gasoline, kerosene and jet fuel. Their concentration in the wastewater may vary from only a few parts per million to as much as 5–10% by volume.

A stable O/W emulsion is a colloidal system of electrically charged oil droplets surrounded by an ionic environment. Violent mixing and shearing of oily wastewater in transfer pumps disperses these minute oil droplets throughout the water. Emulsion stability is maintained by a combination of physical and

Figure 11.1 (*a*) If a few drops of oily water (O/W emulsion) are added to water, they disperse in the water. This is a test to distinguish O/W from W/O emulsions.

chemical mechanisms. These emulsions are similar in behavior to the colloidal systems encountered in swamps (color) and rivers (silt).

One such stabilizing mechanism, ionization, is brought about by the addition of surface-active agents, such as organic materials or cleaners, which aid in maintaining a stable colloidal system. These molecules usually carry an electrical charge and seek out the oil/water interface of the emulsified droplet. Here, the accumulated charges cause the emulsion to be stabilized through repulsion of the commonly-charged droplets. Neutral (nonionic) surfactants can also stabilize an emulsion, since these molecules are bifunctional: one end is soluble in water, and the other end in hydrocarbon, so the molecule bridges the interface and stabilizes it.

Fine, solid particles may stabilize an emulsion if they are of correct size and abundance. In this case, stabilization occurs because the solid particles adsorbed at the oil/water interface tend to reinforce the interfacial film. The dispersed droplets cannot coalesce because of the interference or blocking effect caused by the solids (Figure 11.2).

Emulsions can also be stabilized by friction between the oil and water phases created by vigorous mechanical or physical agitation. Static electrical charges developed by this action tend to collect at the oil/water interface.

An emulsifier is usually a complex molecule, often having a hydrophilic (water-loving) group at one end and a lyophilic (oil loving) group at the other (Figure 11.3). Emulsifiers disperse oil droplets in the water phase because they

Figure 11.1 (*b*) A few drops of this emulsion added to water remained as a separate phase floating on the surface, showing it to be a W/O emulsion.

Figure 11.2 Physical emulsion stabilization by finely divided solids, illustrated with oil-in-water emulsion.

have an affinity for both water and oil that enables them to overcome the natural forces of coalescence.

Most emulsifiers are surfactants having either anionic or nonionic polar groups. Petroleum sulfonates and sulfonated fatty acids are common anionic emulsifiers, and ethoxylated alkyl phenols are common nonionic emulsifiers. Examples of naturally occurring surfactants are organic sulfur compounds, various simple esters, and metal complexes. Alkaline cleaners containing surfactants that emulsify free oil are present in many wastewaters. Table 11.1 lists a variety of emulsifiers for both O/W and W/O systems.

Breaking Oil-in-Water Emulsions

Emulsions may be broken by chemical, electrolytic, or physical methods. The breaking of an emulsion is also called resolution, since the result is to separate the original mixture into its parts. Chemicals are commonly used for the treatment of oily wastewaters, and are also used to enhance mechanical treatment. In breaking emulsions, the stabilizing factors must be neutralized to allow the

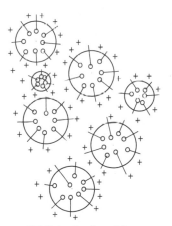

(a) Oil-in-water emulsion

(b) Water-in-oil emulsion

NOTE: Emulsifier molecule shown in simplified form:

Water-soluble end Oil-soluble end
(Hydrophilic group) (Lipophilic group)

Figure 11.3 Chemical stabilization of emulsions by surfactants having hydrophilic and lipophilic groups.

TABLE 11.1   Emulsifying Agents

Oil-in-water type	Water-in-oil type
1. Formation—when soaps are colloidally dispersed in water phase	1. Formation—when soaps are precipitated from aqueous phase

2. Ionic Emulsifiers
   a. Sodium, potassium soaps and sulfides
   b. Sodium naphthenes and cresylates
   c. Precipitated sulfides plus surfactants
   d. Organic amines
	2. Ionic Emulsifiers
	   a. Multivalent metal soaps
	   b. Sulfide ion plus carbon particles
	   c. Multivalent metal oxides
	   d. Mercaptans
	   e. Naphthenic or cresylic acids

3. Electrolytes which favor stability
   a. Salts of univalent cations
   b. Salts of di- and trivalent cations
	3. Electrolytes which favor stability
	   Salts of di- and trivalent cations

emulsified droplets to coalesce. The accumulated electrical charges on the emulsified droplet are neutralized by introducing a charge opposite to that of the droplet (Figure 11.4). Chemical emulsion breakers provide this opposite charge. The dielectric characteristics of water and oil cause emulsified oil droplets to carry negative charges. Therefore, to destabilize an oil-in-water emulsion, a cationic (positive charge) emulsion breaker should be used.

The resolution of an O/W emulsion should ideally yield an oil layer and a water layer. However, such a clear resolution is seldom achieved: there is often a scum, called a rag, at the interface where solids and neutralized emulsifier collect.

The treatment of oily wastewater is normally divided into two steps.

1. *Coagulation.* This is destruction of the emulsifying properties of the surface-active agent or neutralization of the charged oil droplet.

2. *Flocculation.* This is agglomeration of the neutralized droplets into large, separable globules.

Traditionally, sulfuric acid has been used in oily waste treatment plants as the first step in emulsion breaking. Acid converts the carboxyl ion in surfactants to carboxylic acid, allowing the oil droplets to agglomerate. Chemical coagulating

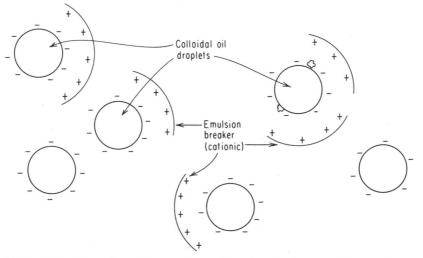

Figure 11.4   The action of a cationic emulsion breaker in neutralizing surface charges on a colloidal oil droplet in oily waste water.

Figure 11.5 The use of organic emulsion breakers in place of alum or salts which form hydrous flocs greatly reduces sludge volume. The oil can be extracted from the sludge.

agents, such as salts of iron or aluminum, can be used in place of acid, with the additional benefit that these aid in agglomeration of the oil droplets. However, the aluminum or iron forms hydroxide sludges that are difficult to dewater. Acids generally break emulsions more effectively than coagulant salts, but the resultant acidic wastewater must be neutralized after oil/water separation.

Organic demulsifiers are extremely effective emulsion breaking agents, giving more consistent results and producing better effluent quality than an inorganic program. In many treatment plants, organic emulsion breakers have replaced traditional alum treatment for exactly those reasons. In addition to yielding a better quality effluent, organic emulsion breakers often require lower dosages than a corresponding inorganic treatment. Organic emulsion breakers reduce the amount of sludge generated in a treatment program by as much as 50–75% (Figure 11.5).

Table 11.2 lists emulsion breakers used in both O/W and W/O treatment programs.

TABLE 11.2 Types of Emulsion Breakers

Main Type	Description	Charge	Used For
Inorganic	Polyvalent metal salts such as alum, $AlCl_3$, $FeCl_3$, $Fe_2(SO_4)_3$	Cationic	O/W
	Mineral acids such as H_2SO_4, HCL, HNO_3	Cationic	O/W and W/O
	Adsorbents (adding solids)— pulverized clay, lime	None	O/W
Organic	Polyamines, polyacrylates and their substituted copolymers	Cationic	O/W
	Alkyl substituted benzene sulfonic acids and their salts	Anionic	W/O
	Alkyl phenolic resins, substituted polyalcohols	Nonionic	W/O

Figure 11.6   The float produced by dissolved air flotation of an oily waste water (O/W) emulsion. *(Courtesy of Infilco Degremont Incorporated.)*

Mechanical O/W treatment methods include flotation (DAF), ultra-filtration (UF), activated carbon adsorption (AC), and coalescence.

In a flotation unit, Figure 11.6, air is dissolved under pressure (40–70 psig) in the liquid to be treated. As the pressure is released, the liquid becomes supersaturated with air and small bubbles form. These bubbles, from 10 to 100 microns in diameter, normally have a slight negative charge. They may collide with suspended particles in the liquid and attach themselves by adhesion, adsorption, or entrapment within the floc. Since the net specific gravity of this air-solid or air-liquid particle combination will be less than that of water, the particle will rise to the surface. There it combines with other particles to form a froth, or float, that can be removed by mechanical skimmers.

There are three types of dissolved air flotation systems, direct aeration, partial aeration, and effluent recirculation. Experience has shown that effluent recirculation is usually the most efficient for oil removal. This involves the pressurization and aeration of a side stream of clarified effluent. This stream is then mixed with the pretreated waste stream in the flotation tank. An oily waste emulsion breaking chemical (organic or inorganic) may be used to destabilize and agglomerate the colloidal oil suspension. The common practice in oily waste treatment plants is to feed the emulsion breaking chemical to the suction side of the lift pump or into a rapid mix tank and an inorganic coagulant aid to the discharge side of the pump. A high molecular weight polymer may be added to the recycle stream prior to entering the flotation unit.

Ultrafiltration consists of forcing an oily emulsion to pass through very small pores (less than 0.005 microns) in a membrane. Only water and dissolved low molecular weight materials can pass through the pore structure of the membrane, leaving a concentrate of the emulsified oil droplets and suspended particles. Plugging does not occur as it can in ordinary filtration because particu-

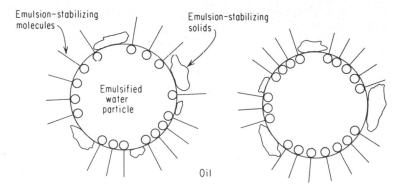

Figure 11.7   Stabilized water-in-oil emulsion.

lates are much larger than the pores and cannot enter the membrane structure.

Activated carbon adsorption has been used to clean up wastewater containing lesser amounts of soluble and emulsified organic contaminants (less than 100 mg/l). This is usually employed as a polishing step.

Coalescers are used where oily water may contain free oil and oil in a weakly emulsified state; examples are tanker ballast and oil field brines. There are a variety of designs, ranging from simple, baffled vessels where coalescence is induced by eddy currents, to rather sophisticated devices using membranes which will allow water to pass through but reject oil.

WATER-IN-OIL EMULSIONS

Water-in-oil emulsions are viscous, concentrated substances formed when oil comes into contact with water and solids. Metal particles and other solids may be coated with surfactants in such a manner that they are preferentially wetted by the oil rather than the water (Figure 11.7). In circumstances where agitation is present, the water becomes dispersed in the oil as a fine emulsion, and these small water droplets together with the oil-coated solids maintain the stability of the emulsion. Many types of water-in-oil or waste oil emulsions are found. Table 11.3 classified some of the more common waste oils according to their relative oil, water and solids content.

TABLE 11.3   Classification of Waste Oils

	Percent Oil	Percent Water	Percent Solids
Refining—crude	90–95	5–10	0–5
Machining—cutting, grinding oil	50–80	20–50	0–20
Waste treatment sludges	40–50	40–50	5–10
Steel mills—rolling oils	80–95	5–20	0–5

W/O Emulsion Stabilizers

Among commonly occurring substances that promote or stabilize W/O emulsions are soaps, sulfonated oils, asphaltic residues, waxes, salt, finely divided coke, sulfides, and mercaptans. Finely divided solids varying in size from colloidal to 100 microns and larger, are particularly effective in stabilizing these emulsions.

The presence of hydrophobic and hydrophilic colloidal solids at the oil/water interface may result in the larger particles aggregating around the dispersed droplets. The presence of these large particles throughout the continuous phase tends to form a complex matrix consisting of solids, oil-in-water, and water-in-oil emulsions existing simultaneously as a stable mixture in which either oil or water may be the continuous phase.

Breaking Water-in-Oil Emulsions

Water-in-oil emulsions can be broken by chemical or physical methods, including heating, centrifugation, and vacuum precoat filtration. Centrifugation breaks oil emulsions by separating the oil and water phases under the influence of centrifugal force (Figure 11.8). Filtration of waste oil emulsions can be accomplished through high rate sand filters (HRF) or diatomaceous earth (DE) filters (Figure 11.9). The operation of these pieces of equipment must be carefully controlled to provide the highest quality of upgraded oil.

Chemical treatment of a waste oil emulsion is directed toward destabilizing the dispersed water droplets and solids or destroying emulsifying agents. Acidification may be effective in breaking W/O emulsions if the acid dissolves some of the solid materials and thus reduces surface tension.

The newest method involves treatment of a W/O emulsion with a demulsifying agent containing both hydrophobic and hydrophilic groups that is able to form a water wettable adsorption complex. The mechanism of W/O emulsion breaking can be best explained by visualizing the displacement of the original emulsifying agent from the interface by a more surface-active demulsifying material. This process can be enhanced by heating to reduce viscosity and increase the solubility and rate of diffusion of the emulsifying agent in the oil phase. Because water droplets in oil tend to be positively charged, these types of emulsions are typically treated with an anionic (negative charge) organic emulsion breaker. Sometimes a combination of acid and organic demulsifying agent provides the best results.

In all cases, the treatment reagents must be thoroughly mixed into the W/O emulsion to provide intimate contact with the emulsified water droplets. Heating the emulsion to 120–180°F often produces rapid separation. Adequate settling time must be allowed to provide for optimum resolution of the oil, water, and solids phases (Figure 11.10).

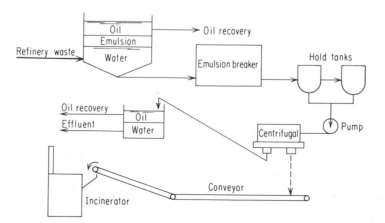

Figure 11.8 The application of a centrifuge in treatment of waste oil (slop oil) in a refinery. *(Courtesy of Bird Machine Company.)*

Figure 11.9 Diatomaceous earth filter of the pressure leaf design used for treating emulsions in oil field flooding operations. *(Courtesy of L*A Water Conditioning Company.)*

INDUSTRIAL SOURCES OF EMULSIONS AND TREATMENT PRACTICES

An industrial activity that requires the use of process oils and water may be susceptible to emulsion formation at any point in its system. The three major industries producing oily waste are petroleum refining, metals manufacturing and machining, and food processing.

Figure 11.10 Breaking a waste oil emulsion with chemical emulsion breaker, showing the effect of increasing chemical dosage on maximizing oil recovery and solids separation.

Hydrocarbon Processing Industry

Petroleum refining operations generate both O/W and W/O emulsions, present in drainage water, spills, separator skimmings, tank bottoms, and various oil recovery traps.

In the petrochemical industry quench waters generated in ethylene and other olefin manufacturing operations may contain mixtures of heavy, middle and light hydrocarbons.

In the processing of crude oil, desalting is used initially to remove corrosive salts carried by the oil. In desalting, water is mixed with crude oil to wash it free of these salts. This forms a water-in-oil emulsion that is resolved in an electrostatic device, usually assisted by demulsifying chemicals. Frequently, however, not all of the emulsion is resolved, and the residue must be separated for further treatment. Often this emulsion is dumped into an oily sewer along with O/W and W/O emulsions formed in crude fractionation, thermal cracking, catalytic cracking, hydrocracking, and other processes. All of these emulsions contain too much water to justify processing, so they are usually dumped into an oily sewer system.

In the oily sewer, these emulsions are stabilized. Oil spills from process and general oil runoff are sent to this sewer along with oily wastewater, storm water, dirt and debris. These components are mixed by pumps and flow turbulence in the sewer to form additional emulsions, or to further stabilize those already formed. The oils making up these emulsions are typically mixtures of light and heavy hydrocarbons.

The oily wastewaters collected from various points throughout the plant are delivered in a sewage system to an API separator. The skimmings from the API separator, which are usually good oil with low levels of solids and water present, may be sent back to the desalter or the coker. The underflow from the separator goes on to dissolved air flotation units (DAF). The underflow (the water) from the DAF unit may flow to a bio-oxidation pond and then to a clarifier before the water is ultimately sent to a river or sewer system (Figure 11.11). Emulsifying agents are not usually found in these O/W emulsions.

Waste oil treatment in refineries may be concerned with two different types of sludges or emulsions: skimmings from the API separator and the DAF units are typically sent to an oily sludge holding tank; the second type of waste oil emulsion in a refinery, leakage from processes, is often collected in various types of traps and drains throughout the plant. This oil may be of high enough quality that it can be blended with crude feedstock and returned to a process desalter or the coker unit.

A common measure of oil quality is the percent bottom sediment and water (BS&W). (Crude feed to a desalter typically has no greater than 5% BS&W.) If the reclaimed oil quality is too poor for use as desalter feed blend, the emulsion may be stored in a separate container or may be mixed with the API and DAF skimmings. These tanks typically have heating and recirculation or other type of mixing capabilities. Often, the fugitive waste oil emulsions can be separated solely by heat and a quiescent settling period. The API and DAF skimmings typically do not respond to this treatment, requiring the addition of a chemical W/O emulsion breaker. In either case, emulsion breakers can be used to effect a more rapid, complete separation of the oil, water and solids phases. Treatment with an organic emulsion breaker involves feeding the chemical to the line while the treatment tank is being filled. This is followed by a quiescent period ranging from one to several days. The separated layers can then be drained. The solids which are not oil-wet can be trucked to landfill. The water, which may contain residual emulsified oil, is recycled back to the head of the oily wastewater treatment system and the recovered oil may be used according to individual plant needs.

Figure 11.11   The application of DAF in a refinery wastewater flow sheet.

Basic Metals Industry

Oily wastes generated in steel mills include both emulsified and non-emulsified, or floating, oils. Oily wastes from hot rolling mills contain primarily lubricating and hydraulic pressure fluids. Wastes from cold strip operations contain rolling oils that were used to lubricate the steel sheet and reduce rust. Oil-in-water emulsions are sprayed on the metal during rolling to act as coolants.

Waste waters from these plants typically have a wide variety of contaminants, and the objectives of treatment include removal of not only oil, but also solids and metal fines. In a typical steel mill waste treatment scheme (Figure 11.12), the plant wastewater enters an equalization tank, where the detention time is a few hours. The water then flows to an air flotation unit, where it may be treated with organic or inorganic coagulants. The skimmings from the flotation unit may be pumped to a storage tank for batch treatment with waste oil emulsion breakers. The underflow from the flotation unit usually passes to further treatment or is recycled.

Waste oil treatment in the primary metal industry is usually more complicated than in a refinery. Chemical emulsion breaking treatment programs often require the addition of acid to dissolve metal fines. In batch treating these emulsions, it is important that the chemical be thoroughly mixed into the emulsion and that heat be applied throughout the treatment and settling stages. After the settling period, the solids and water layers can be disposed of in the same way that refinery rag layers are handled. The oil layer is high quality and may be suitable for use as a boiler fuel blend or may be sold to a re-refiner or oil re-claimer.

Automotive and Machining Industries

Metalworking and metal parts manufacturing plants generate waste streams containing lubricating and cutting oils, lapping and deburring compounds, grinding and other specialty fluids.

Figure 11.12   Typical oil recovery/oily waste treatment plant in a steel mill.

The wastewater generated in these plants contains a wide variety of oils and surfactants, so may require complicated treatment. The wastewater from several different operations often arrives at the treatment plant in separate streams or may be blended in the sewer system (Figure 11.13). All wastes flow to an equalization tank and then through several chemical feed and mix tanks prior to entering a flotation unit. The flotation skimmings are collected in storage tanks and the underflow from the air flotation unit may then pass to final treatment or recycle.

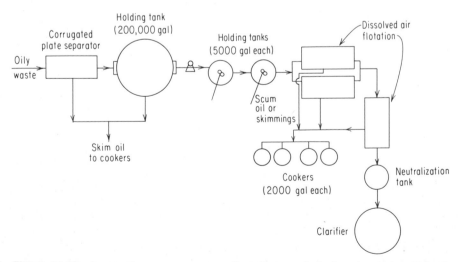

Figure 11.13   Automotive waste treatment flow sheet, typical of engine and machined parts operation.

The flotation skimmings can be pumped to lead-lined cooking tanks where they are treated with acid, an organic waste oil emulsion breaker and a high molecular weight polymer for oil recovery. The rag layer from this treatment is sold to an oil scavenger and the good, recovered oil may be burned as boiler fuel or reused in various plant processes.

Meat and Food Processing

Rendering plants, creameries, bakeries, breweries, and canneries generate emulsions containing natural fats and oils from animal processing and oils from packing and container manufacture. Both of these operations occur on the same premises, and the waste streams may be mixed.

Textiles

Wastewaters from cotton and wool manufacturing plants contain oils and greases from the scouring, desizing and finishing operations. Oily wastewater in the synthetic fibers industry is produced during desizing and scouring. Finishing oils are used to reduce friction and snagging of fibers on spinning machines. These types of oils may also be associated with machine lubricating oils in the plant oily wastewater.

Miscellaneous Industries

Many other industries have processes which may generate oil or oily wastewater such as: paints, surface coatings, and adhesives; oils, fats and waxes; soaps and detergents; dyes and inks; and the leather industry. All have potential emulsion problems that can be solved by one or more emulsion breaking techniques.

Chapter 12
Ion Exchange

Ion exchange removes unwanted ions from a raw water by transferring them to a solid material, called an ion exchanger, which accepts them while giving back an equivalent number of a desirable species stored on the ion exchanger skeleton. The ion exchanger has a limited capacity for storage of ions on its skeleton, called its exchange capacity; because of this, the ion exchanger eventually becomes saturated with unwanted ions. It is then washed with a strong regenerating solution containing the desirable species of ions, and these then replace the accumulated undesirable ions, returning the exchange material to a usable condition. This operation is a cyclic chemical process, and the complete cycle usually includes backwashing, regeneration, rinsing, and service.

The earliest ion exchangers were inorganic sodium aluminosilicates, some of which were manufactured synthetically and others made by processing natural greensand, which is a mineral called zeolite, into more stable, higher capacity forms. Even though these zeolites now have only limited use for water treatment, the name has persisted, and even synthetic organic ion exchangers are often called zeolites.

The ion exchangers used in water conditioning are skeleton-like structures having many ion exchange sites, as shown in Figure 12.1. The insoluble plastic skeleton is an enormously large ion that is electrically charged to hold ions of opposite charge. Exchangers with negatively-charged sites are cation exchangers because they take up positively charged ions. Anion exchangers have positively charged sites and, consequently, take up negative ions. The plastic structure is porous and permeable, so the entire ion exchange particle participates in the process.

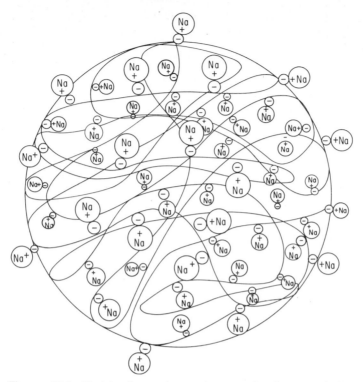

Figure 12.1 Model of a cation exchanger, showing negatively charged exchange sites on the skeleton holding sodium ions like grapes on a vine.

EXCHANGER CAPACITY

Typical exchangers are in the form of beads, having an approximate size of 20–40 mesh (0.8–0.4 mm), as illustrated by Figure 12.2. The chemist expresses the strength of a chemical solution in terms of normality; a 1.0 normal solution contains one gram-equivalent weight of electrolyte in a liter of solution. Ion exchange beads can be considered as solid solutions; the typical cation exchanger

Figure 12.2 Typical commercial exchangers are of two general structures, gel type (left) and macroporous type (right). These are magnifications.

has a normality of approximately 2.0, and the typical strong-base anion exchanger a normality of approximately 1.3. Capacity is also expressed as milliequivalents per milliliter (meq/ml), which is the same as normality; milliequivalents per dry gram (meq/g); and kilograins per cubic foot (kgr/cu ft).

In the early history of zeolite softening, it was common to express water hardness in grains per gallon (gpg) (1 gpg = 17.1 mg/l). Because of this common usage, the capacity of zeolites was rated in kilograins exchange capacity per cubic foot of zeolite, an unfortunately cumbersome term. The factor for conversion of resin normality to kilograins per cubic foot (kgr/cu ft) is approximately 22, so that a cation exchanger with a capacity of 2.0 meq/ml has an exchange capacity of approximately 44 kgr/cu ft.

Most commercial ion exchangers are synthetic plastic materials, such as copolymers of styrene and divinyl benzene (Figure 12.3). There is a fine balance between producing a loosely cross-linked polymer that has free access to water for

(1) Basic monomers

(2) Polymerization of styrene to polystyrene

(3) Copolymerization of styrene and divinylbenzene, showing the role of the DVB in cross-linking the polystyrene chains.

Figure 12.3   The production of a stable ion exchange resin by copolymerization.

rapid reaction but is only slightly soluble, and a tightly cross-linked resin, which would be insoluble, but more difficult to use because of restricted rates of exchange both in exhaustion and regeneration. Water treatment ion exchangers are essentially insoluble and can be expected to last for 5–10 years.

To produce cation exchangers, the plastic is reacted with sulfuric acid, sulfonic groups attaching to each nucleus in the skeleton to provide an exchange site. This produces a strong electrolyte, for which a typical reaction with cations in water is shown below:

$$Na^+ + R \cdot SO_3 \cdot H \rightarrow R \cdot SO_3 \cdot Na + H^+ \tag{1}$$

In this equation, the resin structure is represented by R. The usual convention omits showing the active group $(-SO_3 \cdot H)$ and simply uses the total exchanger molecule, which may be shown as Z (Na_2Z, from the historical usage of the word "zeolite") or X, which is used in this text for the cation exchanger. The above equation is, then, more usually written:

$$2Na^+ + H_2X \rightarrow Na_2X + 2H^+ \tag{2}$$

the X being considered a divalent cation exchange unit. In this example, sodium ions in water are being exchanged for hydrogen ions on the exchanger, a common exchange reaction. This is known as hydrogen cycle operation. On depletion of the hydrogen ion inventory of the exchange resin, called exhaustion, the exchanger is regenerated by an acid wash:

$$2HCl + Na_2X \rightarrow H_2X + 2NaCl \tag{3}$$

Other examples of cation exchange include the following: Hardness removal, with Na-form exchanger, Na_2X:

$$Ca^{++} + Na_2X \rightarrow CaX + 2Na^+ \tag{4}$$

This is known as sodium cycle operation.

Iron removal with Na_2X:

$$Fe^{++} + Na_2X \rightarrow FeX + 2Na^+ \tag{5}$$

Nickel recovery from plating waste by H_2X:

$$Ni^{++} + H_2X \rightarrow NiX + 2H^+ \tag{6}$$

A more realistic example which illustrates an ion exchanger property called selectivity is hydrogen cycle (H-form exchange) processing of a typical water containing a variety of ions:

$$\left.\begin{array}{l} Ca^{++} \\ Mg^{++} \\ Fe^{++} \\ 2Na^+ \\ 2NH_4^+ \end{array}\right\} + H_2X \rightarrow \left\{\begin{array}{l} CaX \\ MgX \\ FeX \\ Na_2X \\ (NH_4)_2X \end{array}\right. + 2H^+ \tag{7}$$

If this ion exchange process continues to exhaustion, the first ions to appear in the effluent will be NH_4^+ and Na^+, and if the exhausted bed is then analyzed, the distribution of ions would be as shown by Figure 12.4. This is due to a selectivity or preference of the cation exchanger for certain ions over others. A typical selectivity list is shown in Table 12.1.

The order of selectivity shown applies to ions in typical water of less than 1000 mg/l TDS. The selectivity is different at high concentrations. For example, in the sodium cycle, the exchanger has a preference for Ca^{+2} over Na^+ at 1000

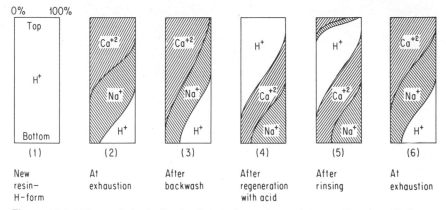

Figure 12.4   Change in ionic distribution during cation exchange—H-cycle, with downward flow of water and acid (cocurrent regeneration).

mg/l; but at 100,000 mg/l its preference is for Na^+ over Ca^{+2} (see Figure 12.5). This is fortunate, as it enhances the efficiency of regeneration with brine.

Returning to the examination of the nature of cation exchangers, there are several materials in addition to the styrene-based material of commercial importance. One is processed greensand—the original zeolite—which is still used effectively for removal of iron and manganese. It can operate only in the sodium cycle over a limited pH range. Another, of increasing importance, is a resin having the carboxyl group (—COOH, with the hydrogen ion exchangeable) as the exchange site. This is called a weak cation exchanger, discussed later

TABLE 12.1   General Order of Ion Selectivity in Water below 1000 mg/l TDS

Cations	Anions
Fe^{+3}	$CrO_4^{-2}*$
Al^{+3}	$SO_4^{-2}*$
Pb^{+2}	$SO_3^{-2}*$
Ba^{+2}	$HPO_4^{-2}*$
Sr^{+2}	CNS^-
Cd^{+2}	CNO^-
Zn^{+2}	NO_3^-
Cu^{+2}	NO_2^-
Fe^{+2}	Br^-
Mn^{+2}	Cl^-
Ca^{+2}	CN^-
Mg^{+2}	HCO_3^-
K^{+1}	$HSiO_3^-$
NH_4^+	OH^-
Na^+	F^-
H^+	
Li^+	

* These may be displaced as they are protonated at low pH to: $HCrO_4^-$, HSO_3^-, $H_2PO_4^-$.

NOTES: Changes in position may occur between products of different manufacture or having slightly different skeletons or exchange groups. In general, selectivity is affected by:
(a) Ionic valence: $3 > 2 > 1$.
(b) Atomic number: $Ba > Sr > Ca > Mg$ in Group IIA.
(c) Hydrated ionic radius: the larger the radius, the lower the selectivity and exchange capacity.

Figure 12.5 Na$^+$/Ca^{+2} equilibria for a sulfonic acid cation exchange resin. *(Courtesy of Rohm & Haas.)*

in a consideration of hydrogen exchange operations. This material is highly selective for H$^+$ and divalent cations with no significant ability to exchange Na$^+$. A third material is a true synthetic zeolite (aluminosilicate) that can be tailored for specific applications (e.g., ammonia removal) and for adsorption of specific molecules (molecular sieves).

ANION EXCHANGERS

Anion exchangers may be produced from a variety of resinous or plastic skeletons, including the same styrene–divinyl benzene copolymer as is used for cation exchangers. As with cation exchangers, two general varieties are used commercially, weak base and strong base exchangers. The functional group of an anion exchanger is an amine, the organic equivalent of ammonia. Weak base exchangers contain a secondary or tertiary amine group, RR'—NH or RR'—N—R', which can adsorb strong acids. Strong base exchangers contain a quarternary amine, R R' R'' R'''N$^+$ · Cl$^-$, which can exchange anions. The most common quarternary resin has the formula, —R·N(CH$_3$)$_3$·Cl, or structurally

$$-\text{C}-\text{C}-\text{C}-\text{C}-$$

$$(\text{CH}_3)-\text{N}^+-(\text{CH}_3)$$
$$(\text{CH}_3) \cdot \text{Cl}^-$$

Weak-base anion exchangers are able to remove only strong mineral acids—HCl, H$_2$SO$_4$, HNO$_3$—with practically no exchange capacity for weak acids—

such as CO_2, SiO_2, and organic acids. The typical reaction is shown as an adsorption, rather than ion exchange process:

$$HCl + A \rightarrow A \cdot HCl \tag{8}$$

(In this text, the letter A represents an anion exchanger.) The exhausted resin is very efficiently regenerated with any alkali, which simply neutralizes the adsorbed acid and releases it as a neutral salt.

Strong-base exchangers are true ion exchange materials. Several typical reactions are:

Dealkalization, with Cl-form exchanger, ACl_2:

$$2HCO_3^- + ACl_2 \rightarrow A(HCO_3)_2 + 2Cl^- \tag{9}$$

Sulfate removal, with Cl-form exchanger:

$$SO_4^{-2} + ACl_2 \rightarrow ASO_4 + 2Cl^- \tag{10}$$

The most common use for strong base exchangers is complete anion removal from hydrogen exchanger effluent, to produce demineralized water:

$$\left.\begin{array}{l} H_2SO_4 \\ 2HCl \\ \\ 2H_2CO_3 \\ 2H_2SiO_3 \end{array}\right\} + A(OH)_2 \rightarrow \left\{\begin{array}{l} A \cdot SO_4 \\ A \cdot Cl_2 \\ \\ A \cdot (HCO_3)_2 \\ A \cdot (HSiO_3)_2 \end{array}\right. + 2H_2O \tag{11}$$

This exchange resin is regenerated with NaOH. In this form, the exchanger can also convert neutral salts to caustic, known as salt-splitting

$$2NaCl + A(OH)_2 \rightarrow ACl_2 + 2NaOH \tag{12}$$

The selectivity of the anion exchanger, also shown in Table 12.1, indicates that silica will leak through the bed first, and the exhausted bed will have the composition shown by Figure 12.6.

PRACTICAL ION EXCHANGE

In the commercial application of ion exchange to water treatment, there are four important principles:

1. Most ion exchange units are simple vessels containing a bed of ion exchange resin operated downflow on a cyclic basis: (a) a unit is operated to a predetermined leakage level, where it is considered to be exhausted; (b) the unit is then regenerated, first by upflow cleaning (backwash) and then by chemical elution, downflow; (c) the resin bed is then rinsed downflow. Because both water and regenerant flow in the same direction, the water leaving the unit is in contact with the resin having the highest level of contaminating ions, so quality and efficiency both suffer.

2. The ion exchange bed has a considerably higher capacity than is used, because uneconomical excesses of regenerating chemical would be required to convert the resin entirely to the desired ion form. For example, the cation resin may have a capacity of 2N (about 44 kgr/cu ft), but only about half of this (20–22 kgr/cu ft) is used for sodium cycle softening. Therefore, there is always a high concentration of contaminating ions, calcium in this case, on the resin as a potential for spoiling the treated water quality.

3. Because of cyclic operation with cocurrent flow of water and regenerant, chemical utilization in regenerating ion exchange resins is usually poor. This

Figure 12.6 Ion distribution during anion exchange demineralization with cocurrent regeneration.

drawback is most pronounced with strong resins—sulfonic-type cation exchangers and quarternary ammonium anion exchangers. For example, in the sodium cycle, if the utilized capacity is 21 kgr (about 3 lb) as $CaCO_3$/cu ft (48 kg/m³) of resin, the salt required is theoretically only $58.5/50 \times 3 = 3.5$ lb NaCl/cu ft. The actual salt consumption is typically 6–10 lb NaCl/cu ft, so the efficiency is about 30–50%. Acid efficiency for hydrogen exchange using a sulfonic-type resin and H_2SO_4 for regeneration, and caustic efficiency for regeneration of strong base anion resins are even poorer, about 20–40%.

However, weak cation resins (carboxylic type) and weak anion resins (amine type) can be operated at close to 100% chemical efficiency.

4. Most ion exchange materials used in water treatment are in the size range of 20–50 mesh, or about 0.5 mm effective size. This makes an ion exchange bed a very effective filter, a characteristic having both advantages and disadvantages. This filtering ability is combined with ion exchange properties in designing industrial condensate polishing systems using ion exchange beds. But the filtering ability also leads to fouling and unpredictable operating runs. Sometimes this is caused by the accumulation of high microbial populations in an exchanger bed, even when operating on a chlorinated municipal water supply.

AN EVOLVING SCIENCE

Because of these limitations, in spite of added capital cost and increased sophistication of equipment, ion exchange designs are changing to reduce chemical cost, improve effluent quality, and reduce pollution created by excessive chemical dosages. These improvements are realized by:

    a. Countercurrent regeneration techniques

    b. Multiple stages of treatment

    c. Use of weak exchangers wherever possible

    d. Pretreatment of water prior to ion exchange (e.g., by lime softening, reverse osmosis) to reduce the ionic load on the ion exchange system

    e. Pretreatment to reduce particulates or soluble organic foulants (e.g., by filtration, adsorption).

In subsequent sections, leakage will be mentioned frequently. The term "leakage" implies a slipping of some of the influent ions into the effluent. In fact, unwanted ions reach the effluent by two different processes (see Figure 12.7*a*):

    1. At the beginning of the softening run (using the Na_2X process as an

example) there is appreciable calcium left in the bottom of the resin bed. Water entering at the top gets completely softened, the only cation being sodium. This softened water, in effect a very dilute brine, regenerates the calcium from the bottom of the bed. So at the beginning of the run the hardness in the effluent is due to calcium residue on the exchanger from the previous run.

2. As the bed becomes exhausted, the calcium contamination at the bottom of the bed decreases and the quality continually improves until true leakage—slippage of incoming Ca^{+2} through the bed into the effluent—begins to appear. The net effect is the leakage curve shown by Figure 12.7b.

This same kind of effect is observed with all exchange processes having co-current exhaustion and regeneration. If the bed is regenerated countercurrent to the water flow, this effect is eliminated and leakage is then due to actual ion slippage. The improvement of both quality and efficiency by counterflow regeneration is strikingly illustrated by Figure 12.8, showing a hydrogen cycle operation with downward service flow and upflow regeneration with sulfuric acid.

A final backwash is another procedure for minimizing leakage.

Slippage is easy to appreciate as one consequence of the limited residence time of the water in the ion exchange bed, typically about one minute.

In an idle unit, there is migration of ions between resin particles. This causes a change of water quality when flow commences again. This migration is also observed during backwash, illustrated in steps (2) and (3) of Figure 12.4.

SODIUM CYCLE EXCHANGE (ZEOLITE SOFTENING)

Zeolite softening is the oldest and simplest of the ion exchange processes. It removes hardness from water, including iron and manganese if these constituents can be kept in the reduced ionic form. When the ion exchange bed is saturated with the hardness constituents, the exchanger is regenerated with sodium chloride brine.

During the processing step—the softening run—the hardness of the raw water may vary and the flow rates through the system may change, but the bed continues to operate effectively to produce a soft water.

Figure 12.7 Leakage through a sodium zeolite softener with cocurrent flows. (*a*) Bed condition during cycle; (*b*) leakage curve.

Figure 12.8 Comparison of results of cocurrent vs. countercurrent regeneration of cation exchange resin. *(Thompson, J., and Reents, A. C., "Counterflow Regeneration," Proceedings of 27th International Water Conference, November 1966.)*

The equipment design is simple, consisting of a steel shell holding the ion exchange bed and provided with piping and valves to permit the essential operations of softening, backwash, brining, and rinsing (Figure 12.9). Instrumentation may be provided to help the operator anticipate exhaustion of the bed, so that the bed can be regenerated before the effluent quality depreciates beyond acceptable limits. Almost all sodium zeolite units include a meter for measuring water flow, usually equipped with an alarm so that when the gallonage corresponding to the capacity of the bed has been reached, the operator will be

Figure 12.9 Cross section of an ion exchange unit, showing design details of internals arranged for cocurrent regeneration. *(Courtesy of The Permutit Company.)*

Figure 12.10 With a multiple-unit system, a full flow of soft water is always available. A single regeneration system serves the battery of units, and individual regenerations are staggered to equalize water quality.

warned of the need to regenerate. More sophisticated units, required by higher quality limits, include automatic hardness analyzers.

Multiple Units

If storage capacity is provided for softened water, a single unit may be adequate for the plant needs. In larger plants it is common to have more than one unit, so that one can be taken out of service for regeneration without interrupting the flow of soft water.

A diagram of a multiple unit system is shown in Figure 12.10. This system uses steel tanks to saturate the brine solution and then to measure it for application to the ion exchange bed. Larger systems, where salt can be more conveniently purchased in truckload quantities than in bags, are designed to have a large concrete salt-saturating basin located adjacent to a track or roadway where brine can be

Figure 12.11 Wet salt storage basin for bulk truckload deliveries of salt. *(Courtesy of Cochrane Division, the Crane Company.)*

Figure 12.12   Multiple-unit sodium zeolite installation for continuous delivery of softened water. *(Courtesy of The Permutit Company.)*

Figure 12.13   Battery of sodium zeolite softeners used in hot process system after lime softening. Designed for automatic operation. *(Courtesy of Cochrane Division, the Crane Company.)*

brought to the plant in bulk and simply dumped into the underground salt storage and brine saturation basin. A typical design of the salt storage facility for these larger installations is shown in Figure 12.11.

Figures 12.12 and 12.13 illustrate several typical installations, the first being a simple zeolite softener treating city water as boiler makeup, and the second a sodium zeolite softener especially designed for high temperature service and installed in a plant to follow a hot process lime softener and filter system.

The chemical reactions for the sodium zeolite process are shown below:
Softening (exhaustion):

$$Ca^{+2} + Na_2X \rightarrow CaX + 2Na^+ \tag{13}$$

$$Mg^{+2} + Na_2X \rightarrow MgX + 2Na^+ \tag{14}$$

NOTE: The selectivity of the exchanger favors Ca^{+2} over Mg^{+2}. Therefore, Mg hardness predominates at the point of breakthrough.
Regeneration (brining):

$$2NaCl + CaX \rightarrow Na_2X + CaCl_2 \tag{15}$$

$$2NaCl + MgX \rightarrow Na_2X + MgCl_2 \tag{16}$$

The amount of salt applied to the individual zeolite bed for regeneration is determined by the acceptable effluent quality limits and the capacity the plant wishes to achieve to properly schedule regeneration of the system based on available labor. The greater the salt dosage, the lower is the hardness leakage and the higher the capacity. However, the higher salt dosage also results in poorer chemical economy and greater quantities of spent brine to be handled through the waste disposal system.

An example is worked out completely in Table 12.2 to give a perspective on the relative size of the equipment, the choice between salt dosage, capacity, and leakage, and the volumes of waste produced.

The zeolite softener simply removes hardness when used for treatment of a raw water supply. A typical analysis showing raw water and treated water is given in Figure 12.14. However, the system is also used for cleanup of process condensates in industrial operations, such as paper mill condensate, chemical plant condensate, and central heating station condensate, where the units are operated at very high flow rates and remove not only traces of hardness that enter the system from leakage of heat exchangers, but also particulate matter, such as corrosion products.

The wastes from regeneration of an ion exchange system are convenient in that they are in solution form. However, they increase the dissolved solids content of the effluent from the waste treatment plant through which they are processed. If this saline water is a problem, it can be treated with lime and soda ash to precipitate the hardness, producing a brine which can then be reused. This process, which converts the liquid saline waste to a solid waste, has been proposed for installations in the Southwest where the spent brine may lower the quality of the receiving streams and where the climatic conditions are favorable for drying of solid waste.

HYDROGEN CYCLE EXCHANGE

The development of ion exchange materials that could be regenerated with acid to exchange hydrogen ions for cations in water provided the first practical chemical process for the removal of sodium, potassium and ammonia, all of whose salts are extremely soluble. The generalized reactions for hydrogen cycle exchange have been given earlier. The following specific reactions and data shown in Figure 12.15 illustrate the process more completely. The effluent is

TABLE 12.2 Sample Calculation of Sodium Exchange System

WATER ANALYSIS—See Figure 12.14. Total hardness = 200 mg/l, allowable leakage = 3 mg/l, TE = 300 mg/l.

PLANT REQUIREMENTS: 1,200,000 gpd = average flow of 1,200,000/1440 = 833 gpm; must accommodate extended peak flow of 1200 gpm.

1. Calculation of required size to handle 1200 gpm. (See Table 12.3.) Use three 10'-0" diameter units.
2. Calculation of required resin volume.
   (a) Required capacity in kilograins:
       Hardness = 200 mg/l; 200/17.1 = 11.7 gr/gal,
       1,200,000 × 11.7/1000 = 14,035 kilograins/day,
       Schedule all 3 units to be regenerated each shift.
       ∴ Required capacity = 14,035/3 = 4678 kgr   total
                                          4678/3 units = 1560 kgr/unit
   (b) Allowable leakage = 3 mg/l
       This leakage can be achieved @ 6 lb NaCl/cu ft.
       (Actual leakage @ 6 lb/cu ft will be only 1.5 mg/l H)

       Capacity at 6 lb/cu ft = 20 kgr/cu ft (Table 12.4)
       ∴ Required resin = 1560/20 = 78 cu ft minimum
   (c) Bed depth: Area of 10'-0" diameter unit = 78.5 sq ft. Therefore, bed would be approximately 1' deep. To achieve the desired leakage, minimum bed depth is 30". Therefore, each unit requires:
       2.5 ft deep × 78.5 ft² area = 196 cubic feet

   (d) The actual regeneration period will be:

$$\frac{196 \text{ cu ft} \times 3 \text{ units} \times 20 \text{ kgr/cu ft}}{14{,}035 \text{ kgr/day}} = 0.84 \text{ day}$$
$$0.84 \times 24 = 20 \text{ hours,}$$

   or one unit will be regenerated every 6 hrs, 40 min
3. Salt consumption @ 6 lb salt—20 kgr/cu ft
   6/20 = 0.3 lb/kgr (2.1 mg/l salt/mg/l hardness),
   14,035 kgr/day × 0.3 lb NaCl/kgr = 4200 lb NaCL,
   this requires bulk deliveries for practical handling by plant labor.

---

acid, it contains carbon dioxide equivalent to the incoming alkalinity, and substantially all of the cations in the influent have been exchanged for hydrogen, except for leakage:

$$Ca(HCO_3)_2 + H_2X \rightarrow CaX + 2H_2O + 2CO_2 \tag{17}$$

$$CaSO_4 + H_2X \rightarrow CaX + H_2SO_4 \tag{18}$$

The strong acidity of the treated water must be corrected to provide a water satisfactory for practically any conventional use. The carbon dioxide is easily removed by degasification, since the equilibrium carbon dioxide concentration corresponding to the typical composition of the atmosphere is less than 1 mg/l. Therefore, the acidity may be neutralized by the addition of alkali, or by anion exchange.

There are several choices for alkalinity neutralization. If the finished water need not be completely softened, the hydrogen exchange effluent can be blended with raw water and the blend degasified, to provide whatever alkalinity is needed in the finished water. Column C of Figure 12.15 gives the analysis of a blend of raw water with hydrogen exchange effluent to produce an alkalinity of 50 mg/l. If the blended water must be completely softened, a sodium zeolite softener can supply the alkalinity for neutralization of the acidity of the hydrogen exchanger effluent, and the analysis will then be that shown by Column D. In both cases the proportion of hydrogen exchanger effluent to be blended is calculated by the following formula:

$$\text{Percent H}_2\text{X} = \frac{\text{alkalinity reduction}}{\text{total electrolyte}} \times 100\%$$

In the example given in Figure 12.15, the blend is:

$$\text{Percent H}_2\text{X} = \frac{200 - 50}{300} \times 100 = 50\%$$

$$\text{Percent raw water or Na}_2\text{X} \qquad = 50\%$$

Another way of neutralizing the acidity in the hydrogen exchanger effluent is to feed an alkaline chemical such as NaOH into the effluent to neutralize the hydrogen ion and to reach the desired alkalinity. This treatment produces the same effluent shown by column D. In this example, the caustic soda dosage would be equal to the 95 mg/l hydrogen ion neutralized plus 50 mg/l desired alkalinity, or 145 mg/l as $CaCO_3$, equivalent to 116 mg/l NaOH.

The major advantage of these variations of the hydrogen cycle process over direct acidification to reduce alkalinity is a reduction of total solids equivalent to alkalinity reduction, as shown by Figure 12.15.

TABLE 12.3   Ion Exchange Flows and Dimensions

Diameter	Area sq ft	Min. Resin cu ft @ 30″	Backwash, gpm †	Backwash, gpm ‡	Backwash, gpm §	Service flow, gpm max.* 1 unit	Service flow, gpm max.* 2 units	Service flow, gpm max.* 3 units
2′-0″	3.14	8	9	19	38	19	25	50
2′-6″	4.91	12	15	30	59	30	40	80
3′-0″	7.07	18	21	42	85	42	56	112
3′-6″	9.62	24	29	58	116	58	77	154
4′-0″	12.6	32	38	75	150	75	100	200
4′-6″	15.9	40	48	95	190	95	130	260
5′-0″	19.6	49	59	118	235	118	160	320
5′-6″	23.8	60	71	143	285	143	190	380
6′-0″	28.3	71	85	170	340	170	230	460
6′-6″	33.2	83	100	200	400	200	270	540
7′-0″	38.5	96	115	230	460	230	310	620
7′-6″	44.2	110	132	265	530	265	350	700
8′-0″	50.3	126	150	300	600	300	400	800
8′-6″	56.8	142	170	340	680	340	450	900
9′-0″	63.6	160	190	380	760	380	500	1000
9′-6″	70.9	176	213	425	850	425	570	1140
10′-0″	78.5	196	235	470	940	470	630	1260
11′-0″	95	240	285	570	1140	570	750	1500

* Service flow is based on rates of 6 gpm/sq ft, single unit maximum rate, and 8 gpm/sq ft short term rate, on multiple units when one unit is out of service for regeneration. To provide a continuous supply of treated water, most plants use two units, so that while one is being regenerated, the other continues to provide finished water. Plants having variable demand store finished water to eliminate surges in flow, minimizing equipment size. Treated water storage permits smaller plants to install only a single unit, relying on stored water to provide requirements during regeneration. This is risky, since it provides no margin for error or for normal maintenance.

† Backwash rate of 3 gpm/sq ft for anion resins at 70°F.

‡ Backwash rate of 6 gpm/sq ft for cation resins at 70°F.

§ Backwash rate of 12 gpm/sq ft for cation resins at 220°F.

TABLE 12.4 Typical Sodium Zeolite Performance

Salt Applied, lb/cu ft	6	8	10	15
Approx. capacity, kgr/cu ft	20	23	25	30
Salt rate, lb/kgr	0.30	0.35	0.40	0.50
mg/l Salt/mg/l hardness	2.1	2.5	2.8	3.5
Hardness leakage, mg/l, at				
100 mg/l total electrolyte	0.1–0.3	0.1–0.2	0.1	0.1
250 mg/l total electrolyte	0.5–2	0.5–1.0	0.3–0.5	0.1–0.2
500 mg/l total electrolyte	3–6	2–4	1–3	0.5–1.0
1000 mg/l total electrolyte	12–25	8–15	5–10	2–4

Identification of Analyses Tabulated Below:

A. Raw Water   D.

B. Softened Water   E.

C.   F.

Constituent	As	A	B	C	D	E	F
Calcium	$CaCO_3$	150	2				
Magnesium	"	50	1				
Sodium	"	100	297				
Total Electrolyte	$CaCO_3$	300	300				
Bicarbonate	$CaCO_3$	200	200				
Carbonate	"	0	0				
Hydroxyl	"	0	0				
Sulfate	"	50	50				
Chloride	"	50	50				
Nitrate	"	0	0				
					N O		
					C H A N G E		
M Alk.	$CaCO_3$	200	200				
P Alk.	"	0	0				
Carbon Dioxide		20	20				
pH		7.4	7.4				
Silica		15	15				
Iron	Fe	0.2	Nil				
Turbidity		Nil	Nil				
TDS *		350	370				
Color		Nil	Nil				

* Note the increase in TDS due to higher equivalent
weight of sodium (23) compared to Ca (20) and Mg (12.2)

Figure 12.14 Expected results of simple sodium zeolite treatment.

Identification of Analyses Tabulated Below:

A. Raw Water

B. H_2X Effluent

C. H_2X + Raw Water Blend

D. H_2X-Na_2X Blend or H_2X + NaOH

E. Neutralization

F.

Constituent	As	A	B	C	D	E	F
Calcium	$CaCO_3$	150	Nil	75	Nil		
Magnesium	"	50	Nil	25	Nil		
Sodium	"	100	5	50	150		
Hydrogen		0	95	0	0		
Total Electrolyte	$CaCO_3$	300	100	150	150		
Bicarbonate	$CaCO_3$	200	0	50	50		
Carbonate	"	0	0	0	0		
Hydroxyl	"	0	0	0	0		
Sulfate	"	50	50	50	50		
Chloride	"	50	50	50	50		
Nitrate	"	0	0	0	0		
M Alk.	$CaCO_3$	200	0	50	50		
P Alk.	"	0	0	0	0		
Carbon Dioxide		20	220	5*	5*		
pH		7.4	2.7	7.4	7.4		
Silica		15	15	15	15		
Iron	Fe	0.2	Nil	Nil	Nil		
Turbidity		Nil	Nil	Nil	Nil		
TDS		350	150	200	200		
Color		Nil	Nil	Nil	Nil		

* After degasification

Figure 12.15   Expected results of split stream treatment.

By far the most common process is the blending of hydrogen exchanger and sodium exchanger effluents, known as split-stream softening (Figure 12.16). A typical split-stream system is shown in Figure 12.17.

Acid Regeneration of Cation Exchangers

In the systems just described, a strong cation resin is usually used with sulfuric acid regeneration. The approximate capacities realized with cocurrent sulfuric acid regeneration of such an exchanger are shown in Table 12.5. The regeneration efficiency is rather poor when compared to theoretical, 0.143 lb/kgr (1 kg/kg).

The development of weak cation (carboxylic) exchangers (discussed later) has diminished the popularity of the split-stream dealkalizer. A layered bed with acid-regenerated carboxylic resin above a salt-regenerated strong cation resin provides advantages in efficiency and reduction of wastes. But the split-stream

Figure 12.16 Schematic showing the blending of acid effluent from H_2X unit with alkaline sodium zeolite effluent through adjustable rate controllers designed to maintain correct blend as flow demand varies.

offers flexibility in dealing with a water supply of variable composition, since the ratio of Na_2X flow to H_2X flow can be adjusted.

The spent regenerant requires careful attention for disposal since it contains a large amount of unused acid plus calcium sulfate at concentrations far above its solubility, creating a potential sludge problem. The use of hydrochloric acid avoids the calcium sulfate precipitation, but in most areas hydrochloric acid is too expensive compared to sulfuric acid.

As shown by Table 12.5, an increase in the amount of acid applied for regeneration produces an increase in capacity, but at the expense of efficiency. A second effect of higher regeneration level is a reduction in leakage. In the hydrogen cycle treatment scheme shown by Figure 12.15, sodium leakage is not critical, since the acid effluent is neutralized by a sodium-based alkali. Therefore it is practical to use only 6 lb/cu ft (96 kg/m³) regeneration level for better acid efficiency. However, as more fully developed later in the text regarding demineralization, the higher dosage of acid may be needed to meet the quality goals of demineralizing systems.

Figure 12.17 Split stream H_2X − Na_2X exchangers softening and dealkalizing a municipal water. The exchangers are fitted for automatic regeneration. *(Courtesy of The Permutit Company.)*

TABLE 12.5   Strong Cation Resin Performance H-Cycle, H₂SO₄ Regeneration

Acid applied, lb/cu ft	6	8
Approx. capacity, kgr/lbs/cu ft		
1. At TE/M ratio − 3.0	12	13.5
lb/kgr	0.5	0.6
parts H₂SO₄/part cations	3.5	4.2
2. At TE/M ratio = 2.0	13.5	16
lb/kgr	0.45	0.5
parts H₂SO₄/part cations	3.2	3.5
3. At TE/M ratio = 1.5	15	17
lb/kgr	0.4	0.47
parts H₂SO₄/part cations	2.8	3.3

NOTES
1. For split-stream dealkalization, use 6 lb H_2SO_4/cu ft.
2. For demineralization:
    (a) 6 lb H_2SO_4/cu ft for mixed bed
    (b) For 2-bed systems, use 6 lb/cu ft, where Na < 50 mg/l, 8 lb/cu ft otherwise.

Using the water analysis of Figure 12.15, data on acid dosage and resulting capacity and sodium leakage with cocurrent regeneration are plotted in Figure 12.18.

Using Weak Cation Exchangers

The utilization of regenerant acid can be considerably improved by incorporating a carboxylic exchanger into the system. In such a system, the carboxylic exchanger bed is sized to react with the alkalinity or the hardness of the incoming water, whichever is the lesser. The strong cation exchanger is then sized to react with the balance of the cations. The carboxylic unit then operates at close to

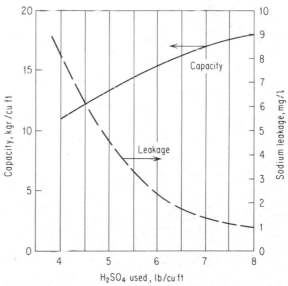

Figure 12.18   Typical performance of H-cycle exchanger with cocurrent flows, sulfonic acid resin.

Milliequivalents alkali added per gram

Figure 12.19 Titration curves of cation exchange resins. *(Courtesy of Rohm & Haas.)*

theoretical efficiency, approximately 0.15 lb/kgr (1.0 kg/kg). The distinctive performance of a carboxylic exchanger is strikingly illustrated by the comparison of acid-base titration curves for carboxylic and sulfonic exchangers, Figure 12.19.

Carboxylic exchangers typically have a capacity as high as 70 kgr/cu ft (3.2 N), but the operating capacity is usually in the range of 20–40 kgr/cu ft (0.9–1.8 N). This compares to a range of only 12–18 kgr/cu ft (0.6–0.9 N) for the strong cation exchanger regenerated with H_2SO_4.

The results of treatment whether using a strong cation resin or a combination of a strong cation resin and a carboxylic resin are the same. The advantage of the carboxylic resin is a reduction in cost by improved acid efficiency and reduced waste treatment load through reduction of excess acid. Against this chemical saving must be balanced the cost of the more sophisticated design required by the use of two resins. Some systems incorporate layered beds of carboxylic and sulfonic resins in the same vessel; these are susceptible to fouling because the carboxylic resin is light and difficult to clean and should be provided with a separate regeneration system to avoid calcium sulfate deposition.

Countercurrent Regeneration of H_2X Units

Another choice is available to improve results, and that is to design the exchanger for countercurrent regeneration.

An excellent example of this is given in Table 12.6. This compares side-by-side performance of two cation exchangers in a Canadian plant, where these units are part of a demineralizing train. One was operated by conventional cocurrent acid regeneration, and the other with countercurrent. The units were operated to produce equal low levels of sodium leakage, using H_2SO_4 for regeneration. The units each contained the same kind of strong cation resin. The remarkable in-

TABLE 12.6 Comparison of Cocurrent to Countercurrent Regeneration of Cation Exchanger

Operating factor	Cocurrent	Countercurrent
Regeneration:		
Acid, lb/cu ft	6.0	3.7
Concentration	2% and 4%	2%
Capacity:		
kgr/cu ft	7.7	14.5
lbs H_2SO_4/kgr	0.78	0.26
Regeneration:		
Acid Consumption, as a percent of theoretical	520%	170%

crease in capacity and regenerant efficiency showed up not only on these cation units, but also on the anion units, which were likewise converted and compared. A second example, where the exchanger was operated on a relatively high solids water, is shown by Figure 12.8.

The countercurrent system is a little more sophisticated, but improved quality and increase in efficiency make this attractive.

ANION EXCHANGE PROCESSES

The nature of anion exchange was briefly introduced earlier, with reference to both the strong and weak base anion exchangers. The first reaction shown for the strong base exchanger involved the removal of alkalinity from water by the exchanger in substitution for chloride ions. This is a simple and practical process for the reduction of alkalinity without the use of acids. Since the exchanger is regenerated with sodium chloride brine, chemical handling is very simple. The chloride-form of the anion exchanger removes sulfate as well as bicarbonate, and because sulfate removal is not usually necessary, this is an added cost to the operation.

In some water treatment operations, the reduction of sulfate by itself may be important, and this can be accomplished in the same fashion. The removal of sulfate is somewhat selective as compared to the reduction of bicarbonate, so the efficiency of this operation is higher than that for the dealkalization process.

Although most plants soften water before dealkalization through an anion exchanger, this is not strictly necessary. For example, cooling tower makeup could be dealkalized through the anion exchanger without prior softening.

By far the most common form in which anion exchangers are used in water treatment is the hydroxide form, with caustic soda being used for regeneration; and the most common process using this form of strong-base resin is demineralization, where the anion exchanger follows the hydrogen-form cation exchanger. In this process, the anions in the cation effluent are exchanged for hydroxide; if there are cations present, such as sodium, the effluent will contain sodium hydroxide, and this is the most prominent factor affecting the quality of finished demineralized water. When demineralized water is used for boiler makeup, silica leakage is of primary interest, and the amount of sodium leakage which occurs proportionately affects silica leakage. Using the water analysis of Figure 12.15 and the sodium leakage through the cation exchange shown by Figure 12.17, the quality of demineralized water that can be produced by a strongly basic anion exchanger is shown in Figure 12.20 for two different levels of acid regeneration of the cation exchanger and varying levels of caustic used for regeneration of the anion exchanger.

A simplified chart of typical performance capacities for strongly basic anion exchangers is listed in Table 12.7.

Process Refinements

If the quality of water as shown by these illustrations is not adequate for the intended service, alternative methods of treatment must be used. The most obvious possibility is the installation of a second stage demineralizer to polish the water produced from the first stage. Another alternative is to use a mixed bed demineralizer either for the primary service or for polishing; in this type of unit, the cation and anion resins are intimately mixed after regeneration, in effect providing hundreds of stages of demineralization (Figure 12.21).

Other choices include improvements in design, such as counterflow regeneration, and reduction of the loading on the ion exchange system by pretreatment.

One of the common procedures for reducing loading on the anion exchanger

Figure 12.20 The effect of caustic regeneration level on capacity and silica leakage in a two-bed, cocurrent demineralizer with degasifier (analyses Figure 12.15).

is the removal of carbon dioxide by degasification so that it need not be removed by ion exchange.

Weakly basic exchangers can be installed in demineralizing systems both to relieve the load on the strong anion exchanger and also to improve the economy of operation. Weakly basic exchangers remove only the strong mineral acids, such as hydrochloric and sulfuric acid, and the alkali used for regeneration neutralizes these adsorbed acids so that the regeneration is close to 100% efficient.

There are numerous possibilities for the design engineer in putting together individual units of a demineralizing system to suit the type of raw water being

Figure 12.21   Mixed bed demineralization. (*a*) Conventional two-bed cation-anion exchangers. (*b*) Multistage demineralization with mixed cation and anion resin beads.

Scheme		Removal		
		Cations	Strong anions	Weak anions
(1) SCR WBR Two bed		By SCR	By WBR	None
(2) ① SCR or ② WCR ① SBR or ② MB Two bed		1. By SCR 2. By WCR + SCR in MB	← By SBR → ← By SBR in MB →	
(3) MB Mixed bed		By SCR	← By SBR →	
(4) SCR WBR SBR Three bed		By SCR	By WBR	By SBR
(5) WCR WBR MB Three bed		By WCR + SCR in MB	By WBR	By SBR in MB
(6) ① SCR or ② WCR DG ① SBR or ② MB Two bed with DG		1. By SCR 2. By WCR + SCR in MB	By SBR By SBR in MB	By DG + SBR By DG + SBR in MB
(7) ① SCR or ② WCR DG WBR ① SBR or ② MB		1. By SCR 2. By WCR + SCR in MB	By WBR By WBR	By DG + SBR By DG + SBR in MB

SCR – strong cation resin; WCR – weak cation resin
SBR – strong base resin; WBR – weak base resin
DG – degasifier; MB – mixed bed

Figure 12.22 Basic types of demineralizers and resins used.

TABLE 12.7   Strong Base Exchange Capacities in Demineralizing
Service (Regenerated with NaOH at 95°F, with 90 minutes
contact time.)

NaOH, lb/cu ft	Cap., kgr/cu ft	lb/kgr	Final SiO$_2$, mg/l
3.5	10	0.35	0.6
5.0	12	0.42	0.3

NOTE: SiO$_2$ leakage is based on anion loading of 100% SiO$_2$, water at 75°F, and final conductivity of 3 micromhos. Prorate to suit actual conditions:

1. If SiO$_2$ in influent to anion unit is only 10% of the total anions, final SiO$_2$ will be only 10% of value shown.

2. If water temperature is 90°F, SiO$_2$ leakage will increase 50%; at 50°F, SiO$_2$ leakage will decrease 50%.

3. If conductivity of finished water exceeds 3 micromhos, SiO$_2$ leakage will increase about 20% for each 5 micromhos increase.

4. In using these data, estimate the amount of water produced from capacity and total anion loading, which is the sum of all anions entering the exchange unit. If there is a degasifier in the system for the reduction of CO$_2$ ahead of the strong base resin, this reduces the load on the strong base resin.

processed, the economics of plant operation, and the ultimate quality demanded by the process use. These are illustrated by Figure 12.22. Some general rules for the selection of individual components of a demineralizing system based chiefly on economics of operation are shown in Table 12.8.

Because the weakly basic exchanger is regenerated simply by neutralization of the adsorbed mineral acids, a variety of alkalies can be used for this operation. The approximate capacity of these exchangers and the kinds of regenerants that may be used are illustrated by Table 12.9.

TABLE 12.8   Demineralizer Unit Selection Chart

Flow rate, gpm	Amount of impurity to be removed, mg/l			Resins required			Units to be used				
	FMA	CO$_2$	SiO$_2$	C	WB	SB		C	DG	A	MB
1. Any	Any	None	None	x	x	—	(1)	x	—	x	—
							(2)	—	—	—	x
2. Any	Any	Any	None	x	x	—	(1)	x	x	x	—
							(2)	—	x	—	x
3. 0–20	Any	Any	Any	x	—	x	(1)	x	—	x	—
							(2)	—	—	—	x
4. 20–50	Any	0–50	Any	x	—	x	(1)	x	—	x	—
							(2)	—	—	—	x
5. Over 100	0–100	Over 100	Any	x	—	x	(1)	x	x	x	—
							(2)	x	x	—	x
6. Over 100	Over 200	Over 100	Any	x	x	x	(1)	x	x	x	—
							(2)	x	x	x	x

NOTES: 1. C = cation, A = anion, DG = degasifier, MB = mixed bed, WB = weak base, SB = strong base, FMA = free mineral acidity (SO$_4$ + Cl + NO$_3$).

2. Numbers in parentheses: (1) multi-bed plant, (2) mixed bed for 1 micromho effluent.

3. Intermediate ranges (50–100 gpm flow, 50–100 mg/l CO$_2$, 100–200 mg/l FMA) require careful evaluation for best balance in capital and operating costs.

TABLE 12.9   Typical Weak Base Exchange Capacities

Chemical	Dosage, lb/cu ft	Capacity, kgr/cu ft	Usage, lb/kgr
NH_3	1.5	20.0	0.08
NaOH	3	21.3	0.14
Na_2CO_3	6.6	19.6	0.34

NOTE: Capacity based on a 1:1 ratio of HCl to H_2SO_4.

Waste Treatment Considerations

A prominent factor in the selection of any ion exchange process is the waste created by regeneration of the ion exchange bed. The waste may be reusable, as in the discharge from the unit during backwashing, or it may be troublesome, as in the case of spent acid from regeneration of a cation exchanger. The proper treatment of these wastes requires an evaluation of each step in the regeneration process to determine the amount and flow rate of the waste from the regeneration step and the concentration of contaminants.

As an example of the importance of studying each step in the regeneration process, when a sodium zeolite system is installed to follow a hot process softener, there is essentially no undesirable material in the backwash from the zeolite, so this entire flow is reclaimed by returning the zeolite backwash to the head of the filters to reclaim both the heat and the water. There may be useful chemical values even in spent regenerants; spent caustic from regeneration of a strong anion exchanger may be used to regenerate the weakly basic anion exchanger. And finally, careful attention should be given to recovery of discharge from the rinsing operation; cation exchanger rinse following acid regeneration has been used as cooling tower makeup to provide alkalinity reduction. Hot zeolite rinse water can be returned to the filter inlet when its hardness reaches the normal inlet hardness level. Spent caustic from anion exchanger regeneration has been used as salt-cake makeup in kraft pulping operations. Under the right circumstances, this could be combined with the spent sulfuric acid.

If no use can be made of the spent regenerants, they must be balanced to produce a neutral effluent that will not upset the overall plant waste treatment system. This may have an influence on such decisions as whether or not to install a degasifier for CO_2 removal and at which efficiency to operate the exchangers. For example, there may be no need to improve the efficiency of anion exchanger regeneration with caustic if the spent acid from regeneration of the cation exchanger is going to require extra alkali for neutralization.

There is a variety to select from in choosing the best ion exchange unit for each particular process. The simplest and most common ion exchange unit is a vertical cylindrical vessel designed for downflow operation and making provision for backwash, chemical injection, rinsing, and normal service operations. Figure 12.9 shows a cutaway of a typical unit for this 4-step cycle. In this system, the chemical regenerant flows downward through the ion exchange bed, and normal flow of process water is also downward.

Countercurrent Regeneration

If the system requires more efficient chemical utilization, countercurrent regeneration can be used. In this case, the service flow may be upward through a vessel that is completely packed with ion exchange resin. The chemical injection is then downward, or countercurrent, followed by rinse in the same direction. This arrangement has no provision for resin backwashing in place, so periodically the resin must be withdrawn from the unit and cleaned in an

Raw water

Upper distributor

Resin

Acid regenerant

To drain

Lower distributor

Figure 12.23 A method of countercurrent regeneration. The regenerant is introduced up-flow, with the resin bed held in place by a downward flow of water. *(Courtesy of Illinois Water Treatment Company.)*

external vessel for return to the system. External cleaning may be required every 50–100 cycles; but to achieve this frequency it is important that the water supply to the system be clear.

Countercurrent can also be achieved with a more conventional design that provides head room for backwashing, as shown by Figure 12.23. In this case, the service flow is downward, with regeneration flow upward. To prevent the bed from expanding during upflow regeneration, a counterflow of water may be required to balance the hydraulic pressure in the system.

The mixed bed demineralizer operates with a charge of cation and anion resin in the same vessel, with sequences shown in Table 12.10. A typical internal construction is shown in Figure 12.24. Units of this kind are used for polishing

Figure 12.24 View of internals of a mixed bed demineralizer looking downward, showing reinforcing needed to prevent distributor damage from resin movement. *(Courtesy of Illinois Water Treatment Company.)*

Figure 12.25 Condensate polisher designed for cleanup of 6000 gpm of utility station condensate. The resin is regenerated by sluicing from the exchangers to separate cleanup vessels. *(Courtesy of Illinois Water Treatment Company.)*

demineralized water produced in a two-bed system, although they are sometimes used as a complete unit by themselves if the water is of relatively good quality so that organic fouling will not be a problem. Mixed bed demineralizers are frequently used in purification of utility plant condensate, in which case the units operate at very high flow rates because of the high purity of the water being treated. This saves on resin investment. The resin is withdrawn from the processing unit for regeneration in external facilities, so the design of the process unit is quite simple. A typical condensate polisher with external regeneration is shown in Figure 12.25.

Earlier it was mentioned that ion exchange is a cyclic operation. One path toward improved chemical efficiency has been the design of a continuous ion exchange system. One such design which has been commercially successful is illustrated by Figure 12.26. One reason for its slow acceptance has been the improvement in chemical regeneration efficiency through operating conventional units in a countercurrent manner. The continuous ion exchange units are considerably more sophisticated than the conventional units, and early designs were often unreliable.

Powdered Resins

Another unique type of ion exchange system involves the depositing of powdered ion exchange resins on the surface of a septum-type filter. The powdered resins are a mixture of regenerated cation and anion resins, so they have some capacity for pickup of ionic materials, but they also perform as excellent filters, lending themselves ideally to the filtration of utility plant condensate. Such a unit, illustrated by Figure 12.27, offers cost savings over conventional ion

Figure 12.26   Typical arrangement of a continuous ion exchange system. *(Courtesy of Himsley Engineering Company.)*

exchange beds with external regeneration, particularly when handling nuclear plant condensate where spent resins must be disposed of because of radioactive contamination. The volume to be handled is generally much less with the powdered resin system than with the packed columns.

Finally, in the preparation of ultra-pure water for such services as transistor manufacture, special ion exchange designs are used where the ion exchange material is in cartridge form and is expendable. A high purity system of this kind might include a primary demineralizer followed by an evaporator, with the distillate being processed through ion exchange cartridges and filtered through membrane filters at the point of use. The many facets of ion exchange technology cannot be explored in a general text on water treatment such as this. The production of ultrahigh purity water and selective ion exchangers are only two aspects of interest to water treatment specialists that require their own field of literature. But one final item of special interest that deserves mention is the availability of an ion exchange material having both cation and anion exchange sites on the same polymer backbone. These sites are weak electrolytes, so they may be regenerated to their weak acid and weak base forms with hot water.

This formula for such an ion exchanger may be represented as

$$\left[\begin{array}{c} \quad\quad\quad NH_2 \\ \quad\quad\quad | \\ -R-R-R-R- \\ \quad | \\ \quad COOH \end{array} \right]_x$$

Figure 12.27 Powdered resin filtration system. Cutaway showing internals of condensate polishing unit (top). Typical installation of filter unit, skid mounted (bottom). *(Courtesy of Graver Water Conditioning Company).*

and the exchange reaction with NaCl in solution is:

When the resin is regenerated with hot water, the NH_2 group becomes basic, and the carboxylic group returns to the acid form:

A schematic diagram showing how such a resin may be used in a continuous ion exchange system for water desalination is shown in Figure 12.28. This process may make it possible to use low-grade industrial heat sources beneficially for the first time. This process should become competitive with other desalination processes with which it is comparable in yield and production of reject brine.

EVALUATION OF ION EXCHANGE RESIN PERFORMANCE

Although water is known as the universal solvent, industrial grade ion exchange materials are relatively impervious to it. However, certain changes appear in the ion exchange material during its lifetime, as it cycles from regenerated to exhausted form, and users of ion exchange materials should budget for a replacement of about 10% per year of cation resin and 20% per year of anion resin.

Capacity Variance Normal

A single ion exchange unit operating on a constant quality influent will show variations in capacity from one run to another, basically due to inability to achieve perfect flow distribution with a flat wave front through the ion exchange bed. Deviations of 5–10% each cycle are not unusual. A steady falloff of capacity, however, is a matter of real concern because it may lower effluent quality, decrease chemical utilization efficiency, and make it difficult for the operator to properly control the system.

A simple reason for loss of capacity may be lost material due to excessive backwash, resin flotation induced by the presence of gas or vapor in the water during backwash, or loss through an internal distributor due to mechanical failure. So, observation of the bed and a periodic measurement of bed level, always done after backwashing and draining at the end of the exhaustion period, is the first step in investigating capacity loss. If the bed is not flat, the causes of disturbances that create the unevenness in the bed should be investigated. While the ion exchange bed is open for inspection, a core sample should be taken for examination. A one-inch diameter copper tube or conduit will extract ample material for examination.

Most capacity problems can be attributed to dirty ion exchange beds, and this is usually caused by improper backwash. For adequate cleaning, the bed should be expanded until it is very close to the backwash offtake in the top of the ion exchange unit, and this requires adjustment of the backwash as water temperature changes. In effect, dirt moves at a higher velocity through the bed than it does when it reaches the bed surface and passes into the freeboard space above the expanded bed. This is why it is important that the expanded bed reach very closely to the level of the backwash offtake.

Even when flow rate is adequate, backwash time may be inadequate. This is particularly true of anion resins, which are commonly backwashed at a flow rate of about 3 gpm/sq ft (0.12 m³/min/m²) corresponding to a rise rate of only about 5 in/min (12.7 cm/min). If the freeboard is 30 in (0.76 m), which is common, it will require at least six minutes before the surface of the bed has expanded to the backwash offtake, and additional time must be allowed for

TABLE 12.10 Sequence of Steps in Regenerating a Mixed Bed Demineralizer

1. Backwash to separate resins with upper layer of anion resin and lower of cation resin.
2. Settle bed.
3. Commence regeneration, with acid upflow through cation bed, caustic downflow through anion bed, and spent liquor withdrawn at interface.
4. Discontinue chemical feed and flush feedlines.
5. Displace chemical from both resin sections.
6. Fast rinse cation section while continuing displacement of anion section.
7. Rinse downflow through both sections.
8. Drain water from freeboard to 3–5″ above bed.
9. Air mix from bottom to fluidize bed.
10. While air mixing, dewater bed through drawoff at the interface collector.
11. Refill unit slowly through bottom distributor.
12. Final rinse downflow of acceptable quality.

the solids accumulated within the bed to be washed free and discharged from the unit.

The second most common cause of erratic capacity is channeling, which can be detected fairly reliably by the surface appearance. If the surface is uneven, it is helpful to probe the surface if there is a supporting bed beneath the ion exchange resin, to see if the supporting bed itself has been upset. The level of the supporting bed can be readily felt by probing with a stiff wire or rod. Some ion exchange units are equipped with underdrain systems having strainer nozzles, and the plugging of these will cause an uneven pattern of distribution; corrosion may actually destroy the threads of these nozzles and cause them to break off, allowing a full flow of water to come through the opening.

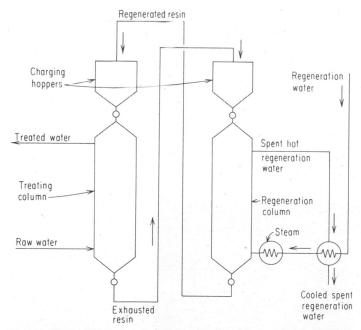

Figure 12.28 Bifunctional resin system for demineralizing brackish water, using heat for regeneration.

Figure 12.29 axes and labels:
- Y-axis: Effluent salinity, % NaCl (0 to 14)
- X-axis: Minutes after start of brining (0 to 70)
- "B" Good elution plug flow
- "A" Poor elution, due to dilution or channeling

Figure 12.29   Evaluating regenerant distribution by elution studies.

Regenerant Concentration Important

Incorrect chemical application is a third important cause of poor resin performance. There is an optimum concentration for each application, so the first
step in investigating this potential cause of trouble is to determine the incoming
concentration of regenerating chemical. If this is correct, then there may be
some problem in the regenerant distribution system or in excessive dilution of
the chemical between the distributor and the bed surface as it passes through
the freeboard. To promote piston-like flow during regeneration, the regenerant
distributor should be no more than three inches above bed level.

Detection of regeneration problems is relatively easy by following an elution
study during the chemical injection period. Samples are taken from the bottom
collector at regular intervals, the solution strength is measured, and the strength
is plotted versus time on a graph. Figure 12.29 shows poor elution characteristics, with an uneven wave front passing down through the bed during
regeneration, evidenced by excessive dilution and departure from piston displacement characteristics. Curve B shows the same unit after correction of the
regeneration procedure.

If none of these factors proves to be the cause of faulty performance, it may
be that the effluent quality is simply being spoiled by bypass of raw water
through a multiport valve or the individual valve system directly into the
effluent. For example, backwash is normally accomplished by using raw water,
and the backwash is fed to the bottom of the unit to the same point where
effluent is normally withdrawn. A leak through the backwash control unit could

Figure   12.30   Gel-type   resin
containing   a   large   amount   of
loose precipitate, indicating improper backwash. This condition
is responsible for most problems with ion exchange systems.

Figure 12.31 Badly cracked gel-type resin. This may be caused by internal precipitate or osmotic shock, the latter being rather common in hot zeolite units if pressure is suddenly released.

cause raw water to appear in the effluent. If there is a multiport valve in the system, this leakage can be verified by taking a sample from the effluent of the multiport valve and comparing this to a sample taken from the bottom header of the ion exchange unit before it approaches the multiport valve connection.

Finally, resin characteristics may have changed to produce poor results. The change may be a physical one, with the development of excessive fines; it may be caused by the accumulation of fouling materials on the surface of the ion exchange resin, with metal oxides commonly found on the cation resin and organic material commonly found within the pores of the anion resin. Or, the resin structure itself may have been attacked by the water environment, most commonly caused by the presence of oxidizing agents.

Troubleshooting Approaches

Sometimes, the cause of trouble can be observed by using a low-power magnifying glass and comparing the resin sample taken from the unit with a sample of fresh material retained from the initial resin shipment. This examination may reveal the presence of excessive fines, fractured particles, or debris in the resin mix or coating the resin particles. Illustrations of these situations are shown in Figures 12.30 through 12.33. If visual observation does not provide the clue, then a complete resin analysis should be undertaken. Three examples of resin analyses are shown in Tables 12.11, 12.12, and 12.13.

The cation resin shown in Table 12.11 was sampled from a sodium zeolite softener, and the analysis is compared to the analysis of new material.

A review of the analysis shows that there are significant changes from new material. Loss in total capacity is caused by breakage of cross-linkages in the polymer with consequent swelling, as shown by increased water content. Increase in water retention from a typical 53 to about 60.5% causes a drop in total

Figure   12.32 Inorganically fouled gel-type resin showing both external and internal fouling. Barium and strontium frequently contribute to this problem in units regenerated with H_2SO_4.

Figure 12.33 External organic and inorganic fouling of gel-type resin.

capacity from 40 kgr/cu ft to 28 kgr/cu ft. Since dry weight capacity (measured in meq/g of oven-dried resin) is almost equal to typical new resin, there has been no loss of ion exchange sites.

The shift of the wet screen analysis from 20 mesh toward 50 mesh indicates either poor sampling (most of the sample from the bed surface) or gradual production of fines. The large proportion of 50 mesh suggests gradual buildup of pressure loss, which may be affecting performance.

Since the increase in water retention is caused by attack of the resin structure at the cross-links, the water supply should be examined to determine the cause of attack. In a hot lime–zeolite system, a usual cause is dissolved oxygen. Catalyzed sodium sulfite may be applied to lime-treated water ahead of the filters and zeolite softeners, and also to the regenerant brine. This resin will continue to perform well to a water retention capacity of about 70%; removing the cause of attack will delay the time when this point is reached. Care should be exercised in backwashing, since the lower density, swollen resin expands more during backwash than heavier, fresh resin.

Anion resins are generally much more sensitive to degradation than cation resins, particularly through irreversible fouling with organic material. The organic material may have been present in the original water supply, but it is often the accumulation of breakdown products from attack of the cation resin preceding it.

Table 12.12 shows the analysis of a strongly basic anion resin from a demineralizer system where the loss of the salt-splitting capacity is very evident. (Salt-splitting is the ability of OH-form anion resin to convert a solution of NaCl to NaOH.)

TABLE 12.11   Cation Resin Evaluation—Styrene-Sulfonic Acid Type

Characteristic	Sample	Typical New
Total capacity (T.C.):		
meq/ml	1.27	1.8
meq/g	4.96	4.9
kgr/cu ft	28	40
Water retention capacity, %	60.5	53
Wet screen analysis:		
% retained on 16 mesh	1.2	4–8
% retained on 20 mesh	14.1	35–45
% retained on 30 mesh	20.3	35–45
% retained on 35 mesh	9.5	7–10
% retained on 40 mesh	11.3	3–8
% retained on 50 mesh	19.1	2–5
% through 50 mesh	24.5	0–1

TABLE 12.12   Anion Resin Evaluation

Characteristic	Sample	Typical
Total capacity (T.C.):		
meq/ml	1.17	1.4
meq/g	2.43	3.0
kgr/cu ft	25	30
Salt-splitting capacity, % of T. C.	17	95–100
Water retention capacity, %	50.0	36–42
Wet screen analysis		
% retained on 16 mesh	0.2	1–3
% retained on 20 mesh	0.2	20–30
% retained on 30 mesh	18.6	40–50
% retained on 35 mesh	58.8	15–25
% retained on 40 mesh	14.4	5–10
% retained on 50 mesh	4.9	2–5
% through 50 mesh	2.7	0–1

This sample shows measurable loss of exchange sites and severe loss of salt-splitting capacity. Even if the water being treated has a low ratio of weak acids to total acids, this reduction of salt-splitting capacity is undoubtedly producing short service runs. The resin appears to have reached the end of its useful life. The water supply should be examined to determine whether this type of anion resin is applicable to this plant. If so, plant records should be examined to determine how long this resin has been in service. After replacement with new resin, a program of annual resin evaluation should be instituted to plan for periodic resin additions or replacement to maintain uniform operating results.

Although screen analysis shows a shift from 20 mesh, there is little evidence of fines. Operating problems are due to loss of resin capacity rather than to hydraulic problems caused by change in particle size.

The analysis of another type of strongly basic anion resin is shown in Table 12.13. In this analysis, reduction in total capacity is insignificant. Loss in salt-splitting capacity, while measurable, should cause little change in operating results, since exchange capacity is in the 10–12 kgr range, and salt-splitting capacity is still approximately 20 kgr. The higher the percentage of weak acids in water, the more pronounced will be the reduction in exchange capacity as salt-splitting capacity is lost. Analysis shows the resin is in good physical and chemical condition; the plant should be performing up to capacity.

TABLE 12.13   Anion Resin Evaluation

Characteristic	Sample	Typical
Total capacity (T.C.):		
meq/ml	1.19	1.3
meq/g	3.57	3.2
kgr/cu ft	26	28
Salt-splitting capacity, % of T.C.	75	95–100
Water retention capacity, %	N.D.	44–48
Wet screen analysis		
% retained on 16 mesh	0.2	1–3
% retained on 20 mesh	19.4	20–30
% retained on 30 mesh	49.1	40–50
% retained on 35 mesh	16.9	15–25
% retained on 40 mesh	10.0	5–10
% retained on 50 mesh	4.0	2–5
% through 50 mesh	0.4	0–1

TABLE 12.14   Ion Exchange Evaluation—Sulfonic Resin, Sodium Form

Total exchange capacity*			Water retention capacity, %	62.3
% of original, when completely			Microscopic examination	
cleaned	71		Bead size	
meq*/ml (wet)	1.34		% Normal	50
kilograins/cu ft	29.2		% Large	—
Salt splitting capacity*			% Small	50
% of original, when completely			Broken beads	
cleaned	—		%	50
meq†/ml (wet)				
Small column capacity*				
Weak acid resin, % of original,				
when completely cleaned	—			
kgr/cu ft	—			
Weak base resin, % of original,				
when completely cleaned	—			
kgr/cu ft	—			

Metal contaminants analysis

Elements (g/cu ft) as such			
Iron (Fe)	20	Magnesium (Mg)	—
Silica (Si)	26	Calcium (Ca)	—
Aluminum (Al)	21	Barium (Ba)	1
Manganese (Mn)	2	Strontium (Sr)	11
Chromium (Cr)	—	Zinc (Zn)	—
Copper (Cu)	—	Chlorine (Cl)	3
Nickel (Ni)	—	Phosphorus (P)	2

Condition of resin	
Chemical	Fair
Physical	Very poor

* meq/ml × 21.8 kgr/cu ft
† Optimum capacity (not operating capacity)

Various forms of analyses are used to evaluate the performance and characteristics of ion exchange materials. These tables list the screen analysis in detail, but this is seldom required. Sometimes of equal importance is the composition of materials coating the resin surface or found loose in the resin bed. Tables 12.14 and 12.15 are representative analyses of cation resins including an assay of the crud contaminating the resin. In neither case was a sample of the original material provided, but observation indicated that it was the typical sulfonated styrene cation exchanger used in most industrial applications.

In the case of Table 12.14, the analysis shows the cation resin to be in poor physical condition, but still having an acceptable chemical composition. There has been an increase in water retention capacity from a normal of 50–53%, showing some decross-linking, but this has not yet reached serious proportions.

The resin sample was observed to be mixed with large amounts of loosely-held particulate matter and fouled with organic substances. The contaminants on the resin include large amounts of silica, moderate amounts of iron, aluminum and strontium, plus small quantities of manganese, barium, chlorine and phosphorus. The accumulation of particulate matter within the resin bed suggests that higher backwash rates may be required to improve performance. Tests of the resin indicated that capacity loss could not be restored by any chemical cleaning procedures, and the loss was caused by the contaminants found on the resin. In this case, even though the resin has not undergone extensive physical degradation, since it cannot be cleaned, replacement is recommended.

In the next example, Table 12.15, the cation resin is in fairly good physical condition, but very poor chemical condition. This cation resin is also mixed with large amounts of loose particulates, and is contaminated with extremely high concentrations of iron, large amounts of chlorine and phosphorus, and moderate amounts of silica and copper.

The water retention capacity has increased to 71.8%, at which point the material is extremely light, difficult to contain during backwash, and subject to early failure at an unpredictable time. The capacity is so low that the resin is essentially of marginal value and should be replaced at an early date. The loss in cross-linkage should be investigated; this particular system is operating on a municipal supply, and free chlorine in the supply water should be measured.

TABLE 12.15   Ion Exchange Evaluation—Softener

Total exchange capacity*		Water retention capacity, %	71.8
% of original, when completely			
cleaned	48	Microscopic examination	
meq†/ml (wet)	0.91	Bead size	
kilograins/cu ft	19.8	% Normal	80
		% Large	—
		% Small	20
		Broken beads	
		%	20

Metal contaminants analysis			
Elements (g/cu ft) as such			
Iron (Fe)	270	Magnesium (Mg)	—
Silica (Si)	6	Calcium (Ca)	—
Aluminum (Al)	—	Barium (Ba)	—
Manganese (Mn)	—	Strontium (Sr)	4
Chromium (Cr)	1	Zinc (Zn)	—
Copper (Cu)	20	Chlorine (Cl)	120
Nickel (Ni)	—	Phosphorus (P)	74
		Lead (Pb)	2

Condition of resin	
Chemical	Very poor
Physical	Poor

* meq/ml × 21.8 kgr/cu ft
† Optimum capacity (not operating capacity)

SUGGESTED READING

Kunin, Robert: *Elements of Ion Exchange*, Reinhold, New York, 1960.
Nordell, Eskel: *Water Treatment for Industrial and Other Uses*, Reinhold, New York, 1961.

Chapter 13
Neutralization

Acid-base reactions are among the most prevalent of the chemical processes used in water conditioning. It is fortunate that commercially available acids and bases are relatively low in cost. Typical costs of acids and bases used in water treatment are shown in Table 13-1, which also indicates the relative value of these materials on an equivalent basis.

In addition to these chemicals, there are chemical wastes having residual acid or base values that can be used for neutralization in waste treatment. For example, pickle liquor from the steel industry is useful both for its acid value and for the iron it contains as a coagulant; sludge from lime–soda water softening is a good source of alkali for neutralization of acid wastes.

Progress in the neutralization of an acid or base is easily measured by pH. However, the practicality of using pH to control the neutralization reaction is greatly influenced by the buffer capacity of the water. For example, it is much easier to neutralize an acidic waste containing hydrochloric acid to a pH of 7.5 with sodium carbonate than with caustic soda. This is illustrated by Figure 13.1.

Treating an acidic wastewater may be relatively easy because the allowable effluent pH range is fairly broad, usually 5–9. However, adjustment of the Stability Index of a water requires controlling pH to a rather narrow range, so the equipment for feeding acid or alkali to achieve a specified Stability Index in process water is generally more sophisticated than equipment used in a wastewater treatment plant.

EXAMPLES OF ACID-BASE REACTIONS

The correction of the Stability Index with lime is shown in Figure 13.2. This is a relatively common problem, although lime is not always used because it is more difficult to handle than liquid caustic or soda ash. When used in large quantities,

TABLE 13.1 Acid and Alkali Costs for Neutralization

Chemical	Specification	Cost,* ¢/lb	Equiv. cost,† $/lb equiv.
Sulfuric acid [H₂SO₄ (Oil of Vitriol)]	66° Be'—93%	2.50‡	1.30
Hydrochloric acid [HCl (muriatic acid)]	20° Be'—32%	1.80‡	2.12
Limestone (CaCO₃)	200 mesh, 93%	0.40‡	0.22
Quicklime (CaO)	Lump, 90%	2.45§	0.76
		1.76‡	0.55
Hydrated lime [Ca(OH)₂]	Pulv, 93%	2.30§	0.92
Soda ash (Na₂CO₃)	Light, 50% Na₂O	5.35§	3.10
		3.50‡	2.03
Caustic soda (NaOH)	Dry	15.5§	6.20
	Dry	14.5¶	5.80
	50% liquid	8.0*	3.20
Ammonia (NH₃)	Liquid	9.0‡	1.53

* Cost is given in cents per pound of product as shipped, not including freight, except for 50% liquid caustic, where cost is ¢/lb NaOH.
† Cost per lb-equivalent is ¢/lb × lb/lb equivalent; lb-equivalent is a lb-mole/valence.
‡ Bulk cost in tank cars, tank trucks, or hopper cars.
§ Cost in bags.
¶ Cost in drums.

it is purchased as pebble lime (quicklime, CaO) and slaked to Ca(OH)₂. A typical feeding system is shown in Figure 13.3. Figure 13.2 shows incremental additions of lime to a water requiring stabilization. The first increment of 6 mg/l is added for neutralization of all of the CO_2: additional lime then converts HCO_3 to CO_3^{-2} in successive steps. The resulting pH and Stability Index at each increment is shown in the same tabulation. These data are plotted in Figure 13.4.

Figure 13.1 Neutralization of acidic waste.

Identification of Analyses Tabulated Below:

A. Hypothetical Water

B. A + 6 mg/l Lime (as CaCO₃)

C. B + 4 mg/l Lime (as CaCO₃)

D. C + 5 mg/l Lime (as CaCO₃)

E. D + 5 mg/l Lime (as CaCO₃)

F. _____

Constituent	As	A	B	C	D	E	F
Calcium	$CaCO_3$	60	66	70	75	80	
Magnesium	"	20	20	20	20	20	
Sodium	"	10	10	10	10	10	
Total Electrolyte	$CaCO_3$	90	96	100	105	110	
Bicarbonate	$CaCO_3$	55	61	57	52	47	
Carbonate	"	0	0	8	18	28	
Hydroxyl	"	0	0	0	0	0	
Sulfate	"	30	30	30	30	30	
Chloride	"	5	5	5	5	5	
Nitrate	"	0	0	0	0	0	
M Alk.	$CaCO_3$	55	61	65	70	75	
P Alk.	"	0	0	4	9	14	
Carbon Dioxide		6	0	0	0	0	
pH		7.3	8.3	8.9	9.3	9.5	
Silica		5	5	5	5	5	
Iron	Fe	0.1	0.1	0.1	0.1	0.1	
Turbidity		0	0	0	0	0	
TDS		100	106	110	115	120	
Color		0					
pH_s @ 70° F		8.25	8.2	8.15	8.05	8.0	
S. I. @ 70° F		9.2	8.05	7.14	6.8	6.5	

Figure 13.2 Correction of stability index with lime. Goal: Stability index (S.I.) of 7.0.

Assuming the goal is a Stability Index of 7, the graph shows that this can be accomplished with approximately 13 mg/l lime as $CaCO_3$, resulting in a pH of approximately 9.1.

The equivalent weight of commercial lime [93% $Ca(OH)_2$] is approximately 40, so that lime as calcium carbonate multiplied by 0.8 gives commercial lime requirements.

Another example of Stability Index correction is the reduction of the scaling tendencies of a lime-softened water, which usually remains supersaturated with calcium carbonate even after filtration. The common practice is to recarbonate by injection of CO_2 gas after the sedimentation basins and ahead of filters (see Figure 13.5). However, the same effect can be achieved by the feeding of sulfuric acid (see Figure 13.6).

The results of sulfuric acid addition and recarbonation are markedly different, as shown by Figures 13.7(a) and (b). These are compared in Figure 13.8. Here the safety features and buffer capacity of recarbonation are apparent when the goal is simply to increase the Stability Index above 6.

(a)

(b)

Figure 13.3 Device for slaking and feeding large quantities of lime in water treatment plants. (a) Photo of slaker-feeder assembly. (b) Cutaway showing details of operation. *(Courtesy of Wallace & Tiernan Division, Pennwalt Corporation.)*

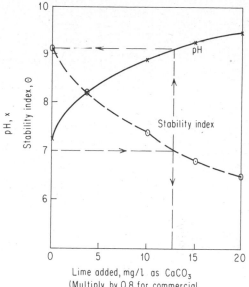

Figure 13.4 Correction of stability index with lime. Goal: S.I. = 7.0 @ 70°F. Required lime = 13 mg/l as $CaCO_3$; 10.4 mg/l as 93% $Ca(OH)_2$. Control point = pH 9.1.

Figure 13.5 Schematic diagram of water flow through recarbonation basin demonstrating how CO_2 bubbles are diffused by the submerged combustion burner at the bottom of the basin, and then further dispersed by the water flow, giving optimum absorption time. *(Courtesy of Ozark-Mahoning Company.)*

Figure 13.6 Adjustable stroke pump with variable-speed DC motor, acid feed proportioned to flow, pH corrected.

Identification of Analyses Tabulated Below:							
A. Hypothetical water				D. $C + 10$ mg/l CO_2 as $CaCO_3$			
B. $A + 10$ mg/l CO_2 as $CaCO_3$				E. $D + 10$ mg/l CO_2 as $CaCO_3$			
C. $B + 10$ mg/l CO_2 as $CaCO_3$				F. $E + 10$ mg/l CO_2 as $CaCO_3$			

Constituent	As	A	B	C	D	E	F
Calcium	$CaCO_3$	140	140	140	140	140	140
Magnesium	"	60	60	60	60	60	60
Sodium	"	20	20	20	20	20	20
Total Electrolyte	$CaCO_3$	220	220	220	220	220	220
Bicarbonate	$CaCO_3$	0	0	10	20	30	40
Carbonate	"	40	50	40	30	20	10
Hydroxyl	"	10	0	0	0	0	0
Sulfate	"	70	70	70	70	70	70
Chloride	"	100	100	100	100	100	100
Nitrate	"						
M Alk.	$CaCO_3$	50	50	50	50	50	50
P Alk.	"	30	25	20	15	10	5
Carbon Dioxide		0	0	0	0	0	0
pH		10.3	10.0	9.8	9.7	9.6	9.5
Silica		10	10	10	10	10	10
Iron	Fe	0	0	0	0	0	0
Turbidity		0	0	0	0	0	0
TDS		250	250	250	250	250	250
Color		0	0	0	0	0	0
pH_s @ $70°F$		7.95	7.95	7.95	7.95	7.95	7.95
S.I. @ $70°F$		5.60	5.95	6.15	6.25	6.35	6.40

Figure 13.7a Correction of stability index with CO_2 (recarbonation of lime-softened water).

Identification of Analyses Tabulated Below:						
A. Hypothetical Water			D. C + 5 mg/1 H_2SO_4 as $CaCO_3$			
B. + 5 mg/1 H_2SO_4 as $CaCO_3$			E. D + 5 mg/1 H_2SO_4 as $CaCO_3$			
C. B + 5 mg/1 H_2SO_4 as $CaCO_3$			F. E + 5 mg/1 H_2SO_4 as $CaCO_3$			

Constituent	As	A	B	C	D	E	F
Calcium	$CaCO_3$	140	140	140	140	140	140
Magnesium	"	60	60	60	60	60	60
Sodium	"	20	20	20	20	20	20
Total Electrolyte	$CaCO_3$	220	220	220	220	220	220
Bicarbonate	$CaCO_3$	0	0	0	5	10	15
Carbonate	"	40	40	40	30	20	10
Hydroxyl	"	10	5	0	0	0	0
Sulfate	"	70	70	70	70	70	70
Chloride	"	100	100	100	100	100	100
Nitrate	"	0	0	0	0	0	0
M Alk.	$CaCO_3$	50	45	40	35	30	25
P Alk.	"	30	25	20	15	10	5
Carbon Dioxide		0	0	0	0		
pH		10.3	10.0	9.9	9.9	9.0	9.6
Silica		10	10	10	10	10	10
Iron	Fe	0	0	0	0	0	0
Turbidity		0	0	0	0	0	0
TDS		250	250	250	250	250	250
Color		0	0	0	0	0	0
pH_s @70° F		7.95	8.0	8.05	8.1	8.2	8.25
S. I. @ 70° F		5.6	6.0	6.2	6.35	6.6	6.9

Figure 13.7b   Correction of stability index with H_2SO_4.

Simple changes in water alkalinity or acidity without regard to Stability Index correction are easily calculated: the reduction of alkalinity, such as application of acid to a sodium zeolite effluent prior to its use as boiler feedwater, requires the addition of 1 mg/l commercial 66° Baumé sulfuric acid for each mg/l of alkalinity reduction needed. An increase in alkalinity requires the addition of 0.8 mg/l caustic or lime for each mg/l alkalinity increase required. These changes in alkalinity are calculated on the basis of calcium carbonate equivalents and then converted to the equivalent weight of the commercial alkali or acid added to the system.

POTENTIAL ENERGY SAVINGS

An example of the reduction of alkalinity with acid in the treatment of boiler makeup is shown in Figure 13.9. In this case, the alkalinity is added to the

Figure 13.8 Comparison of recarbonation to acidification of lime-softened effluent.

makeup system ahead of the zeolite. There is some risk in such an operation because it requires excellent acid feed and control equipment, and protection of the piping between the injection point and the deaerator, since corrosion could introduce objectionable iron. However, often the gain in reduced blowdown, with its attendant heat savings, justifies the installation of sophisticated equipment that can accomplish these results using a basic system already in operation in the power plant. The risk is minimized by adding the acid ahead of rather than downstream of the zeolite softener, since the sodium zeolite could pick up hydrogen ions in the event of accidental overfeed of acid.

An operation of this kind, and even less sensitive situations, requires the installation of properly designed feed systems to avoid the consequences of over- or under-feeding acid. Figure 13.6 illustrates a system that can handle the chemical injection problem by proportioning the flow of chemical to the flow of water to be treated, and correcting the basic dosage with a pH controller, which in this case adjusts the stroke of the pump. In this system, there must be adequate lag built into the mixing chamber in which the pH is measured so that the controller can function properly without overriding or underriding while hunting for the pH setpoint.

Ion exchange has been applied to acid-base neutralization problems in a unique way: Weak base anion exchangers and carboxylic cation exchangers have the ability to pick up acid and release it as a neutral solution in treating a fluctuating wastewater which is periodically acidic and alkaline. If the excess free acid is balanced by the alkalinity, regeneration is unnecessary, and only periodic backwash is needed to keep the system operating. Although more expensive than a chemical feed system for the same purpose, it saves space and eliminates the maintenance costs of equipment and controls inherent in a chemical feeder. This type of system has been used to neutralize spent demineralizer regenerants. Figure 13.10 shows the pH record of the effluent of an ion exchange neutralizer in this kind of service. Although the pH fluctuates, it is kept within limits of 6–9 usually specified in municipal sewer codes.

Identification of Analyses Tabulated Below:

A. Zeolite Softened Makeup (1)   D. Concentrated 10 X in Boiler

B. After H₂SO₄   E.

C. "B" After Deareator * (2)   F.

Constituent	As	A	B	C	D	E	F
Calcium	CaCO₃	Nil	Nil	Nil	Nil		
Magnesium	"	Nil	Nil	Nil	Nil		
Sodium	"	125	125	125	1250		
Total Electrolyte	CaCO₃	125	125	125	1250		
Bicarbonate	CaCO₃	90	30	30	0		
Carbonate	"	0	0	0	50		
Hydroxyl	"	0	0	0	250		
Sulfate	"	15	75	75	750		
Chloride	"	20	20	20	200		
Nitrate	"	0	0	0	0		
M Alk.	CaCO₃	90	30	30	300		
P Alk.	"	0	0	0	275		
Carbon Dioxide		10	70	0	0		
pH		7.1	5.8	8.3	11.7		
Silica		3	3	3	30		
Iron	Fe	0	0	0	0		
Turbidity		0	0	0	0		
TDS		150	150	150	1500		
Color		0	0	0	0		

(1) If max. boiler alkalinity is 300 mg/l max. concentration ratio
is 300/90 = 3.3 ≡ 30% blowdown.
(2) After alkalinity reduction, max. conc. is 10 (column D)
≡ 10% blowdown.
* Not including steam dilution.

Figure 13.9 Alkalinity reduction of boiler makeup.

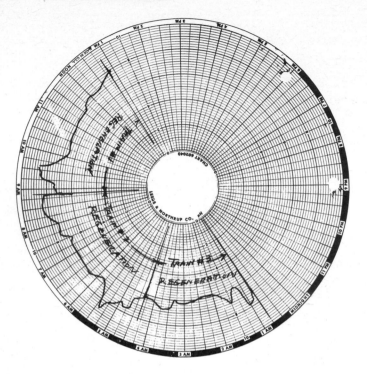

Figure 13.10 Chart of pH recorder monitoring the effluent from an ion exchange neutralizer. *(Courtesy of Cochrane Division, the Crane Company.)*

Chapter 14

Degasification

Water may contain a variety of gases in solution as well as minerals and organic matter. Because oxygen and nitrogen are the predominant gases in the atmosphere, surface water contains these two gases. Carbon dioxide is another common atmospheric gas; its concentration varies from place to place depending to a large extent on industrial activity.

There is an important distinction between oxygen and nitrogen on the one hand and carbon dioxide on the other: the former do not ionize in water, so these molecules exert a gas pressure in solution; carbon dioxide forms carbonic acid, which ionizes in water, so only the unreacted part can exert a gas pressure. At a pH below about 4.5, all of the CO_2 dissolved in water is present as a gas; above about 8.5, all of it is ionized. Other common ionizing gases are H_2S, HCN and NH_3.

The products of respiration influence the composition of gases in water. In surface waters, algae produce oxygen in the presence of sunlight through the photosynthetic reaction of carbon dioxide and water to produce carbohydrates. Bacteria, on the other hand, utilize oxygen in their metabolism and produce CO_2. The action of soil bacteria frequently produces high levels of carbon dioxide in well waters, and deep well waters are usually devoid of oxygen because these bacteria have removed it from the percolating ground water.

HENRY'S LAW

The amount of gas dissolved in water is directly proportional to the partial pressure of that gas in the vapor space above the water/gas interface. This is known as Henry's Law. Another important consideration of gas solubility is Dalton's Law, which states that the total pressure of a mixture of gases is made up of the individual pressures of those gases, and these are in direct relationship to their molar or volume ratios in the vapor space. For example, air normally contains about 80% nitrogen and 20% oxygen by volume and the standard atmospheric pressure is 760 millimeters of mercury. Dalton's Law states that the partial pressure of O_2 in the atmosphere is 152 millimeters $(.20 \times 760)$ and the partial pressure of N_2 is 608 millimeters $(.80 \times 760)$.

Temperature is an important factor in gas solubility; solubility decreases as temperature increases. This is because the increasing temperature results in an increasing vapor pressure of the water itself, so that escaping water molecules at the liquid-gas surface force away other gas molecules.

A final factor important to the solution of gases in water is the diffusion of the gas molecules through water. The rate of diffusion increases with increasing temperature as molecular activity increases and the viscosity of the water decreases.

In the removal of gas from water, the mass transfer principles that apply to the process are analogous to the principles of heat transfer. The rate of gas transfer is directly proportional to three factors as shown by the following equation:

$$Q = Ka\Delta P$$

where Q = quantity of gas transferred (lb/hr)
   K = gas transfer coefficient (lb/hr/sq ft/mm Hg)
   a = area (sq ft)
   ΔP = log mean driving force (mm Hg)

The gas transfer coefficient, K, is a function of both the specific gas being transferred and also the geometry of the system. As noted below, there are various shaped packing materials that can be used in packed towers (Figure 14.1); there is also variety in the designs of diffuser elements and atomizers. At the liquid-gas interface, there is assumed to be a liquid film on one side and a gas film on the other, and these films are affected by the nature of the liquid and the gas, with their combined effects influencing the gas transfer coefficient.

The area factor, a, is the total surface area created in the degasification chamber by packing, by producing numerous fine water droplets, or by forming minute gas bubbles. In the case of tower packing, each size and shape of packing material—raschig rings, berl saddles, spirals—has a definite exposed area:volume relationship. This ratio increases as the size of the packing decreases, but so, too, does the pressure required to force stripping gas through the packing.

The gas driving force can be calculated readily for nonionizing gases. Ionizing

Raschig rings   Berl saddles   Rings with
                                         internal ramps

Telleretts   Pall rings

Figure 14.1   Varieties of common tower packings.

Figure 14.2 Packed column degasifier.

gases often present a difficult problem, because the pH of the system establishes the degree of ionization, and the pH changes as the gas is removed.

DEGASIFICATION DESIGNS

The three types of degasification units commonly used in water treatment are shown in Figures 14.2, 14.3, and 14.4.

The first of these is a packed stripping tower. Water is introduced at the top, sometimes through a spray pipe, and allowed to percolate through the packing against a countercurrent of gas other than the gas being removed. Typically air is used as the stripping gas to remove dissolved gases such as carbon dioxide, ammonia, hydrogen sulfide, or methane.

In the second type of degasifier, water is atomized into an inert gas, which is continually withdrawn as the stripped gas leaves the water surface.

Figure 14.3 Spray-type tower used as a degasifier. This type of design lends itself to ammonia stripping in treating wastewaters.

Figure 14.4 Diffusers used for degasification of water in open, exposed areas.

In the third design, the stripping gas is introduced into the water through submerged diffusers, bubbles its way up through the water, carrying the stripped gas out of the aqueous environment into the atmosphere above.

The packed stripping tower is commonly used in refineries and paper mills for steam stripping of sour condensates. Figure 14.5 shows a refinery application, and Table 14.1 shows the analysis of a sour condensate before and after stripping. The steam consumption for this operation is very high, in the range of 0.5–1.0 lb/gallon. The basic reason is that the gases being removed are ionized, so that they exert only a fraction of the potential vapor pressure that would be available if pH could be properly adjusted. Unfortunately, the ammonia is best removed at a pH over 10 and the H_2S and HCN are best removed at a pH below 6; in the pH range of 7–8, these gases are highly ionized (Figure 14.6). It can be seen from this that a more practical system for stripping sour condensate might be a two-stage operation with alkali added for increasing the pH for ammonia removal in the first tower, and acid added for reduction of pH for stripping of H_2S and HCN in the second tower. There are many other complex reactions occurring in a system like this, for example, the formation of thiocyanates and ferrocyanides, further reducing the potential for gas stripping.

A similar design stripping column is used for the vacuum deaeration of cold water, as illustrated in Figure 14.7. In this kind of unit, vacuum is usually created by steam ejectors. Steam consumption can often be minimized by having two stages of stripping sections in the same column, with a steam jet ejector on each

TABLE 14.1 Refinery Sour Water Stripper

	In	Out
Sulfides, as HS, mg/l	1876	0
Ammonia, as NH_3, mg/l	1480	194
Cyanides, as CN, mg/l	24	2
Phenol, mg/l	102	65
pH	9–9.5	7.5
Temperature	195°F	230°F

Physical Design Data: 60 gpm flow, 3500 lb/hr steam; tower diameter 3′6″, packing 12′ of 1″ Raschig rings.

Reference: API Manual 1969, Chapter 10, Table 10-1.

Figure 14.5 Typical arrangement for stripping column operation processing refinery sour water.

stage. The vacuum produced is calculated to reduce the partial pressure of oxygen to less than 50% of that corresponding to the partial pressure equivalent to the desired effluent oxygen concentration. This type of tower usually uses raschig rings as packing.

Still a third variation in the design of stripping columns is shown in Figure 14.8, which is a stripper using air for stripping out carbon dioxide. This is of fiberglas construction, with raschig ring packing. This unit may also be designed of wood stave construction to eliminate corrosion problems, and the packing itself consists of layers of wooden slats 3–4" apart. The open spacing allows for

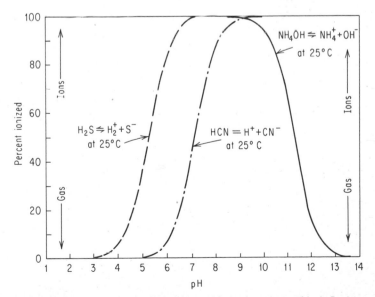

Figure 14.6 Ionization of weak acids and bases in water and its influence on internal gas pressure.

Figure 14.7 Vacuum deacrator at an oil production operation. *(Courtesy of L*A Water Conditioning Company.)*

a low pressure drop through either design of tower, so that the air blower is
seldom required to operate in excess of 3″ H₂O discharge pressure. This provides economical gas removal.

A final design of packed column is one of the oldest devices in water treatment, the tray-type deaerating heater. In this unit, the packing is made up of a
series of stainless steel or cast iron slotted trays, and steam is used both for heating and stripping oxygen out of the water. This design is still very popular in
boiler plants because it is more efficient thermally than the atomizing type
deaerators described below.

Probably the major use for the atomizing-type stripper is as a deaerating
heater in steam power plants. These units atomize the water by the energy of
steam passing through an atomizing nozzle, and the steam both heats and strips
the water of its dissolved oxygen content (Figure 14.9). Since the condensation
of the steam in the vapor space creates the steam flow needed for atomization,
this device requires a temperature difference of at least 50°F between the water
entering the vessel for stripping and the steam. Because of the pressure drop
across the atomizer, this device is less efficient than a tray-type deaerating
heater.

The final design category, submerged diffusion, is seldom used unless certain
space requirements favor it. The gas transfer coefficient is poor, and to be effective there must be some means for continually sweeping the surface of the basin
by adequate ventilation to carry away the stripped gases.

CHEMICAL REMOVAL

While most gas removal in water treatment is done by mechanical action, chemical destruction of these gases is an equally important process. Ion exchange is also effective.

Even at high temperatures, there is some residual dissolved oxygen after water has been deaerated in a power plant deaerator. Sodium sulfite or hydrazine can be fed to the effluent to react against the possibility of accidental oxygen leakage into the system, as shown in the following chemical reactions:

$$2Na_2SO_3 + O_2 \rightarrow 2Na_2SO_4 \tag{1}$$
$$N_2H_4 + O_2 \rightarrow 2H_2O + N_2 \tag{2}$$

Because of the high temperatures found in the feedwater system, oxygen corrosion can be rapid. Catalysts are usually included in the sulfite formulation to assure fast, complete oxygen destruction.

While carbon dioxide can be stripped from water in the free gas form, it can also be neutralized by the application of lime, caustic, or sodium carbonate. The carbon dioxide that escapes with the steam can be neutralized by the application

Figure 14.8   FRP decarbonator. *(Courtesy of The Permutit Company.)*

Figure 14.9 Atomizing-type deaerating heater. *(Courtesy of Cochrane Division, the Crane Company.)*

of amines to the system. In this case, the amine forms a bicarbonate compound, and actually develops some alkalinity in the condensate.

Carbon dioxide is also removed in the anion exchanger of a demineralizer.

Ammonia can be destroyed chemically by chlorination. The initial reaction forms chloramine, and until this material has been completely broken down, the application of chlorine does not produce a free chlorine residual.

$$NH_3 + Cl_2 \rightarrow NH_2Cl + HCl \tag{3}$$
$$2NH_3 + 3Cl_2 \rightarrow N_2 + 6HCl \tag{4}$$

When the ammonia has been completely reacted, then the residual appears: this is called the break point. Ammonia cannot always be destroyed in this fashion, however, since many wastewaters contain organic materials that react with chlorine in preference to the ammonia, so that these may be destroyed before the excess chlorine is available for reacting with the ammonia.

Ammonia can be removed by cation exchange. A type of clay, clinoptilolite, is specific for removal of ammonia in preference to other cations. This has been used in several waste water treatment applications.

Finally, hydrogen sulfide may be destroyed chemically by oxidation with chlorine, or it may be precipitated by application of a heavy metal salt. The chlorination reactions are as follows:

$$H_2S + Cl_2 \rightarrow S + 2HCl \tag{5}$$
$$H_2S + 4Cl_2 + 4H_2O \rightarrow H_2SO_4 + 8HCl \tag{6}$$

Chapter 15
Membrane Separation

The use of semipermeable membranes is a comparatively recent addition to the technology of water renovation or purification. As design engineers strive to perfect these membranes and the techniques of their application, they can look to nature for examples of semipermeable membranes performing aqueous separations both in plant and animal tissues. In a sense, synthetic membrane devices are copying what is taking place in many natural systems: the roots and heartwood of trees and the kidneys and small intestines of animals use membranes for the transfer of nutrients and food to the cells and for removal of waste products.

In purifying by membrane separation, water passes through a membrane as a result of a driving force, or a combination of driving forces, leaving behind some portion of its original impurities as a concentrate. The type of membrane or barrier, the method of application of the driving forces, and the water characteristics determine the amount of impurities removed.

In the past, problems of membrane fouling or degradation and concentrate disposal have kept costs comparatively high and limited application of membrane systems to special situations, such as to cases where the impurities removed had commercial value. More recently, improvements in membranes and application technology and more stringent environmental discharge limits have made membrane separation practical.

FILTRATION

In the simplest membrane separation process, the membrane acts as a porous barrier for filtration. Water is forced through the membrane by a pressure differential across it. The pores in the membrane may be rather large, generally 0.1 micron or larger. When the membrane is used as an analytical device to detect suspended solids in a water sample, a pore size of 0.45 microns is usually used. The membrane can be made of many different materials, such as cellulose acetate. The number of pores per unit surface area and their shape or configuration can vary greatly, influencing production rates and quality. The membrane chemistry and structure are also important factors.

In filtration, suspended solids are removed on the face of the membrane. If the suspended solids are slimy or easily compressed on the surface, the membrane may become clogged much like any other filter medium, and filtration rates may drop to impractical levels; the process must be stopped and the membrane may require replacement. Seldom can the membranes be cleaned by backflushing. Membranes used for filtration remove little colloidal or soluble material. The efficiency with which very fine suspended solids are removed depends primarily on the size and shape of the pores and the type of filter cake developed during filtration.

There may be more than sieve-type action taking place during filtration. The membrane may swell, changing its characteristics, and there may be chemical or electrochemical interactions between the membrane and certain soluble or colloidal substances in the water being filtered.

As with other water filtration processes, filtration rate varies directly with water temperature (inversely with viscosity), and directly with the pressure differential across the membrane.

To make membrane filtration practical, the bulk of the suspended solids should be removed prior to the membrane unit. A typical example of membrane filtration is shown in Figure 15.1, as part of a total system producing ultrapure water for integrated circuit manufacture. The membrane is the last step in the process, removing crud which would be undetected by ordinary analysis, but which could ruin the integrated circuit. The membrane may process over 1000 liters/cm² (250,000 gal/ft²) before plugging in this application, where it would pass less than one liter/cm² (250 gal/ft²) if used to filter samples of many municipal water supplies.

ULTRA-FILTRATION

As the pore sizes in a membrane are made smaller, i.e., much below 0.1 micron, the pressure differential required to produce acceptable flow rates increases substantially. Processes using small pore-sized membranes and increased pressure, called ultra-filtration (UF), generally require pressure differentials in excess of 20 psig (1.4 kg/cm²). The purpose of using a smaller pore size is to remove colloids and certain high molecular weight organic materials from water. However, this small pore size makes the membranes even more susceptible to clogging or blinding than filtration membranes. In certain configurations, UF membranes can be backflushed to solve this problem. UF membranes may be damaged permanently by excessive heat or pressure causing flux to drop drastically.

More pronounced than in straight filtration, the character and form of the UF membrane is critical to the results obtained. To obtain suitable flow rates, the UF semipermeable membrane usually has an extremely thin skin on the surface of a more porous, thicker substrate. This type of membrane is said to be anisotropic. The skin may be only 1–5 microns thick while the substrate may be 25–50 microns thick. Additional mechanical support is usually necessary. The skin and the substrate are often the same material, the skin being modified on the surface of the bulk membrane by treating the surface thermally, mechanically, chemically or by some combination of these.

In addition to possible blinding of the UF membrane, concentration polariza-

Figure 15.1 Ultrapure water is needed in many areas of manufacture of electronic components. The final step in the treatment system shown here is membrane filtration following several stages of ion exchange. *(Courtesy of Bell Laboratories.)*

tion may also affect flux rates. This phenomenon occurring in the water layer adjacent to the membrane surface is the result of a localized increase in the concentration of rejected impurities. This increases the solution density and viscosity at the membrane surface, reducing flow rate. A number of design techniques have been developed to reduce concentration polarization.

Figure 15.2 shows a typical UF installation. This unit is used in the automotive industry to continually filter a special electrodepositing paint from wash water, recovering the paint and preventing a buildup in salinity. It is also used to filter the paint itself from the dip tank to maintain density as paint is exhausted from the paint bath.

DIALYSIS

Although dialysis is seldom used for the purification or renovation of water, it is a membrane separation process that can be used to reclaim strong chemical solutions, preventing their becoming a waste problem. So dialysis is of interest in water technology (Figure 15.3).

In simple dialysis, the driving force is the concentration gradient across the membrane. The membrane has pores through which solutes can diffuse. Ions of large ionic radius diffuse through more slowly than those of smaller radius, so a separation of ionic species is possible. Solute or colloids too large to pass through

Figure 15.2 Ultrafiltration system being used to control density and recover paint solids. *(Courtesy of Abcor, Inc.)*

the pores are retained in the concentrate. Some water may pass through in a direction opposite the flow of ions because of the osmotic pressure.

Even though almost any semipermeable membrane could be used in dialysis, the most commonly used membranes are made of a type of hydrated cellophane. This has been chemically altered to produce the surface properties and pore sizes needed for the specific separation. These membranes may also be stretched

Dialyzate $(1.05Q_L)$ out

Solvent $(1Q_s)$ (Water)

H_2SO_4 125 g/l
Cu   26 g/l
Ni   43 g/l

Membrane

Solvent cell

Liquor cell

Liquor (Q_L) in

Diffusate out $(0.95\ Q_s)$

H_2SO_4 400 g/l
Cu   30 g/l
Ni   45 g/l

H_2SO_4 235 g/l
Cu   2 g/l
Ni   Nil

Figure 15.3 Single dialysis cell separating free acid from a copper refinery liquor. *(From Chamberlin, N. S., and Vromen, B. H., "Make Dialysis Part of Your Unit Operations," Chem. Eng., May 4, 1959.)*

Water passes through porous membrane
tubes, salts stay behind

Q_1
at high pressure
(about 300 psi)
Concentration $= C_i$

$Q_s =$ saline waste
$0.3 - 0.4 Q_i$
at $5 - 70 C_i$

$Q_P =$ product water
$0.6 - 0.7 Q_i$
at $0.1 C_i$

(a) Reverse osmosis (single stage)

H_2 Cl_2

(+)   (−) Saline waste

Cathode   Anode

Membranes

Wash stream

Feed
x mg/l NaCl

Product
(approx. $0.1 \times$ mg/l NaCl)

C = Cation permeable membrane which allows all cations (Na in this illustration)
to pass through but rejects anions.

A = Anion permeable membrane which allows anions (Cl in this illustration)
to pass through but rejects cations.

Figure 15.4 Schematic drawing of a stack of permselective membranes
assembled as an electrodialysis unit.

to change diffusion rates. Selectivity of a given membrane is largely related to its
pore size. All of the problems discussed in connection with other membrane
separation processes are also inherent in dialysis.

In the textile industry, dialyzers have been used to reclaim caustic from mercerizing baths: the NaOH passes through the membrane into the recovery water
flow, and the organic residue is kept in the liquor for disposal.

ELECTRODIALYSIS

In electrodialysis (ED), the driving force is electrical. Semipermeable membranes,
having anion and cation exchange properties, are alternately stacked in a press
with narrow water passageways between them (Figure 15.4). When a direct current is applied to electrodes on either side of the stacked membranes, the anions
migrate toward the anode and the cations toward the cathode. Since the cation
exchange membrane allows only the passage of cations, and the anion exchange
membranes the passage of anions, the alternation of membranes creates concentration and dilution in the alternate compartments of the stack, as shown in the
figure. The flow rate through these narrow compartments or channels, the
number of stacks used, and the amount of driving force or electrical current
applied determine the amount of salt (cations plus anions) removed from the
water.

To minimize current requirements, these channels are made as narrow as possible. As the amount of salt concentration decreases in the product water passageways, its electrical conductivity decreases, and the electrical energy required to remove additional salt increases. If too much current is applied, some electrolysis (formation of H_2 and O_2) will occur, reducing overall efficiency.

Concentration polarization is even more limiting with electrodialysis than with other membrane separation processes. Concentration polarization causes the development of a membrane potential opposite to the applied potential. Concentration polarization and water splitting, mentioned earlier, increase the tendency of scale formation as concentrations of calcium in the brine channels exceed the solubility for calcium carbonate or calcium sulfate, for example.

Calcium carbonate or magnesium hydroxide precipitates are most likely to form at the anion exchange membrane-concentrate interface due to the higher pH (OH ions) there. The development of scale or deposits on the membrane surfaces reduces ion transfer and increases current requirements.

Improvements in membranes and stack designs have helped minimize the effects of concentration polarization. Methods of stabilizing scaling tendencies and cleaning stacks on the run to postpone shutdowns have been devised. Special cells have been designed for individual applications in attempts to increase reliability and reduce cost.

Electrodialysis is used to produce potable water from brackish water (Figure 15.5). One of the largest municipal plants produces over 3.5 mgd (10 m³/min) for the city of Cortu in the Greek Islands. Units are also being installed in utility systems to reprocess cooling tower blowdown (Figure 15.6).

REVERSE OSMOSIS

Osmosis is the process in which a solvent flows across a membrane separating a stronger from a weaker solution; the solvent flows in the direction that will reduce the concentration of the stronger solution. The flow of solvent between

Figure 15.5 Package electrodialysis plant, showing filter on feed, control system, and membrane stacks (left to right). *(Courtesy of Ionics, Inc.)*

Figure 15.6 A cooling-tower circuit with side stream desalting and brine concentration. The figures above will vary depending on makeup water analysis, pretreatment capabilities, metallurgy restrictions of the cooling system, and operating considerations for the higher purity boiler water circuit.

solution compartments can be observed as the liquid in the compartment of stronger solution increases in volume. If these compartments are fitted with standpipes, the flow will continue until the level in the stronger solution compartment is higher than that in the weak by a dimension which equals the osmotic pressure.

In reverse osmosis (RO), a driving force, the differential pressure across the membrane, causes water to flow from the stronger solution to the weaker. Therefore, the pressure required must exceed the osmotic pressure. The differential pressure is often greater than 300 psig (21 kg/cm²) depending on concentration differences. It averages about 10 psi for each 1000 mg/l difference in TDS. The differences are influenced by the types of membranes used. In reverse osmosis, transport of water through the membrane is not the result of flow through definitive pores, at least not pores as commonly conceived. It is the result of diffusion, one molecule at a time, through vacancies in the molecular structure of the membrane material. The vacancies in amorphous polymers are in a state of flux, or are not fixed, while in crystalline materials the vacancies are voids in lattice structures and are essentially fixed in number, position and size. RO membranes are made of amorphous polymers, but usually contain some crystalline or less amorphous regions.

Reverse osmosis has also been called hyperfiltration, indicating its relationship to a high pressure filtration process. However, it should not be confused with ultra-filtration which uses lower applied pressures and different membranes, because ultra-filtration removes essentially no solutes of low to intermediate molecular weight, while reverse osmosis can remove even low molecular weight ionic species.

The salt removal or rejection obtained is primarily a characteristic of the semipermeable membrane. A given membrane may reject one ion more effectively than another; this rejection may be affected by the presence of other ionic species in the water being processed. In general, the greater the water flux through a given type of membrane, the lower the salt rejection—the less salt retained in the concentrate and the more contaminated the product. Conversely, the higher the salt rejection rates, the lower the water flux through the membrane, using the same applied pressure. These properties can be varied by changing the type of polymers used and methods of manufacturing and processing the membranes. As with electrodialysis, potential for concentration polarization, scaling and fouling are serious considerations in designing process units to take advantage of the various membrane materials available.

TYPICAL RO DESIGNS

Membranes are formed into tubes (Figure 15.7), rolled from sheets (Figure 15.8), and made into fine hollow fibers (Figure 15.9). To meet the required rejection rates, the design must maximize the flux rates per unit volume, and minimize problems from concentration polarization, without seriously increasing the energy needed to operate the system.

It is extremely difficult to clean membranes once they are fouled. Pressure cycles help, as do some cleaning agents. Preconditioning water to be processed is almost always required, even if only a filtration step. A Fouling Index has been developed to guide designers in the selection of a pretreatment process.

This is based on the rapidity of plugging of a standard membrane filter. The test water is filtered at constant pressure, and the time required to produce 100 ml of filtrate is determined initially (t_0) and after 15 minutes (t_{15}). The fouling index is then determined from the relation

$$FI = \left(6.7 \quad \frac{t_{15} - t_0}{t_{15}}\right)$$

To avoid fouling of RO membranes, the Fouling Index of the feed should be less than 3. Chemical treatment with polyphosphates is also used to attempt to reduce plugging of RO membranes with precipitates of $CaCO_3$, $CaSO_4$, and $Mg(OH)_2$.

A simple comparison of commonly-used RO membranes is shown in Table 15.1.

Figure 15.7 Tubular design utilizes a cellulose acetate membrane integrally contained on the inner surface of a support tube. Feedwater flows through the tube, purified liquid passes through the tubular membrane, and contaminants remaining inside the tube discharge from the opposite end. A number of membrane-tube units are connected in parallel within a container with manifolds for feed, concentrate and product. (*Courtesy of The Permutit Company.*)

Figure 15.8 Spiral wound RO barriers are modified cellulose acetate sheet-type membranes spirally wound around a permeate collector tube and covered with an outer wrap. Elements are housed in a vessel containing the necessary seals, inlets and outlets. Feedwater passes through the membranes to the collector tube and out of the element. Contaminants are discharged through the concentrate outlet. *(Courtesy of The Permutit Company.)*

Figure 15.9 Fine hollow fiber barriers are bound into a cylindrical bundle containing many square feet of surface area. This assembly is installed in a shell fitted with inlet, concentrate outlet and purified water outlet. Water is under pressure around the fibers, so pure water passes through the fiber walls and flows through the fibers' bore. Reject is discharged through the concentrate outlet. *(Courtesy of The Permutit Company.)*

**TABLE 15.1   RO Membrane Characteristics
(Based on 90% rejection)**

	Type membrane		
	Triacetate hollow fibers	Polyamide hollow fibers	Cellulose acetate spiral wound
Flux at 400 psi, gpd/sq ft	1.5	1.0	15–18
Back pressure, psi	75	50	0
pH range	4–7.5	4–11	4–6.5
Maximum temperature, °F	86	85	85
Cl_2, maximum mg/l	1.0	0.1	1.0
Bio-resistance	Good	Excellent	Fair
Backflushing	Ineffective	Ineffective	Effective

TABLE 15.2   Typical RO Performance

	Constituent, mg/l	
	Raw	Finished
Hardness, as $CaCO_3$	380	20
Alkalinity, as $CaCO_3$	215	16
Total Electrolyte, as $CaCO_3$	445	29
Silica, as SiO_2	25	3
pH	7.2	6.0
CO_2	25	25

TABLE 15.3   Performance of Reverse Osmosis Unit Treating Pulp Paper Mill Wastewater

Constituent (* in mg/l)	February 25, 1976			July 21, 1976		
	Feed	Permeate	Concentrate	Feed	Permeate	Concentrate
Soluble solids*	54,400	372	66,900	47,600	246	61,355
Sodium*	6,500	62	8,000	6,000	58	7,750
BOD_5*	13,900	1,005	17,600	11,467	775	15,900
Color	112,500	65	146,800	83,000	52	108,000
pH	5.8	4.1	—	—	—	—
	(5.5–6.0)	(4.0–4.8)	—	—	—	—

NOTE: Permeate is rejected from plant cycle, producing acceptable waste water for discharge to municipal treatment plant with pH correction.

SOURCE: William R. Nelson, Green Bay Packaging Inc., private communication.

Figure 15.10   RO system processing waste water for recycle of concentrate and for use of permeate for effluent dilution. *(Courtesy of Green Bay Packaging Inc.)*

RO units are finding widespread application in desalination of brackish water for potable or industrial use, pretreatment of fresh water ahead of demineralizers to reduce chemical consumption and minimize production of strong wastes, and treatment of wastewater. There are now a number of municipal RO installations, one of the largest, in Japan, having a capacity of about 5 mgd (13 m³/min).

Results of RO treatment of a water supply to reduce load on a demineralizer are shown in Table 15.2. And the application of RO to wastewater treatment is illustrated by Figure 15.10, an installation in a paper mill designed to reduce TDS in the mill discharge. Operating results from this unit are shown in Table 15.3. A 100 mgd (262 m³/min) desalting plant at Yuma, Arizona will include RO modules of several types for comparison of performance.

Chapter **16**

Aeration

Aeration is the mechanical process of providing intimate contact of air with water. As applied to water treatment, aeration transfers gas molecules, most notably oxygen, from air (gas phase) to water (liquid phase). While dissolving oxygen in water is most often the goal, aeration also includes removal of undesirable gases, such as CO_2 and methane from water, sometimes referred to as degasification.

TADLE 16.1 Aeration Processes in Water and Wastewater Treatment

Process	Simultaneous or subsequent reactions	Results	Examples
Aeration	None	Increase in dissolved oxygen content.	Oxygenation of streams. Post-aeration of sewage plant effluent.
Degasification	Aeration	Increase in dissolved oxygen content; displacement of gaseous or volatile impurities.	Removal of CO_2, H_2S, methane, taste and odor.
Aeration	Chemical oxidation	Oxidation of inorganic impurities; increase in dissolved oxygen content.	Removal of Fe, Mn, H_2S.
Aeration	Biochemical oxidation	Removal of organic impurities by biochemical digestion.	Sewage treatment BOD removal.

Aeration is almost always accompanied by other processes or reactions, which may be physical, chemical, or biochemical in nature. Table 16.1 gives an overview of such processes with the common objectives and results of aeration of water and wastewater.

By far the greatest use for aeration equipment is in the field of biochemical oxidation of organic wastes, domestic or industrial. But, aeration is also used extensively for oxidation of inorganic impurities such as iron, manganese and hydrogen sulfide, and for removal or oxidation of volatile impurities causing odor or bad taste. Aeration simply to increase oxygen content of water is sometimes carried out as the last step in a water or waste treatment plant.

MECHANISM OF AERATION

As a gas, oxygen is slightly soluble in water. At 20°C and sea level, saturation concentration is only 9.5 mg/l. At this concentration, it represents only 0.00095% of the weight of the water. But this concentration, when released as a gas, occupies 6.7 ml, or 0.67%, of the volume of the water which contained it. To correct gas solubility from weight to volume, use

$$ml/l = \frac{22.4}{mol\ wt} \times mg/l$$

As with most gases, solubility of oxygen in water is inversely proportional to temperature. Dissolved solids concentrations also affect DO. Table 16.2 shows solubility of oxygen at various temperatures, elevations (which affect atmospheric pressure), and dissolved solids levels. As these data suggest, saturation values for oxygen in a particular water must be determined by aeration tests. While it is not necessary to obtain data as extensive as those shown in Table 16.2, it is necessary to establish the ratio (beta factor) between oxygen saturation levels in a specific water and in pure water at the same temperature and pressure.

TABLE 16.2 Solubility of O_2 in Water as Influenced by Temperature, Elevation, and Salinity

Temperature		Elevation, ft				Salinity, mg/l*	
°F	°C	0	1000	2000	5000	400	2500
32	0	14.6	14.1	13.6	12.1	14.55	14.25
50	10	11.3	10.9	10.5	9.4	11.25	11.00
68	20	9.2	8.8	8.5	7.6	9.16	8.97
86	30	7.6	7.4	7.1	6.4	7.57	7.40

* These O_2 solubility values are at sea level.

PRINCIPLES OF GAS TRANSFER

Aeration proceeds in three separate steps: (1) Air is brought into intimate contact with water by exposing a large surface area. This is created mechanically in the form of countless drops or small bubbles, depending on the type of aerator used. (2) Gas molecules pass across this surface into the liquid phase. The gas must pass through a thin barrier at the liquid surface, a liquid film, before it reaches the bulk of the liquid phase. The liquid underneath the film quickly becomes saturated with oxygen. (3) Gas molecules diffuse away from the liquid film into the bulk of the liquid until saturation is complete.

It is obvious that a large surface and turbulent conditions, which disrupt the liquid film and agitate the bulk liquid, increase transfer rates.

The rate of oxygen transfer to the liquid body is expressed mathematically by the overall transfer equation:

$$\frac{dc}{dt} = K_L a(C_s - C)$$

This says that the change of oxygen concentration with time, dc/dt, is equal to a transfer coefficient, K_La, times the oxygen deficiency in the liquid. Oxygen deficiency is the difference between saturation concentrations, C_s, and the prevailing oxygen concentration in the water, C, in mg/l. The above equation is rearranged to

$$\frac{dc}{C_s - C} = K_La\ dt$$

and the integrated form is

$$-\ln(C_s - C) = K_Lat$$

Inserting limits gives the equation

$$\ln\frac{C_s - C_0}{C_s - C_t} = K_Lat$$

where C_s = oxygen concentration at saturation
  C_0 = oxygen concentration at time zero
  C_t = oxygen concentration at time t
A plot of $C_s - C_t$ versus time on a semilog graph will yield a straight line with a slope equal to K_La.

Since the oxygen saturation concentrations are dependent on temperature, pressure, and dissolved solids as well as the nature of the solids, the rate of transfer of oxygen into water is also dependent on these variables. To use the equation for design purposes, it is necessary to perform aeration tests and to plot oxygen uptake versus time. When the differences between saturation levels and actual oxygen concentrations are plotted against time on semilog paper, the slope of the line becomes equal to the overall transfer coefficient, K_La (Figure 16.1). An example of such data collection and plotting is shown in Table 16.3.

Figure 16.1 Plot of oxygen deficiency vs. time.

TABLE 16.3   Aeration Test and Sample Calculations for Determination of Alpha Factor

AERATION EQUIPMENT: Diffused aerator; diffuser to be located 12 feet below surface.
TEMPERATURE: 68°F, 20°C
ELEVATION: 1000 feet above sea level

STEP 1:
Aeration Tests
Water
Dissolved oxygen readings, mg/l, and oxygen deficit versus time, minutes, based on saturated DO of 8.8 mg/l:

Time	0	20	40	60	80	100
DO	0	1.6	3.8	5.4	6.5	7.2
Deficit	8.8	7.2	5.0	3.4	2.3	1.6

Deficit plotted versus time on semilog graph (Figure 16.1)
Slope of straight line is equal to K_La for water

Waste
Waste aerated in same equipment as the water, at 25°C
Dissolved oxygen readings and deficit versus time, minutes assuming saturation at 6 hours:

Time	0	20	40	60	80	100
DO	0	1.0	2.7	4	4.8	5.5
Deficit	7.0	6.0	4.3	3	2.2	1.5

STEP 2:
Deficit plotted versus time on semilog graph, Figure 16.1.

STEP 3:
Slope of straight line is equal to K_La
To convert K_La_{25} to K_La_{20}, use the relationship

$$K_La_{25} = K_La_{20} \times 1.02^{(25-20)}$$

For water at 20°C,

$$K_La \text{ water } 20°C = \frac{\log 7.3 - \log 2.35}{1 \text{ hr}} \times 2.3 = 1.132$$

For waste at 25°C,

$$K_La \text{ waste } 25°C = \frac{\log 6.0 - \log 2.15}{1 \text{ hr}} \times 2.3 = 1.025$$

$$K_La \text{ waste } 20°C = \frac{1.025}{1.02^{(25-20)}} = \frac{1.025}{1.10} = 0.93$$

$$\text{Alpha factor} = \frac{K_La \text{ for waste}}{K_La \text{ for water}} = \frac{0.93}{1.132} = 0.82$$

EQUIPMENT

In fresh water treatment, gravity aerators and spray aerators have traditionally been used to remove iron, manganese and hydrogen sulfide. Aeration techniques developed for wastewater treatment are applicable to fresh water, but capacity requirements are generally much greater.

Gravity or cascading aerators often resemble cooling towers, as the water is pumped over the top and allowed to cascade over wooden slats to a sump or basin.

The forced draft aerator is similar to a cooling tower in that air is forced upward against the counterflow of water over wooden slats. The coke-packed aerator, also a gravity flow unit, is popular in iron and manganese removal installations because of its simplicity.

In the area of wastewater treatment, greater capacities and higher efficiencies are required. The most widely-used types of equipment are: diffused aerators, surface aerators (high and low speeds), and submerged turbine aerators.

Figure 16.2 Air diffusers in municipal sewage treatment plant. The diffuser assemblies may be retracted, as in basin on right, for maintenance and to prevent clogging when basin is out of service. *(Courtesy of FMC Corporation.)*

In diffused or submerged aeration, air is forced through a diffuser, releasing small bubbles near the bottom of the aeration vessel. This establishes good contact between the oxygen and water at a pressure above atmospheric. It creates a large liquid-gas interface by producing small diameter bubbles through the small pores of the diffusers (Figure 16.2).

Efficiencies and power requirements for submerged aerators are closely related to the type of diffusers used. These can be porous, nonporous, or perforated pipe. The type of diffuser used is selected on the basis of oxygen transfer characteristics and maintenance requirements.

The porous type diffusers have found most use in municipal waste treatment systems employing conventional activated sludge treatment. Oxygen transfer efficiencies as high as 10–12% may be achieved. The biggest problem is the tendency for clogging from the air side; clogging from the water side can also be a problem if the units are left in the liquor without air being bled through the system.

The nonporous diffusers do not clog as readily from the air side. However, oxygen transfer efficiencies (i.e., the ratio of oxygen absorbed to oxygen applied by pressurized air passing the diffuser) may amount to 4–8%. This means that power requirements may be as high or even higher than with porous diffusers. Nonporous diffusers are usually constructed from nozzles or orifice plates made of metal or plastic.

The simplest type of diffuser is a perforated pipe laid along the bottom of the aeration vessel. This arrangement is used in ponds or narrow aeration tanks.

Mechanical surface type aerators have increased in popularity, especially in industrial waste treatment plants. While submerged aerators bring air into contact with the water, surface aerators operate in a reverse fashion, bringing the water into contact with the atmosphere. Such aerators actually lift large volumes of water above the surface and expose small liquid droplets to the atmosphere (Figure 16.3).

Basically, a surface aerator is a motor-driven impeller located at or beneath

Figure 16.3 Details of construction of a fixed-position surface aerator, shaped to produce high volume pumping and air entrainment. *(Courtesy of Infilco Degremont Inc.)*

the liquid surface, mounted on fixed supports or on pontoons moored to the aeration basin. A draft tube is sometimes used to improve pumping capacity.

Two designs of impellers are used, updraft and plate type vanes. The updraft impeller moves large volumes of water in the upward direction while the plate aerator causes the water to be scattered outward.

A combination surface-submerged aeration device is sometimes used in units designed for high loadings. These are furnished with a diffuser located at the bottom of the aeration tank with an impeller immediately above it. This combina-

(a)   (b)   (c)

Figure 16.4 Flow patterns for (*a*) diffused-air, (*b*) mechanical-aeration, and (*c*) combination turbine and diffuser-ring systems. *(From Chemical Engineering, April 17, 1972, p. 97.)*

Figure 16.5 Horizontal rotors with radial quills circulate and aerate wastewater in these oxidation ditches. *(Courtesy of Lakeside Equipment Company.)*

tion can transfer more oxygen per unit volume than any other device. It is usually applied to deep tanks, complicating maintenance because a steady bearing is required at the bottom.

Typical installations and flow patterns of submerged aerators, and surface and combination aerators are shown in Figure 16.4.

The brush aerator, also a surface unit, transfers oxygen by providing a liquid film on a wetted surface. This unit lends itself to aeration of streams or oxidation ditches. Mounted at a fixed level, it generates moderate turbulence and pumping action, with some spray of liquid from the rotating elements (Figure 16.5).

A summary of oxygen transfer rates of various types of aeration devices is shown in Table 16.4.

SIZING OF AERATION EQUIPMENT

Except in cases of degasification, aeration requirement is a function of degree of oxygen deficiency in the water and the oxygen-consuming reactions taking place. Of the examples given in Table 16.1, oxidation of iron and manganese requires much less oxygen on a pound-per-1000 gallons basis, than biochemical oxidation of organic material (BOD). In addition, BOD concentrations in both industrial

TABLE 16.4 Summary of Aerator Capacities

	Typical ratings, lb O_2/hp-hr
Submerged aerators	
Porous diffusers	4
Non-porous diffusers	1.5
Surface aerators	
Plate	2.0–2.5
Turbine	3.0–3.5*
Propeller	2.5–3.5
Combination aerators	2–3

* Small units may be higher.

and municipal wastewater are generally much higher than the concentration of iron and manganese found in natural waters. Aeration capacity requirements for BOD removal, therefore, far exceed those of any other oxygen-consuming reaction.

The oxidation of both iron and manganese takes place most readily at a pH over 8. Theoretically, 1.0 mg/l O_2 oxidizes approximately 7 mg/l of either Fe^{+2} or Mn^{+2}. Oxidation of these metals requires increasing oxygen concentration to near saturation.

Oxygen requirements for biochemical oxidation processes (BOD removal) are well established for municipal applications. In cases where no industrial wastes are included with the sewage, aeration capacity is strictly a function of loadings and the type of treatment process to be applied. Some plants provide more or less aeration capacity depending on the extent to which the sludge is being aerated and the amount of denitrification required.

In industrial applications, as in municipal, aeration requirements are functions of BOD loadings and extent of sludge oxidation. However, other factors such as variations in loadings and waste composition may also demand greater aeration design capacities. Pilot studies are usually required.

Oxygen transfer rates of aeration devices are expressed in pounds of oxygen per horsepower per hour. Aerator horsepower requirements can be calculated once the loading, flow rates, and oxygen uptake requirements are known. Examples of such calculations are below.

Sizing Aeration Equipment

For simple aeration applications, horsepower requirements are expressed by:

$$hp = \frac{Q \times d \times L}{24 \times q}$$

where Q = flow, mgd
d = density of liquid, 8.34 lbs/gal for water
L = loadings or oxygen demand in mg/l
q = oxygen transfer rate in lbs O_2/hp-hr

Example   For addition of 6 ppm dissolved oxygen to a water stream flowing at 2.5 mgd using an aerator device having a transfer rate equivalent to 2.0 lbs oxygen/hp-hr, power input requirements will be:

$$hp = \frac{2.5 \times 8.34 \times 6}{24 \times 2} = 2.6 \ hp$$

The same equation may be used for biochemical oxidation of soluble BOD.

Example   For oxidation of 240 ppm BOD in a 15 mgd sewage plant, using aeration equipment rated at 2.5 lbs O_2/hp-hr, power input requirements will be:

$$hp = \frac{15 \times 8.34 \times 240}{24 \times 2.5} = 500 \ hp$$

In practice, for reasons of sludge oxidation requirements and overall safety design factors, as much as 50% extra capacity above that required by the soluble BOD may be furnished. Similar considerations apply to industrial installations.

Chapter 17
Adsorption

In typical fresh waters, the bulk of the constituents in a filtered sample are dissolved minerals. There are, however, significant amounts of non-ionic materials present as colloids. Among these are silica, insoluble metal oxides, and organic compounds, such as color and taste- or odor-producing substances.

The division between colloidal matter and particles of larger size in water is arbitrary. The generally accepted upper boundary for a colloid is a diameter of 1.0 micron. Above this size, particles such as fine silt have a measurable settling rate and can be removed by sedimentation, though the period for reducing the concentration to one-half its original may be as long as a week or a month. Particles smaller than 1.0 micron are kept in suspension by the impact of molecules and ions dissolved in the water. The zig-zag movement may be observed under the microscope, and is known as Brownian motion.

As the particle size is reduced below 1.0 micron, the ratio of surface to volume and correspondingly the electrical charge per unit weight increase. This further stabilizes the colloidal matter, preventing sedimentation. The lower limit of colloid size may be considered to be about 1–10 millimicrons (1 millimicron = 0.001 micron, or 10^{-6} millimeter), close to the dimensions of large molecules in solution.

Colloids are further classed as hydrophobic and hydrophilic, the former resisting wetting by water, and the latter being strongly attracted to water and therefore difficult to adsorb. For example, polar materials such as sugar and alcohol are not adsorbed by activated carbon.

Adsorption is the physical adhesion of molecules or colloids to the surfaces of a solid, an adsorbent, without chemical reaction. In some respects, adsorption is similar to coagulation and flocculation. One distinction is that adsorption generally uses an adsorbent solid processed especially for water treatment; in coagulation and flocculation, the adsorbent is produced in situ by the reaction of a chemical, such as alum, with water.

POWDER OR GRANULES

Adsorbents may be either finely powdered materials, applied to water in a clarifier or ahead of the filter, or 0.5–1.0 mm granules contained in a vessel similar to a pressure filter. The most common adsorbent is activated carbon, used both in powdered and granular forms. Other adsorbents include a variety of clays, magnesium oxide, bone char, and activated alumina. Special ion exchange resins are also used.

Since adsorption is a surface reaction, a measure of the effectiveness of an adsorbent is its surface area. For carbon, the total surface area is usually 600–1000 square meters per gram. This surface is negatively charged. In spite of this, the negative charge of most colloids in water does not deter adsorption of high molecular weight materials, as the molecular structure itself becomes the controlling factor as molecular weight increases.

Adsorbents are porous, and the size of the pores is important. This is measured by iodine number, methylene blue number, or molasses number. The iodine number, a simple titration most commonly used, measures pores passing colloids larger than 1 millimicron. For activated carbon, this number has a range of 650–1000.

TASTE AND ODOR CONTROL

Some tastes and odors are caused by mineral constituents in the water. Examples are the salty taste apparent when chlorides are present at 500 mg/l or more, and the "rotten egg" odor caused by hydrogen sulfide in some well waters. However, most objectionable tastes and odors in potable water are caused by biological activity, Table 17.1. Many species of algae, diatoms and actinomycetes produce organic byproducts, such as essential oils, which can be observed by microscopic examination. The release of these materials into water, particularly when large populations of organisms die, produces objectionable tastes and odors. The released oils are negatively-charged colloids.

TABLE 17.1   Sources of Tastes and Odors

Cause	Percent of cases	Treatment, % of plants reporting		
		Carbon	Chlorination	Aeration
Algae*	82	82	15.5	2.5
Decaying vegetation	67	85	13.8	1.2
Trade wastes	38	61	35.7	3.3
Other	23	85	13.2	1.8

* Frequency of occurrence:
    Diatomaceae: Asterionella, Synedra
    Protozoa: Synura, Dinobryon
    Cyanophyceae: Anabaena, Aphanizomenon
    Chlorophyceae: Volvox, Staurastrum
    Fungi: Crenothrix
SOURCE: Sigworth, E. A.: Control of Odor and Taste in Water Supplies, *JAWWA,* 49, 12, December 1957, page 1507.

Usually these effects are seasonal. They are controlled by the addition of powdered activated carbon either to the coagulation basin or immediately ahead of the filters in a typical municipal water plant. If the water supply contains considerable organic matter, the plant may need prechlorination; because chlorine oxidizes activated carbon, the selection of the best point for carbon application must be made carefully. In these cases, it is often best to apply the carbon ahead of the chlorine application point, if possible, allowing 10–15 minutes for adsorption to take place. If applied ahead of the filters, because carbon is so finely divided, it is important that the filters be in good condition so that the carbon will not pass into the effluent. This final application of carbon ahead of filters may remove residual chlorine, so final chlorination after the filters might be required. The carbon dosage may be as high as 50 mg/l if applied prior to clarification; it should not exceed 5 mg/l if applied ahead of filters.

The test for determining the optimum powdered carbon dosage for taste or odor control—or for organic removal—is performed much like a jar test. The procedure for measuring odor is quite elaborate if carried out by APHA Standard Methods; however, practical modifications are possible as long as the basic principles of dilution, avoidance of fatigue, isolation from background odors, and testing by a panel of several analysts are followed. Different amounts of carbon are added to a series of jars, the jars are agitated for a controlled period corresponding to the detention that can be achieved in the plant system, and odors are determined on the treated samples after filtration. If the data, residual odor (X-axis) vs. odor removed/mg/l C (Y-axis), are plotted on log-log paper, a straight line results. Figure 17.1 is a typical plot.

ORGANIC REMOVAL

If the organic content of the water is high, and relatively constant year-round, it becomes more economical to install pressure filters containing granular carbon or resin than to continuously apply the high dosages of powdered carbon needed to accomplish the same purpose. Typical granular carbon is about 8–30 mesh, having an effective size of 0.9 mm and a uniformity coefficient of 1.8.

The packed bed of adsorbent can be regenerated. If the organic material is volatile, the carbon bed may be regenerated by steaming. However, it is more conventional to remove the carbon and reprocess the material through a furnace. In large installations, the furnace is installed as part of the carbon

Figure 17.1 Odor reduction with powdered activated carbon.

Glass tubing

Rubber stopper

Glass or plastic
pipe,1" I.D.

5'

3"

Regenerant inlet
tube detail

3 mm glass beads

Screen

Rubber stopper

Glass tubing

Figure 17.2 Design of resin
bead column for bench studies of
adsorption process.

installation; in smaller installations, the carbon may be discarded, or removed and returned to the manufacturer for reprocessing.

Packed beds of ion exchange resin are regenerated with brine, causing the ion exchange beads to shrink and expel the adsorbed organic matter.

Because adsorption reactions are relatively slow, particularly in cold water, packed beds are usually operated at lower flows than filters and ion exchange systems, usually below 2 gpm per cubic foot. Bed depths over four feet are common so that the retention time in the bed for adsorption may vary from 10 to 30 minutes. In evaluating the performance of granular beds of adsorbent, pilot plant studies are required. If organics are to be removed from a waste stream, the testing program may be extensive, since data must be obtained not only on the removal efficiency of the adsorbent itself, but also on the capability of the exhausted adsorbent to be regenerated.

When carbon is used, regeneration by reburning is a difficult process to evaluate by pilot plant; assistance by the carbon supplier may be needed. On the other hand, the testing of an ion exchange-type adsorbent is simple, since regeneration is accomplished with brine.

DEGREE OF RECOVERY IMPORTANT

The tests should be repeated for a long enough period of time to indicate whether the capacity of the resin is completely reclaimed each regeneration, and therefore, to what extent and how frequently replacement of resin may be necessary. Tests of this kind are usually performed in glass tubes approximately 1 inch in diameter, with a bed of 30 inches of resin adsorbent. The tube is provided with end connections to permit normal downflow processing, backwashing for cleaning, and elution of accumulated organic material with brine. A typical test set up is shown in Figure 17.2.

A plot of organic removal by a packed column of resin, regenerated with brine, is shown in Figure 17.3.

Because the material being removed is colloidal, and the charge on the col-

Figure 17.3   Changes in water quality produced by passage of an organic-containing water through a brine-regenerated organic trap.

loidal matter is influenced by pH, careful control of pH may be needed in the adsorption process. It is possible for a sudden increase in pH to desorb the colloidal matter, rendering the effluent quality poorer than influent.

Although some silica in water exists as the bisilicate ($HSiO_3^-$) anion, it is likely that it is for the most part present as a negatively charged colloid. It can be removed by anion exchange in a demineralizing system, suggesting that it is ionic; it can also be adsorbed on precipitated iron hydroxide and magnesium hydroxide, following an adsorption isotherm, which suggests that it is colloidal.

The only effective adsorbent for silica when treating water at typical surface water temperatures is iron hydroxide produced from using iron salts as a coagulant. Relatively high dosages are required for removal, and achieving these dosages produces high sulfate salts as a byproduct. Nevertheless, in some circumstances this is an effective process.

Silica is also removed in lime softening processes. The magnesium hydroxide precipitated in the process is chiefly responsible for this. The process is inefficient at ambient surface water temperatures in a conventional lime softener with one hour detention, but it becomes quite significant at temperatures of 120–140°F, and very effective at typical hot-process softening temperatures in excess of 220°F. Contact time and density of the adsorbent sludge are important factors.

There is no way to predict with accuracy the effective dosage for silica removal, particularly where iron is used as the coagulant. This may be because there are other competing reactions. However, the jar test is reliable for anticipating the required chemical dosage for silica removal.

A typical isotherm showing the removal of silica at surface water temperatures with ferric sulfate is shown in Figure 17.4. A series of tests using magnesium as the absorbent are plotted in Figure 17.5. In all cases, the amount of magnesium required for precipitation is over twice what would be required if the reaction produced magnesium silicate.

APPLICATIONS OF CARBON FILTERS

Figure 17.6 shows carbon filters in the beverage industry following a lime softener. Accumulated solids require frequent backwash of the carbon filter beds. The density of carbon is only 25–30 lb/cu ft, so backwash rates must be kept low.

Figure 17.4 Removal of silica by ferric sulfate
at river water temperature.

This limits effective cleanup, so the water supply to the carbon bed should be clear.

Not only are the organic contaminants removed from water, but so also is residual chlorine, which is eliminated by the following chemical reaction:

$$2Cl_2 + 2H_2O + C \rightarrow CO_2 + 4HCL \qquad (1)$$

In this chemical reaction, 1 mg/l Cl_2 reduces the alkalinity of the water by about 1.5 mg/l (as $CaCO_3$) by the production of HCl.

In the beverage industry, most bottling plants are under a franchise agreement that requires installation of water treatment facilities to reduce hardness

Figure 17.5 Silica adsorbed by $Mg(OH)_2$ precipitated from Mg^{+2}, 100°C, pH 10.

Figure 17-6 In most beverage plants, the water supply is superchlorinated and lime treated in a cold process softener (in background). Granular carbon filters (foreground) then remove residual taste, odor, and chlorine to produce a water that does not interfere with the desired flavor of the beverage. *(Courtesy of Infilco-Degremont Inc.)*

and alkalinity, often involving cold-lime softening. Frequently high chlorine dosages are applied to insure complete sterilization. If the residual chlorine were not removed, it would destroy some of the organic materials used for flavoring. In the brewing and distillery industries, free chlorine would be objectionable in the fermentation process. So for these operations, the carbon filter is ideal for removing tastes and odors and for de-chlorination. Because the water has been pretreated, the organic load is generally very low. The carbon may operate for six months to two years before exhaustion, and it is often more practical to re-place the carbon bed with new material than to regenerate it.

Organic matter in water can cause permanent fouling of anion resin used in demineralizing service. The water supplied to demineralizers has generally received several steps of pretreatment, so that the application of carbon filters prior to demineralizing is very practical since the water is clear and the organic load is reasonably low. Since chlorine can damage ion exchange resins, carbon has the same advantage in pretreating water for demineralization as in bottling plant operations, since it will de-chlorinate the water as well as remove organics. The carbon filters are backwashed as needed, but regeneration is seldom practiced because of unfavorable economics. The exhaustion of the carbon can be determined by measurement of organic matter in the treated water.

Figure 17.7 A trailer-mounted activated carbon pilot plant used for wastewater treatment studies. *(Courtesy of Illinois Water Treatment Company.)*

WASTEWATER TREATMENT

The removal of organic matter from wastewater is in a completely different category from the earlier examples of carbon treatment, since the organic concentration may be quite high. Most waste treatment plants in larger industries discharging directly to streams remove organic matter biologically in enormous aquariums in which bacterial cultures use dissolved organics as their food. However, bacteria have preferences in food, and those materials not readily digested —called refractory organics—may not be consumed at all. Carbon has the ability to adsorb many of the refractory materials which cannot be digested economically in a biological system. Powdered activated carbon is used in some biological digestion systems. The carbon concentrates the food source so that bacterial colonies clinging to it can more efficiently convert the organic food to biomass or all the way to CO_2.

Because the organic content of waste waters may be several orders of magnitude above that of fresh water, the economics of carbon treatment of waste

Figure 17.8 Carbon contacting and regeneration—process flow diagram with upflow contactors.

waters is vastly different from the treatment of fresh water. It is essential that the carbon system be designed for thermal regeneration. In such a system, the carbon may pick up 0.2–0.4 lb (kg) of organic matter for each pound (kg) of its own weight before needing regeneration. The adsorbed organics are usually burned off in a regeneration furnace. Approximately 5% of the carbon adsorbent is lost on each pass through the furnace. The performance and costs can be evaluated only by pilot plant operations (Figure 17.7).

When carbon beds are used for polishing the effluent from a biological system, the reduction by the biological system of the organic content to levels in the range of 10–20 mg/l organic as COD may permit the installation of conventional downflow carbon filters. However, where the carbon may be required to produce high quality effluent from a fairly high concentration of organic matter in the influent, countercurrent operation is desirable so that the final effluent leaving the carbon bed will be in contact with the freshest carbon. A flow diagram illustrating such a countercurrent system is shown in Figure 17.8.

An activated carbon system has been operating at the South Lake Tahoe sewage plant since 1968 as part of the polishing system following conventional activated sludge sewage treatment. The carbon column is an upflow packed column having a total bed depth of 14 feet (4.2 m) and providing about 20 minutes residence time. The flow sheet for the plant is shown in Figure 17.9. With this system, the water quality at various stages of treatment is shown in Table 17.2. In the operation of this system, approximately 200 lb (90 kg) carbon are regenerated per million gallons (3785 m³) of water treated. The organic material removed corresponds to a carbon loading of 0.4 pounds as COD per pound of carbon regenerated. Activated carbon for organic removal is equally important in industrial waste treatment. The carbon is capable of removing many organic materials that are not biodegradable, as in refinery wastewaters (Figure 17.10). Large plants have their own complete facilities, including regeneration furnaces. Where this may not be economical, the carbon supplier may install the treatment units and provide regeneration as a service (Figure 17.11).

RESIN COLUMNS

Special ion exchange resins have been developed to perform as adsorbents in the removal of organics from water. In the application described earlier, where resin is used to protect a demineralizer against fouling, the equipment utilizing the resin is almost identical to a common ion exchange unit. The resin is sensitive to temperature change, and the slower rates of reaction at low temperatures require that the flow rates be selected for the coldest water anticipated. Similar

Figure 17.9 Tertiary treatment schematic—South Lake Tahoe, California.

TABLE 17.2 Water Quality at Various Stages of Treatment at South Lake Tahoe

Quality parameter	Raw wastewater	Effluent					
		Primary	Secondary	Chemical clarifier	Filter	Carbon	Chlorinated final
BOD (mg/l)	140	100	30		3	1	0.7
COD (mg/l)	280	220	70		25	10	10
SS (mg/l)	230	100	26	10	0	0	0
Turbidity (JTU)	250	150	15	10	0.3	0.3	0.3
MBAS* (mg/l)	7	6	2.0		0.5	0.10	0.10
Phosphorus (mg/l)	12	9	6	0.7	0.10	0.10	0.10
Coliform (MPN)†	50 million	15 million	2.5 million		50	50	<2.0

* Methylene blue active substance: detergents, surfactants
† Most probable number: colonies/100 ml

units have been designed for the extremely high organic loading found in kraft pulp mill wastes, the resins being particularly designed for lignin and similar organics found in these waste waters.

SLURRY SYSTEMS

The adsorption of silica by iron floc or magnesium hydroxide produced by lime softening requires the maintenance of a high sludge density for efficient performance. Of the varieties of coagulation basins available for water treatment, those that provide maximum contact of the water to be treated with dense sludge produce the best silica reduction.

Figure 17.10 A 2000 gpm countercurrent activated carbon system treating refinery wastewater. Each column is 10′-0″ diameter with an overall height of 65′-0″ and bed depth of 45′-0″. A 5′0″ diameter multiple hearth furnace regenerates spent carbon. (*Courtesy Illinois Water Treatment Company.*)

Figure 17.11 A packaged carbon adsorption system with provision for carbon removal for regeneration at a separate servicing facility. *(Courtesy of Calgon Corporation.)*

Of the variety of miscellaneous adsorption processes, in addition to those discussed, fluoride removal is of some importance. Lime precipitation rarely reduces fluoride below 10 mg/l. Further reduction can be obtained by adsorption on magnesium oxide in a slurry-type contactor, or by passage of the fluoride-bearing waste through a column of hydroxyapatite. Experiences with these processes are limited and bench tests must be run to obtain data for design and for estimation of costs.

SUGGESTED READING

American Water Works Association: *Water Quality and Treatment,* McGraw-Hill, New York, 1971.
Baylis, J. R.: *Elimination of Taste and Odor in Water,* McGraw-Hill, New York, 1935.
Hassler, J. W.: *Activated Carbon,* Chemical Publishing Company, New York, 1963.

Chapter 18

Evaporation

Evaporators are widely used in many water treatment operations, such as preparation of boiler feedwater, concentration of diluted liquor, evaporation of sea water to produce fresh water, and concentration of waste liquors to reduce volume for further processing or disposal.

The typical evaporator is like a fire-tube boiler, with the flame replaced by steam or process vapor as the heat source; but, there are significant differences:

    1. The evaporator has a much smaller temperature gradient across the heat transfer surfaces.

    2. It usually holds less liquid.

    3. Evaporator tubes are usually made of special metals (titanium) or alloys (stainless steel), whereas boiler tubes are made of steel.

To transfer heat efficiently at low temperature gradients, the evaporator surfaces must be kept free of deposits, which have an insulating effect. Correct chemical treatment and scheduled cleaning are important.

Every liquid exerts a vapor pressure, the magnitude of which is a measure of its volatility. High vapor pressure liquids evaporate readily, while those with low vapor pressures evaporate more slowly, requiring an increase in temperature to speed the rate. The kinetic energy of all molecules increases with increasing temperature. The rate of evaporation depends on the nature of the substance, the amount of heat energy applied to the liquid, and surface effects.

When a liquid reaches the temperature at which its vapor pressure equals atmospheric pressure, boiling occurs. This is the rapid evaporation from all parts of the liquid mass, with bubbles of vapor forming in the interior and rising to the surface. The pressure within these bubbles equals the vapor pressure of the liquid at that temperature, so the boiling point depends on the external pressure. For example, at sea level, pure water boils at 212°F (100°C) where its vapor pressure is one atmosphere (1 bar), or 14.7 lb/sq in. If the external pressure is reduced, as occurs at elevations above sea level or under vacuum, water boils at a lower temperature.

EFFECT OF SALT CONCENTRATION

Since evaporators may process liquids other than pure water, factors other than atmospheric pressure must also be considered. Soluble salts in the solution decrease the vapor pressure, elevating the boiling point. Therefore, as dilute liquor evaporates and becomes more concentrated, its boiling point rises. Figure 18.1 shows the boiling point elevation as the concentration of a salt increases in aqueous solution.

As water is evaporated from a solution and the liquid becomes more concentrated, it is possible to concentrate to the point where the solubility of the salts is exceeded. This results in precipitation, usually as scale on the heat transfer surfaces. Where water is being evaporated, the scale may consist of salts of calcium, magnesium and silica. This scale severely reduces the heat transfer rate, slowing evaporation and reducing thermal efficiency.

It takes a lot of heat to evaporate water. Raising the temperature of one pound of water 1°F requires 1 Btu; to change that one pound into vapor at atmospheric pressure requires 970 Btu. The high energy requirement for evaporation makes it important that the heat balance of a plant be controlled for maximum use of energy. A typical evaporator usually receives heat from live steam or from steam bled from a turbine.

EVAPORATOR DESIGN

There is a large variety of designs of evaporators, although the majority work on the principle of steam passing on the outside of a series of tubes with water or water solution, either confined or recirculated, flowing as a thin film over the inside of the tubular heating surface. The various types of evaporators are classified according to the way the water is vaporized:

1. *Boiling type.* Evaporators which heat water to the boiling point and evaporate it by applying an external heat source.

2. *Flash type.* Evaporators which superheat water by an external heat source and flash it into vapor.

3. *Compression type.* Evaporators which add energy to water vapor by compression and return this to the evaporator body as the heat source for boiling.

In the submerged tube boiling-type evaporators (Figure 18.2), steam enters a tubular element, boils water, and discharges water vapor from the evaporator shell. The heating elements are usually bundles of tubes of various configura-

Figure 18.1 Effect of solution concentration on atmospheric boiling point using NaCl as an example. For any specific concentration, the solution boiling points at several pressures plotted against the boiling points of water at these same pressures produce a straight line.

Figure 18.2   Simple submerged-tube evaporator.

tions. These may be completely submerged in the water, partially submerged, or arranged so that only a film of water flows across the surfaces. In each design, the space for vapor generation must be ample to avoid steam blanketing to prevent fouling with baked on sludge.

As in a boiler, bleed-off regulates the solids concentration of the boiling liquid. Vapor-purifying devices trap entrained water droplets. This is particularly important where the aim of evaporation, as in most water treatment systems, is to produce high quality distillate. The vapor purifiers are comparable to those in boilers. In addition to the conventional designs, bubble cap purifiers are sometimes used. These return part of the distillate to continually wash fresh vapor.

A boiling-type evaporator with proper disengaging area should produce distillate with less than 1 mg/l total dissolved solids. The quality is affected by the dissolved solids content of boiling water which may be entrained in the vapor discharge. Lower solids levels are attainable with more sophisticated vapor purifiers and conservatively designed evaporator elements. Vapor quality is affected by the CO_2 liberated from the bicarbonate alkalinity, just as in boiler operation.

CONDENSATION

Purified vapor leaving the evaporator is condensed in several ways:

1. In older utility systems where evaporators were used to provide high quality makeup, the vapor was discharged through the deaerating heater and condensed by the boiler feedwater (Figure 18.3). (New utilities use demineralizers instead of evaporators to process makeup.)

2. Vapor may be condensed by a surface condenser if the purified liquid phase is to be kept separated for some reason. Each pound of vapor becomes one pound of distillate in the condenser shell.

3. The vapor may be fed to the tube element of the second evaporator

Figure 18.3   Typical utility-type evaporator operation.

Figure 18.4   Multiple-effect evaporator with condenser.

body, and the vapor from this second unit fed to a third, producing a multiple-effect evaporator (Figure 18.4). In this type of multiple-effect evaporation, vapor from the last unit is liquefied in a condenser. Each pound of fresh steam fed to the first stage theoretically produces one pound of condensate from each stage. In practice, however, a triple-effect evaporator produces about 3.1 lb of total condensate per pound of steam instead of 4.0, the total condensate including that produced by the fresh steam applied to the first effect.

Figure 18.5   Typical sulfate pulping liquor evaporator flowsheet. *(Courtesy of Unitech Division, Ecodyne Corporation.)*

Multiple-effect evaporators are used principally for chemical process operations. Typical of such evaporators are the units found in the pulp industry for the concentration of sulfate black liquor (Figure 18.5).

The primary aim of evaporation in the power plant is to produce boiler makeup of high quality. The chemical treatment program must be designed to produce high-purity vapor while helping to maintain clean heat transfer surfaces. As in boiler water conditioning, the goals of chemical treatment are control of carryover, prevention of deposits, and elimination of corrosion. The makeup to most utility evaporators is pretreated to remove hardness, reduce alkalinity, and eliminate dissolved oxygen. The chemical treatment applied to the evaporator should be controlled to maintain the limits shown in Table 18.1.

TABLE 18.1   Typical Evaporator Controls Following Pretreatment

Reading	Range	Where and how maintained
TDS, mg/l	2500 max	In evaporator, by blowdown
SiO$_2$, mg/l	100 max	In evaporator, by blowdown
Hydroxide, mg/l CaCO$_3$	150–200	In evaporator, by blowdown or by NaOH feed
Dispersant and antifoam		In evaporator, by chemical feed
PO$_4$, mg/l	30–60	In evaporator, by phosphate-organic treatment
SO$_3$	30–60	In evaporator, by chemical feed
pH	8.2–8.6	In vapor, by amine treatment

NOTE: Where there is no pretreatment of evaporator makeup, chemicals should be fed for internal treatment just as for a low pressure boiler, as shown by Table 18.2.

Where there is no pretreatment of the evaporator makeup, then the chemical program should be the same as used for internal treatment of a low pressure boiler, as shown in Table 18.2. Where the feed to the evaporator is brackish or sea water, it is often difficult to maintain a scale-free system even with a good internal treatment program. In such cases, the operation is programmed so that scale is allowed to build up on the heating tubes for a planned period, then the temperature of the system is suddenly dropped, creating a thermal shock that cracks the scale from the tube surface for removal from the bottom of the evaporator. Other evaporators are manufactured with bowed tubes which flex with temperature change, also resulting in scale-cracking and shedding.

TABLE 18.2   Evaporator Controls—Internal Treatment Only

Reading	Range	Where and how maintained
TDS, mg/l	1500 max	In evaporator, by blowdown
SiO$_2$, mg/l	100 max	In evaporator, by blowdown
Hydroxide, mg/l CaCO$_3$	150–250	In evaporator, by blowdown or by chemical feed
Dispersant and antifoam	Trace	In evaporator, by selecting proper treatment combination
PO$_4$, mg/l	0	
pH	8.2–8.6	In vapor, amine treatment
SO$_3$, mg/l		If the evaporator is used intermittently, a residual SO$_3$ of 30–60 mg/l should be maintained to protect the evaporator shell from corrosion

MULTIPLE-EFFECT UNITS

Although multiple-effect evaporators are usually used for process operations, they have a definite tie-in to the utility system. In the pulp industry, five, six,

Figure 18.6 Black liquor evaporator in a kraft pulp mill. Some of the condensate may be recovered for reuse, but much of it is contaminated with sulfur compounds. *(Courtesy of Unitech Division, Ecodyne Corporation.)*

or even seven effect evaporators are used to concentrate water from the pulp washers for recovery of cooking chemicals. The black liquor may be concentrated to approximately 65% total solids, of which about half are organic materials. In this condition, the black liquor can be fired to a black liquor recovery furnace; the organic material supports its own combustion and smelts the cooking liquor salts to a recoverable form. Figure 18.6 shows a typical large installation of such a black liquor evaporator. Fresh steam fed to the first effect produces condensate that can be reused as boiler feedwater. However, the condensate produced in subsequent stages is too contaminated by volatiles for such use, but may be used for brown stock washing, stock dilution, or other purposes. Some of this condensate is so foul that it must be stripped before it can be put into the sewer for treatment in the waste treatment plant. The vapors stripped from the foul condensate may be sent to the lime kiln where the organics responsible for the foul odors are burned.

The bauxite industry also uses multiple-effect evaporators for concentration of sodium aluminate liquors, producing more condensate than required for boiler makeup. However, again the condensate is usually too contaminated to be directly usable as boiler feedwater.

A final example is the beet sugar industry, where syrups are concentrated by evaporation, again producing an excess of condensate over boiler makeup requirements. These condensates are frequently contaminated with sugar, which is very detrimental to boiler operation, and ammonia, which is corrosive to systems that contain auxiliary equipment fabricated of copper alloys.

The advantage of multiple-effect in increasing yield per unit of energy can also be built into two quite different designs of evaporators which bear little resemblance to the standard multiple-effect evaporator. The first of these is the vapor compression still, which was developed initially for sea water evaporation aboard ship (Figure 18.7); and the second is the multi-stage flash evaporator, which has become popular for the production of potable water from brackish or

Figure 18.7   Schematic of vapor compression still.

Figure 18.8   Schematic of multistage flash evaporator.

Figure 18.9   Three flash evaporator modules, each with a capacity of 2.5 mgd, producing potable water for Al Khobar, Saudi Arabia. (*Courtesy of Aqua-Chem Inc.*)

Vapor out

Distillate reflux in

Vapor body

Liquid level

Steam in

Heating element

Condensate out

Weak feed in

Circulation pump

Concentrate waste discharge

Vertical tube forced circulation
(single pass)

Figure 18.10 A type of evaporator design used for concentration of radioactive wastes from nuclear fuel reprocessing. *(Courtesy of Unitech Division, Ecodyne Corporation.)*

sea water (Figure 18.8). Both of these designs work on low temperature differentials and must be kept free of deposits to maintain efficient heat transfer. Flash evaporators having a capacity of 7.5 mgd (20 m³/min) have been installed for municipal water supply in the Middle East, where energy costs are favorable for such an installation (Figure 18.9). Where sea water is being used as the feed, chemical treatment for prevention of calcium carbonate, calcium sulfate, and magnesium hydroxide scales is required. This has usually involved reduction of alkalinity and operation at low pH, but large installations may find pretreatment of the sea water of value. Such pretreatment has been ruled out by the high cost of chemicals and the extra equipment, but the increasing cost of fuel may offset this in the future. Special alloys must be used throughout to counteract the corrosive effects of the concentrated sea water.

Evaporators are finding application in the concentration of wastes to minimize volume, simplify ultimate destruction, or both. Examples include the treatment of radwaste from nuclear power plant operations (Figure 18.10) and concentration of plating wastes (Figure 18.11).

Figure 18.11 Compact evaporator designed for concentration and recovery of plating solutions from rinse water (*Courtesy of Industrial Filter & Pump Manufacturing Company.*)

Chapter 19

Oxidation-Reduction

Fuel burned in air combines with oxygen, and if this fuel is carbon, the complete reaction is:

$$C + O_2 \rightarrow CO_2 \qquad (1)$$

Although this illustration of combustion is an oxidation reaction where carbon combines with oxygen, not all oxidation reactions involve oxygen. In the above reaction it is apparent that there is a change in the valence of carbon from 0 to +4. There is also a change in the valence of each oxygen atom from 0 to −2. The broad interpretation of oxidation is therefore a chemical reaction in which there is an increase in valence (or a loss of electrons). To maintain the electrical neutrality of a system every oxidation must be accompanied by a reduction. Thus, a reduction reaction can be defined as a reaction in which there is a decrease in valence (or a gain of electrons). By these definitions, the following chemical reactions can be identified as oxidation-reduction (redox) reactions:

$$Fe^0 + 2H^+ + 2Cl^- \rightarrow Fe^{+2} + 2Cl^- + H_2^0 \qquad (2)$$

or $\qquad Fe + 2HCl \rightarrow FeCl_2 + H_2$

$$2Cl^0 + 2H^+ + S^{-2} \rightarrow 2H^+ + 2Cl^- + S^0 \qquad (3)$$

or $\qquad Cl_2 + H_2S \rightarrow 2HCl + S$

$$2CrO_4^{-2} + 6Fe^{+2} + 16H^+ \rightarrow 2Cr^{+3} + 6Fe^{+3} + 8H_2O \qquad (4)$$

or $2Na_2CrO_4 + 6FeSO_4 + 8H_2SO_4 \rightarrow Cr_2(SO_4)_3 + 3Fe_2(SO_4)_3 + 2Na_2SO_4 + 8H_2O$

where in the chromate radical (CrO_4), Cr has a valence of +6.

In the first reaction, iron is oxidized and the hydrogen ion is reduced to hydrogen gas; in the second, the sulfide ion is oxidized to free sulfur as the chlorine is reduced to the chloride ion; and in the third reaction, ferrous iron is oxidized to ferric iron as chromate radical is reduced with hexavalent chromium going to trivalent. Another way of showing the first reaction in its separate segments, called half-cell reactions, is as follows:

Oxidation: $$Fe^0 \rightarrow Fe^{+2} + 2e \tag{5}$$

Reduction: $$2e + 2H^+ + 2Cl^- \rightarrow H_2{}^0 + 2Cl^- \tag{6}$$

Redox Reaction: $$2HCl + Fe \rightarrow FeCl_2 + H_2 \tag{7}$$

In each of these half-cell reactions, the material being oxidized is called a reducing agent, and the material being reduced is an ozidizing agent. The relative reactivity of the elements in terms of oxidation/reduction tendencies is illustrated by the Electromotive Series of the elements. The elements above hydrogen in this series will replace hydrogen from water or from acid solutions. For example, the series shows that sodium will react with water at room temperature to evolve hydrogen, and this can be shown as an oxidation-reduction (redox) reaction:

Oxidation: $$2Na^0 \rightarrow 2Na^+ + 2e \tag{8}$$

Reduction: $$2e + 2HOH \rightarrow H_2 + 2OH^- \tag{9}$$

Redox reaction: $$2Na + 2H_2O \rightarrow H_2 + 2NaOH \tag{10}$$

In this reaction, the element sodium (shown here as Na^0) as the reducing agent is oxidized to the sodium ion. Water, then, must be the oxidizing agent in this reaction.

Iron, which is much lower than sodium on the Electromotive Series, also reacts with water, though not so rapidly as to make the generation of hydrogen apparent. However, iron in an overheated superheater tube in a steam boiler will react readily with steam to produce hydrogen in measurable quantities. Although iron will not displace hydrogen from water readily at room temperature, it will very actively produce hydrogen in mineral acids. This is because the hydrogen ions are much more available in acid than they are in water.

Pursuing the Electromotive Series further, mineral acids should have very little effect on copper, since copper is below hydrogen in the series. However, hydrogen gas should reduce the copper in a copper sulfate solution to metallic copper. Because the hydrogen and copper are so close in the Electromotive Series of elements, the reaction is not readily evident. However, iron and copper are relatively far apart, and the reaction of elemental iron with copper sulfate is easily demonstrated; an iron nail in a copper sulfate solution will soon be plated with copper, even at room temperature.

These reactions all demonstrate the close relationship between oxidation-reduction reactions and the Electromotive Series.

The relative strengths of oxidizing and reducing agents are shown in Table 19.1. As an example, this table shows that ferric iron is most readily reduced by sodium, followed by magnesium, aluminum and zinc. Conversely, aluminum is most readily oxidized by chlorine, followed by manganese dioxide, oxygen and cupric ions.

Since oxidation and reduction reactions involve the transfer of electrons, it would be expected that oxidation and reduction reactions occur in an electrolytic cell. In the electrolysis of water, hydrogen is produced at the cathode and oxygen at the anode. Comparable reactions take place in all electrolytic cells—reduction at the cathode and oxidation at the anode. In the electrolysis of brine, the chloride ions lose electrons (oxidize) at the anode, becoming oxidized to chlorine gas; the sodium ions gain electrons (reduce) at the cathode, and immediately react with water to produce hydrogen and caustic soda.

TABLE 19.1   Relative Redox Potentials

↑ Increasing strength of reductant	Reductant	— (– e) → ⇌	Oxidant	↓ Increasing strength of oxidant
	Na	⇌	Na^1	
	Mg	⇌	Mg^{+2}	
	Al	⇌	Al^{+3}	
	Zn	⇌	Zn^{+2}	
	Fe	⇌	Fe^{+2}	
	H$_2$	⇌	2H$^+$	
	Cu	⇌	Cu^{+2}	
	Fe^{+2}	⇌	Fe^{+3}	
	H$_2$O	⇌	O$_2^0$	
	I$_2$	⇌	IO$_3^-$	
	Mn^{+2}	⇌	MnO$_2$	
	Cl$^-$	⇌ ← (+ e) —	Cl^0	

Strong oxidizing agents such as chlorine and chlorine dioxide can be hazardous; if they contact organic matter, such as paper or oil, the reaction is fast and violent. However, in many aqueous solutions, such as a surface water supply saturated with air, the concentration of oxidizing and reducing materials is so low that most redox reactions are extremely slow. The rates of these redox reactions are in no way comparable to the almost instantaneous reaction of acid with alkalinity in water, or lime with carbon dioxide. Many oxidation-reduction reactions must be catalyzed; for example, the removal of dissolved oxygen from water by application of sodium sulfite is barely measurable until a catalyst is added to the water. Similarly, the oxidation of ferrous iron to the insoluble ferric condition is normally very slow, but may be catalyzed by the presence of oxides of manganese.

Even though they are slow there is appreciable energy available in some of the redox reactions that occur in water. It can be shown thermodynamically that the sulfate ion is strong enough to oxidize organic matter in water: this does not occur by a direct route, but Nature carries out the reaction indirectly through microbes. This occurs under anaerobic conditions in well waters, and the result is the production of sulfides by anaerobic bacteria. Most of the oxidation-reduction reactions occurring in natural water systems are biologically mediated.

Because the oxidation and reduction equations for the overall redox reactions involve electron transfer, and since the voltage for these half-cell reactions can be determined, the progress of a redox reaction can be measured by proper instrumentation. The electrical system used for measuring voltage potential uses two electrodes, one being of a noble metal such as gold, and the other being a reference such as a hydrogen electrode or a calomel electrode. The voltage between these electrodes is measured, and as the oxidation-reduction reaction proceeds there is a change in voltage. For example, if a chromate solution is to be reduced using ferrous sulfate, the initial voltage is quite high because of the strong oxidation potential of chromate, and as ferrous sulfate is added the voltage drops, showing an inflection when the reaction is complete. The progress of the reaction is shown in Figure 19.1.

Redox recorders are used industrially to control the addition of oxidants or reductants to a water solution, or to follow the progress of the reaction in the system.

Using thermodynamic and physical chemical data, it is possible to predict the species of oxidizable and reducible matter in water based on redox potential and pH. Such a phase diagram is illustrated in Figure 19.2, showing the distribution

$$Na_2CrO_4 + 6FeSO_4 + 8H_2SO_4 \longrightarrow Cr_2(SO_4)_3 + 3Fe_2(SO_4)_3 + 2Na_2SO_4 + 8H_2O$$

Figure 19.1   Titration of chromate with $FeSO_4$ in acid solution.

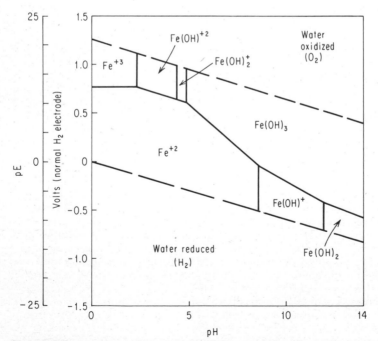

Figure 19.2   Pourbaix diagram for Fe in water based on precipitation of hydroxide forms, at 2×10^{-7} M total Fe. *(From F. E. Clark, TAPPI Journal, 49, 10, 124A, October 1966.)*

of iron in an aqueous system at different pH values and different oxidation potentials.

There is another useful physical chemical notation representing the status of the oxidizing or reducing environment in an aqueous system for individual species that may be oxidized or reduced. This is the concept of pE, which is analogous to pH; like pH, it is a negative logarithm. The value of pE is minus the log of the electrons exchanged in the redox reaction. Although there are no free electrons in the aqueous environment, a number proportional to the number of moles of material being oxidized or reduced can be assigned to the electron transfer. If all oxidation and reduction equations are written with a single electron, an equilibrium can be established for which the constant can be determined. Mathematically, the relative electron activity, pE^0, at which the ionic species being examined are at an activity of unity, is shown as:

$$pE^0 = \log K$$

where K is the equilibrium constant.

Then

$$pE = pE^0 + \log (\text{product/reactant})$$

where pE represents a concentration of the species at other than unit activity.

Using ferric iron as an example, the half-cell reaction is as follows:

$$Fe^{+3} + e = Fe^{+2}$$

$$K = \frac{[Fe^{+2}]}{[Fe^{+3}][e]} = 3.4 \times 10^{13}$$

Using this data, $pE^0 - 12.53$, the level of electron activity at which ferrous and ferric ions are of equal concentration in an oxygen-free environment. When this system is exposed to the environment, the presence of oxygen causes an increase in pE to 16.49, and at this pE value the ferrous ion concentration is reduced to about 10^{-1} of the total iron concentration.

Since there is a relationship between pE, the free energy involved in the electron transfer, the electrode potential, and the equilibrium constant for each redox reaction, it is possible to construct a phase diagram for most redox reactions in natural aqueous environments showing the distribution of species as established by pH and pE. In most natural aquatic environments, the pE can range from a strongly reducing value of -8 (corresponding to a voltage of approximately -0.3) to a strongly oxidizing value of 16 (corresponding to a voltage of approximately 1.0); below the lower limit water would be reduced to produce hydrogen, and above the upper limit water would be oxidized to produce oxygen.

It is important to recognize that although the environment may be strongly oxidizing or reducing, the voltage potential for the half-cell reaction does not influence the rate of reaction, and many such reactions in aqueous systems are very slow unless catalyzed.

The Electromotive Series as summarized in Table 19.1 shows that a substance can be defined as an oxidant or a reductant only in terms of other substances in the aqueous environment. Even though oxidation and reduction are accepted as relative terms, certain chemicals are normally described as oxidizing agents or reducing agents only if they are at the far ends of the series.

The most common oxidizing agents used in water treatment are air, chlorine and chlorine-releasing compounds, oxygen, ozone, hydrogen peroxide, potassium permanganate, chromate salts, and nitrate compounds. Following are five major water conditioning applications using these oxidizing agents.

IRON REMOVAL

Iron may be present in water (a) in colloidal form, (b) as the ferrous iron, or (c) as a chelated compound. The colloidal form can be removed by coagulation, flocculation and precipitation or filtration, and so will not be dealt with here. The chelated form may require oxidation of the organic material composing the chelate so that the iron may then be precipitated for removal. In the ferrous form, iron may be found in certain well waters at concentrations as high as 25 mg/l under anaerobic conditions. The reducing conditions that permit iron to become soluble in well water frequently also produce sulfides. In the treatment of many municipal water supplies containing iron, the raw water is often aerated before being introduced into the clarifier, and this introduction of air is often adequate for the oxidation of soluble iron to the insoluble ferric state. One reason this process may be successful is that the water is then held for 60–90 minutes before being collected at the overflow weirs for filtration, allowing time for the iron to fully oxidize.

Where the amount of iron to be removed is relatively low, on the order of 2–3 mg/l, it may be possible to remove this iron directly on a filter, but this requires a more powerful oxidant than air and the presence of a catalyst, such as manganese, with an increase in pH to a minimum of 8.5. Even with this, the residence time in the filter itself may not be adequate for complete oxidation and iron removal, and a detention tank may be required for this purpose. The oxidation of iron with chlorine and potassium permanganate are shown by the following two reactions:

$$2Fe^{+2} + Cl_2{}^0 \rightarrow 2Fe^{+3} + 2Cl^- \tag{11}$$

(In this reaction, 0.64 mg/l Cl_2 is required for each mg/l Fe.)

$$MnO_4{}^- + 3Fe^{2+} + 2H_2O + 5OH^- \rightarrow MnO_2 + 3Fe(OH)_3 \tag{12}$$

(In this reaction, 0.95 mg/l $KMnO_4$ is required for each mg/l Fe.)

pH has a pronounced effect on iron removal. Although the oxidation potential of both chlorine and permanganate decrease as the pH increases, the rate of reaction increases significantly with increase in pH. Also, the solubility of the oxidized iron decreases as the pH increases.

MANGANESE REMOVAL

The removal of manganese from water is similar to iron removal. A variety of oxides of manganese is produced by chlorine and permanganate oxidation, but these are of little significance in the treatment technology. In most industrial water systems, manganese can be more troublesome than iron at much lower concentrations, so the final filtration process is critical to successful removal of manganese. The effectiveness of removal increases significantly as the pH is raised to about 9.0, and time is even more critical than with iron removal.

REMOVAL OF ORGANIC MATTER

Oxygen and air are seldom used directly for oxidation of organic material, but they are of course used in biologically mediated oxidation systems, such as in the activated sludge process. At high temperatures [about 300°F (150°C) and above] and high pressures air or oxygen injected into a reaction vessel will oxidize appreciable organic matter (the Zimmerman Process). When chlorine is used for oxidation, the results may be disappointing in that chlorine forms substitution products, particularly in reacting with phenols, that may be more objectionable than the original organic molecule. Even when reacting with such a simple organic molecule as methane, the chlorine does not destroy the methane but produces methyl chloride according to the following reaction:

$$Cl_2 + CH_4 \rightarrow CH_2Cl + HCl \tag{13}$$

On the other hand, ozone and permanganate may be used for complete destruction of phenol and simple organic molecules, as shown by the following equations:

$$14O_3 + \underset{\text{phenol}}{C_6H_5OH} \rightarrow 6CO_2 + 3H_2O + 14O_2 \tag{14}$$

In this reaction, 7.2 mg/l ozone is required for each mg/l phenol.

$$4KMnO_4 + \underset{\text{formaldehyde}}{3HCHO} \rightarrow 4MnO_2 + 2K_2CO_3 + CO_2 + 3H_2O \tag{15}$$

In this reaction, 17.5 mg/l permanganate is required for each mg/l of organic carbon (TOC).

Although these reactions take place, the rate is slow and therefore substantial residence time is needed in the reaction vessel.

Phenol can be oxidized by permanganate, but the reaction requires about two hours at a pH of 7 for 90% completion; even with an increase in pH to 9–10, it still takes about 30 minutes for 90% reaction.

CYANIDE REMOVAL

Cyanide can be oxidized to the cyanate form under alkaline conditions both by chlorine and permanganate, according to the following reactions:

$$CN^- + Cl_2^0 + H_2O \rightarrow 2HCl + CNO^- \tag{16}$$

In this reaction 2.75 mg/l chlorine is required for each mg/l CN.

$$3CN^- + 2MnO_4^- + H_2O \rightarrow 2MnO_2 + 3CNO^- + 2OH^- \tag{17}$$

In this reaction 4.1 mg/l $KMnO_4$ is required for each mg/l CN.

Both of these reactions are carried out at a pH greater than 10. In the case of chlorine, it is important to maintain this pH to avoid formation of toxic cyanogen chloride.

Although the cyanate is much less toxic than cyanide, complete destruction is often necessary, requiring further oxidation of the cyanate with chlorine or hypochlorite as shown in equation (18).

$$2CNO^- + 3OCl^- + H_2O \rightarrow N_2 + 3Cl^- + 2HCO_3^- \tag{18}$$

Combined with above reaction, complete destruction of CN to N_2 requires 6.9 mg/l Cl_2 per mg/l CN.

The optimum pH for the second stage of this reaction is approximately 8.5. As in other oxidation reactions, time is an important factor to be studied; the cyanide reactions generally require over ten minutes and an excess of oxidizing agent in order to provide complete destruction.

SULFIDE REMOVAL

In the aeration of sulfide-bearing waters to eliminate odor, some of the sulfide is converted to colloidal sulfur according to the following reaction.

$$2HS^- + O_2 \rightarrow 2S^0 + 2OH^- \tag{19}$$

Sulfides can also be oxidized by chlorine and permanganate according to the following reactions.

$$HS^- + Cl_2 + H_2O \rightarrow 2Cl^- + 2H^+ + S^0 + OH^- \tag{20a}$$

$$S^0 + 3Cl_2^0 + 4H_2O \rightarrow H_2SO_4 + 6HCl \tag{20b}$$

$$2MnO_4^- + 3(HS^-) + H_2O \rightarrow 3(S^0) + 2MnO_2 + 5OH^- \tag{21}$$

In all of the above examples, it is important to recognize that the oxidation was involved with specific individual species in the water. Since the aqueous system contains a variety of species, some of which may participate in the oxidation-reduction reactions, it is clear that predicting the best oxidation material for the reaction, optimum pH, required time for completion, and dosage of the oxidizing agent is impossible. In the final analysis, the examples above simply suggest potential oxidizing materials that might be used; bench testing is needed to evaluate these and others to obtain data to design an effective treatment process.

REDUCING AGENTS

The commercially available reducing agents most commonly used in water treatment are sulfur dioxide, sodium sulfite, and ferrous sulfate or chloride, with occasional use of zinc hydrosulfite, borohydride compounds, hydrogen sulfide, and zinc dust. The most common reductions in water treatment are the scavenging of dissolved oxygen with sodium sulfite, reduction of excess chlorine with sodium sulfite, and the reduction of chromate to its trivalent form. Typical reactions for each of these processes are shown below.

$$O_2 + 2SO_3^{-2} \rightarrow 2SO_4^{-2} \tag{22}$$

In this reaction, 8 mg/l Na_2SO_3 is required for each mg/l O_2.

$$Cl_2 + SO_3^{-2} + H_2O \rightarrow SO_4^{-2} + 2HCl \tag{23}$$

In this reaction, 1.8 mg/l Na_2SO_3 is required for each mg/l chlorine.

$$2Na_2CrO_4 + 6FeSO_4 + 8H_2SO_4$$
$$\rightarrow Cr_2(SO_4)_3 + 3Fe_2(SO_4)_3 + 2Na_2SO_4 + 8H_2O \tag{24}$$

In this reaction 3.94 mg/l $FeSO_4$ are required per mg/l chromate.

In commercial practice, the first reaction, elimination of dissolved oxygen from water, requires the use of a catalyst for practical treatment in a reasonable time; the reduction of chlorine need not be catalyzed.

The reduction of chromate is carried out at a pH of approximately 2.5–3.0 using more than twice the theoretical requirement of reducing agent for completion of the reaction in 15–20 minutes.

It is important to recognize that there are usually species present in water in addition to those represented by the above equations. For example, chromate is a common constituent in industrial recirculating cooling water systems, where it is used as a corrosion inhibitor. In the organic chemicals industry, leakage of organics into the cooling water often results in a reduction of chromate. Recognizing how difficult it is to reduce chromate at concentration levels of 10–20 mg/l with strong reducing agents under controlled conditions, it may be conjectured that the reduction of chromate in a cooling system may be a biologically-mediated reaction.

SUGGESTED READING

Stumm, W., and Morgan, J. J.: *Aquatic Chemistry,* Wiley, New York, 1970.
Weber, W. J., Jr., et al: *Physicochemical Processes for Water Quality Control,* Wiley, New York, 1972.

Chapter **20**

Corrosion Control

Corrosion is Nature's way of returning processed metals, such as steel, copper, and zinc, to their native states as chemical compounds or minerals. For example, iron in its natural state is an oxidized compound (i.e., Fe_2O_3, FeO, Fe_3O_4), but when processed into iron and steel it loses oxygen and becomes elemental iron (Fe^0). In the presence of water and oxygen, Nature relentlessly attacks steel, reverting the elemental iron (Fe^0) back to an oxide, usually some combination of Fe_2O_3 and Fe_3O_4.

Although corrosion is a complicated process, it can be most easily comprehended as an electrochemical reaction involving three steps as shown in Figure 20.1:

1. Loss occurs from that part of the metal called the anodic area (anode). In this case, iron (Fe^0) is lost to the water solution and becomes oxidized to Fe^{+2} ion.

2. As a result of the formation of Fe^{+2}, two electrons are released to flow through the steel to the cathodic area (cathode).

3. Oxygen (O_2) in the water solution moves to the cathode and completes the electric circuit by using the electrons that flow to the cathode to form hydroxyl ions (OH^-) at the surface of the metal. Chemically, the reactions are as follows:

Anodic reaction: $$Fe^0 \rightarrow Fe^{+2} + 2e^- \tag{1}$$

Cathodic reaction: $$\tfrac{1}{2}O_2 + H_2O + 2e^- \rightarrow 2(OH^-) \tag{2}$$

In the absence of oxygen, hydrogen ion (H^+) participates in the reaction at the cathode instead of oxygen, and completes the electrical circuit as follows:

$$2H^+ + 2e^- \rightarrow H_2\uparrow \tag{3}$$

Every metal surface is covered with innumerable small anodes and cathodes as shown in Figure 20.1. These sites usually develop from: (1) surface irregularities

Basic corrosion reaction

$Fe^0 \rightarrow Fe^{+2} + 2e^-$ $1/2\,O_2 + H_2O + 2e^- \rightarrow 2OH^-$ (pH > 4.0)

Corrosion rate is under cathodic control

Figure 20.1 Reactions occurring during the corrosion of steel in the presence of oxygen. The presence of OH⁻ at the cathode can be demonstrated by the pink coloration of phenolphthalein dye.

from forming, extruding, and other metalworking operations; (2) stresses from welding, forming or other work; or (3) compositional differences at the metal surface. In the case of steel, this may be caused by different microstructures; Figure 20.2 is an enlargement of a polished specimen of steel showing ferrite and cementite as two distinctly different components. In brass, the difference may be between the fine crystals of copper and zinc that make up this alloy. Inclusions on or below the metal surface may be the cause of anode-cathode couples. These impurities may have formed when the metal was molten or because impurities were pressed into the surface during the rolling, finishing or shaping operations.

CORROSION RATES

As noted above, three basic steps are necessary for corrosion to proceed. If any step is prevented from occurring, then corrosion stops. The slowest of the three

Figure 20.2 Microstructure of low-carbon steel at 20 × showing background matrix of ferrite (iron, light-colored) containing grains of pearlite (dark colored). The pearlite consists of lamellae of ferrite and cementite (Fe_3C). (*a*) The pearlite is seen to be in layers, created by the extrusion of the metal through a die.

Figure 20.2 (*b*) The larger pearlite grains in this specimen are randomly oriented, and the lamellae of ferrite and cementite can be seen.

steps determines the rate of the overall corrosion process. The cathodic reaction (step 3) is the slowest of the three steps involved in the corrosion of steel so this reaction determines the rate. It is slow because of the difficulty oxygen encounters in diffusing through water. One factor in increasing corrosion, then, is increasing water temperature, which reduces its viscosity and speeds the diffusion of oxygen.

A large cathodic surface area relative to the anodic area allows more oxygen, water and electrons to react, increasing the flow of electrons from the anode to corrode it more rapidly. Conversely, as the cathodic area becomes smaller relative to the anodic area, the corrosion rate decreases.

If, however, the anodic area is reduced with no corresponding decrease in the cathodic area, the same amount of metal will be lost, but from fewer or smaller anodic sites. The corrosion rate will not have been changed because the cathodic surface area has not been reduced, but each anodic site will be deeper. This is a simple explanation for the cause of pitting attack on metals. Pitting is more damaging than general loss over a large anodic area because it leads to rapid metal wall penetration and equipment failure. Figure 20.3 contrasts pitting metal loss to general metal loss from corrosion coupons exposed to similar field environments in cooling systems.

Area ratios as they affect corrosion rate play a significant part in the selection of effective inhibitors to control corrosion. They are also a major consideration in designing equipment to minimize corrosion.

Figure 20.3 (*a*) Surface of corrosion coupon is smooth and cleaned prior to insertion in water line. (*b*) This coupon surface has been uniformly corroded, with some areas of localized attack. (*c*) This coupon surface has been pitted. The weight loss may be lower than (*b*), but failure (penetration) will occur earlier. Depth of pits may be measured by microscope or by a micrometer probe.

(a)

(b)

Figure 20.4   (*a*) Polarization of the cathodic area at lower pH values by H_2 molecules. These may be depolarized by reaction with O_2. (*b*) Polarization of the cathode by an alkaline film highly concentrated in OH^- ions. These may be depolarized by chemical reaction with metal cations causing precipitation, by low pH, or by high-velocity water sweeping the surface.

POLARIZATION-DEPOLARIZATION

As noted earlier, hydroxyl ions (OH^-), hydrogen gas (H_2), or both, are produced at the cathode as a result of the corrosion reaction. If these chemical reaction products remain at the cathode they produce a barrier (Figure 20.4) that slows the movement of oxygen gas or hydrogen ions to the cathode. This barrier becomes a corrosion inhibitor because it insulates or physically separates oxygen in the water and the electrons at the metal surface. The formation of this physical barrier as a result of corrosion is called polarization. The removal or disruption of this barrier exposes the cathode, and corrosion resumes. This action, called depolarization or barrier removal, is enhanced by several factors:

1. Lowering the pH of the water. This increases the concentration of the hydrogen ions reacting with the hydroxyl ions to form water, thereby eliminating the hydroxyl barrier.

2. Increasing the water velocity into the turbulent flow region tends to sweep away hydroxyl ions and hydrogen from the surface of the cathode, thereby depolarizing it.

GALVANIC CORROSION

A special form of the general corrosion reaction is galvanic corrosion. This relatively common form of corrosion results when two dissimilar metals are connected and exposed to a water environment: one metal becomes cathodic and the other anodic, setting up a galvanic cell. For example, when copper and steel are connected in water, steel becomes the anode. It is said to be anodic to the copper which is the cathode. The metal loss occurs at the anode, so the steel corrodes. The same principles of cathode-anode surface area ratios that apply to the general corrosion reaction apply to the galvanic cell: larger cathode—higher corrosion rate; smaller cathode—lower corrosion rate; large anode—general corrosion metal loss; small anode—pitting type attack. The galvanic couple corrosion rate is influenced by the types of metals that are connected. Table 20.1 lists a series of common metals and alloys frequently encountered in water systems. This is quite similar to the electromotive series of elements. The connection of two of these metals in a water environment (a galvanic couple) corrodes the more anodic. For metals close to one another in this series, the corrosion rate

TABLE 20.1   An Approximate Order of Galvanic Cell Corrosion

Electromotive Series of Elements	Galvanic Series of Metals and Alloys		
	Anodic		
Potassium			
Calcium			
Sodium			
Magnesium	Magnesium		
Aluminum	Aluminum		$\uparrow$
Zinc	Zinc and Zn coatings	Al-2s	
	Cadmium and Cd coatings	Aluminum alloys	
Iron	Steel	Al-17s	
	Cast iron	$\downarrow$	
Nickel			
Tin		$\downarrow$	
	Tin $\Big\}$	solders	
Lead	Lead $\Big\}$	$\uparrow$	$\uparrow$
	Ni resist		60–40 brasses
Hydrogen	Chromium	70–30	
		$\downarrow$	
	Nickel $\Big\}$		
	Inconel $\Big\}$	Hastelloys $\uparrow$	
Copper	Copper, bronze		$\uparrow$
	Cupro-nickel, Monel	Stainless steels	
Mercury			
Silver	Titanium	$\downarrow$	
Gold			
	Cathodic		

is less than for metals widely separated. In a galvanic couple, then, corrosion rate is dependent upon:

1. What metals are connected
2. Relative anodic to cathodic surface areas

Figure 20.5 shows extremely severe pitting and metal wall failure. This resulted principally from galvanic attack. The ultra-pure aluminum tube experienced periodic copper plating from trace concentrations of copper in the circulating water which set up the severe galvanic attack. In this case, low flow velocities and inorganic and microbial deposits accentuated the problem.

CONCENTRATION CELL CORROSION

Just as the dissimilar metals noted above generate a galvanic current with a fixed concentration of water, a galvanic current can also be set up when a single metal is exposed to different concentrations (ionic strengths) of water solutions. The attack that occurs at the anode as a result of this mechanism, called concentration cell corrosion, takes place in the more concentrated solution. Con-

Figure 20.5 Severe corrosion of aluminum piping caused by the presence of copper ions in the water in the piping system.

centration cells are the usual cause of the troublesome local etch or pitting type of metal loss.

Concentration cell corrosion may severely shorten equipment life; equipment designed for years of service may fail in days. Generally, this type of corrosion occurs at any site where deposits, poor equipment design, or both, allows a localized concentration of a specific substance—such as NaCl or O_2—to be notably different from the amount found in the bulk of the water environment.

A typical sequence for the deposit-related concentration cell failure shown in Figure 20.6 is as follows: A deposit forms on a metal surface in a cooling water system. In a short time, the oxygen under the deposit is consumed by the normal corrosion reaction. As the oxygen concentration beneath the deposit becomes less than that in the bulk water surrounding the deposit because fresh O_2 is hindered from migrating through the deposit, the area under the deposit becomes anodic to the surrounding area. This unique concentration cell mechanism is called an oxygen differential cell. The corrosion that began as normal corrosion has now changed to a differential cell corrosion mechanism.

The rate of the differential cell reaction is proportional to the difference in concentration between the oxygen under the deposit and that found in the water around the deposit. In most cases, concentration cell corrosion will proceed much faster than the standard corrosion mechanism that originally occurred beneath the deposit and will result in a pitting-type metal loss.

An oxygen differential cell is rarely the sole cause of metal loss under a deposit. Coexisting with most oxygen differential cells are the corresponding chloride and sulfate concentration cells. These coexist because chloride and sulfate ions penetrate the deposit or crevice and concentrate. The deposit behaves like a semipermeable membrane (a Donnan membrane); as the iron ions (Fe^{++}) leave the anodic surface, the $Cl^- + SO_4^=$ anions diffuse through the deposit to maintain neutrality, resulting in a buildup of electrolyte under the deposit. This further accelerates the corrosion already taking place due to the oxygen differential cell.

Anaerobic microbes which can reduce sulfate to sulfides under a deposit, create a very aggressive condition to further accentuate the metal loss.

In summary, deposits can lead to aggravated pitting attack initiated as normal corrosion, but compounded by various concentration cell corrosion mechanisms, which may include microbial involvement. Because these concentration cells and their corrosion products are shielded by deposits, not even the most effective inhibitors can get through to properly protect the metal surface. This emphasizes the importance of maintaining water systems free of deposits.

Other important factors which influence corrosion include the concentration of dissolved solids in water, dissolved gases, and temperature.

DISSOLVED SOLIDS

The influence of dissolved solids on corrosivity is very complex. Not only is the concentration important, but also the species of ions involved. For example, some dissolved solids (such as carbonate and bicarbonate) may reduce corrosion, while others (such as chloride and sulfate) may increase it by interfering with the protective film. Figure 20.7 shows that corrosivity does not increase at a linear rate with increasing total dissolved solids concentrations. In fact, over 5000 mg/l, a further increase in dissolved solids shows progressively less influence on corrosion rate of mild steel.

(a) Debris settles on metal surface.

(b) Oxygen can reach metal only at open surface.

(c) Oxygen continues to depolarize the cathodic area while chloride diffuses into the porous deposit.

(d) The iron within the deposit remains soluble as Fe^{+2} in the absence of O_2; and corrosion increases as ionic strength in the deposit increases.

Figure 20.6 Successive steps in the formation of an oxygen concentration cell as a consequence of deposit on a steel surface in oxygenated water.

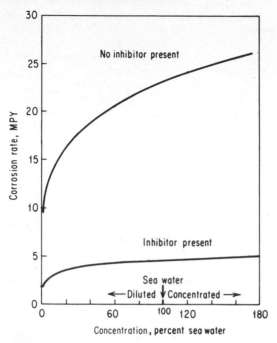

Figure 20.7   Corrosion of mild steel in concentrated and diluted sea water. Rates determined by coupon testing in flowing aerated water at 30°C and pH 7.5. *(M. Mindick, private communication, March 29, 1978.)*

DISSOLVED GASES

CO_2 and O_2 are the major gases of concern in most industrial systems. Increasing the free CO_2 content in water reduces pH and tends to depolarize the cathodic surface area. In a relatively unbuffered condensate, this could produce a low pH and corrosive water. In a buffered water, such as a typical cooling water system, the impact of the increased CO_2 would be less.

As explained earlier, oxygen produces cathodic depolarization by removing the hydrogen produced at the cathode.

Hydrogen sulfide and ammonia are less frequently encountered than oxygen and CO_2, but both exert a strong influence on the corrosion of iron and copper alloys. Hydrogen sulfide is almost always ionized as bisulfide and sulfide ions, which tend to depolarize the anodic area. Ammonia increases the corrosion rate of copper and copper alloys by complexing the copper in the normally protective copper oxide or copper carbonate surface films.

TEMPERATURE

As a general rule, each 15°F (8°C) increase in temperature doubles the rate of chemical reactions. Therefore, temperature increases the speed of corrosion because the cathodic reaction proceeds faster, although not at a rate predicted by the above rule of thumb. This is because the oxygen diffusion rate is also involved in the process. Figure 20.8 represents some of the actual increases in corrosion rate related to temperature.

Figure 20.8 High temperature boosts corrosion except where oxygen is free to escape. (*From "Corrosion Report," Power, December 1956.*)

STRESS CORROSION CRACKING

Metal under tensile stress in a corrosive environment may crack, a type of failure called stress corrosion cracking (Figure 20.9). The metal stress may be applied by any kind of external force which causes stretching or bending; it may also be due to internal stresses locked into the metal during fabrication by rolling, drawing, shaping or welding the metal. The corrosive environment and the stress need not be of any specific minimum value. For stress corrosion cracking to take place, the combined effect of the stress and corrosion causes cracking either with a high stress in a mild corrosive environment or with a mild stress in a highly corrosive environment. At moderate stress and with a mild environment, there may be no failure.

Figure 20.9 Stress corrosion cracking of low-carbon steel. In this case, the specimen examined was taken from an embrittlement detector and illustrates caustic embrittlement. (500×)

If the combined effects are sufficient, generally both intergranular and trans granular cracks develop at right angles to the applied force. Highly corrosive waters tend to encourage randomly oriented cracking.

If the stresses are mechanically applied, this attack may be relieved by removing the applied stress. Where the stress is internal, relief is more difficult, since there is no practical way to locate and measure internal stresses in equipment at a plant site. A reliable means of reducing stress corrosion is to eliminate the corrosive environment or isolate the metal from water, such as by employing coatings. Application of a corrosion inhibitor may also help reduce this type of attack, but this approach is generally impractical because of the very high level of inhibitors required to effectively control the corrosion rate.

To a large extent, proper design and good fabrication procedures must be relied on to produce equipment, piping or structures free of internal stresses. For example, heat treatment after fabrication (stress relief annealing) allows the crystalline structure of the metal to free itself of internal stresses. Even large process vessels are stress relief annealed to guard against stress corrosion cracking.

CAUSTIC EMBRITTLEMENT

Caustic embrittlement is a special type of stress corrosion cracking that sometimes occurs in boilers. At one time, this was a common cause of boiler failure, but improved fabrication practices and better water treatment have made it rare. Three concurrent conditions were found to cause caustic embrittlement:

　　1. A mechanism by which boiler water could concentrate to produce high concentrations of sodium hydroxide.

　　2. At the point of concentration, the boiler metal must be under high stress such as where the boiler tubes are rolled into the drum.

　　3. The boiler water must contain silica, which directs the attack to grain boundaries, leading to intercrystalline attack; and it must be of an embrittling nature. An embrittlement detector can be used to determine if the boiler water is embrittling in character.

CHLORIDE INDUCED STRESS
CORROSION CRACKING

A specific type of stress corrosion cracking is induced by a chloride concentration cell, common with, but not limited to, stainless steels (Figure 20.10). To occur, it requires a chloride concentration and tensile stress focused together to cause both intergranular and transgranular branch type cracking. This produces weakening of the metal and eventual failure. When this type of failure was first experienced, it was thought that chloride concentrations as low as 50–100 mg/l were responsible. But experience indicates that the concentration of chloride in the water contacting the stainless steel is not the critical factor. The main factor is the existence of conditions that allow chloride concentration cells to develop.

In the absence of concentration cells or stress, chloride levels in excess of 1000 mg/l have not caused stainless steel to crack. In fact, some desalination plants, where chloride concentrations exceed 30,000 mg/l have not experienced failures, when properly annealed stainless steel construction was used, and the system kept free of deposits. The key to preventing stress corrosion cracking is eliminating deposits and designing and fabricating stress-relieved equipment that does not allow concentration cells to occur.

Figure 20.10 Chloride stress corrosion cracking of type 316 stainless steel, showing the typical branching of the crack. (150×.)

CORROSION FATIGUE CRACKING

As the name implies, corrosion fatigue cracking is a result of a combination of both a corrosive environment and repeated working of a metal (Figure 20.11). The fatigue is brought on by the routine, cyclic application of stress.

This action occurring repeatedly in a corrosive environment eventually causes the metal to crack. Such failure can occur with any kind of corrosive environment and any type of metal.

The fatigue cracks are normally at right angles to the applied stress and the rate of propagation is dependent on the corrosivity of the water, the degree of stress, and the number of cycles that occur over a given time.

To minimize or prevent this type of attack, it is necessary to locate the source of stress and reduce the cyclic frequency or magnitude. Inhibitors are helpful in reducing the corrosivity at the metal-water interface, thereby minimizing one of the two forces that must be present for this transgranular, D-notched type of failure to propagate.

Corrosion fatigue cracking is more common than stress corrosion cracking.

TUBERCULATION

Tuberculation is the result of a series of circumstances that cause various corrosion processes to produce a unique nodule on steel surfaces. Figure 20.12 shows a cross section of a typical tubercle, with the majority of the mound composed of layers of various forms of iron oxide and corrosion products in laminar form. Initially, metal ions are produced at an anodic site. A high pH, caused by

Figure 20.11 Corrosion fatigue cracks in low-carbon steel. Blunt, wedge-shaped cracks are typical in this kind of failure. (150×)

hydroxyl or carbonate ions, encourages iron to redeposit adjacent to the anodic area. This mechanism continues until the original anodic area is pitted from metal loss, and the pit is filled with porous iron compounds forming a mound, since the byproducts are more voluminous than the original metal. Within the tubercle, the aquatic environment is high in chlorides and sulfates and low in passivating oxygen. As a result, both oxygen differential cells and concentration cells form. Advanced tubercles may contain sulfides or acids.

This type of corrosion is common in systems not properly treated (Figure 20.13). Tubercles greatly increase the resistance to water flow and restrict carrying capacity. Large tubercles may break loose periodically and become lodged in critical passageways, such as heat exchanger water boxes or high pressure descaling sprays in a hot rolling process.

Figure 20.12 Model of a corrosion tubercle, showing the forms of iron oxide found at various layers as influenced by oxidation-reduction potential.

Figure 20.13 Tuberculation of a small-diameter pipe quickly blocks water flow and leads to perforation of the metal wall.

IMPINGEMENT ATTACK

Impingement attack is another type of selective corrosion involving both physical and chemical conditions, which produce a high rate of metal loss and penetration in a localized area. It occurs when a physical force is applied to the metal surface by suspended solids, gas bubbles, or the liquid itself, with sufficient force to wear away the natural or applied passivation film of the metal. This process occurs repeatedly and each occurrence results in the removal of successive metal oxidation layers.

The most easily identified characteristic of impingement attack is the "horseshoe walking upstream" (Figure 20.14). This pattern generally results when deposits on the metal surface create an eddy around an obstruction and debris or bubbles strike the metal around the deposit. A general metal loss or wall thinning indicates abrasive attack from suspended solids.

Cavitation is a special form of impingement attack most often found in pump impellers. This attack results from the collapse of air or vapor bubbles on the metal surface with sufficient force to produce rapid, local metal loss (Figure 20.15).

DEZINCIFICATION

Dezincification is a type of corrosion usually limited to brass. It takes two forms, general and plug type, but the mechanism is believed to be the same. For example, dezincification occurs when zinc and copper are solubilized at the liquid-metal interface, with the zinc being carried off in the liquid medium while the copper replates. The replated copper is soft and lacks the mechanical strength of the original metal. The redeposition accounts for the copper color characteristic of dezincification (Figure 20.16).

General dezincification occurs wherever a large surface of the metal is affected, while plug type is highly localized.

Figure 20.14 Erosion-corrosion, or impingement attack, of brass. Soft metals and alloys are particularly susceptible to this type of corrosion, accelerated by silt or gas bubbles. (12×)

CORROSION INHIBITION

In water distribution systems, related water-using equipment, and boiler and condensate systems, complete corrosion protection of metal and alloys may be impractical. The goal is to control corrosion to tolerable levels by good design, selection of proper materials of construction, and effective water treatment. Levels of corrosion may be expressed as metal loss in mils/year (mpy), a mil being 0.001 in. (0.0025 cm). (1 mpy = 0.025 mm/yr.) In a cooling system, an acceptable loss may be as much as 10–15 mpy (0.25–0.37 mm/yr); in a supercritical boiler it may be zero.

MATERIALS OF CONSTRUCTION

Where practical and economical, use of corrosion resistant materials such as copper, stainless steel, copper-nickel alloys, concrete, and plastic may offer advantages over carbon steel. However, when taking this approach, it is important to thoroughly understand the total system. For example, substituting Admiralty for mild steel in a heat exchanger in a system exposed to ammonia would be a mistake. Substituting a pure aluminum exchanger for aluminum alloy may reduce process side corrosion at the expense of accelerating waterside corrosion. Galvanic couples from mixtures of alloys should be avoided.

Figure 20.15 Cavitation of a bronze pump impeller, common to the operation of a centrifugal pump with a starved suction.

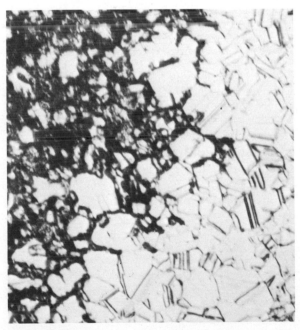

Figure 20.16 Dezincification of brass, showing the selective leaching of zinc and the residue of copper redeposited in the cavity. (100×)

COATINGS AND LININGS

Another practical way to prevent corrosion is to separate a metal from the water with coatings or linings. It is common to coat selected parts of some systems. For example, water boxes and tube sheets in many utilities are coated to minimize galvanic corrosion between these mild steel components and the Admiralty tubes generally employed in the surface condenser. Coatings and liners of various types are also used to prevent water line corrosion in feed tanks and emergency holding tanks. A special plastic sleeve is used in some utilities and industrial plants to prevent impingement attack at the entrance of condenser tubes. But as a general practice, most industrial systems are so widespread and complex that completely coating all piping would be too expensive, and coatings are therefore usually limited to the examples given above.

INSULATION

As noted earlier, the joining of dissimilar metals can lead to galvanic corrosion. If this cannot be corrected by a substitution of materials of construction, and it is essential to use these dissimilar metals in the system, they may be insulated from one another. This can be accomplished by inserting nonconductive materials, such as plastic pipe, between them (Figure 20.17). When this is done, it may be necessary to put an electrical cable as a jumper around the isolated unit, because the system may be used as an electrical ground.

APPLIED CHEMICAL INHIBITORS

In spite of the fact that many options exist to minimize corrosion by improved design or better construction methods, because of economics, the majority of systems are designed and fabricated in such a way that a chemical inhibitor program is needed to control corrosion. This applies to all types of water systems: potable water distribution systems, cooling water systems, boiler water systems, process water, and effluent treatment plants.

In the following discussion, because the greatest use of corrosion inhibitors is in cooling water systems, these will serve as the basis for examples of techniques of corrosion protection. The techniques of controlling corrosion in other environments, such as steam/condensate systems or water distribution headers, are covered elsewhere in this text.

CORROSION INHIBITORS

As noted earlier, all the elements of a corrosion circuit must be completed for corrosion to proceed. This involves, among other things, an anodic and cathodic

Figure 20.17 A method of insulating aluminum equipment from steel piping to prevent galvanic attack.

reaction. Therefore, any chemical applied to the water to stop the anodic reaction will stop corrosion; as a corollary, any material added to reduce the rate-determining cathodic reaction will reduce corrosion.

An effective corrosion control program usually depends on specific inhibitors to stop the anodic reaction, slow the cathodic reaction, or both. Typical inhibitors in use are shown by Table 20.2.

TABLE 20.2 Typical Corrosion Inhibitors

Principally anodic	Principally cathodic	Both anodic and cathodic
Chromate	Calcium carbonate	Organic filming amines
Orthophosphate	Polyphosphonate	
Nitrite	Zinc	
Silicate		

Of the anodic inhibitors, chromate, the most widely used, is a very strong inhibitor. Where many common corrosion inhibitors form a barrier layer on the metal surface, chromate reacts with the metal, forming a comparatively hard film of reduced chromate (Cr_2O_3) and alpha iron. The film formed in this manner is tightly adherent and long lasting. Orthophosphate, also an anodic inhibitor, forms an iron phosphate film, but this is not as tightly adherent or as long lasting as chromate. Nevertheless, when properly established and maintained, ortho-phosphate can be an effective corrosion inhibitor. Ordinarily, nitrite, orthophosphate and silicate receive less consideration than chromate in open re-circulating cooling systems because of costs and technical limitations, including potential for deposits (tricalcium phosphate), nutrient effect on microbes, and limited effectiveness, particularly true of the silicate species. In addition, these inhibitors require closer control than chromates.

Anodic inhibitors carry a risk: if applied in insufficient quantities, they do not properly passivate all anodic sites. Under these circumstances, the few remaining anodic sites become the focal point of all the electron flow to the cathodic reaction area, and deep pitting can result. Therefore, it is important to maintain sufficient quantities of anodic inhibitor in the system at all times.

Cathodic inhibitors generally reduce the corrosion rate by forming a barrier or film at the cathode, restricting the hydrogen ion or oxygen migration to the cathodic surface to complete the corrosion reaction. Since the overall rate is under cathodic control, the corrosion rate is reduced proportionally to the reduction of cathodic surface area.

Cathodic species—zinc, polyphosphate and calcium carbonate— are all considered safe compared to the risks of anodic inhibitors.

ANODIC/CATHODIC INHIBITOR MIXTURES

When inhibitors were first introduced into water systems, they were frequently composed of single active components (e.g., chromate). Over the years, it has been found that some ingredients improve the performances of others, a chemical principle called synergism. For example, chromate used by itself requires 200–300 mg/l CrO_4 to prevent corrosion in an open recirculating system; but, chromate combined with zinc, various organic and inorganic phosphates, or molybdates, provides equal or better results at only 20–30 mg/l CrO_4. Some systems currently operate quite successfully with less than 10 mg/l CrO_4, a feat that would be impossible without effective supplements only recently developed. Currently, chromates are used alone only in unique situations.

ORGANIC FILMERS

These materials are typified by forming filming layers on metal surfaces to separate the water and metal. These include filming amines for condensate systems that work effectively only in significantly reduced oxygen environments and soluble oils that are generally limited to special applications in cooling water systems. These materials form and maintain a dynamic barrier between the water and metal phases to prevent corrosion. This film is generally substantially thicker than the films established with the proper application of inorganic inhibitors such as chromate or zinc. An inherent danger in the filmer approach is that a small break in the continuous film could allow the corrosive agent to be focused on the unprotected area resulting in rapid penetration of the metal.

Another series of inhibitors of note are those applied to reduce copper and copper-alloy corrosion. These include mercaptobenzothiazole, benzotriazole and tolytriazole.

These are organic compounds that react with the metal surface and form protective films on copper and copper alloys. They form an extremely thin film barrier that is not to be compared with the thicker soluble oil type barrier. These materials are receiving more attention in modern treatments as more systems operate under increasingly higher TDS levels, a condition that encourages copper corrosion. Certain organo-phosphorus scale inhibitors used in cooling systems are aggressive to copper-type materials, requiring the addition of a copper inhibitor film when these are used.

SACRIFICIAL ANODES

Sacrificial anodes reduce galvanic attack by providing a metal (usually zinc, but sometimes magnesium) that is higher on the galvanic series than either of the two metals that are found coupled together in a system. The sacrificial anode thereby becomes anodic to both metals and supplies electrons to these cathodic surfaces. Design and placement of these anodes is a science in itself. When properly employed, they can greatly reduce loss of steel from the tube sheet of exchangers employing copper tubes, for example. Sacrificial anodes have helped supplement chemical programs in a variety of cooling water and process water systems.

WATER DISTRIBUTION SYSTEMS

The control of corrosion in water distribution systems presents some difficult problems in economics and water chemistry. In municipal water distribution systems, the choice of treatment chemicals is limited because the treated water must meet potable standards. Many industrial plants have the same problem, because drinking water is often tapped from the general mill supply. A secondary problem is the selection of a chemical for corrosion control that will not be harmful or undesirable in any of the uses of the water in the plant. And economics is an important consideration because the user resists the addition of any appreciable treatment costs to the 10–50 cents per 1,000 gallons that he may already be paying for the water.

Often where a water is corrosive, special materials of construction may be selected for the distribution system. These may include galvanized instead of ordinary steel piping; or it may be necessary to use special pipe such as thin-wall stainless steel tubing, lined pipe or non-metallic pipe.

However, the majority of installations for municipal or mill water distribution use plain steel. This is subject to corrosion, chiefly because of dissolved oxygen, an unfavorable stability index, or both. Corrosion may be aggravated by deposition of suspended solids, which might develop from after-precipitation of a lime treatment or biological activity.

The first step in correcting a distribution system corrosion problem should be a review of the water analysis to see if a change in the stability index would be beneficial. In many cases the corrosion can be brought under control by carrying a positive Langelier Index, or a Stability Index below 6.

Lime is usually fed to the system, since it has the dual effect of increasing calcium and alkalinity. One of the problems with lime, however, is that it may not be readily dissolved. Suspended lime in the system may settle at times of low flow or in areas of low velocity to create concentration cells. Even though it is more troublesome to do so, if proper feeding and dissolution of lime cannot be assured, then caustic soda should be fed and this may be supplemented with calcium chloride to achieve the overall effect of adding lime. If the plant has its own water treatment system, it may be possible to correct the Stability Index ahead of the final filters to avoid after-precipitation of undissolved lime.

If the water in the distribution system has been disinfected and carries a chlorine residual, this helps greatly in controlling corrosion by eliminating the additive effect of microbial activity to the corrosion process.

The conventional chemical treatments used in distribution systems include polyphosphates and silicates.

The exact mechanism by which polyphosphates control corrosion in distribution systems is not well known, but it probably includes dispersancy and the ability of polyphosphates to inhibit calcium carbonate precipitation (threshold treatment). Polyphosphates are usually applied at a dosage of about 2 mg/l. They are not objectionable in potable water, but they do sequester calcium so that polyphosphate-treated waters may not be completely reacted in ion exchange systems. In many cases this is not objectionable, but where high-purity demineralized water is required, the carry through of only 0.1–0.5 mg/l hardness could be objectionable.

Sodium silicates are less frequently used because the dosage required is usually in the range of 8–10 mg/l as SiO_2, requiring a feed of about 20–25 mg/l sodium silicate. Nevertheless, the treatments are effective, and although they may not be economical for treatment of the total water supply, they may be applied instead to points of use along the distribution system where the cost of the treatment can be justified. For example, in soft water areas where water is quite corrosive, such as along the northeastern seaboard, sodium silicate may be used to treat incoming municipal water at shopping centers and commercial buildings.

Zinc is effective in corrosion control of distribution systems just as in cooling water systems. It is usually fed with polyphosphates, but where the polyphosphate is objectionable it may be fed with orthophosphates. Since the orthophosphates are anodic inhibitors and because the level of treatment must be kept quite low to avoid calcium phosphate deposits, a treatment of this kind must be very carefully monitored for potential pitting-type attack. Such treatment may provide general corrosion protection but could lead to localized pitting.

Sacrificial anodes are sometimes used at critical locations in a distribution system where the water is tapped off for once-through cooling of heat exchangers or process equipment. They may also be used in domestic hot water heaters in areas where the municipal supply is unusually aggressive, but it is not economical to treat the total flow.

Since oxygen is a prominent factor in corrosion of steel distribution systems, deaeration may be a practical process for corrosion control. Reduction of O_2 concentration to less than 0.5 mg/l will usually provide adequate protection.

A number of industrial installations have used cold water deaerators (vacuum deaerators) for protection of long pipelines. The cost is usually justified not just on the basis of maintenance cost but also in energy savings, since corrosion control maintains a smooth pipe wall surface, thus reducing pumping power consumption.

MONITORING RESULTS

Most water systems are in continuous use, so it is rare to have access to inspect the actual system to observe or measure corrosion and corrosion inhibition. A number of tools have been developed to measure corrosion by indirect means. Some of the more common of those employed today are outlined below:

Corrosion Coupons   These preweighed metal specimens (Figure 20.18) are normally put into a system for 30–90 days. Following removal, they are cleaned, reweighed and observed. The metal loss (expressed in mpy) and the type of attack (general, pitting) is then determined and reported.

Occasionally, coupons undergo visual evaluation only. Coupon data vary widely based on coupon finish (e.g., polished vs sandblasted), location in the system, length of exposure, type of metallurgy, and type of pretreatment, if any. Corrosion coupons are excellent tools when properly used and evaluated. The outline diagram (Figure 20.19) shows a typical report of a coupon evaluation.

Corrosion Nipples   These are similar to coupons in concept, but are not preweighed, and only visually evaluated. They offer an advantage over a poorly designed and installed corrosion coupon setup that does not take flow velocity into consideration. Generally, however, coupons have more utility because they provide more information if the coupon racks have been properly designed.

A nipple consists of a simple pipe that is installed on a bypass arrangement (Figure 20.20) so that the nipple can be easily removed for inspection at any time.

Corrosion Meters   Corrosion coupons provide long-term data. For more immediate results a corrosion meter can provide a readout in 24 hours or less following initial system insertion. Like the coupon, the corrosion rate is indicated

Figure 20.18a   Installation of corrosion coupon rack. The control valve at left connects to the water line being sampled and is throttled to produce the correct velocity past the coupons, as measured at the overflow (top). The coupons are inserted at each tee.

Figure 20.18b Installation of corrosion coupons.

in mpy. The meter works by measuring an electrical potential across electrodes made of the metal being evaluated.

When allowed to stabilize in the system, the meter illustrated in Figure 20.21 can provide instantaneous corrosion readings. This is useful for optimizing pH, TDS, inhibitor level, chlorine application and other control variables. The more sophisticated meters provide a pitting tendency index, so both the amount of metal loss and type of loss is indicated.

Figure 20.18c Typical coupons after exposure.

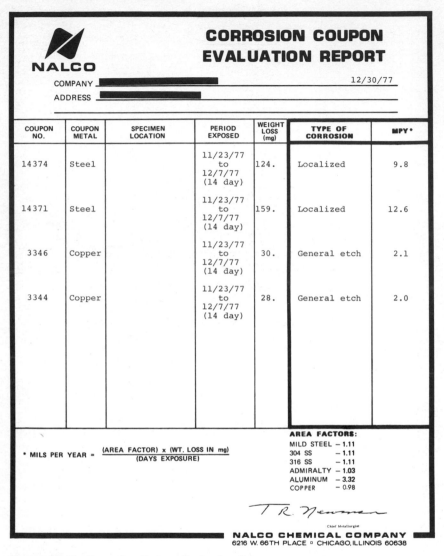

CORROSION COUPON EVALUATION REPORT

COMPANY ▌▌▌▌▌▌▌▌▌▌▌▌▌▌▌▌▌   12/30/77

ADDRESS ▌▌▌▌▌▌▌▌▌▌▌▌▌

COUPON NO.	COUPON METAL	SPECIMEN LOCATION	PERIOD EXPOSED	WEIGHT LOSS (mg)	TYPE OF CORROSION	MPY*
14374	Steel		11/23/77 to 12/7/77 (14 day)	124.	Localized	9.8
14371	Steel		11/23/77 to 12/7/77 (14 day)	159.	Localized	12.6
3346	Copper		11/23/77 to 12/7/77 (14 day)	30.	General etch	2.1
3344	Copper		11/23/77 to 12/7/77 (14 day)	28.	General etch	2.0

$$* \text{ MILS PER YEAR} = \frac{(\text{AREA FACTOR}) \times (\text{WT. LOSS IN mg})}{(\text{DAYS EXPOSURE})}$$

AREA FACTORS:

MILD STEEL — 1.11
304 SS — 1.11
316 SS — 1.11
ADMIRALTY — 1.03
ALUMINUM — 3.32
COPPER — 0.98

T. R. Newman
Chief Metallurgist

NALCO CHEMICAL COMPANY
6216 W. 66TH PLACE □ CHICAGO, ILLINOIS 60638

Figure 20.19   Corrosion Coupon Evaluation Report.

Bypass line used while test nipples are being inspected

Test nipples

Valve 3

Valve 1

Valve 2

Figure 20.20   The use of test nipples, installed in steam or condensate lines, permits both visual inspection of system conditions and a measure of corrosion.

Figure 20.21   Operator connecting a corrosion meter to a permanently installed probe to read corrosion rate of the probe material in the system. (*Courtesy of Magna Instruments, a division of Rohrback Corporation.*)

Although meters provide some unique advantages over coupons, coupons continue to be employed to determine long term effects of water and metal contact under fluctuating system conditions. The coupon and the meter are effective tools that complement one another.

Instantaneous corrosion monitoring has been applied to feed and control the level of inhibitor in cooling water systems. This technology has generally been limited to chromate inhibitors.

Field Evaluation Unit   Figure 20.22 shows a typical field evaluation unit. It has several key points. First, it incorporates a scientifically designed corrosion coupon rack. The flow (and therefore velocity) through the rack is selected and controlled. There are positions for both meter probes and corrosion coupons so that short term and long term corrosion rates can be effectively measured. Second, the unit duplicates heat transfer surfaces. Since temperature or heat flux can have a significant effect on the scaling, fouling or corrosion rates being experienced in a system, monitoring this variable is important. A properly installed unit can provide an excellent readout and visual indication of what is happening in the operating equipment. The Field Evaluation Unit effectively monitors corrosion on both heat transfer and non-heat transfer surfaces under conditions that closely duplicate flow velocities, metallurgy and heat flux of the actual operating system.

Figure 20.22 A field test unit including heat exchanger and coupon rack used for evaluating corrosion inhibitors and the effect of temperature and flow rate on their performance.

Chapter 21
Deposit Control

Deposits, in simplest terms, are an accumulation of sediments or settled solids that drop out at some point in a system where the water velocity falls to a level too low to support the material in the stream. This definition is over-simplified since deposits are usually found to contain—in addition to settled solids—scale, corrosion products, microbial masses, reaction products and oils.

Deposits can occur in any type of water conduit, water using device, or storage tank. They occur in boilers as well as distribution systems and heat exchange equipment. In this book, those deposits forming in cooling systems are examined, and the principles of deposit control in other systems can be surmised from the focus on the fundamentals of deposit formation.

A deposit is seldom composed of one substance, and is almost always an accumulation of materials. For example, silt from makeup water may begin to deposit in a low-flow section of a heat exchanger. If the water is on the border of $CaCO_3$, instability, the settling solids may act as the initiator for the scaling mechanism by further obstructing flow, and a deposit will form. This will then be a combination of silt and scale, and it may form even though the system is being treated for scale control by acid or some other chemical.

Once the deposit forms, dormant microbial organisms may become active, and if the deposit were then analyzed, all three constituents would be found. The difficulty in studying the analysis is deciding the likely order of events. The sequence could have started with microbial activity blocking the flow, causing the co-deposition of the other two constituents. Analyzing deposit mechanisms and devising effective control actions demand a study of the total system. The problem may not be caused by suspended solids alone.

DEPOSIT SOURCES

The source of potential depositing material may be external or internal to the system. One of the most prominent external sources is the water supply itself, which may contain suspended solids, such as silt in a turbid surface water, soluble or precipitated iron, manganese, or carryover from a clarifier or other pretreatment unit.

A second source of depositing materials, particularly in an open circulating cooling system with a cooling tower, is air. Cooling towers act as large air scrubbers, and the water is quite effective in capturing dust, microbes, and other debris from the large volume of air that it contacts. Because the amount of suspended solids in air is always changing, the suspended solids level in the circulating water also changes considerably from time to time; seasonal variations are common, depending on local environmental conditions. Atmospheric sources contribute significantly to deposits in arid sections of the country, near farm lands, and in areas of high prevailing winds.

Cooling towers also scrub industrial gases from air. Ammonia, hydrogen sulfide, sulfur dioxide and others are readily absorbed into water, where they react chemically, changing the water characteristics. Sometimes this change can be so dramatic that scaling, corrosion or microbial masses may suddenly obstruct a system in a matter of days.

Another significant external factor influencing deposits is leakage of process fluids into a water stream. This leakage may contribute directly or indirectly to the deposits. The most common effect is to provide food for microbial growth if the leaking contaminants are organic, such as oil or food substances.

Miscellaneous external sources include water used on pumps in the water circuit and lubricants applied to valves, pump glands and bearings that leak into the water system through these seals.

Internal sources of deposit originate in the circulating water—chemical precipitation, formation of corrosion products, polymerization, and biological growth are examples of these.

Precipitation is usually induced by temperature change or a disturbance in the equilibrium of the system which causes the solubility product of some constituent in the system, such as calcium carbonate, to be exceeded. Steel corrosion products form iron oxides and hydroxides that tend to deposit in the system, particularly on hot surfaces. Polymerization of organic materials is a more nebulous effect; an example of this is the coagulation of proteins which occurs when the temperature of water reaches 140–150°F (60–65°C), the pasteurization range. There may be naturally-occurring proteins in the system brought in with the raw water makeup, or the proteins may be by-products of the metabolism of microbial life in the system. The polymerization of other organic materials may also occur. Finally, biological activity may be encouraged by the nutrients and food substances present in the water.

DEPOSIT APPEARANCE

Because a deposit is frequently sedimentary, it may be found in the system as uncompacted silt in equipment or piping, or it may have hardened as additional chemical or biological activity developed after sedimentation of the initial material. Where biological activity develops rapidly, the deposit may be predominantly organic material from cell substances, and it may be porous or slimy. The deposit may be modified by chemical reactions, particularly if high temperatures prevail which could encourage chemical precipitation or corrosion reactions. At any rate, regardless of the nature of the deposit, because it is basically sedimentary, it usually has a laminar structure which tells something of its history (Figure 21.1).

Figure 21.1 Laminar nature typical of most deposits, indicating variations in the environment. Analysis of each layer is sometimes required to determine all of the reasons for deposit formation.

DEPOSIT IDENTIFICATION

Evaluating the cause of a deposit in a water distribution system requires a complete examination of the water system involved. A flow diagram showing the water circuit, piping, and individual pieces of equipment in the system is required. Flow rates at critical points in the system, temperatures encountered (including seasonal variations), and materials of construction are also important data. The location of the deposit in the system should be indicated on the flow diagram.

Sensual observations are important, particularly those relating to the appearance of the equipment or piping where the deposit was found, the nature of the deposit itself, and samples of water from the system taken at the deposit location. The deposit may have an odor when first removed from the system which may disappear when it reaches the laboratory for analysis. The fresh deposit may feel slimy, yet may lose this characteristic if it dries before reaching the laboratory. So it is important that the person sampling record his own observations of this kind relating to the fresh sample.

Four types of analytical tests are used to supply chemical and biological data to supplement the physical data; a deposit analysis, a complete mineral analysis of the water, a microbial analysis of the system water and a microbial analysis of the deposit (Figures 21.2, 21.3, 21.4, and 21.5).

The water analysis shown in Figure 21.3 indicates that this water is stable as it exists in the river at 50°F (10°C). However, if the water is used for cooling and is heated to 100°F (38°C), the Stability Index shows that $CaCO_3$ will precipitate, which may cement together the settled clay deposits. This indicates that either softening or a scale control chemical treatment should be considered to prevent problems of excessive deposit formation.

Taken together, the deposit analysis and the water analysis may indicate whether the suspended materials present in the water source can create sedimentary type deposits. Confirmation of the role of raw water suspended solids in the formation of the deposit may be further verified by an analysis of the solids themselves. These analyses (Figures 21.6 and 21.7) indicate that this water

NALCO

DEPOSIT ANALYSIS
REPORT

FROM:

Sample Marked: Water Delivery Line

Analysis No.	329757
Date Sampled:	4/22/73
Date Received:	4/29/73
Date Printed:	5/03/73

Physical Appearance: Layered Tan Solid

Inorganics in dried sample

Iron Fe_2O_3	35
Silica (SiO_2)	30
Phosphorus (P_2O_5)	3
Alumina (Al_2O_3)	12
Calcium (CaO)	3
Sulfur (SO_3)	1
Carbonate (CO_3)	0
Loss at $200°C$	16

The following elements were not determined:

Na Mg Zn Cl K Ti V Cr Mn Co Ni Cu Sr Sn Pb

Lab comments:

  No iron present in top layers.

James J Hickey

NALCO CHEMICAL COMPANY
6216 W. 66TH PLACE □ CHICAGO, ILLINOIS 60638

Figure 21.2 Deposit taken from water supply line.

contains a high level of colloidal clay originating in the river supplying the plant. The settleability of these solids may be determined by the Imhoff cone to provide a basis for deciding whether clarification may be necessary.

Figure 21.8 shows a microbiologically-contaminated water source. This level of contamination is common in river waters and some well systems fed by surface waters. The level of microbial contamination in this system indicates the need for a continuous biocidal program to protect the equipment against fouling. For once-through water usage, a low chlorine dosage, and a specific biodispersant should be considered separately or in combination to maintain a clean system. Slime-forming bacteria present a heat transfer problem in all systems where they are found; bacterial slimes have a lower heat transfer capacity than calcium carbonate scale.

In Figure 21.2 the deposit analyzed had a segmented or layered structure, the upper layers of this deposit indicating the high silt content of the system. The high iron content of the lower layers indicates active corrosion occurring below the silt.

Layering is often the result of long-term corrosion, wherein the strata represent changes in distribution of the various forms of iron, as in the development of a long-term corrosion tubercle. Examination of other layered deposits may indicate various periods of process contamination, variations in suspended solids, or lack of pH control of the water system.

Deposits can be analyzed physically as well as chemically. Microscopic examination of a deposit explores the appearance of individual layers. X-ray fluores-

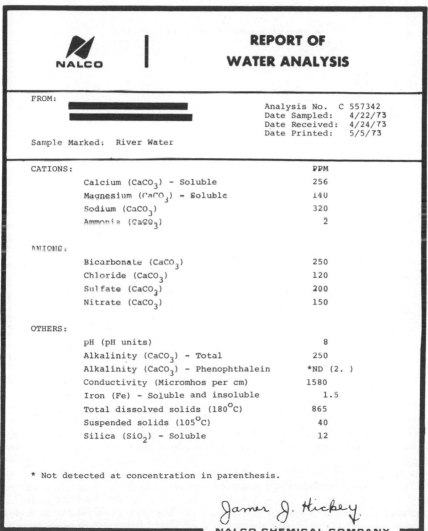

REPORT OF WATER ANALYSIS

NALCO

FROM:

Sample Marked: River Water

Analysis No.   C 557342
Date Sampled: 4/22/73
Date Received: 4/24/73
Date Printed: 5/5/73

CATIONS:		PPM
	Calcium (CaCO$_3$) - Soluble	256
	Magnesium (CaCO$_3$) - Soluble	140
	Sodium (CaCO$_3$)	320
	Ammonia (CaCO$_3$)	2
ANIONS:		
	Bicarbonate (CaCO$_3$)	250
	Chloride (CaCO$_3$)	120
	Sulfate (CaCO$_3$)	200
	Nitrate (CaCO$_3$)	150
OTHERS:		
	pH (pH units)	8
	Alkalinity (CaCO$_3$) - Total	250
	Alkalinity (CaCO$_3$) - Phenophthalein	*ND (2.)
	Conductivity (Micromhos per cm)	1580
	Iron (Fe) - Soluble and insoluble	1.5
	Total dissolved solids (180°C)	865
	Suspended solids (105°C)	40
	Silica (SiO$_2$) - Soluble	12

* Not detected at concentration in parenthesis.

James J. Hickey

NALCO CHEMICAL COMPANY
6216 W. 66TH PLACE · CHICAGO, ILLINOIS 60638

Figure 21.3 Analysis of water from same system as Figure 21.2.

NALCO | **REPORT OF**
MICROBIOLOGICAL ANALYSIS

Company ▓▓▓▓▓▓▓▓▓▓▓▓

Address ▓▓▓▓▓▓▓▓▓

Sample Marked   Condenser Deposit

Analysis No.	007548
Sampling Date	4/22/73
Date Rec'd by NALCO	4/24/73
Date Printed	5/3/73

Physical Appearance   Brown deposit

(All counts express quantity of organisms per ml of sample)

BACTERIA

AEROBIC SLIME FORMING
Non-Sporeforming
Flavobacterium 20,000
Mucoids .... NEG IN 1/1000
Aerobacter .... NEG IN 1/1000
Pseudomonas 35,000,000

Sporeforming
  B. subtilis 200
  B. cereus
  B. megatherium
  B. mycoides 500

ANAEROBIC CORROSIVE
Desulfovibrio 10,000
Clostridia 3,000

IRON DEPOSITING
Sphaerotilus ....
Gallionella .... NONE

OTHER BACTERIA   NONE

TOTAL COUNT   80,000,000

REMARKS:

FUNGI

MOLDS
  Aspergillus 500
  Penicillium ....
  Trichoderma 200
  Alternaria ....
  Mucor   100
YEASTS
  Torula ....
  Monilia .... NONE
  Saccharomyces ....
  Rhodotorula ....

ALGAE

BLUE GREEN .... NONE
  Oscillatoria ....

GREEN
  Chlorococcus ....

DIATOMS ....

OTHER ORGANISMS

Ronald Christensen
Head, Microbiological Laboratory

NALCO CHEMICAL COMPANY
6216 W. 66TH PLACE □ CHICAGO, ILLINOIS 60638

Figure 21.4   Microbial analysis of water from supply line.

cence shows the quantitative levels of specific atoms contained in a deposit. X-ray diffraction techniques determine the crystalline composition of materials within the deposit. A scanning electron microscope with an energy dispersive analysis of X-ray (EDAX) capability can identify elements and provide visual examination of individual deposit layers at high magnification. These examinations are not always necessary, but are valuable aids to solving difficult problems. In instances where microbial activity has been a contributor to deposit formation, regularly scheduled sampling of water from the deposit area for microbiological analysis is necessary to assure that the disinfection program is protecting the system.

Deposit control programs work best when used for preventive rather than corrective purposes. All the tools noted earlier are employed for evaluating the problem. For example, if the survey shows that the concentrations and type of solids introduced into a system are likely to settle at the velocity encountered in the system, then either chemical treatment or a reduction of these solids is necessary, or both. This may take the form of complete treatment of the incoming makeup water. In a recirculating cooling system, it may require the inclusion of a slipstream filter in the loop. If the change in the Stability Index

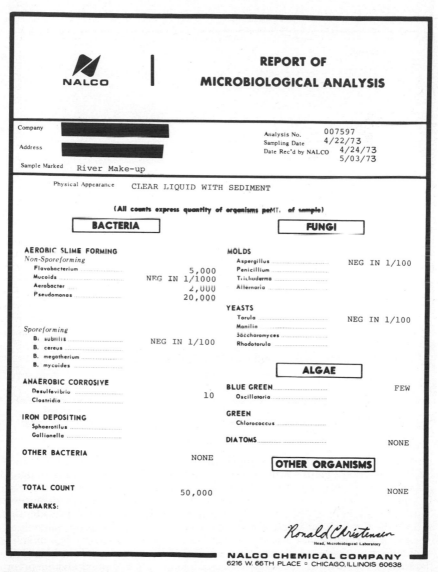

Figure 21.5 Microbial analysis of deposit from condenser cooled by same water supply as Figure 21.3.

REPORT OF
WATER ANALYSIS

NALCO

FROM:

ANALYSIS NO.   P 5390
DATE SAMPLED   8/20/77
DATE RECEIVED   8/23/77
DATE PRINTED   8/26/77

SAMPLE MARKED: River Water

CATIONS:	PPM
CALCIUM ($CaCO_3$) - SOLUBLE	110
MAGNESIUM ($CaCO_3$) - SOLUBLE	58

ANIONS:	
BICARBONATE ALKALINITY ($CaCO_3$)	132
SILICA (SiO_2) - Soluble	6

OTHERS:	
pH (pH UNITS)	7.9
ALKALINITY ($CaCO_3$) - TOTAL	132
ALKALINITY ($CaCO_3$) - PHENOLPHTHALEIN	ND*
ALKALINITY ($CaCO_3$) - P-$BaCl_2$	ND*
CONDUCTIVITY (MICROMHOS PER cm)	260
TURBIDITY (NEPHELOMETRIC TURBIDITY UNITS)	36
CALCIUM ($CaCO_3$) - SOLUBLE AND INSOLUBLE	111
MAGNESIUM ($CaCO_3$) - SOLUBLE AND INSOLUBLE	58
IRON (Fe) - SOLUBLE AND INSOLUBLE	2.3
SUSPENDED SOLIDS	85

*NOT DETECTED (BELOW INDICATED LIMIT OF DETECTION)

James J. Hickey

NALCO CHEMICAL COMPANY
6216 W. 66TH PLACE □ CHICAGO, ILLINOIS 60638

Figure 21.6 Analysis of river water.

resulting from a temperature change is such that it cannot be dealt with employing sequestering agents or dispersants, then the pretreatment system should provide not only for removal of suspended solids, but also softening of the water by lime treatment. Finally, sterilization of the makeup water, either with the clarification/softening operation or separately, should be practiced if microbial activity cannot be kept under control by treatment of the process water itself.

Preventive control may also require modification of the system. For example maintaining solids in suspension may require increasing the velocities through the water circuit by such means as recycling around the equipment with a pump, or agitating the water by injection of air into critical segments of the system at periodic intervals, called "air-rumbling."

TREATMENTS TO CONTROL
SYSTEM DEPOSITS

The first category of deposit control chemicals includes sequestering agents such as polyphosphates, organo-phosphorus compounds, and polymers such as acrylates. These exert a threshold effect reducing the potential for precipitation of iron, manganese and calcium compounds.

The second group is organic dispersants, including organo-phosphorus compounds, surface-active agents, and polyelectrolytes. If the applied dispersant is a charged molecule, such as a polyelectrolyte, it will disperse suspended solids by adsorbing to their surfaces, thus adding an electrostatic charge to the particles, causing them to repel one another. Other dispersants condition the surfaces

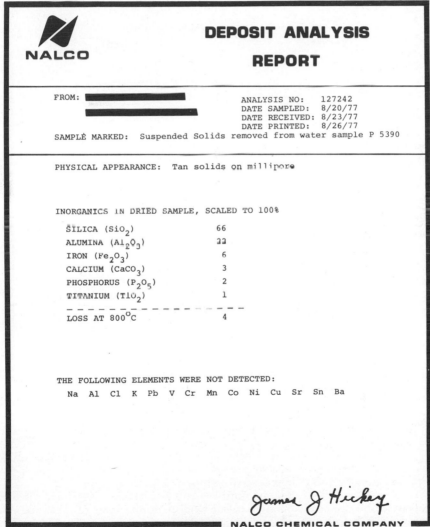

Figure 21.7 Analysis of suspended solids from sample, Figure 21.6.

REPORT OF
MICROBIOLOGICAL ANALYSIS

NALCO

Company	
Address	
Sample Marked	Illinois River Water

Analysis No. 113729
Sampling Date 7/29/77
Date Rec'd by NALCO 8/2/77
Date Printed 8/5/77

Physical Appearance

(All counts express quantity of organisms per ml of sample)

BACTERIA

AEROBIC SLIME FORMING
Non-Sporeforming
Flavobacterium	NEG IN 1/1000	
Mucoids	NEG IN 1/1000	
Aerobacter	NEG IN 1/10	
Pseudomonas	80,000	

E. coli   40

Sporeforming
B. subtilis
B. cereus
B. megatherium
B. mycoides

ANAEROBIC CORROSIVE
Desulfovibrio   100
Clostridia

IRON DEPOSITING   NONE
Sphaerotilus
Gallionella

OTHER BACTERIA   NONE

TOTAL COUNT   320,000

REMARKS:

FUNGI

MOLDS
Aspergillus	NEG IN 1/10
Penicillium	
Trichoderma	
Alternaria	

YEASTS
Torula	NEG IN 1/10
Monilia	
Saccharomyces	
Rhodotorula	

ALGAE

BLUE GREEN   NONE
Oscillatoria

GREEN   NONE
Chlorococcus

DIATOMS   NONE

OTHER ORGANISMS

NONE

Ronald Christensen
Head, Microbiological Laboratory

NALCO CHEMICAL COMPANY
6216 W. 66TH PLACE □ CHICAGO, ILLINOIS 60638

Figure 21.8 Microbial analysis of a contaminated water.

of the suspended solids in other ways to keep them from coagulating and settling.

A third class is compounds having both sequestering and dispersing properties. This category includes organo-phosphorus compounds, inorganic polyphosphates and natural or processed lignins and tannins.

A fourth category of deposit control agents is surface-active chemicals that penetrate and disperse biomasses, called biodispersants. Some of these are also biocides and help kill the slime organisms. Frequently, chlorine is used in conjunction with biodispersants, although other kinds of biocides may also be applied.

(a)

(b)

(c)

(d)

Figure 21.9 Crystal distortion caused by organic treatment chemicals. (All photos 2000×)
(a) CaCO₃ precipitated from a fresh water source. (b) Distortion created by a polyacrylate
treatment. (c) Changes in structure produced by treatment with an organic phosphate.
(d) Changes produced by a combination treatment of polyacrylate/phosphonate at only
0.5 mg/l.

A fifth group includes those chemicals used to modify the crystal structure of
scale. Scale, often mistaken for deposit, is the result of precipitation of the scale
components from a supersaturated solution. Since the presence of particulates
induces precipitation, scale is often one of the fractions in deposits. Chemicals
like tannin, lignin, or their derivatives have been used for many years to prevent
the growth of large crystals. In doing this, although precipitation is not prevented, the material that precipitates is structurally weak—more like a deposit
than a scale. In this respect, these chemicals which distort or modify crystal
growth may also be considered as deposit control agents. These chemicals are
used both in cooling systems and in boilers; they were the first organic treatments used to keep heat exchange surfaces clean. Figure 21.9 shows the typical
development of CaCO₃ crystals and distortion by chemical treatment of the
water.

Chapter **22**

Control of Microbial Activity

All water treatment processes are affected by the presence of microbes. Many oxidation-reduction reactions are biologically mediated. In most cases, microbial effects are detrimental to the water-using process or system. However, certain industrial operations put microbes to work in a useful way: the activated sludge process uses microbes for digestion of organic wastes; microbes are used for the fermentation of beverages; microbial enzymes are useful for leather processing.

Disinfection of municipal drinking water and sterilization of food processing and hospital equipment are examples of applications of biocides (chemicals toxic to microbes) where the goal is to kill all microbes. However, a complete kill is often costly, and not always necessary. Cooling water in utilities, steel mills, refineries, and other industrial plants is treated to control microbe populations at levels that experience has proven to be tolerable to the system without complete sterilization. Papermaking systems, unlike cooling water systems, are designed to operate with large amounts of suspended solids, so the tolerable levels of microbe populations are considerably higher than for cooling water. The tolerable microbe count in a paper mill varies with the type of paper being made and machine operating conditions.

Planning an effective microbial control program for a specific water treatment process requires an examination of:

1. The types of organisms present in the water system and the associated problems they can cause.

2. The population of each type of organism that may be tolerated before causing a significant problem.

Typical microbes encountered in water treatment and the problems they cause are summarized by Table 22.1.

Bacteria, the largest group of troublesome organisms, cause the most varied problems. They are usually classified in water treatment by the types of problems

TABLE 22.1 Typical Microorganisms and Their Associated Problems

Type of organism	Type of problem
A. Bacteria	
1. Slime forming bacteria	Form dense, sticky slime with subsequent fouling. Water flows can be impeded and promotion of other organism growth occurs.
2. Spore forming bacteria	Become inert when their environment becomes hostile to them. However, growth recurs whenever the environment becomes suitable again. Difficult to control if complete kill is required. However, most processes are not affected by sporeformers when the organism is in the spore form.
3. Iron depositing bacteria	Cause the oxidation and subsequent deposition of insoluble iron from soluble iron.
4. Nitrifying bacteria	Generate nitric acid from ammonia contamination. Can cause severe corrosion.
5. Sulfate reducing bacteria	Generate sulfides from sulfates and can cause serious localized corrosion.
6. Anaerobic corrosive bacteria	Create corrosive localized environments by secreting corrosive wastes. They are always found underneath other deposits in oxygen deficient locations.
B. Fungi Yeasts and molds	Cause the degradation of wood in contact with the water system. Cause spots on paper products.
C. Algae	Grow in sunlit areas in dense fibrous mats. Can cause plugging of distribution holes on cooling tower decks or dense growths on reservoirs and evaporation ponds.
D. Protozoa	Grow in almost any water which is contaminated with bacteria; indicate poor disinfection.
E. Higher life forms	Clams and other shell fish plug inlet screens.

they cause: slime-forming bacteria, iron depositors, sulfate reducers, and nitrifying bacteria. Each group has its preferred environment and thrives in specific areas of a water system. Aerobic bacteria, for example, require oxygen, so they are found in aerated waters such as in a cooling tower basin or white water in a paper machine wire pit. Anaerobic bacteria, on the other hand, don't use oxygen and obtain their energy from reactions other than the oxidation of organic substances. The reduction of sulfur in sulfate to the sulfide ion is an example. Since anaerobes don't need oxygen, they are found in oxygen-deficient areas, such as under deposits, in crevices, and in sludges.

Iron-depositors occur in water high in ferrous iron, which they convert to insoluble ferric hydroxide, and which becomes part of the mucilaginous sheath around the cell. These deposit and accelerate corrosion rates, which produces additional soluble iron, further increasing the population of iron depositors in the system. The cycle accelerates until the whole system is plugged with iron deposits (Figure 22.1).

Nitrifying bacteria oxidize ammonia to nitrate. This nitrification reaction sometimes occurs in iron removal filters, accompanied by a reduction of oxygen

Figure 22.1   Iron-depositing bacteria initiated the tuberculation attack of this steel distribution pipe.

Figure 22.2   The development of pits filled with voluminous products of corrosion from the attack of sulfate-reducing bacteria on steel pipe.

Figure 22.3 Electron photomicrograph of *Aerobacter aerogenes,* showing the capsule around the cells and hairlike fimbriae believed to play a part in slime formation. (Picture width is approximately 2 microns.)

Figure 22.4 Microtome of wood section from a cooling tower, showing fungal attack.

and pH. These bacteria are often found in ammonia plants where leakage of ammonia into cooling water encourages their growth. A pH drop caused by the conversion of ammonia to nitrate is often the clue to their presence.

Sulfate-reducing bacteria are found in many systems subject to deposit problems. The sulfides produced are corrosive to most metals used in water systems, including mild steel, stainless steel, and aluminum. Evidence of the sulfate reducers is the unique pit etched on the metal surface, sometimes in the form of concentric rings (Figure 22.2).

Many bacteria secrete a mucilaginous substance that encapsulates the cell Figure 22.3), shielding it from direct contact with water, so that the cell is protected from simple toxic biocides. Control of encapsulated bacteria usually requires both oxidation and dispersion of the protective sheath so that the biocide can reach the cell.

Yeasts and molds can live on dead or inert organic matter. Fungi are often found on wooden structures, such as cooling tower fill and supporting members, and sometimes under bacterial or algal masses. Fungal attack of wood usually means permanent loss of strength of the wood structure, so protection of the wood requires control of fungi from the time the structure is put into service. Periodic testing of the wood to determine its resistance to fungal attack is an important maintenance step. Very thin sections of wood specimens taken from susceptible locations are examined to determine the extent of attack if there has been any (Figure 22.4).

Algae need sunlight to grow, so they are found on open, exposed areas, such as cooling tower decks or on the surface of reservoirs, ponds, and lakes. Most algae grow in dense, fibrous mats that not only plug distribution piping and flumes, but also provide areas for subsequent growth of anaerobic bacteria under the algae deposits.

A century ago, a Danish biologist, Christian Gram, developed a method of staining bacterial cultures as a means of separating them into two broad categories as an aid to identification; those that retain a blue color produced by an iodine treatment are called Gram-positive; those not retaining the blue color and accepting a red dye following iodine treatment are Gram-negative. Most aquatic microbes are Gram-negative. They all are negatively charged colloids (have a negative zeta potential), a property not related to the Gram staining technique. Because they are negatively charged colloids, they are affected by cationic polymers and biocides.

PHYSICAL FACTORS AFFECTING MICROBE GROWTH

Many species of microbes indigenous to soil, water, and vertebrate organisms thrive in a rather broad temperature range of 10–45°C. Nature has produced select organisms that can live at temperatures as low as 0°C and as high as 70°C. Higher temperatures kill all microbes.

Denaturation of proteins, which causes coagulation within the cell, occurs at temperatures below 70°C. Commercial pasteurization is a denaturation process. Milk is usually pasteurized at 63°C by holding that temperature for 30 minutes; if the temperature is raised to 72°C, pasteurization is completed in only 15 seconds. This process kills all disease-producing (pathogenic) organisms but does not produce sterile milk; some microbes remain to cause the milk to spoil in time. Most actively growing microbes of interest in water treatment technology are killed at 70°C in less than five minutes.

Maintaining low temperatures is not an effective means of killing microbes. At 0–5°C, organisms become dormant. Freezing kills many cells, but those that survive are capable of complete recovery from the shock. One procedure used to preserve microbes involves freezing cells rapidly at −70°C and then removing the ice crystals as vapor (sublimation). This process is lyophilization.

Dry heat results in dehydration of all cellular matter and oxidation of intracellular constituents. Sterilization of laboratory media is usually carried out in an autoclave at 121°C. Sterilization of glassware is done with dry heat at 160°C for two hours.

Moisture is required for microorganisms to actively grow. Many species of pathogenic organisms are killed quickly by drying. However, organisms in the spore or cyst state can survive low moisture environments; and, if transported by wind or animals to a location where moisture levels suit them, they revive and form new colonies. To prevent attack by microbes, lumber and other vulnerable materials are dried to less than 20% moisture content.

Organisms containing chlorophyll are able to use the radiant energy of the sun or artificial lighting to convert CO_2 to carbohydrates, which they need for cell synthesis. However, not all radiant energy is useful to the cell and certain frequencies of radiation are harmful. Radiation is therefore one method of microbe control.

Short-wave length forms of energy, such as gamma rays (0.01–1 Å) and X-rays (1–100 Å) are particularly useful. These create free hydrogen and hydroxyl radicals and some peroxides when they pass through the cell, causing cell damage or death. These forms of radiation are hazardous. Energy in the ultraviolet region (100–4000 Å) is also useful for killing microbes. In this case, the energy is absorbed by the nucleic acids, creating chemical reactions that are lethal to the cell. This form of energy, however, has poor penetrating ability, so the use of ultraviolet light for disinfection requires a special design of treatment unit so that the energy does not have to penetrate deeply into the water.

Osmosis is the diffusion of water through a semipermeable membrane separating two solutions of different solute concentrations. The water flows in a direction to equalize the concentrations. When microbes are placed in 10–15% salt solutions or 50–70% sugar solutions, the water inside the cells is extracted by the surrounding medium. This dehydrates the cells so they are unable to grow or are killed. This technique is used commercially to preserve food. Bees use this principle to preserve honey, concentrating it by fanning the comb with their wings.

The interfaces between a liquid and a gas (such as surrounding a bubble of air in water), between two liquids (oil droplets in water), and between a solid and a liquid (sand grains in water) are characterized by unbalanced forces of attraction between the molecules of water at the surface and those in the fluid body. These forces are closely associated with the metabolic processes of the microbe. The cell must be able to accumulate nutrients at its surface for assimilation, and waste products must be eliminated from the cell and carried away. Therefore, the growth and well-being of a cell are influenced by surface forces in the surrounding aquatic environment.

Substances having surface tension depressing effects (surfactants) tend to have a detrimental effect on microbes if the concentration is high enough. These materials can alter cell division, growth, and survival. Surfactants are often used to increase the effectiveness of biocides by dispersing cell colonies and protective sheaths to allow the toxicant to contact the cells. Some toxicants are themselves surface active (such as phenols and quaternaries) and tend to accumulate on cell surfaces by adsorption. This prevents entrance and utilization of food substances by the cell. Quaternaries will sometimes cause leakage of cellular material out of the cell wall by changes in surface tension at the membrane surface.

CHEMICAL FACTORS AFFECTING MICROBIAL GROWTH

Microbes have been found to exist in the broad pH range of 2–13. However, the most common microbes associated with water—algae and bacteria—usually maintain their internal pH at 7, so they prefer a neutral aquatic environment.

Generally, yeasts and molds favor depressed pH, in the range of 3–4. Dilute alum solution is sometimes contaminated by fungi, causing the plugging of alum feed lines and rotameters while at the same time the solution is free of bacterial growth.

Bacteria and fungi can both contribute to industrial problems over a pH range of 5–10. Other chemical factors, discussed in earlier chapters, include the presence of organic matter to serve as food for the microbes, and a supply of the common nutrients such as nitrogen and phosphorus required for cell metabolism.

One of the surprising facts of microbe life is that there is such a profusion and variety of forms that some can almost always be found that will resist damage by, or even thrive on, chemicals that are toxic to animal and plant life. For example, phenol was one of the early chemical biocides used for sterilization in medical practice, yet it is readily digested in activated sludge waste treatment plants. Similarly, some bacteria thrive in wastewaters that contain herbicides, pesticides, cyanide, arsenic compounds, and a great variety of other chemicals normally considered toxic.

METHODS FOR CONTROLLING MICROBIAL ACTIVITY

For practical reasons, in most industrial water systems, only limited use can be made of the physical conditions that affect microbial life. For example, heating water may control microbial activity, but if the water is used for cooling purposes, this is not useful. Radiation is sometimes used, but its adoption on a widespread basis would require the development of more efficient energy sources and better designs of equipment to expose the water to the radiant energy. Among chemical conditions that might be used for microbe control, pH is the only likely candidate for practical results. Even this is limited unless the system water can be kept at a pH over 10. However, pH does have important effects on the performance of biocides, as shown below.

Since neither physical nor chemical conditions can be changed in a practical way to control microbial growth, chemicals must be used as biocides. The two commonly used types are oxidizing and non-oxidizing.

OXIDIZING BIOCIDES

Chlorine gas dissolved in water hydrolyzes rapidly according to the following equation:

$$Cl_2 + H_2O \rightarrow H^+ + Cl^- + HOCl \tag{1}$$

Hydrolysis occurs in less than a second at 65°F (18°C). Hypochlorous acid (HOCl) is the active ingredient formed by this reaction. This weak acid tends to undergo partial dissociation as follows:

$$HOCl \rightleftharpoons H^+ + OCl^- \tag{2}$$

This produces a hypochlorite ion and a hydrogen ion. Depending on pH and concentration, chlorine in water exists as free chlorine gas, hypochlorous acid

Figure 22.5 Distribution of hypochlorite in water as affected by pH.

or hypochlorite ion. Figure 22.5 illustrates the distribution of these components at varying pH values. Above pH 7.5, hypochlorite ions predominate, and they are the exclusive form when the pH exceeds 9. The sum of the hypochlorous acid and hypochlorite ions is defined as free available chlorine. Hypochlorite salts such as calcium hypochlorite ionize in water to yield these two species, depending on pH.

$$Ca(OCl)_2 \rightleftharpoons Ca^{+2} + 2OCl^- \tag{3}$$
$$2OCl^- + H_2O \rightleftharpoons HOCl + OCl^- + OH^- \tag{4}$$

Thus, the same equilibria are established whether elemental chlorine or hypochlorite is used for chlorination.

Liquefied chlorine is available in bulk or in cylinders. A typical installation for feeding chlorine is shown in Figure 22.6a and b.

Chemicals other than chlorine gas that liberate hypochlorite ions are compared to one another in oxidizing power on the basis of "available chlorine." The available chlorine values of a number of disinfectants are shown in Table 22.2.

Chlorine is a strong oxidizing agent capable of reacting with many impurities in water including ammonia, amino acids, proteins, carbonaceous material, Fe^{+2}, Mn^{+2}, S^{-2}, and CN^-.

The amount of chlorine needed to react with these substances is called the chlorine demand. Chlorine reacts with ammonia to form three different chloramines:

$$HOCl + NH_3 \rightarrow NH_2Cl \text{ (monochloramine)} + H_2O \tag{5}$$
$$NH_2Cl + HOCl \rightarrow NHCl_2 \text{ (dichloramine)} + H_2O \tag{6}$$
$$NHCl_2 + HOCl \rightarrow NCl_3 \text{ (trichloramine)} + H_2O \tag{7}$$

These chloramine compounds also have biocidal properties; they are referred to as the combined residual chlorine. In general, the chloramines are slower acting than free residual chlorine, but have the advantage of being more effective at pH values above 10. Chloramines may also be more persistent in a water system.

Breakpoint chlorination is the addition of sufficient chlorine to satisfy the

Figure 22.6a Typical chlorination system. In this plant, eight chlorinators each meter up to 8000 lb Cl_2/day to municipal sewage plant effluent. Each is supplied by a chlorine evaporator (in background, right). (*Courtesy of Wallace & Tiernan.*)

Figure 22.6b Ton cylinders of chlorine are mounted on a scale to monitor consumption by weight loss, and the discharge is converted to Cl_2 gas by the evaporator on the right. The chlorine supply room is isolated from operators in the control room. (*Courtesy of Wallace & Tiernan.*)

Chlorine applied, mg/l
(breakpoint can be estimated at 10 X NH₃, mg/l)

Figure 22.7 Breakpoint chlorination curves showing reaction of Cl₂ with N-compounds.

chlorine demand and produce free residual chlorine. When breakpoint chlorination is used, the ammonia nitrogen content is destroyed and the residual chlorine remaining will be almost entirely free available chlorine (Figure 22.7).

Chlorine also reacts with organic nitrogen in water. This is found in components of living cells, protein, polysaccharides, and amino acids. The toxicity of chlorine is thought to be derived not from the chlorine itself or its release of nascent oxygen, but rather from the reaction of the HOCl with the enzyme system of the cell. The superiority of HOCl over OCl⁻ may be due to the small molecular size and electrical neutrality of HOCl, which allow it to pass through the cell membrane.

On-site production of hypochlorite from sea water or brine is becoming popular as it limits the exposure of operating personnel to chlorine gas or hypochlorite compounds. An installation of such a system is shown in Figure 22.8.

Chlorine reacts with a variety of organic materials, and attention is being directed to the presence of chlorinated compounds in water thought to be produced by chlorination. Chloroform is one of these materials. Because of concern for the potentially adverse physiological effects of these chlorinated compounds, regulatory agencies are severely restricting chlorine applications to large effluent

TABLE 22.2 "Available Chlorine" of Chlorination Chemicals

Material	Percent available Cl₂
Chlorine gas (Cl₂)	100
Chlorine dioxide (ClO₂)	263
Hypochlorites (OCl)	
Calcium, HTH, Ca(OCl)₂	70
Sodium, NaOCl	
Industrial grade	12–15
Domestic grade	3–5
Lithium, LiOCl, laundry grade	35
Chlorinated isocyanuric acid (CONCl)₃	85

Figure 22.8 An electrolytic cell designed to produce chlorine from brine. This unit is generating Cl_2 from sea water for chlorination of sewage plant effluent. *(Courtesy of Electrolytic Systems Division, Diamond Shamrock.)*

flows. For example, treatment of utility station condenser water with chlorine may be limited to a total period of only two hours per day at residuals averaging not over 0.2 mg/l Cl_2

Chlorine dioxide, ClO_2, is used to a limited extent in water treatment for the control of taste and odor problems and for the degradation of phenol. It is used extensively in the pulp and paper industry for bleaching. This compound must be generated from the reaction of chlorine with sodium chlorite as shown:

$$2NaClO_2 + Cl_2 \rightarrow 2ClO_2 + 2NaCl \tag{8}$$

Generally an excess of chlorine is used to drive the reaction to completion. For safety and to preserve its stability, the material is generated on-site. Since chlorine dioxide does not react with ammonia, it is useful in systems containing ammonia.

The next most common oxidizing biocide is ozone, O_3. This is in use commercially throughout Europe and in certain municipalities in the United States for disinfection of potable water. It is also used in certain waste treatment applications to avoid the residual chloramines that result from the usual chlorination of wastewater effluent. Ozone is produced on-site by an electric corona discharge through air or oxygen. A typical ozone generator is shown in Figure 22.9.

Oxidizing biocides such as chlorine, hypochlorites and organochlorine materials will kill all organisms in the system quickly, if the free chlorine comes into direct contact with the organisms long enough and at a strong enough dosage level. They also retain their effectiveness because organisms cannot adapt to or become resistant to chlorine.

However, oxidizing biocides also react with contaminants like H_2S, NH_3, pulp lignins, wood sugars and other organics. This increases the amount of chlorine required for biocidal effects. They are not persistent, and they decay quickly after the chemical feed stops. They do not penetrate slime masses, and lose their effectiveness as pH increases.

So oxidizing biocides require complementary treatments to improve their effectiveness. These include dispersants to remove existing slime masses and to prevent organisms from settling on heat transfer surfaces; penetrants to permeate organic masses and to expose and kill subsurface organisms; and

Figure 22.9   A battery of three 110 lb/day ozonators installed in a municipal plant. These produce O_3 from air. *(Courtesy of Infilco Degremont, Inc.)*

biocides for control of organisms in systems contaminated with H_2S, NH_3, and other reducing agents.

NONOXIDIZING BIOCIDES

Nonoxidizing biocides offer a way to control microbial activity in systems incompatible with chlorine, such as water systems high in organic matter or ammonia. They provide the following features:

1. Activity independent of pH
2. Persistency
3. Control of organisms such as fungi, bacteria, and algae

Since all of these benefits are usually not available from a single penetrating biocide, individual ingredients are formulated into proprietary products designed to increase overall performance in very specific applications, e.g., paper machine systems, open cooling water systems, and process water in food plants.

ORGANO SULFUR COMPOUNDS

Methylene-bis-thiocyanate (MBT), (SCN)—CH_2—(SCN), is a well-known organo sulfur biocide. It is usually recommended for applications in paper mills and cooling systems where effluent limitations are strict, and where control of slime-forming bacteria is the main problem. Holding time and pH affect the half-life of MBT, which hydrolyzes in water to form less toxic substances.

Figure 22.10 illustrates the pH dependency of the half-life of MBT. At a pH of 11, it is destroyed in seconds.

A continuous feed of 1 mg/l to the makeup of a cooling system will control organisms entering with the water. If an alkaline cooling water treatment program is being used, the relatively higher pH will cause the MBT to hydrolyze faster. In most cooling systems, the molecule will eventually be destroyed if holding time is sufficiently long. Most of the degradation products are volatile and are stripped in the tower.

A study to assess the effect of MBT on biological sewage treatment programs indicated that 0.5–2.0 mg/l had no measurable effect on BOD and suspended solids removal. So it is feasible to treat a system with methylene-bis-thiocyanate to control microbes and still have an effluent amenable to biological treatment.

CHLORINATED PHENOLS

These are highly effective against most common organisms, especially fungi and algae. It is common to spray tower fill with chlorinated phenols to increase the lumber's resistance to fungal attack. These compounds can also be used effectively as biocides when fed directly to cooling water. Trichloro- and pentachloro-phenol are commonly used for these applications because of their effectiveness and good cost performance.

However, effectiveness is dependent on pH, with a decrease in activity as pH increases, due to a change from the phenolic to the less active phenate form. At a pH of 9 these compounds are only about 10% as effective as at a pH of 6.

Although chlorinated phenols are less active at higher pH ranges, they can still be effective and sufficiently persistent. Applications of these products on a slug basis normally work best in systems with long holding times and low pH.

Water treated with chlorinated phenols may be added to activated sludge units without causing significant upsets, provided there is equalizing capacity ahead of the treatment units to even out flow and concentration and to provide for measurable decay before introduction into the activated sludge system. Several days detention is usually required. The chlorinated phenols adsorb to a significant extent on the particulate matter and are concentrated for removal with the sludge.

CATIONIC BIOCIDES

If penetration of slime and algae masses is desired along with persistency, then amines and quaternaries (quats) are usually applied. The use of amines or quats with chlorination usually permits the dosage of chlorine to be reduced.

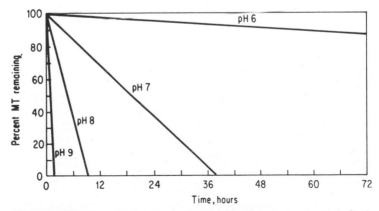

Figure 22.10 Degradation of methylene-bis-thiocyanate at pH 6, 7, 8, and 9.

Many of these biocides are surface-active and therefore can disperse slime masses. This allows chlorine and other toxicants to contact organisms which, under normal circumstances, they would not harm. The "wettability" of organic slime masses is increased so that the toxicants can reach under the mass to get at anaerobic corrosive bacteria.

In a typical amine program in a cooling tower system, a once-per-month slug of an amine biocide at 75 mg/l for 48 hours is used to supplement continuous chlorination at 0.5–1.0 mg/l free residual for 6–8 hours per day.

ORGANOMETALLICS

A typical example of this group of biocides is the compound bis-tributyl tin oxide, $(H_9C_4)_3{\equiv}Sn{-}O{-}Sn{\equiv}(C_4H_9)_3$. This compound is used to control fungi and algae. It also has a tendency to adsorb on surfaces in the system, especially on wood, and therefore, analyses usually do not show tin levels as high as would be expected from dosage calculations. This adsorption provides for residual algae and fungi control after treatment is discontinued. Although its toxicity is greatest on fungi and algae, it also provides good control of anaerobic corrosive bacteria.

MICROBIAL CONTROL PROCEDURES

In systems where microbe populations may be maintained within a certain acceptable control range and complete sterilization is not required, frequent microbe analyses should be run for monitoring the program. Sometimes only total counts are run to indicate overall microbe population levels. However in systems such as industrial recirculating cooling water loops, analyses of more specific organisms are required. Changes in total count do not always indicate changes in fungi, anaerobic bacteria, sulfate-reducing bacteria or algae. Since these organisms can be troublesome, they should be monitored specifically.

In industrial waters, a microbial analysis usually expresses counts per one milliliter sample. Since a billion bacteria weigh on the order of one milligram, a high count of 10,000,000/ml of sample represents only about 10 mg/l of suspended solids.

COOLING WATER SYSTEMS

A typical report of those organisms most commonly found in industrial water systems is shown in Figure 22.11. This analysis is typical of the weekly analyses for microbe counts taken on a cooling system water in an ammonia plant, sampled when the system is under control. The notation "NEG IN 1/1000" means that no organisms were observed in a 1/1000 dilution of the sampled water. The total count is usually higher than the sum of individual aerobic slime-forming bacteria shown above it. This is because there are many more types of aerobic bacteria in cooling water than those specifically reported as troublesome.

Figure 22.12 demonstrates changes in microbe populations produced by an ammonia leak into the cooling water system described above. This sudden influx of nutrient caused aerobic slime formers to multiply. The resulting deposition of these aerobes increased the shelter for anaerobic corrosive bacteria underneath the deposits.

Using analyses such as these, an industrial plant can optimize biocide usages to minimize water treatment costs while preventing unnecessary shutdowns caused by rampant microbial contamination.

NALCO

| | REPORT OF MICROBIOLOGICAL ANALYSIS |

Company ▊▊▊▊▊▊▊

Address ▊▊▊▊▊▊▊

Analysis No.   013756
Sampling Date   11/12/76
Date Rec'd by NALCO 11/18/76

Sample Marked   Cooling Water (under good control)--Ammonia Plant

Physical Appearance   YELLOW LIQUID

(All counts express quantity of organisms per ML of sample)

BACTERIA

AEROBIC SLIME FORMING
Non-Sporeforming

Flavobacterium		50,000
Mucoids (S)	NEG IN	1/1000
Aerobacter		20,000
Pseudomonas		70,000

Sporeforming

B. subtilis	
B. cereus	
B. megatherium	NONE
B. mycoides	

ANAEROBIC CORROSIVE

Desulfovibrio	NONE
Clostridia	

IRON DEPOSITING

Sphaerotilus	NONE
Gallionella	

OTHER BACTERIA   NONE

TOTAL COUNT   500,000

REMARKS:

FUNGI

MOLDS

Aspergillus	
Penicillium	NEG IN 1/10
Trichoderma	
Alternaria	

YEASTS

Torula	
Monilia	NEG IN 1/10
Saccharomyces	
Rhodotorula	

ALGAE

BLUE GREEN

Oscillatoria	NONE

GREEN

Chlorococcus	NONE
DIATOMS	NONE

OTHER ORGANISMS

NONE

Ronald Christensen
Head, Microbiological Laboratory

NALCO CHEMICAL COMPANY
6216 W. 66TH PLACE □ CHICAGO, ILLINOIS 60638

Figure 22.11   Analysis—a cooling system under control.

A common problem in once-through cooling water systems is iron fouling. In many instances the iron fouling is actually a result of contamination with iron-depositing bacteria such as *Sphaerotilus* or *Gallionella*. By routinely monitoring the makeup water with microbiological analyses, potential problems with iron depositors can be anticipated and treatment adjusted before the problem gets out of hand.

Figure 22.13 shows a typical makeup water analysis with iron depositors present. A total count analysis would have indicated this system to be under good control and would have missed the potential for iron fouling from the iron-depositing bacteria.

NALCO | **REPORT OF**
MICROBIOLOGICAL ANALYSIS

Company	▉▉▉▉▉▉▉▉▉		Analysis No.	016801
Address	▉▉▉▉▉▉▉▉▉		Sampling Date	3/23/77
			Date Rec'd by NALCO	4/1/77

Sample Marked (Under upset conditions caused by ammonia leak)--Ammonia Plant

Physical Appearance   YELLOW LIQUID WITH FLOC

(All counts express quantity of organisms per ML of sample)

BACTERIA

AEROBIC SLIME FORMING
Non-Sporeforming
Flavobacterium 200,000
Mucoids .... (S) NEG IN 1/1000
Aerobacter 70,000
Pseudomonas 400,000

Sporeforming
  B. subtilis ....
  B. cereus ....
  B. megatherium ....
  B. mycoides ....

ANAEROBIC CORROSIVE
Desulfovibrio 20
Clostridia ....

IRON DEPOSITING
Sphaerotilus .... NONE
Gallionella ....

OTHER BACTERIA   NONE

TOTAL COUNT   14,000,000

REMARKS:

FUNGI

MOLDS   NEG IN 1/10
Aspergillus ....
Penicillium ....
Trichoderma ....
Alternaria ....

YEASTS   NEG IN 1/10
Torula ....
Monilia............................
Saccharomyces ....
Rhodotorula ....

ALGAE

BLUE GREEN............................... NONE
Oscillatoria............................

GREEN   FEW
Chlorococcus ....

DIATOMS............................... NONE

OTHER ORGANISMS

PROTOZOA   FEW

Ronald Christensen
Head, Microbiological Laboratory

NALCO CHEMICAL COMPANY
6216 W. 66TH PLACE □ CHICAGO, ILLINOIS 60638

Figure 22.12   Analysis—the system in Fig. 22.11 out of control because of an exchanger leak.

PAPER MILL WATER SYSTEMS

In the manufacture of unbleached grades of paper or board, total counts of 30–40 million bacteria per ml can often be tolerated in the system without causing slime problems, because the solids are highly dispersed by residual lignin materials remaining in the system. By contrast, in the production of bleached grades, slimes and other microbial problems would be uncontrollable at such high total counts because of the absence of the dispersive lignins.

The high temperatures of linerboard production systems often allow the machines to run virtually slime-free even though total counts may approach the 30–40,000,000 range. Cylinder machines can tolerate extremely high levels of bacteria because the machines run slowly and are relatively immune to production interruptions from slime. They usually produce heavyweight, multi-ply board which can incorporate slime spots without damage to its properties.

Molds and yeasts are more responsible for slime problems in papermaking systems than are bacteria. Molds create more problems than yeasts because their thread-like, branched form can trap fiber, filler material and debris, and bind them into a tenacious deposit. Yeasts cause more problems than bacteria because they are considerably larger and have a tacky coating around the cell membrane.

Figure 22.14 shows an analysis of a deposit taken from a paper machine frame. The important features of this deposit are the high levels of yeasts, the presence

---

NALCO

REPORT OF
MICROBIOLOGICAL ANALYSIS

Company ▇▇▇▇▇▇▇

Address ▇▇▇▇▇▇▇

Analysis No.	017583
Sampling Date	4/13/77
Date Rec'd by NALCO	4/20/77

Sample Marked   Well Water

Physical Appearance   CLEAR LIQUID

(All counts express quantity of organisms per ML of sample)

BACTERIA		FUNGI	
AEROBIC SLIME FORMING		**MOLDS**	
Non Sporeforming		Aspergillus	NONE
Flavobacterium	NEG IN 1/1000	Penicillium	
Mucoids		Trichoderma	
Aerobacter		Alternaria	
Pseudomonas			
		YEASTS	
		Torula	NONE
		Monilia	
Sporeforming		Saccharomyces	
B. subtilis	NONE	Rhodotorula	
B. cereus			
B. megatherium			
B. mycoides		**ALGAE**	
ANAEROBIC CORROSIVE		**BLUE GREEN**	NONE
Desulfovibrio	10	Oscillatoria	
Clostridia	5		
		GREEN	NONE
IRON DEPOSITING		Chlorococcus	
Sphaerotilus	FEW		
Gallionella		**DIATOMS**	NONE
OTHER BACTERIA	NONE	**OTHER ORGANISMS**	
TOTAL COUNT	NEG IN 1/1000		NONE

REMARKS:

Ronald Christensen
Head, Microbiological Laboratory

NALCO CHEMICAL COMPANY
6216 W. 66TH PLACE □ CHICAGO, ILLINOIS 60638

Figure 22.13   A well water with low counts can still produce troublesome iron growths.

REPORT OF
MICROBIOLOGICAL ANALYSIS

NALCO

Company	Analysis No. 018357
	Sampling Date 4/28/77
Address	Date Rec'd by NALCO 5/2/77

Sample Marked   Tray Deposit (No. 1 Machine)

Physical Appearance   Thin green deposit

(All counts express quantity of organisms per   of sample)

BACTERIA   ### FUNGI

AEROBIC SLIME FORMING
Non-Sporeforming

			MOLDS	
Flavobacterium		1,000,000	Aspergillus	
Mucoids _____(S)	NEG IN 1/1000		Penicillium	
Aerobacter		50,000	Trichoderma	
Pseudomonas		5,000,000	Alternaria	
			Fusarium	100

YEASTS

			Torula	
			Monilia	20,000
Sporeforming			Saccharomyces	
B. subtilis	NEG IN 1/100		Rhodotorula	
B. cereus				
B. megatherium				
B. mycoides				

ALGAE

ANAEROBIC CORROSIVE			**BLUE GREEN**	NONE
Desulfovibrio	10,000		Oscillatoria	
Clostridia	200			
			GREEN	NONE
IRON DEPOSITING			Chlorococcus	
Sphaerotilus	NONE			
Gallionella			**DIATOMS**	NONE

OTHER BACTERIA

OTHER ORGANISMS

*Facultative	NEG IN 1/100	
TOTAL COUNT	56,000,000	Protozoa MANY

REMARKS:

Bacteria	MANY
Fibers	MODERATE

*Either aerobic or anaerobic in original sample

Ronald Christensen
Head, Microbiological Laboratory

NALCO CHEMICAL COMPANY
6216 W. 66TH PLACE □ CHICAGO, ILLINOIS 60638

Figure 22.14   Bioanalysis—paper machine frame.

of anaerobic corrosive bacteria, and the presence of coliform bacteria (*E. Coli*). Deposits caused by aerobic bacteria require total counts many times higher than these, so this is not primarily a bacterial problem. The major culprit is yeast. Corrosion may be a problem in this system because of the high level of anaerobic corrosives associated with the deposits. Protozoa in the deposit are indicators that there are problems in treating the fresh water brought into the mill. Improper chlorination or filtration of the fresh water may be the cause.

Chapter 23
Biological Digestion

In biological digestion, bacteria cultivated under controlled conditions utilize organic matter in the water as their food, making this a useful process for removing certain organic materials from water. Since the process deals with living organisms, every factor influencing the growth and health of the culture must be considered, including an adequate food supply, the availability of nutrients, a temperate climate, and a relatively uniform environment free of temperature shocks and similar disturbances. If the system is aerobic, oxygen must also be available for respiration.

There are many ways of characterizing organic matter in water. The carbonaceous fraction of the total organic matter can be determined (total organic carbon, TOC), and the susceptibility of the organic matter to oxidation by strong oxidizing agents, such as chromic acid, can also be measured (COD). However, the fact that the carbonaceous material can be oxidized is no assurance that the material is a suitable food for bacteria. The ability of bacteria to digest organic matter is measured by the BOD (Biochemical Oxygen Demand) test.

The BOD test uses what is essentially a miniature incubator containing the organic-laden water, saturated with oxygen, a culture of aerobic bacteria, and suitable nutrients. The sample is incubated at 68°F (20°C), usually for five days (BOD_5). Additional information on the nature of the organics may be obtained by incubating a second sample for 20 days. At the end of the incubation period, the oxygen content is measured, and this value is related directly to the respiration of the bacteria and the reduction of organic matter during the test incubation. The organic matter may be metabolized to create new cells, or completely converted to CO_2. The aerobic bacteria used for this test are normally taken from an activated sludge plant, and contain a variety of organisms which have become acclimated to the particular sludge in which they were grown (Figure 23.1).

(a)   (b)

Figure 23.1 (*a*) A variety of microbes develop in an activated sludge system, including filamentous types which interfere with sedimentation. (*b*) When the filamentous organisms (*Sphaerotilus* in this case) predominate, a condition known as sludge bulking develops.

TREATING INDUSTRIAL ORGANICS

In working with a wastewater that contains organic matter from an industrial plant, it is important to acclimate the bacteria to the waste by operating an incubator for a period of about a week to obtain organisms that have adapted to the particular organics to be digested. It is common to find that a standard BOD test may indicate poor biodegradability of an industrial waste simply because the normal sewage organisms used in the test have not become adjusted to the waste. The process of acclimatization results in the elimination of ineffective bacteria and the selection of those organisms that have the ability to digest organic matter that may actually be toxic to many organisms found in a municipal activated sludge.

The more closely the BOD result approaches the COD determination, the more readily is the organic matter in the waste digested by the selected bacteria. A ratio of 0.5, for example, is extremely favorable but bacterial digestion is practical even when the ratio is as low as 0.1–0.2.

A number of industries have developed around biological processes, such as wine and antibiotics, which use fermentation to produce useful products. These industries use pure strains of microbes for a specific purpose. In water treatment processing by biological treatment, except for the seeding of the system during initial startup, the microbial populations that colonize and populate the system include a wide variety of species, many of which enter the system with air or water. The population of the typical activated sludge system is shown by the analysis of Figure 23.2. This population distribution will be maintained fairly uniformly as long as the system in which these organisms live is not upset beyond their ability to cope with changing conditions.

AVAILABLE PROCESSES

Although special organisms or strains are not usually required for water treatment processes, the method of digestion most suited to the organic material in the water will favor the organisms that are most effective in that system. The categories of organisms developing may be correlated to three operating conditions, aerobic, anaerobic, and facultative.

By far the largest category is aerobic, using organisms that require oxygen for their life processes. Facultative systems are selected for certain industrial waste treatment operations and in many of the smaller municipalities. Anaerobic systems are usually confined to strong organic wastes, such as those coming from food processing plants, or accumulated organic sludges from the aerobic process.

An understanding of the growth pattern of bacteria is important to the design of a bacterial digestion system. Bacteria reproduce by fission, one cell splitting to produce two, two producing four, and so on. When there is adequate food supply, this reproduction rate occurs exponentially (Figure 23.3). During

NALCO

REPORT OF
MICROBIOLOGICAL ANALYSIS

Company		Analysis No.	033315
		Sampling Date	3/7/78
Address		Date Rec'd by NALCO	3/7/78

Sample Marked Mixed primary and aeration tank

Physical Appearance Liquid with floc

(All counts express quantity of organisms per ml of sample)

BACTERIA   **FUNGI**

AEROBIC SLIME FORMING

Non-Sporeforming

Flavobacterium	NEG IN 1/1000	
Mucoids (S)	1,000	
Aerobacter	5,000	
Pseudomonas	100,000	
E. coli	10,000	

Sporeforming

B. subtilis	
B. cereus	2,000
B. megatherium	500
B. mycoides	

ANAEROBIC CORROSIVE

Desulfovibrio	1,000
Clostridia	1,000

IRON DEPOSITING

Sphaerotllus	NONE
Gallionella	

OTHER BACTERIA NONE

TOTAL COUNT 700,000

REMARKS:

FUNGI FILAMENTS MANY

MOLDS

Aspergillus	20
Penicillium	
Trichoderma	
Alternaria	

YEASTS

Torula	200
Monilia	1,000
Saccharomyces	
Rhodotorula	

ALGAE

BLUE GREEN

Oscillatoria	FEW
Anabaena	FEW

GREEN NONE

Chlorococcus	

DIATOMS NONE

OTHER ORGANISMS

PROTOZOA FEW

Ronald Christensen
Head, Microbiological Laboratory

NALCO CHEMICAL COMPANY
6216 W. 66TH PLACE □ CHICAGO, ILLINOIS 60638

Figure 23.2 Typical activated sludge organisms.

Figure 23.3 Phases of microorganism development.

this logarithmic growth phase, the cells remain dispersed. The organic material may be synthesized into new cellular material, broken down completely to CO_2 and water, or there may be smaller organic molecules (metabolites) formed from the larger ones. These may eventually be completely digested to CO_2.

As the microbes flourish, the food supply begins to limit further growth, and in this declining growth phase, also shown in Figure 23.3, a change takes place in the microbial population; the colonies of bacteria begin to form settleable biological flocs. Unless additional food is introduced, a third phase, the endogenous growth phase, commences. In this phase, the bacteria become cannibalistic, feed on each other and on dead cellular matter, and once again become highly dispersed. The suspended solids in the system become difficult to settle.

This growth curve teaches that the ratio of food to bacterial population is of major importance in biological digestion processes. This ratio, called the food-to-microorganism (F/M) ratio, can be measured and is an important factor in design and operation of aeration basins, such as activated sludge basins. The food is the BOD of the incoming wastewater; the suspended solids in the incubation basin are mostly attributed to the bacterial population, so the population density is obtained by multiplying the suspended solids concentration in mg/l by the incubator volume. The F/M Ratio is then expressed as follows:

$$F/M = B_i/C_s \times 1/D$$

where B_i = BOD of incoming wastewater, mg/l
C_s = suspended solids in the incubation basin, mg/l (also called mixed liquor suspended solids, MLSS)
D = detention in the incubator, in days
$= \dfrac{\text{incubator volume, in gallons (m}^3)}{\text{flow, in gallons per day (m}^3/\text{d)}}$

Sometimes, instead of using total suspended solids in this ratio, the volatile portion of the suspended solids (MLVSS) may be considered more applicable, particularly if the incoming waste is handled without primary sedimentation to remove inorganic suspended solids. In an activated sludge system in a sewage plant, the volatile suspended solids are usually approximately 70% of the total solids in suspension.

In Figure 23.4, the F/M ratios are plotted to correspond to the approximate boundaries between the logarithmic growth phase, the declining growth phase, and endogenous respiration in aerated basins. In all of the varieties of activated

Figure 23.4   Relationship of bacterial growth phase to food supply in an aerated system.

sludge processes, the aeration devices are usually designed to be capable of maintaining a minimum dissolved oxygen (DO) concentration above 2 mg/l.

TEMPERATURE EFFECTS

A major factor in biological digestion is water temperature, and the daily and seasonal changes that can be anticipated in the biological system. There are two forces at work over the operating temperature range: the first is the competition between psychrophilic, mesophilic, facultative, and thermophilic organisms, each having a preferred temperature range. Second, in the favorable operating range for each of these categories of organisms, the metabolic rate approximately doubles for every 20°F (11°C) temperature increase (Figure 23.5). This points up one of the most serious problems of biological digestion: the fact that the bacterial colonies are almost in a state of suspended animation in the winter if the plant must be shut down and the temperature of the incubation basin drops to 32°F (0°C).

The bacterial colonies favor a pH in the range of 5–9, and are seriously inhibited in their activities if the pH should drop below 5 or exceed 10. pH is only one of the factors that must be evaluated to determine the variability of

Figure   23.5   Temperature change of 20°F alters typical activated sludge microbe metabolism rate by a factor of two up to 80°F. As 32°F approaches, rate nears zero. Above 100°F, activity decreases, and soon thermophilic organisms take over. *(Adapted from Power Special Report "Waste-Water Treatment," June 1967.)*

the waste stream to decide on the need for equalization, or storage capacity, prior to the biological digestion system to avoid upsets in the aquatic environment.

TRACE NUTRIENTS

Finally, the bacterial populations require nutrients in addition to carbonaceous food, as indicated by the empirical chemical formula for bacterial protoplasm, $C_{60}H_{87}O_{23}N_{12}O$. As a rule of thumb, the system requires approximately 5 parts of nitrogen as N and 1 part of phosphorus as P for every 100 parts of BOD in the wastewater. Many wastewaters, particularly municipal sewage, contain the required nitrogen, but industrial wastewater may require supplemental nutrients, usually added as ammonium salts and phosphoric acid.

The phenomenon called sludge bulking is thought to be caused by inadequate nutrient levels, although this is probably an oversimplification of a difficult problem. In sludge bulking, the sludge settles slowly because of the development of filamentous organisms in the biomass. The projecting filaments make the biological floc similar to thistledown, so that it moves with the water currents and resists settling. A bulking sludge produces a high sludge volume index (SVI) and is readily identified in microscopic examination. Other factors that are believed to promote bulking conditions may include low pH, which favors the growth of mold and yeasts; the presence of high concentrations of carbohydrates; and low levels of dissolved oxygen.

BENCH TESTING

In working with a wastewater containing organic matter of an undefined nature, bench testing followed by pilot plant testing is absolutely essential for obtaining data needed to design the biological treatment system. Before this work can commence, the wastewater flow must be studied over a sufficient period of time to indicate the variations that can be expected in composition and temperature so that provisions can be made for equalization, which is usually required. A sampling system should then be installed to withdraw a sample of the wastewater flow at regular intervals, deliver it to a miniature equalization basin, and produce a composite sample of wastewater that is representative of the total flow, and can be drawn on at any time for the bench studies. A water analysis must then be run on the composite sample to determine the mineral analysis and also the organic material as determined by BOD, COD, and TOC. The mineral analysis must include the determination of total nitrogen and phosphorus to determine whether there is a need for nutrient addition. Once this has been done, a miniature biological digestion system (incubator) is set up to operate on a batch basis (Figure 23.6). This consists of a five gallon container with an aeration device, such as an aquarium aerator obtained from a pet supply store. The procedure for running the test is then carried out as outlined in Table 23.1. Feeding waste to the aeration vessel may be on a continuous basis if a suitable laboratory pump is available.

Because the results of a BOD test are not known for five days, it is helpful to establish the ratio of BOD to COD or BOD to TOC prior to beginning the test, and then to use the COD or TOC test to measure the progress of the biological digestion experiment.

SLUDGE ACCLIMATIZATION

The common procedure for sludge acclimatization is to withdraw a sample from the incubator once a shift, at which time the sludge is settled and the

TABLE 23.1   Summary of Bench Scale Biological Treatability Procedure (See Figure 23.6)

AERATION VOLUME:	15 liters of wastewater
FEED PORTION VOLUME:	800 ml
FEEDING PROCEDURE:	Withdraw 1000 ml from aeration chamber. Settle for 30 min in a 1000 ml cylinder. Decant and discard 800 ml. Refill cylinder to 1000 ml with fresh waste and return to aeration vessel.

Phase	Feeding frequency	Average feed rate, ml/hr	Detention time, hr
Acclimatization	Once every 8 hrs	100	150
Sludge buildup	Once every 4 hrs	200	75
Rate studies	Once every 2 hrs*	400	37.5
Rate studies	Hourly	800	18.75
Rate studies	Once every 0.5 hr	1600	9.38

* Feed may be semicontinuous or continuous. Withdrawal can be periodic.

sludge volume measured. This procedure is repeated until the sludge volume has stabilized or is increasing (consult Table 23.1 for feeding procedure). Sludge buildup is accomplished by increasing the feed rate after the period of sludge acclimatization. When sufficient quantities of sludge have been produced, rate studies can commence.

Rate studies can be made at sludge volumes of approximately 200 ml/l. Data such as BOD, TOC, COD, pH, temperature, and total dissolved solids are run on the raw waste and on the supernatant from settling tests. These tests are run for 1–2 weeks at constant feed rates to establish the degree of removal at various detention periods.

A test of this kind with long detention times simulates an extended aeration

Figure 23.6   Equipment for bench scale biological treatment study.

system with an extremely low F/M ratio. As such, it produces BOD reductions that are reproducible on a plant scale only with an extended aeration system. The test, in effect, indicates the maximum biodegradability that can be achieved and the minimum BOD levels that can be reached.

At the conclusion of the test, the mixed liquor in the incubator should be examined to establish the sludge volume index (the Mohlman Index). This index is calculated as follows:

$$\text{SVI} = \frac{C_v}{C_s} \times 1000$$

where C_v = settled volume (Imhoff cone test), ml/l
C_s = mixed liquor suspended solids, mg/l

Therefore,

$$\text{SVI} = \text{ml/mg} \times 1000 = \text{ml/g}.$$

An SVI below 100 implies that the sludge will settle and compact well. If the SVI exceeds about 200, sediment action is slow, and chemical coagulation and flocculation will probably be required in the final clarifier.

Another measure of the performance of a biological digester is the sludge age, which is calculated as follows:

$$\text{Sludge age} = \frac{C_s}{C_i} \times D$$

where C_s = solids in aeration basin, mg/l
C_i = solids entering basin, mg/l
D = detention, in days

For example, if C_s = 3000 mg/l, C_i = 100 mg/l, and D = 0.5 days, SA = 30 × 0.5 = 15 days.

There is no best value for any given process, but there is for each individual plant and this must be determined by experience.

A pilot plant must then be designed to treat this waste and evaluate the numerous combinations of units that can be put together for a complete biological digestion system. The following factors must be considered in choosing between the systems available, and some choices may be quickly discarded without trial or evaluation because they don't meet the needs of the plant:

1. Effluent limitations: These are established by the EPA under the NPDES (National Pollution Discharge Elimination System) program. Does the final BOD achieved by the test meet the requirements?

2. Reliability: This is also established by the NPDES permit, which spells out permissible deviations from average performance and the duration of such excursions.

3. Climatic conditions: Some systems may be rejected because of failure to perform in subzero weather, or because of turnover of the basin with high prevailing winds.

4. Location of residential areas and neighboring industries: This can be particularly significant with odor-bearing wastes.

5. Availability of land for lagooning or land application of liquid waste or sludge.

6. Space available for treatment units.

7. Energy required and available for pumping, aeration, sludge collection, and sludge disposal.

8. Equipment costs and operating costs.

9. Manpower for operation.

Before considering which of the biological systems may be best suited for the waste to be processed, it is important to evaluate the pretreatment steps that might reduce the load on the biological system and simplify its operation. Typical pretreatment steps include grit removal, screening, and primary sedimentation. If the suspended solids concentration is relatively low, below a range of 50–100 mg/l, pretreatment may be unnecessary and the waste may go directly to the biological digester.

AERATED SYSTEMS

By far the largest number of biological systems fall into the category of aerobic digesters, depending on aeration to support oxygen-consuming bacteria. If ample land is available, an aerated lagoon (Figure 23.7) may be the most practical incubator, usually having a detention time of about 30–60 days.

Aeration basins are typically designed for a detention of 12–48 hours, so the F/M ratio is quite low. The aeration devices are usually capable of delivering about 3 lb of oxygen per hour per horsepower applied (1.8 kg/kwhr). Where surface aerators are used, the system operates as a completely mixed basin, and maintaining solids in suspension may require as much as 100 horsepower (75 kw) per million gallons of volume (3780 m³). A modification of the aeration basin is the oxidation ditch.

ACTIVATED SLUDGE PROCESS

The activated sludge system is much more compact, operates at a much higher loading (F/M ratio), and cannot produce quite as efficient reduction of organic matter as the aerated lagoon. Sludge production is significantly greater. This is the system typically used in larger municipal sewage plants, where it operates successfully under a wide range of climatic conditions. Air is usually supplied through subsurface diffusers. In some plants, pure oxygen is supplied instead of air, further reducing the volume of the incubator.

Sludge production is an important aspect of the biological digestion process. Referring to Figure 23.4, in a high rate aeration system, where there is so much food that the bacteria multiply exponentially, much of the food goes to produc-

Figure 23.7 An aerated facultative lagoon for treatment of sewage from a community of approximately 5,000 people. *(Courtesy of Hinde Engineering Company.)*

Figure 23.8 Sludge produced in municipal activated sludge plants as influenced by F/M ratio. *(EPA Report 11010-ESQ-08/71, August, 1971.)*

tion of new cells, so sludge (which is made up almost entirely of biomass) production is high. Conversely, when food is scarce, the bacteria become cannibalistic and cell production is low, so sludge production may actually cease as new cells reach an equilibrium with those consumed. An estimate of sludge production can thus be made on the basis of *F/M* ratio (Figure 23.8).

In the typical municipal sewage plant using activated sludge, shown in Figure 23.9, the waste is first passed through a grit chamber and then clarified in a primary sedimentation basin, where the BOD may be reduced by 35–40% and the suspended solids by about 50%. The sludge in the primary clarifiers may settle to a density in the range of 4–6%. The overflow from a primary clarifier enters the aeration basin, where it may remain under aeration for 6–8 hours. The mixed liquor suspended solids level is typically in the range of 2500–4000 mg/l. The liquor from the aeration basins then flows to a final clarifier, where the biological sludge is settled, and the overflow is disinfected for discharge to the receiving stream. The biological solids in the secondary clarifier, being very light, flocculent colonies, often require chemical treatment for flocculation and sedimentation. The sludge in the secondary clarifier seldom compacts to more than 1.5–2.0% solids.

Using this example, assuming a BOD reduction in the secondary system of 200 mg/l, 8 hours (0.33 day) detention and MLSS of 3000 mg/l, the *F/M* ratio is

$$\frac{200}{3000} \times \frac{1.0}{0.33} = 0.2$$

Figure 23.9 Conventional activated sludge.

Figure 23.10 Extended aeration.

At this ratio, the production of sludge is expected to be 0.3 lb/lb (0.3 kg/kg) BOD removed, equivalent to 60 mg/l (Figure 23.8).

Since the bacteria in the sludge are still active, they are returned to join the primary clarifier effluent entering the aeration basin. The excess production of sludge, which was calculated to be 0.3 lb/lb BOD removed, is drawn off for further processing; it may be joined with the primary sludge or dewatered separately for disposal.

Modifications of the basic system include extended aeration, step aeration and contact stabilization.

In an extended aeration plant (Figure 23.10), the waste stream is fed directly to the aeration basins without primary sedimentation, with the balance of the process being the same as the basic system.

With step aeration (Figure 23.11), secondary biological sludge is introduced at the head of the aeration basin, but the primary clarifier effluent is introduced in portions at several positions along the path through the aeration basin. In this design, the detention is usually reduced to about 3-4 hours.

Contact stabilization (Figure 23.12) is a final modification of the activated sludge process, and here the biological solids are mixed with the clarified sewage for a period of only 30-60 minutes, in which time they act as flocculants for removal of suspended and colloidal matter and for adsorption of soluble organic materials. The collected sludge from the final clarifier is processed through a separate aeration basin in which the adsorbed and entrapped solids are then digested by the biomass.

TRICKLING FILTERS

Competing with the activated sludge process and its modifications is the bio-filter or trickling filter (Figure 23.13). Though the trickling filter does not provide the high degree of organic removal afforded by the activated sludge process, it has advantages in space savings and in its ability to resist upsets. Newer

Figure 23.11 Step aeration.

Figure 23.12 Contact stabilization.

modifications of the biofilter incorporate rotating disks (Figure 23.14). In either of these designs, a gelatinous biological mass forms on the filter surfaces, and this mass digests the organic matter in water passing over the surface. These units do not require air beyond that available to them by natural ventilation. Where the organic concentrations are high, the concentration ahead of the conventional trickling filter is reduced by recycling a portion of the biofilter effluent or the plant effluent. A variety of schemes are available, as shown by Figure 23.15.

The disk-type filters do not require this recycle scheme. If loadings are high, disks can be operated in series, so the organic is reduced in two or three stages. The disk filters are usually housed to minimize evaporative cooling and maintain as favorable an operating temperature as possible.

There is a continual sloughing of organic debris from the surface of the biofilter, requiring final clarification of the wastewater effluent for discharge to a receiving stream. This usually amounts to 0.1–0.3 lb solids per lb BOD removed in a municipal sewage system. Handling industrial wastes, sludge production may be as high as 0.4–0.5 lb/lb BOD removed if the waste is high in carbohydrates, and as low as 0.05–0.1 lb/lb BOD removed if the organics are volatile acids or alcohols.

Figure 23.13 Construction details of a trickling filter showing rotary distributor, underdrain, rock fill, and provision for air ventilation. (*Courtesy of FMC Corporation.*)

Figure 23.14 In this 1.0 mgd sewage treatment plant biological treatment takes place on these assemblies of disks mounted in basins through which pretreated sewage is flowing. A growth of biological gel develops on the rotating disks, providing the mechanism for digestion of organic wastes. *(Courtesy of Autotrol Corporation.)*

ANAEROBIC DIGESTION

Anaerobic processes are sometimes used for highly concentrated organic wastes. The two designs most prominently used are the anaerobic lagoon and the closed digester.

In the anaerobic lagoon, wastes simply enter the digestion basin without addition of air, and the oxygen content is quickly depleted, leading to fermentation. Very commonly, a thick crust forms on the lagoon, preventing oxidation and to some extent confining the odorous gases produced by anaerobic decomposition. In the anaerobic lagoon, carbonaceous material is converted to organic acids and alcohols, and later to methane. The proteinaceous material is converted to ammonia, and sulfates in the water are often reduced to sulfides, the principal source of odor from the system. In processing fruit or vegetable canning wastes, the fermentation may occur so rapidly that the basin does not crust over, because the solids are prevented from agglomerating by the effervescence of the gas produced.

Anaerobic digestion is generally slower than aerobic, and a typical food processing waste may require an anaerobic lagoon with a detention of as much as 30 days for effective operation. For the most part, however, the anaerobic lagoon has been limited in acceptance because of the potential for emission of sulfide odors.

The anaerobic digester is widely used in municipal sewage plants to stabilize the accumulated waste biological solids. These may be treated separately or mixed with primary sludge, depending on the volatile content of the sludge. A typical digester (Figure 23.16) can process these solids to yield a stabilized dewaterable sludge at about 3–4% solids with acceptable odor. The anaerobic digestion produces 70% methane gas that is collected and burned to provide heat to the digester to maintain its temperature at about 90–95°F (32–35°C). The digester is insulated so that this temperature can be maintained for efficient biological activity during the digestion period of 15–20 days. The ammonia and CO_2 produced during digestion yield ammonium bicarbonate in a solution, producing a supernatant from the digester with an alkalinity in the range of

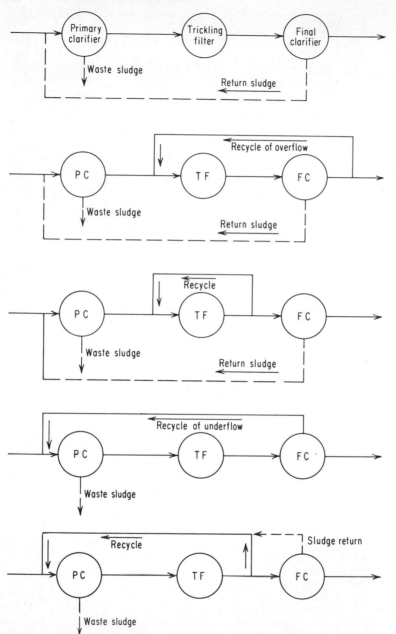

Figure 23.15 Schemes for trickling filter plants based on strength of wastes.

Figure 23.16   Anaerobic digesters operated in series with gas used to heat first stage. Tanks are insulated by earthen backfill.

500–1500 mg/l. This supernatant is usually periodically withdrawn and fed to the aeration basins.

OTHER PROCESSES

Other methods of biological digestion include facultative lagoons, land irrigation, and cooling tower digestion. In the facultative lagoon, usually designed with a retention time in excess of 30 days, anaerobic digestion occurs in the settled sludge layer, and aerobic digestion occurs in the surface water. The lagoon may be 5–10 feet (1.5–3.0 m) deep. The effluent quality is subject to upsets by violent weather conditions and by the development of algal blooms in the summer. The algae play a prominent role in aerobic digestion, but they present difficulty in the production of a clear overflow from the lagoon.

With land irrigation, the soil bacteria become the active agents in the digestion of the organic matter if this is a spray-irrigation type of application. Liquid wastes have been successfully disposed of in this fashion on both forest and crop lands, and the use of wastewater for irrigation will play a prominent role in the future (Figure 23.17).

Figure 23.17   Treated wastewater may be used for irrigation if it is free of heavy metals that might concentrate in food crops. Ridge and furrow irrigation, shown here, is common and relatively inexpensive. (*From EPA Publication 5012, "Environmental Pollution Control Alternatives—Municipal Wastewater."*)

Figure 23.18   Pilot plant designed for biological digestion studies on fresh wastewater at a plant site. This unit can be operated in a variety of modes, including extended aeration, step aeration, and contact stabilization.

In some industrial plants, cooling towers have been used as a kind of combination biofilter and activated sludge system. This requires, of course, the maintenance of active biological populations in the cooling tower, and the goal of biological digestion may not always be consistent with the goal of maintaining clean heat transfer equipment in the plant process areas where the cooling water leaving the tower is used.

In designing the biological digestion system, once the bench studies have been completed and the designer has reviewed the options open for biological treatment, a pilot plant must be set up to obtain the final design criteria for any given wastewater treatment problem. There are numerous handbooks providing rules of thumb that have been used in the past for design of biological treatment systems, but none of these can be relied on without pilot plant experience to determine the degradability of the organic materials in the wastewater under simulated plant conditions. A typical activated sludge pilot plant set up to investigate an industrial wastewater problem is shown in Figure 23.18; Pilot plants such as these must be designed for round-the-clock operation and require as careful attention for their control as a full size wastewater treatment plant. The investment in pilot plant facilities and manpower is paid for in the efficiency and reliability of the final plant.

Chapter **24**

Aluminum Industry

Aluminum manufacture has four distinct phases of production from raw ore to finished products: mining, bauxite refining, reduction, and fabrication. Another category is secondary production by independent scrap recovery plants, but this is similar to recovery operations in the remelt section of the fabrication plant.

MINING

Bauxite is the ore used in the production of aluminum. It is a mixture of aluminum oxide trihydrate and monohydrate, with iron oxides, aluminum silicates, and titanium oxide impurities. The ore usually contains from 5 to 25% moisture, which is removed from imported ores to reduce shipping weight and improve handling. In the U.S. most ore is imported, but some Arkansas bauxite is also processed. Lower grade aluminum minerals, such as kaolin and refuse from coal preparation, are being investigated in a variety of research programs attempting to extract alumina from such alternate sources.

Open pit mining accounts for almost all bauxite production. The overburden is stripped and the ore recovered by drag lines and shovels. The ore is then sized and sent to the bauxite plant where it is stored for blending and later use.

BAUXITE PROCESSING

To utilize the aluminum values in either domestic or imported ores, the alumina in these minerals must be extracted and purified. This is done in alumina refineries, which produce a finished product of calcined alumina, Al_2O_3, necessary for the electrolytic reduction process which is used to produce primary aluminum metal.

Of the nine basic alumina refineries operating in the United States, two are

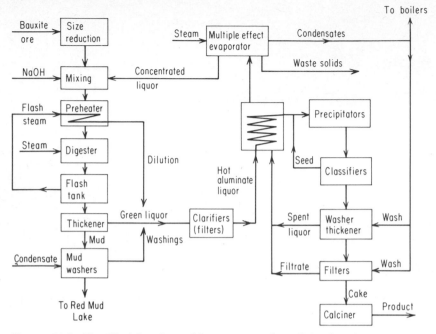

Figure 24.1 Simplified flowsheet of Bayer process for refining bauxite ore.

in Arkansas utilizing domestic bauxite. The others use ores imported from Australia, Jamaica, Africa, and other areas.

In an operation called the Bayer process, raw bauxite is digested at temperatures as high as 475°F (250°C) and pressures up to 500 psi (35 kg/cm²), by caustic solutions to yield a slurry containing sodium aluminate (NaAlO₂), and suspended waste solids called red mud. A process flow sheet is shown in Figure 24.1. To allow efficient recovery and reduction of waste, the red mud is settled or filtered from the dissolved liquor using natural and synthetic flocculants to produce a clear sodium aluminate solution.

The red mud from the first separation step is re-slurried with weak liquor in a washing operation to extract more of the aluminum and alkali values. The most common practice uses a continuous countercurrent decantation (CCD) arrangement with as many as seven washing stages to recover almost all significant alumina and alkali values. The red mud waste is finally discharged to a large mud lake (tailings pond).

After filtration, the pregnant liquor, rich in sodium aluminate, is cooled through heat exchangers to about 120–140°F (50–60°C) prior to entry into precipitation tanks. Here, seed crystals of previously precipitated alumina trihydrate are added and the tanks agitated for a day or two. This hydrolyzes the aluminate to yield alumina trihydrate (aluminum hydroxide), which grows on the seed material. This process is allowed to continue until about half of the alumina values are converted. Further precipitation may result in excessive dropout of impurities, such as silica. The alumina trihydrate slurry is then sent to classification and thickening tanks to separate the trihydrate from the spent liquor. The trihydrate is filtered and calcined to produce anhydrous alumina. Following the removal of the trihydrate crystals, spent liquor is concentrated by evaporators and returned to the beginning of the circuit.

Many Uses for Water

Water enters the process stream primarily as steam or condensate. A small amount of water may be introduced as purified makeup to prepare process reagents such as flocculants or cleaning solutions. Storm water and waste surface water may enter the process as return water from the mud lake. Noncontact cooling water is used for equipment cooling, and finished alumina product cooling. This water may be from an outside source or from the mud lake reservoir (see Figure 24.2).

Once in the process stream, water is used again and again as a solvent, to transport heat or slurry, to wash away impurities, to create vacuum, to generate electricity, and to prepare chemical makeup solutions.

A major input of steam comes from the digestion tanks where the alumina values are dissolved from the ore. As pressure is relieved in flash tanks, the lower pressure steam is liberated with its heating potential. This is used to heat the spent liquor before it joins the fresh bauxite in the digester, thereby recycling heat in a closed loop. Other uses for the steam from the digester flash tanks are in the evaporators concentrating the spent liquor.

Wash water streams vary in composition depending on the product purity required. Condensate is used to wash the precipitate on the trihydrate filters to remove residual impurities. This wash water or other condensate may be used to wash the thickened trihydrate before going to filtration dewatering. Excess condensate beyond that required in steam generation may be used in final red mud washing along with mud lake return water.

Mud lake return water consists of overflow from gravity thickening as well as storm water inflows. The amount varies depending on local conditions. The water contains a low concentration of alumina and caustic values from mud leaching. This proceeds to the last mud thickener where it washes mud underflow from the previous thickener. Increased in alumina and caustic content, it joins the mud from the second previous washing, and so on through the circuit. As it progresses up through the wash train, the alumina and caustic values increase correspondingly. Finally it joins the partially cooled digester discharge where the final increase in alumina content is achieved. This countercurrent decantation process is designed to provide economical recovery of as much alumina and alkali as possible.

Figure 24.2   Water and steam uses in Bayer process.

In addition to its use as an effective solvent, the water serves to transfer solids from unit to unit within the process. This includes not only the bauxite slurry, but the trihydrate and the red mud as well. It also provides a medium for wet grinding of the bauxite ore to the proper particle size for digestion. The use of water as a means of contact cooling of the overhead vapors and barometric condensers allows both the extraction of needed condensate water and also the concentration of process streams. Water use in these barometric condensers may reach 5000–10,000 gallons per ton of product (20–40 m³/t).

Due to process economics, the bulk of the unit process contact effluent streams become intermediate feed streams to the other units, as described. Non-contact streams represent a loss of heat rather than chemical values. These heat values are recovered wherever practical. Even though no significant discharges are planned, water may be lost from any of the following production areas:

1. Drying and calcining.
2. Red mud (evaporation and seepage from lakes or contained as part of the in-place mud content).
3. Evaporation of liquor streams.
4. Sand disposal.
5. Evaporation of washdown water streams.

The complete water use scheme, including the Bayer Process circuit, is shown in Figure 24.2.

ALUMINUM REDUCTION

Aluminum is the most common metallic element in the Earth's crust, comprising about 7.3% expressed in the elemental form, or about 15% in the commonly-occurring oxide form, Al_2O_3. Unlike iron, the next most common element, aluminum was unknown to the ancients, and it was only a century ago that the metal became available in commercial quantity.

As indicated by its position in the Electromotive Series, aluminum is a reactive metal. Because of this, reduction of aluminum oxide by carbon in a furnace, a process which easily produces iron from its ore, is unsuccessful because the aluminum metal produced is vaporized and quickly returns to the oxide form when the reaction is reversed on cooling. Success in producing aluminum from the oxide was finally achieved in 1889 by the discovery of a unique electrochemical process. The process was discovered simultaneously by Hall in the U.S., and Heroult in France.

Alumina produced by the Bayer process previously described is dissolved in a molten bath composed chiefly of cryolite ($3\ NaF \cdot AlF_3$), to which is added fluorspar (CaF_2) and aluminum fluoride (AlF_3). The molten mixture is prepared in an electrolytic cell, called a pot, illustrated by Figure 24.3. A series of carbon anodes project into the bath from above, and the amorphous carbon pot lining, with metal collector bars embedded in it, serves as cathode. The pot lining is encased in insulation and refractory brick surrounded by an outer steel shell. The exact reactions in the cell are not completely understood, but the important result is a reduction of the aluminum oxide by carbon, according to the following reactions:

$$Al_2O_3 + 3C \rightarrow 2Al + 3CO\uparrow \tag{1}$$

$$2Al_2O_3 + 3C \rightarrow 4Al + 3CO_2\uparrow \tag{2}$$

The oxidation occurring at the anode produces a mixture of about 25% CO and 75% CO_2, and this exiting gas mixture carries with it certain volatile fluoride compounds. Carbon is consumed at the rate of about 0.5 lb/lb of aluminum

Figure 24.3 A potline in an aluminum reduction plant. Fumes are withdrawn from each cell and delivered to a scrubber. Fresh anodes are in the rack at the right. The crane moves the tapping device and crucible from cell to cell. *(Courtesy Kaiser Aluminum and Chemical Corporation.)*

produced. Aluminum is produced by reduction at the cathode, and a pool of aluminum metal collects on the bottom of the cell. The passage of current through the cell generates sufficient heat to keep the bath molten and at a temperature of about 1650–1740°F (900–950°C).

Frequent Feeding Necessary

The heat is contained by the insulation of the pot lining material plus a crust which forms on the surface of the bath. Although aluminum oxide is the basic raw material, it makes up less than 8% of the bath, and must be continuously added. A supply of alumina is maintained on the crust where it heats and de-hydrates. The crust is broken periodically and some of the alumina is stirred in to replenish what has been consumed by the reduction process.

Molten aluminum is periodically withdrawn (tapped) from the pot and cast into pigs or into any of various types of ingots. The usual power consumption for aluminum reduction is in the range of 8–10 kW-hr/lb (4 kW-hr/kg) of aluminum produced, so that a pot line of perhaps 200–240 cells producing about 100,000 tons/year of aluminum would have a power requirement of about 250 megawatts. Because of this high electrical power requirement, aluminum reduction plants are usually located near low-cost sources of power. Typically these plants use hydroelectric power or have contracted with nearby utility stations for a significant block of their electrical output. Because direct current is needed for electrolytic cells, a substantial investment is required for electrical facilities to convert the alternating current available from public utilities to direct current.

Because of the high consumption of carbon electrodes, each plant has its own facilities for producing these from mixtures of petroleum coke and pitch. Rather extensive facilities are required for materials handling and processing of the electrodes. A flow sheet of an aluminum reduction plant and an electrode processing plant are shown in Figure 24.4.

Figure 24.4 Flowsheet of aluminum reduction plant and electrode processing plant.

Exhaust Gases

In the reduction process, as indicated by the chemical equation shown earlier, the consumption of the carbon electrodes produces a mixture of carbon monoxide and carbon dioxide. These gases leave the cell and carry with them certain volatile components from the bath, including fluoride compounds. Particulates from the surface of the pot are also entrained with the escaping gases. To control air emissions, there are hoods positioned over each cell and suction is applied to collect the gases. The gases are routed through wet scrubbers to remove both gaseous and particulate materials. Since the fluoride content of the gas stream is valuable, the scrubbing water is often fortified with reactive chemicals, such as sodium aluminate, to produce various mixtures of sodium and aluminum fluorides which can be returned to the bath after concentration and drying.

For air emission control in the electrode processing plant wet scrubbers are sometimes used, and the scrubber water becomes a significant part of the total waste treatment load. But it is more common to control these emissions with dry collectors.

Following the reduction of aluminum in the pot line, the metal is cast either by a continuous casting process or by conventional casting into molds on a casting floor. In continuous casting units, water is used for mold cooling. The requirements for high quality water are much more stringent for the continuous casting operation than for conventional cooling operations. The cooling water may be reclaimed over evaporative cooling towers, and the systems can be troublesome because the water often contains oily mold-release agents. The materials provide food for microbes, making it difficult to keep the cooling system free of slime and other microbial masses.

After casting, the ingots are cooled by air or by water spray, and in some cases the system is designed to produce a very fine spray so that the water is evaporated completely to dryness and leaves no residual wastewater to be dealt with in a treatment system. If an excess of water is required, it will contain suspended solids and oil, and will require treatment for disposal. Air cooling, either alone or combined with a water spray, will undoubtedly find increasing use as a way of minimizing wastewater discharge.

There are various other cooling water applications in the reduction plant. These include water for cooling hydraulic oil, green anodes, and compressors. The plant receives electrical power from a nearby utility at high voltage which must be reduced through transformers. The alternating current at reduced voltage is then converted by mercury arc rectifiers to direct current, which may be as high as 800 volts, based on a loss of about 5 volts at each pot, with the cells of the potline being connected in series. Cooling water is required for components of the rectifier. There is a transformer and rectifier unit for each pot line. Cooling water may also be required for the chlorine compressors, which are used to supply chlorine gas for degassing molten aluminum.

METAL FABRICATION

The aluminum ingot is converted to a wide variety of forms, including sheet, plate, structural shapes, rods and other bar stock, tubes, wire, and foil. Some of these can be extruded by heating the metal to a temperature at which it becomes plastic, but the bulk of production is done in the rolling mill. Since initial rolling is done on hot metal, the hot ingot may be sent directly to the rolling mill, but it is usually passed through furnaces to make certain that the temperature is uniform throughout. Cooling water is applied at the rolls to maintain the proper temperature for rolling, and lubricating oils (called rolling oils) are often applied to the system to facilitate rolling and prevent the development of surface imperfections otherwise caused by the friction of working through the rolls. The roll cooling water is recirculated, and the debris from the rolling operation settled, with facilities also being provided to reclaim the rolling oil wherever possible.

In addition to the cooling water used on the rolls, water may also be required for cooling furnace doors and for typical utilities operations such as compressor jacket cooling and bearing cooling.

Some fabricated shapes may be finished by special chemical treatment, such as the anodizing of aluminum sheet or tube by chromic acid treatment. These finishing operations may generate wastes that require separate treatment before being discharged into the final waste treatment plant.

Most reduction plants purchase their power from utilities so have no need for high pressure boilers. Power may be generated in the bauxite plants where turbines exhaust into the steam line supplying the evaporators. But in the reduction plants, boilers are operated principally for space heating in the winter and for electrode paste heating, so the water treatment systems for these operations are usually quite simple.

In the secondary refinery, aluminum scrap is melted in induction furnaces in operations quite similar to recovery operations in the primary smelter itself where scrap must be reclaimed from butt ends and clippings. In secondary smelters, the nature of the impurities is unknown, so fluxing agents are added to eliminate them. The contaminants are removed as dross from the surface of the molten metal after casting.

SUGGESTED READING

Shreve, R. N.: *Chemical Process Industries*, 3d ed., McGraw-Hill, New York, 1967.

U.S. Environmental Protection Agency: *Development Document for Bauxite Refining*, EPA-440/1-74-019-c, March 1974.

U.S. Environmental Protection Agency: *Development Document for Primary Aluminum Smelting*, EPA-440/1-74-019-d, March 1974.

U.S. Environmental Protection Agency: *Development Document for Secondary Aluminum Smelting*, EPA-440/1-74-019-e, March 1974.

U.S. Environmental Protection Agency: *Economic Analysis of Effluent Guidelines, The Nonferrous Metals Industry (Aluminum)*, EPA-230/2-74-018 (NTIS-PB-239-161), August 1974.

Chapter 25

Automotive Industry

The Automotive and Machinery Industries segment, classified by SIC codes 3400–3799, is composed of a wide variety of manufacturing operations, including (a) automotive (self-propelled) vehicles: farm implements, autos and trucks, construction equipment, and aircraft and aerospace; (b) machinery: appliances, electrical machinery, and fabricated metal products.

There are four basic operations in the manufacture of most of these products: casting (foundry operation, die casting, or investment casting), machining, stamping and fabricating, and final assembly. Although water consumption is relatively modest in each of these operations, water quality is important, and aqueous wastes are quite concentrated.

Some plants may perform just one of the above operations, while others carry out the entire process from casting through assembly at a single integrated plant. Figure 25.1 shows the flow of material for the total operation of an automotive plant.

FOUNDRY OPERATIONS

In the foundry, parts such as crankshafts, engine blocks, and transmissions are cast. In a typical iron foundry, pig iron is purchased from a steel mill and melted in a furnace called a cupola, similar in design to a blast furnace. The iron is mixed in the furnace with a charge of coke and a flux or slag-forming material which may be limestone or fluorspar. Air is blown into the furnace at the tuyeres, as in the blast furnace, and the combustion of the coke melts the charge, with molten iron draining to the bottom and slag floating to the top.

The gases leaving the cupola are combustion products, basically CO_2 with perhaps a small amount of CO, plus a small amount of SO_2, if the coke was made from sulfur-bearing coal. When the charge is dumped into the burden, there is

Figure 25.1   Basic automotive manufacturing.

some breakup of the relatively weaker coke lumps, and there is an initial surge of coke fines into the exit combustion gases. There usually is iron oxide also broken loose from the bars of pig iron, so the discharge from the cupola is high in suspended solids.

To avoid creating an air pollution problem, the foundry may install a baghouse for dry collection of the dust, or a wet scrubber. If the latter is installed, this becomes the principal use of the water in the foundry operation. A typical foundry operation is shown in Figure 25.2.

Because the products of combustion are acidic, the pH of the scrubber water is generally quite low. Figure 25.3 shows a pH chart taken from a recorder sampling scrubber water. The effect of opening and closing the charging door is to dilute the stack gases, which is apparent on the strip chart.

A second use of water in the foundry is for cooling the cupola shell. This is usually done by direct spraying of the steel shell with water through a circumferential pipe at the top of the cupola. This water may be collected at the bottom

Figure 25.2 Water circuit in a grey iron foundry with wet scrubbers.

of the cupola, pumped over a cooling tower and returned to the top of the cupola. Most foundries adjust pH and add a corrosion inhibitor to protect the cupola shell

A third use for water is in the granulation of slag tapped from the cupola. The molten slag collects in the granulation tank, and the slag grains are removed by flights up a ramp and discarded into a totebox.

Figure 25.3 Strip charts showing pH variations in Venturi scrubber effluent.

Most foundries encounter dust problems in the preparation of sand molds and the breakup of the sand from the finished casting, where the material is crushed for return to the molding room. A variety of chemicals may be mixed with the sand to produce the green mold, which must be cured before molten metal is poured into it. Phenolic compounds are sometimes used in preparing the mold, so phenol may be present in the foundry wastewater both from this source and also from the coke charged to the cupola. Oils may also be used in the preparation of the mold, and these volatilize during the baking of the mold and must be collected by a wet scrubber. Depending on the operations, there may be individual wet scrubbers at the cupola, the sand mold, and the shakeout room, or wastewater from these areas may be combined prior to treatment.

Table 25.1 shows the analysis of a foundry wastewater related to the installation illustrated in Figure 25.2. The oil content was quite high, but there was no evidence of free oil in the sample. This is a common occurrence where the bulk of suspended solids consists of carbon and iron oxide, as in foundry operations. After the treatment of this particular wastewater, the oil content was reduced to less than 50 mg/l, suspended solids to about 56 mg/l, and phenol to 0.5 mg/l. The collected solids were vacuum filtered for disposal, and the oil content of the dry cake was about 15%.

There is often some fluoride present in the wastewater, which may be introduced by volatilization into the cupola stack gas or may be dissolved from the slag in the granulation tank. Since most foundries discharge into a city sewer before the water eventually reaches a watercourse, the amount of fluoride is not usually so high as to require special treatment.

There is evaporation of the scrubber water, leading to concentration, so that chemical treatment is usually required for control of scale and corrosion in the recirculating system, and special alloys are often required for the circuits of a multiple-circuit washer where the pH may become very low.

MACHINING

Rough cast parts are sent to parts and accessories plants to be machined. Figure 25.4 shows the typical operations in a plant that machines parts for and assembles car engines. Major operations include machining, cleaning, engine testing (hydro-test), and waste treatment.

Rather than a single assembly line for the machining operation, a series of small lines is set up for each part and department. Each department performs its own particular machining operations on the subassemblies, and each of these may require a specific type of machine coolant, varying from a water-base material to a heavy sulfur oil. These coolants provide lubricity and cooling to the metal and tool used to shape it. Many of these oils contain emulsifiers that readily create O/W emulsions when mixed with water.

Soluble oil coolants are usually maintained at 5–15% oil concentration and stored in central sumps. The oil is recirculated through screens or filters to the

TABLE 25.1   Analysis of a Typical Foundry Wastewater

Constituent	mg/l
Total dissolved solids	770
Suspended solids	1900
Extractables (oil and grease)	290
Phenols*	1.5
pH	7.6

* Present in the coke and also in core binders.

1. MACHINED

2. CLEANED

3. PAINTED
(if appropriate)

4. ASSEMBLED

5. READY FOR
   FINAL
   ASSEMBLY
   IN CAR

Figure 25.4 Typical operations in an engine plant.

machine tool and back to the sump. At the machine the soluble oil absorbs heat and picks up metal fines and hydraulic oil from leaks. Plants will normally dump the entire coolant system periodically because of bacterial buildup or because the emulsion is no longer stable. It is good practice to add biocide to control bacterial activity, but even this cannot extend coolant life indefinitely.

A recent development has been the introduction of synthetic and semi-synthetic coolants. The synthetic coolants contain no oil, while the semi-synthetics contain some oil but less than soluble oil coolants. These have some advantages over soluble oils on the machine; however, they are still in the developmental stage.

City water or clarified plant water is usually used to make up the coolants. If high hardness levels are found in the makeup water, soft water is sometimes advantageous because calcium ions tend to destabilize the emulsions, especially if the coolant concentrates. Removing the calcium and magnesium extends the stability of the soluble oils.

PARTS CLEANING

The other major operation in the machinery plant is cleaning. The parts must be cleaned before and after machining to remove dirt, rust preventive, and coolant.

Chemical cleaners are used, usually alkaline and detergent types. Anionic phosphate cleaners had been used extensively in the past, but have been greatly reduced. Nonionic surfactants have become quite popular. The cleaner usage is substantial since the cleaners are continually depleted and fresh chemicals are needed to maintain the strength necessary for effective performance.

In the machine shop, blowdown from the parts cleaners comprises roughly 80% of the flow to the waste treatment plant. Because a primary function of the cleaner is to remove coolant, blowdown usually contains 500–4000 mg/l oil. These wastes are emulsions stabilized by the surfactants in the coolant and in the cleaners. Other flows to the waste plant include soluble oil dumps, other cleaners such as floor cleaners, cooling water from a variety of sources (such as air conditioning systems), boiler blowdown, hydraulic oil leaks and spills, and storm water.

Occasionally, changing from soluble oil to a synthetic coolant has caused problems in the waste treatment plant when acid and alum were being used for emulsion breaking. Organic emulsion breakers have proved more effective in removing oil from the effluent under a wide variety of coolant selections. However, reduction of soluble BOD by alum or organic emulsion breakers is usually very limited. BOD loadings to the waste plant may, in fact, increase since the synthetics usually have a higher BOD than soluble oils.

Another factor that can have an impact on the quality of the waste treatment plant effluent is cleaner usage. Excessive cleaner usage, especially of certain strong nonionic cleaners, can increase dosages in the waste treatment plant or even make the waste virtually untreatable. Volume and type of cleaner should be balanced against the impact on both the cost and quality of the waste treatment plant operation.

TABLE 25.2   Raw Waste from Machining Operations

Constituent	mg/l
Hexane extraction	4000
P alkalinity (as $CaCO_3$)	424
Total alkalinity (as $CaCO_3$)	708
Suspended solids	300
Fe (total)	4
TDS	1500
pH	10.4
Ca hardness (as $CaCO_3$)	20
Total hardness (as $CaCO_3$)	26
Total PO_4	3.0

Table 25.2 shows a typical analysis of the untreated effluent from a machining plant. Basically the effluent is an oil-in-water emulsion. This analysis does not include free or floating oils.

Machining plants use cooling water for air conditioning, powerhouse diesel generators and compressors, hydraulic oil coolers, and furnace cooling if the plant is involved in heat treatments, such as annealing.

Each plant, depending on what it manufactures, may have its own unique uses for cooling water. For example, engine plants typically hydrotest the assembled engine on a dynamometer before shipment. A typical test system is shown in Figure 25.5. On the tube side or closed side, the heat exchanger takes the place of a radiator. Soluble oil-type products are used on the closed side if the engine is going to be drained before shipment. These products lay down a film that prevents flash corrosion. If the engine is not going to be drained, either soluble oil or conventional corrosion inhibitors can be used, depending on the manufacturer's restrictions.

Figure 25.5   Cooling water circuit for hydrotesting finished engines.

A typical boiler plant generates an average of 2 million lb/day of 150 psi steam, primarily for winter heat, but some steam is also used to heat various cleaner baths, so there is a light boiler load in the summer. If the plant has a forging operation, steam may also be used to drive the hammers (Figure 25.6). Zeolites seem to be the most common method of softening, with average feedwater hardness being 1–2 mg/l. Figure 25.7 is a diagram of a typical boiler plant.

WATER-WASHED PAINT SPRAY BOOTHS

Some machinery plants (such as engine plants) have small spray booths where primer is sprayed on parts. These small booths experience the same maintenance problems as larger ones, such as those used to paint car bodies, and they require chemical treatment. They are not as important to production, so they are frequently poorly maintained.

Since spray booths are so widely used throughout the automotive and machinery industries, a description is given here to illustrate the type of water technology required for successful operation. Goals of the water treatment program are to (1) keep the water circuit free of deposits, (2) make the paint overspray collected in the water non-sticky and readily removable from the water, (3) minimize backsection deposits to prevent obstructing flow of paint-laden air from the

Figure 25.6 A large steam-operated forging hammer. The dies and sow block have been removed for routine maintenance. *(Courtesy of Forging Industry Association.)*

Figure 25.7 The boiler house in an automotive plant is simple and reliable.

booth, (4) minimize contaminants in the air discharged to the outside so it will not create an air pollution problem, and (5) minimize booth maintenance.

Figure 25.8 illustrates a typical paint spray unit for small parts, such as would be found in the machinery plants. The conveyor carrying the parts to be painted passes in front of the wet wall, and the operator sprays paint on the parts as they pass by, with the excess or overspray being collected on the film of water flowing down the wet wall. The water must be chemically conditioned so that the pigment and the excess vehicle and solvent are killed and do not form a sticky mass that would be difficult to remove from the pan. Water is continually withdrawn and recirculated to the spray header, which provides scrubbing of the discharge of ventilating air before water drains back down the wet wall.

The large paint spray booths used in the automobile assembly shops are illustrated in Figures 25.9 and 25.10. Operators work inside these booths, applying paint to the car body. The floor of these units is grating supported above a water basin, and falling paint deposits on the water while other paint particles are carried by the air flow into the water curtain either on the wet walls or into the wall cavity, or back section, where additional sprays scrub the flow of air.

DETACKIFYING PAINT

Properly treated water will collect the pigment and organic components of the paint and condition these so that they are not tacky, producing a sludge which can be readily handled without sticking to the scrapers or flights used for its removal. The material which carries up into the back section is scrubbed out and killed by properly treated water wash so that deposits do not form in this relatively constricted wall cavity. If the water is not properly treated, particles penetrate the water curtain, build deposits in the back sections, and go out the stack as particulate emissions. In addition to the air pollution problem, extensive maintenance is required to remove the deposits in the back sections, on the eliminators, on the fan blades, and in the basin below the grating to keep the booth operating so that it provides safety to the operator and a clean discharge to the outside air.

Paint spray booths are in some respects like an air washer, in that the spray water may evaporate and cause concentration of dissolved solids or water may be condensed from the air and there may be a continual dilution of the spray water. This means that a check on total dissolved solids, pH, and alkalinity is required periodically to keep the system under good control.

Recirculation volumes on washers of this type are high—about 10,000 gpm for a typical body spray booth and 500–1000 gpm for a parts spray booth. The water retention time in the system is relatively low, perhaps only 2–3 minutes. The basin is usually dumped at the end of the shift. The actual water makeup requirements are difficult to estimate because they depend on the evaporation rate and the frequency of dumping, which are unique for each installation.

STAMPING

In the stamping operation, the first step is to loosen mill scale from the metal surface in preparation for stamping by passing the strip steel through a flex roller (Figure 25.11). This flex roller bends and flexes the steel through a series of rollers. Wash oil is brushed on during the flexing operation to remove the mill scale and dirt.

The flexed steel is cut to size and then stamped to the desired shape by large hydraulic presses. Drawing oil is sprayed on the dies to aid in stamping.

The stamped part is further cut and trimmed to the precise size; and the drawing oil, cutting oil, and dirt are removed in a parts washer, creating an oily waste-

Figure 25.8 Small parts paint spray booth.

water. The part may then be welded or primed depending on the manufacturing requirements. The assembled part is then ready for shipment to the assembly plant. Finished products from stamping and fabrication plants include doors, floor pans, trunks, hoods, and fenders.

The flows from stamping and fabrication are usually quite low (50,000 gpd) and consist of oily wastes from the parts washers, cooling water blowdown, and blowdown from the spray booths. The wastewater contains 100–500 mg/l oil and can be effectively treated with O/W emulsion breakers. Occasionally, wash oil, hydraulic oil, and drawing oil are dumped to the waste plant, but most plants try to segregate these relatively clean oils from the wastewater for recovery or sale.

PLATING WASTES

Where plating of parts is a major operation, waste treatment plants are designed to remove heavy metals. Traditional treatments of reduction and pH adjustment to remove the metal as the hydroxide are commonly used. A typical heavy metal removal plant is shown in Figure 25.12. Destruction of cyanide may also be required.

Economics may justify heavy metal recovery, most frequently by an ion ex-

EXHAUST
STACK

EXHAUST FAN

AIR FILTERS

GRATING

WATER NOZZLE —
SPRAY FORMS
WATER CURTAIN

BACK SECTION
PANEL

ELIMINATORS

PAN

ASSEMBLY LINE
CONVEYOR

BACK SECTION

Figure 25.9 Automotive paint spray booth.

Figure 25.10 Cross section of automobile paint spray booth.

Figure 25.11   Fabricating and stamping.

change operation. Nickel is easily reclaimed from rinse tanks following nickel plating on H-form cation resin, with the Ni-rich regenerant returned to the plating tank. Chromate is also recoverable, but not in a form useful in the plating operation.

Plating is as much an art as a science. Parts to be plated require careful cleaning and rinsing, often with soft water to avoid spotting. The plating baths are precisely controlled and may require demineralized water makeup. A typical plating line is shown in Figure 25.13.

Painting is increasingly important in the metal fabrication plants as the efforts to stop body corrosion increase. Zinc-rich primers are sprayed on the interiors of doors, fenders and other areas that are enclosed after assembly to improve corrosion protection. This operation is carried out in the same type of spray booth as described earlier.

Utilities, such as steam and cooling water, are much the same in stamping and fabrication as described for the machining operation.

ASSEMBLY PLANTS

Figure 25.14 shows a typical flow diagram for an assembly plant. These plants receive all of the parts and sub-assemblies produced in supplier plants and as-

Figure 25.12   Heavy metals precipitation in a metal finishing shop using sulfide precipitation. Freshly prepared iron sulfide slurry is normally fed to the neutralized waste at the precipitator inlet, but may be fed ahead of the filter where the nature of the waste better suits this alternative.

semble them into a finished car. Major operations include welding, bonderizing, painting, and assembly.

In the assembly plant, the sheet metal is welded to the frame and floor pan to construct the shell of the car. During the welding operation, the welder tips are cooled by recirculating water. The most common problem in this closed cooling system is fouling, plugging the tips with corrosion products. If the water flow is reduced by plugging, the tips may melt, causing a shutdown of the assembly line. Filtration and chemical treatment with soluble oil products and conventional corrosion inhibitors minimize this corrosion and plugging.

In the bonderizing step, a metal phosphate layer, such as zinc phosphate, is

Figure 25.13   Flowsheet of a chrome plating line including cleaning step and three stages of metal deposition.

Figure 25.14 Process flow in an automobile assembly plant.

applied to the metal surfaces to provide corrosion protection and a surface for the paint finish. Figure 25.15 shows a typical phosphatizing operation consisting of cleaning, rinsing, phosphating, rinsing, and sealing with chromic acid. After bonderizing, many plants use a process to electrostatically deposit a primer coat of paint on the metal surface by dipping the electrically-charged metal into a vat of water-base paint. The oppositely charged paint particles are attracted evenly to the metal surface (see Figure 25.16). Makeup to this system is demineralized so that the bath conductivity can be controlled.

In this process, the bath tends to heat up. The paint is cooled below 90°F (32°C) through a heat exchanger by either a chiller or open recirculating cooling tower system. After the electrostatic dip, the painted car is baked in an oven to set the finish. The exhaust gases from the ovens pass through heat exchangers

Figure 25.15 Phosphating and electrocoating lines.

to recover heat by warming the oven makeup air. These exchangers foul with paint residue and require frequent cleaning.

Periodically, concentrated rinse water from electrostatic coating is dumped to the waste plant. These dumps can upset the waste plant by introducing waste that is difficult to treat. If the pH of the paint is lowered to less than 4.0, gumballs form and plug the lines and pumps.

Most vehicle assembly plants have the type of wet spray booths described earlier. Their utility services are comparable to those found in the machining plants.

There are two specific miscellaneous water uses in the assembly plant: (1) The assembled car is passed through a spray to test for leaks. Fluorescent dye is put in the water so a black light will clearly reveal leaks. Wetting agents are also added to make the test more severe and to prevent water spots. (2) The final process is a typical car wash operation. Various soaps are added to help clean the car.

TABLE 25.3 Summary of Water Uses

	Foundry	Machining	Fabricating and stamping	Assembly
Cooling	Cupola walls Cupola wet cap Slag granulator Comfort Compressors Furnace walls	Engine testing Oil coolers Comfort Compressors	Stamping Welder Comfort Compressors	Welder ELPO Comfort Compressors
Boilers	Makeup Wet scrubbers	Makeup Wet scrubbers	Makeup Wet scrubbers	Fuel Internal
Cleaning		Makeup Rinse	Makeup Rinse	Makeup Rinse
Spray booths		Makeup	Makeup	Makeup
Plating			Makeup Rinse	

Figure 25.16 Electrocoating process for automobile bodies.

Wastes from assembly plants are usually quite dilute. Typical contaminants are paint solids, oil, BOD, suspended solids, zinc, chrome, and phosphate. Coagulants and O/W emulsion breakers work well on these waters. Water comes from spray booths, stripping tanks, phosphatizing, wet sanding, car wash, cooling water, water leak test, and various parts washers. Typical flows range from 500,000 to 1,000,000 gpd.

Table 25.3 summarizes water uses in the major automotive manufacturing steps.

Chapter 26

Chemical Industry

The chemical elements can be combined in such a variety of ways that it is not surprising that the chemical industry is the most diverse of all industrial operations. Even when the number of elements that can take part in a reaction is limited, as with hydrogen, carbon and oxygen, the combinations can produce an endless array of products.

Over 10,000 products are produced by the chemical industry, most of which are used to make other products of which the public is for the most part unaware. Even foods and beverages can be considered to be mixtures of chemical substances.

The government has broken down the chemical industry by its method of standard industrial classification coding. But there are other ways of categorizing it, including tonnage, dollar value, and the position the chemicals may occupy on the path between raw materials and consumer products. Using the latter method of classification, Table 26.1 shows the wide variety of chemical products, of which the fifth category covers those finally reaching the consumer market.

PROCESS COOLING IS MAJOR H_2O USE

The industry is a major user of water, as shown by Table 26.2. The greatest use is for cooling process equipment. Many chemical reactions generate heat, and the reaction vessel is cooled so that the temperature is controlled at the desired limit and the reaction does not get out of control. Other chemical reactions require heat, and most chemical plants provide this with their own steam. If the steam is used only for low temperature process heat, the plant may operate a low pressure boiler; but if the plant requires a great deal of electrical energy as well as heat, it is common to install high pressure boilers to generate power through steam turbines, with the turbines exhausting into a process steam line,

TABLE 26.1   Varieties of Chemical Products

Class of chemicals	Examples
1. Heavy Chemicals	Sulfur, sulfuric acid, lime, soda ash, ammonia, hydrochloric acid, caustic soda, methane, alum, chlorine, potash, salt, borax, phosphoric acid
2. Intermediates	Acrylic acid, acrylonitrile, cyclic compounds, unsaturated compounds, aldehydes, ketones, alcohols
3. Finished Products—for fabrication or blending	Polyethylene, polyacrylamide, nylon, sodium phosphate, pigments, fertilizers, explosives, solvents
4. Specialty Products—for industrial and agricultural use	Corrosion inhibitors, coatings, herbicides, pesticides, food additives, inks, adhesives, dyes, cleaners
5. Consumer Products	Fabrics, paints, drugs, cosmetics, detergents, toilet preparations, sterilizing agents, baking preparations, photographic products

with perhaps some of the steam going directly to a turbine condenser. Table 26.2 shows the requirements both for boiler feedwater and also for cooling of the turbine condenser.

Cooling water is usually reclaimed by use of cooling towers, so the requirements for makeup water are minimized. Most heat exchangers use water on the tube side. However, in some chemical processes, it is more suitable to have water on the shell side with process liquor on the tube side. In this design, the water velocity is low compared to conventional practice, and suspended solids in the cooling water can create deposit problems.

Another large use of water is for process applications, which may include hydraulic conveying, hydraulic classification, washing, and equipment cleanup. Some water may become part of the finished product. Finally, provision is made in most chemical plants for fire protection, which usually requires water either applied directly, as a fog, or as a component of foam.

Chemical plant operations are classified into unit operations (such as evaporation, drying, crystallization) and unit processes (such as monomer production, sulfuric acid production, or catalytic cracking—all involving a number of unit operations). Because each chemical manufacturing plant differs so much from its neighbors, it is simpler to examine the water and steam requirements of unit operations than to attempt to assess water and steam requirements for different classifications of chemical manufacturing plants.

In most chemical operations, there are processing steps involved in preparing the raw materials for the reaction that produces the finished product. The raw materials may be crushed and then conveyed by water to classification devices, such as screens, which may be operated either wet or dry. Soluble raw materials may be dissolved in water, or if gases, absorbed in water to facilitate the chemical reaction. The quality of water may be important; for example, it may contain iron, which could catalyze a reaction, discolor the finished product, or precipitate to produce a turbid product.

After preparation, the ingredients may be charged to a reactor. This may be done batchwise or continuously, depending on the volume of throughput, the value of the products being handled, and the economics of the alternative designs. If the reaction is endothermic, the reactor is usually heated with steam; if the reaction is exothermic, the reactor is designed so the mixture must be heated to a certain level before the reaction will occur, and thereafter the reaction may become exothermic and cooling will be required. Figure 26.1 illustrates a reac-

TABLE 26.2   Water Use in the Chemical Industry

Industry			Annual water use in billions of gallons				
Category	Value of shipments[a]	Number of plants[b]	Total intake[c]	Process cooling[d]	Condenser cooling[e]	Process	Boiler feed[e]
281—Industrial Inorganic Chem.	4.6	344	592	98	19	62	7
282—Plastics & Synthetics	8.4	189	540	93	11	55	12
283—Drugs	6.0	97	NR	7	Nil	5	0.9
284—Soaps & Detergents	5.4	109	31	3	Nil	1	0.3
285—Paints & Coatings	0.7	36	NR	0.7	Nil	0.1	Nil
286—Industrial Organic Chem.	10.7	291	1316	681	316	77	18
287—Agricultural Chemicals	2.1	126	221	41	NR	16	NR
28—TOTAL	39.7	1343	2927	929	348	227	44

[a] In billions of dollars
[b] Number reporting to census
[c] Fresh water only
[d] Total water for process cooling
[e] Total water for turbine condensing
[f] Boiler feed plus miscellaneous uses
NR = not reported
SOURCE: 1972 Census of Manufactures, Department of Commerce.

Figure 26.1   A reaction vessel designed both for heating and cooling of process materials.

Feed

Countercurrent rinses

Solids discharge

Mother liquor

Figure 26.2 A pusher-type centrifuge designed for countercurrent rinsing of solids for liquor recovery. *(Courtesy of Sharples-Stokes Division, Pennwalt Corporation.)*

tion vessel designed for both heating and cooling. The polymerization of organic materials is an example of a reaction requiring initial heating, followed by cooling to maintain a control temperature.

The chemical reaction does not always take place in such a sophisticated reactor; it often occurs in a simple sedimentation vessel similar to that used for lime softening of water.

Once the chemical reaction has taken place, additional processing is usually required to remove unreacted raw materials or unwanted byproducts. When these impurities are solids, typical solids/liquids separation processes are used. Depending on the nature of the solids to be removed, the choice may be sedimentation, filtration, or centrifugation. The solids removed are often washed for recovery of values in the liquor mixed with these sloids (Figure 26.2).

Figure 26.3 Energy changes accompany many chemical separation processes, requiring heating or cooling of the process liquor. In this large crystallizer, ammonium sulfate is produced at a rate of 600 tons per day. *(Courtesy of Whiting Corporation.)*

Figure 26.4 Simplified flowsheet of alum manufacture uses several unit processes.

If the impurities are not solids, then the final separation may require extraction with a solvent, which may be water if the process fluid is hydrocarbon. Or the separation may be achieved by an operation involving a phase change such as evaporation, distillation, crystallization, or drying. In all of these operations energy is applied to produce the separation, and cooling water may be used on condensers or reflux heat exchangers (Figure 26.3).

PROCESS FLOWSHEETS

A simple example showing how these unit operations are assembled into a complete process and how water and steam are used is the manufacture of alum, shown in the flow sheet of Figure 26.4. In the preparation of raw materials, the bauxite is crushed and ground in the dry form and fed into the first reaction vessel, where it meets concentrated sulfuric acid and is diluted with washings from later operations. The mixture is heated with steam so that the reaction can take place rapidly, iron is removed as an impurity, and the liquor is fed to a clarifier, where a flocculant is added. The underflow solids are pumped to a two-stage washing system, where the alum liquor is recovered by having these solids washed with condensate. The overflow liquor is further concentrated in an open evaporator, and the concentrate is then discharged onto a cooling floor where crystallization occurs. As seen in this flow sheet, the reaction takes place in relatively simple and compact vessels and the balance of the equipment is for preparing the raw materials, and finishing the product to meet the required specifications. Steam is required for the operation, and the condensate produced is used as the wash water in processing the waste solids.

A second example, where the preparation of raw materials and separation and purification of the final product is more extensive is shown in Figure 26.5, relating to the manufacture of sodium chromate from chromite ore.

A good example of the complexity of the petrochemical industry is the manu-

Figure 26.5 A variety of unit processes are used in this scheme for production of sodium chromate and by-product salt cake from chromite ore.

facture of synthetic rubber, illustrated by Figure 26.6. In this illustration, the raw materials are intermediates or specialty chemicals, the equipment for carrying out the reaction is quite complex, and the final processing steps are equally complicated. There is extensive use of steam and water throughout the process.

There are many other processes used in the chemical industry, such as electrolysis and ion exchange, also using water and steam extensively; the earlier illustrations serve the purpose of pointing out the diversity of operations in the chemical industry and the widespread use of both water and steam in almost every operation.

ENVIRONMENTAL EFFECTS

The problems of water pollution control are particularly complicated in the chemical industry. The flow charts have shown how widely water and steam are used in all kinds of operations, and each point of use represents a possibility for contamination with the raw material, intermediate, or finished product at that point.

It is usually less expensive to design the process to prevent contamination and to install equipment to recycle and recover chemicals than it is to remove or neutralize the contamination after the fact in a waste treatment plant. For example, if the waste solids produced in the alum process, Figure 26.4, still contain too much liquor to be acceptable as landfill, a third washing stage may be added. In the removal of unreacted raw materials from a finished liquid organic com-

Figure 26.6 In petrochemical processes, a large variety of sophisticated units may be required, as in this flowsheet for production of synthetic rubber. (*From Chemical Engineering, pp. 121–126, Feb. 22, 1960.*)

**TABLE 26.3 Waste Profiles of Selected Organics in Water
(Based on oxygen demand*)**

Chemical	BOD	COD	Theoretical O_2 demand
Acids			
Acetic	0.34–0.88	1.01	1.07
Benzoic	1.37	1.95	1.97
Formic	0.15–0.27	—	0.35
Maleic	0.38	0.83	0.83
Alcohols			
n-Amyl Alcohol	1.6	—	2.72
n-Butyl Alcohol	1.5–2.0	1.90	2.59
Ethyl Alcohol	1.0–1.5	2.0	2.1
Methyl Alcohol	0.6–1.1	1.5	1.6
Phenol	1.6	—	2.4
Isopropyl Alcohol	1.45	1.61	2.40
Aldehydes			
Formaldehyde	0.6–1.07	1.06	1.07
Furfural	0.77	—	1.66
Ketones—Acetone	0.5–1.0	1.12	2.20
Ether			
Ethyl Ether	0.03	—	2.59
Cyclic Compounds			
Aniline	1.5	—	3.09
Benzene	0	0.25	3.07
Monochlorbenzene	0.03	0.41	2.06
Toluene	0	0.7	3.13
Xylene	0	—	3.16

* Given in gm O_2/gm of chemical

pound, the installation of additional trays in the distillation column to recover the unreacted material may be much more practical than permitting the material to be discharged as a vapor or condensed in a barometric condenser, either of which represents a pollution problem.

As a general rule, if a chemical plant is producing inorganic chemicals, precipitation and solids/liquids separation equipment are usually used for the waste treatment operation; if handling organic chemicals, removal of organics by adsorption on activated carbon or by digestion in an activated sludge system is almost always required. The organic residues present a difficult problem in that many of them are not easily digested by bacteria, and sometimes a combination of bacterial digestion plus activated carbon adsorption is required.

Table 26.3 lists a few organic compounds found in wastes from chemical plants where these materials are manufactured. For the organic acids and alcohols shown on this list, the BOD is usually over 50% of the COD or the theoretical oxygen demand, and such wastes are amenable to biological digestion in an activated sludge system. Benzene and its close relatives are usually impervious to biological attack and must be removed by stripping, adsorption, or both. So in many organic chemical plants, if a wide variety of compounds across the spectrum of active groups—alcohols, aldehydes, aromatics—is present, the waste may require both biological and activated carbon treatments.

In any case, the pollution control engineer must be aware of all raw materials, intermediates, and finished products produced, recognizing that they may be found in the effluent. He should be familiar with the toxicological properties and tolerance levels of each, and their potential effect on the receiving stream or the waste treatment plant.

SUGGESTED READING

Shreve, R. H.: *Chemical Process Industries*, 3d ed., McGraw-Hill, New York, 1967.

U.S. Environmental Protection Agency: *Development Document for the Major Inorganic Products*, EPA-440/1-74-007-a, March 1974.

U.S. Environmental Protection Agency: *Development Document for the Major Organic Products*, EPA-440/1-74-009-a, March 1974.

U.S. Environmental Protection Agency, *Development Document for the Synthetic Resins*, EPA-440/1-74-010-a, March 1974.

Chapter 27

Coke Industry

An essential raw material for the iron blast furance and the cast iron foundry is coke, which is produced from coal in the United States at a rate of 60–70 million tons per year. Coke is the source of both energy and carbon for chemical reduction in the blast furnace, in which it is used at a rate of approximately 0.5 ton per ton of finished iron. In foundry cupolas it is used as a fuel for melting pig iron.

Blast furnace coke is manufactured from carefully blended stocks of high and low volatility coals. The mix is ground, charged to a furnace, and heated for approximately 18 hours at about 1800–2000°F (980–1100°C) to drive off moisture and volatile matter. At the end of the coking period, incandescent coke is pushed from the furnace into receiving cars, quenched with water, and sent to the blast furnace or to other industrial uses. The finished product is controlled by careful selection of raw materials and through the process steps to produce a carbonaceous product strong enough to avoid crushing in the blast furnace or cupola, and pure enough to avoid transmitting unwanted impurities to the product of the blast furnace or cupola.

Another variety of coke, produced by the petroleum refinery, is used for other purposes, such as electrode manufacture. This is considered a refinery operation and is not included here as part of the coke industry.

Because coal is a heterogenous mixture of amorphous carbon and a variety of organic chemicals and inorganic minerals (ash) the coking process yields not only coke but also a variety of by-products, as shown by Table 27.1. The integrated coke plant is usually broken down into two major areas, the coke plant itself, and the by-product plant, which recovers tar, ammonium sulfate, and light oils. The by-products plant refines the light oils to produce such valuable organic chemicals as benzene, toluene, xylene, and naphthalene.

TABLE 27.1   Products of Coke Plant Operation
[Based on 1 ton of coal (0.91 kkg)]

Coke oven gas	10,000–12,000 cu ft (283–340 m³)
Coke	1,400 lb (640 kg)
Ammonium sulfate	25 lb (11 kg)
Tar	10 gal (38 l)
Light oil	2–4 gal (7–15 l)

COKE PLANT

A large inventory of high and low volatile coals is maintained at the plant site, partly for economic reasons and partly to permit blending of incoming coal to minimize variations in composition and to permit exercising quality control over the charge, and therefore the finished product. A typical coke plant processes 2000–4000 tons (1800–3600 t) of coal per day and may stockpile a 30–60 day supply. The several grades of coal are blended, crushed to about 50 mesh, and transferred to a storage bin for charging.

The coking operation is carried out in a battery of 10–100 individual ovens designed to provide relatively uniform production of finished products and to recover heat in a way that minimizes fuel requirements. Of the 10,000–12,000 cu ft of gas produced per ton of coal charged (315–630 m³/t) about 40–50% is returned as fuel to the coke ovens. Figure 27.1 is a simple schematic of a coke oven showing the oven itself and the regenerative brickwork used to reclaim heat and minimize fuel consumption.

The oven chamber is wider at the discharge end so that when the coke is pushed from the oven it will not bind. Typically, the oven is approximately 35 ft (10 m) long, 10–15 ft (3–4.5 m) high, and 10–20 in. (25–50 cm) at the pusher end and about 2–3 in. (5–7 cm) wider at the discharge end.

The blended, crushed coal charge is fed to the ovens by a charging car mounted on the coke oven battery and traveling from one oven to the other as needed (Figure 27.2). The cycle of charging, coking, and discharging is illustrated in Figure 27.3. To minimize air pollution during charging, new plants are being constructed to provide charging through a pipeline carrying preheated coal in a fluidized condition.

During the coking period, the coke oven gas is collected through ascension pipes at the top of the oven, scrubbed in the gas collecting main with weak ammonia liquor to remove tar, and discharged to the by-products recovery operation. The heating gas is burned and the products of combustion pass through flues on both sides of the oven, finally passing through a regenerator. When the regenerator becomes hot, the flue gas is diverted to a second regenerator, and the first, heated regenerator is then used to preheat air to conserve fuel. The flue gas temperature is carefully controlled to avoid overheating the coke charge.

At the completion of coking, the oven is isolated from the gas main, and the incandescent coke is pushed into rail cars for prompt transfer to a quenching tower. Here, quench water showers the coke to cool it and prevent further loss by combustion.

BY-PRODUCT RECOVERY

The coke oven gas is then processed for recovery of valuable by-products as shown by the flow diagram in Figure 27.4 Depending on the capacity of the plant and the value of the by-products, each coke plant may decide on the extent to which recovery is economical. The diagram shown represents complete recovery, but this may not be practiced in every plant.

Figure 27.1 Coke oven, showing complex arrangement of flues for heating the oven to convert coal to coke, and regenerative brickwork for heat recovery. (*Copyright 1964 by United States Steel Corporation.*)

Figure 27.2   Car riding the top of the coke oven battery to charge coal to the ovens. *(Copyright 1964 by United States Steel Corporation.)*

The gas is first cooled by spraying with weak ammonia liquor. In a secondary loop, the weak ammonia liquor is then cooled either by heat exchangers or by an open recirculation system incorporating a cooling tower. Since the spray cooling condenses the moisture originally in the coal, there is an increase in the volume of the weak ammonia liquor. Some liquor is bled off at a steady rate to maintain the material balance of the system. The gas is compressed and then passes to a tar precipitator, an electrostatic device for tar removal. The tar from the precipitator is combined with that decanted from the weak ammonia liquor and is a useful by-product, going into roofing pitch, asphalt shingles, and other products.

Following cooling, ammonia is removed from the coke oven gas by washing with a recirculating sulfuric acid solution. This liquor is sent to crystallizers for the production of ammonium sulfate. The gas is then sent through a final cooler where it is contacted with cool water to reduce the temperature to less than 68°F (20°C) so that the wash water will recover naphthalene from the gas. The cool gas is then washed with a wash oil, which extracts additional by-product hydrocarbons. Finally, the gas is sent to a scrubber for reduction of sulfur which may be required to meet air emission standards when it is used as fuel.

The wash oil containing hydrocarbons may then be processed for separation of benzene, toluene and xylene, as illustrated by the flow sheet in Figure 27.5.

UTILITY REQUIREMENTS

Because of the availability of excess by-product gas, the coke plant usually produces its own steam to drive turbines used for compressing the gas. The plant may also generate electric power for its own needs. Usually the turbine exhaust steam is used in the distillation required to separate benzene, toluene, and xylene.

Appreciable water is needed by the coke plant, principally for gas cooling. This may come to approximately 1000–2000 gal/ton (4–8 m³/t) of product. In

CHARGING, LEVELING AND PUSHING OPERATIONS
IN ONE COKING CYCLE OF A BY-PRODUCT COKE OVEN

A. THE CHARGING LARRY, WITH HOPPERS CONTAINING MEASURED AMOUNTS OF COAL, IS IN POSITION OVER CHARGING HOLES FROM WHICH COVERS HAVE BEEN REMOVED. THE PUSHER HAS BEEN MOVED INTO POSITION.

B. THE COAL FROM THE LARRY HOPPERS HAS DROPPED INTO THE OVEN CHAMBER, FORMING PEAKED PILES.

C. THE LEVELING DOOR AT THE TOP OF THE OVEN DOOR ON THE PUSHER SIDE HAS BEEN OPENED, AND THE LEVELING BAR ON THE PUSHER HAS BEEN MOVED BACK AND FORTH ACROSS THE PEAKED COAL PILES TO LEVEL THEM. THE BAR NEXT IS WITHDRAWN FROM THE OVEN, THE LEVELING DOOR AND CHARGING HOLES ARE CLOSED, AND THE COKING OPERATION BEGINS.

D. COKING OF THE COAL ORIGINALLY CHARGED INTO THE OVEN HAS BEEN COMPLETED (IN ABOUT 18 HOURS) AND THE OVEN IS READY TO BE "PUSHED." THE OVEN DOORS ARE REMOVED FROM EACH END, AND THE PUSHER, COKE GUIDE AND QUENCHING CAR ARE MOVED INTO POSITION.

E. THE RAM OF THE PUSHER ADVANCES TO PUSH THE INCANDESCENT COKE OUT OF THE OVEN, THROUGH THE COKE GUIDE AND INTO THE QUENCHING CAR.

Figure 27.3 Cycle of coke oven production. *(Copyright 1964 by United States Steel Corporation.)*

Figure 27.4 Flow sheet of coke oven gas cooling and recovery plant. *(From PB 249-661, "Water Pollution Abatement Technology: Capabilities and Cost, Iron and Steel Industry," National Technical Information Service, Springfield, Va.)*

Figure 27.5 Processing of wash oil to yield benzene, toluene, and x-lene *(From PB 249-661, "Water Pollution Abatement Technology, Capabilities and Cost, Iron and Steel Industry," National Technical Information Service, Springfield, Va.)*

Figure 27.6 Emissions from the coke oven discharged during the pushing operation are captured by this specially designed mobile unit that transports the coke to the quench tower. *(Courtesy of The Alliance Machine Company-Hartung Kuhn & Company.)*

addition to gas cooling, water is used for coke quenching and for cooling of utility auxiliaries, such as air compressors and pump glands.

As in many hydrocarbon processing plants, process water becomes contaminated not only with oil but also with ammonia, phenol, cyanide, and thiocyanates. The major sources of wastewater are (a) the weak ammonia liquor from the primary coolers, (b) blowdown from cooling towers used either directly or indirectly for gas cooling, (c) contaminated condensate from steam distillation of some of the hydrocarbon fractions, (d) storage tank water draw, and (e) storm water. Strong wastes that may be segregated for separate disposal include acid and caustic used in light oil processing, spent soda ash solution from the sulfur removal tower, and excess liquors from the ammonium sulfate recovery process.

BIOLOGICAL TREATMENT

The weak ammonia liquor may be segregated for separate treatment through a biological system, which has proved to be an effective method for reduction of both phenol and cyanide.

Because of the relatively high requirement for quenching water, about 150–200 gal/ton (0.6–0.8 m³/t) of coke, this has usually been used as a point for disposal of the stronger wastes, such as excess weak ammonia liquor, which would otherwise be difficult to process to a level acceptable for final discharge to a receiving stream. There is considerable heat in the coke pushed from the oven, and some plants reclaim this heat by using air cooling rather than water quenching. This preheats the air and reduces fuel consumption.

The problems of both air and water pollution control are formidable in the coke plant, being complicated by the nature of the raw materials, the design of the coke ovens, and the economics of by-product recovery. Each plant requires individual study to arrive at the best solution. Solving the problems will require revolutionary developments in technology, both in terms of pollution control facilities and also modification of the process itself. For example, coke oven fumes released during the pushing step are being captured by special emission control cars positioned on the rails at the oven being discharged (Figure 27.6). Where the coke plant is part of a steel mill, there may be opportunities for disposal of some wastes through steel mill operations such as slag quenching.

SUGGESTED READING

McGannon, H. E., (ed.): *The Making, Shaping and Treating of Steel*, 8th ed., United States Steel Corporation. 1964.
Shreve, R. N.: *Chemical Process Industries*, 3d ed., McGraw-Hill, New York, 1967.

Chapter 28

Food Processing Industry

Because of its intimate connection with the public health, the food industry has had a long history of surveillance of its activities by local, state, and federal agencies. Congress passed the original Food & Drug Act in 1906. That Act, with subsequent legislation, controls not only the chemicals that are directly added to food—salt, seasonings, and preservatives—but also such chemicals as sizing in food wrap that may indirectly become food additives by contacting food.

In addition to the close control of the FDA, additional surveillance is imposed on meat and poultry processing plants through the U.S. Department of Agriculture. No chemical can be brought into a meat or poultry processing plant unless approved by the USDA for its intended use, such as equipment cleaning or water treatment

Because of this close regulation, the choices of chemicals used in water or wastewater treatment may be more limited in the food industry than in other major water-consuming industries.

There are many segments of the food processing industry, of which the major water-using categories include sugar cane and beet processing, beverage manufacturing, fruit and vegetable processing, meat and poultry, grain processing, fats and oils, and dairy products. The water consumptions of these segments are shown in Table 28.1.

Although there are wide variations in the process steps in each of these industry segments, there are a number of common unit operations. The distribution of water in the plant can be put into three categories: process water, cooling water, and boiler feedwater. The percentage distribution varies considerably from a high of about 60% used for processing in the meat and poultry industry, to a low of only 15% in the sugar industry. However, 75% of the water used in the sugar industry is for cooling purposes (and later becomes process water), with only 25% being used in the meat and poultry industry. Most food processing

TABLE 28.1   Water Usages in Food Processing*

Industry segment	Gross use	Water flows, MGD intake	Discharge
Sugar	1061	545	518
Beverages	797	275	226
Fruit and vegetables	620	348	324
Meat and poultry	458	296	288
Grain processing	386	218	199
Fats and oils	358	107	89
Dairy products	218	119	111

* 1972 Census of Manufactures, U.S. Department of Commerce Publication MC72 (SR-4), Water Use in Manufacturing.

plants generate steam for cooking or processing, and water used for boiler makeup ranges from about 6% of the total usage in fruit and vegetable processing, to about 15% in the fats and oils segment.

Process water uses include: washing of raw materials and process equipment; conveying products from one process area to another; dissolving or extracting; and addition to the finished product. Cooling water may be used to operate refrigeration equipment, to condense steam from evaporators or turbines, or to cool process equipment such as compressors, cookers, and engine jackets.

Steam may be generated for cooking, for heating evaporators, or for space heating. In some industries enough steam is required to justify installation of a turbine to extract power from the steam before it is sent to process. If the steam can come into direct contact with food, there are strict limits on chemicals used for both steam and boiler water treatment, and on their maximum concentrations.

Knowing the processing operations in a food plant is helpful to an understanding of water use; water may be used sequentially for several purposes. For example, in the sugar industry, which has a very high requirement for condenser cooling water because of the evaporation and concentration of syrups, this cooling water is used for washing cane brought in from the fields before it is discharged, and it is categorized as cooling water rather than process water.

Because the problems of cooling water and boiler water treatment in the food industry are similar to other industries, this chapter will deal specifically with process water, with some consideration of its contamination and final treatment for disposal.

THE SUGAR INDUSTRY

There are many process steps in the sugar industry (some of which are similar to corn processing). As the largest food processing water user with a variety of process operations, the sugar processing industry offers a good example of water use in food processing.

Sugar (sucrose), a chemical classified as a disaccharide with the formula $C_{12}H_{22}O_{11}$, is derived from two major crops, sugar cane and sugar beets. Cane is cultivated in tropical and semi-tropical climates (e.g., Puerto Rico, Florida), while beets are raised in temperate climates (Idaho, California). In the United States, about 7 million tons of sugar are produced annually compared to world production of 75 million tons each year. In the United States the major sugar cane producers are Louisiana and Florida with Hawaii and Texas also important contributors. Beet sugar production is principally in the western and northwestern states. Cane exceeds beet sugar production. Because these crops spoil rapidly, they cannot be stored and the production of sugar is seasonal, with a mill operating a production campaign of about 120 days geared to the plant harvest.

Sucrose, which constitutes up to 20% of the weight of the cane or beet, is readily degraded by bacterial action. The first step in the degradation is the production of invert sugars, fructose and glucose:

$$C_{12}H_{22}O_{11} + H_2O \rightarrow C_6H_{12}O_6 + C_6H_{12}O_6 \qquad (1)$$
$$\text{sucrose} \qquad\qquad \text{fructose} \quad \text{glucose}$$

The second step is the production of lactic acid ($C_3H_6O_4$) under the conditions prevailing in beet sugar manufacture, or dextran ($C_6H_{10}O_5$) under the conditions common in the cane sugar mills. Since this degradation is primarily caused by bacteria, it is important to maintain control of microbial organisms throughout the mill to avoid loss of production of sucrose. Microbial activity also causes processing difficulties, such as filter blinding, slime formation, and odors.

A basic flow diagram applying to cane and beet sugar processing is shown in Figure 28.1.

As the crops arrive at the mill they contain soil and trash accumulated during the harvesting operation. In the case of cane sugar harvested by pushers, similar to bulldozers, the refuse may constitute as much as 10–25% of the weight of material delivered to the mill. This is not merely inert material; it represents a major source of bacterial inoculation since soil organisms are present with appreciable fecal matter from birds, rodents, and other small animals that live on the crop lands. Because of this, washing is a critical operation to the preparation of raw materials going to further extraction processes. On the other hand, washing should not be excessive, as this leads to loss of sucrose in the wash water.

After washing, sucrose is extracted from the raw material. In cane sugar mills, this is usually done by crushing and milling the washed, cut cane stalks, producing a juice containing approximately 12–15% sucrose. In the beet sugar industry, the beets are sliced into long, narrow pieces (cossettes), and the sucrose extracted by washing with water in diffusers at about 160°F (70°C). There is grow-

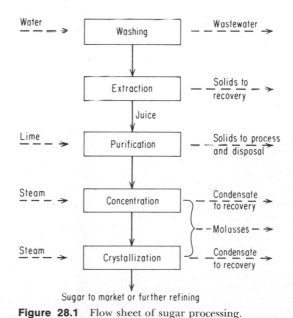

Figure 28.1 Flow sheet of sugar processing.

ing interest in the use of diffusers in place of crushers and mills in cane processing to reduce maintenance costs and improve yield.

The cane stalks are pressed after initial crushing and milling to reclaim as much sugar as possible, and the remaining solids (called bagasse) are usually burned in boilers to generate steam. Bagasse may also be used as a raw material for such products as insulation board or acoustical tile. In the beet sugar industry, the beet pulp residue is quite high in protein, and it may be mixed with some of the plant production of molasses for cattle feed.

As with most other natural products, there are a variety of chemicals other than sucrose in the cane and beets. These must be removed to maximize the yield of sugar, minimize the production of molasses, and reduce taste, color, and odor producing impurities. Lime is used to precipitate these impurities, and the lime mud is removed by conventional solids/liquid separation devices. The mud is washed to reclaim as much sugar as possible, and it may then be (a) reburned to produce fresh lime, (b) returned to the fields for its fertilizer value (it often contains significant phosphate), or (c) sent to landfill.

The purified juice must be concentrated to produce a thick syrup, the form of sugar often used by the beverage industry, or to produce a crystalline product. The juice is concentrated by evaporation. Since it contains calcium from the lime treatment, a common problem in the industry is the formation of scale in the pans (simple steam-jacketed evaporators) or in the multiple effect evaporators. Another common problem is foaming as the juices become concentrated during evaporation.

The flow sheet of a cane sugar mill producing raw sugar is shown in Figure 28.2. There is widespread use of steam throughout the plant, so the boiler house is a significant factor in economical production of sugar. Many sugar mills operate intermediate pressure boilers and produce electrical power through turbo generators, taking extraction steam from the turbines for operation of pans, evaporators, and crystallizers, and in many cases taking part of the steam through the turbine to a condenser. Cooling water from both turbine and evaporator condensers may then be used as process water.

Because the operation of a multiple effect evaporator produces more water as condensate than it consumes as steam, there is usually an excess of condensate available as boiler feedwater. This condensate often presents special problems in that it is likely to be high in ammonia, and it may periodically contain sucrose or invert sugar. The introduction of sugar into the boiler quickly produces an acid condition, so careful monitoring of the condensate system for sugar content is important to the protection of the boiler system.

The pollution control problems of the sugar mills are unusual because of the seasonal nature of the industry. The campaign is usually during the dry months, when streams cannot assimilate any excess organic loading. So the mills minimize discharge flows by recycling as completely as possible, and the wastewaters are treated biologically and impounded for solar evaporation or controlled discharge when stream flows return to acceptable rates.

THE BEVERAGE INDUSTRY

This segment of the food industry is another major consumer of water, some of which becomes part of the final product. The balance is used for washing of bottles and containers, cooling of compressors and refrigeration equipment, and makeup to boilers producing steam used for cooking, evaporation, heating of pasteurizers, and space heating.

The water used in the product must, of course, be potable; in addition, there are standards within the industry related to the effect of water quality on the

Figure 28.2 Process flow chart of cane sugar mill. *(Courtesy of Rio Grande Valley Sugar Growers, Inc.)*

taste of the finished beverage. In the soft drink industry, for example, it is common to lime soften the water for hardness and alkalinity reduction, since alkalinity destroys the flavor of acidic fruit extracts. In the lime softeners, breakpoint chlorination is also practiced. The finished water is filtered and then passed through activated carbon as a final precaution for the removal of chlorine and any residual tastes or odors. Most soft drink bottling plants have hot water boilers to provide the heat required for bottle and can washing.

Breweries and distilleries, on the other hand, operate their own steam plants because steam is required for cooking and for the operation of evaporators. In many of these plants, steam passes through turbines to generate power, exhausting to lower pressures for process operations. The unit operations in these plants are quite similar to those found in the chemical industry in principle, but special designs enable the equipment to be readily cleaned to prevent microbial contamination of the product and to avoid risks to the public health.

Special designs of piping and fittings, such as long-sweep pipe elbows, are used throughout the food industry because of this need for sanitation (Figure 28.3). Highly polished stainless steel, monel, or chrome-plated steel eliminates scratches, nicks and crevices which could offer a home for bacterial growths. The careful cleaning of equipment after each use creates a special problem of pollution control in that spent chemical cleaners, especially those containing biocides, often interfere with the performance of pollution control equipment.

Figure 28.3 A filter installation typical of the food and beverage industry practices. Note the use of special stainless steel piping and fittings. *(Courtesy of Croll-Reynolds Engineering Company, Inc.)*

Figure 28.4   The flow of product and water through a pasteurizer for careful control of beverage temperatures. Flows are cascaded for energy recovery. (*Courtesy of Barry-Wehmiller Company.*)

Two water-using systems are unique to the food industry and require special attention to water quality: these are the bottle and container washing systems and the pasteurizer.

In the bottle washing operation, both cleaning and sterilization are required, so detergents and biocides are applied to match the severity of the problem. If the bottle washer is handling returnable bottles, since there is no way of knowing what might have been in the bottles when in the hands of the public, it is important to use effective cleaning chemicals. These are quite alkaline. Because of this, it is beneficial to have zeolite softened water for washing and rinsing as this reduces the demand for detergents and also greatly facilitates the drainage of the bottle after rinsing for spot free surfaces.

When strongly alkaline cleaners are used, these provide a biocidal effect that depends both on the length of time the chemical is in contact with the bottle, and the causticity of the cleaning solution. Even with this protection, however, chlorine is often applied to the final rinse water to insure sterility.

In the pasteurizing operation, as practiced in breweries, the bottled product is moved through the pasteurizer, passing first through a chilling zone to halt the growth of specific spoilage organisms. A controlled temperature water bath then slowly brings the beverage to approximately 160°F (70°C) and holds it for the time required to insure that the entire contents of the bottle have been pasteurized. Usually two heating stages are used to prevent thermal shock and bottle breakage. The bottle is then moved into a chilling compartment before leaving the pasteurizer for packaging. It is useful to have zeolite softened water for this operation also, to avoid spotting the bottles or cans. The temperature in the pasteurizing section is maintained by circulating hot water; and the chilling sections (also staged to avoid thermal shock) may be tied into a cooling tower and supplemented with a closed chilled-water system (Figure 28.4), although once-through cooling water is still widely used.

In the event of bottle breakage, these water systems are inoculated with nutrients (the beverage), and microbial activity may quickly get out of hand. Biocides or chlorine-biodispersant treatments are used to keep this under control.

For the most part, beverage industry wastewaters are handled by municipal sewage systems. This may require the plant to install equalization facilities to unify the composition and flow rate. In-house handling of strong wastes, such as chemical cleaners, may also be necessary to make the equalization program effective.

A number of large distilleries provide their own independent waste treatment facilities, usually conventional biological treatment.

FRUIT AND VEGETABLE PROCESSING

Just as with fluming of sugar beets in the sugar industry, traditionally, water has been the media of in-plant conveyance of most fruits and vegetables in this industry segment. Not only has this choice been economical, but also it provides additional benefits in prewashing and cooling. However, due to the pollution load that results from fluming, new methods of conveyance (air, vacuum, and mechanical) are now becoming more common, so washing and rinsing, which may require as much as 50% of the total water used in process operations, is a separate step. Grading and sizing are sometimes accomplished simultaneously with washing.

After the fruits and vegetables are washed, peels are removed in a variety of ways. Steaming or soaking in caustic solutions are the most common, but air and mechanical peeling are also used. Dry caustic peeling of potatoes is gaining acceptance within the industry as a means of greatly reducing pollution loads.

Water blanching is generally used for vegetable processing to remove air and to leach solubles before canning. Steam blanching of vegetables is usually used to destroy enzymes before freezing or dehydration. The blanching effluent stream contributes a significant portion of the total pollution load in canning operations.

In most canneries, the cans are filled with uncooked food and then passed through a steam exhaust box to eliminate air preceding the can sealing operation. The food is then cooked in the cans by direct contact of steam in retorts, which are pressure cookers in which cans are stacked in racks. After cooking, large volumes of water are required to cool the cans as they pass through cooling water canals. For continuous production, horizontal rotary cookers may be used in place of retorts and cooling canals, with steam cooking in the first cylindrical shell and water cooling in the second. Even larger continuous units are available to process up to 50,000 cans on a two-hour cycle including preheat, steaming, cascade cooling, and final cooling.

A number of food products are cooked before they are bottled or canned, and many of these, such as catsup, require concentration through evaporation of water from the juice. So, there are many varieties of processing units used in the fruit and vegetable processing industry, including jacketed cookers and evaporators. All of this food processing equipment must be kept clean, usually by sanitizing with chlorinated water or detergents.

Like most food industries, the fruit and vegetable processors are trying to adopt dry cleaning methods to reduce the pollutant loading on effluent water. This pollution loading varies enormously from one type of product to another. For example, in the processing of asparagus, the BOD and suspended solids are usually below 100 mg/l, whereas in the production of whole kernel corn, the BOD and suspended solids may be several thousand mg/l. The solid wastes also vary considerably from one material to another.

Although many canneries are served by municipal sewage systems, many also operate their own waste treatment facilities. Those in farm areas where land is available have been successful in using spray irrigation as a means of disposal, often accomplishing as high as 99% BOD removal. One reason spray irrigation has been effective in the canning industry is because of the seasonal nature of its operations, permitting discharge during dry weather and avoiding the problems of freezing that would occur with a year-round operation of spray facilities in cold climates. A flow diagram of such a facility is shown in Figure 28.5.

Although activated sludge is an effective treatment process, strong waste from food processing may be fermented prior to final aerobic digestion to improve overall BOD reduction. This is especially useful in handling fruit processing

Figure 28.5 Spray distribution of food processing wastes to sloped grassland with collection of treated runoff. This system is very efficient in temperate climates. (*Courtesy of U.S. Environmental Protection Agency.*)

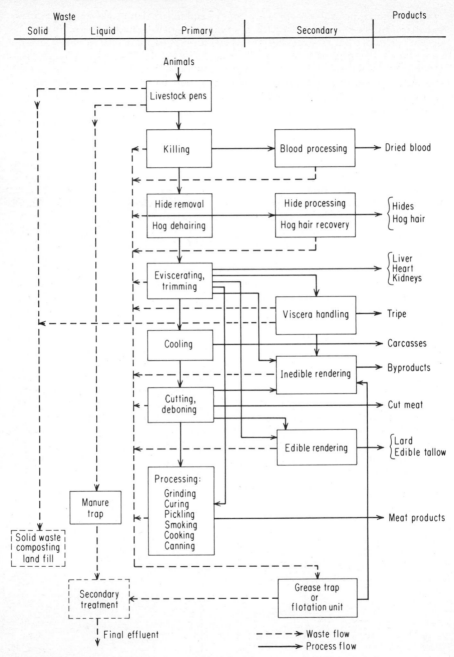

Figure 28.6   Flow chart for a packinghouse. *(EPA Contract No. 68-01-0031.)*

wastes because anaerobic fermentation proceeds rapidly and greatly reduces the load on the aerobic polishing unit.

MEAT AND POULTRY

A generation ago, Carl Sandburg called Chicago "hog butcher for the world;" today its great stockyards are almost empty. Economics and environmental control problems have moved the meat industry closer to the animals' grazing lands and feedlots. There, the packing houses purchase live animals, weigh them, and keep them for several hours or overnight in "cow palaces," or holding pens, for processing.

The diverse steps in meat processing are shown by the flow sheet in Figure 28.6. Poultry processing is illustrated by Figure 28.7.

In the first step of meat processing, animals are stunned by electrical, mechanical, or sometimes chemical means before slaughter. Large packing houses can slaughter over 300 cattle or almost 1000 hogs per hour, while giant poultry processors can kill almost 500 broilers per minute. Water is used sparingly on the kill floor; there are two separate drains so that the blood can be reclaimed for further processing without being diluted by cleanup water.

Blood is either processed on-site or sold to renderers for processing. This consists of evaporating the water from the colloidal solids by "dry cooking" in a steam-jacketed vessel or by direct steam contact. The coagulated blood solids are then dewatered to about 57% moisture either by solids/liquid separation or further evaporation. The water from this process (serum water) carries a heavy pollutant load. Blood processing is a heavy contributor to air pollution also. The final product, blood meal, rich in amino acids, is sold as a nutrient to poultry and hog feeders.

Cattle hides are removed from carcasses, and these "green hides" are usually cured on-site by salting and stacking for 14 days or by soaking in a brine solution, which takes about 18 hours. The brine solution is filtered for recycle to remove horn and flesh particles, hair and other solids, and discarded after a few days use. After curing and sorting, the hides are sent out for tanning.

Most hogs are processed without skinning; hair is removed by soaking in 140°F water, usually containing a surfactant, and then processing through a dehairer, a device using rubber hair scrapers with copious sprays of hot water. A gas singer burns remaining hair from the carcass before further processing.

Hair is usually further processed by a caustic soak followed by steam cooking to produce a high protein animal feed supplement called hair meal.

Large volumes of water are used as the cattle and hog carcasses are cut and processed. Viscera are removed and conveyed by water to edible and inedible product processing.

Federally inspected and approved fat removed from the meat is rendered to make fine cosmetics and lard. This process of edible rendering is a "wet process." Live steam is injected into a pressure vessel and the fat is released to float on the condensate (stick water). The stick water is high in BOD and extractables, and constitutes a high loading on the waste treatment plant.

Most inedible rendering is accomplished dry. Ground offal is introduced into a steam-jacketed vessel, where water is evaporated under a slight vacuum. The cooked products are tallow and bone meal.

In basic operations, poultry and hog processing are similar. Scalding tanks are used to enhance feather removal; and the production of feather meal is similar to hair meal. Large amounts of water are used throughout the process.

Because of the high BOD of meat processing wastes, water pollution control is somewhat unusual in that anaerobic digestion is frequently used prior to aerobic digestion. A crust develops on the anaerobic lagoon which normally controls the odors often associated with anaerobic fermentation. Pretreatment by equalization, screening, and flotation is essential to good control of the operation. The digester loading is typically about 0.2 lb BOD/day/cu ft of digester volume. The wastewater is usually warm, about 80–100°F (27–38°C), which is beneficial, as anaerobic digestion is greatly hindered at low temperatures. Detention may be 12–24 hours. This combination of anaerobic-aerobic digestion followed by sedimentation usually results in 90% BOD reduction in the first stage and over 98% overall (Figure 28.8).

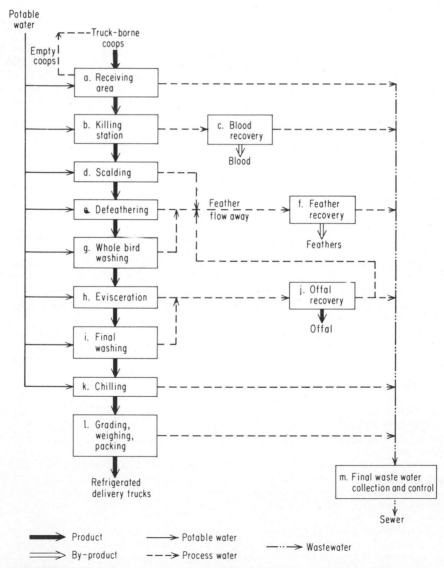

Figure 28.7 Flow chart of poultry processing plant. *(Courtesy of U.S. Environmental Protection Agency.)*

(a)

(b)

Figure 28.8 Meat processing waste treatment. (a) Flow schematic; (b) aerial view. *(From EPA 625/3-74-003, "Water Treatment: Upgrading Meat Packing Facilities to Reduce Pollution," October 1973, U.S. Environmental Protection Agency, Technology Transfer.)*

Many packing plants discharging to city sewage plants are required to provide pretreatment (equalization, screening, grease removal) to reduce the load and equalize the composition of wastes to avoid upsetting the municipal plant operations.

SUGGESTED READING

Lund, H. F., (ed.): *Industrial Pollution Control Handbook,* McGraw-Hill, New York, 1971.

Shreve, R. N.: *Chemical Process Industries,* 3d ed., McGraw-Hill, New York, 1967.

U.S. Environmental Protection Agency: *Development Document for Beet Sugar,* EPA-440/1-74-002-b, March 1974.

U.S. Environmental Protection Agency, *Development Document for Cane Sugar Refining,* EPA-440/1-74-002-c, March 1974.

U.S. Environmental Protection Agency: *Development Document for Red Meat Processing,* EPA-440/1-74-012-a, March 1974.

U.S. Environmental Protection Agency, *Development Document for the Apple, Citrus and Potato Processing Segment,* EPA-440/1-74-027-a, March 1974.

Chapter 29

Mining

Water uses in the mining and mineral processing industries may be divided into two parts. The first includes all uses of water and its treatment for removing the mineral from its surroundings, both in underground environments and also in surface stripping operations. The second deals with the processing of these recovered mineral ores. During these operations the beneficial mineral that has been mined is separated from valueless companion materials, normally by grinding and processing fine ore particles as a slurry. Water is used to prepare the slurry and to transport the mineral during this processing operation. Both aspects of water usage—in mining and in mineral processing—will be discussed here.

The most widespread use of water in underground mining operations is for dust control. Most automatic mining equipment includes an integral water spray system. Spray nozzles are supplied by a water hose coupling at the rear of the mining machine. The spray nozzles are set up to provide a water curtain around the area being mined when the mechanized drill, cutter, or continuous miner is in operation, thereby confining the dust at the face (Figure 29.1).

One of the major problems with such underground water systems is clogging of nozzles by scale and dirt particles in the water supply. Usually some type of strainer or filter immediately ahead of the mining equipment traps these particles to prevent their reaching the small nozzle orifices. Often, stabilization reagents are added to this water line to prevent scale formation if the water is hard or contains iron or manganese.

Another use for underground water is hydraulic mining. With this technique, water under high pressure is directed toward the face of the mine. The energy of the water stream breaks the mineral from the mine wall and washes it into a collection system. This type of mining may gain popularity as it becomes better understood. Currently its main use has been in the coal industry and to a limited

Figure 29.1   This continuous coal-mining machine is equipped with water spray nozzles to suppress dust at the working surface. *(Courtesy of Lee-Norse Company.)*

extent the uranium industry. The cutting action of the water stream can be enhanced by coalescing the water into a very narrow stream, focusing its energy on the selected area of the mine face. Certain types of water soluble polymers are used to give this cohesiveness to the water stream, thereby increasing mining efficiency.

UNDERGROUND WATER

In these examples of underground water use—dust control and hydraulic mining—it may be necessary to pump fresh water underground. However, in most instances there is already extensive underground seepage, and it is necessary to remove this from the mine to continue efficient operations. This water must often be pumped over appreciable distances from the mine floor to the surface for disposal. In many cases, it contains significant concentrations of dissolved solids leached from geological formations. It may be acidic due to the types of minerals it has contacted. In the coal industry, reactions with forms of iron pyrites intimately mixed with the coal produce an acidic water, and treatment of acid mine drainage is a serious problem for this industry (Figure 29.2).

Figure 29.2   Flowsheet of a treatment system to handle about 300 gpm of coal mine drainage having an acidity of 1600 mg/l. Sludge recycle is essential to production of a dense, settleable precipitate.

Bacterial action is believed to be responsible for the production of acid from the pyritic material, and the result is a water often at a pH below 3, containing up to 1000 mg/l Fe and with sulfate concentrations as high as 4000 mg/l. Not only is the cost of treatment a burden, but the by-product lime sludge is also a serious problem, often requiring large land areas for sludge impoundment.

It is often necessary to chemically treat underground water to prevent attack on pipes and pumps used to transport it to the surface. In many cases the water has run through muddy areas and picked up a significant load of suspended solids, making it necessary to provide flocculation and coagulation of the solids prior to pumping the water to the surface.

Once at the surface, this drainage water is often added to the general water system for the mineral processing plant. Occasionally it requires further treatment to adjust pH or remove suspended solids precipitated upon exposure to the air. After pH adjustment with lime, most heavy metals precipitate. Settling basins are then required to clarify the water prior to discharge or recycle into the general plant water system.

Often in underground mining, a shaft or tunnel provides the approach to the ore body to be mined. As ore is withdrawn and the cavity (stope) becomes enlarged, it becomes necessary to re-grade the floor of the stope at frequent intervals to make the mine face accessible to the miners and their machines and drills.

So, where the method of stope mining is practiced, tailings from the mineral processing plant are often used as backfill to provide the floor for the rising stope. These tailings compact in the stope, and water drains from beneath. This water is often the predominant portion of the mine drainage discussed earlier, which must be clarified before being pumped to the surface. Flocculant addition to the tailings often improves drainage and provides a more compact backfill in the stope area.

Very few minerals are mined and used directly without further treatment. The raw ore is either physically or chemically processed to remove the inert materials (gangue) from the desired mineral. This is normally done in a wet milling operation. In wet milling, the ore is crushed, slurried with water, and subjected to several techniques capable of separating the valued mineral from the gangue.

COAL PROCESSING

In the coal industry, various types of shale and clay are produced as a mixture with the coal. To increase the heating value of the coal and to reduce the hauling cost, a complex process of coal washing is normally used to reduce the total ash content. In this process the coal is graded to a certain size, usually less than six inches, and then fed into a slurry bath in which the density of the media is closely controlled. The coal floats in this heavy media bath while the heavier rock sinks to the bottom.

Following this heavy media separation all the floated material is again sized by vibrating screens for further purification. The smaller-sized fractions may be processed by shaking tables, hydrocyclones, or froth flotation. In each of these steps, coal is recovered and dried prior to shipment. The refuse is dewatered as well as possible by screens.

However, the final water effluent, after the larger materials have been removed, usually contains a significant concentration of very fine refuse in suspension. This might include some coal not recovered during the washing operations. Primarily, however, it contains sand and small pieces of rock and clay in a slurry of 3–15% solids. To close the coal preparation plant water system and minimize or eliminate effluent flow, it is necessary to dewater this refuse slurry as efficiently as possible. Normally a thickener is used to compact

Figure 29.3   Flowsheet of coal washing and drying plant. (*Reprinted from* Coal Age, *January 1976. Copyright McGraw-Hill, Inc.*)

the solids into a mud of 30–40% solids by weight. The overflow from the thickener is normally of good enough quality to be reused in the coal washing plant.

FURTHER DEWATERING

The underflow slurry from the thickener is still pumpable, but not yet suitable for final discharge. In the past, this slurry was discharged into tailings ponds and lagoons and allowed to settle under its own gravity. Today, coal washing plants are closing their plant water systems entirely, requiring them to further dewater the refuse slurry to a dry, handleable form. The moisture must be reduced so that the refuse is dry enough to be trucked to a disposal site to be used as landfill.

Several techniques can accomplish this: vacuum filtration, centrifugation, and vibrating refuse screens. The key is to dewater the refuse slurry to the point where there is no subsequent water runoff when the dry solids are disposed of.

A complete water circuit for a modern coal washing plant is shown in Figure 29.3. Analyses of a typical makeup water and concentrated circuit waters are shown in Figure 29.4. There is a consistent increase in sodium, sulfate, and chloride. Lime is often added to the circuit to offset the development of acidity.

Identification of Analyses Tabulated Below:

A. Plant A--makeup   D. "B" recirculated water

B. "A" recirculated water   E. Plant C--makeup

C. Plant B--makeup   F. "C" recirculated water

Constituent	As	A	B	C	D	E	F
Calcium	CaCO₃	74	350	60	44	490	950
Magnesium	"	31	190	22	14	140	340
Sodium	"	644	1368	260	528	79	161
Total Electrolyte	CaCO₃	749	1908	342	586	709	1451
Bicarbonate	CaCO₃	170	18	88	118	220	0
Carbonate	"	0	0	0	0	0	0
Hydroxyl	"	0	0	0	0	0	0
Sulfate	"	9	290	230	410	450	1400
Chloride	"	570	1600	24	58	39	51
Nitrate	"						
M Alk.	CaCO₃	170	18	88	118	220	0
P Alk.	"	0	0	0	0	0	0
Carbon Dioxide							
pH		7.8	7.3	8.0	7.8	7.6	4.0
Silica	SiO₂	16	2	3	4	15	23
Iron	Fe	0.2	1.5	5	28	0.1	0.7
Turbidity							
TDS (Conductivity)		1500	3800	650	1200	1200	2200
Color							

Figure 29.4 Selected coal mine analyses.

METAL-CONTAINING MINERALS

In the base metal industries, such as copper, lead-zinc and iron ore processing, it is necessary to grind the mineral to such a fine size as to produce discrete particles of metal-rich minerals and quartz, feldspar and other worthless materials. In the copper, lead and zinc industries, the liberated metal-rich particle normally consists of a sulfide mineral, which is then amenable to separation and recovery by froth flotation techniques. In the iron ore or taconite industry, the iron is present as the mineral magnetite, $FeO \cdot Fe_2O_3$, which lends itself to separation by magnetic techniques. To recover minerals by either flotation or magnetic separation, the ore is ground in a wet condition to improve efficiency. Large volumes of water are used to slurry the dry ore.

During the hard rock grinding process, steel balls and rods are used to pulverize the mineral ore (Figure 29.5). In these mills, the grinding media is consumed at the rate of about one pound steel per ton of ore. This metal loss is due to physical abrasion and chemical corrosion. Chemical inhibitors can effectively reduce the rate of corrosion and subsequent wear of the steel balls and rods.

After separating the desirable mineral from the tailings, the final slurry is sent to a tailings thickener just as in the coal washing operation. Again, the tailings slurry is thickened in the thickener and the clarified water returned to the processing plant for reuse. The underflow slurry may be disposed of in large open tailings ponds where natural evaporation and seepage occur. If there is any significant breakout of free water in the tailings pond, this water is either discharged to a stream or recycled to the main plant water system.

The flow sheet for a copper mining operation is shown in Figure 29.6, including both the crushing and concentration steps.

In all thickening operations, the large demand for clear water and the size limitations of thickeners and settling ponds make it necessary to use synthetic flocculants and coagulants to aid in the settling process. These synthetic separation aids enable the plant to obtain all the desired recycled water necessary along with increased compaction and dewatering of the refuse solids. The size of thickeners and settling ponds is clearly illustrated in Figure 29.7, an aerial view of a copper mine in a mountainous area of Arizona.

However, no matter how efficient the thickening operation may be, a certain amount of process water always is lost to tailings with the slurry solids. Consequently it is necessary to add a quantity of fresh makeup water to maintain the balance of the plant water system.

In certain industries, such as copper, lead, and zinc where the sulfide minerals

Figure 29.5 Fine copper ore is ground in these ball mills, each 16′-6″ diameter by 19′ long. Each mill is driven by a 3000-hp motor. *(Courtesy of Duval Corporation, Stearns-Roger, Incorporated, and Ray Manley Photography.)*

Figure 29.6 Copper ore processing flowsheet. (*a*) Crushing sequence; (*b*) concentrating sequence.

are floated at high pH, the addition of fresh makeup water containing significant calcium and magnesium hardness can result in unstable water (a low Ryznar Index, high Langelier Index). The refuse slurry which is clarified in the thickener contains sufficient alkalinity to react with the fresh calcium and magnesium added with the makeup water. Therefore, it is advantageous to add the makeup to the clarified recycled water in a vessel where precipitation of carbonates and hydroxides will not pose a major scaling problem. It has been found that addition of makeup directly to the thickener eliminates most problems.

However, it is also necessary to stabilize this combined water prior to sending it back to the plant. If this is not done, a significant buildup of scale can form in storage tanks as well as pipes and pump parts, causing problems and increasing plant maintenance. Analysis of makeup and recirculated process water from several copper mills is shown in Figure 29.8.

Figure 29.7   Aerial view of Duval copper mining operation, Suaharita, Arizona. *(Courtesy of Duval Corporation, Stearns-Roger, Incorporated, and Ray Manley Photography.)*

MINERAL LEACHING

Other mineral industries use aqueous solutions to leach or dissolve the desired mineral from its ore. Included among these industries are uranium, bauxite for the recovery of alumina, soda ash for the recovery of sodium carbonate, potash for the recovery of potassium, and phosphate rock which processes naturally-occurring phosphate ore to phosphoric acid for fertilizer intermediates. Aqueous solutions containing various leaching materials (acids, alkalies, or brines) dissolve the valuable mineral from the undesirable constituents in the ore. In most operations of this type, a series of countercurrent decantation (CCD) thickeners are used to recover as much soluble mineral as possible from the mud refuse. Flocculants are required in this process to compact the mud levels to the greatest extent and to yield as clear a pregnant liquor as possible for ultimate mineral recovery.

In several of these industries, process steam is required to supply the heat necessary for maximum leaching. Operations of this type require an effective boiler water treatment program to maintain maximum efficiencies. In those metal industries in which smelters are used to reduce the ore to its elemental form, waste heat boilers are used to convert heat from smelter gases into steam.

Mill		Ca	P	M	O	pH	CO_3	HCO_3	TDS
A.	Makeup	65	4	136	0	8.7	8	128	300
	Clarified	1410	280	360	200	11.1	160	0	3000
B.	Makeup	60	20	115	0	8.4	40	75	270
	Clarified	1890	560	630	490	11.7	140	0	2000
C.	Makeup	—	12	60	0	8.1	24	36	580
	Clarified	—	214	254	164	11.5	90	0	1300

Figure 29.8   Water quality comparison of fresh makeup water and recirculated mill process water for several western copper concentrators.

These waste heat units gather additional heat energy by cooling the sides of the furnaces and other liquid metal transferring vessels. The steam generated by the process heat is then utilized for power generation as well as other process purposes.

Associated also with these heavily process-oriented industries are significant cooling water applications. For instance, in many of the metal sulfide smelting operations, acid plants have been built to recover the sulfur dioxide from waste gases. These recovery plants yield sulfuric acid, which can in turn be used to leach other types of metal mineral ores. Cooling water is a major problem for these satellite plants because of the salinity of the limited water sources in mining areas and the atmospheric contamination.

In summary, the mineral processing industry is continuing to close as many of its water systems as possible. To a great extent this industry has grown up with the philosophy of water recovery, having been forced for many years to reuse water because of its large water requirements for milling and mineral processing. Many of these plants are in water-short areas of the country. Consequently most mineral processing plants have always had thickeners to clarify their plant waste waters (Figure 29.7). What is planned is to further dewater the thickener under-flow slurries to produce dry, handleable solids as required for landfill, completely closing the system. Large tailings ponds are still used in the western states where enough land is available for long-term sedimentation. In these tailings ponds, the natural process of evaporation usually produces a dry, disposable refuse material.

The mineral processing industry needs all the clear water it can obtain for use in the processing of its ores. It will continue to improve its techniques for the recycling of its process waters. The primary objective is clarity. It is necessary to remove suspended solids to convert the waste water to a usable quality for further mineral slurrying. Often pH control is necessary. Consequently, the addition of acid or alkali to the recycled water is necessary to bring the water into balance for scale and corrosion control. In most cases very little is done to reduce dissolved minerals in the effluent. The addition of fresh makeup water at a continuous rate momentarily dilutes the buildup of dissolved minerals. But in a closed system, there is a large increase in dissolved solids in the circuit, and the only point of discharge of these solids is in the water lost with the final tailings discharge to landfill. The main water treatment process in the mineral processing industry is solids/liquids separation in the tailings system (Figure 29.9). The effective use of synthetic polymers to improve solids/liquids separation efficiency enables the mineral processing industry to conserve water and minimize the strain on the environment.

SLURRY CONVEYING

One water-related operation in the mining industry that is advancing rapidly is hydraulic transport of minerals. Several pipelines are already in operation, the most notable being the Black Mesa coal pipeline feeding an electric generating station in Nevada. There are many indications that additional slurry pipelines will be needed to transport minerals such as coal and iron ore. The major concern in such slurry pipelines is that water is removed from the environment at one location and transported to another. Some slurry pipelines proposed for the more arid regions of Montana and Wyoming have encountered public opposition because they represent an export of water from the region. Perhaps this may be resolved by intermittent use of the pipeline to return water and refuse to their original source.

The pipeline system lends itself to some interesting water treatment problems.

Figure 29.9   Tailings clarifier-thickeners at a large western copper concentrator.

Of course, a chemical that could be added to the slurry while it is in the pipeline to increase the pumping efficiency could be of importance to the operation. Various materials which exhibit friction-reducing tendencies are being evaluated. In addition, there are usually periods when the pipeline is idle, normally filled with water. Under such conditions, corrosion begins to take place under the layer of solids on the bottom. Therefore, it is necessary to chemically treat these water slugs used to fill the gaps in the line between various quantities of the mineral slurries, to prevent this corrosive action. Because of the huge volumes of water involved, economics of this once-through system are of great concern.

Chapter **30**

Pulp and Paper Industry

Primitive people over countless ages communicated with each other or expressed themselves by audible sounds and visible symbols carved in wood or stone, impressed in clay, or painted on the walls of caves. As society progressed, these sounds and signs developed into language; symbols became alphabets, and records of important events could then be written on clay tablets. The Egyptians simplified record-keeping with the introduction of papyrus sheets, formed from the reeds of the papyrus plant, about 3000 B.C. The word paper is derived from papyrus.

During later periods of civilization, scribes kept handwritten records on parchment and hand-formed paper, chiefly for the ruling classes. The hope of written communication for the masses first came with the development of the printing press about 500 years ago. This created a demand for paper, so varieties of fibers and process methods were vigorously investigated for use in paper manufacture. In the early days of the American colonies, the fibers were obtained from rags; but by the nineteenth century, demand for paper increased beyond the ability of rags to supply the need, and wood fibers began to find use in paper pulp.

The pulp and paper industry has since grown to produce not only paper for records, documents, and books, but also heavier grades for packaging, and plain and corrugated liner board for shipping containers, such as drums and cartons. Despite the relative light weight of the finished product, pulp and paper constitute one of the major tonnage products in the United States; it may soon challenge the output of the steel industry in annual production. The production of the major varieties of paper and board are shown in Table 30.1.

Paper is almost entirely derived from wood today, and since only about half of the weight of timber brought to the pulp mill is cellulose, researchers over the years have actively sought uses for the remaining 30–50% released during chemical pulping. They have developed a variety of byproducts which include

TABLE 30.1   Past and Projected Production, thousand tons/year

		1974	1980	1985
A.	**Paper**			
	1. Newsprint	3,300	3,864	4,315
	2. Printing and writing	13,500	13,616	14,168
	3. Packaging and converting	5,900	6,228	6,532
	4. Tissue	3,900	3,956	4,048
	Total	26,600	27,664	29,063
B.	**Paperboard**			
	1. Unbleached kraft	12,800	14,168	15,640
	2. Bleached kraft	3,700	3,864	4,232
	3. Recycled board	8,100	8,280	8,556
	4. Semi-chemical	4,000	4,048	4,416
	Total	28,600	30,360	32,844
C.	**Building paper and board**			
	1. Construction paper	1,900	2,070	2,144
	2. Construction board	3,400	3,663	3,876
	Total	5,300	5,733	6,020
D.	**Total machine dried pulp**			
	1. Dissolving pulp	1,700	1,638	1,619
	2. Paper grade (mkt. pulp)	5,500	5,580	6,247
	Total	7,200	7,218	7,866
Total industry		67,700	70,975	75,793

turpentine for the paint and coatings industry, tall oil for the manufacture of chemical intermediates, ligno-sulfonates as surface active agents and dispersants, and such other products as yeast, vanillin, acetic acid, activated carbon, and alcohol. Table 30.2 shows the major categories of the components of wood.

NON-PAPER PRODUCTS

Subsidiary operations in many pulp and paper mills include the manufacture of plywood, particle board, and chipboard, and the production of alpha cellulose, which is a dissolving pulp used in the manufacture of cellulose acetate.

Probably no industry has done as much in reclaiming waste products as the pulp and paper industry. Scrap paper is collected, sorted into grades for reprocessing, and converted into new grades of tissue, book stock, container board, and other useful forms. Approximately 20% of the output of the paper industry is reused by secondary fibers processing plants.

TABLE 30.2   Components of Wood Substance

Total wood substance	100%
Steam or solvent extractable	5%
Extractive free wood (including 0.5% inorganic)	95%
Mild oxidation yields soluble lignin	25%
Holocellulose (total polysaccharide)	70%
Dilute alkali extraction yields hemicelluloses	20%
Net wood cellulose	50%

WATER: A BASIC RAW MATERIAL

The manufacture of pulp and paper requires large volumes of water. Since its earliest days, the industry has located almost exclusively along major rivers. The first mills used water not only to make pulp and paper but also for hydraulic power, by damming the stream to produce the head needed to drive water wheels which operated the grinding stones to convert wood to pulp. Many modern mills are located at the site of these early mills and continue to use hydraulic power for operation of grinders or of hydroelectric turbines.

The water required by a modern pulp/paper mill varies considerably with the pulping process, the availability of water, the bleaching sequence, and restrictions on wastewater discharge. Table 30.3 shows the water requirements for older and newer mills, based on the type of production.

TABLE 30.3 Net Water Use (Effluent Flow) from the Manufacturing of Pulp and Paper Products

	Typical gal/ton	New mills, gal/ton
Pulp manufacturing process:		
a. Unbleached kraft	15,000–40,000	20,000
b. Kraft bleaching	15,000–35,000	20,000
c. Unbleached sulfite	15,000–50,000	25,000
d. Sulfite bleaching	30,000–50,000	40,000
e. Semi-chemical	8,000–40,000	10,000
f. Deinked	20,000–35,000	25,000
g. Groundwood	3,000–48,000	4,000
h. Soda pulp	60,000–80,000	65,000
Paper manufacture:		
a. Fine paper	8,000–40,000	10,000
b. Book or publication grades	10,000–35,000	12,000
c. Tissue	7,000–45,000	15,000
d. Kraft papers	2,000–10,000	5,000
e. Paperboard	2,000–15,000	8,000

The pulp and paper industry is a large user of water because the pulp is washed with water at several points in the process, and water is used to convey the pulp fibers from their initial production in the pulp mill through various refining operations, and finally to the paper machine, where it may be introduced to the forming wire at a slurry concentration which is 99% water and only 1% fiber (called 1% consistency in paper mill terminology). Whereas older mills used as much as 50,000 gallons per ton of finished paper product, modern mills have closed up their systems to reduce the amount of water required and therefore the volume of waste to be treated. In a modern unbleached pulp/paper mill, producing linerboard, the consumption may be as low as 10,000 gallons per ton, and in a bleached pulp/paper mill the requirement may be approximately 15–20,000 gallons per ton. So, in a mill producing about 1000 tons per day, which is typical of southeastern U.S. kraft mills, the water treatment plant may be required to produce about 20 mgd of mill water for process and boiler makeup.

Of the variety of pulping operations in use throughout the world, most fall into one of three categories: mechanical pulp, chemical pulp, or secondary fiber (reclaimed paper).

For most types of timber used to supply the pulp mill, the logs are cut to a convenient length and debarked in a device such as the barking drum shown in Figure 30.1. Since the bark is a significant portion of the raw material, the water

Figure 30.1   Bark is removed from cut wood in this rotating debarking drum.

used in the debarking operation is recycled and the bark removed, dewatered, pressed, and used as fuel for steam generation in specially designed bark-boilers. Excess water from this operation is often high in BOD, because of the wood sugar extracted in the debarking process, and high in coliform organisms from the exposure of the tree to animal life both in the forest and in the wood yard.

GROUNDWOOD PULP

In the production of mechanical pulp, logs are loaded into the magazine of a grinder (Figure 30.2) in which they are pressed against a grinding wheel. Abrasion separates the bundles of fibers into individual strands, and except for a relatively small percentage of organic matter extracted during the grinding operation, the lignin which holds the fibers together remains in the finished pulp, so that the pulp yield is quite high. The yield varies with the type of wood being ground, but is generally on the order of 90%; that is, 90% of the weight of wood fed to the grinder becomes pulp available for paper manufacture.

   Although the organic material extracted from the wood fiber during grinding is a small percentage of the fiber weight, it is a significant addition to the water; so the water wasted from the groundwood pulping operation is quite high in organic matter.

   Paper produced from groundwood pulp is weak and has poor aging properties. For that reason it is used for manufacture of newsprint, where strength and aging properties are not critical factors. Even with newsprint, to provide the strength needed on a modern printing press, some chemical pulp, usually about 15%, is blended into the groundwood pulp to produce a satisfactory sheet.

THERMOMECHANICAL PULPING

Thermomechanical pulping (TMP) is a new process producing a mechanical pulp superior to groundwood in strength. Used in newsprint, it permits a reduction of chemical pulp in the furnish, at the same time producing a stronger sheet. But its major contribution to the industry is its ability to reduce chemical and water usage, with carrythrough benefits in waste treatment, while producing a pulp comparable to chemical pulp in many respects.

   In the TMP process (Figure 30.3), wood chips are washed with recycled water,

LOADING FLOOR

COUNTING
DEVICE

MAGAZINE

STONE

PRESSURE FOOT
HYDRAULIC CYLINDER

DAM
SLUICE

Figure 30.2 Logs are forced against a grinding stone to produce groundwood pulp. *(From Pulp and Paper Science and Technology, vol. 1: Pulp, McGraw-Hill, 1962.)*

Screw feeder
Chips are compressed into a steam-tight plug prior to entering the preheater. Air is removed and chip moisture equalized

Impregnator
For certain applications, water and/or chemicals can be absorbed quickly and uniformly into the chips for chemical pretreatment of both softwoods and hardwood.

Pressurized refiner
Equipped with inner and refinining zones independently adjustable during operation for more accurate refining.

Preheater
Steaming time is controlled accurately by a gamma ray level gauge in the preheater. Uniform heating improves pulp quality. No fresh steam is required.

Figure 30.3 Components of a thermomechanical pulping system with provision for chemical pretreatment. *(Courtesy of American Defibrator Inc.)*

which may be white water or filtrate containing pulping chemical residues. This is macerated in a screw press to a homogeneous slush, and passed continuously through a steam-heated digester. This softens the fibers and permits them to separate later at boundaries which are relatively free of lignin. This improves refining, conducted in three stages following the digester. The refined pulp is screened, cleaned, and adjusted to the required consistency for bleaching. As with groundwood, hydrosulfite is the bleaching chemical.

CHEMICAL PULPING

To improve the qualities of pulp fiber, early research workers developed chemical processes to dissolve the lignin and other organic materials holding the fibers together, releasing the fibers without extensive mechanical working. There is a continual development of new modifications to these basic chemical processes to meet modern needs for high quality product and minimum wastewater contamination.

TABLE 30.4   Chemical Pulping Processes

pH environment	Acid	Neutral	Alkaline
Anionic species	SO_2, HSO_3^-	HSO_3^-, SO_3^{-2}, HCO_3^-, and CO_3^{-2}	HS^-, S^{-2}, and OH^-
Cationic species and process designation	(1) H^+—acid sulfite (2) Na^+—sodium base (3) NH_4^+—ammonium base (4) Ca^{+2}—calcium base (5) Mg^{+2}—magnesium base	Na^+ (1) Neutral sulfite (2) Neutral sulfite— semichemical (3) Chemiground*	Na^+ (1) Kraft (2) Kraft— semi- chemical*

* In these processes, liquor is used to soften the wood before grinding.

The basic chemical processes in use today are categorized as acid, neutral, or alkaline pulp processes, as shown by Table 30.4.

In all of the chemical pulping processes, a chemical solution is prepared and fed to a digester, a vessel in which it is mixed with wood that has been cut into chips to permit the liquor to penetrate effectively and produce a uniform pulp. The mixture is then cooked for a specified period at the optimum temperature for the particular process and the type of wood being pulped. Most digesters operate on a batch basis, but there is increasing use of continuous digestion processes.

At the conclusion of the digestion period, the contents of the digester are dumped into a blow pit. Because the liquor is at a high temperature, steam and volatile components from the wood flash off. These are condensed, and organic byproducts may be produced from the condensed liquid. The quenching of the vapor provides heat for process water and also controls air pollution by concentrating and collecting sulfur compounds for burning.

RECOVERING PROCESS INGREDIENTS

The pulp from the blow pit is washed to remove the chemicals; the pulp then goes to further processing and the wash water containing the chemicals is usually reclaimed. Because the liquor contains organic matter extracted from the wood, when concentrated by evaporation the organic material reaches a concentration level that permits the liquor to be sprayed into a furnace for burning, the combustion of organic matter providing the Btu's for evaporation of the liquor to dryness. The chemicals in the liquor become molten, and the molten products (smelt) collect at the bottom of the furnace for recovery. This recovery procedure does not apply to calcium-base cooking liquors. Since there is no practical way to recover the calcium-base liquor, the calcium-base sulfite process has practically disappeared. Magnesium-base liquors are recovered, but not exactly as described above.

Chemical recovery has been in operation for many years in the kraft process, because the process would not be economical without such recovery. The chemicals recovered are returned to the process through a chemical recovery operation which will be described later. The chemicals recovered from the NSSC process (neutral sulfite—semi-chemical) cannot be used directly again in the process, but can be used as makeup to a kraft mill. Because of this, many pulp mills have both kraft and a semi-chemical process; if the pulp mill is strictly a NSSC mill, it may recover its chemicals in a dry bead form, providing a product which can be supplied to a nearby kraft mill.

Because these pulping operations use sulfur-containing chemicals, many of which have a high odor level, sophisticated processing equipment is required to avoid leakage, which could result in air pollution. These sulfur compounds have a high oxygen demand, so it is equally important to avoid leakage of pulping liquors to the sewer, where they would impose a load on the waste treatment plant. Not only do these liquors have a high chemical oxygen demand (COD), but they also contain the organics extracted from the wood, and are therefore high in BOD.

The yield from chemical pulping is considerably less than from a groundwood operation, where the organic remains attached to the cellulose fiber. The extraction of lignin and hemicellulose is so effective in chemical pulping that the kraft process has a yield on the order of less than 50% compared to a semi-chemical pulping yield of about 70% and the groundwood pulp yield of about 90%.

THE KRAFT PROCESS

As an example of the chemical pulping operation, the kraft process, which produces about 75% of the total pulp output of the United States, is illustrated by Figure 30.4. In this process, chips and white liquor are measured into a digester, and the mixture is then brought up to about 350°F either by direct steam injection or by recirculation of liquor through a steam-heated exchanger on the side of the digester. At the completion of the cooking period, which may take 2½–3 hours, the contents of the digester are dumped to the blow pit, the vapors from which are used for heating water, and in the process turpentine may be recovered, a significant byproduct in pulping softwood. Non-condensible gases, such as H_2S and SO_2, are released for separate treatment to control sulfurous emissions.

The pulp is sent to the brown stock washers to remove the excess chemical which may lower pulp quality. There are usually three stages of washing (Figure 30.5) with water flowing countercurrent to the pulp, picking up pulping chemical to become a weak black liquor containing approximately 3–5% total solids. This liquor is concentrated to over 55% total solids in an evaporator

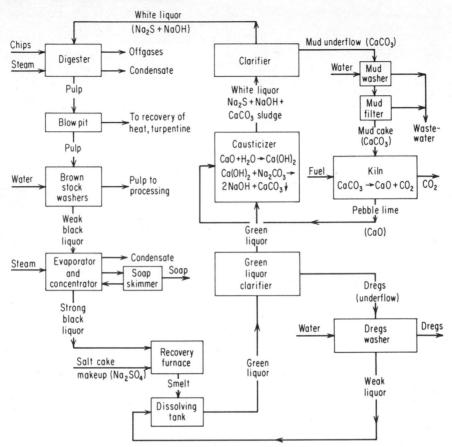

Figure 30.4 Kraft process flowsheet.

Figure 30.5 A typical brown stock washing system.

producing a strong black liquor so high in organic solids that it will burn when sprayed into the recovery furnace. Salt cake (the industry term for Na_2SO_4) is also added to the recovery furnace to provide makeup to the sulfur-bearing liquor to account for losses at various points in the circuit. In the recovery furnace, the sulfate is reduced to sulfide and some of the caustic is converted to carbonate by contact with the CO_2-containing gases produced from combustion of the organic matter. These materials become molten at the furnace temperatures, and the molten salts, called smelt, drain down the furnace tubes and collect at the bottom of the furnace. They are tapped off into the smelt dissolving tank.

GREEN LIQUOR PROCESSING

Recovered weak liquor quenches and dissolves the smelt, producing green liquor that must be clarified before it can be regenerated. The dregs from the clarifier contain valuable chemical, so they are washed and the weak liquor returned to the dissolving tank. The green liquor, which contains sodium carbonate, is then causticized by the addition of lime, converting the sodium carbonate to sodium hydroxide and producing calcium carbonate precipitate. The product of the liming operation is white liquor, which must be clarified before it can be returned to the digester. The mud produced from the clarifier is almost entirely calcium carbonate. This is washed and filtered, and the cake is fed to a kiln, which burns the calcium carbonate to calcium oxide for recycle.

The operation of a modern kraft mill is so tight that the amount of salt cake required for makeup to account for liquor losses is typically in the range of only 25–50 pounds per ton of pulp. The condensates produced at the digester and evaporator vary in quality: those produced directly from the condensation of boiler house steam can usually be returned to the boiler plant, but even here, careful monitoring is required to make certain that leakage does not occur in the system to spoil the condensate and cause problems with steam generation. Other condensates may be used for pulp washing and other washing operations. The poorest grade of condensate from the evaporator, sour condensate, must be stripped of its volatile sulfur compounds, and it usually remains so badly contaminated that it must be sent to the waste treatment plant. It is a major source of problems in the operation of the waste treatment plant.

Using the kraft mill as a pattern, Figures 30.6 and 30.7 show the chemical pulping for the magnesium-base sulfite process and for the neutral sulfite-semichemical process respectively. The sources of wastewater contamination in these circuits are similar to those found in the kraft mill.

Pulp Processing

In the chemical pulping operation itself, the major items of equipment are the digester, the blow pit, vapor recovery, and pulp washers.

These are the basic units shown on the reference diagrams of chemical pulping operations. Contamination of steam condensate or water with pulping liquors can occur in the digester, except where direct injection of steam into the digester may be practiced. Two types of digesters are shown in Figures 30.8 and 30.9, the former is a batch type digester in the kraft industry, where the liquor is externally circulated through a heat exchanger in which leakage of liquor into the condensate is always a potential threat. The second illustration shows a continuous digester, which also has external heat exchangers for heating of liquor or wash water with steam, again providing potential for leakage of contaminants into steam condensate.

The washers shown in Figure 30.5 were originally designed only to improve

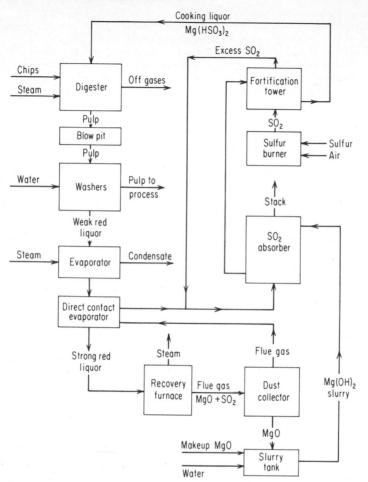

Figure 30.6   Magnesium base sulfite pulp flowsheet.

pulp quality by removing excess liquor. By operating the wash water counter-current to the pulp flow, recovery of relatively strong liquor was also possible. With the attention today on minimizing wastewater discharge, the pulp washer also provides a potential point of reusing excess water from the paper mill or contaminated condensates from the pulp mill. In recycling these wastewaters to the washer, the original intent of washing to produce an acceptable pulp must be kept in mind; for example, certain pulp mill condensates are so badly con-taminated with odorous sulfur compounds that they are unacceptable for pulp washing because they impart this odor to the finished pulp, and it persists even in the finished paper sheet.

After the pulp has been washed and the liquor reclaimed, there are a variety of devices for purifying the pulp to the extent necessary for its end use in paper, board, or chemical manufacture. The major devices are thickeners, refiners, screens and cleaners.

Some of these devices require that the pulp be diluted before it can be pro-cessed and others require that the pulp be thickened. This change in con-sistency may be done in storage vessels, called stock chests, or directly by in-line mixing if dilution is the effect to be achieved. However, where concentration

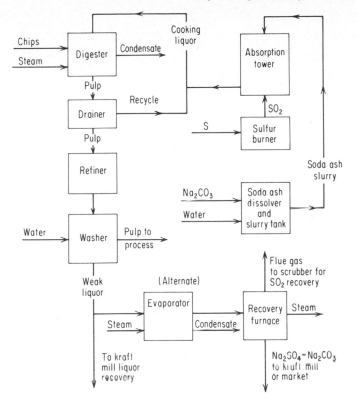

Figure 30.7 NSSC pulping process.

of the pulp is required, the pulp must be passed over a thickener (Figure 30.10) for removal of water. The water recovered from this thickening operation is recycled to the most convenient point in the pulping system.

Refiners are somewhat related to grinders, providing mechanical force to abrade the pulp fibers and reduce them to individual strands of cellulose. The two most common types of refiners are disk refiners (Figure 30.11) and Jordans (Figure 30.12). Screens are used to classify pulp fibers to a certain size, with the oversize particles being returned for reprocessing; screens are also used for the removal of undesirable materials from the pulp, such as knots and non-cellulose debris (Figure 30.13).

Centrifugal cleaners are hydraulic cyclones that separate pulp fibers both on the basis of density and size. The more dense or oversize materials are sent to the periphery of the cyclone, and the acceptable fiber fraction is withdrawn from the center of the cyclone. Very often three stages of centrifugal cleaning are involved (Figure 30.14). The rejects from the first stage go to the second, rejects from the second go to the third, and rejects from the third are wasted or returned to a point where their values may be reclaimed, such as in the barking drum where some waste cellulose particles may remain with the bark to be reclaimed in the bark boiler.

These basic units are put together in a pulp mill in different ways depending on nature of the wood being pulped, the pulping process, and the type of paper or board being manufactured. Typical schematics for a groundwood mill, kraft mill, and semi-chemical mill are given in Figures 30.15, 30.16, and 30.17.

Cooling liquor

Chips from silo

Vent to heat recovery

Heater

Steam

Condensate

Stock pump

To blow tank and washers

Figure 30.8 In this batch digester, chips are cooked over a 60 to 90 minute cycle, and the pulp product is drawn off for washing and further processing.

BLEACHING

If the final product is a bleached grade of paper or board, bleaching is done in the pulp mill. Chlorine and chlorine compounds are most commonly used for bleaching kraft pulp, but oxygen bleaching is assuming increasing importance in the industry. Typically, bleaching is accomplished in several stages, with the residues of the bleaching operation extracted from the pulp between these

Chips in

Chips

Silo

Hot liquor manifolds

Chip impregnation

Steam heating

Chip feeder

Cooking

Steaming vessel

Pressure feeder

Pulp washing

Liquor pump for chip conveying

Cooling

Cooking liquor makeup

Pulp to blow tank

Figure 30.9 Continuous digester used in the manufacture of kraft pulp.

Figure 30.10   Removal of excess water is often needed for pulp storage. This process is called deckering. These two types of deckers are commonly used for increasing consistency. (Top) This drum filter is thickening kraft fiber. (Bottom) Fiber dewatered through this vertical, slotted-screen decker is seen tumbling into the pulp discharge flume. *(Courtesy of Dorr-Oliver Incorporated.)*

Figure 30.11   (Top) In the disk refiner stock flows between rotating grooved plates, which separate bundles into individual fibers. (Bottom) Details of disk design. *(Courtesy of Bolton-Emerson.)*

stages. A common example would be chlorination followed by caustic extraction as the first part of the sequence; this would be followed by hypochlorite bleaching, also followed by caustic extraction, with a final treatment with chlorine dioxide. In pulp mill terminology, this would be identified as CEHED bleaching. There is as yet no practical way to reclaim the materials extracted from the pulp during the bleaching operation, and these liquors constitute one of the major pollution problems in the pulp mill. This production of strong wastes from the bleaching operation is shown in a typical bleaching sequence diagram, Figure 30.18.

When oxygen is included in the sequence, it is the first stage and replaces chlorination and extraction, significantly reducing the concentration of wastes and the load on the waste treatment plant.

Figure 30.12 In the Jordan refiner, stock is forced between a rotating plug and a stator, both of which have grooved surfaces or blades to break up fiber bundles.

Other bleaching agents include zinc hydrosulfite, which is used for bleaching groundwood pulp, sulfur dioxide alone, or chlorination followed by sulfur dioxide.

PROBLEMS CREATED BY WATER

There are a variety of water related problems in the pulp mill in addition to those already mentioned. These include contamination of steam condensate, discharge of concentrated wastes that cannot be recovered, and non-recoverable water containing organic matter and other reducing chemicals that produce a load on the waste treatment plant. One of the principal problems is foaming, induced by the surface-active nature of some of the organic matter extracted from the wood. Chemicals for foam control are commonly required at the screens and washers to maintain production capacity.

A more difficult problem to control is the production of scale in evaporators, where the gradual increase in concentration of both inorganic and organic solids causes the solubility limit of calcium sulfate and other materials to be exceeded.

Figure 30.13 Rotary screens can handle large flows and classify fibers by their size. These screens are installed ahead of a bleached kraft foodboard machine. *(Courtesy of Black Clawson Company.)*

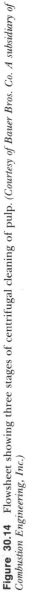

Figure 30.14 Flowsheet showing three stages of centrifugal cleaning of pulp. *(Courtesy of Bauer Bros. Co. A subsidiary of Combustion Engineering, Inc.)*

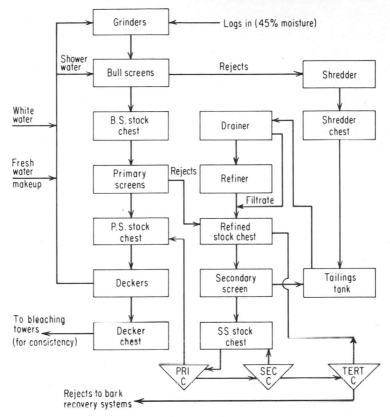

Figure 30.15 Groundwood mill process flowsheet.

It is common practice to boil out an evaporator with water on a scheduled basis to keep this under control. Sometimes the water used for boilout can be reclaimed if it is sufficiently concentrated to justify putting into the evaporator circuit; some of the water used for this operation, however, must be wasted and this imposes a load on the waste treatment plant.

As in so many other industrial operations using water, corrosion is a constant threat; for the most part this is kept under control by the selection of suitable alloys or plastics, but even alloys may be subject to corrosion where microbial activity may cause slime deposits. Fortunately many of the circuits are relatively hot, which in itself prevents slime growths, but microbial activity frequently develops in the cooler areas of the pulp mill system.

SECONDARY FIBER RECOVERY

Waste paper and board make up a major raw material resource for the paper industry. These wastes are sorted, and the choice between the different grades and their prices determines how they are reprocessed and the type of finished sheet produced and its cost. There are about 40–50 grades varying in quality from clean clippings from a paper converted (such as envelope stock) to newsprint and used paper bags. The poorest grade is unsorted (Mixed Grade No. 2).

The raw stock is reduced to slurry by agitating with hot water in a mixing

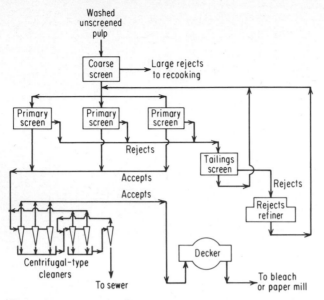

Figure 30.16   Kraft mill process flowsheet.

Figure 30.17   NSSC process flowsheet.

Figure 30.18   Kraft mill pulp bleaching, CEDED sequence.

tank (Figure 30.19). Strings, bailing wire, paper clips and miscellaneous debris are separated at this point. If the stock is printed matter and the finished pulp must be equivalent to virgin pulp, it is de-inked. This operation involves heating the stock to about 150°F and adding chemical agents to release the ink from the fiber. Following this, the stock is screened and washed, either by flotation (Figure 30.20) or over side-hill washers. At this point, clay and other filler, which can amount to as much as 15% of the weight of the raw stock, are separated and removed from the system with the ink. These separated wastes present a difficult disposal problem as these solids are hard to dewater. The dewatered cake can be used as landfill, which may still present a problem since land disposal sites near plants are becoming scarce.

The secondary fiber pulp may go directly to a cylinder machine for manu-facture of corrugating medium. It may be bleached and dyed for the manu-

Figure 30.19   Hydrapulper.
(Courtesy of Black Clawson Com-pany.)

Figure 30.20 Flotation by dispersed air separates ink sludge released from recoverable fiber by deinking chemicals. *(Courtesy of Voith-Morden, Inc.)*

facture of tissue and toweling. Other products of secondary fiber processing include newsprint and writing papers. The same kinds of screens, thickeners, and cleaners may be used in processing reclaimed paper/board as are used in a mill processing virgin pulp, as described later.

WATER REMOVAL FROM PULP

The finished pulp is sent to the paper mill for conversion to paper or board. Dilution water, the majority of which comes from the paper machine wire pit, reduces the consistency of the pulp to less than 1%, and often below 0.5%, ahead of the paper machine. To convert this to the finished sheet, the 99.0–99.5% water must be reduced to produce a sheet usually containing less than 6% water.

The least costly way to remove water from the pulp is by drainage through a screen or wire, and this forms the basic part of most paper machine designs. Thereafter, water is removed at increasing increments of cost, first by vacuum, then by pressing, then by the blotting and pressing action of a felt blanket, and finally by evaporation as the sheet is carried over a multitude of stacks of steam-heated drums.

FOURDRINIER MACHINE

The most common paper machine is the fourdrinier, illustrated in Figure 30.21. The water that drains through the endless wire belt is collected in a pit and returned to the flow of incoming pulp stock to maintain the consistency at the feed point (the headbox) at a constant value. Sizing chemicals may be added to the stock at the headbox to produce certain desired sheet qualities. Since the water from the wire pit, called white water, is continuously recirculated, the addition of soluble chemicals, or chemicals that form soluble byproducts, results in a gradual increase in the dissolved solids in the white water. The white water also contains fibers which escape capture on the sheet. Excess white water is bled from the system, usually passed through a device for reclaiming fibers (called a saveall) and returned upstream in the process, often as far upstream as the pulp mill.

The sheet leaving the fourdrinier machine, called the wet web, may contain 2–4 lb of water per pound of fiber (33–20% consistency). It has very poor strength, so a very delicate balance of output from the fourdrinier machine and throughput at the press rolls is necessary to keep the wet web from breaking. The sheet leaves the felt section at a moisture content of only 20–40%, and the long stacks of drying rolls evaporate this moisture, delivering the sheet to a final calender stack for smoothing, and then to the reel as a finished product with a moisture content of less than 6%. The overall schematic diagram of the paper machine and the drying section is shown in Figure 30.22.

In some paper mills, the paper may be treated on a special size press located at some point midway between the ends of the drying rolls.

As in the pulp mill, sometimes centrifugal cleaners are installed on the paper machine system for purification of the recycled white water. There are a number of kinds of savealls used for recovering fiber from excess white water, a common one being a dissolved air flotation clarifier. A unit of this type will typically re-

Figure 30.21 Fourdrinier paper machine installation looking from headbox toward dryer section.

Figure 30.22   Simplified flow diagram of a fourdrinier paper machine. *(From Pulp and Paper Science and Technology, vol. 2: Paper, McGraw-Hill, 1962.)*

duce suspended fiber from a concentration of 200–300 mg/l to a residual of 25–50 mg/l producing a float with a consistency of approximately 5%.

CYLINDER MACHINE

Another common type of paper machine is the cylinder machine, commonly found in smaller mills and often used for the production of heavier grades of paper board. A typical cylinder machine is shown in Figure 30.23. The finished sheet leaving the cylinder machine is processed similarly to the sheet leaving the fourdrinier, by a battery of steam-heated dryer rolls. Heavier board may be dewatered on a single dryer drum, the Yankee dryer (Figure 30.24).

On both types of machines the sheet must be trimmed to an exact width depending on customer requirements, and the trim is collected for repulping. This material and broke, the term for excess product which cannot be handled at the reel, are fed to a beater (Figure 30.25), where they are mixed with white water to produce a pulp of a consistency which can be returned to the pulp mill or held in a stock chest until it can be returned to the paper machine system.

MICROBIAL ACTIVITY

Given the conditions of organic fiber, cellulose, residual organics extracted from the wood, and warm, oxygenated water in the white water circuit, bacterial growths become one of the major problems of paper manufacture. If these growths are not controlled, slimes form in the paper machine system and periodically break loose to enter the circuit, find their way through the headbox onto the paper machine, and develop as imperfections in the finished sheet. Equally important, these growths lead to corrosive attack even in stainless steel alloy systems. Therefore, one of the major problems in paper manufacture is microbial control with chemicals that are effective and at the same time safe to handle.

The trend toward tightening up the paper system to reduce water consumption has resulted in the buildup in the content of both inorganic and organic solids in the white water system, accentuating the problems of slime control and corrosion control. Figure 30.26 shows the results of corrosive attack of stainless steel caused by slime formation and the action of anaerobic bacteria at the slime/metal interface. Figure 30.27 shows sheet imperfections caused by bacterial colonies in the white water system. Foaming is another water-related problem that has been accentuated by the closing up of the paper mill white water circuit.

Because water is so important to the pulp and paper industry, it is common to find in modern pulp and paper mills a water treatment plant as sophisticated as a municipal plant treating potable water. The quality of water required in the process varies with the grades of paper being produced and the specifications for these grades. These are generally summarized by Table 30.5. The standards shown in this table have been subject to considerable exceptions in past practice, and may be revised in the future as the industry learns what it can do with higher concentrations in the process water stream as mill systems are tightened to reduce discharge.

DESIGNING FOR THE FUTURE

Unfortunately, there is scanty data to guide the designer of a new mill in the quality standards required for makeup water, which must be satisfactory not only in producing products that meet market standards, but also in conditioning

Figure 30.23 Furnish in five forming vats is picked up by the bottom felt of this cylinder machine. Water is removed from the cardboard by suction and by pressing and bloting. The finished board is 5-ply, often distinguishable because of the variation in the pulps in each forming vat.

Figure 30.24 Yankee dryer. *(Courtesy of AER Corporation.)*

the water to render it neither corrosive nor scale-forming under the wide variety of situations occurring in the pulp and paper mill.

For the most part, water treatment plants for new mills are designed based on past experiences and operating practices that may be quite different from the experiences the mill will encounter as pollution control restrictions become increasingly strict. One of the consequences of stricter discharge regulations may be a relaxation in product quality; for example, brightness has been associated with quality of fine paper, and there is little doubt that the brightness achievable today is beyond what is required for legibility of books and documents. This brightness is achieved at the expense of more severe chemical treatments in processing which add to the pollution load. A relaxation in brightness standards for paper products, then, would seem consistent with the goals of reducing the pollution load on the waste treatment plant.

Providing a general idea on the various uses of water in a typical pulp and paper mill, Table 30.6 shows both the volume required and the wastes produced in a typical 500 ton/day kraft mill with conventional chlorine and hypochlorite bleaching.

WASTE TREATMENT

The points of waste production will be apparent from a study of the flow sheets of the different pulp and paper manufacturing operations. In the present state of the art, most mills have tightened up their water systems to reduce discharge, but have not done so to the extent that dissolved solids build up over 5000 mg/l. There is substantial flow of excess water carrying with it the rejects from pulp cleaning, excess pulping liquor which could not be reclaimed, dregs from the chemical recovery area, materials extracted from the pulp during bleaching, and

Figure 30.25 (Top) The hollander beater was an early device for refining pulp, and is still used in many mills for repulping broke. (Bottom) Plant installation.

Figure 30.26 Corrosion of stainless steel sieve in a paper mill caused by sulfate-reducing bacteria.

Figure 30.27 Sheet imperfections are caused by sloughing of slime mass into machine system. In this photo, the removal of the slime mass during calendering left a hole in the sheet.

excess clay and filler not retained by the sheet. Since a good portion of the wastes are organic materials extracted from the wood, the BOD of the combined wastes is usually quite high—on the order of 50–150 lb/ton of product, or typically in the range of 100–300 mg/l. Suspended solids levels may be as low as 50% of the BOD values. Because this is not greatly different from municipal sewage plant loadings, the type of waste treatment facility installed in a pulp and paper mill is generally quite comparable to what is found in municipal treatment plants. Table 30.7 shows the range of suspended solids and BOD loadings found in a variety of pulp and paper manufacturing operations. Figure 30.28 shows the lay-

TABLE 30.5 Process Water Quality Standards

Substance, mg/l	Fine paper	Kraft paper (bleached)	Ground-wood papers	Soda and sulfate pulp
Turbidity as SiO_2	10	40	50	25
Color in platinum units	5	25	30	5
Total hardness as $CaCO_3$	100	100	200	100
Calcium hardness as $CaCO_3$	50	—	—	50
Alkalinity to methyl orange as $CaCO_3$	75	75	150	75
Iron as Fe	0.1	0.2	0.3	0.1
Manganese as Mn	0.05	0.1	0.1	0.05
Residual chlorine as Cl_2	2.0			
Silica (soluble) as SiO_2	20	50	50	20
Total dissolved solids	200	300	500	250
Free carbon dioxide as CO_2	10	10	10	10
Chlorides as Cl	—	200	75	75
Magnesium hardness as $CaCO_3$	—	—	—	50

From TAPPI Monograph No. 18.

TABLE 30.6   Effluents from a Typical 500 tpd Kraft Mill (built in 1960–1965 period)

Process	Effluent, gal/ton	Suspended solids, lb/ton	BOD$_5$, lb/ton
1. Debarking	2,640	31	7
2. Cooking and washing	264	—	9
3. Screening and cleaning	26,400	31	20
4. Bleaching			
a. Acid	15,800	6	22
b. caustic	10,500	3	11
5. Pulp sheet formation	1,050	2	—
6. Evaporation	1,850	0.2	30
7. Causticizing	1,320	0.2	—
8. Recovery furnace	3,960	0.2	—
Total	83,784	73.6	99

out of a bleached kraft mill using current technology for wastewater treatment for discharge to a nearby receiving stream. In this particular plant, the primary clarifiers handle only those wastes carrying over 50 mg/l suspended solids. After clarifying these wastes, the effluent is combined with the remaining low solids streams (such as bleach plant effluent) and treated in an extended aeration plant for biological reduction of organic solids. The digested waste is then processed through a final clarifier for discharge to the receiving water. Table 30.8 shows the analysis of the raw waste streams and the final effluent. The design of a treatment system of this type requires months of pilot plant study to determine the range of waste concentrations to be anticipated, to evaluate the performance of the aerobic digestion system under a broad range of temperatures and pH

Figure 30.28 Typical layout of waste treatment system for a bleached kraft mill.

TABLE 30.7   Sources of Solids in an Integrated Mill

Area	Suspended solids, mg/l	Dissolved solids,* mg/l
Woodroom	500–700	700–800
Pulp mill (bleach plant)		
Caustic extract	60–80	4000
Acid extract	60–80	1500
Total	200–250	1800
Recovery plant	3000	3000
Paper machines	400–700	300–400

* Increase over solids level in mill water.

values, and a study of the optimum procedures for dewatering and disposal of waste sludges.

Not only are large volumes of water needed for process, but also for the generation of steam. The pulp and paper industry is energy intensive, and the organic matter (such as bark and lignin) extracted from the wood fits into the overall planning and design of a steam generation system to utilize these wastes

Figure 30.29 Hypothetical steam flows in a kraft pulp/paper mill. Distribution varies somewhat seasonally as air and water temperatures change.

TABLE 30.8   Integrated Pulp/Paper Mill Waste Treatment

Constituent	Inlet *	Inlet †	Lagoon feed	Final effluent‡
Suspended Solids, mg/l	530	140	400	210
Alkalinity, mg/l as $CaCO_3$	224	(760)§	324	32
pH	7.6	2.3	7.2	6.3
BOD, mg/l as O_2	233	136	154	11
COD, mg/l as O_2	930	750	790	350
TOC, mg/l as C	270	230	260	110
Conductance, μm	1200	6400	1700	1700

* Fiber-containing streams from paper mill
† Lower suspended solids streams from pulp mill
‡ Without chemical coagulation
§ Acidity

as a fuel source. Because large volumes of steam are needed on the paper machines, particularly the drying rolls, the industry optimizes the heat balance by condensing turbine exhaust on the machines, making it economical for the industry to produce its own electrical power.

A flow diagram and heat balance of a steam generation plant in a typical kraft mill is shown in Figure 30.29. In an integrated kraft pulp/paper mill, a steam plant of this type will produce in the range of 5,000–10,000 pounds of steam per ton of production. The operation of the utilities system is so critical to the production process that the profit or loss of a mill requires efficient performance of the utility plant.

SUGGESTED READING

Lund, H. F., (ed.): *Industrial Pollution Control Handbook,* McGraw-Hill, New York, 1971.
Shreve, R. N.: *Chemical Process Industries,* 3d ed., McGraw-Hill, New York. 1967.
U.S. Environmental Protection Agency, *Development Document for Unbleached Kraft & Semichemical Pulp,* EPA-440/1-74-025-a, May 1974.

Chapter 31

Petroleum Industry

Petroleum refining is one of the major manufacturing industries in the United States, producing more than 75% of the petroleum products consumed in this country. Ninety percent of these are fuels supplying over 46% of the country's energy needs. Plastics, solvents, asphalt, lubricants, and intermediate chemicals are among the more than 3,000 products made from petroleum.

Petroleum refining is a continuous operation incorporating a number of interrelated process units. It is one of the largest "wet" processing industries in the United States.

Because it is used in the refinery for heating, cooling and processing, water is an important factor in process operations. A refinery may draw water from a variety of sources, and the treatment processes used to condition this water vary accordingly. Little or no treatment may be required for some well waters, while other water sources may require an extensive plant incorporating clarification, softening, and filtration. The types of water treatment problems here are much the same as in other industrial applications. In general, the basic water flow scheme is illustrated in Figure 31.1.

After initial processing, the water is usually divided into several streams for use throughout the refinery. At most locations, this water can be used directly as cooling tower makeup, with little or no further pretreatment. However, an extensive treatment scheme is usually necessary to produce the high quality water required for boiler feed.

Figure 31.2 shows a typical water handling system designed for a large refinery utilizing a surface water source as plant makeup.

Refinery processes are net consumers of heat, to the extent that 10–15% of the heat equivalent of the incoming crude is used in the refinery operations. This is provided by refinery by-products, including off-gases, residual oil, and coke, in many cases supplemented by natural gas. A typical process heat balance is shown by Figure 31.3. This does not include heat recovered in process-heat boilers.

Figure 31.1 Water uses in a typical 150,000 BPD refinery.

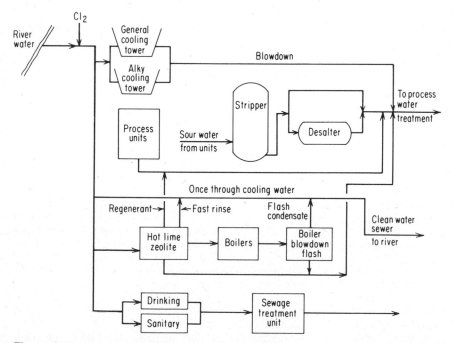

Figure 31.2 Water conditioning system treating surface water for refinery usage.

Source of energy	Percent of total heat
Crude oil	Nil
Distillate oils	1.6
Residual oil	9.0
LPG	1.3
Natural gas	36.2
Refinery gas	35.1
Coke	13.1
Steam (purchased)	1.1
Electricity (purchased)	2.6

Total heat requirement is approximately 674,000 Btu/bbl of crude processed.
SOURCE: From U.S. Bureau of Mines.

Figure 31.3 Refinery process heat balance.

PROCESS OPERATIONS

The refining of petroleum products and petrochemicals involves two basic operations: physical change, or separation processes; and chemical change, or conversion processes. A refinery is a conglomerate of manufacturing plants, the number varying with the variety of products produced. The bulk of these products (kerosenes, fuel oils, lubricating oils, and waxes) are fractions originally present in and subsequently separated from the crude petroleum. Some of these are purified and supplemented with non-petroleum materials to enhance their usefulness. For example, soap is added to lubricating oil to make grease. A refinery with half a dozen processes, including distillation and cracking, can produce gasoline, kerosene, and fuel oils. The manufacture of solvents requires two or three more processes; lubricating oil production, at least five more; waxes another two or more. Asphalts, greases, coke, gear oils, liquefied petroleum gases, alkylate, and all the other kinds of products that can be made would require as many as 50 different processes. Figure 31.4 is an overall flow diagram for a generalized refinery production scheme.

As previously mentioned, refining is basically concerned with separation and conversion processes, carried out by individual unit operations. Basic to most of these are furnaces, heaters, and heat exchangers, and distillation and extraction columns. Heat exchangers are typically of shell and tube design, often utilizing incoming hydrocarbon feedstock as a cooling medium for hot products. If additional cooling is required—trim cooling—this is done with water.

Distillation and extraction are usually the principal techniques in product separation. Distillation separates various hydrocarbon mixtures into components having different boiling points. In extraction, hydrocarbons are separated based on their different solubilities in a specific solvent. In some unit operations, filters are used to remove suspended contaminants from the hydrocarbon stream, such as catalyst fines and inorganic precipitates.

Distillation Figure 31.5 illustrates a typical distillation column (pipe still). Preheated crude is charged into the bottom of a distillation column at a pressure slightly above atmospheric and the vapors rise through the column, contacting a down flow stream (reflux). As a result, the lightest materials concentrate at the top of the column, the heaviest materials at the bottom, and intermediate materials in between. Desired products are withdrawn at appropriate points. Because the lighter products (as vapor) must pass through the heavier products (as liquid) and must be in equilibrium with them at each point in the column,

Figure 31.4 Generalized flowchart for petroleum refining. (*From Shreve, R. N., Chemical Process Industries, 3d ed., McGraw-Hill, New York, 1967.*)

Figure 31.5 Distillation column with sidestream steam stripper.

each stream contains some very volatile, low-molecular-weight components (light ends).

As indicated in Figure 31.5, steam strippers are sometimes used to remove light ends from a sidestream. The sidestream is fed to the top of the stripper; countercurrent steam strips out the light ends and carries them back to the main column.

The wastes from crude oil fractionation, and in general from most distillation columns, come from three sources. The first is the water drawn from the overhead accumulator prior to recirculation or transfer of the hydrocarbons to another fractionator. The water that separates from the hydrocarbons in these accumulators is usually drawn off and discharged to the oily sewer system. This water can be a major source of sulfides, especially when sour crudes are being processed; it may also contain significant amounts of oil, chlorides, mercaptans, and phenols. A second significant waste source is discharge from oil sampling lines; this oil should be separable, but may form emulsions in the sewer. A third possible waste source is the stable oil emulsion formed in barometric condensers used to produce a vacuum in some distillation units (Figure 31.6).

In vacuum towers a steam jet ejector is the most widely used method for creating a vacuum. The steam and other vapors removed from the fractionator must be condensed, and the liquid removed prior to discharge of the vapor to the atmosphere.

The barometric condenser condenses the steam jet by a water spray in a closed chamber, and the water drains down the barometric leg. The organics, oils, and steam condensate are intimately mixed in a large volume of cooling water, which tends to form difficult-to-handle emulsions. Newer refineries use surface condensers instead of barometric condensers. These units consist of a series of

Figure 31.6 Barometric condenser.

shell and tube exchangers in which the condensibles are removed, and the water used for cooling does not come into direct contact with the condensate (Figure 31.7). The water discharge from the distillation operation is sent to the refinery waste plant, sometimes through a separate gravity oil separation unit.

Thermal Cracking and Related Subprocesses   In thermal cracking units, heavy oil fractions are broken down into lighter fractions by application of heat at high pressure, but without the use of a catalyst. Production of gasoline is low, but middle distillates and stable fuel oils are high. Visbreaking and coking, the

Figure 31.7 Tubular process steam condenser.

Figure 31.8 A thermal cracking process treating topped crude (Universal Oil Products process). *(From Shreve, R. N., Chemical Process Industries, 3d ed., McGraw-Hill, New York, 1967.)*

two major types of thermal cracking, maximize the production of catalytic cracking feedstocks, indirectly increasing gasoline production.

Oil feed is heated in a furnace to cracking temperatures and the cracked products are separated in a fractionator (Figure 31.8). The heat breaks the bonds holding the large molecules together, and under certain conditions, some of the resulting smaller molecules may recombine into larger molecules again. The products of this second reaction may then decompose into smaller molecules depending on the time they are held at cracking temperatures.

Visbreaking is a mild form of thermal cracking; it causes little reduction in boiling point, but significantly lowers viscosity. The feed is heated, cracked slightly in a furnace, quenched with light gas oil, and flashed in the bottom of a fractionator. Gas, gasoline, and furnace oil fractions are drawn off, and the heavier fractions are recycled.

Residual oils may be cracked to form coke as well as the usual gaseous and liquid products. The most widely used process, known as delayed coking (Figure 31.9) accounts for about 75% of the total oil coking capacity.

Thermal cracking units require cooling water and steam on the fractionating towers used to separate products. Some towers employ steam stripping of a sidestream to remove light ends, requiring an overhead condenser and accumulator system for product/wastewater separation. Wastewater usually contains various oil fractions and may be high in pH, BOD, COD, NH_3, phenol, and sul-

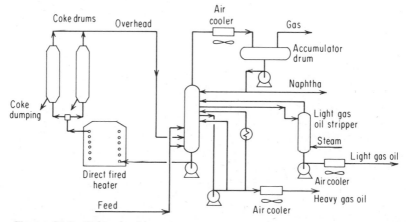

Figure 31.9 Delayed coking process.

Figure 31.10   Fluid catalytic cracking unit.

fides. Another important water use area is the high pressure water sprays used for coke removal in delayed coking. Several refiners have instituted water recycle clarification systems to minimize water discharge from these coking units.

Catalytic Cracking   The fluid catalytic cracking process is the most widely used refining process (Figure 31.10). A large mass of finely powdered catalyst contacts the vaporized oil in the processing unit. The catalyst particles are of such a size that when aerated or "fluffed up" with air or hydrocarbon vapor, they behave like a fluid and can be moved through pipes and control valves.

In the catalytic cracking process, vaporized feed and fluidized catalyst flow together into a reaction chamber. The cracked vapors from the reactor pass upward through a cyclone separator which removes entrained catalyst. The product vapors then enter a fractionator, where the desired products are removed and heavier fractions recycled to the reactor. Spent catalyst passes from the separation vessel, downward through a steam stripper, and into the regenerator where carbon deposits are burned off. The regenerated catalyst again mixes with the incoming charge stream to repeat the cycle. Combustion in the regenerator is restricted to prevent inactivating the catalyst. This incomplete combustion produces a preponderance of CO over CO_2. Significant amounts of hydrocarbons and other substances also remain unburned in the combustion gases. The CO and hydrocarbons in the exhaust make it a useful fuel. Most refineries burn this exhaust gas in specially designed carbon monoxide (CO) boilers to generate steam. The gas burned in the CO-boiler carries a significant amount of residual catalyst fines, which can cause furnace deposits.

The catalytic cracker is one of the largest producers of "sour water" in the refinery, coming from the steam strippers and overhead accumulators on the product fractionators. The major pollutants resulting from catalytic cracking operations are BOD, oil, sulfides, phenols, ammonia, and cyanide.

Catalytic Reforming   In catalytic reforming (Figure 31.11), the object is to convert straight chain into cyclic molecules (aromatics of high octane). So reforming is essential to production of high octane gasoline. Platforming, the most widely used reforming process, includes three sections: (1) in the reactor heater section, the charge plus recycle gas are heated and passed through reactors containing platinum catalyst; (2) the separator drum separates gas from liquid, the gas being compressed for recycling; and (3) the stabilizer section corrects the separated liquid to the desired vapor pressure.

Figure 31.11 Catalytic reforming process.

The predominant reforming reaction is dehydrogenation of naphthenes, or removal of hydrogen from the molecule. Important secondary reactions involve rearrangement of paraffin molecules. All of these result in a product with higher octane ratings than the reactants. Platinum and molybdenum are the most widely used catalysts, with platinum predominating because it gives better octane yields. Because platinum catalysts are poisoned by arsenic, sulfur and nitrogen compounds, feedstocks usually are treated with hydrogen gas (hydrotreated) before being charged to the reforming unit. This produces hydrogen compounds, such as H_2S, which can be removed from the hydrocarbon stream.

Reforming is a relatively clean process. The volume of wastewater flow and the pollutant concentrations are small.

Alkylation The amalgamation of small hydrocarbon molecules to produce larger molecules is known as alkylation (Figure 31.12). In the refinery, this reaction is carried out between isobutane (an isoparaffin) and propylene, pentylenes, and in particular, butylenes (olefins). The product is called alkylate. The olefin-isobutane feed is combined with the fractionator recycle and charged to a reactor (contactor) containing an acid catalyst at a controlled temperature.

Figure 31.12 Alkylation process using sulfuric acid. (*Adapted from Hengstebeck, R. J., Petroleum Processing, McGraw-Hill, New York, 1959.*)

Aluminum chloride, sulfuric acid, and hydrofluoric acid are common acid catalysts. The contents of the contactor are circulated at high velocities to expose a large surface area between the reacting hydrocarbons and the acid catalyst. Acid is separated from the hydrocarbons in a recovery section downstream and recirculated to the reactor. The hydrocarbon stream is washed with caustic and water before going to the fractionating sections. Isobutane is recirculated to the reactor feed, and alkylate is drawn from the bottom of the last fractionator (debutanizer).

Acid may contaminate the cooling water should heat exchangers leak. Water drawn from the overhead accumulators contains varying amounts of oil, sulfides, and other contaminants, but these are not a major source of waste in this subprocess. The wastes from the reactor contain spent acids which refineries may process to recover clean acids, or may sell. Occasionally, some leakage to the sewer or cooling system does occur. The major contaminant entering the sewer from a sulfuric acid alkylation unit is spent caustic from neutralization of the hydrocarbon stream leaving the reactor.

Hydrofluoric acid alkylation units do not have spent acid or spent caustic waste streams. Any leaks or spills that involve loss of fluoride constitute a serious and difficult waste problem.

Sulfuric alkylation units usually have a chilled water refrigeration system with several compressors which have critical shell side cooling water on inter and after coolers.

Hydrotreating   Hydrotreating is mild hydrogenation (Figure 31.13) that removes sulfur, nitrogen, oxygen, and halogens from a hydrocarbon feed and converts olefins (unsaturated hydrocarbons) to saturated hydrocarbons. Petroleum feedstocks ranging from light naphthas to lubricating oils are hydrogen treated. The major application of hydrotreating has been removing sulfur from feeds to catalytic reformers to prevent catalyst poisoning. Each of the different types of hydrotreaters, which vary in the selection of catalyst, incorporates a reactor and a separator. The oil feed, preheated to 400–700°F (204–371°C), passes through a fixed bed reactor where it combines with hydrogen in the presence of a regenerable metal oxide catalyst at 200–500 psig (14–35 kg/cm²). The product stream is cooled before entering a separator where excess hydrogen gas is separated for use in other operations. After separation, the product is steam stripped for removal of residual hydrogen sulfide.

Major wastewater streams come from overhead accumulators on fractionators and steam strippers, and sour water stripper bottoms. The major pollutants are sulfides and ammonia. Phenols may also be present, if the boiling range of the hydrocarbon feed is high enough.

Figure 31.13 Hydrotreating process.

600 psi at 700°F

Boiler feedwater

Back pressure turbines

Condensing turbine

2-CO boilers

Process heat boiler

Aux. fuel boiler

Condensate for desuperheat

150 psi   150 psi

Heat load   DAH   Process heat boilers   Heat load   Stripping steam

Receiver   BFP   Clean condensate   Sour condensate

40% condensate returns

60% treated makeup   Main deaerator   Sour water stripper   Desalter

To waste treatment

Figure 31.14 Process steam uses and condensate recovery in a typical utility.

UTILITY SYSTEMS

The steam generating system is the heart of the refinery operation, since steam is a major source of energy in the refinery. It is used to drive pumps and compressors, to heat process streams, and to strip sour water. Few refineries generate electricity, but typically produce 10% of their motive power requirement. A typical water balance is shown by Figure 31.14.

The pretreatment of boiler feedwater is one of the most important steps in efficient boiler operation. The specific pretreatment scheme for a steam generating system is dependent on such factors as boiler design, steam requirements, heat balance, outside power costs, and further expansion. Many refineries use hot process softeners, filters, and ion exchange trains.

Additional steam is generated in heat recovery and process-heat boilers. These boilers can be found throughout the refinery at the various process units. Process heat boilers often resemble shell and tube heat exchangers in design. In most refineries, the steam generated by the process usually condenses as an acceptable quality condensate for return to the boiler that produced it. The major concern in these systems is prevention of corrosion in the condensate system, particularly at the point of initial steam condensation. In addition, depending on the pressure of the system, a condensate polishing unit may be installed to remove oil, corrosion products, or both, prior to returning this water to the boiler.

COOLING WATER SYSTEMS

As stated earlier, the cooling requirements of a refinery demand a large volume of water. It has been estimated that 80–85% of the total water requirements are for cooling if cooling towers are used for water conservation. The cooling systems in a refinery are similar to those found in many manufacturing plants, involving once-through, open recirculating, and closed cooling circuits. While each of these systems can be found in the refinery, the open recirculating system serves the greatest demand for process cooling. Once-through cooling is becoming rare except for coastal installations designed to use sea water.

REFINERY POLLUTION CONTROL— WASTE TREATMENT

Broadly speaking, a refinery wastewater system consists of:

1. A drainage and collection system.

2. Gravity type oil water separators and auxiliaries required to remove oil and sediment.

3. Treatment units or disposal facilities to handle segregated chemical solutions and other process wastes and to control the effects of pollutants that have toxic properties.

Figure 31.15 is a generalized list of wastewater sources and their segregation into the various sewer systems provided to optimize reuse and reduce overall treatment volumes to a minimum. The oil-free sewer collects wastewaters that have not contacted oil and that are not subject to any other contamination for which treatment must be provided.

Since these waters seldom contain significant oil contamination, they may bypass API separators and some may discharge directly into the refinery outfall line. However, if collected in a common sewer, this flow is usually mixed with oily waste after API separators for a common treatment.

The oily cooling water sewer system is intended to handle waters that are expected to be subject to minor oil contamination from leaks in heat exchange

Figure 31.15 Suggested scheme of collection and treatment of refinery wastewaters.

equipment or from spills. In the absence of contamination by chemicals or fine solids which tend to cause emulsions, separation of the oil from the water can be readily accomplished.

Barometric condenser cooling water subject to contamination by easily separable oil, but not containing emulsified oil, may also be included in this system.

The process water sewer system collects most wastewaters that come into direct contact with oil or that are subject to emulsified oil contamination or to chemicals limited by the plant discharge permit. Water from the process water sewer system is treated in an oil-water separator, and pollutants remaining after gravity separation are reduced by secondary treatment methods.

Separator skimmings, which are generally referred to as a slop oil, require treatment before they can be reused because they contain an excess of solids and water. Solids and water contents in excess of 1% generally interfere with processing.

The sanitary sewer system collects only raw sanitary sewage and conveys it to municipal sewers or to refinery treatment facilities. State or local regulations usually determine the sanitary disposal requirements. Raw sewage can be used for seeding refinery biological treatment units.

Special systems include those required for the separate collection and handling of certain wastes having physical or chemical properties that cause undesirable effects in the refinery drainage system, oil-water separators, or secondary treatment facilities. Spent solutions of acids and caustic, foul condensates, and degraded solvents are examples of such wastes.

Main wastewater treatment systems separate pollutants from the water by physical, chemical, or biological means. Primary treatment consists of physical, and often chemical, processes. Primary treatment separates the gross waste load of oil and suspended solids from the water. Secondary treatment removes much of the remaining organic and dissolved solid pollutants by biological treatment, which consumes and oxidizes organic matter.

There are a few physical, chemical or biological methods known as tertiary treatment, including activated carbon adsorption and filtration. As pollution control regulations become more stringent, tertiary treatment methods will become more common.

Sour Water Stripping

Many wastewater effluents from petroleum refining processes originate from the use of steam within the processes. The subsequent condensation of the steam usually occurs simultaneously with the condensation of hydrocarbon liquids and in the presence of a hydrocarbon vapor phase that often contains H_2S, NH_3, HCN, phenols, and mercaptans. After separation from the hydrocarbon liquid, the condensed steam contains oil and a mixture of these contaminants. These wastewaters are typically called sour waters or foul waters because of the unpleasant odor characteristic of dissolved hydrogen sulfide.

The amounts of these contaminants in a sour water stream depend on the type of refining process from which the stream originated, as well as the feedstock to that process and the pressure level at which the steam was condensed within the process. The contaminant concentrations in typical sour waters will usually be 50–10,000 mg/l H_2S, 50–7,000 mg/l NH_3, and 10–700 mg/l phenolics.

The principal contaminants in sour waters are hydrogen sulfide and ammonia, ionized as HS^{-1} and NH_4^{+1}, respectively. These can be removed by single-step steam stripping, which is a simple form of distillation for the removal of dissolved gases or other volatile compounds from liquids. Stripping is rather inefficient and requires large volumes of steam because these ionized substances exert very little gas pressure unless the pH is adjusted. Stripping also removes phenolics to some extent, but the amount of phenolics removed may vary from 0 to 65%.

Effluent water from a sour water stripper is often used as makeup to the desalter. Refiners are investigating new schemes for incorporating portions of this water into refinery utilities systems.

Spent Caustic Treatment

Alkaline solutions are used to wash refinery gases and light products; the spent solutions, generally classified as sulfidic or phenolic, contain varying quantities of sulfides, sulfates, phenolates, naphthenates, sulfonates, mercaptides and other organic and inorganic compounds. These compounds are often removed before the spent caustic solutions are added to refinery effluent. Spent caustics usually originate as batch dumps, and the batches may be combined and equalized before being treated or discharged to the general refinery wastewaters.

Spent caustic solutions can be treated by neutralization with spent acid or flue gas, although some phenolic caustics are sold untreated for their recoverable phenol value. Neutralization with spent acid is carried to a pH of 5 to insure maximum liberation of hydrogen sulfide and acid oils.

In the treatment of spent caustic solutions by flue gas, hydroxides are converted to carbonates. Sulfides, mercaptides, phenolates, and other basic salts are converted to hydrogen sulfide, phenols and mercaptans at the low pH conditions caused by the flue gas stripping. Phenols can be removed and used as a fuel or can be sold. Hydrogen sulfide and mercaptans are usually stripped and burned in a heater. Some sulfur is recovered from stripper gases. The treated solution will contain mixtures of carbonates, sulfates, sulfides, thiosulfates, and some phenolic compounds. Reaction time of 16–24 hours is required for the neutralization of caustic solution with flue gas.

SUGGESTED READING

Lund, H. F., (ed.): *Industrial Pollution Control Handbook,* McGraw-Hill, New York, 1971.

Shreve, R. N.: *Chemical Process Industries,* 3d ed., McGraw-Hill, New York, 1967.

U.S. Environmental Protection Agency: *Development Document for the Petroleum Refining Industry,* EPA-440/1-74-014-a, April 1974.

Chapter 32
Steel Industry

Iron and steel making use more water than any other manufacturing industry. A U.S. survey disclosed that the industry water usage was about 5 bgd (13,100 m³/min) of cooling water and 3.5 bgd of process water. Approximately 2 bgd of this water required some form of chemical treatment to make it suitable for use. Of the 3.5 bgd of water that was used in processes, about 65% required some form of treatment before being discharged. As a rough estimate for an integrated mill, 120 tons of water are used for every ton of steel produced (Figure 32.1). A summary of cooling water uses is given in Table 32.1.

BLAST FURNACE OPERATIONS

The blast furnace is the heart of the iron-making process. Iron ore, coke, and limestone are charged by a skip car to the top of a furnace. Most furnaces range from 16–28 ft (4.9–8.5 m) in diameter and may be 100 ft (30.5 m) tall. The raw materials, fed in layers to the furnace, are iron ore or pellets, coke, and limestone. In the lower portion of the furnace, hot blast air is injected through a

Figure 32.1 To produce 1 ton of finished iron, the blast furnace requires 120 tons of water.

TABLE 32.1   Cooling Water Use in an Integrated Steel Mill

	gal/ton	m³/kkg
1. Blast furnace	8,000	33
2. Basic oxygen furnace	700	3
3. Open hearth furnace	3,600	15
4. Electric arc furnace	2,600	11
5. Continuous casting	4,200	18
6. Bar mills (hot)	1,000	4
7. Plate mills	4,080	16
8. Pipe mills	24,800	103
9. Cold sheet mills	3,360	14
10. Hot sheet mills	16,000	66
11. By-product coke plant	4,500	19
12. Sinter strands	350	1.5

series of circumferential openings called tuyeres, at about 30–35 psi (2 bars) and 1800°F (985°C). The air flows upward through the burden of raw materials in the furnace, and gas exits the furnace top at 4–5 psi (0.3 bars).

Coke (carbon) reacts with Fe_3O_4 and Fe_2O_3 in the furnace, releasing the iron and producing CO and CO_2 gas. The iron sinks to the furnace hearth where the original impurities in the charge combine with the lime, forming slag, which floats to the top of the iron. The gas leaving the top of the furnace carries fine dust, which is separated and recovered in collection equipment. The combustible exhaust is used in reheating stoves and in generating steam at boiler houses. The iron and slag are periodically tapped and collected in special rail cars every two to six hours, depending upon furnace conditions.

To keep this large furnace working efficiently, much of the equipment connected with the furnace uses cooling water at various points. A modern blast furnace requires 1000–15,000 gpm (63–950 l/sec) of cooling water. Figure 32.2 illustrates the overall dimensions and general cooling water utilization for a typical blast furnace. This generalized drawing shows that the blast furnace may be constructed in two ways: water sprays may provide cooling water on the outer shell of the furnace, as illustrated on the left side; or, as illustrated on the right side, the furnace may contain stack plates and bosh plates which are hollow passages for cooling water built into the furnace wall. The primary task of the cooling water on the stack area is to prolong the life of the refractory inside the furnace. The stack area uses about one-third of the cooling water flow through the furnace.

Where plates are used, these are generally connected vertically in a series of 4–7 plates with water flow of 15–50 gpm (1–3 l/sec) in each series. Temperature rises 12–25°F (7–14°C) throughout the series. The cooling demand for the refractory decreases as height above the ground increases.

Figure 32.3 shows a hearth and bosh section of the blast furnace. Here, too, either sprays or plates may be used for cooling. The bosh area reaches the maximum furnace temperature, ranging up to 3500°F (1950°C). At this point cooling requirements for the furnace are most critical.

The left-hand side of Figure 32.2 indicates a carbon or closed bosh arrangement. Here, the water sprays are directed at steel plates containing the carbon brick of the bosh area. It may be seen that the spray water is collected in an angular trough directly above the tuyere zone. Also, a stack trough is indicated just at the top of the mantle line. Cooling water from the blast furnace is generally collected in a circular trough surrounding the furnace itself. On the right-hand side of Figure 32.2, a cooling plate arrangement is indicated. Again, plates in

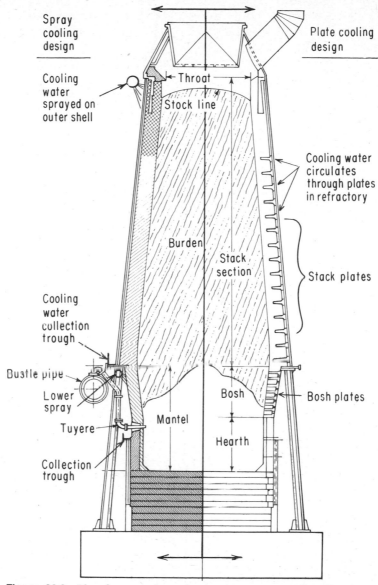

Spray cooling design

Cooling water sprayed on outer shell

Plate cooling design

Throat

Stock line

Cooling water circulates through plates in refractory

Burden

Stack section

Stack plates

Cooling water collection trough

Bustle pipe

Lower spray

Tuyere

Mantel

Bosh

Bosh plates

Hearth

Collection trough

Figure 32.2   Blast furnace schematic, showing two types of cooling-water systems.

this area may be connected in a series of 4–6 plates with a temperature rise of 12–25°F (7–14°C).

The cooling water in the lower section or hearth is not shown on the drawing. Normally, large diameter steel pipes run directly through this area to provide cooling. Stack and bosh cooling equipment is easily accessible and changeable at failure. However, should pipes in the hearth area fail, it is impossible to

Figure 32.3   Blast furnace—wind blowing area with plates used for bosh cooling. *(Copyright 1971 by United States Steel Corporation.)*

remove and replace them without major overhaul of the furnace. Figure 32.2 also shows the area in which the molten metal and slag reside. Molten materials are generally not allowed to reach a higher level than just below the tuyeres.

In the tuyere area air preheated in stoves is blown into the furnace. The tuyeres are copper-jacketed nozzles with cooling water in the jackets. Heat exchange rates are high, so it is important that the cooling system be protected from fouling or plugging to maintain adequate heat transfer.

The valves controlling the flow of hot blast air from the stoves to the furnace must also be cooled to prevent failure or jamming.

The basic problem of water chemistry for all of these systems is protection from corrosion, scale, and fouling from silt or microbiological growths. One of these or any combination may exist within a cooling system at any time.

EXHAUST GAS TREATMENT

Hot air blown through the furnace is changed in composition and expands in volume. The exit gas velocity is high and entrains solids, principally burden fines —ore, coke, and limestone. This dirty gas passes through a dry dust collector, where a majority of the heavier solids are removed, and then proceeds to a wet scrubbing system. Scrubbing water and the dirty gas collide in a venturi or orifice system where almost all suspended solids are removed—usually over 99%. The scrubbed gas has a Btu value of 85–100 Btu per standard cubic foot (1950 cal/m^3) and is used for heating stoves or firing boiler house furnaces.

The scrubber water containing high concentrations of suspended solids, from 500 to as high as 10,000 mg/l, is normally sent to a thickener or clarifier. Here, the solids are settled, and the effluent water is either sent to the receiving stream, sometimes after additional treatment, or recycled (Figure 32.4).

The heaviest concentrations of solids settled from the water are normally iron, silica, and limestone. Soluble impurities usually include ammonia, phenols and cyanide. The chemistry of the scrubbing water continually varies as it is being exposed to hot, dusty gas and then cooled and clarified before recycle. Cooling towers are often used to reduce temperature after the water contacts the hot gas. Evaporation of pure water vapor in the cooling tower concentrates dissolved solids within the water and affects its chemical balance. This must be taken into account when planning a proper cooling water program, as blowdown is required to control the salinity of the recirculating water, and chemical treatment is needed for control of scale, deposits, and corrosion.

Additional water is used for slag granulation or for slag cooling. Where the water is recycled within a slag pit area, there is usually a high potential for deposition occurring within the recycling lines and pumps, and the water chemistry of these systems must be continually monitored.

There are a number of boiler houses in a steel mill complex, and the boiler house in the blast furnace area is one of the most important. Most of these installations have 900 psi boilers, but some of the older plants continue to operate a few 450–600 psi boilers with the higher pressure units. A major use for steam is to operate turbines, which drive the large turbo-compressors delivering air to the blast furnaces. A typical turbo-compressor discharges 100,000 scfm (2830 m³) air at a pressure of 30–35 psi (2 bars), requiring a steam turbine using about 350,000 lb/hr (160,000 kg/hr) steam at 900 psi (60 bars). These turbines operate on a condensing cycle, but some low pressure steam may be extracted for operation of auxiliaries, such as fans, pumps, and compressors in the utility area.

STEEL PRODUCTION

Steel is manufactured from iron—the blast furnace product—by three different methods: the basic oxygen process, the open hearth process, and the electric arc process. The objective of each is to reduce impurities; for example, the 4% carbon content of the iron is reduced to about 0.2% in the steel product, depending on the metallurgical specifications of individual orders.

Basic Oxygen Process

In the basic oxygen method, the mixture of hot metal from the blast furnace (usually 50–60% of the total charge), scrap steel, and slag conditioning materials, such as lime and fluorspar, are charged to the furnace (Figure 32.5). Oxygen at a rate of 15,000–20,000 cfm is injected through a lance lowered into the vessel only

Figure 32.4 A clarifier-thickener of this design treats blast furnace gas scrubber water for removal and recovery of solids. (*Courtesy of Inland Steel Company.*)

Figure 32.5   Hot metal is being poured from the ladle into the tilted BOF furnace as the first step in the steel-making process. *(Courtesy of Baumco Gesellschaft fur Anlangenstechnik mbH, Essen, West Germany.)*

inches above the raw materials. The oxygen blowing period continues for 20–25 minutes to melt and burn off impurities.

A typical BOF vessel has a 100–300 ton (90–270 kkg) capacity and produces steel in about 45 minutes. The vessel capacity is usually filled before the blowing of oxygen to allow space for the violent reactions to occur.In the Q-BOPS system the oxygen is blown through the bottom of the vessel, working through the materials and thus reducing the amount of violent splashing.

There are several water uses in the basic oxygen unit. First, the oxygen lance must be water cooled. In most plants this is a closed recirculating cooling water system. In most of these closed systems, the lance water flows through the shell side of a heat exchanger, with cooling water on the tube side of the exchanger.

Because of the high heat release, gases leaving the furnace hood during the oxygen blow are very hot. The hood is usually cooled with water recirculating through the hood panels. There are several systems where boilers are installed in the hood area for waste heat recovery and cooling of the gases.

As the gases leave the hood area, they can be further cooled by a wet scrubber

Figure 32.6 Basic oxygen furnace, showing major water uses for cooling and scrubbing. As different materials are added to the vessel during a heat, the composition of the scrubber water varies. (*From EPA 440/1-74-024a, "Development Document for Effluent Limitations Guidelines and New Source Performance Standards for the Steel Making Segment of the Iron and Steel Manufacturing Point Source Category."*)

and cooling system which requires large volumes of water (Figure 32.6). This water is then sent to clarifier-thickeners for sedimentation of the solids, and the water can then be recycled or discharged. There is a wide swing in water composition through the entire heat, as shown by a pH record of the effluent. Those systems not using wet gas scrubbers normally have electrostatic precipitators.

Open-Hearth Process

In the open-hearth process (Figure 32.7) the same basic materials used in the BOF process are charged to the open hearth furnace. Hot metal is not as essential to the open hearth as to the basic oxygen unit. These furnaces normally produce 100–600 tons (90–540 kkg) of steel per heat over a period of 6–12 hours.

In the open hearth furnaces, oxygen lance cooling is also required, similar to the BOF process. In addition, cooling water in the range of 750–1500 gpm (2.7–5.4 m³/min) is required to cool the skewback channels and doors in the furnace.

Recirculating wash water from open hearth scrubbers is usually acidic so that special materials of construction are required in closing up these systems. However, because the pH of the circulated water is in the range of 2.5–3.0, this system can be completely closed without fear of scale. The only water loss is that present in the sludge or filter cake.

Electric Furnace Process

The third method of steel making is the electric furnace process (Figure 32.8), which can produce either the common grades of low carbon steel, or, by charging with alloying materials, special steel such as stainless or tool steel. Electric furnaces normally operate on scrap and have the advantage of being adaptable to almost any part of the country, close to special markets. Because they are not dependent upon the hot iron from a blast furnace for their production, they are not tied down to the traditional steel centers.

Most electric arc furnaces are equipped with water cooled doors. Water cooling is applied also to the roof ring, the electrode ring, and the electrode clamps.

While most electric furnace operations use baghouses to clean their gases, there are plants using wet gas scrubbers.

CONTINUOUS CASTING

Continuous casting (Figure 32.9) was developed to reduce the overall cost of steel manufacturing by eliminating several steps in conventional steel preparation such as ingot teeming, soaking, and blooming. Continuous casting is the process of continuously pouring molten metal from a ladle into the complex casting equipment which distributes the liquid, shapes it, cools it, and cuts it to the desired length. The casting is continuous as long as the ladle has available metal. Should one ladle follow another without interruption, the process is called "piggy-backing a cast."

Correct water treatment and distribution is critical to continuous casting. Steel leaving the ladle at about 2800°F (1550°C) is poured into a trough called a tundish. The bottom of the tundish has one or more openings through which the molten steel is distributed to form slabs or billets in the forming area called the mold. The mold is a water-cooled copper jacket providing for high heat exchange rates. At the start of a cast, a dummy bar is moved close to the top of the mold to completely seal the interior. As the cast starts, this bar is slowly lowered to receive molten metal, and the cooling effect of the water-jacketed

Figure 32.7 Open-hearth furnace operation, showing water used for cooling and scrubbing. (*Adapted from EPA 440/1-74-024a, "Development Document for Effluent Limitations Guidelines and New Source Performance Standards for the Steel Making Segment of the Iron and Steel Manufacturing Point Source Category."*)

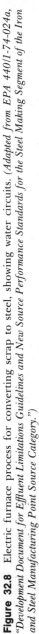

Figure 32.8 Electric furnace process for converting scrap to steel, showing water circuits. (*Adapted from EPA 440/1-74-024a, "Development Document for Effluent Limitations Guidelines and New Source Performance Standards for the Steel Making Segment of the Iron and Steel Manufacturing Point Source Category."*)

Figure 32.9 Continuous casting of slabs or billets.

mold starts the formation of a metal skin. Proceeding through the length of the mold a distance of 30"–36" (1 m), the dummy bar and skin-contained metal are exposed to a series of direct contact water sprays which complete the job of solidifying the steel. As solidification is completed, the dummy bar is cut from the formed metal and removed. The continuously-moving, completely-formed billet or slab then moves through guides to the straightening rolls and onto the runoff table for cutting to specific lengths.

The crucial point in this process is the copper water-cooled mold which forms the initial skin. Unless the skin is formed quickly and uniformly, a breakout will occur, shutting down the operation. The most reliable cooling water program uses the highest quality water available in a closed loop with a secondary open cooling loop. Condensate, high purity boiler feedwater, or low hardness waters have been used as makeup. Hardness levels should never exceed 10 mg/l. Since the system is closed, there is little loss and the best corrosion inhibitors and dispersants can be used.

Spray water that contacts the billet or the slab becomes contaminated with iron oxide particles as the hot metal is oxidized. This water is normally processed in a filtration system for solids removal, recirculated through heat exchange equipment, and recycled to the sprays. The sprays must be kept from plugging at all times because the flow of water to the billet or slab being cooled must be uniform at all points.

Auxiliary mechanical equipment of the continuous casting machine is also water cooled. This may have a separate cooling water system, or it may be consolidated with the spray cooling water systems.

THE HOT-MILL ROLLING OPERATION

The hot mill (Figure 32.10) produces such products as sheets, plates, bars, rods, and structural shapes. This operation is the largest user of water in the steel

Figure 32.10 Hot mill rolling plate for further reduction through a hot strip mill. *(Courtesy of Tippins Machinery Company, Inc.)*

mill, a reasonable use being about 7500 gallons per ton of hot metal rolled (31 m³/kkg).

The first step in rolling is heating the steel billet or slab in a reheat furnace to as high as 2350°F (1300°C). Cooling water must be used to cool the doors and frames in some of the reheat furnaces, and this may be either once-through or recirculated. As the heated billet or slab leaves the furnace, high pressure descaling water up to 2000 psi (135 bars) is blasted onto the surface to remove any oxide scale so that no imperfections are caused by rolling this debris into the metal.

Water is also used for roll cooling and for spraying directly onto the steel prior to its being handled at the end of the machine. A high speed sheet mill operates in the range of 4000–6000 feet per minute (1220–1830 m/min); and a high speed rod or wire mill operates at 8000–9000 fpm (2440–2750 m/min). As water passes over the hot metal from rolling station to rolling station, the oxides washed from the metal are carried to a scale pit. There is a wide particle size range in the operation of descaling as the slab or billet is going through the mill. Larger particles are removed during the initial rolling (the roughing end), and very fine particles are washed off in the final rolling operations (the finishing end).

Much of the scale encountered in the scale pit can be removed with clam-type diggers, electromagnets, or traveling screen grates, but the fine-sized particles are normally separated by coagulation in water clarification equipment. Most new plants recycle the water used on the hot strip mills (Figure 32.11).

When the water is recycled through the mill, attention must be given to potential problems of scale, corrosion, fouling, and microbial activity. This is especially true for water going to the high pressure sprays. Heat removal may be required for controlling the work environment.

Considerable amounts of water are used for cooling electric motor systems in many of these mills. The motor driven rolls keep the product moving to its end point. There can be as many as 300–400 motors at an installation.

COLD ROLLING MILLS

Cold rolling mills are divided into two categories: single stand, and multi-stand, where steel is rolled in tandem. Because the steel is cold, it is hard to work, so the cold rolling requires lubricant in water (soluble oil) not only to cool, but to give a good finish to the steel. Water properties to be controlled in this operation include total suspended solids, iron, and oil. There are two systems for feeding lubricant and water in a cold rolling operation: recirculating and once-through.

Recirculating System

In the recirculating system a weak emulsion of oil and water circulates to the roll for cooling and lubrication of the sheet, collects under the roll and passes through the treatment process. The emulsion is carried from the first stand to the second, third, and fourth. Fresh water is used only on the first and last stands. The spent liquid is normally collected, and an emulsion breaker is used to free the oil. The solids are settled and reclaimed for the iron content, and the oil is reclaimed and reused (Figure 32.12).

Water treatment for these systems consists of sedimentation, flocculation, filtration, and air flotation. The flows from these operations vary from 200 to 1500 gallons per ton of steel processed (0.8–6 m³/kkg).

Figure 32.11   Hot strip mill, showing recycle of clarified water for roll cooling and scale removal.

Figure 32.12 Cold rolling mill with recirculated water containing rolling oil emulsion. Provision is made for periodic treatment of spent rolling oil emulsions.

Once-through System

Another cold rolling operation using direct application of oil is the once-through system, used on thin gauge material such as tin plate. The usual treatment system serves a multi-stand mill, having 2–5 stands. A 5–10% oil-in-water emulsion is applied to the steel at the first four stands, while a detergent solution is applied at the last stand. A once-through system is used for this service since the water must be kept clear. The wastewater, which contains a significant amount of oil, goes to a treatment system that includes an air flotation unit with oil skimmer, chemical treatment, aeration tanks, flocculating tank, and a settling basin or a clarifier.

Emulsion breaking chemicals may be required for efficient treatment of this waste. The oil is reclaimed and reused, while the sludge is disposed of as landfill.

HEAT TREATMENT

To produce special physical properties in certain grades of steel, the metal passes through a series of heat treatment operations including heating in a furnace, annealing at a carefully controlled temperature for a specified period of time, quenching in water or oil, and final cooling in air.

Generally, the temperatures in the annealing furnaces are not so high as to require water cooling of the furnace elements, but some cooling may be needed in special cases. The temperature of the quench oil or water quenching tank must be carefully controlled; so the coolant in the quench tank is usually recirculated through a heat exchanger to remove the heat brought into the system from hot metal. Oil discharge such as could arise by overflowing the quench oil system or by rupture of a tube in the oil-water heat exchanger, must be guarded against. Oil is generally the only likely contaminant to arise in the heat treatment area.

SINTERING

Sintering is a process that recovers solid residues from scrubbers and clarifiers. This process includes collection of useful materials such as iron ore fines, mill scale, limestone, flue dust, and coke fines (Figure 32.13).

The various materials are mixed in controlled proportions with a fixed amount of moisture then distributed onto a permeable grate and passed through to an oil- or gas-fired furnace (ignition furnace). Combustion air is drawn downward through the bed. After a short ignition period the firing of the bed surface is discontinued, and a narrow combustion zone moves downward through the bed, with each layer in turn heating to 2200–2250°F (1204–1228°C). In advance of the combustion zone, moisture and volatiles vaporize. In the combustion zone bonding of the particles occurs, and a strong agglomerate is formed.

Most of the heat from the combustion zone is absorbed by drying, calcining, and preheating the lower layers of the bed. When the combustion zone reaches the base of the sinter mix, the process is complete. The sinter cake is tipped from the grate and broken up. After screening, the undersize is recycled, and the remaining sinter is sent to the blast furnace.

Water is added to the sinter mix, to control moisture at 5–8%. Water is also sprayed for dust control in the plant, and at the many conveyor transfer points where raw materials are moved from storage areas to the sinter line (strand).

Many plants scrub the sinter furnace exhaust gases to remove entrained solids. The scrubber water usually requires treatment by coagulation to remove

Figure 32.13 Schematic of sinter plant showing wet and dry dust collection. (*From EPA 440/1-74-024a, "Development Document for Effluent Limitation Guidelines and New Source Performance Standards for the Steel Making Segment of the Iron and Steel Manufacturing Point Source Category.*")

suspended solids; chemical conditioning to control scale, corrosion and fouling; and removal of pollutants prior to discharge.

ACID PICKLING

The treatment of steel in an acid bath, known as pickling (Figure 32.14), removes oxide from the metal surface and produces a bright steel stripped down to bare metal and suitable for finishing operations, such as plating, galvanizing, or coating. Both sulfuric and hydrochloric acids are used, with the latter growing in popularity as more byproduct hydrochloric acid becomes available from the chemical industry. With either acid, disposal of spent pickle liquor is a serious problem.

Pickling may be either batch or continuous. Usually, the acid is prepared at about 5–15% strength, depending upon the work to be processed in the pickle tank and the type of acid used for pickling. As the acid works on the oxide surface, there is a gradual buildup of iron in the pickle solution and a depletion of the acid. When the iron content reaches a level that slows the pickling operation, the bath is either dumped or reprocessed. In some pickling operations, acid is continually withdrawn in order to hold a fairly constant ratio of iron to free acid in the pickle bath, thereby maintaining uniform pickling conditions for all the steel passing through. The metal leaving the pickle bath carries some of the liquor with it into the subsequent rinsing and neutralizing operations. The loss of acid by dragout varies with the type of work, the shape of the products being pickled, and the speed of the operation. It can run as high as 20% of the acid used. Appreciable rinse water must be put into the rinse tank and withdrawn continuously for discharge to a treatment facility.

SLAG PLANT

Various useful products are recovered from slag, some being produced from the slag in a molten form, and others after solidification.

Molten blast furnace slag can be quenched with water to produce lightweight expanded aggregate for the manufacture of cinder block. It can also be spun into mineral wool insulation. Solid air-cooled slag is crushed to various sizes for use as a track ballast, highway foundation, and similar structural material.

In plants handling slag there is normally airborne dust that tends to cake on conveyor belts or interfere with proper operation of mechanical equipment. Water washing of the air is sometimes practiced, or water may be used for washing conveyor belting, creating a high suspended solids wastewater.

BOF, open hearth, and electric furnace slags are very high in iron. Therefore, they are usually broken up and reclaimed for charging to the blast furnace.

UTILITIES

Because of the useful combustible gases produced at the coke ovens and the blast furnaces, steel mills are able to produce a large percentage of their total power requirements by burning this fuel in boiler houses. In addition to boilers directly fired with these byproduct fuels, other boilers reclaim heat from gases discharged from the open hearth furnaces, the BOF shop, and the engines that operate on coke-oven gas.

The steam generated by these boilers is used throughout the complex for driving turbines, powering presses and forges, and providing heat wherever it may be required. Some of this steam may be treated with steam cylinder oil

Figure 32.14   Acid pickling of steel sheet.

ahead of steam engines and presses, producing an oily condensate that requires treatment prior to disposal.

In addition to production of power from steam, some byproduct gases are used in gas engines to produce electrical power or mechanical energy directly for such uses as compressing air for the blast furnaces. Other utilities include air compressors, vacuum pumps, and pump stations to supply the enormous quantities of air and water needed for the operation.

The water requirements for these utilities in the steel mill are similar to those of other industries. High quality water must be produced for makeup to the steam generators, and these in turn concentrate the water, which is then removed by blowdown at a relatively high salinity level. The water treatment facilities required for producing this high quality water generate their own wastes, such as lime sludge from lime softening operations, brine from zeolite softening operations, or spent acid and caustic from demineralizer regeneration.

Cooling water is used by these utilities for such purposes as condensing turbine exhaust, cooling compressor jackets, cooling bearings on various types of powerhouse auxiliaries, and conveying ashes from coal fired furnaces.

SUGGESTED READING

Lund, H. F., (ed.): *Industrial Pollution Control Handbook,* McGraw-Hill, New York, 1971.
McGannon, H. E., (ed.): *The Making, Shaping and Treating of Steel,* 8th ed., United States Steel Corporation, 1964.
U.S. Environmental Protection Agency: *Development Document for Steel Making,* EPA-440/1-74-024-a, June 1974.

Chapter 33

Textile Industry

All finished textile products, whether clothing, carpeting or tire cord, have their origin in wool, cotton, synthetic fibers, or combinations of these. These fibers are processed to make them suitable for their end uses. These processes include: removal of natural impurities from wool and cotton (dirt, grit, grease); removal of process impurities (sizing, metallic contaminants); and finishing, to impart particular qualities of appearance, feel, and durability.

COTTON

The three basic steps in processing cotton (Figure 33.1) are spinning, weaving and finishing. Cotton spinning and weaving are dry processes. Foreign matter is removed from the raw cotton by opening and cleaning, picking, carding, and combing. The individual fibers are joined, straightened, spun into thread, and wound on spools.

To improve strength and stiffness of lengthwise (warp) yarn, it is passed through a sizing solution that controls abrasion and reduces friction. Starch, polyvinyl acetate (PVA) and carboxymethyl cellulose (CMC) are the sizing agents. This yarn is woven into cloth known as greige goods, which is sent to the finishing mill to process into salable products.

The finishing process, mostly wet, begins with the removal of sizing, natural wax, pectins, alcohols, dirt, oil and grease to prepare the cloth for the following steps:

Singeing—The cloth passes between heated plates or rollers, or across an open gas flame to burn off loose fibers. Sparks are extinguished as the cloth passes through a water box.

Desizing—Starch is solubilized by enzymes or acid by a 3–12 hour soaking. Excess liquor is removed. The cloth is then fresh-water rinsed and processed through a caustic or penetrant bath.

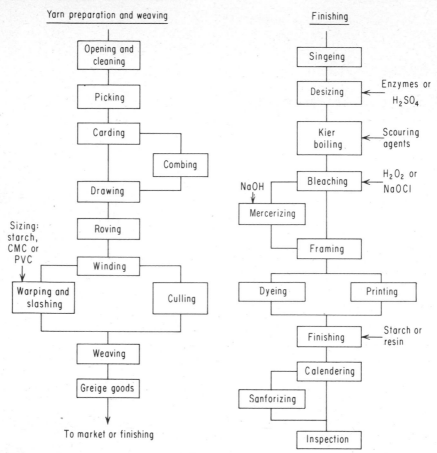

Figure 33.1 Cotton processing flowsheet.

Caustic Scouring—Greige goods are cooked to remove cotton wax, dirt, and grease. The cotton cloth is saturated with liquor consisting of caustic soda, soda ash, pine oil soap, and surfactants and scoured in a steam bath for one hour. Finally, the cloth is rinsed to remove the scour liquor. This develops a yellow, absorbent pure cellulose fiber.

Bleaching—Peroxide, hypochlorite or chlorine in combination with sodium silicate and caustic soda are applied as bleach liquor, and the cloth passes into a steam chamber (J-Box) for approximately one hour. The bleached cloth is rinsed in water and stored for further processing.

Mercerization—Bleached cloth may be mercerized to swell the fiber, thus improving luster, dye affinity and strength. In mercerization, the cloth is carried through a caustic soda solution (20–25% NaOH) while under tension, then through a water rinse, acid dip and final water wash.

Dyeing—Many different chemicals are used for dyeing:

a. Direct dyes are applied directly to the cloth.

b. Vat dyes and sulfur dyes are applied to cloth in a reduced state and then oxidized.

c. Developed dyes and naphthol dyes are applied to cloth and developed with a secondary chemical.

d. *Aniline black dye* is oxidized on the cloth by air or steam.

Printing—This process imparts a colored pattern or design to the cloth by a roller or screen print machine. The colors are fixed by steaming or other treatment.

Final Finishing—This process involves sizing (starch or resin), waterproofing, fireproofing, or preshrinking.

WOOL

Raw wool, a protein (keratin), contains glandular secretions (suint and wool grease) and feces from the sheep, plus dirt, straw, and vegetable matter. Residues of treatments applied for disease control or for identification of the animal may also be present. Wool is normally insoluble in water, but above 250°F (121°C) some fractions dissolve. Wool fiber expands upon wetting, but contracts to its original size when dried. Being amphoteric, wool is damaged by caustic or acid solutions, so special care must be taken when subjecting it to such treatments in processing.

Wool Processing

Sorting and Blending—Raw fibers are sorted into lots according to fineness and length. Fibers from different lots are blended to maintain uniformity.

Scouring and Desuinting—Foreign matter is removed by washing with soaps, alkalies, or other chemicals, or by solvent extraction. Scouring the fleece reduces weight by 35–65%. The extracted material is processed to recover lanolin.

Washing—The scour is followed by a clean water rinse.

Carding—The wool fibers are disengaged and rearranged into a web.

Oiling—An antistatic agent is applied to the fibers.

Backwashing—Removing oil that has been put into worsted stock in the blending, oiling, and mixing operations.

Gilling—A special procedure for carding which separates the long, choice fibers of the same length from the shorter fibers.

Top Dyeing—The application of a tint to the choice, long fibers (called "wool top") used for production of worsted, a tightly spun yarn. The tinting is for identification only.

Roving—Narrow strips of web are gently meshed together and wound onto spools for the spinning frames.

Spinning—The rovings are drawn through small rollers which further extend the web by pulling the fibers apart lengthwise.

Winding—The spun rovings are twisted and wound onto bobbins as finished yarn.

Figure 33.2 outlines the wool processing flow diagram.

Scouring (or slashing) prepares the wool for weaving. In detergent scouring, the predominant method, the wool is treated in successive bowls with capacities of 1,000 to 3,000 gallons (3.8–10 m^3) each. The first bowl is used for steeping (desuinting); the next two contain soap alkali for grease removal; and the final bowls are for rinsing.

Batch or continuous solvent scouring produces less water pollution than detergent scouring. Grease laden solvent is distilled to recover the solvent. A final detergent washing removes residual solvent and grease.

Dyeing is performed in open or pressure type machines. The pollution loading is related to the dye used.

Fulling is a process of shrinking the woven fabric by subjecting it to moisture, heat, and friction to produce a felt-like texture. Soap is the felting agent and water is evaporated during the process. Following fulling the wool cloth contains

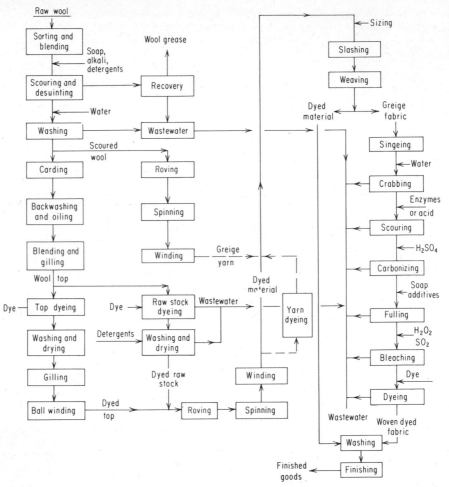

Figure 33.2   Wool processing flowsheet.

considerable process chemical and must be washed. The cloth passes through a "first soap," is squeezed between rollers, washed in a "second soap," and finally rinsed in a water bath.

In the carbonizing process for removing residual impurities, the wool fabric is impregnated with 4–6% sulfuric acid and oven dried at 212–220°F (100–105°C). The evaporation of the water concentrates the acid, charring organic contaminants. Rollers crush the charred matter, which is then removed by a mechanical dusting machine. The cloth is rinsed, neutralized by soda ash solution, washed again, and dried. Sulfur dioxide or hydrogen peroxide bleaches the natural yellow tint of the wool to white.

SYNTHETICS

The most common synthetic fibers are cellulose base (acetate/rayon) and polymer base (acrylic, nylon, polyester and orlon). Spun yarn is processed like natural fibers, requiring size to impart strength and to provide a protective coating for weaving. Continuous filament yarn requires less sizing.

Static charges build up on synthetic yarn during most processing steps so antistatic oils and lubricants are applied to the fiber before weaving. These include polyvinyl alcohol, styrene based resins, polyalkylene glycols, gelatin, and polyvinyl acetate.

Synthetic fabric finishing processes are similar to those used with cotton, and include scouring (removal of process chemicals from weaving), initial rinsing, bleaching, second rinsing, dyeing, and final finishing (waterproofing, shrink proofing, etc.).

WATER USES IN THE TEXTILE INDUSTRY

Clean air, free from debris, and controlled at precise temperature and humidity levels is vital to textile processing. The industry is one of the largest users of air-washing equipment to clean and temper air in the processing areas. Tempering requires heating in the winter and cooling in the summer.

Air washers are used throughout cotton mills producing woven fabric; in blending plants where cotton is blended with synthetic staple into yarn and then woven; and in synthetic fiber plants. Air washers also find extensive use in knitting plants, including hosiery and carpet mills. The material removed from the air is transferred to the water, so there are many problems requiring water treatment technology.

The cooling capacity for a typical textile refrigeration unit is 300–1200 tons, depending on the size of the plant. Total plant capacity may be from 300 tons in a very small mill up to 18,000 tons. In large plants, the total tonnage may be supplied by a single cooling tower circuit and a single chilled water system. However, in most cases there are several smaller systems. The tonnage and number of air conditioning systems operating in a plant depend on the combination of textile processes.

New textile plants are designed to consolidate chilled water systems into as few independent units as possible to maximize efficiency and reduce maintenance.

Chilled water is piped around the average textile plant for use in air washers, process heat exchangers, and small office air conditioning units. By far, the largest user of chilled water is the air washer. The average plant with 1,200 tons to 2,400 tons of air conditioning capacity may have six to eight air washers.

When refrigeration units are operating during warm weather (Figure 33.3), air washer units are supplied with chilled water, 40–50°F (5–10°C). Most textile chilled water systems have high level float switches on the chilled water sumps. During summer operation, when the chilled water is dehumidifying plant air, the volume of water in the chilled water system increases as water condenses from the makeup air. When this occurs, the level in the sump rises until it hits a limit switch which diverts excess chilled water (which is essentially condensate) to the cooling tower as makeup. This procedure conserves treatment chemicals, water, and energy, avoiding wasting excess chilled water and increasing the efficiency of the condenser unit.

Chilled water sumps contain filters for suspended solids removal. Many potential fouling problems in the air washer systems can be avoided by removing suspended solids in the chilled water sump in this manner.

In plants where refrigeration is not required during winter months (Figure 33.4), washers operate independently, continually recirculating water from the sump through the spray nozzles. During these months, there is usually evaporation in the air washer system, eliminating overflow and requiring makeup.

In a typical textile mill air washer, air entering from the plant first passes through a fine mesh screen or drum roll filter to remove lint, dust, oil and other debris. Some units have moving paper media while others have stationary syn-

Figure 33.3   Typical textile air washer system—summer operation.

thetic media which is replaced two or three times per year. Some large rotating drum filters have vacuum attachments to continually remove contaminants from the filter medium. A knitting plant or a package dyeing plant with winding operations has oil in the air. However, lint is the major problem in cotton mills.

Most textile air washer systems automatically blend outside air with in-plant air. The temperature and humidity needs may vary from one department to another in the same plant, requiring separate chilled water systems.

The mixture of air enters the washing section where several vertical headers with spray nozzles are spaced evenly across the area of air flow. The nozzles spray water against each other so that the incoming air must pass through a barrier of water droplets two or three feet thick.

The spray nozzle headers are connected to a recirculating pump that has a capacity of 250–1200 gpm (1–5 m³/min). The main pump located at the chilled water sump continually supplies each individual air washer sump. Overflow and gravity return the water to the main refrigeration unit and chilled water sump. Capacities of air washer sump pans range from 600 to 2500 gallons (2–10 m³).

After the spray section of the washer unit, the air passes through mist elimi-nator blades to remove moisture. Some washers are designed with steam reheat coils to temper the cooled air to suit a particular textile process. Bypass ductwork is sometimes designed into a unit to allow for simple heating of the air without washing. Large fans or blowers take the air from the end of the washer unit and distribute it through the plant ductwork.

Most textile mills use compressed air to control water atomizers and for other purposes. Cooling water must be supplied to the air compressor heads, oil coolers, and aftercoolers. The cooling water may come from the main cooling tower system in large plants where there are several air conditioning units, or there may be a separate small tower provided for these units.

The few plants set up for once-through cooling water on air compressor systems conserve this by sending the spent water into one of the cooling towers during summer operation as makeup.

Some air washer units, particularly in synthetics plants, do not use chilled water for the washing process. The eliminator sections of these washers are followed by steam reheat coils, and chilled water coils to adequately control temperature and humidity.

Roto-spray systems, similar in principle to the packaged air washer units, are housed in a cylindrical casing slightly larger than the supply ductwork, and are generally located on the roof of the mill. They have stationary spray nozzles and rotating eliminator blades that look like the compressor stages in a gas turbine. There is very little water in these units, and they are somewhat difficult to treat because the dirt is concentrated in a small amount of water.

AIR WASHER MAINTENANCE

Air washers are periodically shut down and washed out to control the severe fouling and deposition problems that occur. The frequency of shutdown and washout depends on the type of textile process being run, and the severity of the problem. It may be weekly in some plants, while in others 5–6 week intervals between washouts may be acceptable.

The high degree of recirculation in air washers leads to a variety of water problems including slime formation, deposits, corrosion and odors. The major part of most deposits is microbial (slime masses). Microbial activity produces a

Figure 33.4 Typical textile air washer system—winter operation.

sticky slime that combines with dirt, corrosion products and crystalline matter to form hard encrusted deposits above the water level and thick slimy masses below the water on metal surfaces inside the washer. Controlling microbial growth in a chilled water or air washer system is the key to an effective treatment program. Microbe growth also causes odors, carryover, encrustation, and corrosion under deposits. Oil and other organic matter picked up from the plant air provide food for these microbes. Even though some removal of oil may be accomplished with air filters, residual oil will be present in the washer.

Carryover caused by foaming or by biological growth on eliminator blades disrupts air flow and allows solids to pass into plant ductwork. This can cause a variety of problems in the plant from spotting of the product to disrupting the temperature and humidity controls. Severe damage can be done to the plant ductwork. Most textile plant ductwork contains a mat of lint and fiber. When this becomes wet, it becomes encrusted with the dirt present in the washer water and severe corrosion can result.

Corrosion is most severe in textile air washer and chilled water systems during summer operations when the water in the systems deconcentrates. Chiller tube sheets and heads are the most vulnerable areas. Dirt, fiber, oil, and microbiological deposits combine in some cases to totally slime over areas of the tube sheet. Severe pitting occurs under deposits of this nature. Corrosion inside the air washer units themselves may occur on any mild steel structures.

DEVELOPING A TREATMENT PROGRAM

A complete equipment survey and a thorough understanding of equipment operations is needed to design an effective water treatment program for air washer and chilled water systems.

The selection of an effective biocide and dispersant is generally the starting point in developing a water treatment program for air washers and chilled water systems. Corrosion control is closely related to the effectiveness of the microbicide and dispersant. There are no easy answers to the selection of a corrosion inhibitor for air washer and chilled water systems due to the differences between textile plants. The most important part of controlling corrosion is keeping the system clean.

The static charge on textile fiber as it passes through the various textile processes has a great deal to do with their efficiency. For example, if a carding machine is processing staple that has just been brought in from a cold warehouse, the fibers will be negatively charged and will stick to the steel rolls of the card machine rather than smoothly rolling into a sliver of yarn. Fibers that develop too great a negative charge on spinning frames are subject to excessive breaks. Quaternary ammonium compounds may be used to control static charges in air, because they have the added benefits of being good biocides and cleaning agents.

Steam generation facilities in a textile plant will normally be quite simple. Condensate is usually not more than 25% of total feedwater. The boilers are generally low pressure and the steam is rarely used for power generation except in the largest integrated mills.

Effluent treatment may be quite complicated because of the residues of processing chemicals present in the raw wastewater. In-plant containment and process modifications are increasingly necessary to meet effluent restrictions. Typical wastewater characteristics are listed in Table 33.1.

A treatment scheme for a large finishing plant is shown in Figure 33.5. The large equalization basin is provided to even out changes in composition and

TABLE 33.1 Representative Mill Average Raw Waste Characteristics for Various Textile Operations

Variable	Wool and animal hair scouring	Wool dyeing and finishing	Cotton and synthetic woven fabric finishing	Cotton and synthetic knit fabric finishing	Dyeing and Printing of carpet (cotton, wool, syn.)	Cotton and syn. raw stock and yarn dyeing
Water use (gal/lb)	4.3	40	13.5	18	8.3	18
Production (med. size)	80	2–20	6–180	8–40	60	60
1000 lb/day		3–20	7–15	9–60		
BOD$_5$	4740–6220	150–700	250–850	100–650	144–630	75–340
	5480	300	550	250	340	200
TSS	5000–24,500	45–300	45–475	40–485	75–150	25–75
	7500	130	185	300	120	50
COD	29,600–31,300	280–5000	425–1440	450–1440	570–1360	220–1010
	30,500	1041	850	850	925	524
Oil and grease	5000–5600					
	5340					
Total chromium	0.05	4	0.04	0.05	NI	0.013
Phenol	1.50	0.5	0.04	0.27	NI	0.12
Sulfide	0.20	0.1	2.72	0.2	NI	NI
Color (ADMI)	2000	500–1700	325	400	600	600
pH (units)	6–9	6–11	7–11	6–9	6–9	7–12

NI: No Information Available

NOTE: All above, except color and pH, are reported in mg/l; ranges and medians are given.

Source: Lockwood Green Engineers, Inc. "Textile Industry Technology and Costs of Wastewater Control," National Comm. on Water Quality Contract WQSACo-21, June 1975.

Figure 33.5   Cotton finishing mill effluent treatment scheme.

temperature, and to reduce the heat load on the aeration basin. In some plants the presence of strong waste (caustic from mercerizing, dyes, sizing agents) requires segregation and separate treatment of these streams. Activated carbon has been used as part of the treatment where dyes are a problem.

SUGGESTED READING

Shreve, R. N.: *Chemical Process Industries,* 3d ed., McGraw-Hill, New York, 1967.
U.S. Environmental Protection Agency: *Development Document for the Textile Mills,* EPA-440/1-74-022-a, June 1974.

Chapter 34
Utilities

Steam-electric power generating plants are the largest industrial users of water in the United States. The Federal Power Commission 1970 National Power Survey reported that utilities cooling water constituted 80% of all such water usage, or approximately one-third of the nation's total water withdrawals. About 70% of the water withdrawals by utilities is fresh water. The balance is saline water used by generating stations in coastal regions.

The laws of thermodynamics limit the amount of the energy in fuel that can be converted to work by a steam turbine. More than 50% of the initially available heat remains in the exhaust steam leaving the turbine, and most of this is rejected to cooling water and then lost to the surrounding environment. Cooling water required for condensing the turbine exhaust steam in a 1000 MW (1,000,000 kW) plant is about 400,000 gpm (1500 m³/min).

By comparison, other water requirements for steam-electric plants are small. These include replacement of blowdown and other losses from the steam cycle, ash transport (in fossil-fueled plants), equipment cleaning, and domestic uses.

A high percentage of the cooling water is returned directly to its source, because once-through cooling is used in plants having about 70% of the currently installed generating capacity in the United States. Because the condenser outlet water is typically 5–25°F (3–14°C) warmer than the inlet, heat is the principal concern in discharges of utility cooling water. A goal of U.S. environmental policy is elimination of thermal discharges by utilities to receiving waters by July 1, 1981, with some exceptions.

The difference between total water withdrawal and wastewater discharge is mostly evaporation. Evaporation occurs principally from ponds and cooling towers used in recirculating cooling water systems; there is also some from the surfaces of ash settling ponds. Minor water losses can also occur by seepage into the ground from unlined ponds, and in wet ash or water treatment sludges hauled from the plant.

Figure 34.1   This utility system incorporates both a nuclear unit (left) and a coal fired unit (right) at the same site. *(Courtesy of Carolina Power & Light Company.)*

Utility wastewater contaminants include suspended solids, metals such as iron and copper, acids and alkalies from water treating and metal cleaning operations, oil and grease. Less likely to become a water contaminant, but of special environmental concern, are polychlorinated byphenyl compounds (PCB's) used as transformer fluids, now being replaced by safer materials.

THE PROCESS: ENERGY CONVERSION

In steam-electric power production (Figure 34.1), the chemical energy of fossil fuels or the nuclear energy of fissionable materials is converted to heat for generation of steam that is then converted to mechanical energy in a turbine coupled to an electrical generator. Exhaust steam is condensed and returned to the boiler.

Within the fluid (water-steam) cycle of a steam-electric plant, the theoretical efficiency at which heat in the steam can be converted in a turbine to work is shown by:

$$\text{Percent theoretical efficiency} = \frac{T_1 - T_2}{T_1} \times 100$$

where T_1 = absolute temperature of the turbine inlet steam.
  T_2 = absolute temperature of the turbine exhaust steam.

Thus, the greatest efficiency is achieved by providing the highest inlet steam temperature (T_1) and lowest exhaust temperature (T_2) practical for a given boiler-turbine-condenser system.

In practice, upper temperatures are limited by the strength of metals available for boiler and superheater construction; strength falls off rapidly as temperature exceeds 900°F (480°C, 1360°R). Upper temperatures are generally limited to a maximum of about 1100°F (590°C, 1560°R). A significant temperature difference is required to cause heat to flow from the exhaust steam to the cooling medium circulated through the condenser. The practical effect is that lower steam temperatures (T_2) on condensing turbines typically range 80–120°F (27°–49°C, 540–580°R), even with cooling water at 40°F (4°C) in the winter. Within these upper and lower temperatures, then, the best theoretical efficiency would be calculated as:

$$\text{Theoretical efficiency} = \frac{1560 - 540}{1560} \times 100 = 65.4\%$$

Achievable efficiencies are considerably lower than theoretical both for the fluid cycle and for the generating plant as a whole. Significant energy is lost in overcoming fluid and mechanical friction. Sizable amounts of energy are consumed in the operation of the plant's feedwater pumps, boiler draft fans, and other auxiliaries. A power plant's pollution control equipment, required to meet air emission and water discharge standards, can consume as much as 10% of the electrical output. Actual steam-electric plant overall efficiencies range from 32 to 39%.

POWER CYCLE

The energy flow through the water-steam phase changes in a steam-electric plant is called the Rankine Cycle, having four basic stages: boiler, turbine, condenser and feedwater pump.

The Rankine Cycle may be illustrated by several kinds of diagrams. Figure 34.2 shows that cycle, relating the change in temperature of the fluid to its entropy at each stage in the cycle. Entropy is a measure of that portion of the heat received by a cycle that cannot be converted into work due to random motion of the gas (steam) molecules. Entropy is expressed mathematically as the ratio of heat content to temperature.

To achieve the highest possible thermodynamic efficiency, modern fossil-fuel power cycles use steam superheaters and reheaters to raise average temperatures (T_1) of steam flowing through the turbine. Condensers operating at high vacuum permit expansion of steam to the lowest possible exhaust temperature (T_2). And to further recover as much heat as possible, partially expanded steam is extracted from the turbine at various points for heating feedwater (called

a to b: Liquid heating and compression (feedwater pump).
b to e: Reversible heat addition in feedwater heaters (b to c), boiler (c to d) and superheater (d to e).
e to f: Steam expansion and conversion of heat energy to work.
f to a: Reversible rejection of unavailable heat to cooling water "sink".

Figure 34.2   Steps in the Rankine cycle from the introduction of water as a liquid into the system, through its phase change to steam which produces work in a turbine, to the condensing of the exhaust vapor to water again for return to the boiler.

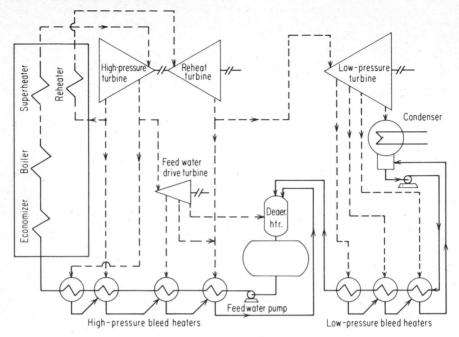

Single reheat, 8-stage regenerative feed heating, 3515 psia, 1000°F/1000°F steam

Figure 34.3   The addition of steam reheat and regenerative feedwater heating to increase efficiency.

"regenerative heating"). Figure 34.3 illustrates a cycle having these components, and Figure 34.4 illustrates their effect on a temperature-entropy diagram of the cycle.

Nuclear steam-electric plants of the light water reactor types, typical in U.S. commercial service, cannot deliver steam at the temperatures achieved in fossil fueled units. Nuclear pressurized water reactors (PWR) (Figure 34.5) employing once-through steam generators achieve only a relatively small degree of steam superheat [30–60°F (17°–34°C)]. But in PWR cycles employing recirculating U-tube steam generators, and in boiling water reactor (BWR) cycles (Figure 34.6) there is no superheat. For this reason, nuclear power cycles are limited to efficiencies of about 32%, compared to 36–39% for fossil fueled cycles, since more heat is lost to the condenser cooling water.

In fossil fueled units, further improvements in thermodynamic efficiency are achieved by economizers and air heaters installed in the path of the exit flue gas between the boiler and stack. Economizers transfer heat from the exit gases to the feedwater; air heaters transfer some of the residual stack gas heat to the boiler combustion air supply.

For still higher efficiencies, where suitable fuels are available, some steam-electric plants combine the operation of a combustion gas driven turbine with that of a steam turbine. In such combined cycle generating plants (Figure 34.7), the hot gases of combustion, such as from a jet aircraft engine—are first utilized for spinning the gas-driven turbine; and the turbine exhaust gas, still containing considerable heat, is then used in a boiler-superheater unit to produce steam to drive a steam turbine.

The heat energy equivalent of one electrical kilowatt hour is 3413 Btu. At 32% overall thermodynamic efficiency, the heat rate for a generating station would be:

$$\frac{3413}{0.32} = 10{,}700 \text{ Btu/kw-hr}$$

If an efficiency of 40% could be achieved, the station heat rate would be only 8,533 Btu/kw-hr—requiring about 20% less fuel for a given output.

WATER: THE WORKING FLUID

In steam-electric power cycles, water is subjected to wide variations in temperature and pressure in the cyclic sequences of compression, heating, expansion and heat rejection. Temperatures may range from 70 to 1200°F, with pressures from 0.5 to 5000 psia.

As shown by the diagram in Figure 34.8, steam density approaches that of water as pressure increases, until the critical pressure is reached at 3208 psia. Above this pressure exists a supercritical fluid which cannot be considered either steam or water. Boilers operating over 3208 psia are called supercritical units.

In cycles operating at pressures below critical where steam density is less than

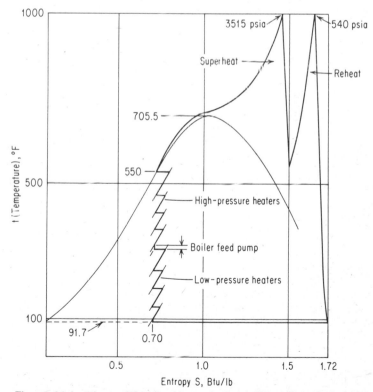

Figure 34.4 The modified Rankine cycle showing the effect of reheating steam and adding feedwater heaters to the cycle. (*Adapted from Steam/Its Generation and Use, Babcock & Wilcox Company, 1972.*)

Figure 34.5 PWR nuclear power cycle showing major components and typical pressures and temperatures. *(Adapted from The Effects of Water Quality on the Performance of Modern Power Plants, Klein and Goldstein, NACE 1968 Conference.)*

Figure 34.6 Diagram of a BWR nuclear power cycle showing major components and typical pressures and temperatures. *(Adapted from The Effects of Water Quality on the Performance of Modern Power Plants, Klein and Goldstein, NACE 1968 Conference.)*

Figure 34.7 Combined cycle gas turbine-steam plant. *(From Power Special Report, Gas Turbines, December, 1963.)*

that of water, phase changes occur from water to steam and then from steam back to water. While there are advantages favoring drum type boilers (Figure 34.9) for most subcritical pressure cycles, once-through boilers are sometimes used because of lower initial costs.

Drum type boilers have two major advantages in subcritical steam generation. First, they can produce high purity steam with less stringent feedwater quality requirements. Mechanical disengagement of steam from the recirculating water leaves most of the undesirable solids behind in the boiler water. And because boiler internal recirculation rates are about four times the rate of steam flow from the boiler, the fluid rising to the steam drum from the generating tubes will be about 75% water. This means that superheated steam, in which some boiler water impurities would become soluble, cannot exist in the boiler drum. Secondly, since the recirculating mixture in the boiler tubes is primarily water, more efficient heat transfer and tube metal cooling occurs than when steam alone flows through the tubes.

In subcritical once-through boilers, a complete phase change occurs with water entering at one end and superheated steam leaving at the other. There is no recirculation within the unit, nor is there a drum for mechanical steam-water separation. Boiler blowdown is impossible, so to prevent deposition of solids

Figure 34.8 As boiler pressure increases, steam density and water density, which are greatly different at atmospheric pressure, approach each other, becoming equal at 3208 psi, the critical pressure.

Figure 34.9 The basic differences between (a) drum-type and (b) once-through steam generators.

in the system beyond the point of water-steam phase change requires stringent feedwater quality requirements—considerably higher than for drum type boilers.

For cycles operating above critical pressure, no phase change occurs, so no steam-water separation is possible. Thus, at supercritical pressures, all steam generators are once-through. Universal Pressure Boilers are once-through boilers suitable for use at pressures above or below critical. From the standpoint of tube metal alloy and thickness requirements, they are economically most practical for operation in the range of about 2000 to 3000 psi.

In higher subcritical pressure cycles (2750–2850 psia), the margin between feedwater quality requirements of drum and once-through boilers is somewhat lessened. At such pressures, effective mechanical steam-water separation is an advantage provided by drum type boilers. But the advantage is limited by the increase in the solubility of water contaminants in the steam, as the densities of steam and water approach each other (Figure 34.8). The solids dissolved in steam cannot be removed by mechanical separation devices in a boiler drum. For high pressure utility boilers, therefore, the concentration of solids in steam is determined to an important extent by their steam-water solubility ratios at the operating pressure. Silica is a notable example (Figure 34.10).

If solids concentrations in the steam were to average 30 ppb (μg/l), for example, a 200 megawatt turbine would receive more than 200 lbs/yr (91 kg/yr) of potential depositing solids. The portion that would deposit in the turbine and the portion that would remain in the steam to recycle to the boiler is not accurately predictable. But, to avoid excessive turbine fouling, experience has shown the necessity of keeping total salt concentrations in the steam below 50 ppb (μg/l) with silica not to exceed 20 ppb (μg/l). Further, to minimize any potential for stress corrosion cracking of turbine members, the steam solids should be free of sodium hydroxide.

In nuclear power cycles, water purity is important for a different reason. Although H_2O becomes only slightly radioactive under neutron flux, producing only short-lived isotopes, the response of materials in the water under flux is of concern. Naturally occurring cobalt, for example, would be an extremely undesirable constituent of primary coolant water passing through the reactor core in either BWR or PWR cycles. The product would be highly radioactive, emitting high energy gamma rays during subsequent decay. So cobalt must be avoided in such systems. Since most other metals also produce radioactive isotopes under neutron flux, the tolerance for water corrosion products is limited in nuclear cycles for operating and maintenance safety.

Although the required degree of purity varies for different cycles, relatively high purity water is required for all modern power cycles. Many water constituents today must be measured and controlled at parts per billion (ppb, or μg/l) concentration levels compared to their measurement and control at parts per million (mg/l) concentrations in the lower pressure cycles that were once common.

However, make-up water of the purity required can be produced reliably and at reasonable cost by ion exchange, evaporation and other pretreatment methods. But, because make-up water volumes are usually only 1% or less of total feedwater in typical power cycles, the major problem has become keeping the water pure after it has entered the cycle.

The two main potentials for contamination of high purity water are corrosion and in-leakage. Corrosion represents not only metal damage, but also contamination of the system water with corrosion products. Low purity water enters the cycle at points of high vacuum (e.g., the surface condenser), and this in-leakage is a second major source of contamination. Careful design and selection of materials of construction minimize the occurrence of these problems.

WATER CHEMISTRY IN FOSSIL-FUELED PLANTS

Apart from steam quality considerations, a major goal of cycle water chemistry and treatment control is the prevention of tube metal failures in high pressure steam generators.

Because make-up water is deionized and essentially free of measurable hardness and other solids, tube failure due to water side scale and deposits is

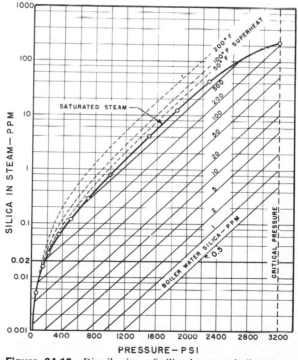

Figure 34.10 Distribution of silica between boiler water and steam.

Figure 34.11 Typical chemical concentrate (ductile gouging) type attack located downstream of a weld with backing ring.

far less likely to occur in utility plants than in lower pressure industrial boilers. Instead, in power plant drum type boilers, tube metal failures are more commonly due to a highly localized "crater" or "ductile gouging" form of water side corrosion, and to water side hydrogen penetration and embrittlement of carbon steel.

The "ductile gouging" form of corrosion is a chemical attack characterized by irregular craters in the tube wall. The tube fails when wall thickness at the point of wastage is insufficient to withstand the internal pressures (Figure 34.11). The most common chemical agent in this form of attack is sodium hydroxide. Even with a bulk boiler water free of NaOH as determined by usual methods of testing, a porous deposit on the tube wall provides a mechanism for concentrating chemical in contact with the tube surface to several thousand mg/l. Sodium hydroxide concentrates in this manner and reacts first with the magnetite tube surface and then with the elemental iron of the tube to form soluble sodium-iron complexes:

$$4NaOH + Fe_3O_4 \rightarrow 2NaFeO_2 + Na_2FeO_2 + H_2O \qquad (1)$$

$$Fe + NaOH + H_2O \rightarrow NaFeO_2 + 3H \qquad (2)$$

The parent tube metal is thus exposed to react with water to reform protective magnetite,

$$3Fe + 4H_2O \rightarrow Fe_3O_4 + 8H \qquad (3)$$

In either case, localized wastage of tube metal occurs and hydrogen is produced as a reaction product. The atomic hydrogen thus produced is capable of intergranular penetration of steel and of reaction with carbon in the steel to form methane gas:

$$4H + C \rightarrow CH_4 \qquad (4)$$

Not only is the steel thus weakened by decarburization along its grain boundaries (Figure 34.12), but the formation of methane develops pressure between grains in the steel microstructure, producing discontinuous intergranular cracks. The end result is failure of the tube wall when such intergranular decarburiza-

Figure 34.12 Attack of boiler steel caused by hydrogen generation, leading to decarburization and fissure formation. (Left) Typical microstructure of pearlite colonies in a ferrite matrix. Etchant: picral. (500×) (Right) Intergranular microcracks and decarburization near fracture surface of actual hydrogen damage failure. Etchant: picral. (500×)

tion and microfissuring have sufficiently reduced its strength. Although some water side wastage of metal may have occurred in the corrosion reaction that produced the hydrogen, hydrogen damage normally results in thick-edged fracture before the wall thickness is reduced to the point that stress rupture would have occurred. In such thick-edged or "brittle" fracture failures, it is not uncommon for an entire irregularly shaped "window" to be blown out of an affected tube.

In summary, the major causes of ductile gouging and hydrogen damage of carbon steel tubes are (1) a chemical agent that will be corrosive if sufficiently concentrated, and (2) a concentrating mechanism.

There are several mechanisms capable of producing high localized salt concentrations. Any condition of heat input in excess of the cooling capacity of the flow of fluid circulating through a tube can result in film boiling on the metal surface, with evaporative concentration of salts occurring. Localized pressure differentials, as created by high velocity through a tube restriction such as welding back-up ring, can result in small pockets of "flashing" water, concentrating salts on the downstream side of the restriction. The mechanism most commonly occurring is that of pre-boiler corrosion, with pick-up of metals and the subsequent deposition of these on heated boiler tube surfaces, where they function as porous membranes. Evaporation beneath the deposit draws in boiler water to replace evaporation loss, but prevents solids from leaving the area.

To prevent such corrosion and hydrogen damage, either all concentration mechanisms must be eliminated, or potentially corrosive chemical agents must be excluded from the boiler water. Since porous deposits of pre-boiler corrosion products create the most common mechanism for chemical concentration, strict attention to protection of pre-boiler metal surfaces is critical.

A significant characteristic of modern utility cycles is the high ratio of pre-boiler surface area to that in the boiler itself. While a ratio of about 0.3 would be typical in a 750 psi system, a ratio of about 1.3 would be typical at 2800 psi. This is a reflection of the multiple stages of regenerative feedwater heating commonly employed to increase cycle efficiency. To the water engineer, the higher ratio means that the area from which metals can be picked up is larger than the area on which they are likely to deposit.

Metals used in fabrication of condensers, low pressure heaters and high pressure heaters are commonly cast iron, stainless steels, and alloys of copper, such as brass and monel. Thus, iron and copper are the principal contaminants likely to be acquired by feedwater enroute to the steam generator.

Feedwater pH is an important factor in minimizing pre-boiler corrosion of metals. For iron and its alloys, although a minimum pH of 8.5 might be acceptable, feedwater pH values in the range of 9.2 to 9.6 are considered optimum. For copper and its alloys, feedwater pH values generally should be in the range of 8.5 to 9.2. A compromise feedwater pH control range of 8.8 to 9.2 is usually established where both metals are present.

Volatile alkalies such as ammonia and amines that will not contribute dissolved solids are commonly used for pH control in this portion of the cycle.

Feedwater oxygen also has a great bearing on pre-boiler corrosion and contamination; an oxygen level of 5 ppb or less is usually specified. The largest potential for oxygen admission occurs in the high vacuum portions of the cycle. Oxygen can be reduced to low levels mechanically, either in deaerating type surface condensers or in separate deaerators located ahead of high pressure feedwater pumps. For removal of residual oxygen, hydrazine may be injected continuously immediately downstream of the condenser. Hydrazine is a chemical oxygen scavenger that introduces no solids to the cycle. Its concentration is controlled in the range of 10–20 ppb in the feedwater, usually measured at the economizer inlet.

Ammonia, an important factor in pre-boiler pickup of copper, is generally present in power cycles, either due to direct addition or decomposition of chemicals such as hydrazine or amines that have been added to the system. It can also result from thermal decomposition of organic matter in cooling water entering the cycle through condenser leaks.

In sufficient concentrations, ammonia reacts directly with copper to form soluble complexes or it can contribute to stress corrosion cracking of copper alloy tubes. Even at lower concentrations, ammonia can react with protective copper oxides on the water side of condenser and heater tube surfaces, exposing parent metal to wastage by reaction with oxygen in the feedwater. To minimize copper attack, most operators limit cycle ammonia concentrations to about 0.1–0.3 mg/l. These limits can be met by carefully controlling chemical additions to the cycle and by proper regeneration of condensate polishers. Where ammonia concentrations build up beyond the desired maximum, deconcentration may require temporarily dumping the normally recycled aftercooler drains (Figure 34.13) where ammonia concentrates.

Good design calls for careful selection of materials of construction to withstand the environment of the pre-boiler systems. Condenser tubes in fresh water coolant service are commonly brass and stainless steel. These materials are also common in low pressure stage heaters, except for supercritical pressure cycles where even minute concentrations of copper can cause serious turbine fouling problems; this requires the use of carbon steel. High pressure stage heaters are fabricated of copper-nickel alloys and carbon steel.

It is now standard practice to reduce metallic "crud" in utility feedwater by polishing the condensate through a filter of mixed cation and anion exchange resins. Filtration removes the insoluble crud and ion exchange removes any dissolved contaminants that have entered the cycle by inleakage.

As shown in Figure 34.14, polishers are generally located between the condenser and the first feedwater stage heater, since a large part of the vulnerable pre-boiler metal surface area is in the condenser and on the steam side of stage heaters cascading drips back to the condenser. This placement protects high temperature feedwater heaters, the steam generator, and the turbine from

Figure 34.13 Noncondensible gases, including air from inleakage and NH₃ from steam cycle, are removed by ejection and inter- and after-condensers. Final drips may be reclaimed or discarded if contamination levels are too high.

deposit-forming contaminants. Temperature limitations on ion exchange resin control location of polishers in the cycle: regenerable polishers can withstand only about 120°F (48°C), so must be confined to the condenser; powdered resin units may be placed in higher temperature locations, but still in the lower pressure stage heater train.

For best cost performance, regenerable mixed bed polishers are commonly operated at service flow rates over 50 gpm/ft² (2 m³/min/m²), about ten times the rate employed in raw water demineralization. To avoid any possibility of contaminating cycle water with regenerant chemicals, resins are removed from the polisher for external regeneration and periodic cleaning.

Non-regenerable, powdered resin polishers have found wide acceptance in

Figure 34.14 Power cycle with full flow condensate polishing.

utility systems. The finely ground resin particles provide good filtration and excellent kinetics for ion exchange. This type of condensate polisher is typically operated at service flow rates of about 4 gpm/sq ft. During cycle cleanup, such as during start up, an inexpensive cellulosic filter aid may be included in the powdered resin mixture. In any case, when the resins become fouled or exhausted, they are discarded, usually every 3 or 4 weeks.

For either regenerable or non-regenerable polishers, the cation exchange resin can be used in ammoniated form to prevent removal of ammonia from the cycle. Anion resins are in the hydroxide form.

Virtually all once-through boilers, because of their especially high water purity requirements, employ polishing of total feedwater.

In drum type boiler systems where water purity is less critical, condensate polishing may not be economically justifiable for normal day-to-day operations. But even in these systems, condensate polishing may be worthwhile to protect the boiler and turbine from the high levels of crud and silica common during initial start-up and subsequent restarts. A polisher can greatly shorten the pre-circulation time, and often pay for itself in the cost of purchased power that would otherwise be necessary during the start-up period.

Condensate polishing eliminates most deposit-forming materials that create chemical concentration mechanisms in steam generator tubes, but such measures are never completely effective. Long term accumulations of such deposits, principally iron and copper oxides, on boiler tube surfaces are removed by periodic cleaning. Utility boilers are generally considered "clean" with deposit weights less than 15 g/sq ft (1.5 g/m²) of tube area. Subcritical pressure boilers are considered dirty when accumulations exceed 40 g/sq ft. Supercritical boilers are considered very dirty at accumulations over 25 g/sq ft. Power boilers with normal feedwater conditions may be routinely chemically cleaned every four years. Longer intervals may allow otherwise soft deposits to harden and become tenacious and difficult to remove.

Corrosion and hydrogen damage of boiler tubes are not likely to occur where rigorous control of pre-boiler chemistry, condensate polishing and periodic cleaning keeps boiler surfaces clean. But because clean tube surfaces cannot be assured at all times and conditions other than water side deposits can create chemical concentration mechanisms, it is general utility practice also to exclude sources of potentially aggressive free sodium hydroxide from the boiler water.

Corrosion of boiler steel is also a function of pH (Figure 34.15), and pH values ideally should fall within a general range of 9.0 to 11.0. But a safe value must be achieved without producing measurable residuals of sodium hydroxide. In utility practice, this is accomplished either with a selection of sodium phosphate salts or with a "zero solids" treatment using all-volatile chemicals.

Sodium phosphates provide the desired pH in boiler water, while avoiding the presence of free sodium hydroxide, as shown by these hydrolysis reactions:

$$\underset{\text{(trisodium phosphate)}}{Na_3PO_4} \rightleftharpoons 3Na^+ + PO_4^{-3} \tag{5}$$

$$Na_3PO_4 + H_2O \rightleftharpoons Na_2HPO_4 + NaOH \tag{6}$$

$$\underset{\text{(disodium phosphate)}}{Na_2HPO_4} \rightleftharpoons 2Na^+ + HPO_4^{-2} \tag{7}$$

$$\updownarrow$$

$$H^+ + PO_4^{-3}$$

$$Na_2HPO_4 + H_2O \rightleftharpoons NaH_2PO_4 + NaOH \tag{8}$$

$$\underset{\text{(monosodium phosphate)}}{NaH_2PO_4} \rightleftharpoons Na^+ + H_2PO_4^- \tag{9}$$

$$\updownarrow$$

$$H^+ + HPO_4^{-2}$$

Figure 34.15   Attack on steel at 590°F (310°C) by water of varying pH.

The phosphates used are blends of disodium and trisodium salts of phosphoric acid. The species of phosphate present will depend upon pH, as shown in Figure 34.16. This plot shows that phosphates exist almost entirely in the dibasic ion form (HPO_4^{-2}) within the pH range of 9.0–11.0 considered optimum for boiler steel.

Note that pH is measured on a cooled sample, and equilibrium pH values in the boiler are somewhat different.

Where the sodium (Na) to phosphate (PO_4) mole ratio in pure water is 3 to 1, for Na_3PO_4, the relationship of pH to phosphate ion concentration will be as shown on the so-called "coordinated phosphate" curve (Figure 34.17).

Controlling pH solely by sodium phosphate hydrolysis, bulk boiler water pH should never accidently increase to levels aggressive to boiler steel. Reaction (6) shows that the hydrolysis reaction of trisodium phosphate is self-limiting; as pH rises above 10.0, generation of hydroxide ions by hydrolysis decreases. It is theoretically impossible for a solution of Na_3PO_4 to reach a pH much above 12.0. If the Na_3PO_4 solution were to concentrate to 10,000 mg/l, the pH would be 12.

Figure 34.16 The distribution of different ionic species of phosphate at various pH values.

Figure 34.17 Equilibrium between PO$_4$ and pH defining the coordinated phosphate boundary. *(Adapted from Combustion, pp. 45–52, October 1962.)*

Sodium hydroxide generated solely by this hydrolysis reaction is sometimes called "captive"; it will be "taken back" and revert to Na$_3$PO$_4$ at any sites of localized evaporative concentration.

In Reaction (6), if water were to be removed by evaporation, the equilibrium would be forced to the left. Upon evaporation to complete dryness, the residue would contain Na$_3$PO$_4$, free of NaOH. But incomplete evaporation, the more likely condition beneath a porous deposit, produces a liquid beneath the deposit rich in sodium hydroxide, especially if incipient localized corrosion were already occurring. Thus, maintaining a 3 to 1 sodium:phosphate ratio in the boiler water may not provide positive protection against caustic concentrate type corrosion damage.

Many utility operators have adopted a modified form of coordinated phosphate control calling for maintenance of a Na:PO$_4$ ratio not over 2.6, corresponding to a 3:2 blend of trisodium and disodium phosphate. The control diagram shown in Figure 34.18 shows the differing hydrolysis effects of different sodium phosphates in selectively adjusting pH, PO$_4$, or both to keep coordinates within the desired range.

The all-volatile treatment (AVT) method uses only nitrogen-hydrogen compounds such as ammonia and hydrazine, so no solids are added. This is mandatory in once-through steam generators. Even in drum type boilers, volatile treatment offers protection against superheater and turbine deposits that might otherwise occur with carryover of boiler water containing dissolved solids.

A disadvantage of all-volatile treatment for drum type boilers is that the boiler water is unbuffered and thus subject to extensive and rapid pH excursions in the event of feedwater contamination. There is no tolerance for condenser coolant inleakage unless condensate polishing is provided.

Contaminant salts entering the cycle from other sources may produce acids (H$^+$) or alkalies (OH$^-$) capable of being concentrated locally to corrosive levels. Typical contaminant sources are (1) condenser leakage; (2) treated make-up water contamination by evaporator carryover or demineralizer leakage; (3) regenerant contamination from ion exchange units; or (4) incomplete removal of chemical cleaning solvents or alkalies. Of these, condenser leakage is the most significant.

Boiler tube hydrogen damage as a result of condenser leakage is particularly likely to occur where the cooling water is brackish. The reactions of contaminants such as calcium chloride and magnesium chloride in boiler water, after depletion of any soluble phosphates, are:

$$MgCl_2 + 2HOH \rightarrow Mg(OH)_2 + 2HCl \tag{10}$$

$$CaCl_2 + 2HOH \rightarrow Ca(OH)_2 + 2HCl \tag{11}$$

In high purity, unbuffered boiler water, very small cooling water leaks can reduce pH to 4.0 or less. Where the acid is then concentrated locally within a deposit at a tube surface, corrosion and hydrogen damage proceed rapidly.

While protection is afforded by condensate polishers, strict surveillance of condenser leakage is prudent for drum type boiler cycles without polishers. As a general rule, leaks causing 0.5 mg/l feedwater concentrations can usually be accommodated in normal operation without serious difficulty: feedwater concentrations of 2.0 mg/l may be tolerated for short periods; but immediate boiler shutdown is usual when a condenser leak produces concentrations greater than 2.0 mg/l. Immediate boiler shutdown is always indicated where acceptable boiler water pH cannot be maintained.

The necessary continuous surveillance of condenser leaks usually relies on so-called "cation conductivity" monitoring, which effectively senses concentration changes as small as 20 ppb (μg/l). In this method, a condensate sample passes through a column of acid-form cation resin to convert sulfate, chloride and nitrate salts to more electrically conductive sulfuric, hydrochloric and nitric acid. The conductivity is then measured in the resin treated sample.

Monitors for silica and sodium are alternative devices for detection of condenser leaks. Against background concentrations commonly encountered in turbine condensates, available monitoring equipment can reliably detect changes of 5 ppb or less in either of these contaminants.

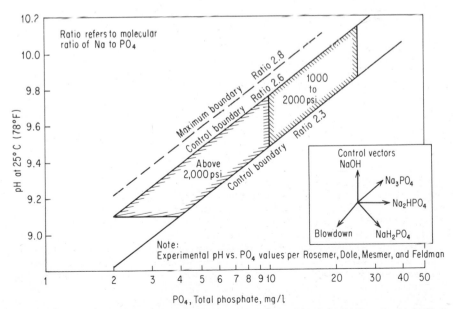

Figure 34.18 Suggested coordinated phosphate control target for high-pressure boilers.

WATER CHEMISTRY IN
NUCLEAR FUELED PLANTS

The nuclear pressurized water reactor (PWR) (Figure 34.5) has two major water systems:

1. The primary loop, or reactor coolant system
2. The secondary loop, or steam generator-turbine cycle

Components of the primary loop are the reactor vessel, a pressurizer, steam generators (heat exchangers), and circulating pump. In the primary loop, water temperature is allowed to rise only about 50°F (28°C) passing through the reactor, so recirculation rates are quite high to absorb the amount of heat generated. Pressure of the recirculating water is kept high enough to keep the water from boiling. The pressurizer maintains this pressure and absorbs changes in volume produced by changes in temperature. For maximum corrosion resistance, wetted surfaces in the primary loop are usually stainless steel or nickel-based alloys.

High purity must be maintained in the primary loop water to minimize fouling of reactor and exchanger heat transfer surfaces and to avoid contaminants that could form undesirable radioactive isotopes under neutron flux. Controlled additions and removals of boric acid in the primary loop water provide the correct concentration of neutron-absorbing boron needed to control neutron flux and energy transfer. Chemicals such as lithium hydroxide, forming relatively safe radioisotopes under neutron flux, are used for pH control in the primary loop.

Under nuclear radiation in passage through the reactor, some of the primary loop water is decomposed into hydrogen and oxygen as follows:

$$H_2O \rightarrow H_2 + \frac{1}{2}O_2 \tag{12}$$

To suppress oxygen generation and to scavenge oxygen entering the system, hydrogen gas is commonly added. Primary loop water purity is usually maintained by continuously passing a portion of the circulating water through a mixed bed demineralizer. These generally utilize anion resins in the borate form, to avoid removal of boron from the water. As impurities accumulate, these resins tend to become radioactive and regeneration becomes impractical. Consequently, the resins are eventually disposed of as a solid radwaste.

Two basic heat exchanger designs are employed as secondary loop steam generators in PWR systems. The recirculating U-tube type (Figure 34.19), is analogous to a drum type boiler in a fossil fueled system. Having an internal recirculation rate of 3 to 4 times the steam flow, the unit provides mechanical steam-water separation and continuous blowdown. But it differs from fossil fueled boilers in that there is no provision for superheating the steam.

The other PWR heat exchanger design (Figure 34.20), provides once-through type steam generation. The heat exchanger is baffled so that incoming feedwater first flows down through an outer annulus in which it is heated to saturation temperature, and then it is converted totally to steam and is slightly superheated in a single upward shellside pass through the tube bundle. Depending on load, up to about 60°F (34°C) superheat can be achieved.

Either type steam generator requires maximum corrosion resistance on the primary side, so tube materials are commonly a special nickel-iron-chromium alloy. Carbon steel shells are generally used, although those parts of the shell surface constituting the primary coolant inlet and outlet plenums are clad on the coolant water side.

For recirculating U-tube type PWR steam generators, the all volatile treatment (AVT) method is preferred to coordinated phosphate treatment. In once-through type PWR steam generators, of course, AVT is automatically required.

Steam outlet

Secondary separator

Primary separator

Recirculated water

Water level

Downcomer area

U tubes

Steaming area

Annular wrapper (downcomer)

Divider plates

Feedwater inlet

Preheater

Coolant chamber

Primary coolant nozzle

Coolant outlet return to core

Coolant inlet from core

Figure 34.19 PWR vertical U-tube recirculating-type steam generator with integral feedwater preheater.

In the nuclear boiling water reactor (BWR) (Figure 34.21), boiling occurs in the reactor itself. The same water serves as the cycle working fluid, the reactor coolant, and the nuclear reaction moderator. Boiling water reactors are comparable to drum type boilers. A portion of the water passing through the core is converted to steam. The steam-water mixture is then separated, with the steam going to the turbine and boiler water returning through circulating pumps to the core inlet.

An important aspect of BWR operation is the effect on the working fluid of direct exposure to nuclear radiation. Some of the water is decomposed into hydrogen and oxygen. It is not possible to inject hydrogen as in the PWR because of the need for continuous removal of all non-condensible gases at the condenser to maintain the vacuum required for turbine efficiency. Thus, steam produced by a BWR reactor contains high concentrations of oxygen, a strong factor in corrosion.

Nitrogen entering the cycle by air inleakage or decomposition of nitrogenous compounds can react to form nitric acid:

$$5O_2 + 2N_2 + 2H_2O \rightarrow 4HNO_3 \tag{13}$$

Additives for pH control and oxygen scavenging, such as amines and hydrazine, are not usable in BWR cycles because they are subject to nuclear decomposition. Thus, corrosion control relies primarily on the corrosion resistant materials used throughout the cycle.

Metallic contaminants in the cycle water, either from condenser leakage or from corrosion of system metals, are subject to stringent limitation to avoid formation of hazardous isotopes and to avoid deposition of crud on the core heat transfer surfaces. Copper is specifically limited because of its tendency to foul the orifices of the core water distributor. Make-up water is demineralized to

Reactor coolant inlet

Manway

Tubesheet
Coolant flows
through tubes

Auxiliary feedwater inlet

Upper annular baffle

Tube support plates

Steam outlet

Divider

Feedwater inlet

Annular space for
feedwater preheating

Lower annular baffle

Steaming area
between tubes

Manway

Tubesheet

Reactor coolant outlet

Return to core

Manway

Drain

Inspection port

Figure 34.20   PWR once-through-type steam generator. *(Adapted from Steam/Its Generation and Use, Babcock & Wilcox Company, 1972.)*

less than 1.0 micromho/cm specific conductivity and 10 ppb (μg/l) silica. Full flow condensate demineralization is then employed to maintain cycle water purity at limits established by the reactor manufacturer. Typical limits are: 30 ppb total metals, 2 ppb Cu, 2 ppb Cl, and 0.1 micromho/cm @ 25°C. Resultant feedwater is essentially neutral, with pH equal to 7.

Where deep bed demineralizers are used in BWR condensate polishing, resins are usually sluiced to external vessels for scrubbing and regeneration. The regenerant wastes generally contain low-level radioactivity which requires processing in the liquid radwaste system. Where non-regenerable powdered resin units are used for polishing, the spent, sluiced resin must be processed.

CONDENSER COOLING WATER

As previously discussed, the thermal efficiency of modern fossil-fueled steam electric plants averages about 34%. The largest part of the loss, equal to about

50% of the heat released by the fuel, is rejected at the condenser. Nuclear-fueled plants, averaging about 32% efficiency, lose even more heat at the condenser. Heat rejected at the condenser is transferred to cooling water, which subsequently releases this heat to the environment.

Although water circulating through the tubes of a surface condenser is called cooling water, it is important to recognize that there is no cooling of the vapor or condensate. The circulating water simply absorbs the heat of vaporization of steam leaving the turbine, converting it to liquid at the same temperature. For this reason, the term "condenser water" is sometimes preferred to "cooling water."

The primary function of a surface condenser is to maximize cycle efficiency by allowing steam to expand through the turbine to the lowest possible exhaust temperature. Just as in a boiler drum, the temperature of steam and water in a condenser is directly related to pressure. At 102°F, for example, the corresponding saturated steam pressure is about 1.0 psia (51.7 mm Hg); this is also expressed as a vacuum of about 27.89 inches of mercury (705 mm Hg). At this vacuum, one pound of steam occupies 331.1 cu ft; when condensed it occupies only 0.016 cu ft, about 0.005% of the original steam volume.

Non-condensible gases (air, ammonia) in the condenser reduce the vacuum achievable, so such gases are continuously removed by mechanical vacuum pumps or steam jet eductors (Figure 34.22).

The ability of a surface condenser to provide the lowest possible backpressure for a given load and cooling water temperature is adversely affected by such things as:

1. Waterside scaling and fouling of condenser tube surfaces
2. Partial blockage of cooling water flow through the tubes
3. Inadequate removal of non-condensible gases
4. Faulty distribution of exhaust steam

Waterside scaling and fouling are probably the most common causes of impaired condenser performance.

The effect of a 1.0" Hg rise in backpressure in a 500 MW plant is illustrated in Figure 34.23. At constant steam rate, electrical output would be reduced by about 13 MW, a loss of 2.5%. This 13 MW represents about $1.25 million in plant investment. Effective condenser water treatment is a very important factor in preventing such losses.

Figure 34.21   In the BWR nuclear plant, steam is generated in the same vessel that contains the fuel elements, as shown in this simplified diagram.

Figure 34.22 Two-pass surface condenser with provision for reversing water flow for backwashing tubes and waterbox. Inter and after condenser drips normally return to the hotwell.

Five basic types of condenser water systems are used in utility stations:
1. Once-through cooling
2. Cooling lake and cooling pond systems
3. Spray ponds
4. Wet cooling tower systems
5. Wet dry combination cooling tower systems

In once-through cooling, water passes once through the condenser and returns to its source at a higher temperature. Because residence time and temperature are low, scaling is usually not a problem. The principal fouling problems are usually related to microbial activity and silt deposition. Regularly scheduled chlorination microbial control usually achieves a moderate increase in condenser cleanliness for several hours. Application of a biodispersant with each application of chlorine can increase both the magnitude and duration of this improvement (Figure 34.24). By increasing the effectiveness of chlorine, such biodispersants also can reduce the dosage of chlorine, helping the plant meet discharge regulations.

Corrosion inhibitors are rarely required in fresh water once-through systems. But for protection of copper alloy tubes (e.g., aluminum-brass) in sea water

500 MW Generation—Coal Fired		
(where unit rating permits fixed load maintenance)		
Back pressure, in Hg (abs)	Gross turbine unit	Heat rates (total)
1.5	7,600 Btu/kWh	3.8×10^9 Btu/hr
2.5	7,800 Btu/kWh	3.9×10^9 Btu/hr
(A) Rise 1.0	200 Btu/kWh	0.1×10^9 Btu/hr
(B) Additional fuel Btu (at 90% boiler efficiency) = ...0.11×19^9 Btu/hr		
(C) Additional fuel cost (at $1.00/million Btu) = ...$110/hr		
		$2,640/day
Plus additional fuel cost caused by increased load on auxiliaries.		

Figure 34.23 The effect of turbine back pressure increase on plant efficiency.

Treatment*	C.F. improvement	
	Highest percent	Duration
0.05 mg/l Cl₂ residual plus 15 mg/l biodispersant	7.24%	6.5 hours
12.12 mg/l Cl₂ residual plus 5 mg/l biodispersant	2.61%	6.0 hours
12.40 mg/l Cl₂ residual alone no biodispersant	0.55%	2.0 hours

* Short duration treatment applications with system blowdown closed off until chlorine residual gone.

Figure 34.24 Condenser tube cleanliness factor improvement through the use of a biodispersant. *(Source: Nalco Research Report Serial No. 1642, June, 1977, re: field evaluation data obtained at Duane Arnold Nuclear Center of Iowa Electric Light & Power Company.)*

once-through systems, low dosages of ferrous sulfate are sometimes applied intermittently to the condenser inlet water to provide a protective film of iron oxide on the tube internal surfaces. The cost effect of the film in reducing heat transfer must be balanced against the benefit of reduced corrosion.

With the advent of environmental regulations restricting thermal discharges, some once-through systems have been modified so that the condenser outlet water passes over a "helper" cooling tower or through a tempering canal with floating spray modules to dissipate heat before discharge. Since such "helper" additions follow the condenser, chlorination-dispersant treatment of the water is the same as for conventional once-through systems.

Cooling water may be discharged to cooling lakes, manmade impoundments created by damming a stream. Condenser water is recirculated through the lake, and heat is dissipated primarily by surface evaporation. The lake receives makeup from rainfall and runoff from its drainage area. Cooling lakes make possible high cooling water withdrawal from streams too small to provide such cooling capacity on a once-through basis. Water treatment practices and discharge limitations are generally the same for these cooling lakes as for once-through cooling.

By contrast "cooling ponds" are defined as impoundments that do not impede the flow of a navigable stream. They are usually constructed along a stream from which makeup water may be pumped to meet evaporative losses not replaced by rainfall or runoff from surrounding drainage areas. Cooling ponds contained within earthen levees at levels above the surface water are said to be "perched." The area required for natural evaporation is typically on the order of 1.0 to 1.5 acres (0.4–0.6 ha) per megawatt of capacity. A pond typically provides detention of about 5 to 15 days to produce the necessary heat dissipation.

Blowdown from cooling ponds is comprised of bottom seepage and controlled overflow to the source stream. Because of the large rainfall-receiving surface areas, concentration ratios are typically quite low, up to about 1.5 times source concentration. But even such low concentration increases may be significant in terms of reduced $CaCO_3$ solubilities, so condenser tubes on pond systems are more likely to scale than they do on once-through cooling systems. Sulfuric acid may be fed to maintain pH below saturation values (pH_s). Scale inhibitors and dispersants are sometimes required in conjunction with acid feed for complete scale prevention.

A significant aspect of cooling ponds is that they promote "homes" for a variety of aquatic organisms. They often support large fish populations. Specific biodispersants in conjunction with periodic feed for chlorine may be needed to keep condenser tubes free of biological slimes initiated by the microorganisms of the food chain supported by the pond.

Spray ponds promote evaporation by mechanically dispersing water into sheets and droplets, dissipating heat effectively so that less pond area is required. Evaporation is mechanically promoted, so it is less dependent on climatological conditions. Recirculating water treatment requirements generally correspond more closely to those of evaporative (wet) cooling towers than to cooling ponds or lakes.

Where large cooling ponds or spray ponds are impractical, cooling towers are installed to reduce thermal pollution of receiving waterways. To comply with restrictions on thermal discharge, blowdown is taken from the tower basin, having the lowest temperature of the recirculating system.

An important advantage of wet cooling towers is their ability to significantly reduce raw water withdrawal and waste water discharge (Table 34.1).

TABLE 34.1   Water Flows for 1000-MW Plant Cooling System
[Based on 20°F (11°C) temperature rise]

	Once-through cooling system	Wet cooling tower recirculating system
Condenser flow, gpm	400,000	400,000
Evaporative conc. ratio	1×	5×
Make-up water, gpm	400,000	10,000
Discharge water, gpm	400,000	2,000

Because drift (entrainment of fine mist) from a cooling tower is part of blowdown, the net discharge to the receiving stream in this example would be about 10 to 200 gpm less than the 2000 gpm shown.

With the constraints of environmental limitations on concentrations of chlorine and other chemicals that may be discharged in blowdown, cooling tower recirculating water treatment practices for stream-electric plants are generally as described elsewhere in this text for industrial plants.

With the increased planning for maximum water conservation, coal-fired plants may substitute cooling tower blowdown for raw water for ash sluicing. Some sluice water is evaporated by the heat of bottom ash, and a small amount is retained by the ash, so the final volume of waste water for disposal is further reduced.

Zero discharge of tower blowdown may be impractical and unnecessary environmentally in most parts of the country, but strategies for approaching this goal have been devised for arid regions where adequate land is available. In such cases, tower blowdown may be routed to on-site solar evaporation ponds.

Various processes for side stream treatment of cooling water and for blowdown concentration reduce discharge volume and required evaporation pond areas. One such conceptual system is illustrated in Figure 34.25. Although side stream processing can control concentrations of potentially scale forming ions, high salinity in the recirculating water is characteristic of these treatment schemes. The effects of high dissolved solids in cooling tower drift and on surrounding vegetation and structures must be considered. Also, the significantly greater impact of condenser leaks on the chemistry of the boiler water cycle must be provided for.

Moisture "plumes" emanate from cooling tower stacks like clouds under many weather conditions, literally dominating the atmosphere in the immediate

Figure 34.25 Simplified schematic of process to recover cooling water by side-stream treatment and desalination to yield only a concentrated brine.

vicinity. One means of eliminating plumes is to use non-evaporative dry cooling towers. In dry cooling towers (Figure 34.26), heat is transferred from the recirculating water to the air by convection rather than by evaporation.

Since dry cooling tower performance is controlled by ambient air dry bulb temperature, rather than by lower wet bulb temperatures, turbine backpressures are higher for dry tower systems than for wet towers, so cycle efficiencies are poorer.

But combinations of wet and dry cooling towers may be used to advantage (Figure 34.27) to alleviate plume problems with minimum loss of cycle efficiency. And, since dry towers handle their part of the heat load without evaporation, overall makeup and blowdown volumes are less for wet-dry cooling tower combinations. Systems may be set up with the recirculating water flowing either in series or parallel through the wet and dry towers. Designs usually provide for a means of totally or partially bypassing either air flow or recirculating water flow selectively around either the wet or dry tower, as may be required to optimize plant efficiency for varying plume abatement and water conservation requirements. Figure 34.28 diagrams a system with provision for water bypass. Figure 34.29 illustrates an integral wet-cooling tower unit with provision for adjusting the balance of air flows through the wet and dry sections. Recirculating

Figure 34.26 Dry cooling towers can be used in water-short areas, but users usually pay a penalty in energy loss where air temperatures are high. *(From Power Special Report, "Cooling Towers," March 1973.)*

Figure 34.27 At this utility station a large combination wet-dry tower is used to cool condenser water. *(Courtesy of the Public Service Company of New Mexico.)*

water treatment practices for wet-dry cooling tower systems are essentially the same as for straight wet cooling tower systems. As load is shifted from wet to dry cooling, less dirt is washed out of the air to contaminate the recirculating water.

Closed recirculating water systems handle a variety of cooling requirements in utility stations, avoiding introduction of outside contaminants that might foul heat exchanger surfaces. Systems of this type are sometimes used for cooling the hydrogen circulated for electrical generator cooling. They also may be used for after-cooling of compressed air, jacket cooling for standby diesel engines,

Figure 34.28 Bypass permits optimum use of wet and dry cooling towers. *(From Combustion, pp. 23–27, October 1976.)*

WARM DRY
EFFLUENT

FAN

DAMPERS

D.E.'S

HEAT
EXCHANGER

FILL

COLD WATER

HOT
WATER

AIR
FLOW

AIR
FLOW

INTAKE
LOUVERS

Figure 34.29 Integral wet/dry cooling tower with damper control (D.E.'s—drift eliminators). *(From Reisman, J. I. and Ovard, J. D. Cooling Towers and the Environment—An Overview, Proc. of the American Power Conference, vol. 35, 1973.)*

and for certain lube oil cooling requirements. In nuclear plants, closed recirculating cooling water systems are commonly used to handle heat loads from the reactor vessel shielding, primary coolant pump seal housings, and other heat loads within the reactor building.

MISCELLANEOUS WATER USES

Another major water use in coal-fired power plants, and to a lesser extent in oil-fired plants, is for ash transport. The solids that fall to the bottom of the boiler furnace (bottom ash) are invariably cooled and conveyed from the boiler by water. The solid products of combustion (fly ash) in the flue gas that do not deposit in the boiler convection passes or air heater, are subsequently removed by electrostatic precipitators, bag filters and wet scrubbers. Fly ash accumulations are removed from these devices either by water or by mechanical or pneumatic means.

The quantity of water required for ash sluicing varies with design factors such as method of firing and nature of the coal. For a typical 1,000 MW coal-fired plant, it amounts to about 10 mgd (26.2 m³/min).

For molten slag tap or "wet bottom" boiler, where water is used to quench

Figure 34.30 The suspension firing of coal produces slag in a variety of forms, including these microspheres, which float to the surface of wet ash collection ponds. (Left) Random spheres; (Right) broken shell.

molten ash, heat pick up can be in the range of 10^6 Btu per ton of bottom ash. Suspended solids in bottom ash water are of concern if they are difficult to settle. Coagulants may be needed to reduce supernatant turbidity. Dissolved solids contribution to the sluice water from the ash is relatively small.

By contrast, fly ash is much more leachable and may contribute on the order of 50–300 mg/l dissolved solids to its transport water. Fly ash often contains hollow microspheres (Figure 34.30), which are difficult to separate from sluice water by sedimentation. So, dry transport systems are often used to handle it.

In oil-fired plants, ash is produced in comparatively small quantities. Bottom ash removal from the boiler by fireside washing and sluicing may be needed only occasionally. Oil ash generally does not settle in ponds as well as coal ash. While ash pond overflow waters have many of the same characteristics as in coal-fired plants, high concentrations of vanadium may be present, originating as an ash constituent of some fuel oils. Bottom ash in some oil-fired plants is removed by dry collection rather than by water sluicing.

Where there is a market for the bottom ash, or where insufficient land is available for settling, dewatering bins can be used and the dewatered ash trucked away. Water drainage from dewatering bins or the supernatant from ash ponds can be recycled to the sluice pumps. Makeup to such recycle systems is required for replacement of evaporative losses and moisure that leaves with the dewatered ash. Because of the poor liquids/solids separation of the buoyant fly ash, however, recycle systems are generally not suitable where fly ash is sluiced to the same dewatering point as bottom ash.

Chemical coagulants and flocculants are useful in the treatment of ash transport waters, to reduce suspended solids to acceptable levels for recycle or final discharge.

In some utility plants firing high sulfur coal, water is also used in wet scrubber type flue gas desulfurization (FGD) systems. Most FGD systems in U.S. power plants use a wet scrubbing process in which the reactive component of the sorbent is not regenerated. Most commonly, sulfur dioxide in the flue gas is reacted with slurries of lime or limestone to form calcium sulfites and sulfates. Sludge from the process, consisting of fly ash and water in addition to the calcium precipitates, is usually piped to large settling ponds. Supernatant water from the ponds is reclaimed and recycled to the process. The ponded sludge retains a quicksand-like character limiting any future use of the pond land area. Makeup water requirements for such systems may be in the range of 0.75 to 1.0 gpm/MW of generation rate.

A smaller number of non-regenerable FGD systems, are of the double-alkali type. In this process, flue gas is scrubbed with a solution of sodium hydroxide, to form sodium sulfite and sodium bisulfite. The scrubbing solution is then reacted with lime, precipitating sludges similar to those with lime as the primary sorbent, restoring the sodium hydroxide for reuse in the process. Although the absorbing medium is thus "regenerated," this process is still categorized as non-regenerable because the sulfur scrubbed from the flue gas is not recovered.

Steam-electric power plants are subject to federal, state and local water pollution control regulations. Where these regulatory bodies differ on specific limitations for a given pollutant, the more stringent regulations generally apply. Some state and local regulations limit certain pollutants not limited by federal guidelines.

Figure 34.31 Water reuse and effluent treatment scheme for a coal-fired steam electric plant.

TABLE 34.2   Major Wastewater Sources and Contaminants in Fossil-fueled Steam-Electric Generating Plants

Source	Principal contaminants
Ash sluicing system	TSS,[a] TDS,[b] heat, oil
Low-volume wastes[c]	TSS, TDS, pH, oil
Metal-cleaning wastes[d]	TSS, TDS, pH, iron, copper, other metals, oil
Boiler blowdown	TSS, iron, copper, oil
Main condensers, once-through cooling	Heat, residual chlorine
Main condensers, recirculating-water blowdown	Residual chlorine, Zn, Cr, P and other corrosion inhibitors
Area runoff[e]	TSS, TDS, pH, oil
Intake water traveling screens and strainers	Solids (debris)

[a] TSS—total suspended solids.
[b] TDS—total dissolved solids.
[c] Low volume wastes—collectively including wastes from ion exchange systems regeneration, evaporator blowdown, flue-gas wet scrubbers, floor drainage, cooling-tower basin cleaning, blowdown from recirculating house service water systems.
[d] Metal cleaning wastes—including waterborne wastes from boiler tube cleaning, boiler fireside cleaning, air preheater cleaning.
[e] Area runoff—including rainfall runoff from storage of coal, ash and other materials.

A significant feature of pollution control regulations for steam-electric plants is that specific discharge limitations relate to individual processes and sources within the plant rather than to the combined discharge. Thus, no credits accrue from combining or diluting one in-plant waste stream with another. For example, the total weight discharge per day of iron originating in boiler blowdown may not exceed the actual daily flow of boiler blowdown times the permissible concentration limit of iron.

A simplified tabulation of steam-electric plant wastewaters and their contaminant characteristics, by source categories, is shown in Table 34.2.

Principles of water recycle, reuse and effluent treatment for steam-electric plants are generally the same as for other process industries. Figure 34.31 illustrates one reuse and effluent treatment scheme for a coal fired plant. In this illustration, bottom ash transport water is recycled. Fly ash is separately handled in a dry system.

For nuclear power plants, a principle of special importance is the segregation of dissimilar wastes. High purity (low conductivity) wastewaters are kept separate from low purity (higher conductivity) waters to facilitate reclamation and recycle of the high purity waters. Chemical wastes, including ion exchange regenerants and chemical cleaning wastes, should be segregated from detergent wastes because of their differing requirements for final treatment before discharge or reuse.

SUGGESTED READINGS

Babcock & Wilcox Company: *Steam/Its Generation and Use*, 1972.
Federal Power Commission: *Steam-Electric Plant Air And Water Quality Control Data*, FPC-S-229, February, 1973.
Federal Power Commission: *Steam-Electric Plant Air And Water Quality Control Data*, FPC-S/253, January, 1976.
Federal Register: *Steam-Electric Power Generating Point Source Category, Effluent Guidelines And Standards*, Vol. 39, Number 196, October 8, 1974.

Klein, H. A.: *Use of Coordinated Phosphate Treatment To Prevent Caustic Corrosion In High Pressure Boilers,* Combustion, October, 1962.

Landon, R. D., and Houx, J. R., Jr.: *Plume Abatement And Water Conservation With The Wet-Dry Cooling Tower,* Proc. of the American Power Conference, Vol. 35, 1973.

deLorenzi, O. (editor): *Combustion Engineering,* The Riverside Press, Cambridge, Mass., 1947.

Skrotzky, B. G. A.: *Basic Thermodynamics, Elements of Energy,* McGraw-Hill, New York, 1963.

U.S. Environmental Protection Agency: *Development Document for Steam Electric Power Generating,* EPA-440/1-74-029a, October 1974.

U.S. Environmental Protection Agency, *Economic Report for Steam Electric.* NTIS-PB-239315/AS.

Chapter 35
Municipal Water

Communities differ widely in character and size, but all have the common concerns of finding, treating and distributing water for industrial, commercial, and residential use. Residential uses include washing, transporting wastes, drinking, food preparation, watering lawns and gardens, heating and cooling, and fire protection. It is estimated that public water utilities in the United States deliver over 30 billion gallons of water daily (bgd) (79×10^3 m³/min) with approximately 19 bgd (50×10^3 m³/min) being used for residential purposes. Household use is about 100 gallons per day (0.38 m³/d) per person, of which less than one percent is consumed, yet the water quality established by potable standards is imposed on the entire supply.

Water has been treated for thousands of years by a variety of processes, though procedures that produce safe potable water were not developed until the 19th century. This resulted from serious epidemics of diseases related to sewage-contaminated water. It was discovered that chlorine was effective as a disinfectant in destroying pathogenic (disease causing) organisms. Maintaining a chlorine residual in the distribution system produced a safe water and protected against harmful contamination. Many countries use chlorination today; others use ozone as a disinfecting agent.

Chlorine and other disinfectants can react with trace organics found in many water sources; their by-products may be objectionable in taste or odor, and some may be harmful. Physiological effects of potentially harmful substances are continually scrutinized by the Federal Government under authority of the Toxic Substances Act.

Because water is so basic to life, public interest in governing water quality has been strong. This has created a demand for modern treatment plants, trained operators, and careful surveillance of chemical treatment and water quality.

Consumption of water per capita ranges from approximately 100 gallons/day

(0.38 m³/d) in very small municipalities, to about 200 gallons/day (0.76 m³/d) in larger systems having greater industrial and commercial demand. Water use primarily depends on the availability of water resources, climatic and seasonal variations, and the cost of the finished water. Where water is scarce, it is used only for essential purposes. Where cost is a prominent factor, it primarily restricts non-essential uses of water, such as lawn watering, since essential uses will be served regardless of cost.

Over the years, water quality standards have become more stringent due to public demand and concern for the effects of specific contaminants. In addition to health-related aspects of contaminants, there are also considerations of palatability.

Prior to 1975, the 1962 United States Public Health Service Standards were the quality criteria for the production of potable water. During 1975, the United States Environmental Protection Agency was mandated to institute a new system of quality regulations by the Safe Drinking Water Act (Public Law 93-523). The interim primary (enforceable) standards were then promulgated to become effective in July 1977. Additional regulations may be anticipated if national testing programs detect harmful contaminants for which regulation is necessary. Current standards are listed in Tables 35.1(A) and (B), which includes the limits recommended by the World Health Organization.

TABLE 35.1A   U.S. Drinking Water Standards

Constituent	Recommended limit, mg/l	Federal mandatory limit, mg/l
Alkyl benzene sulfonate (ABS)	0.5	—
Arsenic (As)	0.01	0.05
Barium (Ba)	—	1.0
Cadmium (Cd) —		0.01
Carbon chloroform extract (CCE)	0.2	—
Chloride	250	—
Chromium (total) (Cr)	—	0.05
Copper (Cu)	1.0	—
Cyanide (CN)	0.01	—
Fluoride (F)	0.6–0.9*	1.4–2.4†
Iron (Fe)	0.3	—
Lead (Pb)	—	0.05
Manganese (Mn)	0.05	—
Nitrate (NO₃)	45	45
Phenols	0.001	—
Selenium (Se)	—	0.01
Silver (Ag)	—	0.05
Sulfate (SO₄)	250	—
Total dissolved solids (TDS)	500	—
Zinc (Zn)	5	—
Mercury (Hg)	—	0.002
Turbidity (Nephelometric procedure)		1 NTU—monthly average 5 NTU—average of two consecutive days (5 NTU—monthly average may apply at state option)
Radioactivity (natural)	—	Gross Alpha 15 pCi/l
Radioactivity (manmade)	—	Gross Beta 50 pCi/l Tritium 20,000 pCi/l Strontium 90 8 pCi/l

* Depending upon ambient air temperature
† Depending upon temperature

TABLE 35.1B   World Health Organization Drinking Water Standards

Constituent, mg/l	1950 international			1961 European	
	Permissible limit	Excessive limit	Maximum limit	Recommended limit	Tolerance limit
Ammonia	—	—	—	0.5	—
Arsenic	—	—	0.2	—	0.2
Cadmium	—	—	—	—	0.05
Calcium	75	200	—	—	—
Chloride	200	600	—	350	—
Chromium (+6)	—	—	0.05	—	0.05
Copper	1.0	1.5	—	0.05*	—
Cyanide	—	—	0.01	—	0.01
Fluoride	—	—	—	1.5	—
Iron	0.3	1.0	—	0.1	—
Lead	—	—	0.1	—	0.1
Magnesium	50	150	—	125†	—
Manganese	0.1	0.5	—	0.1	—
Nitrate	—	—	—	50	—
Oxygen	—	—	—	5.0	—
Phenols	0.001	0.002	—	0.001	—
Selenium	—	—	0.05	—	0.05
Sulfate	200	400	—	250	—
Total solids	500	1500	—	—	—
Zinc	5.0	15.0	—	5.0	—

* May be higher for new piping
† If 250 mg/l SO_4 is present, Mg not to exceed 30 mg/l

In addition to the Primary (enforceable) regulations, there are Secondary (desirable) goals which are to serve as objectives for the industry. Local regulations or objectives may be even more stringent as determined by the individual communities.

RAW WATER CHARACTERISTICS

Raw water characteristics vary widely, the major differences being between surface and ground water, hard and soft water, and river water compared to reservoir water. These differences present varying needs for algae control, turbidity removal, softening, water stabilization, and disinfection. Highly polluted waters have additional requirements to remove organics. Certain waters have undesirable inorganic constituents as well.

Generally, water supplies within a defined geological region are similar. There has been a trend to surface water because of its availability and to minimize the risks of earth subsidence due to uncontrolled ground water withdrawal.

A raw water with a constant low turbidity has more treatment options than one of high or variable turbidity. The presence of color in many low alkalinity waters requires special treatment consideration. Corrosion control will become more important as water quality is monitored to meet the secondary standards in the Safe Drinking Water Act.

In some cases, the requirements of the Safe Drinking Water Act will necessitate a change to a more acceptable water source. The implementation of the Safe Drinking Water Act will also result in the consolidation of many small water suppliers into larger regional systems to take advantage of the economy of scale. This will also allow for the funding of more sophisticated monitoring and treatment requirements.

TABLE 35.2 Typical Water Impurities and Common Methods of Treatment

Typical treatment	Surface						Ground				Surface or ground			
	Turbidity	Taste and odors	Hardness	Color	Iron/manganese	Algae	Hardness	Iron/manganese	H_2S	Bacteria/virus	Heavy metals	Organics	Corrosion	Scale
Preaeration		X			X			X	X					
Filtration only with or without chemicals	X			X	X	X		X						
Ion exchange			X		X		X	X						
Single or two-stage precipitation softening	X	X	X	X	X	X	X	X						
Chemical clarification and filtration	X	X	X	X	X	X	X	X						
Oxidation		X		X	X	X		X	X	X	X	X		
Chlorination		X		X	X	X		X	X	X	X	X		
Adsorption		X		X								X		
Phosphates													X	
Zinc phosphates													X	X

TYPICAL TREATMENT SCHEMES

The type of treatment practiced at a given municipality depends largely on the raw water characteristics. Wherever possible, water resources are acquired and maintained to require a minimum amount of treatment, thereby reducing the capital and operating costs to the municipality. In Table 35.2 are shown the common impurities found in raw water supplies and examples of the general types of treatments that can be employed. Which treatment is optimum depends on local conditions and the level of impurity.

A simple summary of various processes used for treating municipal water is shown in Figure 35.1. By far the largest number of municipalities simply use the scheme shown by flow path No. 1, with water being taken from a well, sterilized by chlorination and pumped directly to the distribution system. Most systems like this are small and often operate with only part-time surveillance. Each state is responsible for reviewing the quality of the water both chemically and bacteriologically. In some cases with this scheme a chemical such as polyphosphate may be applied for final stabilization to minimize either scale or corrosion. If the water is undesirable for household use, the individual homeowner then has the responsibility of meeting his own needs by installing a zeolite water softener or an activated carbon filter.

The second flow path shows only the addition of a filtering system. In some old plants, the slow sand filter is still used for this purpose. The rapid sand filter is now more commonly used. Because the sand filter is limited in its ability to handle suspended solids, this system is usually applied only to impounded waters of excellent quality where post-chlorination can assure a safe potable water. The filter may also be installed to clarify shallow well water where suspended iron may be an occasional problem. There are risks in this kind of system, however, because the filter does no more than remove suspended solids, which are seldom the only problem with a raw water supply.

The third flow path shows the addition of an aerator prior to the filter for

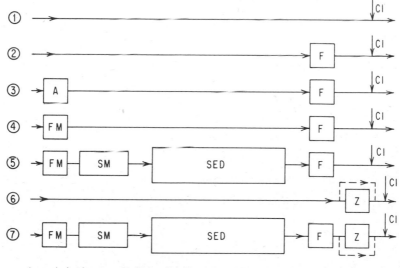

Legend: A – Aerator, F – Filter, FM – Fast mix, SM – Slow mix, SED – Sedimentation basin, Z – Zeolite, Cl – Chlorination

Figure 35.1 Simplified schematic of municipal water treatment flowsheets.

removal of tastes and odors and for oxidation of iron. Usually this is followed by lime for pH increase to about 8.0–8.5, and a flocculant, since the iron precipitate is usually colloidal.

In modern practice, the minimum equipment is usually considered to be that shown by flow path No. 4, and this is usually confined to impounded waters where there will be consistently low suspended solids depending on the seasonal presence of algae and where final disinfection can assure a safe finished water for the municipality.

In handling surface waters that contain significant suspended solids, the fast mix devices of flow path No. 4 are followed by a slow mix flocculator and a sedimentation basin in flow path No. 5, providing the detention for settling of most of the flocculated solids so that the load on the filter is measurably reduced. The detention can also provide for disinfection of raw water, with chlorine being added with or ahead of the coagulation chemicals to relieve the final chlorine demand. The prechlorination step may also improve flocculation by destroying some organic contaminants. This also keeps the settled solids from becoming septic and rising to the surface as gas forms.

In some cases where the water is already clear, the major problem may be caused by calcium and magnesium. In flow path No. 6, this water is softened through zeolite softeners. Some of the water is bypassed so that the effluent may have a hardness controlled at 100–150 mg/l. Often the cost of municipal zeolite softening is more than paid for by the savings to the individual homeowner in areas where the water is so hard that most of the homes would be provided with individual zeolite units. A side benefit is reduced discharge of regenerant brine by the more efficient municipal plant.

The final flow pattern No. 7 includes not only clarification of the surface water, but also final softening by passing a portion of the effluent through a zeolite unit. In this scheme, the sedimentation tank may provide for lime softening as well as clarification, to reduce the load on the zeolite unit.

There are various other combinations of individual treatment processes incorporated into an overall treatment scheme, but the principles are generally little different from those illustrated.

Several municipal water treatment schemes are described below, with a tabulation of water quality and a line diagram of each system.

Case History—Topeka, Kansas (Figure 35.2)

The Topeka water department has demonstrated the value of continuing research in improving water treatment results. Lengthy investigations on the bench and in the plant have produced significant changes in the process for treating the Kansas River water.

The Kansas River, though largely impounded, experiences significant variations in silt content. This previously caused plant upsets and large variations in chemical consumption for clarification, softening, and precipitation. After studying various approaches to reducing high raw water turbidities, the Topeka water department installed a large presedimentation basin. This basin utilizes a cationic polymer coagulant to remove the incoming silt, allowing its return to the river in a natural state. The significance of this pretreatment shows in reduced chemical usage and sludge production (Figure 35.3). A reduction in the noncarbonate hardness will reduce soda ash requirements correspondingly. Table 35.3 shows raw and finished water analyses.

Case History—Park Forest, Illinois (Figure 35.4)

The village of Park Forest, Illinois, produces potable water in a plant utilizing precipitation softening in conjunction with zeolite softening to give a stable,

Figure 35.2   Topeka, Kansas, process flowsheet.

moderately soft water. In the process, hard well water is first aerated to drive off dissolved CO_2 and reduce lime demand. As the water flows to two sludge blanket softeners, lime and liquid sodium aluminate are added for softening and clarification. The softened water, unstable at this point, is recarbonated with CO_2. Phosphate is also added to stabilize the water and prevent scale formation in the system. Following rapid sand filtration, a portion of the water is softened further by sodium zeolite. The two water streams are then blended to give the desired finished water characteristics (Table 35.4). Chlorine and fluoride are added before entering the distribution system. Relatively simple control is possible with this system due to the uniformity of the well water supply with regard to both mineral content and temperature.

Case History—Daytona Beach, Florida (Figure 35.5)

The Daytona Beach water plant uses lime softening to treat a ground water supply for potable use. Lime and chlorine are applied to the raw water along with a controlled return of filter backwash water. The backwash water helps seed the softening process. A high molecular weight anionic flocculant is used to

Figure 35.3   Chlorine dosage as influenced by turbidity and pretreatment program.

TABLE 35.3 Typical Water Characteristics—Topeka, Kansas

	Original process*				Present process			
River turbidity (JTU)	190	605	1020	2000	190	605	1020	2000
River color, APHA	4	5	6	10	4	5	6	10
Polymer, mg/l					1	3	2	4
Presedimentation turbidity	160	370	520	600	13	13	36	40
Primary alum, mg/l	15	27	27	30				3
Activated silica, mg/l	2	2	2	2				2
1st sed. turbidity	3	9	10	20	1	1	2	2
1st sed. color	2	3	3	5	1	1	1	1
Prechlorine, mg/l	7.8	14.4	16.8	21.6	5.4	5.4	6.0	7.2
Post-chlorine, mg/l	1.9	2.8	2.6	2.0	1.4	1.6	1.4	1.2
Hardness								
Raw water, mg/l			129				129	
Finished water, mg/l			156				118	

* Step-wise additions to the plant made it possible to compare these processes under identical inlet conditions.

improve settling. This method replaced the previous use of alum and activated silica because it resulted in lower cost and reduced sludge volume (Table 35.5).

Case History—Niagara Falls, New York (Figure 35.6)

The Niagara Falls, New York, water plant is a conventional clarification plant, typical of those designed to treat low turbidity water sources, such as lake or reservoir supplies. The Niagara River receives low turbidity water from Lake Erie. To minimize sludge production, instead of adding alum alone to form the typical large floc structure, the plant restricts the alum dosage to that needed to form a tiny pinpoint floc. The object is to make the solids filterable, not necessarily settleable. A typical dosage is 2–4 mg/l alum and 0.25–0.5 mg/l polymer coagulant. When the plant operates on alum alone, the dosage is 8–12 mg/l. Filter runs of 50–72 hours are achieved with either program. Floc penetration and solids loading on the filters are greater with alum-polymer than with alum alone, but total sludge volume is less (Table 35.6).

Case History—San Diego, California (Figure 35.7)

San Diego's municipal water is produced by three plants of conventional design. These treat Colorado River water drawn from impoundments which also receive runoff from the local watershed (Table 35.7). Although there are seasonal changes in composition, on a daily basis the raw water is relatively consistent in quality, with the only major variation being temperature. Periodically, copper sulfate is used for algae control in the reservoirs.

Figure 35.4 Park Forest, Illinois, process flowsheet.

TABLE 35.4 Typical Water Characteristics—Park Forest, Illinois

| | Hardness (mg/l, as $CaCO_3$) | | | Alkalinity | | | Dissolved | |
	Ca	Mg	Total	P	M	O	solids	pH
Well water	256	232	488	0	360		630	7.1
Precipitation softened	70	170	240	48	90	6	351	9.8
Zeolite softened			6	0	86		405	8.4
Finished blend	36	100	136	0	80		370	8.1

WATER TREATMENT PLANT BY-PRODUCT DISPOSAL

In the water treatment process, by-product solids produced by the removal of contaminants from the raw water become a secondary disposal problem. To minimize the costs of sludge handling, the volume of sludge produced should be reduced as much as practicable.

Reduction of the weight of solids removed from the raw water is impossible, of course, if the quality goals are to be achieved. Any weight reduction then must come from the reduction of chemicals added for coagulation and floc formation. In addition to this weight reduction, the type of sludge produced should be controlled, if possible, to produce a minimum volume, and to yield a compact sludge that is easy to dewater and dispose of. In general, this may be accomplished by reduction or elimination of inorganic salts which tend to produce a light, fluffy sludge not readily dewatered. This may require partial or complete replacement of the metal salt by organic polymers. In many cases, the addition of a clay nucleating agent allows the complete replacement of the salt, producing an easily dewatered sludge suitable for direct landfill.

Where possible, low turbidity water should be clarified by filtration processes rather than coagulation/sedimentation processes. This may significantly reduce the amount of sludge produced while maintaining water quality. Many plants with low raw water turbidity practicing conventional coagulation/sedimentation processes apply chemical solids that far exceed the amount of suspended solids present in the raw water to be clarified.

Sludge from precipitation softening processes usually cannot be reduced significantly in weight, since they are primarily a result of the insolubilization of dissolved hardness rather than the addition of unnecessary chemicals. Where softening is achieved by ion exchange, it is possible to reclaim the salt values from spent regeneration solutions while producing a solid waste consisting of calcium and magnesium salts. The recycled salt brine can then be used for subsequent regeneration.

Once the water treatment chemistry has been investigated to determine the optimum process producing the least amount of by-product sludge, consideration then focuses on the type of disposal process needed to handle the solids. Where applicable, the potential use of by-product material by a local industry

Figure 35.5 Daytona Beach, Florida, process flowsheet.

TABLE 35.5   Typical Water Characteristics—Daytona Beach, Florida

	Raw	Finished
Alkalinity (as $CaCO_3$)	290	42
Total Hardness (as $CaCO_3$)	324	74
Calcium Hardness (as $CaCO_3$)	287	42
Magnesium Hardness (as $CaCO_3$)	37	32
CO_2	30	
pH	7.35	8.9
Temperature, °C	23	23

should be considered. This may include such diverse activities as brick manufacturing, wallboard production and agriculture. The alkali value of lime sludge may be valuable to neutralize acidic wastes, such as pickle liquor in a steel mill. Finding practical uses for sludge not only reduces the sludge handling cost, but also eliminates the need for landfill of the solid material.

Disposal of sludge by retention in sludge lagoons appears, at first, to be the obvious solution to a sludge disposal problem. Unfortunately, this often is simply a delaying process. Ultimately, the sludge must again be handled if the lagoon must be reclaimed. Lagoons may provide interim storage for a dewatering system which continuously withdraws sludge from the lagoon at a controlled rate, optimizing the design of the dewatering device. This also provides a means to completely flush sedimentation basins in older plants not equipped for continuous sludge withdrawal. Where land is readily available, sludge lagoons may provide an economical method of sludge drying, providing the lagoon depth is not excessive and climatic conditions are favorable.

Sand drying beds have proven acceptable for dewatering water plant sludges. In warmer climates, they may be used year around; in cold climates, the sand beds are usually used in summer to dewater sludge accumulated throughout the year. Coupled with high-molecular weight flocculants, sand bed dewatering provides a practical, inexpensive method of sludge dewatering. It requires little attention by operators and consumes very little energy. Sludge harvesting methods should be considered in designing the beds so that mechanical equipment can be used.

Dewatering by centrifugation has gained popularity due to the compact nature of the equipment and its ability to be operated with relatively little operator attention. Special attention must be given to the details of equipment design to minimize internal abrasion by grit, which leads to costly maintenance. This equipment is able to handle wide variations in feed solids without significant upsets in production.

While vacuum filters have been investigated by some plants, there does not appear to be a widespread use of this equipment to dewater water clarification sludges.

Figure 35.6   Niagara Falls, New York, process flowsheet.

TABLE 35.6   Typical Water Characteristics—Niagara Falls, New York

	Turbidity	pH	M alkalinity	Total hardness
Raw	3	8.3	92	132
Finished	<.3	7.6	90	132

Figure 35.7   San Diego, California, process flowsheet.

TABLE 35.7   Typical Water Characteristics—San Diego, California

	JTU	Alkalinity	Hardness	pH
Raw water	2.0	119	332	8.1
Finished water	0.2	120	338	8.2

The plate and frame filter press has been successfully adapted to dewatering municipal water plant sludge. To properly assess this process, both capital and operational costs must be compared to the alternative methods. In some cases, very high doses of filler, such as diatomaceous earth, lime or fly ash, have been required to produce an acceptable cake. Early designs required considerable manpower per unit of dry cake production, but newer designs have improved upon this.

The belt press includes several varieties of designs of screens or cloths on a conveyor device to reduce sludge volume. Often the solids are discharged as a paste. In some cases, additional stages use press rolls to squeeze out more water and produce a more concentrated cake for disposal.

Filter backwash water, containing relatively little solids, requires separate treatment. In many cases it is possible to simply pump the backwash water directly to the head of the plant without upsetting the normal clarification process. To facilitate this, it is desirable to add a cationic polymer coagulant directly to the recycle stream during the time the backwash waste is being returned. This agglomerates the solids and prevents them from upsetting the clarification process. The backwash flow rate is often so high that direct return to the sedimentation basin may create a momentary overload. This can be controlled by an intermediate equalizing basin. Where sedimentation basins are not employed, the use of decant tanks to concentrate the sludge, followed by sand bed dewatering, should prove adequate.

SUGGESTED READING

American Water Works Association: *Water Quality & Treatment,* 3d ed., McGraw-Hill, 1971.

Chapter 36

Municipal Sewage Treatment

While municipal sewage treatment is a well-established practice, it is an area of water treatment experiencing revolutionary changes because of increasingly stringent effluent quality limitations and the potential value of treated effluent as a source of water for industry, agriculture and municipalities. Until a few years ago, plants were designed to remove 30–40% of the undesirable impurities before discharge into the receiving body of water. There were no real limits on effluent quality as long as the discharge was chlorinated and met bacterial count standards. Municipal sewage plant operators had only minimal training, but, fortunately, many of them were able to learn from experience and became knowledgeable in their plants' operations. With the growing sophistication of modern plants designed to meet stringent goals, training programs in sewage plant operation have become available to supplement on-the-job training for upgrading personnel.

Sewage treatment refers to the processing of primarily domestic sewage produced by typical community and household activities. In rural areas the characteristics of raw sewage tend to adhere to this definition. As cities become larger and more industrialized, the waste volume and characteristics of one particular industry may affect sewage composition. In addition, sewage may be from combined or separate sanitary sewer systems. With combined systems, storm water drains into the sewer lines to become part of the total flow to the sewage treatment plant. Such uncontrolled surges in flow can be very disruptive to the process of sewage treatment, severely limiting the plant's ability to remove pollutants. Future practice aims toward segregating storm water flow in sewer systems separate from those used to collect sanitary waste. This will materially reduce and control the flow entering the treatment plant, thereby increasing its ability to maintain adequate treatment. Storm water retention basins are being built in many cities to even out the severe surges caused by storm water, allowing a more reasonable chance of processing the extra volume.

Figure 36.1 Diurnal variation in sewage flow.

Even with storm water segregation, it appears that the treatment of storm water itself to remove undesirable contaminants may become a requirement for many areas. This is due to its sudden detrimental effect on the receiving streams. In densely populated and highly industrialized areas, storm water may be more polluted than domestic sewage.

Because sewage flow patterns are directly related to residential water use, there are wide variations in inflow during the day, the week, and even the season. Figure 36.1 indicates the degree of variation throughout the day caused by typical residential use patterns. During the week, flows will vary due to other factors, such as the traditional Monday washday. Seasonal variations also affect separate sanitary sewers due to the impact of storm water caused by damaged sewer pipe (infiltration), and sump pump operation. While combined sewer systems are mostly influenced by sudden downpours (inflow), separate systems are affected over a broader period of time due to the slower drainage of water from the saturated soil. After a considerable dry spell, the soil acts as a sponge, reducing the impact of short infrequent showers.

EFFLUENT STANDARDS

The establishment and enforcement of effluent regulations has progressed rapidly as a result of the Clean Water Act (Public Law 92–500). Just as each industrial plant outfall has its National Pollution Discharge Elimination System (NPDES) permit, so do municipal plants. All municipal plants must practice a minimum of secondary sewage treatment prior to discharge into receiving streams. Secondary treatment restricts the effluent to 30 mg/l suspended solids and 30 mg/l BOD, and requires that it be chlorinated to destroy pathogens. While this standard may require some years to achieve, it provides an immediate objective to design engineers upgrading existing plants and installing facilities where none presently exist.

For many waterways, additional, more restrictive standards are imposed due to the particular needs of the receiving stream, defined by its category of usage. A stream used only for navigational purposes may not require elaborate treatment of waste discharges. On the other hand, a receiving body of water used as a source of potable water or for swimming may have very restrictive effluent standards. Regional and local regulations may increase in importance as the Environmental Protection Agency reviews the receiving waters and classifies them based on present and future needs. Some streams may periodically fail to meet the stream standards set for them, usually in temperature, dissolved oxygen, BOD and suspended solids. These streams are termed "quality limited."

A plant discharging into a quality limited stream may be required to produce a better effluent than the typical industry standard.

In some cases, the sewage plant effluent may become high enough in quality to permit recycling into the municipal water supply system for reuse. When this is done, safeguards must be instituted to protect the public health. In many cases, sewage plant effluent is used for irrigation of parks, roadways, and agricultural areas because of its nutrient value, further reducing the impact on a receiving stream.

TYPICAL WASTEWATER TREATMENT PROCESSES

Wastewater treatment practices vary in the type of equipment used and in treatment sequences. Most plants fall into a few basic categories, as shown by the simplified flow sheets in Figure 36.2. While these flow sheets show the basic unit operations that make up the total process, they do not include supplemental treatments such as ammonia stripping or selective ion exchange. These additional processes develop from individual plant needs related to sewage characteristics and flow and the effluent limitations to be met. Since the Clean Water Act requires all plants to practice secondary treatment, only those treatment schemes that include secondary treatment are shown. Stabilization ponds, which provide treatment for smaller municipalities, are omitted. Here, the wastewater is contained in a pond for long periods of time during which useful bacteria and algae consume undesirable pollutants. Shown are the most common unit processes of sewage treatment in municipal plants.

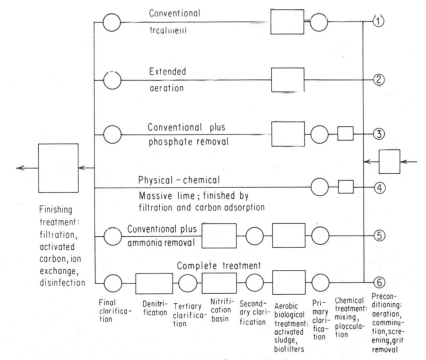

Figure 36.2 Typical processes available for municipal sewage treatment.

Pretreatment

Pretreatment of sewage consists of screening to remove larger solids; or comminution, to shred debris. This is followed by grit removal to settle out the heavy grit particles. Often the waste is pre-aerated, to add dissolved oxygen to the wastewater stream and prevent the odors of anaerobic decomposition.

Extended Aeration

This process takes raw sewage directly into an aerated mix tank for eight hours or more to provide bacteria with optimum conditions to consume the BOD present in the wastewater. The effluent from this mix tank goes to a sedimentation tank where the flocculated colonies of organisms are settled to produce a clear overflow. A portion of the settled microbial floc is returned to the headworks and a portion sent to sludge disposal. The clear effluent is then directed to final treatment such as disinfection, perhaps passing through a final polishing filter. This method of treatment is particularly suited to plants that have a low concentration of settleable solids in the raw sewage. It minimizes the number of unit operations involved in smaller plants.

Conventional Primary-Secondary Treatment

In this process, used by most plants in the United States, the raw waste is first directed to a primary clarifier where settleable solids are removed, reducing the load on subsequent treatment units. Colloidal solids and soluble BOD then leave the primary clarifier for the secondary portion of the plant. This secondary unit may be either a trickling filter or, more commonly, an activated sludge basin. Other devices having fixed position bacterial slime in contact with flowing sewage are similar to trickling filters. These include packed beds and rotating disk media. As in all activated sludge processes, the organisms consume biodegradable organics. After a period of time the organisms and wastewater flow on to the clarifier for separation; with the activated sludge processes, the sludge organisms are returned to the head of the secondary system and a portion wasted to sludge processing. The effluent then goes to final treatment for disinfection and perhaps filtration.

Secondary Treatment with Nitrification

The early stages of this process are similar to conventional secondary treatment. The later stage, nitrification, is the process of converting ammonia and nitrite to nitrate. This is usually done in a separate biological reactor before final clarification. Nitrification may occur in a suspended biological reactor containing specific organisms that use ammonia and nitrite in their metabolism. Following nitrification, a clarifier settles and returns the biological solids to the preceding unit to maintain the nitrification organisms at the proper activity level. Waste sludge is disposed to sludge processing. Disinfection and filtration may also be utilized. Reducing the levels of ammonia and nitrite produces an effluent more compatible to the aquatic life in the receiving stream.

Nitrification/Dentrification

In this process, a continuation of the previous process, nitrates are converted to molecular nitrogen by means of still another biological reactor. This reactor contains organisms that can utilize the combined oxygen from the nitrates and release nitrogen gas. Following clarification the organisms may or may not be returned to the biological reactor depending on the process used. Final filtration and disinfection are utilized as before. The removal of nitrogen can reduce the potential for algal blooms in the receiving water if nitrogen is the limiting nutrient.

Physical-Chemical Treatment

In this process, raw sewage is taken into a rapid mix and flocculation zone where a large dosage of chemicals is added to produce massive chemical coagulation and flocculation. Lime is commonly applied to achieve maximum absorption of impurities in the flocculation process. Following a clarifier to remove the precipitated and coagulated solids, the waste water is filtered to remove residual suspended solids prior to entering a carbon adsorption column. The carbon adsorption column reduces residual organics to a low level. Following this, the effluent is disinfected before entering the receiving stream. In some cases the lime-treated effluent is air stripped of free ammonia before entering subsequent stages in the process. This process is effective where significant amounts of organics can be settled ahead of the carbon bed.

Nutrient Removal

Removal of nutrient usually refers to phosphorus, but may include nitrogen. The objective is to reduce the content to a level that will inhibit eutrophication of the receiving body of water. It has been determined that when either nitrogen or phosphorus is reduced to low levels, algae growth can be controlled to prevent the massive algal blooms that give rise to eutrophication. A study may be necessary to determine which nutrient is limiting, reducing the cost of waste treatment, since only that nutrient need be removed.

Phosphorus is removed by precipitation with calcium at high pH to precipitate calcium phosphate, or with aluminum or iron salts to precipitate phosphorus as the metal phosphate. In either case, phosphorus can be removed to a level preventing troublesome amounts from entering the receiving stream. Consideration must be given to the form of phosphate present in the wastewater. Phosphorus in the orthophosphate form reacts completely with the precipitant; polyphosphate is not completely removed. Some plants have been provided with clarifiers specifically designed for the purpose of precipitating phosphorus, though this often is unnecessary. Where lime treatment is used, it may be added to the primary clarifier if sufficient flocculation time is available to complete the chemical reactions.

Underflow pumps must be sized so that the solids precipitated may be removed effectively from the primary clarifier. Metal salts may be added either ahead of the primary clarifier or into the activated sludge tank prior to its discharge into the biological clarifier. The contained metal hydroxide and metal phosphate sludge does not inhibit biological reactions, providing the pH is in the 7–10 range.

The most efficient performance of metal salts is usually in the activated sludge tanks, where polyphosphate has had time for conversion to the ortho form. Regardless of the chemical used or selection of a reaction site, it is helpful to add an anionic polymer flocculant to the stream as it enters the clarifier for more complete removal of suspended materials and reduction of chemical dosage for effective clarification. This will minimize the volume of waste chemical sludge generated. Without anionic flocculants, significantly more metal salt is required to achieve acceptable results.

Ammonia removal may be practiced by nitrification/denitrification. Other ways to remove ammonia nitrogen include: lime treatment to achieve a high pH followed by air stripping of the ammonia from the waste stream; and ion exchange, where the stream is passed through a bed of clinoptilolite clay, which has a specific affinity for ammonia.

(a)

(b)

Figure 36.3 (a) South Buffalo creek—original flowsheet. (b) Current flowsheet showing improvements in basic process and addition of tertiary treatment.

DISINFECTION

While disinfection may take various forms, chlorine application to a detention basin providing at least 15 minutes reaction time has usually been used for this purpose. In some cases, dechlorination may follow to remove any trace amounts of residual chlorine that might be toxic to stream organisms. Because of concern for the production of chlorinated organics, which might also be toxic, other methods of disinfection are gaining popularity. Ozonation is becoming more practical as improvements in equipment design continue to reduce costs. Further research is needed to define the potential hazards of byproducts of the oxidation of organic materials with chlorine and ozone.

Several plants shown in Figures 36.3 and 36.4 are examples of conventional systems which were upgraded to meet increasingly stringent effluent quality goals.

PLANT PROCESS CHANGES CAUSED BY GROWTH AND INDUSTRIALIZATION

The South Buffalo Creek treatment plant in Greensboro, N.C. (Figure 36.3a) is an example of the impact of industrial and urban growth on both plant size and preferred treatment processes. When originally designed in the early 1930's, domestic sewage was by far the largest portion of the raw sewage. The design flow of 3.25 mgd (8.5 m³/min) was sufficient for an ultimate population of 37,000. The plant performance was adequate during the next few years with 90% BOD removal. By the late 50's industrial discharges had begun to change the character of the raw waste. The industries discharging to the system included textile, meat packing, chemical processing, poultry processing and metal plating. By the mid-60's the industrial BOD contribution had risen to over 65%. Although treatment plant improvements had been made, they were generally expansions of existing equipment. In the mid-60's, a major change in the method of treatment was initiated. This included conversion of trickling filters to activated sludge aeration basins. However, some of the trickling filters were retained

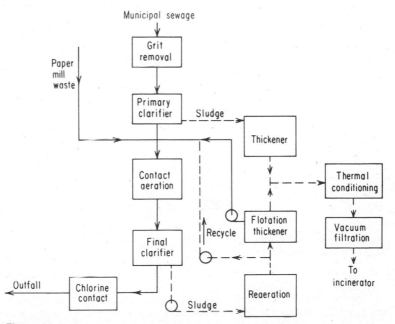

Figure 36.4 Joint municipal-industrial waste treatment facility at Green Bay, Wisconsin.

to serve as roughing filters ahead of the activated sludge basins. This allowed more effective handling of load surges and also protected the activated sludge organisms critical to effective plant performance. By these changes, plant efficiency of 70% BOD removal was increased above 90% again.

Additional plant improvements (Figure 36.3b) will achieve the increased removal efficiencies required for local stream standards while at the same time improving odor control around the plant. Effluent BOD of 15 mg/l and suspended solids of 10 mg/l represent over 98% removal. Phosphorus removal is also practiced.

This is a rather typical case history as it illustrates the steady growth in water consumption, the continual improvements required to meet new standards and the relatively long time needed to implement changes because of problems of funding, design and construction.

MUNICIPALITY AND INDUSTRY JOIN FORCES TO TREAT WASTES MORE ECONOMICALLY

In Green Bay, Wisconsin, the cooperation and planning of industry and government has produced a unique municipal-industrial waste treatment plant. In working out the project, the Green Bay Metropolitan Sewerage District and two paper mills found that it was less expensive and more efficient to treat a complex combined waste than the separate individual plant wastes. In the process (Figure 36.4), the municipal and paper mill wastes are collected and proportioned into the plant process by separate pumping systems. The municipal wastes undergo preliminary treatment to remove grit and settleable solids before entering the secondary treatment phase. Mill wastes, however, do not contain appreciable settleable material so they go directly to secondary treatment. Hydraulic design for the plant is based on a nominal flow of 52 mgd (137 m³/min) with a peak flow of 172 mgd (450 m³/min). To treat this complex and variable waste, the process flow sheet was kept as flexible as possible. The plant can segregate the secondary portion into four separate treatment systems. While the contact stabilization process was chosen for its adaptability to the anticipated changes, the contact basin can receive feed in either slug flow, step feed or complete mix modes. The flows within the plant are monitored and can be proportioned by a computer in the main control room.

Nutrient removal is practiced by using alum and anionic flocculant for optimum settling. While phosphorus nutrient should generally be available somewhat in excess of that required for biological metabolism, provisions were made to allow phosphorus addition if required due to the nutrient-deficient nature of the paper mill wastes.

Excess activated sludge from the plant is thickened by air flotation and then thermally conditioned to give a sterilized sludge. Currently, this sludge is vacuum filtered and incinerated, producing steam from a waste heat boiler. The sludge may also be disposed of on land depending on prevailing conditions.

SEWAGE PLANT EFFLUENT IS FED TO WATER FACTORY 21

An example of more complete purification of municipal wastewater is found in Orange County, California, Water Factory 21. This easily expandable plant combines physical/chemical treated sewage with desalted ocean water to give a high quality product water. This is used as injection water, both to prevent sea water intrusion and to recharge the ground water aquifer.

In this plant, the first step is treatment of the secondary effluent of the Orange

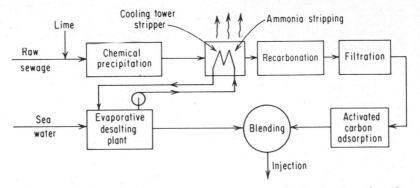

Figure 36.5 Combined tertiary sewage treatment and desalination plant for underground injection at Orange County, California.

County Sanitation District. The process (Figure 36.5) involves chemical clarification with lime to precipitate solids and to liberate ammonia-nitrogen, which is then air stripped. The stripping towers were designed to enhance the removal of ammonia and also provide cooling for the adjacent desalting plant. The absorbed heat improves ammonia stripping efficiency.

Following ammonia stripping and recarbonation, the wastewater is filtered prior to entering carbon absorption columns. The water is then chlorinated to produce a water acceptable for drinking, although it is high in dissolved solids. To remedy this deficiency the water factory also processes an equal amount of sea water using an advanced vertical tube evaporator. The desalted water is also of excellent quality except for its corrosive character due to very low dissolved solids and lack of hardness. When blended (see Table 36.1) the two streams produce a water that is acceptable for drinking at a cost comparable to development of natural water sources.

TABLE 36.1 Quality of Reclaimed Wastewater in Orange County, California

	Concentrations, mg/l			
Constituent	Wastewater before treatment	Reclamation plant product	Desalted seawater	Blended product water
Total dissolved solids	1300	1100	25	540
Total hardness	400	200	1	110
Sodium	220	220	7	110
Sulfate	250	250	1	125
Chloride	240	240	10	120

SOURCE: Courtney R. Chandler, "Water Factory 21," *NWSA Journal,* July 1974, p. 26.

When further expanded to full capacity this facility will provide the flow of water necessary to maintain an effective hydraulic barrier against seawater intrusion.

WORLD'S LARGEST TREATMENT PLANT

The largest sewage treatment plant in the world is the West-Southwest plant of the Chicago, Illinois, Metropolitan Sanitary District with a capacity of 1.44 bgd (3800 m³/min). This plant processes its own sludge plus that produced at another

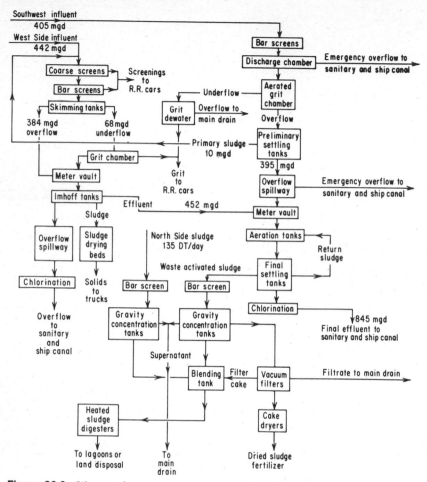

Figure 36.6 West southwest sewage treatment plant of the Metropolitan Sanitary District of Greater Chicago—schematic of wastewater flow.

location. The flow diagram for this plant is shown in Figure 36.6. Table 36.2 compares certain characteristics of Chicago's municipal water supply, which originates in Lake Michigan, and the sewage plant effluent. The treated effluent discharges to the sanitary and barge canal, which joins the Des Plaines River, which eventually drains into the Mississippi River.

The Metropolitan Sanitary District of Greater Chicago (MSDGC) has undertaken an extensive strip mine reclamation project in north-central Illinois using waste sludge from the West-Southwest plant. This project has significantly advanced the knowledge of land applications of municipal sewage sludge.

The MSDGC has also moved forward in the area of storm water retention by designing an extensive network of large diameter collection mains under the city. These tunnels are to store runoff during rain to be pumped later for processing in the existing treatment facilities.

TABLE 36.2 Water Quality Changes from Urban Use

Constituents	Chicago tap water	Raw sewage*	Final effluent*
Total solids, mg/l	164	644	
Suspended solids	Nil	294	9.0
BOD		181	7.0
Ammonia nitrogen		6.8	1.8
Oil/grease, hexane soluble		60	19
pH	7.8	7.3	7.6

* Averages for December 1976.

BY-PRODUCT WASTES

In the treatment of municipal wastewater, some contaminants are actually consumed, but a significant portion simply are converted to solid wastes. When they are removed from the water, they become by-product sludge, which must be disposed of.

The first step in disposal is to stabilize the sludge to eliminate odors and pathogenic organisms. Most plants use aerobic or anaerobic digesters to accomplish this. Following stabilization, the sludge is concentrated and dewatered prior to final disposal in a landfill or by incineration. New processes are being continually investigated to use this waste sludge. It has been used for years as a lawn and agricultural soil supplement. It also finds use as a fuel and as a raw material for conversion to activated carbon.

Sludge is often concentrated before dewatering to permit more efficient utilization of the final dewatering equipment. This is particularly true in the case of waste activated sludge, which may contain only 0.5–1.5% solids. The position of the sludge concentrator will vary, though when used to concentrate waste activated sludge, it is generally ahead of the digester to provide a concentrated feed. In some cases this is the final sludge processing step prior to landfill of digested sludge where the higher moisture does not represent significant haulage costs. The equipment used may vary greatly from plant to plant, though it would be one of the following:

Thickeners The common thickener is a gravity sedimentation tank with very slowly moving rakes surmounted by pickets. Sludge is fed to a centerwell and the movement of the pickets assists in sludge compaction. The purpose is to increase sludge density, thereby minimizing sludge volume and increasing detention in the sludge digester. Usually the thickener is used to densify activated sludge prior to digestion. Thickeners can be very troublesome because the overflow goes back to the primary, and is often the largest source of solids fed to the primary clarifier. The thickener is likely to carry over badly if there are unusual temperature changes or if the sludge becomes septic and floats because of gasification. Chemical treatment is often helpful in controlling solids carryover.

Elutriation This sludge washing process is sometimes used to reduce the ammonia and organic content of the sludge to increase the effectiveness of chemicals used for subsequent dewatering. Sludge passes in one direction through two stages of thickeners, with final effluent moving in the opposite direction to wash it. About 1–2 parts of washwater are mixed with one part of sludge in each thickener, and the sludge is settled before passing on to the next unit.

Flotation This process is an improvement over gravity thickening because it provides a greater difference in density between water and rising air-entrained sludge than is usually possible between water and sinking sludge floc. Usually final effluent is pressurized with air at 60–75 psi (4.2–5.3 kg/cm²) and then mixed with sludge.

Pressure on the mixture is suddenly released, allowing minute air bubbles to attach to the sludge particles and cause them to rise as a blanket of froth. The froth is scraped from the surface, flows down a ramp, and is then pumped at 4–6% solids to the digester or directly to a dewatering system. Chemicals aid in forming a cohesive froth and in improving the quality of the separated water, which is returned to the headworks.

Drainage Concentrators   There are two types of equipment available in this area. One is a twin-drum type unit with sludge fed to the inside allowing water to drain through a cloth covering on the drum. Others are simple top-loaded belt screens which allow drainage of water by gravity, later assisted by pressure rolls.

Digester   Digestion applies to the bacterial system of sludge destruction, traditionally anaerobic sludge digestion, although there is a growing use of aerobic sludge digesters because they usually have fewer operating problems. In many cases, though, aerobic digesters produce a very thin sludge (less than 1% solids), which is hard to dispose of. The anaerobic digester is a large fermentation vat. Several units may be used for flexibility and to keep within practical size limits. The digester stores and ferments sludge during an approximately 30-day detention period, and yields a stabilized sludge—that is, it will no longer support active bacterial growth, so odor-production is negligible.

Anaerobic digested sludge is drawn off periodically for final disposal, generally at a concentration of 4–7% solids. The sludge is almost black and has a musty or earthy odor. The anaerobic activity generates gas, a mixture chiefly of ammonia (NH_3), methane (CH_4), carbon dioxide (CO_2), and some sulfide (H_2S). This combustible gas is burned in furnaces to heat sludge recirculated through the furnace from the digester. In some plants this is an indirect exchange of heat, the fuel heating water in a closed loop, which in turn heats the sludge. This maintains the anaerobic process at optimum temperature—usually about 90°F (32°C). To maintain a uniform temperature, the digester must be insulated.

Some systems use several digesters in series, the first unit operated at 90°F (32°C) and actively undergoing digestion and the secondary unit operating at ambient temperature, usually 70–80°F (21–27°C), so that the sludge no longer ferments thus allowing clearer separation of sludge and supernatant.

As fresh sludge is fed to the digester, to make room for it, thickened digested sludge is withdrawn for disposal and supernatant must also be drawn off. The drawdown of supernatant is usually returned to the raw sewage line intermittently. The supernatant contains a high level of suspended solids and is also highly alkaline, since digestion produces NH_3 and CO_2 which form NH_4HCO_3, producing an alkalinity of 1200–1500 mg/l. Therefore, this intermittent return of highly alkaline supernatant can be a disruptive factor in a good chemical coagulation program in the primary clarifier.

Vacuum Filter   This consists of a vat, which receives the sludge feed, and a horizontal drum with a filtering surface partially submerged in the sludge. An internal piping system draws filtrate through the filter surface and discharges it to a receiver and then draws air through the cake formed on the filter surface. A "doctor blade" or similar device scrapes, blows, or otherwise disengages the cake from the drum and onto a conveyor. Considerable art is involved in filter operation, usually requiring an operator to be on hand at all times for adjustment as sludge density or quality changes. Chemicals are usually required to properly condition the sludge for efficient vacuum filter operation.

A pretreatment device flocculates the sludge before it is fed to the filter vat or pan. Variables are many, including feed sludge density, sludge flow rate, drum submergence, drum speed, flocculating drum detention time and agitation, vat agitation, and vacuum. Filter cloth—including type of fabric and weave—is another variable, though not one that is readily changed. Chemicals are used to increase production, clarify filtrate, or increase cake solids. The filtrate returns to the headworks. Cake is disposed of by incineration or hauling, so maximum density is desired to reduce final disposal costs. The cake may contain as low as 14% solids (typical of thickened waste activated) to as much as 25% (typical of mixtures of primary and digested sludges). In smaller plants, filters may be operated intermittently, often only on the day shift.

Centrifuge   This dewatering device is generally a horizontal, solid bowl centrifugal separator operating at 1000–6000 rpm and having an internal screw conveyor (scroll) to separate and withdraw the centrifuged sludge from the slurry pool. Variables include bowl speed, differential speed between bowl and scroll, feed solids and flow rate, pool depth, and chemical application point. Chemicals needed to control both cake density and centrate clarity are fed internally through a special injection pipe or to the sludge feed itself or both. In small plants, centrifuges, like filters, may be operated only intermittently.

Roll Presses   Many of these units are primarily designed for sludge concentration. Some can be considered as dewatering devices due to their ability to provide cake solids in excess of 12–13%. This is done by a series of opposing rollers which squeeze additional moisture out of the cake.

Filter Presses   This equipment has demonstrated its ability to provide high solids cake. The sludge is processed through a series of plate-and-frame sections with filter cloth inserted over the plate. A filter aid such as lime or fly ash is used, and the sludge is pumped at 100–150 psi ($7–10.5$ kg/cm^2) until the frame is full of compressed cake. The plates and frames are then separated to allow the cake to fall out.

Sludge Beds   These are a series of rectangular earthen basins underlain with a tile collector, above which is a graded gravel drainage and collection layer 12 in. (30 cm) deep, topped by sand 9 in. (23 cm) deep. Sludge is applied by gravity, usually through a simple standpipe. The sludge fills the bed to a level of about 9–12 in. (23–30 cm) above the sand surface. After filling, the bed is quiescent until water drains into the underdrain system, usually 18–24 hours. Moisture then evaporates leaving a cracked surface within 3–4 weeks, depending on weather, sludge conditioning and initial sludge density. A relatively dry cake (24% solids) is finally harvested for disposal as land dressing. Chemical conditioning speeds drainage and facilitates drying, reducing time between harvesting. Sludge beds are used extensively by small plants.

SLUDGE DISPOSAL

Sludge disposal is becoming more important each year because of the amount of sludge generated by improved and expanded treatment processes. Many smaller towns simply pile the sludge near the plant and allow local residents to take it as a fertilizer. Some cities process the sludge to salable fertilizer. In an increasing number of cases, land is purchased for large scale disposal of sludge with the growing of crops being incidental to the operation. Long term effects on the soil must be studied for each new situation.

Many cities use incinerators to dispose of sludge generated from sewage. Sometimes sludge is combined with garbage for incineration. Because of energy considerations, emphasis is being placed on power generation in newer units.

Chapter **37**

Commercial, Institutional, and Residential Water Treatment

This chapter covers the special requirements in treating water for non-industrial facilities such as office buildings, hospitals, apartments, schools, universities, department store chains, hotels/motels, shopping centers, and commercial enterprises such as laundries. The systems in such establishments that require water treatment are heating, air conditioning, and domestic water.

In some respects the water problems encountered in buildings and institutions are similar to those in industrial plants. The consequences of improper water treatment may be even more critical to a hospital or apartment complex than to a large industrial plant, since human health and comfort may be at stake.

Designers of modern commercial, institutional, and residential facilities are well aware of the importance of water treatment. They provide sophisticated chemical feeding and control systems for these installations (Figure 37.1), which are designed to use the same kinds of chemicals as industrial systems. The operating personnel in charge are skilled in the operation of mechanical systems, and are well trained in proper chemical control testing.

Older, smaller facilities may lack good feed systems and skilled personnel. This requires some modification of the chemical program: simple feeders are devised to apply multipurpose chemical formulas, containing a variety of ingredients for controlling any of the problems that might be encountered (Figure 37.2).

HEATING SYSTEMS

Heating systems using water are of two basic designs: (1) steam boilers, and (2) hot water "boilers." Steam boilers are usually package-type firetube design operating at less than 150 psi (10 bars) (Figure 37.3).

These boilers are usually gas- or oil-fired, but occasionally an electrically heated boiler is found. Fuel oils can range from No. 2 to No. 6, including mix-

Figure 37.1 In most modern buildings, chemical treatment of water for heating or cooling is automated for simple, reliable control.

tures of several grades. Many boilers contain burners designed to burn either gas or fuel oil, a useful feature in areas where shortages of either fuel can occur. Coal-fired boilers in commercial buildings and institutions are rare.

In heating applications the steam generated in these boilers is used in one of two ways: (1) directly; i.e., circulated throughout the building, where the heat is

Figure 37.2 Where there are multiple units to be treated, a simple feeder charged with briquetted chemical is often more practical than individual mechanical feeders.

Figure 37.3 A typical packaged steam generator with complete fireside and waterside controls. *(Courtesy of Cleaver Brooks, division of Aqua-Chem, Inc.)*

extracted through radiators and the condensate is returned to the boiler to be used as feedwater; (2) indirectly; i.e., passed through a heat exchanger located relatively close to the boiler, with the condensate returning to the boiler. The other side of the heat exchanger is part of a closed heating water loop which extends throughout the building. The water heated by the steam is pumped around the loop, giving up its heat through radiators, mixing boxes and other types of heat exchangers.

The steam generated in these boilers can have other uses, such as humidification, dishwashing, food preparation, and sterilization in autoclaves (hospitals).

Chemical water treatment in these boilers is similar to that used in most industrial boilers. A careful study must be made of the uses to which the steam is put so that acceptable, safe treatment chemicals can be used. If any part of the steam contacts food, for example, FDA-approved chemicals must be used. If the steam is used for humidification, care must be taken that condensate corrosion inhibitors be safe and odor-free.

Scale, Corrosion, and Foam

The chemical products used should control scale, corrosion and foaming in the boiler, and corrosion in the condensate system. The types of products used are similar to those used in industrial systems; however, they are often blended and packaged so as to be convenient and easy to handle, feed and control.

Hot water "boilers" are really misnamed since they do not boil water and produce no steam. They heat water to 180–500°F (82–260°C) in a vessel almost identical to a steam boiler. The heated water is circulated through the building to various heat exchangers and radiators and back to the boiler.

In addition to hot water boilers, which use gas or fuel oil for heat, there are also electric boilers. These use either enclosed, clad type immersion heaters, or resistance heaters, which operate by a flow of current between electrodes in the boiler water, which is conductive because of its mineral content.

These systems are designed to be closed, so theoretically there should be no makeup water required, but normally a small amount is required to replace that lost by leakage of liquid or vapor. In these systems, the primary concern is prevention of corrosion. Scale formation, although not usually a major factor, can also occur in hot water boilers. This may be caused by a combination of high hardness water, used to fill the system initially and to provide makeup, and the high temperature of the boiler tube surfaces. The gradual accumulation of calcium and alkalinity precipitates $CaCO_3$.

In addition to corrosion and scaling, foaming can also occur. This can lead to severe cavitation-erosion in recirculating pump impellers, caused by the impingement of foam bubbles on the metal at high velocity. The preferred chemical treatment in hot water boilers is a borate/nitrite based product. Such products contain a mixture of corrosion inhibitors to protect steel, aluminum, copper, and admiralty; a scale control agent; and high and low temperature antifoams. This treatment is initially charged at high dosage levels for maximum protection. Since hot water boiler systems have little makeup and the chemicals are relatively stable, only small additions of treatment are required thereafter to maintain protection.

Occasionally, hot water systems require high makeup, caused by excessive leaks of water or vapor from the system. In some cases these systems are very extensive, such as in a university complex with a major portion of the system buried underground. This makes repair of leaks costly compared to the cost of makeup water, so the system has to be treated accordingly. Maintaining high level dosages of a borate/nitrite based inhibitor becomes prohibitive economically. Under these conditions less expensive treatments are used. These still provide acceptable protection, but need more attention for control of chemicals. Into this category fall sodium silicate treatments, combination hydrazine/amine programs and glassy phosphate treatments.

AIR CONDITIONING SYSTEMS

Most large buildings, shopping centers and similar installations use water-cooled air conditioning units. These fall into three categories:

Figure 37.4 Packaged water chiller, using a reciprocating-type compressor. *(Courtesy of The Trane Company.)*

Figure 37.5 A centrifugal-type compressor is used in this package refrigeration unit. *(Courtesy of The Trane Company.)*

1. Reciprocating compressor units, usually electrically driven and using Freon* as the refrigerant.

2. Centrifugal compressor units, driven by electric motor, steam turbine, or gas engine, also use Freon as refrigerant.

3. Absorption refrigeration units, in which the refrigerant (water) is absorbed in concentrated lithium bromide solution, and then evaporated by steam (Figure 37.6).

In the reciprocating and centrifugal systems, the hot compressed refrigerant vapor first passes through a water-cooled condenser (usually a shell-and-tube type heat exchanger) where it is cooled and condensed into a liquid. From there it passes into an evaporator (commonly called a chiller) where it expands under reduced pressure into a cool vapor. The vapor is used to extract heat and is then recompressed, repeating the cycle (Figure 37.7).

The water used to cool the refrigerant in the condenser is itself cooled in a typical cooling tower, and then recycled back to the condenser. Typically, water enters the condenser at 80–90°F (28–32°C), and leaves at 90–100°F (32–38°C). This is known as the open recirculating portion of the cooling water system, since the cooling tower is open to the atmosphere.

The evaporator, or chiller, also a shell-and-tube type heat exchanger, provides chilled water for air conditioning systems. When the condensed refrigerant leaves the condenser, it has been cooled, but is still at a high pressure. When it enters the tube side of the chiller, it expands to vapor in passing through an

* Registered trademark of the E. I. du Pont de Nemours & Co.

Figure 37.6 An absorption-type refrigeration system. *(Courtesy of The Trane Company.)*

orifice or valve into the low pressure (or suction) side of the cycle. The heat required for this vaporization is extracted from the relatively warm [55°F (13°C)] chilled water entering the shell side. This cools the chilled water to about 45°F (8°C) for circulation throughout the building to provide air conditioning. The air being cooled warms this water back to 55°F (13°C), for return to the chiller. The chilled water system is not open to the atmosphere, and is known as a closed recirculating system (Figure 37.8).

In simple terms, the heat within a building is absorbed by the chilled water,

Figure 37.7 Typical air conditioner schematic.

Figure 37.8 Schematic of all components of a complete air-conditioning system.

which then gives up this heat to the refrigerant in the chiller. The refrigerant is then compressed and passed into the condenser, giving up the heat to the open recirculating cooling water. The cooling water then gives up this heat to the atmosphere as it evaporates while passing through the cooling tower. An air conditioning system is nothing more than a mechanism designed to move heat from inside the building to the outside.

Steam absorption units are more complicated in their operation. They use water as a refrigerant, a lithium bromide solution as refrigerant absorber, and steam as a heat source to evaporate the water (Figure 37.9). Absorption units use condensers, cooled by water from a cooling tower, and chillers to provide chilled water for air conditioning. From the water treatment point of view, the operating principles of the open recirculating and chilled water systems are the same in all of the above systems.

In order for water cooled air conditioning systems to operate at design efficiency, careful attention must be paid to the condition of both the open recirculating water and the chilled water. The chemical makeup of water varies widely, depending on the source. Even water from the same metropolitan area can have a wide variation. For example, Chicago's municipal water, obtained

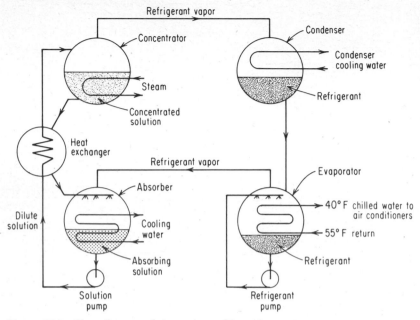

Figure 37.9   Flow diagram of absorption refrigeration system.

from Lake Michigan, has approximately 120 mg/l hardness, but many suburban communities outside Chicago obtain their water from wells, typically with hardness in the 300–500 mg/l range. In some areas of the country, such as the Eastern Seaboard and the Pacific Northwest, waters of exceptionally low hardness are common.

Problems that can occur on the water side of air conditioning systems are:

1. Formation of scale, especially on heat transfer tubes
2. Corrosion of the metals used in the system
3. Microbial fouling
4. Fouling due to dirt and silt accumulation

As with industrial heat exchangers, scale and fouling deposits cause poor heat transfer through the exchanger tubes, reducing efficiency and increasing energy costs. Corrosion causes failure of the system parts, resulting in expensive repair or replacement.

Water treatment procedures for these systems are the same as for industrial systems. Scale and corrosion control in open recirculating systems are maintained either by: (1) keeping the water in a nonscaling condition by using acid to lower the pH, and adding chromate to prevent corrosion, or (2) keeping the water in an equilibrium alkaline condition, and preventing scale by the addition of organo-phosphate sequestering agents. In some cases, where corrosive conditions also exist, corrosion inhibitors are added: zinc may be added to protect mild steel, and organic nitrogen compounds may be added for copper protection.

In systems where concentration results in a pH of 8.5 or above and sufficient alkalinity is present, the addition of corrosion inhibitors may not be necessary. Corrosion coupons at critical spots in the system can be inserted to provide the data to determine whether inhibitors are needed.

Some cooling towers are located in areas where appreciable quantities of airborne dirt and silt are drawn into the recirculating water. These impurities become suspended in the water, and tend to settle out in areas of low velocity, such as in heat exchangers. In addition to impeding heat transfer, settled sludge causes corrosion and encourages microbial activity underneath these deposits. A dispersant may be added to keep the particulates in suspension, until they are eventually removed from the system with the blowdown water. Dispersants are available as separate products, or they can be included in the formulation of multi-purpose products which also contain scale and corrosion inhibitors.

Problems can be caused by aerobic slime-forming microorganisms, anaerobic bacteria, molds, yeasts and algae. Slime-forming bacteria cause loss of heat transfer efficiency in condensers; in severe cases they can completely block the flow of water through the tubes.

Anaerobic bacteria generally grow under deposits in areas where no oxygen is available. These produce corrosive byproducts such as hydrogen sulfide, which can eat holes in piping quite rapidly. Algae growth on tower decks and other areas exposed to sunlight can become so severe as to plug the drain holes on the tower deck. The application of microbial control chemicals is essential to correct these problems.

Closed chilled water recirculating systems, like closed hot water systems, are generally not susceptible to scale formation, since little or no evaporation occurs in a properly operating system. However, leaks and evaporation can result in scale formation. The primary goals in treating these systems are to prevent metal corrosion, to control anaerobic microorganisms, and to prevent foaming.

The preferred chemical treatment for corrosion, scale and foaming is the same as for hot water boilers—a borate/nitrite based formulation containing scale control agents and antifoams.

Life cannot exist in hot water systems, because of the high temperatures involved; but microbes can and do grow in chilled water systems. Typical examples are nitrate-reducing and sulfate-reducing bacteria. The end result of the activity of these microbes is corrosion of the system metal, which can become severe. Proper control is maintained by periodic analysis of the water and by the application of biocides when necessary.

In colder climates, the addition of ethylene-glycol antifreeze solutions to both hot and chilled water systems is common. The chemical treatment selected must be compatible with the antifreeze. For example, borate/nitrate based inhibitors are usually compatible, while chromate based inhibitors are not.

An example of an institutional air conditioning system is shown in Figure 37.10, representing a typical hospital installation. The completely automated chemical feed system for the open cooling tower is shown in Figure 37.11.

DOMESTIC WATER

Domestic water is that used for drinking, cooking, bathing, washing of dishes and clothes, toilet flushing and lawn or garden sprinkling. It is usually municipal water, but may be from private wells. Because of the large size of modern buildings, hot water is often recirculated throughout the building from large holding tanks.

Domestic cold water problems are limited to corrosion of the water piping and holding tanks. Domestic hot water problems include both scale and corrosion. Tastes and odors may be the cause of occasional complaints, but these are not major problems because they do not involve equipment damage and they apply to a very small percentage of the total water used.

The corrosion in both hot and cold systems is caused by (1) water that is

Figure 37.10 These two large centrifugal chilling machines provide for the air conditioning of an entire hospital. *(Courtesy of Carrier Corporation.)*

naturally corrosive as supplied to the building, and (2) the use of a zeolite softener, which replaces Mg and Ca ions with Na ions, creating a more corrosive soft water.

Scale in hot water systems occurs in the hot water heater tubes, and is caused by the precipitation of $CaCO_3$, which becomes less soluble as the temperature rises. At present there are no Federal regulations governing the use of chemicals. In potable water systems within buildings, the accepted practice is to use only those chemicals that are approved for use in municipal water supplies. These chemicals are usually polyphosphates, sodium silicates, or combinations thereof. These products provide both scale and corrosion protection. These chemicals are applied through the simple feeder shown in Figure 37.2.

WASTE TREATMENT

In the building and institutional field, most individual installations discharge their wastes into the municipal sewer system. In some water-short areas, such as Los Angeles, noncontaminated wastes may be segregated from contaminated waste, such as domestic sewage, for recovery and return to the potable water source.

There are certain commercial operations, such as laundries, where strong

Figure 37.11 An automated feed and control system for an air conditioner cooling tower.

Second stage aeration
chamber

Return sludge
lift controls

Air lift
to decant
supernatant to
first stage

Comminutor

Raw
sewage
inlet

Air
diffusers

Air
diffusers

Aerobic
sludge
digestion
chamber

First stage aeration
chamber for raw sewage

Aerated waste
offtake to final
clarifier

Treated
effluent

Shell of
final clarifier

Figure 37.12 Typical packaged sewage treatment plant used by institutions and commercial centers not served by a municipal sewage plant. *(Courtesy of Smith & Loveless Division, Ecodyne Corporation.)*

wastes are given special treatment before discharge. In the case of laundries, the cost of special treatment is partly offset by heat recovery and use of rinse water in the washing cycle. The recovered water contains both valuable heat and unspent detergent. Some institutions, such as hospitals and hotels/motels, operate their own laundries, but dilution with wastewater is usually adequate to produce a combined effluent meeting local discharge standards, which usually apply to oils, pH, BOD and suspended solids.

Some shopping centers, resort hotels, hospitals, and similar establishments may not have access to municipal sewers. These are required to install waste treatment facilities to meet the same standards applied to municipal sewage plant effluents. An illustration of a complete packaged sewage treatment facility serving such an installation is shown in Figure 37.12.

Chapter 38

Cooling Water Treatment

Most of the water employed for industrial purposes is used for cooling a product or process. The availability of water in most industrialized areas and its high heat capacity have made water the favored heat transfer medium in industrial and utility type applications. Direct air cooling is finding increasing use, particularly in water-short areas, but is still far behind water in total numbers of applications and total heat transfer loading.

During recent years, the use of water for cooling has come under increasing scrutiny from both environmental and conservational points of view and as a result, cooling water use patterns are changing and will continue to do so. For example, many systems pass cooling water through the plant system only once, and return it to the watershed. This creates a high water withdrawal rate and adds heat to the receiving stream. On the other hand, cooling towers permit reusing water to such a large extent that most modern evaporative cooling systems employing cooling towers reduce stream withdrawal rates by over 90%. This substantially reduces the heat input to the stream, but not to the environment, since the heat is transferred to the air.

These changes in cooling water system design and operation have a profound impact on the chemistry of water as it influences corrosion, deposition, and fouling potential in the system. This chapter reviews the industrial operations which use water for cooling purposes, the problems of corrosion, scale and fouling in these systems and how these affect plant production through loss of heat transfer, equipment failures, or both. In addition, various cooling water treatment concepts are examined and the control procedures required for their success are discussed.

HEAT TRANSFER

Heat transfer is simply the movement of heat from one body to another, the hotter being the source, and the cooler the receiver. In cooling water systems, the product or process being cooled is the source, and cooling water the receiver.

Cooling water usually does not contact the source directly; the two materials are usually separated by a barrier that is a good conductor of heat, usually a metal. The barrier that allows heat to pass from the source to the receiver is called the heat transfer surface, and the assembly of barriers in a containment vessel is a heat exchanger.

In many industrial heat exchangers both the source and receiver are liquids. If the source is steam or other vapor that is liquefied, the heat exchanger is called a condenser; if the receiver is a liquid that is vaporized, the exchanger is called an evaporator.

The simplest type of heat exchanger consists of a tube or pipe located concentrically inside another—the shell. This is called a double pipe exchanger (Figure 38.1). In this simple exchanger, process liquid flows through the inner tube and cooling water through the annulus between the tubes. Heat flows across the metal wall separating the fluids. Since both fluids pass through the exchanger only once, the arrangement is called a single-pass heat exchanger. If both liquids flow in the same direction, the exchanger is parallel or cocurrent flow; if they move in opposite directions, the exchanger is a counter-current type.

Progressing from this exchanger, more sophisticated units are designed to improve the efficiency of the heat exchange process. Figure 38.2 shows a shell and tube exchanger. Receiver and source could be located on either side of the barrier.

Another simple heat exchange device is the jacketed vessel, with cooling water passing through the space between the double walls of a chemical reaction vessel, removing heat from the process. This design is like a thermos bottle, but in this case, the double wall is used for heat removal instead of insulation.

Removing Undesirable Heat

Once a receiver completes its job and cools the source, it contains heat that must be dissipated. This is accomplished by transferring heat to the environment. In once-through systems cool water is withdrawn, heated, and returned to a receiving stream, which subsequently becomes warmer. In this type of system each pound (0.454 kg) of cooling water is heated 1°F (0.56°C) for each Btu (0.252 cal) removed from the source.

In open recirculating systems, water is evaporated; this phase change from liquid to gas discharges heat to the atmosphere instead of to a stream. Evaporating water dissipates about 1000 Btu's per pound (555 cal/kg) of water converted to vapor. When evaporation is used in the cooling process, it can dissipate

Figure 38.1 Double-pipe heat-exchanger units like this may be assembled from a number of common modules to provide the necessary heat transfer rate.

Two-pass head   Four-pass head

Legend: ●—Flowing away, ⊙—Flowing toward

(a)

(b)

Figure 38.2   Simple detail of shell-and-tube heat exchanger. The water box may be designed for as many as eight passes, and a variety of configurations of shell-side baffles may be used to improve heat transfer. (a) Several water box arrangements for tube-side cooling. (b) Assembly of simple two-pass exchanger with U-tubes.

50–100 times more heat to the environment per unit of water than a nonevaporative system. (This is explained in more detail in a later section of this chapter).

Sensible Heat Transfer

The two most common ways heat is transferred from a source to a receiver in the heat exchange process are conduction and convection. Heat flows from a hot source through a heat exchange surface to the other side by conduction. Heat is then removed from this hot surface by direct contact with cooling water also by conduction. Subsequently this heated water then mixes with other cooler water in a heat transfer process called convection.

The five factors controlling conductive heat transfer are:

1. The heat transfer characteristics (thermal conductivity) of the barrier.
2. The thickness of the heat transfer barrier.
3. The surface area of the barrier.
4. The temperature difference between the source and the cooling water (the driving force).
5. Insulating deposits on either side of the barrier.

Of these five factors, the first three are inherent in the design of the exchanger. Items four and five are operational characteristics that change depending on the conditions of service. Deposits on either side of a metal barrier have a lower thermal conductivity than the metal itself, so the rate of heat conduction is reduced by any deposit. For example, a buildup of 0.1 in. (0.25 cm) of calcium carbonate scale on a heat exchanger tube wall may reduce the rate of heat transfer by as much as 40%.

This reduction means that the cooling water may not remove sufficent heat from the source as required by the process. Therefore, production must be slowed or the flow of cooling water must be increased to maintain the same cooling rate that prevailed before fouling developed. Frequently the latter is not possible.

Heat Exchanger Design

In the simple, single-pass heat exchanger noted earlier (Figure 38.1), both fluids pass through the exchanger only once, so this is known as a single-pass exchanger. The countercurrent arrangement in which source and receiver liquids flow in opposite directions is superior to the cocurrent design because it provides a greater driving force (measured as a mean temperature difference) for the same terminal temperatures; less surface area can transfer the same amount of heat. Counterflow shell-and-tube exchangers are thus more commonly found because more heat can be transferred for a given set of conditions.

The principal disadvantage of the double-pipe exchanger is the small heat transfer surface provided by a single tube relative to the total space required for installation. To offset this limitation, modern exchangers increase the effective heat transfer surface area by using multiple tubes in the shell. This allows more intimate contact between the source and receiver. Also, most industrial heat exchangers employ multiple pass designs. Both of these techniques combine efficient heat transfer with practical equipment sizing. Figure 38.2 shows a double-tube pass, single-shell pass exchanger. In almost all units of this kind, water flows inside the tubes, with process fluids on the shell side, outside the tubes. However, there are notable exceptions, and any investigation of heat exchanger performance must begin with identification of the shell side and tube side fluids. For convenience, this text concentrates on conventional flow, with cooling water in the tubes and process fluid in the shell.

In the design of heat exchangers, the engineer obtains from handbooks heat transfer rates in Btu per hour per square foot of surface, per inch of barrier thickness, per degree of temperature difference, or $U_1 = $ Btu/hr/sq ft/in./°F (cal/hr/m²/cm/°C). For a given heat exchange tube size, which may be standardized in specific designs such as condensers, since the wall thickness of the tube is known, the transfer rate may be shortened to

$$U_2 = \text{Btu/hr/sq ft/°F}$$
$$= (\text{cal/hr/m}^2\text{/°C})$$

The expression may be further reduced for fixed process temperature conditions to

$$U_3 = \text{Btu/hr/sq ft}$$
$$= (\text{cal/hr/m}^2)$$

And finally, a given exchanger in a fixed application which shows little change in temperature conditions may simply be rated in total heat transfer in Btu/hr (cal/hr). If the heat flux in Btu/hr falls off, then an investigation is needed to determine if this is due to changed temperature conditions, insulating deposits, plugged tubes or some other factor.

In most process heat exchangers, heat flux averages 5000–6000 Btu/hr/sq ft (120–150 cal/hr/m²). However, heat flux in some exchangers exceeds 30,000 Btu/hr/sq ft (750 cal/hr/m²) when vapor is condensed on the process side. Transfer rates also vary considerably with water flow velocities (Figure 38.3).

Cooling water temperature varies across the cross section of a tube, the hottest water being that contacting the tube wall. The temperature of the tube wall, called the skin temperature, is important in designing chemical treatment programs. For example, where high skin temperatures occur [above 200°F (93°C)] the plant can find the most probable locations for scale formation and corro-

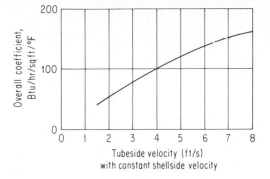

Figure 38.3 Heat transfer co-efficients change with velocity, both on shell side and tube side. Uniform shell-side velocity cannot be achieved because of limitations in geometry.

sion. Many compounds found in water-formed deposits are less soluble at increased temperatures, and corrosion reactions proceed faster at elevated temperatures.

Tube-side cooling water velocity is usually maintained above 2–3 ft/sec (0.6–0.9 m/sec) to as high as 7–8 ft/sec (2.1–2.4 m/sec) to help keep the tube walls free of suspended solids deposition. Lower velocities encourage tube deposits to form by the settling out of suspended solids. In a bundle of tubes, perhaps only one tube may have a low velocity due to plugging or poor distribution.

Occasionally, high pressures on the process side make it more economical to design the exchanger with cooling water on the shell side. One major problem in such exchangers is the low flow velocities frequently encountered around baffles, tube supports and tube sheets even when the average flow velocity through the shell appears acceptable. These low velocity areas greatly increase the potential for deposits and rapid metal deterioration. For example, mild steel exchangers with water on the shell side have been known to fail from perforations in as little as three months, even in the presence of a strong corrosion inhibitor like chromate.

There are three basic types of cooling water systems: once-through, closed recirculating (nonevaporative), and open recirculating (evaporative).

Once-through Cooling

Once-through water is taken from the plant supply, passed through the cooling system and returned to the receiving body of water. Heat has been picked up from the source. The chief characteristic of once-through water systems is the relatively large quantity of water that is usually used for cooling. A simple flow diagram for a once-through cooling water system is shown in Figure 38.4.

The principal water side problems encountered in once-through cooling systems are:

Corrosion is a function of water characteristics and the metals in the system. Corrosion causes premature metal failures; deposits of corrosion products reduce both heat transfer and flow rates.

Scale is caused by precipitation of compounds that become insoluble at higher temperatures, such as calcium carbonate. Scale interferes with heat transfer and reduces flow.

Fouling results from the settling out of suspended solids, corrosion products, and microbial masses. Fouling has the same effect on the system as scaling, but fouling also promotes severe corrosion under deposits.

The treatment of once-through cooling water follows the basic principles used in solving all cooling water problems. The first step is to properly identify the

Figure 38.4 Typical once-through cooling in a small industrial plant.

problem as scale, corrosion, fouling or combinations of these factors. The next step is a thorough survey to understand both the process and water side of the system. This establishes the system design, operating characteristics, and water chemistry, important considerations for selecting and applying a reliable, economical treatment program. Special considerations are given to systems restricted to specific treatments; the potential for cross-contamination of water with process or product may not permit employing the most effective treatment. Some once-through systems use plant water for drinking as well as cooling, thereby requiring chemicals that are safe for potable use.

A typical chemical treatment program for corrosion control may use various types of inorganic phosphates alone or synergized with zinc, other inorganic ions, or silicates. When applied at the low levels required for economical treatment of once-through systems, these materials form no visible film on the metal surface; nevertheless, they can reduce the corrosion rate by as much as 90% over non-treated systems. Corrosion protection is provided because the chemicals act at the point of potential metal loss, hindering the corrosion reaction and thereby reducing the amount of metal removed from the surface.

Where scale is a problem, it is most often calcium carbonate resulting from a change in the stability index of the water. Other frequently encountered scales involve iron and manganese.

There are two basic approaches to the prevention of calcium carbonate scale on heat transfer surfaces and in distribution lines:

1. Interfere with the potentially scaling ions and prevent crystal growth. Inorganic polyphosphates and organophosphorus compounds are normally used alone or together for this purpose (threshold treatment). Occasionally acid is used to adjust the stability index of the water thereby preventing $CaCO_3$ scale. Acid will not control iron and manganese scales. It usually is not the most economical method to treat high volume once-through systems for prevention of $CaCO_3$ scale.

2. Condition crystal nuclei to prevent their growth on heat transfer surfaces and transmission lines. This process of crystal modification uses various acrylate type compounds, phosphate compounds—both organic and inorganic—and natural organics.

Fouling, the deposition of particulate matter or microbial masses, is a complex mechanism governed by variables such as particle size and charge; water velocity, composition, and temperature; and bacterial populations. One approach to handling this problem is to condition the foulants as they develop by applying various compounds of acrylates, sequestering agents, natural organics, organo-phosphorus materials, and specific bacterial control agents and then flushing the conditioned material out of the system. The success of this approach depends on adequate water velocities throughout the system. Low velocity areas, such as in shell side exchangers, reactor jackets, and compressor jackets, are likely to accumulate some sludge and may not be amenable to protection.

A second approach involves dispersing the suspended solids into very tiny particles thereby preventing their agglomeration into sufficiently large particles that would readily settle out of the water. These small particles can be more easily carried through the system. The choice of the best dispersant for this purpose depends on the problem to be solved. Each potential depositing material (sand, silt, clay, corrosion products) requires a specific chemical applied at a dosage sufficient to disperse the specific foulant. Chemicals frequently used include surfactants, acrylates, high and low molecular weight anionic, cationic and nonionic polymers, sequestering agents, and organo-phosphorus compounds.

Most fouling problems in all types of cooling systems are complicated by microbial activity. Slime deposits on tubes not only interfere with efficient heat transfer, but act as a trap to enmesh suspended solids, further impeding heat transfer. In addition, by-products of bacterial metabolism influence water chemistry, including the tendency for scale to form or metal to corrode. Proper use of biocides and biodispersants can be a major step toward solving a once-through fouling problem.

Rarely do corrosion, scale, and fouling occur independently of one another. Usually two or all develop together to cause loss of heat transfer and premature metal loss. For example, microbial fouling can cause scaling and corrosion to occur; corrosion can contribute to iron fouling and encourage more corrosion to occur. To break this cycle, proper problem identification is important for selecting and applying a practical, economical solution to any deposit problem.

Closed Recirculating Systems

A closed recirculating system is one in which the water is circulated in a closed loop with negligible evaporation or exposure to the atmosphere or other influences that would affect the chemistry of the water in the system. These usually require high chemical treatment levels, and since water losses are negligible these levels are economical. High quality makeup water is generally used for best system operation. These systems are frequently employed for critical cooling applications such as continuous casters in the steel industry where the slightest deposit from any source could cause equipment failure.

Figure 38.5 shows a simplified closed recirculating system. Heat is transferred to the closed cooling water loop by typical heat exchange equipment and is removed from the closed system loop by a second exchange of heat from the closed loop to a secondary cooling water cycle. The secondary loop could use either evaporative or once-through water cooling, or air cooling.

Velocity of water in closed systems is generally in the 3–5 ft/sec (0.9–1.5 m/sec) range. Temperature rise usually averages 10–15°F (6–9°C), although some systems can exceed this substantially. Generally closed systems require

Figure 38.5 For many critical applications of heat transfer, water in a closed loop is used for fail-safe chemical control, and this is cooled by an open system.

Open loop   Closed loop

little or no makeup water except for pump seal leaks, expansion tank over-flows, and surface evaporation from system vents. This periodic makeup requires regular analysis for control of correct treatment chemical residuals.

Closed systems usually contain a combination of different metals which provide a high potential for galvanic corrosion. The potential for dissolved oxygen attack is generally quite low in closed systems because of the small amount of makeup water—the main oxygen source. However, in systems that require substantial makeup due to loss of water from leaks, oxygen is continually supplied and oxygen corrosion presents a serious problem. Oxygen can, at elevated temperatures or at points of high heat transfer, cause severe pitting corrosion.

Since relatively little makeup is added to most closed recirculating systems, it is practical and desirable to maintain the system in a corrosion-free condition. This is normally achieved by applying chromates, nitrite/nitrate-based inhibitors or soluble oil-type treatments.

Theoretically, scale should be a minor problem in a closed system since the water is not concentrated by evaporation. In a tightly closed system, none of the common scale-forming constituents deposit on metal surfaces to interfere with heat transfer or encourage corrosion.

With high makeup rates, however, additional scale forms with each new increment of water added so that in time, scale becomes significant. In addition, there is opportunity for sludge, rust, and suspended solids to drop out at low flow points and bake on heat transfer surfaces to form a hard deposit. Therefore, scale retardants and dispersants are usually included as part of a closed system treatment program where makeup rates are high. Often soft water or condensate is used for makeup to closed systems depending on the characteristics of the system being protected.

Because water circulating through a closed system is not exposed to the atmosphere, fouling by airborne silt and sand is rare. However, fouling by microbial masses may occur in closed systems where makeup rate is significant or process leaks encourage bacterial growths. These are controlled with biological control agents formulated to be compatible with the chemical treatments and operating conditions found in closed systems.

It is desirable as a part of routine maintenance to flush closed water systems with high pressure, high velocity water to remove accumulated debris if makeup rates are high.

Open Recirculating Systems

An open recirculating system incorporates a cooling tower or evaporation pond to dissipate the heat it removes from the process or product. An open recirculating system (Figure 38.6) takes water from a cooling tower basin or pond, passes it through process equipment requiring cooling, and then returns the water through the evaporation unit, where the water evaporated cools the water that remains. The open recirculating system repeats this process of reuse, taking in sufficient fresh water makeup to balance the water evaporated and that blown down from the system to control the chemical character of the recirculating water. This greatly reduces water demand (e.g., withdrawal from a river) and discharge, as shown by Figure 38.7.

The following definitions are used to explain the operation of an evaporative system and to permit the plant operator to calculate performance. Figure 38.6 helps to clarify these definitions.

1. *Recirculation rate* (Q_c). The flow of cooling water being pumped through the entire plant cooling loop, usually cooling a number of exchangers. Q_c can usually be estimated from the recirculating pump nameplate data; however, actual measurements are more accurate. The actual recirculation is seldom more than the name plate data and frequently may be 10–20% less. A pump curve,

Figure 38.6 Evaporative cooling system using a cooling tower. Water and solids balances are shown.

usually available from the manufacturer, plots recirculating flow against head; a pressure gauge on the pump discharge should provide a reasonably accurate estimate of flow.

2. *Temperature differential* (ΔT). This term refers to the difference between the average water temperature returning to the tower from the plant exchangers (T_2) and the average water temperature following evaporation (T_1) (tower basin).

3. *Evaporation* (E). The water lost to the atmosphere in the cooling process [gpm (m³/min)]. The evaporation rate is dependent on the amount of water being cooled (Q_c) and the temperature differential, ΔT. As a rule of thumb, for each 10°F (5.6°C) temperature drop across the evaporation process, 1% of the recirculation rate (Q_c) is evaporated. Therefore, a 20°F (11.2°C) ΔT across a cooling tower produces an evaporation loss of 2% of the recirculation rate ($0.02\ Q_c = E$).

$$E = Q_c \times \frac{(T_2 - T_1)}{1000}$$

$$E = Q_c \times \frac{(T_2 - T_1)}{560} \qquad \text{(Metric)}$$

The amount of evaporation that can take place over a given tower is limited by the relative humidity of the air. Relative humidity is determined by measuring the wet and dry bulb temperatures of the air.

4. *Concentration ratio* (CR). Makeup to a recirculating cooling water system contains dissolved impurities. The evaporating water produces pure H_2O vapor, leaving behind these impurities. The ratio of the concentrations of salts in the circulating water (C_B) to those of the makeup (C_M) is the concentration ratio.

$$CR = C_B/C_M$$

Since the input solids must equal the output solids,

$$M \times C_M = B \times C_B$$

where M is the makeup flow and B represents loss of concentrated water. Therefore, the concentration ratio is also

$$CR = M/B$$

The CR should be calculated for a number of individual components in the water because of interferences:

a. The CR would be abnormally high if based on a constituent added to the system. For example, SO_4^{-2} is increased where sulfuric acid is added for pH or

Figure 38.7 Reduction of makeup flow by concentration in an evaporative cooling system.

alkalinity control; Cl^- is increased by chlorination; SO_4^{-2} may also be increased if the plant atmosphere contains SO_2 from combustion gases.

b. The *CR* would be abnormally low if based on a constituent which precipitates from the system. For example, Ca^{+2} is decreased if $CaCO_3$ or $CaSO_4$ scale is forming; SiO_2 is decreased if it precipitates or is removed by adsorption on iron precipitates.

Because of this, it is useful to calculate the *CR* for each constituent in the complete water analysis. As shown in Figure 38.7, even a small degree of concentration enormously reduces water demand, and the greater the *CR*, the lower the demand as the evaporation rate is approached as a limit.

5. *Makeup* (*M*). The flow of water required to replace the water lost by evaporation plus that being lost through blowdown, tower drift, and other miscellaneous losses. It is usually measured by a flow meter; if not it may be calculated as shown below:

$$M = E \times \left(\frac{CR}{CR - 1} \right)$$

6. *Blowdown* (*B*). Since pure water vapor is discharged by evaporation, the dissolved and suspended solids left behind concentrate. If there were no water loss other than evaporation, these solids would concentrate to brine, causing massive scale and corrosion. To balance this, regulated flow is bled from the circulating system. This blowdown (B_R) is calculated and controlled to remove solids at the same rate at which they are introduced by the makeup.

There are other non-regulated losses from the system. One is drift (B_D); the other is leakage (B_L), sometimes deliberate but usually accidental. These are included in the total blowdown calculation,

$$B = B_R + B_D + B_L$$

Blowdown is related to other factors thus:

$$B = M - E,$$

and
$$B = M/CR$$

7. *Drift* (B_D). Even though evaporating water is pure, some water droplets escape as mist through the evaporation equipment. In modern cooling towers, very intricate mist and drift eliminators may be added to reduce this droplet loss to about 0.0005% of the recirculation rate. A more usual drift loss in conventional cooling towers is in the range of 0.05–0.2% loss based on the recirculation rate. Since drift contains dissolved solids it is really a portion of the blowdown. In the absence of a controlled blowdown, as when the blowdown valve is deliberately closed, drift establishes the maximum concentration ratio in the absence of other system losses.

8. *System losses* (B_L). Circulating water may be lost in the plant through pump or valve leaks; by tap off for once-through cooling of pump glands, compressor jackets or bearings; or draw-off for such uses as equipment or floor area washup when the cooling water line happens to be close to where water is needed. In many plants, miscellaneous draw off of recirculating cooling water is so great that it is impossible to build up the concentration ratio over 1.2–1.5. This severely limits the selection of an economical chemical treatment program and prevents effective conservation of water.

9. *Holding capacity of system* (V). Usually most of the water in a system is contained in the cooling tower basin or spray pond. An approximation of the holding capacity can be obtained by calculating the volume of water in the basin and adding an extra 20–30% for the water contained in the lines and equipment. Additional increases may be required if the system has an unusually large number of open box condensers, jacketed vessels, or furnaces with substantial water holding capacity.

10. *Time/cycle* (t).   One cycle (c) is defined as the time required for water to make one trip around the circulating loop. This time is a function of the holding capacity and the recirculation rate.

$$t = V/Q_c$$

11. *Holding time index* (HTI).   The holding time index is an expression of the half-life of a treatment chemical added to an evaporative cooling system. Mathematically, this index represents the time required to dilute an added chemical to 50% of its original concentration after the chemical addition is discontinued. It is also the time required to concentrate the makeup solids by a factor of 2. This is an important factor in setting control limits where chemical feed may be interrupted. It is also important for establishing an effective dosage for biological control agents, which are slug fed into the system. A dilution curve for a chemical slug fed into a cooling tower system is illustrated by Figure 38.8.

Calculation of Holding Time Index   The following data are required: recirculation rate, temperature drop, concentration ratio and holding capacity of the system.

1. Calculate the time/cycle, t.

2. From Table 38.1 determine the number of cycles (c) required to reach the prevailing concentration ratio, based on the temperature drop through the tower or spray pond.

3. Multiply this by the time/cycle to get the holding time index expressed in minutes, then divide by 60 or 1440 to convert to hours or days respectively.

The following example illustrates this calculation:

a. Recirculation rate: Pump data shows a recirculation rate of 5500 gpm (21 m³/min). Use 5000 gpm (19 m³/min) as a good estimate of actual recirculation.

b. Temperature drop:

$$105°F - 85°F = 20°F$$
$$(41°C - 30°C = 11°C)$$

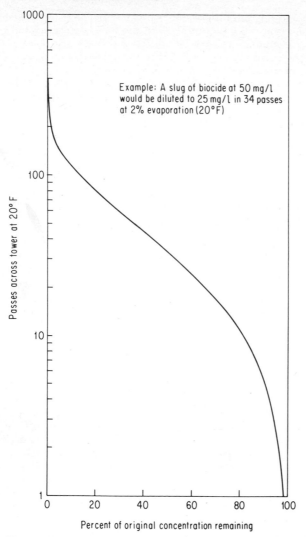

Example: A slug of biocide at 50 mg/l would be diluted to 25 mg/l in 34 passes at 2% evaporation (20°F)

Figure 38.8   The effect of time and makeup dilution on slug application of a chemical to an evaporative cooling-water system.

c. Evaporation loss: 20°F (11°C) is equivalent to 2% evaporation loss:

$$0.02 \times 5000 = 100 \text{ gal/min evaporation loss}$$
$$(0.02 \times 19 = 0.38 \text{ m}^3/\text{min evaporation loss})$$

d. Concentration ratio (see analyses on Figure 38.9): Tests on the makeup and recirculating water show concentration ratios of 2.8 to 8.3.

The approximate concentration ratio is 3.0 based on magnesium and silica, since magnesium and silica remain soluble at the prevailing pH and concentration conditions. Chlorine and sulfuric acid are both being added to the system and thereby eliminate the use of Cl^- and SO_4^{-2} as valid *CR* indicators.

TABLE 38.1 Cycles Required to Concentrate in the Absence of Blowdown

Concentration ratio	Temperature drop through tower		
	10°	20°	30°
1.1	6.5 cycles	3.2 cycles	2.1 cycles
1.3	20.2	10.2	7.0
1.5	34.5	17.2	11.7
1.8	55	28	19
2.0	69	34	23
2.5	105	52	35
3.0	138	70	47
3.5	174	87	58
4.0	208	104	70
4.5	241	120	81
5.0	324	162	93

e. Makeup:

$$M = E \times \left(\frac{CR}{CR - 1} \right)$$

$$M = 100 \times \frac{3}{2} = 150 \text{ gpm}$$

$$(M = 0.38 \times \frac{3}{2} = 0.57 \text{ m}^3/\text{min})$$

f Holding capacity of the system: Basin contains 72,000 gal (284 m³). The total holding capacity of the system is estimated to be 100,000 gal (379 m³).

g. Time/cycle:

$$t = \frac{100,000}{5000} = 20 \text{ min}$$

$$\left(t = \frac{379 \text{ m}^3}{19 \text{ m}^3/\text{min}} = 20 \text{ min} \right)$$

h. Holding time index: If CR = 3, and $\Delta T = 20°F$ (11°C), Table 38.1 shows average cycles at 70; at 70 cycles,

$$\text{HTI} = 70 \times 20 = 1400 \text{ min, or 23 hr}$$

If the blowdown rate is known, a simplified version may also be used to calculate holding time index:

$$\text{HTI} = 0.693 \times \frac{\text{holding capacity (gal)}}{\text{blowdown (gal/min)}}$$

$$\text{HTI} = 0.693 \times \frac{100,000}{50} = 1385 \text{ min}$$

where $0.693 = \ln 2.0$, a number related to the half life in the earlier definition.

Cooling Towers

Cooling towers are designed to evaporate water by intimate contact of water with air. Cooling towers are classified by the method used to induce air flow (natural or mechanical draft) and by the direction of air flow (either counterflow or crossflow relative to the downward flow of water).

Identification of Analyses Tabulated Below:

A. Raw water   D. _____

B. Recirculated cooling water   E. _____

C. Concentration ratios   F. _____

Constituent	As	A	B	C	D	E	F
Calcium	CaCO₃	182	526	2.8			
Magnesium	"	78	240	3.1			
Sodium (by difference)	"	40	120				
Total Electrolyte	CaCO₃	305	886	2.9			
Bicarbonate	CaCO₃	190	80				
Carbonate	"	0	0				
Hydroxyl	"	0	0				
Sulfate	"	84	696	8.3*			
Chloride	"	29	94	3.2*			
Nitrate	"	2	6				
Chromate		0	10	--			
M Alk.	CaCO₃	190	80				
P Alk.	"	TR	0				
Carbon Dioxide		TR					
pH		8.3	7.5				
Silica		22	68	3.1			
Iron	Fe	0.3					
Turbidity		10					
TDS		360	ND				
Color		Nil					
* Not valid, since Cl₂ and H₂SO₄ are being fed.							

Figure 38.9 Concentration ratios in an evaporative cooling system.

Natural Draft Towers—In natural draft towers, air flow depends on the surrounding atmosphere, which establishes the difference in densities between the warmer air inside the tower and the external atmosphere; wind velocity also affects performance. Most natural draft towers in modern utility service are of hyperbolic design (Figure 38.10), which has been used for many years in European installations. These tall towers provide cooling without fan power, and they also minimize plume problems and drift.

Mechanical Draft Towers—Mechanical draft cooling towers use fans to move air instead of depending on natural draft or wind. This speeds the cooling process and increases the efficiency of the tower by increasing the air velocity over droplets of water falling through the tower. Mechanical towers can, therefore, evaporate much more water than natural draft towers of the same size.

There are two designs of mechanical draft towers, forced and induced draft. In forced draft towers (Figure 38.11) fans mounted on the side of the tower

Figure 38.10 Hyperbolic towers cooling condenser water in a utility station. *(Courtesy of The Marley Company.)*

Figure 38.11 Forced-draft tower design. This design was widely used prior to development of the induced-draft design. Fans and motors are conveniently located for maintenance.

Figure 38.12   Induced-draft tower design, with crossflow of air through tower packing. Air enters the tower louvers and is well distributed. *(Courtesy of The Marley Company.)*

force air horizontally through the tower packing, producing intimate mixing of air with the falling water.

Induced draft cooling towers (Figure 38.12) are either counterflow or crossflow with fans on top pulling cooling air up through or horizontally across the falling water. The choice between forced draft and induced draft is based on engineering considerations that take prevailing weather patterns into account. A major consideration is to avoid recirculation of the warm air discharge, which would greatly reduce tower performance. The main advantage of a counterflow tower is that the coldest water contacts the driest air, providing the most efficient evaporation sequence.

TREATMENT AND CONTROL

Every cooling water system presents a unique combination of equipment, water chemistry, blowdown and control considerations. Proper selection of a sound cooling water treatment program requires collecting a considerable amount of information. This is often a painstaking task because of the complexity of the mechanical equipment involved and the variations encountered in operating conditions. Figure 38.13 and Table 38.2 show an example of a system survey, divided into five major categories: (1) cooling system data, (2) cooling water chemistry, (3) heat transfer data, (4) effluent considerations, (5) present treatment and control methods.

Cooling System Data   This section identifies physical aspects of the system such as number and type of heat exchangers, materials of construction of exchangers and piping, type of tower, maximum temperatures of the water and process, tower operating temperatures, and system characteristics such as velocities, makeup, bleed-off and holding time index. This section should be supplemented with the process flow and water flow diagram as well as complete specifications on critical heat exchangers.

Cooling Water Chemistry   This section identifies the chemical environment of the system. The information is divided into the chemistry of the makeup and recirculating water, including a description of pretreatment processes and sources and types of contamination of the recirculating water. Causes of poor makeup water quality and persistent sources of contamination should be examined; these are critical to the treatment program, so the possibility of correction is a decisive factor in program selection.

Heat Transfer Data This survey section is organized into four parts:

1. *Results monitoring,* defining how heat transfer is evaluated, including the use of corrosion coupons and test heat exchangers; data on plant heat exchangers, permitting calculation and monitoring of heat transfer rates.

2. *Control methods,* indicating how heat transfer is controlled. For example, a common method in many plants is to throttle cooling water entering certain heat exchangers in the winter to prevent overcooling of the process. However, throttling reduces velocities and promotes fouling which leads to a loss of heat transfer that cannot always be recovered by reopening the throttled valve. Alternate control methods, such as water recycle or process stream bypass should be considered in preference to throttling water flow.

1. COOLING SYSTEM DATA		2. COOLING WATER CHEMISTRY				3. HEAT TRANSFER DATA		
M E T A L L S	Tubes	CS, Adm, SS	PPM	MAKE-UP	RECIRC. WATER	P L A N T	D A T A	Include Temperature, Pressures, Vacuum, Cleanliness Factors, heat transfer coefficients, etc.)
	Tube Sheets	CS, SS	TDS	330	1680	M O N I T O R I N G		Temperature, pressure
	Lines	CS	SS or JTU	22	86			
	Coils	CS	H as CaCO₃	182	960	T O O L S	U S E D	Include Methods, Location of Tools, (Temperature, Pressure, Velocity), Typical Results, etc.
V E L O C	Min.	2.5	HCa as CaCO₃	102	590			
Ft Sec	Max.	7 +	Mg as CaCO₃	80	370			
	Avg.	3.0	P as CaCO₃	0	0	C O N T R O L	M E T H O D	Include Throttling of Cooling Water, Throttling of Process By-Passes – (Used to Control Temperature for Methods, etc.)
MAX. TEMP °F.	Process Side	510°F	M Alk.	1 511	50			
	Water Side	120°F	Cl as NaCl	116	620			
N U M B E R O F S	Tube & Shell	55	SO₄ as Na₂SO₄			C O M M E N T S		Include Condition of Heat Transfer Equipment, Amount, Type and Location of Deposits, Condition of Tower, Etc.
	Baro-metric		Total PO₄	0.4	2.0	P R E S E N T		Fouling present in heat exchangers.
	Annular Space		Ortho PO₄	0.4	2.0			Moderate tuberculation in last
	Open Box		SiO₂	2-10	10-50			passes of exchangers and water
	Other		Total Fe	0.1	0.6			boxes.
	No Exch. with Water Shell Side	6	Sol. Fe	0.1	0.4			
T Y P E	T O W E R	Deck Open or Closed	Open	Total Al₂O₃	0.4	2.0	C L E A N I N G	P R O C E D U R E	Include On-Stream and Turnaround Cleaning Methods, and Frequency
		Nat. or Mech. Draft	Mech.	Sol. Al₂O₃	0.4	1.8			Annual turnaround. Refinery has
	Side Stream Filter Yes/No	No	pH	7.3	7.1			been replacing admiralty bundles
	Recirc. Rate GPM	46,000		MAKE-UP WATER PRETREATMENT				with mild steel due to process
	Holding Capacity Gal.	600,000	Include Source, Pretreatment Method, All Chemicals, Results					side corrosion.
T O W E R S	T E M P	Max. Return °F.	115°F	Des Plaines				
		Max. Supply °F.	85°F	River with trav-				4. PLANT EFFLUENT CONSIDERATIONS
		ΔT °F.	30°F	eling screens		Where is Bleed-Off Discharged	To API separator and waste
	Avg. No. Cycles	5.7		CONTAMINATION OF RECIRCULATING WATER		Present Waste Treatment	treatment plant.
	Holding Time Index in Hours	28.9	Include Source, Type, Amount, and Frequency			CrO₄, Zn, PO₄ Removal Capabilities of present waste water facilities	Combining blowdown with other
	Bleed-Off GPM	359	Hydrocarbons, H₂S				effluent streams reduces chromate
	Make-Up GPM	1436	(periodic leaks)			Plant Eff. Limits on CrO₄, Zn, PO₄	No limits

5. PRESENT TREATMENT AND CONTROL METHODS											
pH		CORROSION AND SCALE INHIBITOR		DISPERSANT		BIOCIDE		CHLORINE		CONTROLS	
Type Acid & Strength	66°	Product		Product		Product	None	Form, Gas Liq, Pulv.	Gas	Cycles of Concentration	
Slug/Cont. or Auto	H₂SO₄	Slug/Cont. or Auto	Cont.	Slug/Cont. or Auto	Slug	Slug/Cont. or Auto		Slug/Cont. or Auto	Slug	Actual No. Desired No.	5.7	6
Desired pH Range	6-7	Desired ppm Range	40-45	Desired ppm Range	50 ppm	Frequency		Frequency	m/w/f		Makeup	Bleed
Actual pH Range	5-8	Actual ppm Range	20-50	Actual ppm Range	3 hrs	Residual Time		Residual Time	1 ppm for 4 hours	Metered Yes/No	Yes	Yes
Lbs/Day	Slug	Lbs/Day	255	Lbs/Day	104	Lbs/Appli.		Lbs/Day		Controled Yes/No	Yes	Yes

Figure 38.13 General data required in making a cooling system survey. Supporting data include flow diagrams and tabulation of individual heat exchangers (Table 38.2).

TABLE 38.2 Performance Data for Individual Heat Exchangers Tabulated on General Survey (Figure 38.13)

		General			Cooling water				Process side				Materials of construction			
Exc. number	Nomenclature	Shell side or tube side cooling water	Heat flux	Number of passes	Velocity	Max exit temp, °F	ΔT across Exc.	Pressure	Product nomenclature	Max. inlet temp, °F	Design outlet temp, °F	Pressure	Tubes	Channel	Head	Sheet
	FCC															
307	Compressor inlet stage cooler	Tube	9,475	1	3	100	5	35	Hydrocarbon vapor	262	154	70	Adm	CS	CS	Adm
309	Compressor seal oil cooler	Tube	6,000	2	5.5	120	10	35	Oil	245	159	25	Adm	CS	CS	Adm
314	Compressor seal oil cooler	Tube	3,780	2	6.5	120	8	40	Oil	245	159	25	SS	SS	SS	SS
316*	Bearing lube oil cooler	Shell	4,600	2	4.5	120	10	35	Oil	230	159	30	SS	SS	SS	SS
322	Main overhead trim cooler	Tube	12,000	4	3.0	135	25	30	Hydrocarbon vapor	510	154	120	CS	CS	CS	CS
330	Main air blower lube system	Tube	8,750	2	6.5	118	12	40	Oil	225	154	40	CS	CS	CS	CS
333	Main air blower turbine exhaust	Shell	10,250	1	2.5	125	10	40	Air	320	115	65	Adm	CS	CS	CS
337	Main air blower turbine gland cooler	Shell	8,000	1	5.0	115	5	40	Air	200	110	40	CS	CS	CS	CS

* Information was taken from the most critical exchanger in a series of similar exchangers.

3. *Present conditions,* defining the physical conditions of the heat exchange equipment inspected during the survey, supplemented by the analysis of significant deposits. This information provides a basis for recommendations for cleaning, preconditioning of metal surfaces, and application of chemicals for proper system maintenance.

4. *Cleaning procedure.* This includes mechanical and chemical cleaning procedures currently employed.

Plant Effluent Considerations Some cooling systems are bled off directly into a receiving stream; others are discharged to various kinds of waste treatment processes; and some discharge to municipal sewage systems. Each imposes considerations on the choice and application of a chemical treatment program.

Control Monitoring and Followup Chemical control, monitoring of results, and corrective action are required for an effective cooling water treatment program. A wide variety of analytical tools and monitoring devices are available to aid in developing and maintaining a chemical program that will provide an efficient operation.

The goal of analysis and monitoring is to identify potential problems before they occur. The major diagnostic tools include:

1. Water analyses (on-site and laboratory)
2. Deposit analyses (organic, inorganic, and microbial)
3. Corrosion and deposition monitoring devices
4. Metallographic analyses
5. Microbial analyses

CORROSION CONTROL

Corrosion in recirculating cooling water systems is controlled by employing one or more of four major inhibitors and a variety of minor supplements. The four basic inhibitors are chromate, zinc, orthophosphate and polyphosphate. Minor supplements include molybdate, nitrite, nitrate, various organic nitrogen compounds, silicate, and natural organics.

The earliest chemicals for treating recirculating cooling waters were inorganic polyphosphates and natural organic materials. The concept was to add a small amount of acid to control the stability index to a slightly scale-forming value.

Polyphosphate and natural organic materials were added to the program to provide both corrosion protection and scale inhibition. The scale inhibition stemmed from the use of the polyphosphate as a threshold treatment. In addition, the polyphosphate combined with calcium to form a cathodic inhibitor that reduced the corrosion rate. The natural organic material tended to keep the metal surface relatively clean and aid the inhibitor in establishing a protective film. It also dispersed suspended solids, and modified calcium carbonate and tricalcium phosphate precipitates if these tended to develop on hot surfaces.

This concept of cooling water treatment is still used today in many operating systems. However, a critical aspect of this treatment approach is the potential reversion of the polyphosphate to orthophosphate; if this occurs, the resulting orthophosphate combines with calcium, forming tricalcium phosphate. This can be very troublesome if the amount precipitated is large. To minimize this, the water is kept at a relatively low pH. With this system, pH is difficult to control.

The next cooling water treatment was chromate, an exceptionally reliable corrosion inhibitor. Initially, chromate was applied at very high dosages, frequently in the range of 200–300 mg/l as CrO_4. Acid was added to the system to lower the pH to between 6 and 7, preventing calcium carbonate from precipitating. This treatment was quite effective in both scale inhibition and corrosion protection, but one shortcoming was that pitting attack tended to occur if the chromate residual became low. It was found that if chromate were combined with other inhibitors, particularly cathodic types (e.g., zinc and polyphosphate), the chromate level could be reduced to 20–30 mg/l CrO_4 with better results than obtained at 200–300 mg/l CrO_4 used alone. The synergized chromate approach also employed acid, frequently controlling the pH to 6–7. An additional advantage of synergized chromate was the margin of safety provided against pitting attack should the chromate be momentarily underfed.

These synergized chromate formulations are still considered among the best corrosion inhibitors in use today. However, increasing environmental pressures are forcing the development of innovative synergized chromate formulations that permit carrying chromate levels in a recirculating system substantially below 10 mg/l CrO_4 while continuing to provide acceptable corrosion protection. To achieve results with this approach the system pH must be controlled precisely, and dispersants and biocides used to keep the system clean. An obvious limitation to this approach is that the reservoir of protection available with the higher CrO_4 levels does not exist. Therefore, process contamination, uncontrolled microbial activity, fouling, and deposition will disrupt the system much more quickly than at the more traditional 20–30 mg/l CrO_4 levels.

Although chromate has done an outstanding job for years, increasing environmental concerns have brought pressure on research into new corrosion inhibitors with potentially less environmental impact. An early result of such research was the development of organo-zinc combinations. Since zinc, a cathodic inhibitor, has a lower film strength than chromate, the pH of the system for an organo-zinc program was increased to between 7 and 8 to make the water less corrosive, allowing the zinc to form a satisfactory inhibitor barrier. The organic portion of the treatment was a dispersant to keep the system free of deposits, thereby encouraging formation of an adequate zinc film. In addition to dispersancy, certain types of organics increased zinc solubility at the higher pH required for this method of treatment. These programs were adequate in many industrial plants, but because the inhibitor film at the operating pH was not as effective as a chromate film, these programs did not substantially replace traditional chromate type treatments.

Subsequently, an innovative concept in cooling water chemistry arrived with the introduction of organo-phosphorus compounds. Like inorganic polyphosphates, these prevent scale formation by the threshold effect. However, there the similarity ends; inorganic polyphosphates easily revert to orthophosphate, with increasing holding time, temperature, and microbiological attack. Organo-phosphorus compounds do not revert under normal cooling tower conditions except under severe microbiological attack. Further, unlike the inorganic polyphosphates, the organophosphorus compounds are generally able to inhibit precipitation of calcium carbonate and other scale-forming species at a higher pH and alkalinity than tolerated by the inorganic polyphosphates. This development opened the door to what is now known as the alkaline approach to treating cooling water systems.

The basic treatment concept is to raise the pH of the operating system to 7.5–9.0, thereby substantially reducing the natural corrosivity of the recirculating water. An organo-phosphorus compound is then added to the system to prevent calcium carbonate from forming. This approach relies on the natural alkalinity of the water and pH elevation to inhibit corrosion.

Experience has shown that although the higher pH provides a less corrosive water, frequently this reduction is not of sufficient magnitude to protect all mild steel systems, especially mild steel heat exchangers with high heat flux or low flow velocities. These systems still require supplementing the organo-phos-

TABLE 38.3 **Important Cooling Water Variables**

Variable	Effects
Ca, Mg	Define scaling tendency of water
M, pH, T	Define concentrations of carbonate and bicarbonate, and solubility of calcium carbonate
SO_4, SiO_2	Must be controlled to prevent sulfate and silicate scales
Suspended solids	Cause fouling, require dispersants
Contaminants: Hydrocarbons, glycols, NH_3, SO_2, H_2S	Cause fouling and microbial growth, high chlorine demand, precipitate chemical treatments

phorus materials with applied corrosion inhibitors like zinc, orthophosphate, polyphosphate, chromate, or combinations of these.

The significant advantage provided by organo-phosphorus compounds over earlier treatments is that the reduced corrosivity of the water allows lower residuals of applied inhibitors to be maintained while achieving acceptable corrosion rates. Another particular advantage of the alkaline concept of treatment is the substantial reduction or occasional elimination of acid feed. This, of course, depends on the chemistry of the system.

Table 38.3 lists some of the more important variables that must be controlled in cooling systems. Calcium and magnesium hardness define the scaling tendency of the water. Total alkalinity, pH and temperature define the concentrations of carbonate and bicarbonate ions in the water, and also the solubility of calcium carbonate. All of these must be controlled within acceptable ranges for each system to insure scale-free operation. Concentrations of sulfate and silica must also be controlled at reasonable levels to prevent formation of gypsum and silica scale.

Many systems contain suspended solids which concentrate in the tower and cause fouling. Dispersants may be used to control this once the problem has been properly defined. Some of the solids may come from the makeup, some may be washed from the air, and some may be precipitation products or microbial masses. If the suspended solids are excessive, as evidenced by plugged tubes, a filter system must be added to the circuit to filter a portion of the circulating water, approximately equal to the evaporation rate.

Table 38.4 lists some of the major chemical components available for cooling water treatment. In using this chart it should be noted that no one of these is useful by itself. For example, good corrosion control is difficult or impossible in a dirty, scaled system. Good scale and fouling control to maintain clean surfaces minimizes the dosage of corrosion inhibitors. Many chemicals help to solve more than one problem, as shown in Table 38.4. Whether or not a particular chemical is the best choice for a given system depends on the specific conditions in that system.

FOULING CONTROL

Deposit control in cooling water systems is absolutely essential for maintenance of heat transfer rates. However, control of deposits is often more difficult in alkaline systems than in lower pH systems. The makeup water may contain dissolved solids, organic matter and suspended solids, any of which can contribute to fouling. A system may become grossly contaminated with microbes; for example, makeup water with a high BOD, such as a recycled municipal or in-

TABLE 38.4   Chemical Components of Cooling Water Treatments

Chemical treatments	Problems			
	Corrosion	Scaling	Fouling	Microbes
Chromates	x			
Zinc	x			
Molybdates	x			
Silicates	x			
Polyphosphates	x	x		
Polyol esters		x	x	
Phosphonates		x	x	
Natural organics		x	x	
Polyacrylates		x	x	
Non-oxidizing biocides			x	x
Chlorine				x
Ozone				x

dustrial effluent, is particularly susceptible to fouling from slime-forming bacteria.

Table 38.5 shows some sources of foulants in a typical recirculating system. The raw water and air inoculate a system with colloidal organic matter, silt, soluble iron and microbes. Hydrogen sulfide, sulfur dioxide and ammonia may enter from the plant atmosphere.

Referring to Table 38.4, most of the commonly used scale control chemicals also control fouling, but they are not all equally good at dispersing all kinds of deposits. The selection of the proper dispersant for any operating system is based on actual analysis of a deposit. Natural and synthetic organics, including sulfonated lignins, tannins, and surface-active agents are generally applied for dispersing hydrous oxides and organic deposits. Materials of the acrylate family are dispersants for silt, sand, hard iron oxides and other inorganic deposits. Organo-phosphorus compounds, including polyol esters and phosphonates, are dispersants for calcium carbonate and calcium sulfate precipitates. However, once deposits form, any scale removing action by these dispersants takes place slowly, so the best approach is to prevent the scale from forming in the first place.

MICROBIAL CONTROL

Microbial deposits present a special case of fouling. Treatment often requires biocides to kill microbe colonies and dispersants to loosen and wash them away. The most common biocide employed in all systems is chlorine. Chlorine is believed to be less effective above a pH of 8 than below 7 because of the well-

TABLE 38.5   Sources of Fouling Deposits

Raw water	Airborne	Recirculating water
Colloidal organics	Dirt	Scale: $CaCO_3$, $CaSO_4$, $MgSiO_3$
Silt, dirt	Reactive gases— H_2S, SO_2, NH_3	Corrosion products: Fe_2O_3
Soluble iron		Process leaks— hydrocarbons, sulfides
Microbial contamination	Microbial contamination	Microbial deposits

known hypochlorite equilibrium. Nevertheless it is still an effective biocide and is indispensable to many cooling water treatment programs.

There are problems associated with the use of chlorine. It can react with some organic materials, particularly phenolic compounds, to form reaction products that are non-biodegradable or refractory, presenting potential effluent problems. Generally speaking, chlorine can be applied to most recirculating systems without danger of tower lumber delignification if free chlorine residuals do not exceed 1 mg/l. It is seldom necessary to continually carry a free chlorine residual over 0.2–0.3 mg/l to control microbial growths in most systems.

Although chlorine is an excellent killing agent, there are some notable limitations to chlorine that require the use of nonoxidizing biocides in most systems. Chlorine is not a penetrant so it may achieve a surface kill on a microbial deposit, but will not penetrate the slime layer to remove and kill organisms underneath. This is in direct contrast to the non-oxidizing biocides and selective biodispersants which do have penetrating ability.

Chapter **39**

Boiler Water Treatment

Of the many uses for energy in the United States today—in industry, in transportation, in homes and commercial buildings—the largest portion is directed toward producing steam through the combustion of fossil fuels. Utilities account for the greatest share of this, but industrial plants also produce enormous quantities of steam for process uses, often generating electrical power through turbines as a byproduct.

The treatment of water for steam generation is one of the most sophisticated branches of water chemistry. An understanding of the fundamentals of boiler water chemistry is essential to the power engineer who continually strives to increase the efficiency of the boilers and steam-using equipment in his plant.

The pressure and design of a boiler determine the quality of water it requires for steam generation. Municipal or plant water of good quality for domestic use is seldom good enough for boiler feedwater. These sources of makeup are nearly always treated to reduce contaminants to acceptable levels; in addition, corrective chemicals are added to the treated water to counteract any adverse effects of the remaining trace contaminants. The sequence of treatment depends on the type and concentration of contaminants found in the water supply and the desired quality of the finished water to avoid the three major boiler system problems—deposits, corrosion and carryover.

Deposits, particularly scale, can form on any water-washed equipment surface—especially on boiler tubes—as the equilibrium conditions in the water contacting these surfaces are upset by an external force, such as heat. Each contaminant has a definite solubility in water, and will precipitate when this has been exceeded. If the water is in contact with a hot surface and the solubility of the contaminant is lower at higher temperatures, the precipitate will form on the surface, causing scale. The most common components of boiler deposits are calcium phosphate, calcium carbonate (in low pressure boilers), magnesium

TABLE 39.1   Expected Composition of Boiler Sludge

Constituent	Coagulation-type treatment	PO₄ residual treatment
Calcium carbonate	High	Usually less than 5%
Calcium phosphate	Usually less than 15%	High
Calcium silicate	Usually less than 3%	Trace or none
Calcium sulfate	None	None
Calcium hydroxide	None	None
Loss on ignition	Usually less than 5%	Usually 8–12% except higher in very pure feedwaters
Magnesium phosphate	None	Usually less than 5% except in some high-pressure boilers
Magnesium hydroxide	Moderate	Moderate
Magnesium silicate	Moderate	Moderate
Silica	Usually less than 10%	Usually less than 10%
Alumina	Less than 10%	Usually less than 10%
Oil	None	None
Iron oxide	Usually less than 5%	Usually less than 5% except in high purity feedwaters
Sodium salts	Usually less than 1.5%	Usually less than 1.5%
Copper	Trace	Usually low
Other metals	Trace	Low

hydroxide, magnesium silicate, various forms of iron oxide, silica adsorbed on the previously mentioned precipitates, and alumina (see Table 39.1). If phosphate salts are used to treat the boiler water, calcium will preferentially precipitate as the phosphate before precipitating as the carbonate, and calcium phosphate becomes the most prominent feature of the deposit.

At the high temperatures found in a boiler, deposits are a serious problem, causing poor heat transfer and a potential for boiler tube failure. In low pressure boilers with low heat transfer rates, deposits may build up to a point where they completely occlude the boiler tube. At higher heat transfer rates, and in high pressure boilers, the problem is more severe: at temperatures in the 900–1350°F (482–732°C) range, carbon steel begins to deteriorate. Figure 39.1 shows the normal structure of carbon steel boiler tubes and Figure 39.2 illustrates the spheroidization of carbon and successive changes in structure, which begin to

Figure 39.1   Normal   structure of low-carbon boiler steel.

Figure 39.2 Above 800°F, the carbon begins to form spheroids and grain growth develops.

take place above 800°F (427°C), weakening the metal. Temperatures within the boiler furnace are considerably above this critical temperature range. Water circulating through the tubes normally conducts heat away from the metal, preventing the tube from reaching this range. Deposits insulate the tube, reducing the rate at which this heat can be removed (Figure 39.3); this leads to overheating and eventual tube failure (Figure 39.4). If the deposit is not thick enough to cause such a failure, it can still cause a substantial loss in efficiency and disruption of the heat transfer load in other sections of the boiler.

Figure 39.3 Deposits on the waterside of a boiler tube insulate the metal from the cooling effect of water flow. The metal on the fireside may then become overheated. (*Adapted from Jacklin, C., "Deposits in Boilers," Industrial and Engineering Chemistry, May 1954.*)

Figure 39.4 A typical tube failure caused by overheating.

Deposits may be scale, precipitated in-situ on a heated surface, or previously-precipitated chemicals, often in the form of sludge. These drop out of water in low velocity areas, compacting to form a dense agglomerate similar to scale, but retaining the features of the original precipitates. In the operation of most industrial boilers, it is seldom possible to avoid formation of some type of precipitate at some time. There are almost always some particulates in the circulating boiler water which can deposit in low velocity sections, such as the mud drum. The exception would be high purity systems, such as utility boilers, which remain relatively free of particulates except under conditions where the system may become temporarily upset.

The second major water-related boiler problem is corrosion, the most common example being the attack of steel by oxygen. This occurs in water supply systems, preboiler systems, boilers, condensate return lines, and in virtually any portion of the utility system where oxygen is present. Oxygen attack is accelerated by high temperature and by low pH. A less prevalent type of corrosion is alkali attack, which may occur in high pressure boilers where caustic can concentrate in a local area of steam bubble formation because of presence of porous deposits.

Some feedwater treatment chemicals, such as chelants, if not properly applied, can corrode feedwater piping, control valves, and even the boiler internals.

While the elimination of oxygen from boiler feedwater is the major step in

Figure 39.5 This instrument is used to monitor corrosion-produced hydrogen concentrations in steam.

controlling boiler corrosion, corrosion can still occur. An example is the direct attack by steam of the boiler steel surface at elevated temperatures, according to the following reaction:

$$4H_2O + 3Fe \rightarrow Fe_3O_4 + 4H_2 \uparrow \tag{1}$$

This attack can occur at steam-blanketed boiler surfaces where restricted boiler water flow causes overheating. It may also occur in superheater tubes subjected to overheating. Since this corrosion reaction produces hydrogen, a device for analyzing hydrogen in steam, Figure 39.5, is useful as a corrosion monitor.

The third major problem related to boiler operations is carryover from the boiler into the steam system. This may be a mechanical effect, such as boiler water spraying around a broken baffle; it may be due to the volatility of certain boiler water salts, such as silica and sodium compounds; or it may be caused by foaming. Carryover is most often a mechanical problem, and the chemicals found in the steam are those originally present in the boiler water, plus the volatile components that distill from the boiler even in the absence of spray.

There are three basic means for keeping these major problems under control:

1. *External Treatment* of the water—makeup, condensate, or both—before it enters the boiler, to reduce or eliminate chemicals (such as hardness or silica), gases or solids.

2. *Internal Treatment* of the boiler feedwater, boiler water, steam, or condensate with corrective chemicals.

3. *Blowdown*—Control of the concentration of chemicals in the boiler water by bleeding off a portion of the water in the boiler.

EXTERNAL TREATMENT

Most of the unit operations of water treatment (Table 39.2) can be used alone or in combination with others to adapt any water supply to any boiler system. The suitability of the processes available is judged by the results they produce and the costs involved.

The boiler treatment program aims at control of seven broad classifications of impurities: suspended solids, hardness, alkalinity, silica, total dissolved solids (TDS), organic matter, and gases. The extent to which each of the unit processes applicable to boiler makeup treatment, as described in earlier chapters, reduces or removes these impurities in summarized by Table 39.2.

Suspended Solids

The removal of suspended solids is accomplished by coagulation/flocculation, filtration, or precipitation. Other unit processes, except direct reaction, usually require prior removal of solids. For example, water to be processed by ion exchange should contain less than 10 mg/l suspended solids to avoid fouling of the exchanger and operating problems.

Hardness

A number of unit operations remove calcium and magnesium from water, as summarized by Table 39.2. Sodium exchange removes hardness and does nothing else; other processes provide additional benefits. Figure 39.6 compares these softening processes, showing the additional reduction of other impurities that may occur. Differences between softening processes are summarized in Table 39.3.

Alkalinity

— *why.*

It is desirable to have some alkalinity in boiler water, so complete removal of alkalinity from boiler makeup is seldom practiced except in demineralization.

TABLE 39.2 Boiler Makeup Treatment Processes

Impurity to be removed	Direct addition Note 1	Coagulation/ flocculation	Solids/ liquid separation	Precipitation	Adsorption	Ion exchange	Evaporation	Degasification	Membrane separation
Suspended Solids	NA	10 mg/l	<1 mg/l	10 mg/l	←— These processes require pretreatment for suspended solids removal —→				
Hardness	NA	NA	NA	Partial Removal Note 2	NA	0–2% Note 3	NA	Note 5	↕ (arrow)
Alkalinity	Can be decreased to 0 or increased as needed	Note 7	NA	Partial Removal Note 2	NA	Note 8	NA	NA	
Silica	NA	Slight Removal	Slight Removal	Partial Removal Note 9	Partial Removal Note 9	Note 10	Note 4	NA	Note 6
Dissolved Solids (TDS)	May increase Note 11	NA	NA	Partial Removal Note 2	NA	Note 12	↕ (arrow)	NA	
Organics	Note 13	Partial Removal Note 13	NA	Partial Removal Note 13	5–10%	Partial Removal Note 14	NA	NA	
Gases	Can be decreased to 0	May increase Note 8	NA	Note 15	Note 16	Note 8		Note 17	

NOTES TO TABLE 39.2:

1. Direct addition is the application of a chemical directly to water, where the byproducts remain in solution.

2. In the precipitation process, hardness can be reduced by a controlled amount, depending on the lime dosage. In partial lime softening, only the Ca is removed. This is accomplished by adding just enough lime to react with bicarbonate alkalinity plus free CO_2. The Ca hardness after treatment is approximately 35 mg/l cold or 15–20 mg/l hot, if the raw water calcium exceeds the calcium; if the raw water alkalinity exceeds the calcium, then the CO_3 concentration of the treated water is 35 mg/l cold, 15–20 mg/l hot. The reduction of calcium equals the reduction of alkalinity, since $CaCO_3$ forms as a precipitate. More complete hardness removal requires adding enough lime to react with the magnesium as well as the bicarbonate alkalinity and the free CO_2. In this case, if the alkalinity of the raw water exceeds the total hardness, the Ca residual is approximately

35 mg/l cold, 15–20 mg/l hot; if the hardness exceeds the alkalinity, then the CO_3 after treatment is 35 mg/l cold, 15–20 mg/l hot. The residual magnesium is approximately 30 ppm cold, 2–3 mg/l hot, when excess lime is added to produce a hydroxide alkalinity of 10 mg/l. The reduction of total solids equals the hardness reduction with coincident reduction of silica and organic matter.

3. The residuals after ion exchange vary with the water analysis, the regenerant dosage and application method, and the arrangement of the units in the system. Typical leakages through a sodium exchanger regenerated with brine are shown in the chapter on ion exchange.

4. Makeup to an evaporator is usually treated either ahead of the evaporator or in the evaporator body; the concentrated water is similar to boiler water, and the chemical treatment program is like boiler treatment.

5. If water is degasified for CO_2 removal, the chemical balance may be disturbed and hardness may precipitate in the degasifier.

6. In the membrane process, incoming solids remain in the saline stream unless removed by pretreatment. The degree of purification varies with water analysis and membrane characteristics, such as ion selectivity.

7. Alkalinity may be reduced by coagulation with alum or iron salts; it may be increased by aluminate; it may remain constant if the dosages of alum and aluminate are balanced.

8. Alkalinity is reduced by blending the effluents of sodium and hydrogen zeolite units (split-stream treatment). It can be reduced to any desired residual. The alkalinity reduction produces an equivalent concentration of CO_2 gas, which can be degassed to 5–10 mg/l at ambient temperature or to zero at 212°F (100°C).

9. The residual silica can be predicted from the water analysis and the dosage of adsorbent applied in the treatment process. Residuals range from 90% in cold process to as little as 5% in hot process, depending on the adsorbent added or on the magnesium precipitated by lime softening.

10. Silica is removed in ion exchange processes only by strong base anion resins regenerated with caustic. If the anion resin unit follows a sodium zeolite, the residual may be 10% of the feed; if the anion unit is part of a demineralizer, residuals as low as 0.01 mg/l can be achieved.

11. Some reactions, such as that between sodium sulfite and oxygen, produce a soluble byproduct (sodium sulfate) which increases TDS.

12. The reduction of dissolved solids by ion exchange varies with different cation and anion exchange processes. With sodium zeolite treatment, TDS is unchanged on a $CaCO_3$ equivalent basis; with split stream hydrogen zeolite, H_2X, TDS reduction equals the alkalinity reduction; with a demineralizer, removal is essentially complete and the residuals depend on the combination of units in the system.

13. Organic matter is reduced by both coagulation/flocculation or lime softening. Organic color over 50 mg/l interferes with lime softening unless counteracted by adsorption on carbon or by chemical oxidation. It is usual to obtain about 30% removal of organic matter in cold clarification or lime softening, and 50% removal in hot process precipitation. These removal efficiencies vary with the selection of coagulants, chlorine, permanganate, or powdered activated carbon.

14. Special ion exchange resins (like activated carbon) can be used to remove color. However, organic matter tends to accumulate irreversibly on anion resins, presenting serious operating problems. Organic matter should be removed ahead of a demineralizing system. Organic matter also interferes with membrane processes.

15. Carbon dioxide is removed by lime in cold process softeners and by degasification in the spray section of hot process softeners, which also reduce dissolved oxygen to a residual of about 0.5 mg/l. H_2S may be removed by adding a heavy metal precipitant such as an iron or zinc salt.

16. Taste and odor producing gases can be removed by activated carbon. Carbon also removes excess chlorine, through a chemical reaction.

17. Degasifiers using air for stripping reduce CO_2 and H_2S by 90–95% if the pH is kept below 7. Vacuum deaerators do as well on CO_2 and H_2S and also reduce dissolved O_2 to less than 1.0 mg/l. Steam-heated deaerators will remove all free CO_2 and reduce dissolved O_2 to 0.005 mg/l.

Identification of Analyses Tabulated Below:

A. Raw Water   D. Split-Stream + Degasifier

B. Simple Na₂Z Softening   E. Partial Lime-Cold

C. Na₂Z + Acid + Degasifier   F. Hot Lime-Zeolite

Constituent	As	A	B	C	D	E	F
Calcium	CaCO₃	115	Nil	Nil	Nil	35	Nil
Magnesium	"	45	Nil	Nil	Nil	40	Nil
Sodium	"	60	220	220	105	60	115
Total Electrolyte	CaCO₃	220	220	220	105	135	115
Bicarbonate	CaCO₃	135	135	20	20	15	0
Carbonate	"	0	0	0	0	35	20
Hydroxyl	"	0	0	0	0	0	10
Sulfate	"	65	65	180	65	65	65
Chloride	"	20	20	20	20	20	20
Nitrate	"	0	0	0	0	0	0
M Alk.	CaCO₃	135	135	20	20	50	30
P Alk.	"	0	0	0	0	18	20
Carbon Dioxide		10	10	5	5	0	0
pH		7.3	7.3	6.8	6.8	9.8	10.3
Silica		10	10	10	10	9	1
Iron	Fe	0	0	0	0	0	0
Turbidity		Nil	Nil	Nil	Nil	Nil	Nil
TDS (estimated)		275	290	290	170	190	155
Color		0	0	0	0	0	0
Total Hardness		160	Nil	Nil	Nil	75	Nil

Figure 39.6 A comparison of water softening processes.

Some alkalinity is also needed to provide optimum pH in the feedwater to prevent corrosion of piping and equipment.

The makeup alkalinity may be present as HCO_3^-, $CO_3^=$, or OH^-. If the makeup is city water that has been zeolite softened, alkalinity is usually in the bicarbonate (HCO_3^-) form; if lime softened, it is mostly carbonate ($CO_3^=$), but the water may also contain some hydroxide (OH^-). When bicarbonates and carbonates are exposed to boiler temperatures, they break down to release CO_2:

$$2NaHCO_3 \rightarrow Na_2CO_3 + H_2O + CO_2 \uparrow \qquad (2)$$

The sodium carbonate then breaks down further to caustic:

$$Na_2CO_3 + H_2O \rightarrow 2NaOH + CO_2 \uparrow \qquad (3)$$

The carbon dioxide gas redissolves when the steam condenses, producing corrosive carbonic acid:

$$CO_2 + H_2O \rightleftharpoons H_2CO_3 \rightleftharpoons H^+ + HCO_3^- \qquad (4)$$

ZEOLITE

TABLE 39.3 Water Softening Process Summary
(Summary of Figure 39.6)

Process	Residuals, mg/l			
	Hardness	Alkalinity	Silica	TDS
Original water	160	135	10	275
Sodium exchange	Nil	135	10	290
Sodium exchange and acid	Nil	20	10	290
Split stream	Nil	20	10	170
Partial lime (cold)	75	50	9	190
Hot lime–zeolite	Nil	30	1	155

The amount of CO_2 generated is proportional to the alkalinity. For a given alkalinity twice as much CO_2 is formed from HCO_3^- as from $CO_3^=$ because the bicarbonate breakdown is the sum of both reactions (2) and (3) above. The carbonic acid is usually neutralized by chemical treatment of the steam—either directly or indirectly through the boiler—to produce a condensate pH in the range of 8.5–9.0. Reduction of feedwater alkalinity is desirable, then, to minimize CO_2 formation and reduce chemical treatment costs.

The hydroxide produced by the breakdown of HCO_3^- and $CO_3^=$ is beneficial for precipitation of magnesium, to provide a good environment for sludge conditioning, and to minimize SiO_2 carryover. However, too high an excess of caustic can be corrosive, particularly if localized concentration can occur. The breakdown of HCO_3^- is complete, but not all the $CO_3^=$ converts to caustic. The conversion varies from one boiler to another and increases with temperature. As a general rule, at 600 psi 65–85% of boiler water alkalinity is NaOH, the remainder Na_2CO_3. (This is based on the equilibrium in the cooled sample of boiler water.)

The degree of alkalinity reduction is therefore dictated by boiler water control limits and steam quality goals. The best unit process for alkalinity reduction may be chosen for the other benefits it provides as well as its efficiency in alkalinity reduction. Figure 39.7 compares alkalinity reduction processes and their supplemental benefits. The major differences between these processes are summarized in Table 39.4.

Silica

The permissible concentrations of silica in boiler water at various operating pressures are given in Table 39.5. Silica reduction is not always necessary, especially in the absence of a condensing turbine. Low concentrations of silica can sometimes produce sticky sludge in low pressure boilers treated with phosphate. A makeup treatment process may be selected to provide just the

TABLE 39.4 Alkalinity Reduction Processes
(Summary of Figure 39.7)

Process	Residuals, mg/l			
	Alkalinity	Hardness	Silica	TDS
Original water	135	160	10	275
Direct acid addition	20	160	10	290
Split stream	20	Nil	10	170
Na_2X and anion (Cl)	20	Nil	10	290
Cold lime	50	75	9	190
Hot lime–zeolite	30	Nil	1	155

Identification of Analyses Tabulated Below:

A. Raw Water

B. Direct H_2SO_4 + Degasifier

C. Split-Stream + Degasifier

D. Na_2Z + Chloride Anion Exchanger

E. Partial Lime-Cold

F. Hot Lime Zeolite

Constituent	As	A	B	C	D	E	F
Calcium	CaCO₃	115	115	Nil	Nil	35	Nil
Magnesium	"	45	45	Nil	Nil	40	Nil
Sodium	"	60	60	105	220	60	115
Total Electrolyte	CaCO₃	220	220	105	220	135	115
Bicarbonate	CaCO₃	135	20	20	20	15	0
Carbonate	"	0	0	0	0	35	20
Hydroxyl	"	0	0	0	0	0	10
Sulfate	"	65	180	65	5	65	65
Chloride	"	20	20	20	195	20	20
Nitrate	"	0	0	0	0	0	0
M Alk. (Total Alk.)	CaCO₃	135	20	20	20	50	30
P Alk.	"	0	0	0	0	18	20
Carbon Dioxide		10	5	5	5	0	0
pH		7.3	6.8	6.8	6.8	9.8	10.3
Silica		10	10	10	10	9	1
Iron	Fe	0	0	0	0	0	0
Turbidity		Nil	Nil	Nil	Nil	Nil	Nil
TDS (estimated)		275	290	170	290	190	165
Color		0	0	0	0	0	0

Figure 39.7 A comparison of processes for alkalinity reduction.

TABLE 39.5 Silica Concentration in Boiler Water

Drum pressure, psig	Silica Concentration, mg/l	
	*	†
0–300	150	150
301–450	90	90
451–600	40	55
601–750	30	35
751–900	20	20
901–1000	8	15

* Recommended limits.
† Concentration producing 0.02 mg/l SiO_2 in saturated steam at upper pressure limit.

Identification of Analyses Tabulated Below:

A. Raw Water

B. Cold Lime with FeCl$_3$

C. Cold Lime-Soda

D. Lime-Soda @ 220°F

E. Na$_2$Z + A.OH + H$_2$SO$_4$

F. Demineralization

Constituent	As	A	B	C	D	E	F
Calcium	CaCO$_3$	115	70	35	15	Nil	Nil
Magnesium	"	45	40	30	2	Nil	Nil
Sodium	"	60	60	85	108	220	1-2
Total Electrolyte	CaCO$_3$	220	170	150	125	220	1-2
Bicarbonate	CaCO$_3$	135	0	0	0	0	1-2
Carbonate	"	0	35	35	30	20	0
Hydroxyl	"	0	0	30	10	0	0
Sulfate	"	65	65	65	65	180	0
Chloride	"	20	70	20	20	20	0
Nitrate	"	0	0	0	0	0	0
M Alk.	CaCO$_3$	135	35	65	40	20	1-2
P Alk.	"	0	18	48	25	10	0
Carbon Dioxide		10	0	0	0	0	Nil
pH		7.3	10.0	10.8	10.3	10.0	7-8
Silica		10	6	7-8	1	0.5-1	0.05
Iron	Fe	0	0	0	0	0	0
Turbidity		Nil	Nil	Nil	Nil	Nil	Nil
TDS (estimated)		275	225	210	145	290	1-2
Color		0	0	0	0	0	0

Figure 39.8 A comparison of processes for silica reduction.

proper degree of silica reduction required by the steam system. Figure 39.8 shows the treatment results achieved by the various silica removal processes; the influence of each of these processes on other feedwater contaminants is summarized in Table 39.6.

Total Dissolved Solids

Some treatment processes increase dissolved solids by adding soluble by-products to water; sodium zeolite softening increases solids by virtue of adding an ion (sodium) having a higher equivalent weight (23) than the calcium (20) or magnesium (12.2) removed from the raw water. Processes to reduce dissolved solids achieve various degrees of success. Usually, reduction of dissolved solids is accomplished by a reduction of several individual contaminants. Table 39.7 summarizes the analyses of effluents produced by processes which reduce dissolved solids.

**TABLE 39.6   Silica Reduction Processes
(Summary of Figure 39.8)**

Process	Residuals, mg/l			
	Silica	Hardness	Alkalinity	TDS
Original water	10	160	135	275
Cold lime and iron salts	6	110	35	225
Cold lime–soda	7–8	65	65	210
Hot lime–soda	1	17	40	145
Na_2X + anion exchanger	1	Nil	20	290
Demineralization	0.05	Nil	1–2	1–2

Organic Matter

Organic matter as a general classification is only a qualitative term. It includes a wide variety of compounds that are seldom analyzed as specific materials. Problems in boiler systems attributed to organic matter have often been traced to organic materials from plant processes in returned condensate, rather than makeup water contaminants.

Dissolved Gases

Degasifiers are commonly used to remove gas mechanically rather than chemically. Blower types are used for CO_2 removal at ambient temperatures following acid or hydrogen-exchange units. Vacuum degasifiers provide the same extent of CO_2 removal, but also reduce O_2 to less than 0.5–1.0 mg/l, offering corrosion protection, especially if the vacuum degasifier is part of a demineralizing system. Steam-scrubbing degasifiers, called deaerating heaters, usually produce an effluent free of CO_2 with O_2 concentrations in the range of 0.005–0.01 mg/l. Direct reaction of this low residual with catalyzed sulfite or hydrazine eliminates O_2 completely to prevent pre-boiler corrosion.

In addition to makeup treatment, acceptable feedwater quality may require cleanup of condensate to protect the boiler system, particularly if there is process condensate containing oil. Boilers requiring high quality demineralized water also demand high quality condensate. Some plants operate both high and low pressure boilers; high quality feedwater for the high pressure boilers may be provided entirely by a demineralizer, with lower quality condensate segregated for return to the low pressure boilers.

Septum filters are usually selected for oily condensate treatment. A cellulose-type filter aid (processed wood pulp) is applied both as a precoat and a body feed. The temperature should be less than 200°F (93°C) to avoid degradation of the filter aid. Anthracite filters precoated with a floc produced from alum and sodium aluminate are also effective. However, the pH of the condensate

**TABLE 39.7   Reduction of Total Dissolved Solids
(Summary of Tables 39.3, 39.4, and 39.6)**

Process	Residuals, mg/l			
	TDS	Hardness	Alkalinity	Silica
Original water	275	160	135	10
Split stream	170	Nil	20	10
Partial cold lime	190	75	50	9
Hot lime–soda	145	17	40	1
Hot lime–zeolite	155	Nil	30	1
Demineralization	1–2	Nil	1–2	0.05

must be controlled in the range of 7–8 to avoid solubilizing the alumina floc. Condensate contaminated with corrosion products and inleakage of hard water is cleaned up through specially designed, high-flow rate sodium exchangers (Figure 39.9). These have been used to process condensate at temperatures up to 300°F (149°C).

Heavily contaminated process condensates, such as those produced in kraft pulp mills and petroleum refineries, present special problems in use as boiler feedwater. Their composition is usually variable and may include complex organic compounds and unusual ions such as cyanide, thiocyanate, and sulfide. The treatment program cannot be selected simply on the basis of the condensate analysis; research on the bench and by pilot plant operation may be required.

INTERNAL TREATMENT

Scale formation within a boiler is controlled by one of four chemical programs: coagulation (carbonate), phosphate residual, chelation, or coordinated phosphate.

Coagulation Program

In this process, sodium carbonate, sodium hydroxide, or both are added to the boiler water to supplement the alkalinity supplied by the makeup, which is not softened. The carbonate causes deliberate precipitation of calcium carbonate under favorable, controlled conditions, preventing deposition at some subsequent point as scale. Under alkaline conditions, magnesium and silica are also precipitated as magnesium hydroxide and magnesium silicate. There is usually a fairly high concentration of suspended solids in the boiler water, and the precipitation occurs on these solids. This method of treatment is only used with boilers using high hardness feed water and operating below 250 psi.

Phosphate Program

Where the boiler pressure is above 250 psi, high concentrations of sludge are undesirable. In these boilers, feedwater hardness should be limited to 60 mg/l, and phosphate programs are preferred. Phosphate is also a common treatment below 250 psi with soft makeup.

A sodium phosphate compound is fed either to the boiler feedwater or to the boiler drum, depending on water analysis and the pre-boiler auxiliaries, to form an insoluble precipitate, principally hydroxyapatite, $Ca_{10}(PO_4)_6(OH)_2$. Magnesium and silica are precipitated as magnesium hydroxide, magnesium silicate (often combined as $3MgO \cdot 2SiO_2 \cdot 2H_2O$), or calcium silicate. The alkalinity of the makeup is usually adequate to produce the OH^- for the magnesium precipitation.

Chelant Programs

A chelant is a molecule similar to an ion exchanger; it is low in molecular weight and soluble in water. The sodium salts of ethylene diamine tetraacetic acid (EDTA) and nitrilotriacetic acid (NTA) are the chelating agents most commonly used for internal boiler treatment. These chelate (form complex ions with) calcium and magnesium. Because the resulting complex is soluble, this treatment is advantageous in minimizing blowdown. The higher cost compared to phosphate usually limits the use of chelants to feedwaters having low hardness. There is the risk that breakdown of the organic molecule at higher temperatures could create a potential problem of control that could result in corrosion, so chelant programs are usually limited to boilers operating below 1500 psi (100 bars). The addition of polymers as scale control agents increases the effectiveness of chelant programs.

Figure 39.9 An ion exchange system designed for treating chemical plant condensate: (Top) exchange units; (Bottom) control panel. *(Courtesy of Dow Chemical Company.)*

Figure 39.10 The effect of organic treatment—in this case tannin—on the nature of CaCO₃ crystals.

Carbonate crystals
formed by heating water

Crystals altered by
50 ppm tannin

It also reduces the corrosion potential by reducing the chelant dosage below theoretical requirements, so that there is no chelant residual in the boiler water.

Coordinated Phosphate Program

In high pressure, high heat transfer rate boilers, the internal treatment program must contribute little or no solids. The potential for caustic attack of boiler metal increases with increasing pressure, so free caustic alkalinity must be minimized. The coordinated phosphate program is chosen for these conditions. This differs from the standard program in that the phosphate is added to provide a controlled pH range in the boiler water as well as to react with calcium if hardness should enter the boiler. Trisodium phosphate hydrolyzes to produce hydroxide ions:

$$Na_3PO_4 + H_2O \rightleftharpoons 3Na^+ + OH^- + HPO_4^{-2} \tag{5}$$

This cannot occur with the ionization of disodium and monosodium phosphate:

$$Na_2HPO_4 \rightleftharpoons 2Na^+ + HPO_4^{-2} \tag{6}$$

$$NaH_2PO_4 \rightleftharpoons Na^+ + H^+ + HPO_4^{-2} \tag{7}$$

The program is controlled by feeding combinations of disodium phosphate with trisodium or monosodium phosphate to produce an optimum pH without the presence of free OH⁻. To successfully control a coordinated phosphate program, the feedwater must be extremely pure and of consistent quality.

In addition to controlling scale and deposits, internal treatment must also control carryover, defined as entrainment of boiler water into the steam. Boiler salts carried as a mist may subsequently deposit in the superheater, causing tube failures, or deposit on the blades of a turbine. They may also contaminate a process in which the steam is used. Since a high percentage of carryover is caused by foaming, this problem is usually solved by the addition of antifoam to the boiler feedwater.

Sludge in boiler water may settle to form deposits, which are as serious a problem as scale. Chemicals are used to condition boiler water particulates so that they do not form large crystalline precipitates; smaller particles will remain dispersed at the velocities encountered in the boiler circuit. At lower pressures both the coagulation and phosphate residual programs incorporate sludge conditioning agents for this purpose. A variety of natural organic materials are used, including starches, tannins, and lignins. Figure 39.10 shows the effect of tannin in stunting the growth of CaCO₃ crystals; Figure 39.11 illustrates the effectiveness of tannin in preventing CaCO₃ scale in 250 psi (17 bars) experimental boilers by this ability to control crystal growth and disperse the precipitated CaCO₃.

250 psi Calcium
carbonate deposits

250 psi 34 ppm
Tannin-type organic

Figure 39.11 In early experimental boiler studies, the value of tannin in controlling deposits on boiler surfaces was clearly shown.

At intermediate pressures, chemically reacted lignins are widely used. Figure 39.12 shows the approximate molecular configuration of a lignin processed for high temperature stability. Its effectiveness in controlling calcium phosphate scale and magnetic iron oxide deposits at 1500 psi (100 bars) is shown in Figures 39.13 and 39.14.

At intermediate pressures, heat-stable polymers such as anionic carboxylates are also used as effective dispersants. An alkaline environment generally increases the effectiveness of all of these dispersants.

Somewhat related to carryover, in that steam quality is affected, is the discharge of contaminants that volatilize under boiler operating conditions. The major volatiles are CO_2, created by the breakdown of carbonate and bicarbonate mentioned earlier, and SiO_2. Although the CO_2 can be neutralized, it is prudent to reduce feedwater alkalinity to minimize its formation. For all practical purposes, external treatment for silica reduction and blowdown are the only means to avoid excessive SiO_2 discharges for protection of turbine blading. Hydroxyl alkalinity helps reduce silica volatility.

Oxygen is the chief culprit in boiler systems corrosion. Deaeration reduces this to a low concentration in the pre-boiler system, but does not completely eliminate it. Application of sulfite or hydrazine after deaeration scavenges the remaining O_2 and maintains a reducing condition in the boiler water. An advantage of hydrazine is that it is discharged into the steam to become available in the condensate as protection against oxygen corrosion in the return system. If oxygen is present, ammonia can attack copper alloys in condensers and stage heaters. The removal of NH_3 by external treatment may be necessary. The corrosive aspects of

Figure 39.12 Because tannins lose effectiveness at higher temperatures, other organics were developed. This is the structure of lignin processed for deposit control in higher-pressure boilers.

Figure 39.13 The effectiveness of a lignin derivative in controlling calcium phosphate scale at 1500 psi is shown here.

1500 psi
Calcium phosphate
scale

1500 psi
34 ppm lignin
derivative

CO_2 have already been mentioned in relation to condensate systems. The beneficial and detrimental aspects of NaOH in the boiler circuit in relation to corrosion control have also been discussed earlier.

BLOWDOWN

Boiler feedwater, regardless of the type of treatment used to process the makeup, still contains measurable concentrations of impurities. In some plants, contaminated condensate contributes to feedwater impurities. Internal boiler water treatment chemicals also add to the level of solids in the boiler water.

When steam is generated, essentially pure H_2O vapor is discharged from the boiler, leaving the solids introduced in the feedwater to remain in the boiler circuits. The net result of impurities being continuously added and pure water being withdrawn is a steady increase in the level of dissolved solids in the boiler water. There is a limit to the concentration of each component of the boiler water. To prevent exceeding these concentration limits, boiler water is withdrawn as blowdown and discharged to waste. Figure 39.15 illustrates a material balance for a boiler, showing that the blowdown must be adjusted so that solids leaving the boiler equal those entering and the concentration is maintained at the predetermined limits.

One way of looking at boiler blowdown is to consider it a process of diluting boiler water solids by withdrawing boiler water from the system at a rate that induces a flow of feedwater into the boiler in excess of steam demand.

Figure 39.14 The effectiveness of a lignin derivative in controlling iron deposits at 1500 psi. Left, no treatment; right, with organic treatment.

1500 psi
Magnetic iron oxide
deposits

1500 psi
34 ppm lignin
derivative

Figure 39.15   How boiler water solids are controlled by blow-down.

There are two separate blowdown points in every boiler system. One accommodates the blowdown flow that is controlled to regulate the dissolved solids or other factors in the boiler water. The other is an intermittent or mass blowdown, usually from the mud drum or waterwall headers, which is operated intermittently at reduced boiler load to rid the boiler of accumulated settled solids in relatively stagnant areas. The following discussion of blowdown will be confined only to that used for adjusting boiler water dissolved solids concentrations.

Blowdown may be either intermittent or continuous. If intermittent, the boiler is allowed to concentrate to a level acceptable for the particular boiler design and pressure. When this concentration level is reached, the blowdown valve is opened for a short period of time to reduce the concentration of impurities, and the boiler is then allowed to reconcentrate until the control limits are again reached. In continuous blowdown, on the other hand, the blowdown valve is kept open at a fixed setting to remove water at a steady rate, maintaining a relatively constant boiler water concentration. Since the average concentration level in a boiler blown

Figure 39.16   Schematic of industrial boiler system.

down intermittently is substantially less than that maintained by continuous blowdown, intermittent blowdown is less efficient—more costly—than continuous blowdown.

Figure 39.16 is a schematic diagram of a typical industrial boiler plant that discharges steam to a turbine, with part of the steam being condensed in the condenser and the remainder extracted for a process use where the steam may be lost or the condensate become so contaminated that it must be wasted. With reference to this diagram, the following relationships apply in determining blowdown losses:

1. $M \times C_M = F \times C_F = B_1 \times C_{B1}$
2. $M + C + D = F = S + B$ (all in lb/hr) (or kg/hr)
3. $M = L + B_2$ (all in lb/hr) (or kg/hr)
4. $CR_F = \dfrac{C_{B_1}}{C_F} = \dfrac{F}{B_1}$ $CR_M = \dfrac{C_{B_1}}{C_M} = \dfrac{M}{B_1}$
5. $F = S \times \dfrac{CR_F}{CR_F - 1}$
6. $B_1 = F/CR_F$
7. Percent blowdown $= \dfrac{100}{CR}$

where B_1 = boiler blowdown flow containing C_{B1} mg/l solids
     B_2 = blowdown flow from flash tank
    CR = concentration ratio; CR_F is concentration ratio based on feedwater;
          CR_M is based on makeup
     C = returned condensate flow, assumed to be free of solids
     D = steam flow used for deaeration
     F = feedwater flow containing C_F mg/l solids
     L = loss of steam or condensate
     M = makeup flow containing C_M mg/l solids
     S = steam flow

It is common to express blowdown as a percentage of feedwater. However, this may give the utilities engineer a false sense of security. If the plant has 80% condensate return and 20% makeup, a 5% blowdown would appear satisfactory, but it indicates that the makeup is being concentrated only four times—of the four units of makeup entering the boiler, one unit is being thrown away. Perhaps that is as much usage as can be made of that particular quality makeup, but the operator should be aware of it.

Since the main purpose of blowdown control is to reach the maximum permissible concentrations for best boiler efficiency without exceeding concentrations that would harm the system, the first step in developing a blowdown control program is to establish allowable limits. The conventional limits recommended to provide boiler cleanliness and adequate steam quality are shown in Tables 39.8 and 39.9. These cover most situations encountered in industrial boiler operations, but not the coagulation treatment used in low pressure boilers. With the coagulation treatment, total dissolved solids are usually limited to 3500 mg/l, and adequate alkalinity is maintained to provide the carbonate for calcium precipitation and the hydroxide for magnesium precipitation. These levels can be established only after the nature of the makeup treatment system has been considered.

As shown by Tables 39.8 and 39.9 the limits on such things as total dissolved solids, silica, and alkalinity are basically related to the amounts of these materials entering with the makeup water; these concentrations can be adjusted by blowdown, but also by some adjustment in the makeup treatment system if that flex-

TABLE 39.8   Optimum Boiler Water Control Limits*
Drum-type Boilers Using Softened (Not Deionized) Feedwaters

	Pressure, psi					
	150	300	600	900	1200	1500
TDS (max.)	4000	3500	3000	2000	500	300
Phosphate (as PO_4)†	30–60	30–60	20–40	15–20	10–15	5–10
Hydroxide (as $CaCO_3$)	300–400	250–300	150–200	120–150	100–120	80–100
Sulfite	30–60	30–40	20–30	15–20	10–15	5–10
Silica (as SiO_2) max. ‡	100	50	30	10	5	3
Total Iron (as Fe) max.	10	5	3	2	2	1
Organics	70–100	70–100	70–100	50–70	50–70	50–70

* Heat release below 150,000 Btu/hr/sq. ft.

† Where conditions warrant, chelants (EDTA or NTA) may be used in place of phosphates to achieve a hardness-solubilizing rather than a hardness-precipitating effect. In certain programs, phosphate and chelant are used together. Where chelant residuals are to be maintained, recommended boiler water control limits are: (1) boiler pressure below 400 psi, 4–8 mg/l; (2) 401–600 psi, 3–6 mg/l; (3) 601–1000 psi, 3–5 mg/l (all residuals are as $CaCO_3$).

‡ See Table 39.5 for intermediate pressure.

ibility is provided. On the other hand, such constituents as phosphate, organics, and sulfite are introduced as internal treatment chemicals, and their concentration can be adjusted both by blowdown and by rate of application.

For purposes of illustrating the calculation of boiler blowdown related to the concentrations, a 900 psi (40 bars) boiler system in a paper mill is used as an example. The steam goes both to a condensing turbine and a back pressure turbine, with 50% condensate return. The makeup is treated by hot lime–zeolite softening, and, after treatment, has a total dissolved solids concentration of 150 mg/l, silica of 3 mg/l, and total alkalinity of 20 mg/l. Table 39.10 summarizes the conditions established in this example.

With a silica concentration of 1.5 mg/l in the feedwater and an allowable limit of only 10 mg/l in the boiler water, silica is the controlling factor and sets the concentration ratio (based on feedwater) at 6.7. Since the water could be concentrated to a factor of 10 based on total dissolved solids, there is incentive for additional silica reduction in the hot process unit. If the addition of dolomitic lime would permit a reduction from 3 mg/l shown to less than 2 mg/l in the makeup, the blowdown rate could be reduced from 15% to 10%.

A second example explores the use of a simple sodium zeolite softener to treat city water as makeup for a 300 psi boiler. The water analyses in Figure 39.17 show the results of treating the city water through a zeolite softener, and the allowable concentrations in a 300 psi (20 bars) boiler. The concentration ratio is calculated for each of the constituents to be controlled; the lowest CR determines the blowdown rate. In this example, the lowest ratio is 2.5, applying to alkalinity. So the blowdown rate, controlled by alkalinity, would be:

$$\text{Percent blowdown} = \frac{100}{2.5} = 40\%$$

This is a high blowdown loss, expressed as a percentage of makeup. However, in a small plant that generates less than 50,000 lb/hr (22,700 kg/hr) of steam with less than 10–20% makeup, this process might be acceptable just for its simplicity and low cost. Larger plants would find this high blowdown loss unacceptable.

Two processes are explored to modify the sodium zeolite system to reduce alkalinity, Figure 39.18 shows these two modifications, sodium zeolite plus acid, and split-stream treatment. Both of these significantly reduce alkalinity and blowdown. The first process increases the critical CR to 12.5, so blowdown would be controlled by alkalinity at a level close to the optimum TDS. Further reduction in blowdown is achieved by using split-stream treatment, since TDS is reduced as well as alkalinity. At these low levels, silica becomes controlling at a

TABLE 39.9 Optimum Boiler Water Control Limits*
Drum-type Boilers Using High Purity (Deionized) Feedwaters

		Pressure, psi				
	Up to 600	900†	1200†	1500	1800	2400
TDS (max.)	Use same optimum	500	300	200	100	50
Phosphate (as PO₄)	limits as for soft (not	15–25	15–25	5–10	5–10	5–10
pH	deionized) feedwaters	9.8–10.2	9.8–10.2	9.4–9.7	9.4–9.7	9.4–9.7
Silica (as SiO₂)		10	5	2	1	0.25
Total iron (as Fe)		2	2	1	0.5	0.2
Hydrazine (as N₂H₄)		.04–.06 ‡	.04–.06 ‡	.04–.06‡	.04–.06‡	.04–.06‡

* Heat release below 150,000 Btu/hr/sq. ft.

† For most boilers installed before 1950, and for boilers installed since but not having waterwall heat transfer rates conducive to DNB (departure from nucleate boiling) under anticipated operating conditions, control limits applicable for softened (not deionized) feedwaters may be used.

‡ Hydrazine residuals in feedwater just ahead of boiler, e.g., at economizer inlet.

blowdown of 6% of makeup. Capital cost and operating cost figures are needed to decide whether the reduction in blowdown from 8% achieved with the first process to 6%, which can be reached with the split-stream treatment, is justified. The split-stream process is more costly and it creates a secondary problem— disposal of spent regenerant acid.

These examples show that concentration ratios are determined by chemical analyses. Since blowdown rate is never measured, but most plants meter both makeup and feedwater as well as steam, the chemical determination of concentration ratio is the most accurate means of determining blowdown loss. It is apparent that careful sampling of both the feedwater and makeup is required to properly control blowdown and be able to determine blowdown rate. The boiler water must be cool before it can be analyzed, and leakage in the cooler could affect the composition of the boiler water. The boiler water sample is usually taken from the blowdown collection pipe in the boiler drum, and if this is not properly designed, the blowdown sample may be non-representative. An example of this is the accumulation of steam bubbles within the blowdown line which are then condensed through the sample cooler and dilute the boiler water.

Although one of several boiler water constituents may determine the required blowdown rate—for example, silica—it is general practice to determine all of the critical concentrations in the boiler on a regular basis. Each of these can then be related to the total dissolved solids as measured by a conductivity instrument, and the actual control of blowdown can then be related to conductivity for simplicity of control. The chloride test is another simple test to use for controlling blowdown.

TABLE 39.10 Summary of Controls
(All concentrations in mg/l)

Factor	Makeup	Feedwater	Boiler limit (*)	Max CR_F
TDS	150	75	2000	26.7
SiO₂	3	1.5	10	6.7
Alkalinity	20	10	150†	15

* From Table 39.8

† Assuming 90% of boiler alkalinity is hydroxyl, an average hydroxyl alkalinity of 135 mg/l (Table 39.8) corresponds to an average total alkalinity of 150 mg/l. Since silica is controlling, the blowdown rate is:

$$\text{Blowdown} = \frac{100}{\text{CR}_F} = 15\% \text{ of feedwater}$$

Identification of Analyses Tabulated Below:							
A. City Water				D. Concentration Ratios			
B. Na₂Z Effluent				E. Blowdown, % of Makeup			
C. Boiler Limits				F.			

Constituent	As	A	B	C	D	E	F
Calcium	CaCO₃	75	Nil				
Magnesium	"	45	Nil				
Sodium	"	20	140				
Total Electrolyte	CaCO₃	140	140				
Bicarbonate	CaCO₃	100	100				
Carbonate	"	0	0				
Hydroxyl	"	0	0	225			
Sulfate	"	10	10				
Chloride	"	30	30				
Nitrate	"	0	0				
M Alk.	CaCO₃	100	100	250	2.5	40%	
P Alk.	"	Tr	Tr	238			
Carbon Dioxide		0	0				
pH		8.2	8.2				
Silica		3	3	50	16.7	6%	
Iron	Fe	0	0				
Turbidity		0	0				
TDS		160	185	2000	10.8	9.2	
Color		0	0				

Figure 39.17 Simple zeolite softening for a 300-psi boiler.

The continuous blowdown withdrawal pipe should be located in the boiler drum in the area where the risers return to release steam behind baffles (Figure 39.19). It should never be located where it can remove feedwater and fresh chemicals that have not reacted. The holes in the collecting pipe should face upwards so that the pipe cannot become steam-bound, restricting the rate of blowdown withdrawal and interfering with testing.

The valve controlling boiler blowdown is usually calibrated so that the operator can make a simple adjustment if his tests indicate that a change in blowdown rate is required. Because the boiler operates at constant pressure and the blowdown discharges to constant pressure, this is a very reliable and reproducible method of control. The control valve can be designed for automatic actuation by a conductivity recorder.

Most plants have installed systems to recover heat from boiler drum blowdown. In smaller plants, the blowdown may go directly through a heat exchanger, where the heat of the blowdown water is transferred to makeup ahead of the deaerating heater. In larger plants, blowdown is directed to a flash tank equalized to a process steam line, for example, operating at 15 psig (1 bar). In rare cases, a high pressure boiler may be blown down into a low pressure boiler to obtain additional concentrations and steam, or it may be blown down to an evaporator in a utility station. In some plants, more than one flash tank is used, depending on the heat balance and the optimum recovery achievable in that plant.

The amount of steam produced by blowdown to a flash tank can be calculated by using the chart illustrated in Figure 39.20. Several typical blowdown arrangements are shown in Figures 39.21 and 39.22. Where the heat is recovered through a heat exchanger, the exchanger is normally designed to reduce the blowdown temperature to within $10-20°F(6-11°C)$ of the cooling water, which is usually makeup water.

Identification of Analyses Tabulated Below:

A. City Water   D. Boiler Limits @ 300 psi

B. Na_2Z + Acid + Degasifier   E. CR for "B" @ 300 psi

C. Split-Stream + Degasifier   F. CR for "C" @ 300 psi

Constituent	As	A	B	C	D	E	F
Calcium	$CaCO_3$	75	Nil	Nil			
Magnesium	"	45	Nil	Nil			
Sodium	"	20	140	55			
Total Electrolyte	$CaCO_3$	140	140	55			
Bicarbonate	$CaCO_3$	100	20	15			
Carbonate	"	0	0	0			
Hydroxyl	"	0	0	0	225		
Sulfate	"	10	90	10			
Chloride	"	30	30	30			
Nitrate	"	0	0	0			
M Alk.	$CaCO_3$	100	20	15	250	12.5	16.7
P Alk.	"	Tr	0	0	238		
Carbon Dioxide		Tr	5	5			
pH		8.2	7.0	6.6			
Silica		3	3	3	50	16.7	16.7
Iron	Fe	0	0	0			
Turbidity		0	0	0			
TDS		160	160	75	2000	12.5	26.6
Color		0	0	0			

Figure 39.18   Reducing alkalinity to reduce blowdown.

(a) Top view of boiler drum

(b) End view of boiler drum

Figure 39.19   Typical continuous blowdown location.

BOILER TYPES

A boiler is a vessel in which water is continuously vaporized into steam by the application of heat. A primary objective in designing a boiler is to provide for the greatest possible efficiency in absorption of heat. Other objectives are production of pure steam and safe, reliable operation.

Variations in the design of steam generators are almost without limit. This is partly because each new development in improving the quality of boiler makeup

Figure 39.20   The production of flash steam from boiler blowdown.

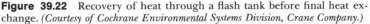

Ⓐ Gate valve normally open (wide)

Ⓑ Gate valve slightly open (cracked)

Ⓒ Gate valve normally closed

Figure 39.21 Recovery of heat from a continuous boiler blowdown line with a heat exchanger. *(Courtesy of Cochrane Environmental Systems Division, Crane Company.)*

has influenced the boiler designer to make the steam generator more compact and efficient.

Design variations occur because of the numerous factors involved in selection and operation of a steam generator: these include capacity, types of fuel available, burner design, pressure and temperature conditions, feedwater quality, load variations anticipated, and space available for the installation.

Each of these factors affects the way steam bubbles form and the mechanism of

Figure 39.22 Recovery of heat through a flash tank before final heat exchange. *(Courtesy of Cochrane Environmental Systems Division, Crane Company.)*

Circular deposits
·conforms to point
of departure
of steam bubble

Circular formation
completely filled
with scale

Figure 39.23 The progression
of initial scale formation.

boiler water concentration at the metal surface. Figure 39.23 shows how scale
initially forms as a ring at the point of bubble formation, and how this ring completely fills with scale if the chemical environment is not properly controlled.

Boilers are of two general designs, firetube and watertube. In firetube boilers
the flame and hot gases are confined within tubes arranged in a bundle within a
water drum. Water circulates on the outside of these tubes (Figure 39.24). As the
water changes to steam, it rises to the top of the boiler drum and exits through a
steam header. Firetube boilers are efficient steam generators for steam requirements below 150,000 lb/hr (68,000 kg/hr) and 150 psi (10 bars). Higher pressure and greater capacity require thicker plates and tube walls in this design, so
watertube boilers are more economical for conditions above these limits.

The watertube boiler differs from the firetube in that the flame and hot combustion gases flow across the outside of the tubes and water is circulated within
the tubes. Combustion of the fuel occurs in a furnace and some of the water
tubes usually form the furnace walls.

Figure 39.24 Water circulation in a firetube boiler.

Figure 39.25 Water circulation in a watertube boiler. The reduction in circulation ratio as boiler pressure increases is shown on the graph. Note also the reduction in available head for a short package boiler (3000 mm = 10 ft high) compared to a tall field erected boiler 100 ft high. *(Courtesy of Combustion Engineering.)*

In a simple watertube circuit (Figure 39.25) steam bubbles form on the heated side of the tubes. The resulting steam-water mixture has a density below that of the cooler water on the unheated side and rises, creating a circulation through the system. The steam bubbles rise until they reach the steam drum where steam is released from the water into the vapor space.

Natural circulation boilers—where circulation is induced by density differences—usually have many parallel circuits. Those sections of tubes in which

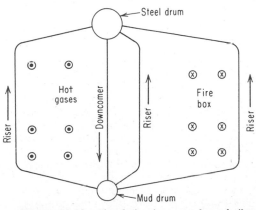

Figure 39.26 Circulation in a two-drum boiler.

Figure 39.27 Pumps assist in circulating water through a boiler when natural circulation is restricted by pressure or elevation.

heated water rises to the steam drum are called risers and those through which the cooler water descends are downcomers. Circulation usually occurs between several drums. The steam drum at the top separates steam from water; the mud drum at the bottom separates suspended solids and sludge from water. A schematic of such a boiler design showing risers, downcomers, and the location of the steam and mud drums is given in Figure 39.26. These basic items are found in all natural circulation boilers regardless of the details of boiler design.

In forced circulation boilers, a pump provides the water circulation (Figure 39.27). This is a more positive control of the circulation pattern than that created simply by density difference. This is important if the boiler may operate over a wide capacity range. If space requirements limit the height of a boiler installation, the density differences available to create natural circulation become small and forced circulation becomes advantageous. It is also advantageous at high pressures as the difference in density between steam and water diminishes. Once-through boilers are special designs for utility operation.

Increased boiler efficiency can be obtained by bringing water into close contact with the source of heat. Tubes are built into the boiler furnace to absorb the greatest amount of heat possible. Usually the entire firebox, called the radiant section, is surrounded by water wall tubes, through which water circulates (Figure 39.28). Connections between various tube sections of the boiler are accomplished by headers, named for their location, such as water wall headers or drum headers.

Steam quality is of paramount importance in most operations if high turbine performance and long equipment life are to be achieved. Boiler water is separated from steam by cyclone separators and steam scrubbers located in the steam drum (Figure 39.29). Steam entering the steam drum is directed first toward the cyclone separator by baffles. The cyclones force the steam into spiral motion on its path toward the exit at the top of the separator, and centrifugal force separates the water from the steam. The purified steam exits at the top of the separator, while the heavier water drains out the bottom and reenters the boiler drum.

After passing through the cyclone separators, final removal of entrained water from the steam is accomplished by secondary steam scrubbers. These consist of baffles that change the direction of the steam so that water impinging on them drains back to the steam drum. The final steam should have less than 0.1–0.5% entrained water, depending on the design and effectiveness of the separators.

The presence of entrained moisture determines steam quality. A steam quality of 95% means the steam contains 5% moisture. This may be measured thermodynamically by a device called a throttling calorimeter, but can be determined much more accurately by detecting the solids in the entrained moisture. Since the bulk of the boiler solids are sodium salts, an ion electrode specifically measuring sodium is used. This measures the sodium content of a sample of condensed steam.

Figure 39.30 shows a plot of sodium content in steam leaving a 250 psi (17 bars) boiler, and how the sodium level, which reflects entrained boiler water, is influenced by boiler operating conditions. A plot of steam demand shows the

Figure 39.28   In this boiler, the radiant section of the furnace is cooled by wall tubes in which steam is generated. In this design, the tangential location of burners produces a turbulence that promotes efficient combustion. *(Courtesy of Combustion Engineering.)*

FINAL SCREEN DRYERS

CENTRIFUGAL SEPARATORS

STATIONARY
SPINNER
VANES

NORMAL
WATER
LEVEL

CONTINUOUS
BLOWDOWN
PIPING

FEEDWATER
PIPE

Figure 39.29   In the steam drum, water is removed by cyclone separators followed by screen dryers. *(Courtesy of Combustion Engineering.)*

sudden surges which produced gross carryover. Assuming the boiler water contains 500 mg/l Na, a sodium content of 50 μg/l Na in the steam indicates the following moisture content of the steam:

$$\text{Percent moisture} = \frac{\mu g/l \text{ Na in steam}}{mg/l \text{ Na in boiler}} \times 10$$

$$= \frac{50 \times 10}{500} = 1.0\%$$

With demineralized make-up, potassium may be the predominant boiler cation, so the test procedure must take this into account.

The average efficiency of a watertube boiler producing saturated steam is about 85%. Most of the heat loss is via hot stack gases and radiation. Improved efficiency can be achieved by adding heat recovery devices.

Table 39.11 shows a typical survey of energy losses in a simple industrial boiler plant. This is a 250 psi oil-fired boiler delivering saturated steam for a process having no heat recovery devices. In this example, the plant has already achieved its optimum water conditions with a blowdown of only 3.5%, and increased efficiency with the existing design is achievable only by a change in firing conditions. However, appreciable energy could be recovered if the plant were retrofitted with heat recovery auxiliaries.

A thermodynamic gain in efficiency can be obtained by raising the temperature of the steam above its saturation point. This is accomplished by passing the

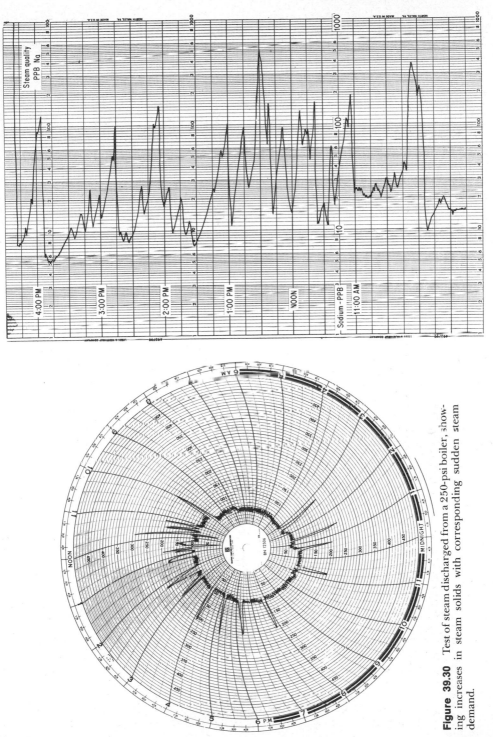

Figure 39.30   Test of steam discharged from a 250-psi boiler, showing increases in steam solids with corresponding sudden steam demand.

TABLE 39.11   Distribution of Boiler Losses
(All figures in millions of Btu/day)

	Actual loss	Potential	Saving
Blowdown	170.0	17.0	none
Stack heat	287.0	275.5	11.5
Excess air	96.9	49.8	47.1
Total	401.0	342.4	58.6

steam through a series of tubes, called superheaters, located in the radiant section of the boiler (Figure 39.31). Similarly, steam that has only a portion of its heat content removed and is at a reduced pressure can be reheated to a temperature close to its initial temperature and reused. This is accomplished in a bundle of tubes called reheaters, also located in the radiant section.

A substantial gain in efficiency can be achieved by raising the temperature of the feedwater entering the boiler to that approaching boiler water temperature

Figure 39.31   Additional heat can be put into saturated steam after leaving the boiler drum by a heat exchanger called a superheater, shown here in a furnace designed to burn CO produced in oil refineries as a by-product of catalytic cracking. *(Courtesy of Combustion Engineering.)*

Figure 39.32 Heat in the stack gases is transferred to feedwater in the economizer, and also may be recovered by preheating combustion air. The heat-exchange bundle (left) is mounted in the stack (right). *(Courtesy of General Resource Corporation.)*

by recovering heat from the hot flue gases before they are discharged up the stack to the atmosphere. This heating of the feedwater, as shown in Figure 39.32, occurs in the economizer.

Similarly, air needed for combustion in the furnace can reclaim additional heat from the flue gas by passing through a series of tubes called air heaters. These are usually located immediately after the economizer. The relative increase in heat absorption gained by adding these heat recovery auxiliaries is shown by Figure 39.33.

Watertube boilers may be of the horizontal straight tube design or the bent tube design. The horizontal straight tube boiler is made up of banks of tubes, usually staggered as shown in Figure 39.34 and inclined at an angle of about 15° to promote circulation. The ends of the tubes are expanded into headers, which provide for circulation between the tubes and the steam drum. The drum may either be longitudinal or crosswise with reference to the axis of the tube bank. The advantages of the straight tube boilers include: visibility through the tubes for inspection, ease of tube replacement, low head room, and accessibility of all components for inspection and gas-side cleaning by hand if necessary during operation. Some of the inherent disadvantages are: difficult access because of the many hand hole caps and gaskets that must be removed, replaced, and tightened; limited steam disengaging surfaces with poor separation of steam and water at high steaming rates; and limited steaming rates caused by relatively low circulation and poor distribution.

The horizontal straight tube boiler is limited to production of approximately 10,000 lb/hr of steam per foot of boiler width.

The bent tube design is a multi-drum boiler with the mud drum at the bottom, the additional drums, all called steam drums, being located at the top. Figures 39.35 and 39.36 show a two-drum and a three-drum bent water tube boiler. Tubes in the bent tube boiler are either inclined or arranged in vertical banks within the combustion space or made up as a water wall assembly, backed with

Relative heat transfer surface

Relative heat absorbed

Percent

Percent

Air heater

Economizer

Superheater

Boiler bank

Furnace water walls

Figure 39.33 This diagram shows the relative heat transfer duties of different sections of a steam generator. *(Reprinted with permission from Power Special Report, "Steam Generation," June 1964.)*

refractories. The bent tube boiler is a rapid steamer, with quick response to fluctuating loads because of its small water volume relative to its generating capacity. Advantages of the bent tube boiler include: greater economy in fabrication and operation, accessibility for inspection, cleaning, and maintenance, and ability to operate at higher steaming rates and deliver drier steam.

Figure 39.34 Inclined horizontal tubes are used for steam generation in this boiler design with box headers at each end connected to the boiler drum. This unit was designed for marine service. *(Courtesy of Babcock & Wilcox Company.)*

Figure 39.35 Two-drum bent-tube boiler with waterwall tubes absorbing heat in the radiant section of the furnace. *(Courtesy of Babcock & Wilcox Company.)*

Bent tube boilers are usually classified further into the number of drums and the arrangement of the tubing within the boiler (Figure 39.37). The three major classifications are:

Type A   This unit consists of one steam drum and two mud drums or headers arranged in an A-pattern with the steam drum at the apex and the headers at the bottom. Bottom blowdown is required from both headers.

Type D   The steam drum and mud drum are located directly above one another and off to one side of the furnace in a D-pattern (Figure 39.44). A series of tubes run vertically between the mud drum and the steam drum. The rest of the

Figure 39.36 Three-drum bent-tube boiler, common in older plants and widely used before the development of waterwall tube designs.

Forced draft fan

Figure 39.37 Schematic of drum and tube arrangements for types A, D, and O bent-tube boiler designs. (*a*) A-type, with large upper drum for effective water-steam separation, and lower drums (headers) for circulation. (*b*) D-type, with steaming tubes discharging near water line, provide more effective feedwater and blowdown piping locations. (*c*) O-type, similar to A-type in circulation pattern with risers entering center of steam drum.

tubes extend horizontally from the steam and mud drums to the furnace wall, at which point they become water wall tubes.

Type O In this arrangement the steam drum is also located directly above the mud drum, but both are located in the center of the boiler, and the connecting tubes are in an O-pattern.

Depending on the size and the complexity of the boiler, it may be erected on-site, or it may be preassembled at the manufacturer's plant. Because the package boilers are usually smaller, they employ high heat transfer rates to obtain the required steaming capacity. For this reason, they may require closer control of boiler water treatment and operation than the field-erected units.

Environmental factors and fuel availability are certain to influence boiler designs of the future. For example, fluidized bed combustion is one possibility for solving the environmental problems of burning coal. It may present new problems in the steam generation section of the system, but even so, the basic principles of boiler water chemistry will still apply.

There are a number of aspects of boiler design that influence the selection and control of the internal treatment program. The first involves the mixing and distribution of chemicals and feedwater. In many boilers, location of feedwater piping, chemical distribution, and blowdown lines have been more a matter of convenience in design and fabrication than of purpose. It is essential for boiler water, feedwater, and treatment chemicals to mix before the cooler water descends into the downcomers and is then heated in the radiant section. Improper mixing may produce scale in the downcomers and hinder sludge conditioning.

With increasing use of demineralized water even for intermediate pressure boilers (600–900 psi), the major impurities in the feedwater are no longer introduced by the makeup, but rather by the returned condensate, principally as corrosion products.

These corrosion products are not solubilized by chelates and are difficult to disperse. If they deposit, boiler salts may concentrate under them, because they are relatively porous and permit boiler water to enter with only steam escaping. This may lead to caustic attack. To prevent this, boilers should be cleaned on a set frequency.

The likelihood of alkalinity attack is increased by variable loads and firing conditions, which cause flexing and cracking of the normal dense magnetite film on the boiler metal, exposing fresh metal to attack.

In forced circulation boilers, there is a tendency for deposits to form on the downstream side of flow control orifices. To avoid this, feedwater should be free of deposit-forming material, especially corrosion products, so that a chemical program can be applied successfully. Condensate polishing may be required since the condensate is the source of the corrosion products. Steam separators are essential to production of acceptable steam and their deterioration will depreciate steam quality.

Boilers are often damaged by corrosion during out-of-service periods. Idle boilers are very vulnerable to attack when air contacts moist metal surfaces. To prevent this corrosion, the boiler metal must be protected either by (1) keeping the surfaces completely dry or by (2) excluding all air from the boiler by completely filling it with properly treated water. Because of variations in boiler design, there is no single, detailed procedure that covers all steps in boiler lay-up, including both chemical and mechanical aspects. The basic principles in protecting boilers against corrosion are simple.

There are two basic ways of laying up boilers—wet and dry. In storing a boiler dry, trays of moisture absorbing chemicals, such as quicklime, are distributed on trays in the boiler drum (or drums) and the boiler is sealed. The alternate method, wet storage, involves forcing air out of the boiler by completely filling it to overflowing with water which has been specially treated. Nitrogen gas under slight pressure can also be used to displace air and blanket the boiler surfaces. Special consideration must be given to protecting superheaters during lay-up, particularly the non-drainable type.

The choice between the wet and dry methods of lay-up depends to a great extent on how long the boiler is to be out of service. Dry lay-up is preferable for long outages; the wet method has the advantage of permitting the boiler to be returned to service on reasonably short notice. It is a good idea to drain, flush and inspect a boiler prior to any lay-up. When time does not permit this, the boiler may be stored wet without first draining it. In this case the chemical treatment for lay-up—including catalyzed sulfite, caustic and organic dispersants — are injected into the boiler just before it comes off the line.

TYPES OF STEAM-USING EQUIPMENT

Steam is a convenient form in which to package energy because it has a high heat content and can be generated at one point and distributed to many different energy-using units throughout a plant. The steam may be used for its heating effect or for motive power.

In heating applications heat transfer may be by direct contact of steam with a fluid, or with a solid object, as in steam cleaning of oily parts. The most common application of direct contact heating is the deaerating feedwater heater in a boiler plant. In this case, the steam serves not only to heat the water at the most efficient point in the feedwater system, but it also acts as an inert gas to strip oxygen and carbon dioxide from the feedwater and carry these non-condensible gases out of the system; the deaerating heater is a sophisticated degasifier. Steam is used in a more primitive way for sparging and heating a variety of liquids, from food products to wastewaters.

Another example of direct contact of steam with another fluid is the thermocompressor, where high pressure steam may be used to boost low pressure steam to a higher pressure where it can be used. For example, an industrial plant will often have an excess of low pressure steam at 5–15 psi. This plant may need 50–100 psi steam for dryers, reboilers, or some other use where higher temperature is needed. A thermocompressor could boost the 5–15 psi steam to 50–100 psi by using live steam directly from the boiler on the jet of the thermocompressor.

Most heating applications are indirect, with a heat transfer surface between the steam and the fluid to be heated. These units are called surface heat exchangers and include a wide variety of devices such as condensers, stage heaters, process heat exchangers, reboilers, evaporators, and space heaters.

The most common surface heat exchanger, the shell-and-tube type, transfers heat from steam or another hot fluid to a colder fluid principally by conduction across a metal tube-wall separating the two. The rate of heat transfer depends on the temperature difference between the fluids, the metal surface area and thickness, and the conductivity of the metal itself. Shell-and-tube heat exchangers can be of several designs. The more complex designs are usually more efficient, but may be more costly and more difficult to clean and maintain.

Closed feedwater heaters, also called stage heaters, are heat exchangers used in steam plants to increase thermal efficiency by raising the temperature of the feedwater as close to boiler temperature as possible with extracted or exhausted steam. A utility system may have as many as 12 feedwater heaters, although it is more common to find eight, the choice being based on the most practical heat balance. Figure 39.38 shows the straight condensing feedwater heater; steam is always on the shell side, with feedwater passing through the tubes. Carbon-steel is used for construction of shells, heads, and tube sheets in most feedwater heaters. In high pressure heaters, tubes may be constructed of carbon steel, monel, or cupronickel; low pressure heaters are commonly fabricated with carbon steel, stainless steel, admiralty, or 90-10 cupronickel tubes.

The surface condenser is a special design of shell-and-tube heat exchanger operating under a vacuum created by condensing steam exhausted from a turbine or from process equipment such as multiple-effect evaporators in bauxite processing plants, kraft pulp mills, and sugar refineries. Air ejectors or mechanical pumps remove non-condensible gases, such as O_2, CO_2, and NH_3, from the vapor space. Utility condensers usually include a degassing or deaerating section in the hotwell to assist in the removal of non-condensibles. Figure 39.39 illustrates a typical utility-type surface condenser.

The cooling water flowing through the condenser tubes may or may not be

Figure 39.38   Straight condensing feedwater heater.

Figure 39.39 Typical surface condenser design. (*Courtesy of Basco Division, American Precision Industries.*)

makeup or feedwater. In a utility, there is no way to reclaim this heat because the cooling water requirements are so much greater than makeup needs. However, many industrial plants, such as steel mills, pulp/paper mills, need relatively large volumes of makeup, and condenser cooling water may be used for this purpose if the recovered heat is usable; it may be recoverable in the winter, but not in the summer, which is often the case for pulp/paper mills.

Reboilers are tubular heat exchangers commonly used in petroleum refineries, usually inserted in the bottom of a distillation column where the tubes are surrounded with hydrocarbon being processed, and steam is supplied to a headbox from which it passes into the tubes. This is one of several process applications where steam flows inside rather than outside the tube bundle.

Space heaters are widely used for comfort heating of offices, shops, and plants. If steam is available, it is often used in tubes within the space heater.

There is a large variety of steam-jacketed processing equipment in industry, including kettles in the food industry, reactors in the chemical industry, rotary drum dryers, and evaporators. The latter usually comprise a series of vessels containing reboiler elements, with a condenser and a heat exchanger for optimum thermal efficiency. Many of these process vessels are operated intermittently, but some of the more sophisticated, such as the continuous digester in the pulp industry, operate on a continuous basis.

It is unusual to find deposits in most steam process equipment, particularly if the equipment is in continuous, steady operation; but deposits do occasionally occur. They usually develop because of inleakage into the steam side from the process side of the vessel, caused by the vacuum that develops during shutdown drawing in contaminants through a leaky tube. Gross carryover of boiler solids with periodic wetting and drying in the process equipment may also cause deposits as the solids concentrate.

A much more common problem with process equipment is corrosion, often due to inleakage of oxygen caused by vacuum during shutdown or under throttle steam conditions. Concentration of CO_2 also occurs with improper devices for temperature or pressure control. This shows up quickly as a localized drop in condensate pH where the CO_2 is allowed to concentrate. Ammonia attacks copper alloys, in areas of O_2 inleakage, particularly where conditions permit its concentration beyond the initial NH_3 concentration in the steam itself.

The major use for steam is motive power, since this is its sole use in the utility industry, which is the largest consumer of energy in most industrialized countries. Even in moderate-sized industrial plants where the chief reason for generating steam is for process requirements, the steam may be put through a turbine at high pressure, with the exhaust steam then being used for the process needs. Turbines are the major prime movers because they are compact and efficient and require little maintenance; however, reciprocating piston steam engines are still found in many older plants throughout the world. These prime movers may be used for direct drive of pumps, compressors, and other mechanical devices, or they may be connected to a generator to supply electrical energy for motor-driven devices and other electrical accessories.

STEAM USED FOR POWER

The development of the modern steam turbine was a monumental engineering achievement—first, for the designer who was able to translate the complex mathematics of thermodynamics into blueprints, and second, for the builder who could convert the intricate design into precise shapes for manufacture almost on a mass production basis. In the simple, single stage turbine, steam is directed through a series of carefully shaped nozzles onto blades, or buckets, fixed at the circumference of the disk attached to the turbine shaft. This is known as the impulse stage. As the steam leaves the rotating blades, a second set of stationary nozzles may be used to collect it and redirect it onto a second set of blades, in which case the set of nozzles and blades is called a reaction stage. Most turbines contain multiple stages, some impulse and some reaction, depending entirely on the duty required of it and the balance of cost and performance. A simple single stage turbine is shown in Figure 39.40, and a multiple-stage utility-type turbine is shown in Figure 39.41.

There are two basic categories of steam turbine operation: condensing, where exhaust steam discharges to a condenser at subatmospheric pressure; and non-condensing, where steam exhausts into process steam headers under pressure (e.g., 100 psi is common in the paper industry). Turbine operation and design are further classified as to the flow of steam through the turbine: flow patterns include straight flow, reheat, automatic extraction, and non-automatic extraction.

In straight flow systems (Figure 39.42), steam at full throttle is directed by nozzles through the entire bank of turbine stages to exhaust. Reheat turbines (Figure 39.43) gain efficiency by discharging steam at an intermediate stage for reheat in the boiler furnace, with the higher temperature steam being returned to the next stage of the turbine for further work. In automatic expansion, steam is extracted from the main flow at one or more points for process use, with the balance passing through to exhaust (Figure 39.44). Non-automatic turbines bleed steam at one or more stages for feedwater heating (Figure 39.45).

The most troublesome type of turbine problem related to water treatment and boiler operation is the accumulation of material on the turbine blading. This may be either inorganic, which is most common, or organic. Some of the volatile materials released from the boiler may condense as the pressure and temperature drop as the steam passes through the turbine. Silica has been mentioned as one of the components of boiler water that can volatilize, and it is one of the principal contributors to turbine deposits; it tends to deposit on lower pressure stages of the turbine, usually at 50 psi or below. The silica limits set for boiler water assume that the steam will be passed through turbines. If the turbine exhausts at 100 psi, there may be no problem in carrying higher silica concentrations than those recommended in Tables 39.8 and 39.9. The relationship between silica in boiler water and silica in steam has been carefully studied, and it is possible to predict the point at which silica will sublime.

Turbine deposits may originate from organic materials in the boiler steam as

Figure 39.40 This simple, solid wheel turbine is commonly used to drive auxiliary equipment such as boiler feed pumps and rotary compressors. Cutaway, left; plant installation, right. (*Courtesy of Terry Corporation.*)

Figure 39.41 This large turbogenerator is typical of nuclear plant units. The cutaway section shows high-pressure and low-pressure turbine blades. *(Courtesy of General Electric Company.)*

Figure 39.42 Straight-flow turbine. *(Figures 39.42 through 39.45 from Power Special Report, "Steam Turbines," June 1962.)*

Figure 39.43 Reheat   turbine.

Figure 39.44 Single automatic extraction.

well as inorganic materials. Usually these are caused by process leaks into the condensate system, but they may also originate in the raw water either from naturally occurring organic materials or from organic wastes discharged into the water source from industrial plants or from municipal sewage treatment plants.

There are numerous additional uses for steam in industrial operation. Many fabrication shops use steam for operation of forges, hammers, and presses. The steam cylinders usually require saturated or slightly wet steam, and are lubricated with specially compounded oil, so in plants of this kind it is common to find oil in the exhaust steam and condensate. Steam jet ejectors with barometric condensers are frequently used to produce vacuum for such diverse purposes as degassing steel and distilling heavy hydrocarbon fractions.

CONDENSATE RETURN

Condensate produced when steam is used in any kind of process is seldom cooled measurably below the steam temperature. Because it is hot, close to the steam temperature, the collection system and piping used to handle it must be carefully selected. The piping is generally larger than that used for cold water because pressure drop will cause steam to flash from the flowing condensate, choking the pipe and restricting flow.

Condensate may be picked up by a pump for boosting to the best point of return, or it may be delivered to a point of lower pressure simply by the pressure gradient.

Turbine condensate is normally collected in a hotwell, and a level is maintained in the hotwell so that the pump transferring the turbine condensate to the deaerator will have adequate net positive suction head. The level in the hotwell is maintained by returning some of the pump discharge, depending on load fluctuations.

Process condensate is also usually returned by pumps to the deaerating heater. Condensate receivers collect the process condensate and maintain level control so that the pump handling the hot condensate will have adequate suction head.

Figure 39.45 Single nonautomatic extraction.

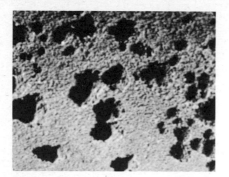

Figure 39.46 Condensate line pitting caused by oxygen and carbon dioxide.

Even so, special designs of centrifugal pumps are usually required for handling hot condensate. Condensate systems can become quite sophisticated, as in a paper mill, where condensate from high pressure dryer rolls may be flashed to lower pressure steam in the condensate system and then routed to another dryer section.

Stage heater condensates are normally handled by gravity, returning to a lower pressure stage heater, the deaerator, or even the condenser hotwell.

Once the condensate has been collected, the proper point of return must be decided upon. In the utility station, the entire flow of condensate may be polished through some type of ion exchange system before being returned to the deaerating heater. In industrial plants, if the condensate is contaminated it will be sent to a treatment plant before returning to the deaerator. For the most part, condensates are returned to the deaerating element itself, as they may contain dissolved oxygen and other gases; however, high pressure returns free of dissolved oxygen may be sent directly to the storage section of the deaerating heater to flash and supply steam for the deaerating operation.

For the most part, the condensate handling system is of ordinary carbon steel construction, although pump impellers, valve trim, and heat exchange tubes are usually of copper alloys. Because condensate is usually hot, if corrosive agents are present, the rate of corrosion will usually be greater than what would be expected in cold water. The principal agents of corrosion are carbon dioxide and oxygen. The CO_2 is normally produced by the breakdown of alkalinity in the boiler and the oxygen may be drawn into the system by inleakage of air or of water contain-

Figure 39.47 Uniform CO_2 attack below water line in a condensate pipe.

Figure 39.48 Attack of copper alloy by ammonia in a stage heater.

ing dissolved oxygen (pump sealing water, for example). Inspection of the condensate piping provides a good clue as to the cause of corrosion, as shown in Figures 39.46 and 39.47.

The principal cause of corrosion of copper alloys is ammonia in systems containing O_2 (Figure 39.48).

Without adequate treatment of the steam, the pH of condensate would normally be low because of the presence of carbon dioxide. The application of volatile alkaline amines will control attack by neutralizing carbonic acid, thus raising the pH value of the system. In a tight system, the neutralizing amine is often adequate for the complete corrosion control program. However, many systems are operated intermittently or under throttling (flow-restricting) conditions where oxygen inleakage can occur. At these higher levels of oxygen, neutralization is inadequate as the sole protective measure against corrosion of steel piping. In such cases, volatile filming amines are added to the steam, which upon condensing produce a waxy substance on the metal and provide a barrier between the flowing condensate and the pipe wall so that corrosion cannot occur. Figure 39.49 illustrates the action of filming corrosion inhibitors in a condensate system.

Hydrazine may be used both for pH correction and oxygen scavenging, but it becomes uneconomical when high levels of carbon dioxide and oxygen occur, a common condition in most industrial operations.

In plants where gross contamination occurs, the source and cause should be located and corrected. An example of such an occurrence is the use of steam for producing hot water through a heat exchanger. The industrial operation may require the hot water at a specific temperature, 150°F for example, and a thermostatic element is installed in the water line to regulate the steam flow into the heat exchanger according to water flow and exit temperature. At low water flows where the steam demand is low, the steam admission valve may be so fully-throttled that there is actually a vacuum in the vapor space. Most of these systems are designed for pressure operation, and under vacuum air leakage is common. If a neutralizing amine is used in a system of this kind, it may be easy to locate inleakage of this sort because the air in the industrial atmosphere will contain enough CO_2 to drop the pH of the condensate at that particular point. So a way to find the source of air inleakage in a complex industrial plant is to sample con-

Figure 39.49 Filming inhibitors coat condensate piping with a non-wettable film, protecting the metal surface from corrosive attack.

densate at all sources and compare the pH of the sample condensate with the pH of a condensed steam sample or a sample of condensate known to be free of atmospheric contamination.

Where attack of copper alloy has been found to be caused by ammonia, filming inhibitors will usually prevent further attack by preventing O_2 from reaching the surface. If the ammonia concentration is high, reduction of ammonia in the pretreatment system should be considered.

Neutralizing Amines

The most commonly used neutralizing inhibitors are amines such as morpholine, cyclohexylamine, and diethylaminoethanol. The ability of each product mentioned to enter the condensate or water phase is indicated by its vapor-to-liquid distribution ratio. This ratio compares the concentration of amine in the vapor phase to the concentration in the water phase.

Product	Vapor to liquid distribution ratio
Morpholine	0.4 to 1
Cyclohexylamine	4.0 to 1
Diethylaminoethanol	1.7 to 1

In order to neutralize carbonic acid, the amine must be present in the water phase. The distribution ratio indicates the preference of an amine for the water phase or the vapor phase. An amine such as morpholine, preferring the water phase, will be present in the initially formed condensate at high temperatures. On the other hand, cyclohexylamine tends to remain with the steam to enter the condensate as the temperatures decrease.

Because of their differing vapor-to-liquid distribution ratios, two or more such amines may be used together to provide effective neutralization programs for complex systems.

Neutralizing amines are fed to the feedwater, boiler steam drum, or steam header. They are controlled by monitoring the returned condensate pH from samples taken at the beginning, middle, and end of a condensate system.

Filming Inhibitors

Inhibitors used to film condensate systems are amines with chain-like molecules. One end of each molecule is hydrophilic (loves water), and the other end is hydrophobic (hates water). The hydrophilic end attaches to the metal, leaving the other end to repel water. As the molecules accumulate, the surface becomes nonwettable. The film, therefore, provides a barrier against metal attack by water containing carbon dioxide, oxygen, or ammonia. Since the molecules also repel each other, they don't tend to build up layers or thick films. Instead they remain a mono-molecular, protective film.

A film one molecule thick actually improves heat transfer in condensers, dryers, and other heat-exchange equipment. By promoting drop-wise condensation, an insulating water film between the water and metal surface is prevented.

Good distribution of filming inhibitors is of prime importance in preventing condensate corrosion. Protection depends on the maintenance of a continuous film. Since steam and condensate can wash away the film, it must be constantly repaired by continuous feed of the inhibitor.

Octadecylamine and certain of its salts were the first chemicals to be used as filming inhibitors in steam-condensate systems. However, because of their wax-like nature (whether supplied in flake or emulsion form), it was difficult to put these chemicals into uniform solutions for feeding. A relatively narrow condensate pH range of 6.5–8.0 is required for the octadecylamine to form a film and to remain on the metal surface. To overcome these limitations molecules formulated specifically for boiler plant conditions have been developed as alternatives to octadecylamine.

Most filming inhibitors can be fed into the boiler system at several locations: they can be pumped into the feedlines, directly to the boiler steam drum, or into the main superheated steam header. If only the process equipment needs protection, the inhibitor may be conveniently fed into the desuperheating water at the process steam header. Regardless of the feedpoint, however, the inhibitor should be fed continuously for best results. Dosages are not based on oxygen or carbon dioxide content of the steam. The amount of inhibitor required is set according to the system's surface area. Creation of an effective film is a physical process, highly dependent on flow rates, feeding, and testing techniques.

EVALUATING RESULTS

There are several good ways of finding out how much corrosion is occurring in a system and how effective a prevention program is:

Test nipples The use of test nipples, installed in steam or condensate lines, permits both visual inspection of system conditions and a measure of corrosion. The nipple can be weighed before and after the test interval to determine weight loss due to corrosion.

Test coupons—have also been used to evaluate condensate corrosion conditions. Preweighed coupons in holders are inserted in condensate lines. After an arbitrary time interval (usually at least 30 days), the coupons are removed, cleaned, and reweighed. The difference in original and final weights, when coupon surface area and exposure time are known, gives an indication of rate of metal loss due to corrosion. It should be noted, however, that such test coupons usually cannot identify bottom "grooving" and threaded-joint corrosion as they occur in actual piping.

Testing for corrosion products (iron and copper) in condensate is a preferred and widely used means of observing corrosion trends. Since metal corrosion products in condensate are mainly present as insoluble particulates rather than in dissolved form, methods of sampling that insure representative and proportional collection of particulates are important.

A general level of corrosion products in the 0–50 μg/l range indicates the system is in control. Because of the problem of sampling error when looking for this small quantity of particulates, a relatively large amount of sample needs to be run. Two accepted methods used are:

1. Visual estimation of iron concentration based on the degree of discoloration of a membrane filter through which a known volume of condensate is passed. Estimation is made by comparing the membrane pad, after filtration of the sample, with prepared standard pads having color equivalents of specific iron values.

2. Very precise quantitative determinations of total iron and copper values are easily made by the Analex method. In this procedure, a sample stream of condensate is allowed to flow through a small plastic cartridge containing a high-purity filter of ion exchange materials for a period of 7–30 days. Particulates are captured by filtration, while dissolved solids are retained by ion exchange. By a unique laboratory process, the total weight of each metal is calculated. A series of successive Analex analyses gives a complete and accurate picture of condensate corrosion trends. Normally, when inhibitors are used in a system previously untreated, the corrosion products observed in the condensate will increase temporarily. Most inhibitors have a "detergent effect" and tend to slough off old oxides. This must be taken into consideration when evaluating test results.

SURVEYING A BOILER SYSTEM

The purpose of surveying a boiler system is to develop physical and chemical data defining the system and its relationship to plant operations with the goal of operating at peak efficiency with minimum maintenance. Physical or mechanical data cover the various types of equipment in the system water supply and treatment equipment, steam-consuming units, condensate handling, preboiler auxiliaries, and the boiler itself. Heat balance data are also included. The chemical data include analyses of all water streams of significance—raw water, condensate streams, treated water, boiler feedwater, boiler water, and wastes. This extensive data gathering is necessary because each boiler system is unique and the optimum performance standards change as new equipment is added, water supplies are changed, and relative costs of fuel, capital equipment, and labor shift.

Making a complete power plant survey requires review of six specific sources of information:

1. Utilities system flow diagram

2. Descriptions of the mechanical equipment and water systems, including physical dimensions and capacities

3. Analyses and flow records of steam and all water sources in the boiler system, including wastes

4. Deposit analyses from past boiler inspections

5. Metallographic analyses of any deteriorated boiler tubes, condenser tubes, pump impellers, piping, or other specimens of metal failures

6. Operating log sheets and service reports

Power Plant Flow Diagram

The flow diagram showing the utility system and all its parts traces water from its source through the pretreatment plant and then into the feedwater system, where it joins the condensate. It shows the path of the feedwater to the boilers,

Figure 39.50 Industrial plant boiler house diagram showing pretreatment, process steam use, and condensate return.

and the distribution of steam to turbines and process. The flow diagram incorporates all steam-using process equipment and the returned condensate flow. Figure 39.50 shows an example of a utilities diagram. A diagram like this should be prepared or checked by the investigator by touring the plant and interviewing operating personnel. Blueprints may not give a current picture because many of these are prepared at the time of construction, and may not have been revised as changes were made after startup.

While preparing the flow diagram of the system, data related to that system should be collected. Figure 39.51 shows a typical plant survey form that is used in recording data of the utility system shown in Figure 39.50.

The survey now requires updated water analyses of all the sources contributing to the boiler feedwater, including raw water, clarified and filtered water, zeolite-treated water, individual condensate returns, and the feedwater itself.

Discretion must be used when deciding how complete an analysis is required of each of these samples. For example, if the water supply is colored, but there is no evidence of problems having developed in the plant from organic materials, there is no need to determine organic matter using such tests as BOD, COD, or TOC, on any of the sampling points along the makeup path. If there is occasional hardness leakage into the condensate, the only analyses which may be needed at the condensate sampling points would be total hardness, iron, pH, and conductivity. The troublesome point in a condensate system can often be detected by filtering the individual samples through membrane filters and com-

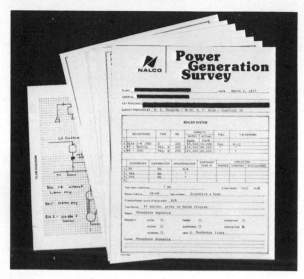

Figure 39.51   Plant survery data required for evaluation of
an industrial steam/condensate system.

paring the filter pads based on the filtration of a uniform sample volume, 500
ml, for example.

On the other hand, condensate being sewered may require rather sophisticated analysis to determine its suitability for boiler feedwater. It may contain
chemical contamination from processing operations, oil, high concentrations
of dissolved gases such as NH_3 and HCN, and high levels of various suspended
solids such as corrosion products or debris.

Determining the flows of the many streams usually requires ingenuity on the
part of the investigator, because for the most part, flow meters are found only
on the clarifier inlet, the individual zeolite units, total feedwater to the boiler,
and total steam production. Determining the ratio of condensate to makeup is
relatively easy, since the condensate in most plants is quite pure compared to the
makeup, and conductivity is a simple means of determining the ratio. However, where the plant has a demineralizer, metered flows must be used since the
makeup is then as high in quality as the condensate. In determining the ratio
of various condensate streams to one another, sometimes temperature differences provide a handy means of making the calculation. For example, in the
illustration used here, the temperature of the turbine condensate will probably
be about 100°F (38°C), with the process condensate coming back at about 200°F
(93°C). The actual temperatures can be measured, and the temperatures of the
combined condensates determined for calculating the ratios.

The most difficult sampling is the steam itself, because a representative sample
is hard to obtain without making special provisions for it. Figure 39.52 indicates
the recommended procedure for sampling steam and condensing this for
analysis. The analysis may only require a determination of pH to establish the
level produced by the application of a neutralizing amine as a benchmark for
interpreting the pH of samples of condensate. On the other hand, steam sampling is extremely valuable as a means of locating sources of trouble in a system.

Figure 39.53 shows data obtained from the use of a hydrogen analyzer
(Figure 39.6) to determine the hydrogen level in a steam produced from a
boiler having process contaminated feedwater. The corrosion action within

the boiler caused by destruction of the protective film of magnetite produced hydrogen directly from the attack of the boiler steel, which is easily observed on the hydrogen analyzer chart.

A common method for determining steam quality is by use of the specific ion electrode for sodium. Since the salts dissolved in the boiler water are sodium salts, the presence of sodium in the steam sample is a direct indication of carryover. Figure 39.30, discussed earlier, shows the chart of such a steam analysis in a plant where periodic carryover was occurring.

If the survey is being conducted to improve the efficiency of the steam plant, special attention must be given to two major water-related operations, the boiler blowdown losses and condensate losses. The boiler blowdown can be cal-

Figure 39.52 Recommended scheme for sampling saturated steam for quality monitoring. Superheated steam requires a modified nozzle to recirculate a portion of the condensed sample for desuperheating. *(From ASTM Standard Method D 1066-69.)*

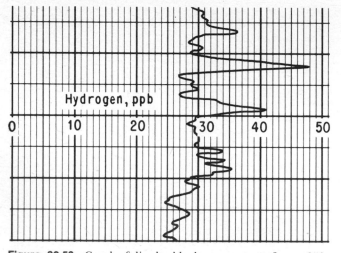

Figure 39.53 Graph of dissolved hydrogen in steam from a 250-psi industrial boiler. A careful study detected periodic contamination of condensate by perchloroethylene that hydrolyzed to HCl in the boiler, generating hydrogen.

culated from chemical ratios. Condensate losses will then be determined as the difference between makeup and feedwater, which are usually metered quantities. Of course, a complete study of the boiler plant is needed to establish the actual operating efficiency, the water-related factors being only part of the energy losses. A typical energy survey for a small plant has been shown earlier in Table 39.11.

Recommendations for improvement may include such steps as changing the combustion conditions in the boiler to reduce excess air; reduction in blowdown; and a plan for increasing the amount of condensate return by either condensate treatment or simply a repiping of condensate that had been lost to a sewer.

The next item on the survey agenda is the collection of deposit analyses from past boiler inspections. Again, discretion is needed in deciding how extensive these analyses need be. Typical analyses have been given earlier in this chapter. For the most part, chemical analyses are adequate for evaluating the problem, but in some cases the crystallographic structure, which must be determined by X-ray, will also be needed. Table 39.12 shows the analysis of a deposit as determined both by chemical analysis and by X-ray diffraction. A great deal can be gained by having the observation of the person collecting the sample recorded as part of the data. For example, the physical appearance of the sample as taken from the site can be valuable information. Many deposits show a laminar structure, indicating periodic changes in the water environment forming the deposit. If the problem should require such painstaking investigation, the individual layers can be analyzed to piece together a story of the causes of variable environmental conditions. If a deposit has been found in the superheater tube, it is often enough simply to know whether the deposit is water soluble or not. So there is considerable judgment required on the part of the investigator to decide what is really needed in analyzing deposits found in various parts of the water circuit.

Metallographic evaluation of specimens of failed tubes, pump parts, or process equipment is a valuable technique for determining the cause of failure so that the program can be modified or changed to correct the cause of failure. A complete history of the failed section is needed, showing its location in the boiler circuit or in the process equipment and the conditions prevailing at the time of failure. As part of the metallographic study, any deposits found on the specimen are analyzed as additional clues to the cause of failure. Figure 39.54 illustrates the section of a failed superheater tube. The section of the tube opposite the failure was of normal structure (pearlitic). The change in metal structure under conditions of overheat are seen in the second section of this illustration, and the nature of the metal at final failure is shown in the third panel, where the overheated metal was actually cooled as the steam rushed through the rupture. This rapid cooling caused quenching of the overheated metal to produce the crystalline structure seen in the third panel. This failure was caused by gradual accumulation of deposits within the superheater tube due to improper layup procedures when the boiler was shut down. During layup, corrosion of the internal tube surfaces occurred, and the corrosion products led to ultimate failure of the tube by insulating the tube surface from normal heat transfer rates.

Finally, the investigator should review all operating log sheets and service reports related to the utility system. There will be found the record of normal and abnormal conditions which were observed day-to-day by the plant operators, and such items as repeated failure of a chemical pump, for example, can be extremely valuable information in pinpointing the cause of plant problems. If a plant has a boiler water consultant, service calls are usually carefully re-

(a)

(b)

(c)

Figure 39.54   Failure of a superheater tube (a). The normal pearlitic structure (Fig. 39.1) was changed by overheating (b). The bursting of the tube cooled the overheated metal to produce the quenched structure (c).

TABLE 39.12 Elemental and X-ray Diffraction Analyses of Brown Deposit from a Steam Drum

Elemental analysis			
Inorganics in dried sample (scaled to 100 percent)		Major calculated combinations (weight percent)	
Iron (Fe_2O_3)	64	Net loss at 800°C	19
Magnesium (MgO)	10	Magnetic iron oxide	51
Calcium (CaO)	8	Magnesium silicate	13
Silicon (SiO_2)	8	Basic calcium phosphate	8
Phosphorus (P_2O_5)	4	Calcium sulfate	4
Sulfur (SO_3)	4	Magnesium sulfate	2
Manganese (MnO_2)	1	Magnesium oxide	1
Carbonate (CO_2)	0		

The following elements were absent (below detection limit):
Na, Al, Cl, K, Ti, V, Cr, Co, Ni, Cu, Zn, Sr, Sn, Ba, Pb.

Loss at 800°C: 19%; $CHCl_3$ extractables: 0%.

X-ray analysis	
X-ray diffraction indicates the presence of the following:	
Fe_3O_4	Magnetite
Fe_2O_3	Hematite
MgO	Periclase (probably)
$Ca(OH)_2 : 3Ca_3(PO_4)_2$	Hydroxylapatite (possibly)

corded and provide another source of information for investigation. A service of this type not only serves to check on the accuracy of the chemical tests conducted by the operators on a routine basis, but it should provide recommendations for improvement in operations based on the experience and judgment of a person who has serviced many plants and can provide recommendations for continual upgrading of the plant based on knowledge of progress made in the water treatment industry at a variety of locations.

Chapter 40

Effluent Treatment

Effluent water quality criteria are no longer matters of local agreements between regional regulatory agencies and industries; they are established by state and federal statutes. In considering effluent treatment for discharge into a receiving stream or lake, each plant outfall must be considered individually as each requires a separate discharge permit from the Environmental Protection Agency (EPA). This is because the effluent characteristics vary widely; even in the same industry plants having the same capacity and processes may produce effluents of widely different quality and quantity. This may be due to differences in raw material composition, sources of plant water supply, water use and recycle, geographic location, or age of the facility.

Sources of Effluent

Data on raw water consumption may not provide accurate information as to the quantity of effluent that will require treatment. Instantaneous plant effluent flows can be as small as 10% or over 200% of the incoming supply rate. Even on a daily average, the effluent may be only 20% of the raw water supply due to evaporation losses, or may exceed the raw water flow on a rainy day (Figure 40.1). To obtain information regarding type of treatment and equipment size requirements, all sources of water must be examined.

Although normally containing little contamination after the initial flow, storm water runoff can contribute significant volume to the plant effluent. Along the Gulf Coast, where precipitation may exceed 60 inches (150 cm) per year, plants must consider runoff in their treatment plans. In other areas, climatic conditions may provide a means to eliminate storm water discharge by favorable evaporation rates. Storm water may be collected and impounded as a good plant water source—often much lower in dissolved solids than the normal supply; in-

Figure 40.1 The effect of storm water on plant effluent flow rate. 1 and 2 are peaks caused by rainfall.

stead of being a discharge load, the storm water can become a benefit. For example, a refinery on a 500-acre (200 ha) site in an area where annual rainfall is 36 in. (90 cm) discharges an average storm water flow of 1.5 mgd (2.62 m³/min). A significant portion of this may be reclaimable if provisions are made to collect it during the rainy season.

The quantity of wastewater flow can be influenced by infiltration of groundwater into the sewer system, especially during the rainy season. Sewers located below the groundwater table or near stream beds may have continual infiltration entering through poorly constructed joints, leaking manholes or manhole covers. Along the seacoast, the rate of infiltration may be influenced by tides. Rates of infiltration range from 15,000 to 50,000 gallons per day per mile (35–120 m³/km) of sewer.

WATER USE AND CONTAMINATION

Discharge patterns are normally determined by examining individual process water uses. Process waters may be required for washing, rinsing, direct contact cooling, solution makeup, chemical reactions, process condensation and gas scrubbing operations. Spent process waters normally generate the largest load of contamination in plant effluents on a daily average basis. This is usually caused by inadvertent leakage of process liquors into the water system. Individual process water uses within a plant may also produce contaminant discharges that may be incompatible in a combined industrial-municipal treatment system.

Contamination may occur from spills and leaks of process or product liquors from manufacturing operations. The volume from spills is usually low in comparison to total water used, but due to high concentration, its loss to the sewer often produces a significant impact on the waste treatment operation. Similarly, storage and transport of raw material or product may require attention as a potential source of contamination. In analyzing wastewaters, it should be assumed that raw materials and products in the process area may somehow find their way into the sewer, and these should be sought in the analysis if they are objectionable contaminants.

Maintenance operations from cleanup and repair of equipment, tankage, and tank trucks or cars also produce concentrated wastes.

UTILITY SYSTEMS

Additional wastes are generated in preparing raw water for use in the plant's utility system. The water treatment plant must dispose of suspended or dissolved solids removed from the supply water as well as chemicals added for treatment. These wastes may discharge on a continuous or batch basis to the plant sewer from clarifiers, filters, softeners and demineralizers.

The plant's utility system discharges less water than it receives. Steam is lost to the atmosphere, but the greatest evaporation loss occurs over cooling towers, when these provide the main source of heat removal. To control the buildup of undesirable materials in its water systems caused by evaporation, the utilities plant removes a small portion of water from the boilers or cooling systems as blowdown. The blowdown may be only 5–10% of boiler and cooling tower makeup, accounting for the large "shrinkage" between raw water and effluent flows. This blowdown contributes some salinity to the effluent since it has been concentrated by evaporation, and also contains chemicals that have been added to control corrosion, scaling and fouling. A typical water balance of a refinery having an evaporative cooling system shows a 60–80% loss of water because of evaporation in the plant.

Finally, plant washrooms and dining facilities generate sanitary wastes. If these are not sent to a municipal treatment system, on-site treatment must be provided for disposal.

PLANT SURVEY

Industrial waste treatment planning begins with a review of plant plot plan and sewer diagram. The plot plan provides general information showing plant size, storage of raw materials, intermediates and finished products, manufacturing operations, materials flow, water supply and effluent disposal sites. The sewer drawings show sewer and manhole locations, floor drains, separated waste collection systems, downspouts and storm drains and any existing effluent treatment facilities. A review of these drawings and available rainfall data will give a picture of sewer loadings, including storm water and plant wastewater.

A valuable reference to possible contaminant discharges is a review of purchase order records, chemical inventories used in conjunction with manufacturing operations, and final production. Discrepancies between input and output provide insights into the types and probable quantities of contaminants that may be present in the plant effluent (Table 40.1).

The potential for disposing of spent chemicals by dumps to the plant sewer or other careless practices must be considered and fail-safe procedures developed to prevent such occurrences.

Inspection of the manufacturing facilities should follow the review of drawings. This tour should focus on water use and resulting waste discharges from each process to identify problems not readily evident by data review alone.

TABLE 40.1   Raw Materials List for a Small Plant Producing Textile Chemicals*

Acids (sulfuric, stearic, oleic)
Aluminum stearate
Alcohols (isopropyl, methyl, butyl)
Butyl carbitol
Chlorinated phenols
Formaldehyde
Kerosene
Mineral oil
Monoethanolamine
Oils (pine, peanut, castor)
Polyethylene
Sodium chloride, perborate, tripolyphosphate, hydroxide
Soap flakes
Tallow
Tapioca flour
Waxes (petroleum and synthetic)

* These chemicals include detergents, softeners, wetting agents, and sizes. All of these are potential wastewater pollutants.

Excess water usage, faulty control, poor housekeeping, and inadequate equipment are common examples of factors contributing to unnecessary contaminant discharges. The inspection offers the opportunity of correcting and preventing contaminant discharges at the source rather than removing the contaminant "after the fact" in the plant effluent. Critical to reducing pollution in a plant is a program to make employees as aware of pollution as they are of safety. As with a successful plant safety program, employee awareness requires continual communication by posters and training sessions.

The plant tour should also include an inspection of existing waste treatment facilities to obtain operating data and equipment sizes. In some plants, night operations may differ from day operations, so the inspection of each shift may be required.

ASSESSING WASTE FLOWS AND QUALITY

Of prime importance is the record of volumes of water requiring treatment. Flow of total plant discharge as well as individual process wastes must be measured. Many plants have permanent flow monitoring devices to meter total plant effluent. However, individual process area flow measurements are also necessary. To provide realistic data on flows to be treated, measurements should be taken over as long a period as practical to show what flow variations must be accommodated in a waste treatment unit (Figure 40.2).

Chemical characteristics of the wastewater and quantity of contaminants present must be established. These are dependent on the raw water supply itself, the water treatment processes, the concentration through utility use, contaminants added in the process operation, or chemicals lost from manufacturing and inventory. Besides the probable contaminants identified through raw materials use, additional types of contaminants may be present as byproducts from the plant processes or as trace contamination in raw materials. Each industry has its own wastewater profile. For example, petrochemical production, petroleum refining, and iron and steel manufacturing produce contaminants such as cyanide, phenols, ammonia and sulfides at different concentrations and ratios. A guide to determining probable contaminants in industrial wastes may be found in numerous EPA-funded studies that were used to establish criteria for effluent compliance by each major industry. Some of this data is summarized by Table 40.2.

SAMPLING AND ANALYSIS

After determining the contaminants to be analyzed for, sampling of the plant streams, both in selected manufacturing areas and in plant outfalls, can proceed to define contaminant loading. The sampling schedule should uncover average contaminant discharges as well as peaks from cyclic or batch operations and process variables. In conjunction with the sampling, continuous monitoring of pH, temperature, and conductivity further define variations in wastewater characteristics (Figure 40.3). Existing waste treatment facilities should also be sampled to establish unit loadings, operating conditions, and contaminant removal efficiencies.

A summary of the raw data may be prepared to show a breakdown of contaminants and flows making up the total plant discharge, focusing on contributions from the various processes and manufacturing areas.

CONSERVATION TO MINIMIZE
EFFLUENT LOADING

At this point if it appears that a relatively large volume of water may require treatment, consideration is given to reducing plant water use. The first area for water conservation is usually process water where water use often exceeds equipment requirements. Secondly, waters identified as mildly contaminated but acceptable for direct reuse in a process not requiring high quality should be segregated for recovery. The third area considered is substitution of recirculating water systems for once-through indirect or direct contact cooling waters. In the steel and petroleum industries, these can make up as much as 90% of total water use.

By simply providing additional rinse tanks with a countercurrent flow of rinse water, metal plating and finishing plants may reduce rinse water require-

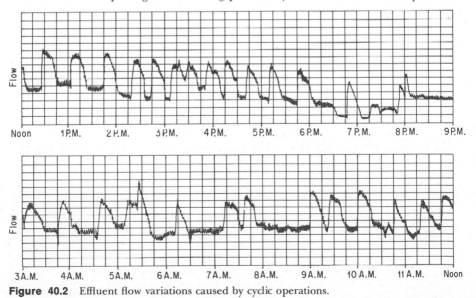

Figure 40.2 Effluent flow variations caused by cyclic operations.

TABLE 40.2 Raw Wastewater Profiles for Selected Industries

Contaminants	Industry									
	Aluminum	Automotive	Chemical	Coke	Food	Mining	Paper	Petroleum	Steel	Textile
Suspended solids	M	M	C	M	M	M	M	C	M	C
Salinity	C	C	C	M	V	M	C	C	C	C
pH variations	C	M	M	M	V	M	M	C	C	C
Oil & grease	C	M	M	M	V	V	I	M	M	C
Settleable solids	M	M	C	M	M	M	M	C	M	C
BOD	V	M	M	M	M	C	M	M	V	M
COD	V	M	M	M	C	I	M	M	V	M
Heat	C	I	V	C	C	I	C	C	M	M
Color	V	V	V	M	C	V	M	I	I	M
Odor	I	I	C	C	C	V	C	C	M	C
Heavy metals	C	C	V	I	I	M	V	V	M	I
Cyanides	I	V	V	M	I	V	I	C	V	I
Thiocyanates	I	I	V	M	I	I	I	C	V	I
Chromates	C	C	C	I	I	I	I	V	V	V
Phosphates	I	C	V	I	V	V	V	V	I	V
Fluorides	C	I	V	V	I	V	I	C	V	I
Ammonia	C	I	V	M	V	I	V	M	V	I
Organics (general)	I	M	M	M	M	I	M	C	V	M
Phenolics	I	I	V	M	I	I	M	C	V	I
Pesticides, biocides	I	I	V	I	I	I	C	C	I	I
Surfactants	V	M	V	I	C	V	V	C	I	C

M = major factor
C = contributes to the problem
I = insignificant
V = varies in the industry, may contribute

Figure 40.3 Conductivity and pH record of a mill outfall, showing discharges at about 1 A.M. and 4–5 P.M., events repeated each day. This is an old city sewer passing through the mill, and investigation disclosed dumps of spent alkali by a neighboring plant.

ments by over 75% (Figures 40.4 and 40.5). Installation of water pretreatment or side stream treatment to remove objectionable contaminants from recirculating cooling systems can extend cooling water use and reduce blowdown.

Evaluation of the survey data may show that a single process or manufacturing area discharges the bulk of the most significant contaminants present in the total plant discharge. Individualized in-plant treatment of that particular source may be warranted. In plating shops this is usually required because treatment of individual contaminants such as cyanide or hexavalent chromium requires chemical reactions incompatible with one another. Poor maintenance practices may cause unnecessary contamination; improved practices and installation of containments for spills and leaks can reduce contamination. Figure 40.6 shows a scheme for containment of strong wastes for recovery or separate disposal.

If possible, sanitary wastes should be collected and sent to a municipal

Figure 40.4   Counterflow rinsing in a metals finishing shop saves water.

treatment plant. An alternate would be to provide septic tanks for the sanitary waste and discharge into a drainage field if volume is small and ground conditions permit. The septic tank discharge may also be chlorinated and then mixed with the plant's process wastes.

REVIEW OF EXISTING FACILITIES

Some industrial discharges contain colloidal solids or emulsified oils that are difficult to remove and may carry through the waste treatment unit. Coagulants are required to destablize these suspensions and allow the particles to float or sink. A common problem in waste treatment units is short-circuiting of the wastewater flow, caused by poor distribution of inflow and discharge, tilted

Figure 40.5   Ratio of rinse water to dragout flow rates.

Figure 40.6 Diking for containment of strong wastes for separate treatment.

overflow weirs, or other poor design features. Installation of baffles or redesign of distributor and collector manifolds may alleviate the problem and allow effective use of the total unit.

Not to be overlooked in the plant survey is the adequacy of existing equipment for treating the average wastewater flow. If clarifiers are found to have a high hydraulic loading, reduction in water usage or the addition of properly sized equipment would be required.

Biological waste treatment units are very sensitive to wastewater conditions. Ineffective contaminant removals can result from one or several factors such as variable flow; too high or low an organic loading; low dissolved oxygen levels; inadequate mixing; insufficient nitrogen or phosphorus nutrient levels; presence of toxic compounds; erratic changes in waste composition, pH or temperature; and growth of undesirable filamentous bacteria or fungi. The ineffective treatment may also be related to inadequate design, such as insufficient aeration capacity or detention time and inadequate solids/liquid separation facilities. A biosystem operation may be optimized by careful review of all operating variables and institution of proper controls.

Although biological waste treatment can effectively reduce organics, microbial growths occurring in other types of waste treatment units may hinder overall treatment efficiency. These growths can produce non-flocculating solids or odorous gases that prevent effective sedimentation and cause fouling or plugging of equipment. They may be controlled by preventing accumulations in dead spaces, elimination or control of their source of food, and application of biocides.

Through the plant tour and review of survey data, it is often possible to reduce both the volume of water and quantity of contaminants that require final treatment. Plants having existing waste treatment systems may find that the in-plant contaminant reduction, segregation, or water reuse studies provide the means for sufficient improvement to achieve current effluent compliance. The improvements may be realized by reduction of water use with resultant increase in residence time.

Control or replacement of chemicals at the process source may eliminate the need for a particular waste treatment process, such as activated carbon for removal of refractory organics. Segregation or in-plant treatment of certain contaminants may prevent adverse effects that can occur with mixtures of different process streams, such as the complexing of metals from one stream with cyanides from another, and solids density loss by mixing a turbid stream with an oily stream.

PROCESS MODIFICATION

One alternative for eliminating or reducing process wastes involves the modification or elimination of steps producing these wastes. For example, the peeling process is one of the greatest sources of waste in most fruit and vegetable processing plants. Research has been directed toward modifying the peeling process so the peel waste can be removed without excessive use of water. One such process modification is the "dry" caustic peeling process for potatoes. In the conventional steam or hot lye peeling processes, potato peels may contribute up to 80% of the total effluent BOD. The new dry caustic peeling method collects peels and caustic as a solid residue, preventing their entrance into plant wastewaters.

In a chemical plant, additional stages of separation to improve product yield from evaporators, washers, filters, or crystallizers may reduce loss of product to the sewer. Often these additional stages are not economical in terms of product recovery costs, but they pay out in reducing final effluent treatment costs.

If possible, the in-plant or waste treatment improvements should be accomplished prior to making final plans for additional facilities. With completion of this program, the total plant discharge should be recharacterized in terms of both flow and contaminant concentrations to reveal the extent of the improvements as well as the contaminants still requiring reduction. Since the wastewater is likely to contain an array of contaminants of various concentrations, a single treatment process usually will not effectively remove each contaminant to the required levels for discharge to a receiving stream. If the plant has no existing waste treatment facilities, a system of two or more stages may be required.

The purpose of the first stage (referred to as primary) or an intermediate stage treatment process would be to remove or reduce contaminants that would interfere or overload a subsequent treatment unit operation (secondary or advanced waste treatment stage).

With the final wastewater characteristics and effluent quality requirements established, the selection of the treatment program may be initiated. The first step is to define the progressive stages of treatment required to obtain the final waste quality goals. The designer should prepare a preliminary schematic flow sheet listing each sequential process treatment step. Perhaps available technology may offer several choices of methods as alternate schematic flow sheets for comparison.

Preliminary evaluation of the possible treatment schemes in terms of estimated installed cost, system limitations, complexity of controls, area and manpower requirements, and flexibility for future needs may decide the final treatment selection or simplify the choices considerably.

A pilot study to simulate the waste process is required to generate the necessary design information. This may be performed by laboratory bench tests or pilot-scale equipment. Bench scale studies are quicker and easier to perform, and may be used to screen and define chemical treatment requirements, and determine contaminant removal efficiency. Obtaining a representative sample is critical for reliable results. The bench test should be performed on composites and various grab samples to determine reliability and establish the ability to obtain repetitive results.

Pilot plant studies should be undertaken where influent waste fluctuations are present and must be considered in the process performance. The pilot studies should include a continuous flow evaluation, preferably on a slipstream of the actual waste flow. The study should continue for a long enough time to include all the major variables encountered in the plant, and to provide sufficient data for design purposes. In some pilot scale studies, such as biological treatment, an acclimatization period is required to obtain reliable, steady-state conditions (Figure 40.7).

These studies determine the quantity of solid wastes generated by the proposed treatment. In many industrial wastewater treatment applications, from simple operations such as food processing to the complex processes of a petrochemical plant, solid waste handling and disposal can present a formidable technical and economic problem. In some cases a chemical wastewater treatment program may be modified to reduce solids generation. For example, this could involve replacing inorganic coagulants with organic polyelectrolytes to minimize sludge formation. Sources of excess solids may be located and brought under control. Reduction of chemical losses in the process operations may significantly reduce sludge production. This is particularly true in metallic waste treatment where lime is often used for neutralization-precipitation.

If solids are difficult to remove in a wastewater clarifier, they will more than likely be difficult to dewater. These sludges will often require chemical sludge conditioning and specialized processing such as precoat vacuum or pressure filtration. Inorganic sludge conditioning chemicals and precoat materials contribute to operating cost not only from a raw materials standpoint but also from rehandling, since their use contributes to the final volume, thereby increasing ultimate disposal or haul-out costs.

In dealing with in-plant or "end-of-pipe" treatment, consideration must be given to ultimate disposal of the contaminants removed from the wastewater. Volatile ingredients may cause air pollution, and sludges may contain materials that would not be acceptable for landfill due to possible water or soil contamination

Figure 40.7 Bench-scale biological studies require frequent attention to observe and record data, during and following the period of acclimatization.

SURVEILLANCE OF PROGRAM

To insure consistent compliance with effluent restrictions, not only a well-designed but also a well-operated facility is necessary. In dealing with chemical waste treatment, over- or under-feed of chemicals will result in inefficiency and poor quality. Chemical feed rates should be verified periodically by jar or laboratory tests. Also of importance with chemical feeds is correct application point and uninterrupted feed.

Most regulatory agencies require routine scheduled analyses for effluent compliance purposes. The critical effluent analyses should also be checked on the raw waste flow to adjust unit operations accordingly. The frequency of such tests is based on influent waste variation.

In many instances, on-line monitors are desirable to provide a continuous record of effluent quality and to adjust chemical additions and equipment performance as necessary to maintain optimum conditions. These devices can warn the operator if a test is out of its control range. The monitoring devices should be cleaned and calibrated as directed by the equipment supplier and the schedule adjusted through experience.

In addition to control analyses normally required on waste treatment effluents, regulatory agencies may require biological monitoring for discharges to receiving streams or bodies of water designated for wildlife or recreational activities. One form of this monitoring may be performance of toxicity measurements. These may expose indigenous fish species to controlled dilutions of waste or, in cages, to the receiving stream below the plant outfall. Total counts of various aquatic organisms above and below the outfall are sometimes preferable. A change in the variety of species and the populations of each provides information on the influence of the plant wastewater on the receiving stream.

The industrial discharge may comply with applicable criteria but still contain compounds harmful to the aquatic organisms or wildlife exposed to the receiving stream. Another form of monitoring related to biological activity of discharges into surface waters is dissolved oxygen sag measurements downstream of discharges. The temperature, residual organic and dissolved solids content may produce a reduction in oxygen levels essential to fish life.

Chapter 41

Wet Gas Scrubbing

Wet scrubbers use a liquid to remove solid, liquid or gaseous contaminants from a gas stream. The scrubbing liquid performs this separation by dissolving, trapping, or chemically reacting with the contaminant.

Scrubbers are used extensively to control air polluting emissions. So many different scrubber configurations have been used that there is some confusion as to whether they all belong in the same category. In some references, for example, the definition of a scrubber may be restricted to certain design criteria, such as whether the units are open or packed. In this text, any device fitting the definition of the first sentence is a wet scrubber.

Scrubber systems can be designed to remove entrained particulate materials such as dust, fly ash, or metal oxides, or to remove gases, such as oxides of sulfur (SO_x), from a flue gas stream to meet air emission standards.

PARTICLE COLLECTION CONCEPTS

In scrubbing particulate matter from gases, the principal concern is usually removal of particles smaller than 10 microns. Larger particles are relatively easy to separate. The successful design and operation of wet scrubbers depends on knowing the size, composition and derivation of the particles to be collected.

Figure 41.1 shows estimated size for some common pollutants. Just as fine particles in water (colloids) carry a charge of static electricity, so do colloidal particles in the fumes and dust, defined as aerosols. If these particles carry no charge, they may be deliberately charged to assist removal by special separators called electrostatic precipitators.

Among the particulates (term for the suspended solid materials) collected by wet scrubbers are dispersion aerosols from processes such as grinding, solid and liquid atomization, and transport of suspended powders by air currents or

Figure 41.1   A comparison of the size of particles present in air emissions.

vibration. Dispersion aerosols are usually coarse and contain a wide range of particle sizes. Dispersion aerosols consisting of individual or slightly aggregated, irregularly formed particles are called dusts.

Condensation aerosols are formed when supersaturated vapors condense or when gases react chemically, forming a nonvolatile product. These aerosols are usually smaller than one micron. In condensed aerosols, solid particles are often loose aggregates of a large number of primary particles of crystalline or spherical form. Condensation aerosols with a solid dispersed phase or a solid-liquid dispersion phase are classed as smokes or fumes. Aerosols which include a liquid dispersion phase are called mists. This classification usually applies regardless of particle size, and differentiation is sometimes difficult.

In practice, a combination of dispersion and condensation aerosols is encountered. Different size particles behave differently because of such physical properties as light scattering, evaporation rates and particle movement. The choice of the best device for particle removal from gas is affected by these differences. Particle sizes, volumes, and weights may be obtained by microscopic sizing and density estimation.

PARTICULATE EMISSIONS

Limits on particulate emissions (smoke, mist, dust) are usually established in four ways:

1. *Emission rate.* The maximum weight that can be legally emitted, lb/hr (kg/hr). This may be expressed as the rate for a specific industry in production terms, e.g., lb/hr/ton (kg/hr/kkg) of pulp.

2. *Maximum concentration* of particulate matter in the gas stream released, e.g., g/m³, grains/cubic foot, or lb/1000 lb gas.

3. *Maximum opacity* of the gas stream emitted, usually measured by observation and comparison to empirical standards (Ringlemann numbers).

4. *Corrected emission rate* is tied to an air quality standard by a formula based on atmospheric dispersion considerations.

Often, several particular emission regulations are enforced simultaneously. If all four types of restrictions are employed, a plant might pass on emission rate and concentration, but fail on opacity. This is an understandable situation, since large particles are the major contributors to weight while smaller particles, in the 0.1–2.0 micron range, are the major contributors to opacity.

The addition of chemical additives to the scrubber water to capture particles in the 0.1–2.0 micron range is often an economical way to meet air quality standards, particularly when compared to the cost of modifications and additions to equipment.

The wet scrubbers discussed in this chapter use water to remove particulates, gases, or both from industrial gas streams or stacks. Water chemistry is often extremely complicated in these scrubber systems because of the variety of operations occurring simultaneously in the scrubber environment.

1. *Heat transfer.* The gas and water are often at different temperatures, so heat will be transferred in the scrubbing process.

2. *Evaporation/condensation.* The gas may be hot and saturated with water vapor. Contact with colder water will dehumidify the gas, and the scrubbing water will be diluted with condensate. If the stack gas is hot and dry, the scrubber water will evaporate, as in a cooling tower, and become concentrated.

3. *Mass transfer.* The gas may contain water-soluble solids or gases that will dissolve in the scrubber water. The water may transfer gases to the gas stream also. For example, the water may be recycled over a cooling tower, becoming saturated with O_2 and N_2, later releasing these to the gas stream.

4. *Scaling.* As the scrubber water is heated or increases in pH, alkalinity, or sulfate-sulfite content, precipitation of $CaCO_3$, $CaSO_4$, or $CaSO_3$ may occur and the scrubber may become scaled.

5. *Corrosion.* This is a common and troublesome problem encountered in most wet scrubbers.

6. *Fouling.* This may occur from the coagulation of the particulate being removed or from microbial activity. Many industrial gas streams contain organics that supply food to microbes.

PRINCIPLES OF OPERATION

Scrubber manufacturers offer a bewildering array of products. Scrubbers are available in a wide range of designs, sizes, and performance capabilities. Some are designed primarily for collection of particles and others for mass transfer (gas removal by a chemical reaction). As good liquid-gas contact is needed for both operations, all scrubbers can collect both particles and gases to some extent. The degree to which the particle collection and mass transfer characteristics of a scrubber can be utilized determines the applicability of the scrubber for each specific purification problem. Figure 41.2 shows the commonly accepted domain of wet scrubbers, based on particle size, relative to other competitive devices.

Figure 41.2 General scheme of application of wet scrubbers compared to competitive devices.

Figure 41.3   Performance range of scrubbing devices.

Figure 41.3 shows the relative particulate removal efficiency of the more common types.

Particle size is one of the most important factors affecting removal efficiency, larger particles being much more easily removed. Submicron particles (1 micron = 10^{-6} meters) are the most difficult to remove.

All wet particle scrubbers operate on the same basic aerodynamic principle. A simple analogy: If water droplets of basketball size were projected to collide with gas-stream particles the size of BB's the statistical chances of collision are small. As the size of the droplets is reduced to more nearly the size of the particles, the chances of collision improve. Studies have shown that a surface film surrounding a water droplet has an approximate thickness of 1/200 of its diameter. A BB (the particle in flight) having a diameter less than 1/200 the diameter of the basketball will flow through the streamline film around the basketball without collision (Figure 41.4). But if the droplet were a baseball instead of a basketball, collision would occur. A 0.5 micron fume particle requires water droplets smaller than 100 microns (200×0.5) for adequate collection. Efficient scrubbing, therefore, requires atomizing the liquid to a fineness related to particle size to afford maximum contact with the particles to be captured.

(a)

(b)

Figure 41.4   The effect of relative droplet size to dust size in the process of particulate capture.

The probability of a droplet hitting the dust particles is proportional to the dust concentration; a ball would be less likely to hit a single BB than a swarm of them. To equalize these factors, scrubbers are regulated as to the volume of gas to be scrubbed (measured by pressure drop of the gas stream), and water to be sprayed (measured by hydraulic pressure at the spray nozzles).

The scrubbing chamber's height and diameter are also tailored to the known characteristics of the gas.

CATEGORIZING WET SCRUBBERS

Wet scrubbers differ principally in their methods of effecting contact between the recirculating liquid and the gas stream. Techniques employed include injecting the liquid into collection chambers as a spray, flowing the liquid into chambers over weirs, bubbling gas through trays or beds containing the liquid, and atomization of the liquid by injection into a rapidly moving gas stream.

One way of categorizing wet scrubbers is by their energy requirements. Some require high energy to perform their task while others require very little. Generally speaking, low energy scrubbers are used for removal of large particulate matter and gaseous contaminants. They rely on high liquid to gas ratios and contact time in the scrubber to increase removal efficiency. High energy scrubbers are used for the removal of very small particulates (1 micron and less).

They depend on high gas velocity for atomization to form small liquid droplets, with maximum impact between water droplets and particulate matter

A second way of categorizing wet scrubbers is based on their selectivity toward either gaseous contaminants or particulate matter. Scrubbers designed primarily for removal of gas are called mass transfer scrubbers or gas absorbers; those designed for removal of particulate are called wet particle scrubbers.

GAS ABSORPTION SCRUBBERS

Gas absorbers, the first category, are designed to maximize contact time and surface area between the scrubbing liquid and the gas. This provides maximum opportunity for liquid/gas chemical reactions to occur. Absorption scrubbers usually have low energy requirements. The types most commonly used are the packed bed, moving bed, impingement, and plate type scrubbers. Although wet particle scrubbers will also provide mass transfer removal of some gases, these four types of absorption scrubbers will do the job more completely and with greater efficiency.

Mass transfer (gas absorption) reactions require long residence times because the contaminants must first be absorbed by the scrubbing liquor and then react chemically to form a product that remains in the liquid phase.

PACKED TOWER

The packed tower (packed bed) consists of a vertical vessel containing packing materials such as rings, saddles, or tellerettes (Figure 41.5). Water is sprayed across the top of the bed and trickles through the packing material. Gas enters near the bottom and contaminants are removed as the gas stream moves upward through the waterwashed packing.

The cleaned gas stream passes through a mist eliminator near the top where entrained moisture is removed prior to discharge. Scrubbing liquor is collected at the bottom. A portion is usually recycled to the inlet, and the balance discharged to the sewer.

Although flows can also be cocurrent or crosscurrent, the countercurrent type

Figure 41.5 Packed tower and types of packing.

is the most widely used. Packed beds have long been used for gas absorption operations because they are able to reduce odor and pollutant gases to low residual concentrations. The limiting factor is economics. As better separation is called for, beds require greater packing depth and operate with higher pressure drops. Gases entering a packed bed should not be heavily laden with solid particles as these cause clogging of the packing material. Pressure drop is typically 0.5 inches of H_2O per foot of packing (4 cm H_2O/m).

Typical applications include rendering plants, food processing plants, sewage treatment plants, and metal pickling plants.

MOVING BED SCRUBBERS

The moving bed wet scrubbers are well suited for high heat transfer and mass transfer rates (Figure 41.6). They are able to handle viscous liquids and heavy slurries without plugging. They accomplish this by using lightweight sphere packing that is free to move between upper and lower retaining grids. Counter-current gas and liquid flows cause the spheres to move in a random, turbulent motion, causing intimate mixing of the liquid and gas.

In addition to excellent gas/liquid contact, the turbulence provides continuous cleaning of the moving spheres to minimize plugging or channeling of the bed.

Moving bed scrubbers are useful to absorb gas and remove particulates simultaneously. This type of scrubber is especially suited for use with gases containing viscous or gummy substances, which would result in plugging of conventional packed bed scrubbers.

Efficiency is good for collection of particles larger than one micron. Both particle collection and gas absorption efficiency may be increased by employing several stages in series. Pressure drop is typically 0.2–0.5″ H_2O per stage.

TURBULENT CONTACT ABSORBER (TCA)

The turbulent contact absorber (Figure 41.7) was developed as an extension of the moving bed scrubber, the difference being the increased turbulence of the TCA unit, resulting from using fewer spheres per unit volume. The TCA enhances the beneficial characteristics of the moving bed scrubber and permits high liquid and gas flows.

Plate Scrubbers

A plate scrubber consists of a tower having plates (trays) mounted inside (Figure 41.8). Liquid introduced at the top flows successively across each plate as it moves downward. Gas passing upward through the openings in each plate mixes with the liquid flowing over it. The gas/liquid contact causes gas absorption or particle removal. A plate scrubber is named for the type of plates it contains: if the plates are sieves, it is called a sieve plate tower.

Impingement Scrubbers

In some designs, impingement baffles are placed a short distance above each perforation on a sieve plate to form an impingement plate to increase turbulence and enhance gas/particle/liquid interaction (Figure 41.9). The impingement baffles are below the liquid level. Pressure drop is about 1–2″ H₂O for each plate.

WET PARTICLE SCRUBBERS

The four basic factors determining the efficiency of wet particle scrubbers are:
1. Water surface area
2. Liquid to gas ratio
3. Particle size and scrubber energy
4. Particulate affinity for water (wettability)

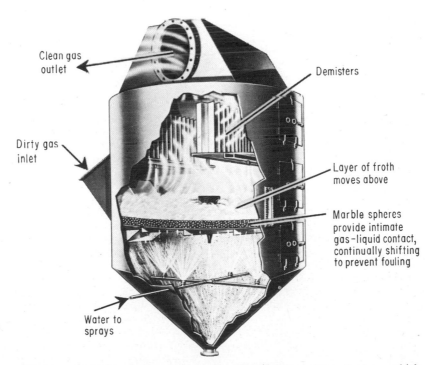

Figure 41.6 Moving bed scrubber, using a lightweight packing of spheres which continually shift, preventing plugging with deposits. *(Courtesy of Environeering, Inc.)*

Figure 41.7 Turbulent contact absorber, another type of moving-bed scrubber. *(Courtesy of Air Correction Division, UOP Inc.)*

Anything mechanical or chemical that causes the water spray nozzles to form smaller water droplets with a larger surface area increases the collision rate between the particulate in the gas phase and the water, resulting in increased particulate removal.

The second way to increase the collision rate is to pump more water through the scrubber. Increasing the liquid/gas ratio is an inefficient means of increasing the surface area of water. Usually, it is more economical to increase the effective liquid/gas ratio by causing smaller droplets to form mechanically or chemically.

The force with which particulate matter strikes the water is a third factor in scrubber performance. Since a liquid film barrier separates particulate in the gas phase from the water, a particle must have enough energy to force its way into the water droplet to be captured. Smaller particles require more energy than larger ones because they have a lower mass and strike the barrier with less momentum than larger particles moving at the same velocity. So, higher energy is required for scrubbing small particles than for large particles.

A higher energy must also be expended to scrub a particle that is hydrophobic (repelled by water) than a similar size particle that is attracted to water—and most particulates in the gas stream are hydrophobic. Increasing the mechanical energy of a wet scrubber increases its ability to remove smaller, and more hydrophobic particulates.

Another means for increasing the removal of these particles is by chemical reduction of surface tension, increasing the wetting power of the water.

Either a high energy or low energy scrubber may be used for removal of particulates from gas streams, the choice depending on the size of the particles. Low energy scrubbers, such as the spray tower and wet cyclone, may be used for particles over 5 microns. For particles smaller than 5 microns, a high energy scrubber such as a venturi or a venturi ejector provides more complete removal. Many wet scrubbing systems, such as those cleaning steel mill blast furnace gas, employ a low energy scrubber followed by a high energy scrubber. The function of the low energy scrubber is to cool the gas (reduce volume) and remove large particles, thereby reducing the load on the high energy venturi scrubber. This also reduces the size and power of the induced draft fan, because the cooling effect reduces gas volume.

Spray Towers

The spray tower collects particles or gases on liquid droplets produced by spray nozzle atomization. The characteristics of the droplets are determined by the design of the nozzle. The sprays are directed into a chamber shaped to conduct the gas to the atomized droplets. Spray towers can be used for both mass transfer and particle collection. Their low pressure drop, 1–2″ H_2O, and high water rate make them the least expensive of the mass transfer scrubbers. Spray chambers are most applicable for removal of large particles, gas cooling, humidification or dehumidification, and the removal of gases with high liquid solubilities.

Wet Cyclones

Wet cyclone scrubbers (Figure 41.10) are effective for removing dusts and liquid aerosols. A finely atomized water spray contacts the gas stream, which enters tangentially at the bottom to pursue a spiral path upwards. The atomized droplets are caught in the spinning gas stream, and swept by centrifugal force across to the walls of the cylinder, colliding with, absorbing, and collecting the dust or fume particles enroute. The scrubbing liquid and particles drain down

Figure 41.8 The plate scrubber provides intimate gas/liquid contact. The flat plates are kept relatively free of deposits in most applications by turbulence. (*Courtesy of Koch Engineering Company, Inc.*)

Figure 41.9 An impingement scrubber uses a perforated plate to promote gas/liquid contact with impingement baffles over the perforations to atomize the water. *(Courtesy of W. W. Sly Manufacturing Company.)*

Figure 41.10 The wet cyclone scrubber. *(Courtesy of Ceilcote Company, a unit of General Signal.)*

Figure 41.11 A venturi scrubber with variable throat to accommodate changes in gas flow. *(Courtesy of FMC Corporation.)*

the wall to the bottom, and clean gas leaves through the top. The higher pressure drop, 6–8″ of H_2O, increases energy costs over those for a spray tower.

Venturi Scrubbers

Venturi scrubbers (Figure 41.11) are best suited for removal of 0.05–5 micron particulates such as those created by condensation of a liquid or metallic vapor or by a chemical reaction forming a mist or fume. Typical examples are ammonium chloride fumes from steel galvanizing, phosphorus pentoxide fumes from phosphoric acid concentration, mists from dry ice plants, and zinc oxide fumes from reverberatory furnaces.

These aerosols are removed by passing the gas and water streams cocurrently through the extremely small throat section of a venturi. As the velocity is accelerated in the throat, the liquid breaks up into extremely fine drops. High gas velocities, ranging from 200–400 ft/sec, make the relative velocity between gas and liquid high enough to cause good liquid atomization and particle collection. The liquid drops collide with and remove the particles in the gas stream and the drops then agglomerate for separation from the gas. The cleaned gas stream then passes through a separator to eliminate entrained liquid.

Venturi scrubbers require high pressure drops (5–100″ H_2O). Pressure drop must be increased as the particle size becomes smaller to assure adequate removal.

Venturi scrubbers can also be used for removing soluble gases. However, such applications are limited to situations where small particulates are also present, because the high energy requirements for operating venturi scrubbers make them costly for controlling gaseous pollutants.

Several modifications of the basic venturi scrubber are available to meet specific requirements of the size and type of particle to be removed. Low, medium, or high energy venturi scrubbers are available, with energy requirements directly related to the pressure drop needed for removal of submicron particulates.

Many venturi scrubbers have a variable throat to allow for change in load. Also, at a fixed load, as the throat is decreased in size, velocity increases, resulting in increased pressure drop and better efficiency in removing submicron particles.

Venturi scrubbers use several methods to atomize the scrubbing water. In the most common, liquid is sprayed through jets across the venturi throat (Figure 41.11). This provides effective removal of submicron dust, fume, and mist particles, and is the first choice for the majority of applications. In another common venturi, the flooded wall type, the scrubbing liquid is introduced tangentially at the top, as shown in Figure 41.12. It spirals down the converging walls to the throat in a continuous film. At the entrance of the throat, it forms a curtain of liquid in the gas stream. The impaction of the gas into this curtain atomizes the liquid. Further impaction and agglomeration occur in the diverging section.

This type of venturi scrubber is recommended for hard-to-handle situations: removal of "sticky" solids from gases; recycling of dirty water where water supplies are limited; and recovery of process materials in concentrated form.

Another common type is the flooded disc scrubber, in which liquid is introduced to a disc slightly upstream of the venturi throat. This liquid flows to the edge of the disc and is atomized by the high velocity gas stream.

Figure 41.13 shows an ejector venturi which uses high pressure spray nozzles

Figure 41.12 In this venturi scrubber design, the water is atomized and it flows down a spiral path toward the venturi throat.

Water
inlet

Gas
inlet

Ejector jet

Diffuser tube

Gas and
liquid out

Figure 41.13 Water creates the energy for this ejector venturi scrubber.

to collect particulates, absorb gases, and move the gas. It derives its energy from the high pressure liquid, while the regular venturi derives most of its energy from the high gas velocity produced by the induced draft fan. An induced draft fan may or may not be required depending on the ejector venturi being used.

There is a high velocity difference between the liquid droplets and the gas; this affects particle separation. Collection efficiency is generally high for solid particles larger than one micron. Mass transfer is affected by the cocurrent flow of the gas-liquid. Energy consumption is relatively high because of pumping costs.

Ejector venturis may be used alone or as the first stage of a more complex system. The principal collection mechanism in this type of scrubber is inertial impaction, which is effected by liquid drops. Particle adherence upon striking the droplets is dependent upon the wettability of the particles. Because scrubbing liquid is usually recirculated, nozzles must be capable of handling a high solids concentration.

WET ELECTROSTATIC PRECIPITATORS

Water can also be used with electrostatic precipitation to improve removal of particulates. In this type of system, water is continually recirculated over the plates and discharged to an ash sluice pond or thickener to be clarified for reuse.

WATERSIDE PROBLEMS

Operating conditions in the scrubber may produce a severely corrosive or scaling water, depending on the gas stream being scrubbed and on the nature of any chemicals being added to the water. Many systems use lime/limestone slurries to react with SO_2, forming insoluble compounds to be removed in a thickener. The problems encountered in wet scrubber operation parallel those found in an open recirculating cooling water system, but the scrubber water is often more saline.

Chemical treatment programs for wet scrubber systems are designed to:

1. Maintain clean nozzles and collection surfaces, preventing deposit or scale buildup, thus helping to maintain unit efficiency.

2. Improve particulate capture or, for gas removal, mass transfer.

3. Control corrosion in the scrubber and recirculating water system.

Water problems in scrubbers range from scale and deposits to corrosion and waste disposal. Depending on the moisture level or dewpoint of the gas stream, gas cooling can result in evaporation or condensation, leading to concentration or dilution of scrubber water.

If the gas stream is above the dewpoint, recycling water for wet scrubbing results in evaporation and concentration of the scrubber water, adding to corrosion and scale problems inherent with the gases or particulates removed from the gas stream. However, in some systems the gas contains substantial water vapor, so condensation with resultant dilution of the recycle water may occur. This tends to lessen the potential for scale, deposits, and corrosion. Dilution is less common than concentration.

Each scrubbing system must be considered individually due to the wide variety of construction materials available, including mild and stainless steels, copper and nickel alloys, fiberglass, PVC, ceramics, lead, and refractories, to name a few. Many manufacturers construct scrubbers of alloyed metals and nonmetallic materials to avoid corrosion problems, but still encounter the problems of scale and deposition. The same techniques and principles used for corrosion and deposit control in cooling systems apply to scrubbers.

Scrubber systems that operate under low pH conditions usually have deposits that are primarily particulates removed from the gas. Those systems that operate at a pH greater than 7.0 will normally yield scale deposits produced from water reactions, or scale and suspended solids combined.

However, even high pH systems of this type will sometimes yield deposits that are primarily particulates removed from the gas. It is difficult to generalize regarding composition of deposits because of the wide variability of scrubber designs, process gases, and water characteristics. The most commonly encountered deposits are calcium carbonate, calcium sulfate, lime [$Ca(OH)_2$], iron oxide, carbon black (soot), oils and greases, aluminosilicates (clays), and metal sulfides. Deposits, like corrosion, can plague virtually every section of the scrubber sys-

TABLE 41.1 Typical Deposit Analyses*,†

	Sugar mill scrubber supply line	Electric utility demister scrubber	Process scrubber—calcium carbide	Coke gas scrubber—fan blade deposit	Blast furnace scrubber—return to furnace
Calcium (as CaO)	60	49	36.4	33	52
Iron (as Fe_2O_3)	1		2.6	5	9
Carbonate (as CO_2)	2	16		0	21
Sulfur (as SO_3)	36	32		44	4
Silicon (as SiO_2)	1	2	2	4	6
Aluminum (as Al_2O_3)	1	1		1	3
Chlorine (as Cl)	0	0		2	
Sodium (as Na_2O)	0	0		5	
Magnesium (as MgO)	0	0	58.5	5	1
Loss at 800°C	14	16	60	67	23
Carbon	0	0	5	62	5
Hydrocarbons	0	0	19		

* Inorganics in dried sample scaled to 100%.

† All figures in %.

tem—from the inlet gas ports to the induced draft fan and stack. Deposits usually form at the venturi throat, trays and packing in gas absorbers, liquid recycle lines and pumps, mist eliminators, induced draft fans, and clarifier supply lines.

The deposit analyses shown in Table 41.1 illustrate the primary components of deposits removed from different types of scrubbers to illustrate the wide diversity from one industry to another. These analyses show that deposit compositions vary widely, with calcium occurring most frequently.

Chemical treatment for scale and deposit control is effective in controlling the majority of deposits, but it must be individualized for each scrubbing system due to variation in deposition problems.

WASTE TREATMENT

Since the basic function of the wet scrubber is to remove contaminants from process and combustion gases, once the scrubber liquid has done its job, the disposal of contaminants transferred to the water must be considered. For the small plant, this may entail merely discharging a bleed-off of recycle water to the sanitary sewer. The larger plant may be required to install an in-plant clarification system. There are two basic types: the first is the full-flow, inline clarifier which clarifies all scrubber water after it has made one pass through the scrubber.

Water is recycled from the clarifier to the scrubber for further reuse. Problems are usually less severe with this type of unit because suspended solids are usually maintained at a fairly low level. This type of system is in many respects comparable to a once-through system. The second basic type of clarifier is that used for clarification of a blowdown sidestream from the recycle system prior to discharge. Problems are normally more severe with this type of system.

Scrubbing liquid that contains high BOD, heavy metals, or toxic matter may require additional treatment, such as biological oxidation, prior to discharge.

AUXILIARY EQUIPMENT

Although the wet scrubber is the heart of the gas cleaning system, auxiliary equipment is required to help the scrubber work efficiently. Auxiliary equipment may be categorized as follows:

1. *Dust catchers* remove gross solids to prevent overloading the scrubber.

2. *Gas quenchers* cool high temperature (over 1000°F) gas and reduce evaporation in the scrubber.

3. *Entrainment separators* (demisters) reduce water droplets in the exit gas.

4. *Gas cooling towers* reduce plume discharge.

5. *Water cooling towers, cooling ponds,* or *spray ponds* facilitate optimum water recycle and minimize makeup.

6. *Induced draft fan* moves gas from the scrubber to the discharge vent or stack.

7. *Forced draft fans* move gas to the scrubber and through to the vent or stack.

8. *Gas reheat system* reduces plume discharge by raising the dewpoint of the gas.

9. *Clarifiers, thickeners, and settling ponds* facilitate recycle and recover solids for disposal or reuse.

10. *Sludge dewatering devices* to consolidate recovered solids.

SELECTED GAS SCRUBBING SYSTEMS

This section presents examples of gas scrubbing systems used in the electric utility, steel, and paper industries, including the basic types of scrubbers and auxiliary systems used in these applications and the nature of the waterside problems.

REMOVAL OF PARTICULATE (FLY ASH) AND SO$_2$ FROM FLUE GAS

Although several different scrubbing systems are available for this application in the utility industry, the process using limestone has been selected to illustrate many of the aspects of wet scrubbing previously discussed.

Figure 41.14 shows the limestone scrubbing process for removal of SO$_2$ from boiler flue gas. Two venturi/absorber scrubber modules, the heart of the system, are used to treat the entire flow of flue gas. This system is designed to be added to an existing conventional stack-gas cleaning system.

Limestone stored in silos discharges through a gravimetric feeder, a wet ball mill and classification system. Limestone slurry at 20% solids leaves the milling system and is stored for transfer to the scrubber modules as needed.

Each scrubber unit consists of (1) a variable-throat venturi that removes fly ash and provides an initial stage of SO$_2$ removal, followed by (2), a countercurrent tray absorber. Sprays in the venturi and the absorber drain into separate reaction tanks, where chemical reactions are allowed to go to completion before the slurry is returned to the scrubber.

Spent slurry from the scrubber, principally calcium sulfite (CaSO$_3$), is pumped to a thickener. Clarified water from this unit is discharged to a pond and returned to the reaction tanks. Thickener underflow is pumped to a sludge-treatment plant, where fly ash and other dry additives are blended to modify the gel-like sludge to produce a stable landfill.

Cleaned flue gases leaving each absorber pass through a bare-tube steam-coil reheater and then to a booster fan. Both booster fans discharge into ID fan in-

Figure 41.14   Utility stack gas scrubbing system. *(From Power, September 1974.)*

Figure 41.15   Blast furnace gas scrubbing system.

lets. An electrostatic precipitator ahead of the scrubbers serves to remove the bulk of fly ash initially. In case of scrubber system malfunction, a bypass of the precipitator discharge goes directly to the stack.

Major control functions, including limestone feed rate, venturi spray liquor rate, venturi differential pressure, slurry solids concentration, and milling system operation, are handled automatically from the boiler control room.

Primary waterside problems are scale and deposits in the venturi scrubbers, gas absorbers, and venturi and absorber recirculation lines and pumps.

STEEL MILL FLUE GAS SCRUBBERS

Wet scrubbers are commonly employed by the steel industry for scrubbing gases produced by the blast furnace and basic oxygen furnace (BOF). A diagram and description of each will be presented to show how the basic scrubber and auxiliary equipment may be combined to meet effluent gas requirements.

Blast furnace gas contains CO and is used for combustion in boilers. This requires the effluent gas to be clean and cooled to reduce gas volumes and moisture content prior to combustion. Prior cooling and reduction in gas volume results in substantial savings in delivery costs through the extensive distribution system throughout the mill. Since the primary objective of cleaning blast furnace gas is to produce dust free, cooled gas to be used as fuel for the boilers, the scrubbing system is designed as shown in Figure 41.15.

Effective removal of a mixture of coarse and fine dust from a very dusty gas necessitates the use of a dust catcher and a multi-venturi scrubbing system. Effective cooling requires the use of a gas cooling tower prior to effluent gas discharge to the boiler.

The dust catcher is merely a settling chamber to remove large particles and reduce loading on the venturi scrubbers. The gas passes through both a primary venturi (with separator) and a secondary venturi for even more effective particulate removal. Then the gas passes through the entrainment separator/gas cooling tower combination. The cleaned, cooled gas is then sent to furnaces. Adequate cooling is required to reduce the moisture level of the gas to avoid problems in distribution lines and funaces, especially in winter.

The recycle water collected from the first venturi, containing a high level of particulates, is sent directly to a clarifier-thickener. The recycle water collected from the separator is recirculated to the first venturi scrubber. Makeup water is added at the clarifier, and the combined overflow is recycled to the secondary venturi. So the cleanest water contacts the cleanest gas, and works its way back to the first venturi and then to the clarifier. Water can be recycled from the thickener to the scrubber or may be used for some other purpose such as slag quenching.

A conventional cooling tower is normally used for removal of heat from the gas cooling tower water or scrubber water. The design of the tower makes it possible to keep the cooling water and the venturi scrubber water separate.

The scrubber water generally contains considerable hardness and alkalinity from the lime fines in the burden in the blast furnace. Consequently, scale is frequently encountered. Deposits of iron oxide and unburned carbon are also a concern in many systems. Deposition problems are most frequently encountered in the primary venturi nozzles and throat region, where the gas contains the highest level of particulates, and in the lines and pumps going to and from the thickener. However, deposition can occur in both venturi scrubbers, the separators, the gas cooling tower, or the scrubber recycle lines and pumps.

Clarification is another major problem area since inadequate liquids/solids separation results in poor water quality of the clarifier overflow.

The objective of BOF gas cleaning is to produce effluent acceptable for discharge into the environment, since the cleaned BOF gas cannot be reused. As a result, the gas scrubber system for a BOF, shown in Figure 41.16, is somewhat different from the system used for blast furnace gas cleaning. The blast furnace dust catcher is replaced by a quenching system and the primary and secondary venturi replaced by a single venturi scrubber.

The function of the quencher is to substantially reduce gas temperatures, by 1000–1500°F (560–840°C), and to reduce gas volumes and resultant fan size and power requirements. A secondary function is to remove dust and particulates greater than 10 microns. This particulate is collected in the scrubber and sent to the solids removal system and thickener. The humidified, cooled gas then passes through the venturi, flooded elbow, separator, and gas cooler prior to discharge up the stack.

The BOF recycle water from the clarifier is pumped to the venturi scrubber, collected in the separator, pumped to the quencher, collected in the scrubber,

Figure 41.16 BOF scrubbing system.

Figure 41.17   Kraft black liquor recovery boiler flue-gas scrubber.

and transferred to the thickener system for clarification and reuse. A cooling tower is then used for removal of waste heat from the gas cooling tower water.

Scale is normally the primary problem in most BOF scrubber systems Calcium and alkalinity levels vary, but are usually not as high as in a blast furnace scrubbing system. Scaling potential is severe in a BOF scrubber because pH occasionally gets as high as 11.0 during lime addition to the converter during a blow. The pH in the thickener is generally more consistent than in the scrubbing water due to equalization in the thickener.

Problem locations in the scrubber system are similar to the blast furnace circuit.

PULP/PAPER WET SCRUBBERS

The most common applications for wet scrubbers in the pulp and paper industry are for coal-fired, bark-fired (hog fuel), and recovery boiler flue gases, and lime kiln recovery operations. The type of wet scrubber that finds the greatest application is the venturi with cyclonic separator combination, or electrostatic/wet cyclone combination. The recovery boiler flue gas scrubber uses a wet cyclonic separator in combination with an electrostatic precipitator (Figure 41.17), while the other processes use the venturi/cyclone combination.

The venturi/cyclone or cyclone scrubbers are very basic systems that suffer from the standard problems associated with wet scrubbing systems—deposition and scaling. Calcium carbonate scaling potential is most severe in the lime kiln scrubber because of the CaO and $CaCO_3$ particulate in the effluent gas. Problems in thickener operation are similar to those encountered in the utility and steel industries.

Chapter **42**

Agricultural Uses of Water

More fresh water is used for agriculture in the United States than for all indus-trial purposes, including utility cooling water. By far the largest portion of this is for irrigation, the principal focus of this chapter. Farm uses include water supply for livestock and domestic use, and water for farm equipment, particu-larly for diesel engine cooling, and preparation of agricultural chemical solutions, such as fertilizers and herbicides.

Both surface and underground sources are drawn on for agricultural water supply; the greatest volume is from surface sources, but the largest number of installations use well water. An example of surface water use is western irrigation with Colorado River water. Land flooding for leaching and irrigation in that area has become so widespread that it has affected the salinity of the Colorado River, requiring the United States to desalinate the river to meet its obligations to its downstream neighbor, Mexico.

CROP IRRIGATION

Although some crops along the eastern seaboard are irrigated, the major appli-cations of irrigation water are in states where both rainfall and water are rela-tively scarce, i.e., west of the Mississippi River. Because of this, there is growing use of reclaimed wastewater for crop irrigation. For many years, the entire dis-charge of the sewage treatment plant at Lubbock, Texas, has been used for irrigation of cotton. But the use of municipal sewage plant effluent for irrigation of food crops is a more sensitive problem and requires careful evaluation of such potential problems as the heavy metals content of the wastewater, the pres-ence of pathogenic organisms, and the effect of each of these on the crops.

Irrigation water must be pumped from the source and passed through some type of distribution system, either open or closed. Many distribution systems are

Figure 42.1 Overhead irrigation systems distribute water over broad expanses of cropland, slowly moving across the fields to optimize water used. *(Courtesy of Valmont Industries, Inc.)*

open ditches and flumes that develop problems of biological growths, plugging with sediment, seepage into the ground (which is usually the highest portion of the water lost en route to the point of use), and evaporation loss.

The problems in closed distribution systems are discussed elsewhere in this text; they are categorized as corrosion, scaling, and deposits caused by sediment or microbial activity. Precipitation may occur in the distribution system if ammonia is added to the irrigation water as a fertilizer.

Many irrigation systems use plastic pipe because of its light weight and easy assembly. Corrosion in such pipelines is not a problem. After reaching the point of use, the water is fed into an irrigation system which may be of the gravity, sprinkler, or drip type. With the gravity system, fields may be completely flooded, as for rice cultivation; or the irrigation water may flow across a sloping field. The bulk of irrigation water today is handled by gravity.

Sprinkler irrigation systems include overhead application, which is commonly used on crops like alfalfa. Overhead spray systems are designed to cover single fields having a diameter of as much as 2500 ft (750 m), Figure 42.1. The second basic type of spray system uses low trajectory sprinklers. Citrus crops may use this design to confine wetting to the soil, leaving the foliage dry. There is considerable evaporation loss in the use of spray irrigation because of the large water surface area produced by the spray mechanisms. This evaporation also produces cooling, which may present a problem of thermal stress to the plant.

The final category of irrigation, drip irrigation, has been developed to meet the needs of agriculture in water-short areas where evaporation losses cannot be tolerated. A controlled volume of water is delivered to each unit under cultivation at predetermined rates, using the device shown in Figure 42.2. Since the flow rate per unit is small, this type of system must be kept completely free of silt or slimes produced by microbial activity to prevent clogging orifices that control the rate of flow to each site.

THE NATURE OF SOIL

Soil is a miraculous mixture of inorganic materials produced by the weathering of rocks and clays, and organic material produced by the decomposition of

Figure 42.2 In drip irrigation, this emitter reduces water pressure by frictional resistance through a long helical path so the emission hole can be as large as possible to avoid plugging.

vegetation. Physical stresses, produced by diurnal temperature changes or seasonal freezing and thawing assisted by erosion from wind and storms, cause exfoliation of exposed rocks, breaking them down into fine particles. The solvent action of water produces a similar effect by selectively dissolving oxides, carbonates, and feldspar, releasing the particles of less soluble material. The effect of both of these weathering reactions is to produce silt and sand, which is washed into the valleys to deposit with other soil-forming materials.

Clays are broken down in a somewhat similar fashion, yet they still bring their swelling properties and their ion-exchange capacity to the soil mixture. Finally, high-molecular-weight organic materials, such as humic acid, fulvic acid, and polysaccharides, with lower molecular weight materials such as protein, are broken down by bacterial action. Just as with the organic components in colored water, these colloidal materials carry a charge that is neutralized as their ion exchange sites take up calcium, magnesium, and iron, causing flocculation and sedimentation of the organic material with the sand and silt.

In this soil mixture, the clay is usually of small particle size, less than 5 microns. Silt is normally in the range of 5–50 microns, and sand may be found in particle sizes from 50 microns to 2 millimeters.

TABLE 42.1 Selected Soil Analyses

Property	Sample		
	A	B	C
Organic matter, %	0.9	1.0	1.4
Ca, ppm*	1600	700	2000
Mg, ppm	150	160	440
K, ppm	210	71	397
P, ppm	103	9	135
pH	7.9	6.2	7.4
H^+, Meq/100 g	0.0	0.7	0.0
Cation exchange cap., Meq/100 g	9.8	5.7	14.7
Sand, %	68.0	74.0	58.8
Silt, %	27.2	17.2	33.2
Clay, %	4.8	8.8	8.8

* mg/kg of soil

Clay<0.005 mm; Silt=0.005 mm – 0.05 mm; Sand=0.05 mm – 2.0 mm

Figure 42.3 United States Department of Agriculture soil classification.

The properties of several soils are shown in Table 42.1, and a diagram that defines the various descriptive categories of soil is shown in Figure 42.3. Voids containing air and moisture occupy about 50% of the soil volume, an important fact in understanding the environment of soil bacteria and the capillary effects that not only retain soil moisture, but at times provide water to the root zone from the water table far below the plant.

The moisture content of the soil is measured by a tensiometer. If the void space is saturated with water, the instrument reads zero; as the soil drains and air occupies an increasing portion of the voids a suction effect is produced, and the instrument dial (a vacuum gauge) shows increasing levels of vacuum. The dial is calibrated in units of barometric pressure (bars), and a reading of 70 centibars usually warns of the soil becoming too dry and requiring irrigation. A tensiometer may be used to automatically control the irrigation system; it may initiate water flow at 30–40 centibars and discontinue flow at 10–20 centibars, for example.

MEASURABLE SOIL CHARACTERISTICS

Although many properties of soil are classified subjectively, such as friability, many other properties can be measured quite precisely. These include the permeability of the soil, its swelling properties, its ion exchange capacity, and the conductivity of the water extract. The pH of the water extract is also an important property as this influences the selection and dosage of chemicals used for soil conditioning.

The plant growing in any soil, properly irrigated and exposed to sunlight, combines carbon dioxide and water to produce carbohydrates and oxygen according to the following reaction.

$$CO_2 + H_2O \xrightarrow[\text{chlorophyll}]{\text{sunlight}} CH_2O + O_2 \qquad (1)$$

This reaction shows that 60% of the weight of carbohydrate originated with water. In other words, the water required to produce the carbohydrate in a bushel of wheat, weighing about 60 lb (27 kg) is about 40 lb (18 kg). Considerably more water is applied to the plant than is converted to carbohydrate, because of transpiration (the plant's equivalent of perspiration) from the foliage, and drainage of excess water past the root zone. The transpiration process takes pure water vapor from the plant's system, leaving behind a more concentrated fluid. In other words, the plant acts as an evaporator, the evaporation providing cooling to the skin just as perspiration does for animals.

Another important fact about the photosynthesis reaction is that it requires chlorophyll as a catalyst. Magnesium is needed to produce the chlorophyll molecule, and this must be taken into the plant fluids through the roots by some process of selection. The plant also requires many other materials for cell synthesis, including phosphorus, potassium, nitrogen, and sulfur. Depending on the type of plant, certain trace elements are needed for nutrition, and these too must come from the water-soil environment. Plants irrigated with municipal sewage plant effluent show uptakes of heavy metals, including potentially toxic materials such as lead and zinc. But these may become concentrated in the stalk, the leaves, or the roots and may not become a part of the fruit. Each of these problems has to be investigated selectively to determine the effect of heavy metals in municipal sewage on specific food crops.

Soil bacteria are partly responsible for solubilizing the required nutrients for transfer across the outer skin of the roots into the plant fluids. For the most part, these are aerobic organisms, so the creation of anaerobic conditions which could be caused by poor drainage or by irrigation with wastewaters high in organic food substances could be detrimental to the plant.

CONCENTRATION EFFECTS

Since the plant foliage evaporates water, the plant fluids become quite concentrated relative to ground water. Osmotic pressure then causes water to pass across the root surfaces from the soil, and this leaves a more concentrated water in the root zone. If the salinity of the water in the root zone becomes too high, the osmotic flow may reverse, and the plant can become dehydrated as it passes water into the soil. The relative salt tolerance of a scattered grouping of crops is shown by Table 42.2, based on the conductivity of a paste prepared from a soil sample.

In addition to the concentration effects caused by transpiration of water from the plant and osmotic flow, there are other factors affecting the composition of water held in the root zone. A prominent force changing this composition is the capillary action of the soil, causing water to rise to the surface crust to be evaporated to the atmosphere. As water is concentrated, whether by transpiration, osmosis, or evaporation, two important indexes of water quality are affected: the Stability Index changes (either the Langelier Index or the Stiff-Davis Index), and the sodium adsorption ratio (SAR) changes. This ratio is defined as

$$SAR = \frac{Na}{\sqrt{\dfrac{Ca + Mg}{2}}}$$

TABLE 42.2   Tolerance of Certain Crops to Salinity

High tolerance (10,000–16,000 micromhos)	Moderate tolerance (4,000–10,000 micromhos)	Low tolerance (below 4000 micromhos)
Barley	Alfalfa	Celery
Sugar Beet	Rye	Green beans
Cotton	Wheat	Field beans
Spinach	Oats	Citrus crops
	Rice	
	Corn	
	Potatoes	
	Carrots	

SOURCE: Water Quality Criteria, 1972. EPA publication R.3-73-033. Original data by Salinity Laboratory Staff, USDA 1953.

where ionic concentrations are in equivalents per million, or milliequivalents/liter (mg/l divided by eq wt).

The clay component of soil has ion exchange properties which play an important role in holding trace metals for the plant to use as they may be needed. The clay component may also include swelling clays, such as bentonite. A high SAR value affects the plant itself, the clay minerals with ion exchange capacities (causing the trace metals to be regenerated off the clay particle), and dispersion and swelling of the clay, reducing its permeability (drainage ability).

There are some general rules about the suitability of irrigation water for certain crops. For example, the SAR limit for certain fruits may be only four, whereas grain and alfalfa may tolerate an SAR as high as 18. However, it is not the irrigation water itself that is of greatest concern, but rather the nature of the water at the root zone, which has been affected by concentration and often by precipitation of calcium carbonate. Figure 42.4 is an illustration of what may happen to irrigation water in concentrating by a factor of four in the root zone. The SAR of the Colorado River at Parker Dam is given as 2.52, and the Langelier Index is +1.05. In the second column of the tabulation, this water has been concentrated four times, which is a typical concentration ratio for soil water about twelve inches below the ground level. The Langlier Index has increased to +2.3 and the SAR is now 5.04. Several processes are going on in the root zone which affect the actual composition, including precipitation of calcium carbonate and respiration of soil organisms to produce CO_2. In the third column, it is assumed that the Langelier Index has reached equilibrium by precipitation of calcium carbonate and by the production of 65 mg/l of CO_2 by bacterial respiration. Because of the precipitation of calcium carbonate, the sodium adsorption ratio has increased almost to six.

A modification of the Langelier Index has been proposed to provide a means of estimating the sodium adsorption ratio of the soil moisture based on the SAR of the irrigation water and the concentration ratio. These relationships are shown below:

1. $pH_c = pK_2 - pK_c + p(Ca + Mg) + p\ Alk$
2. $PI\ (Precipitation\ Index) = pH_{se} - pH_c$
3. $SAR_{se} = SAR_w \sqrt{CR} \cdot (1 + PI)$

where pH_c = equilibrium pH of irrigation water at $CaCO_3$ saturation
pK_2 = $-\log K_2$, second dissociation constant of H_2CO_3

Identification of Analyses Tabulated Below:

A. <u>Colorado River at Parker Dam</u> D. _____

B. <u>"A" at 4 concentrations</u> E. _____

C. <u>"B" assuming CaCO₃ precipitation</u> F. _____

Constituent	As	A	B	C	D	E	F
Calcium	CaCO₃	198	792	512			
Magnesium	''	105	420	420			
Sodium	''	220	880	880			
Total Electrolyte	CaCO₃	523	2092	1812			
Bicarbonate	CaCO₃	113	452	200			
Carbonate	''	7	28	0			
Hydroxyl	''	0	0	0			
Sulfate	''	302	1208	1208			
Chloride	''	100	400	400			
Nitrate	''	Nil	Nil	Nil			
Fluoride		1	4	4			
M Alk.	CaCO₃	120	480	200			
P Alk.	''	4	16	0			
Carbon Dioxide		0	0	65			
pH		8.40	8.4	6.65			
pH_s @ 100°F		7.35	6.1	6.65			
Silica							
Iron	Fe						
Langelier Index		+1.05	+2.3	0.0			
Turbidity							
TDS		661	2644	2364			
Color							
SAR		2.52	5.04	5.8			

Figure 42.4 An example of changes in SAR as ground water becomes concentrated.

pK_c $= -\log K_c$, equilibrium constant for $CaCO_3$
$p(Ca + Mg)$ $= -\log (Ca + Mg)$, the total hardness
p Alk $= -\log$ Alk, total alkalinity
CR $=$ concentration ratio
se $=$ soil extract
w $=$ irrigation water

As shown above, this modified index assumes the precipitation of magnesium as well as calcium in the soil as the imbibed water in the root zone concentrates. It also assumes the ability to accurately measure the pH of the water in the root zone.

Of course, one means of controlling the concentration effect is to leach the soil by applying an excess of water to dilute the concentrate. But, in many areas where irrigation is practiced, there is a shortage of water and concentration

TABLE 42.3 Recommended Maximum Concentrations of Trace Elements in Irrigation Waters*

Element	For waters used continuously on all soil, mg/l	For use up to 20 years on fine textured soils of pH 6.0 to 8.5, mg/l
Aluminum	5.0	20.0
Arsenic	0.10	2.0
Beryllium	0.10	0.50
Boron	0.75	2.0
Cadmium	0.010	0.050
Chromium	0.10	1.0
Cobalt	0.050	5.0
Copper	0.20	5.0
Fluoride	1.0	15.0
Iron	5.0	20.0
Lead	5.0	10.0
Lithium	2.5†	2.5†
Manganese	0.20	10.0
Molybdenum	0.010	0.050†
Nickel	0.20	2.0
Selenium	0.020	0.020
Tin†		
Titanium‡		
Tungsten§		
Vanadium	0.10	1.0
Zinc	2.0	10.0

* These levels will normally not adversely affect plants or soils.
† Recommended maximum concentration for irrigating citrus is 0.075 mg/l.
‡ See Water Quality Criteria, EPA Publication R.3-73-033, 1972, pp. 337–353, for a discussion of these elements.
§ For only acid fine textured soils or acid soils with relatively high iron oxide contents.

control by leaching may be impractical. If soil drainage is poor, excess water may simply flood the voids and restrict air supply to soil organisms.

In some areas where irrigation is practiced, there are times when ground water may rise from the water table to supply the root zone. The compatibility of the concentrated irrigation water with the ground water may become a problem if precipitation occurs and reduces soil permeability.

CONDITIONING IRRIGATION WATER

Quality standards have been recommended for irrigation that are as complete as those issued for potable water. Table 42.3 lists recommended maximum levels of trace constituents in irrigation water.

In addition to these general recommendations, further preferred limits for salinity and important elements such as boron have been proposed for specific types of crops.

Because of the large volume of water used for crop irrigation generally, water treatment for removal of specific constituents has historically been considered uneconomical. For the most part, the only treatment being practiced is threshold treatment for (1) scale control in distribution systems, and (2) to prevent calcium carbonate precipitation in flume water to which ammonia has been added as a fertilizer. The addition of ammonia to irrigation water with a positive Langelier Index may cause calcium carbonate to precipitate, but this can be controlled by the use of polyphosphates. In the newer drip-irrigation systems, where very small volumes of water are brought to individual plants, because of the small flow through the individual distribution units, plugging is an ever-present threat. Clarification, treatment with dispersants, application of biocides, or a combination of these may be necessary to keep the system functioning.

The use of municipal sewage plant effluent for irrigation of croplands can serve both the municipality and agricultural interests. Spray irrigation has proved to be an effective tertiary treatment for both municipal and certain industrial wastes—such as food processing wastes. There will undoubtedly be increased use of waste effluents for irrigation, and the savings to the waste plant operator in not having to install exotic tertiary treatment facilities may justify additional treatment of some kind in the waste plant if the quality of the effluent must be upgraded to meet limitations on such constituents as heavy metals.

The desalination of the Colorado River to upgrade its quality to meet the needs of the Mexican farmers suggests that there will be growing consideration of desalination processes as water quality in water-short areas continues to depreciate and the value of crops increases.

SUGGESTED READING

Water Quality Criteria—1972, A Report of the Committee on Water Quality, Environmental Studies Board, EPA Publication R3-73-033, March 1973.
Salinity Laboratory Staff (1954), U.S. Dept. of Agriculture: "Diagnosis and Improvement of Saline and Alkaline Soils," Handbook 60, U.S. Government Printing Office, Washington, D.C.
Bower, C.A., Walcox, L.V., Akin G.W., and Keyes, M.C.: "Precipitation and Solution of Calcium Carbonate in Irrigation Operations," Soil Science Society of America, Proceedings 29 (1) and 93-94 (1965).
Stumm, W., and Morgan, J.J.: "Aquatic Chemistry," John Wiley & Sons, Inc., 1970.
Croneis, C., and Krumbein, W.C.: "Rocks and Minerals," in "The Crust of the Earth," Rapport, S. and Wright, H., The New American Library, 1955.
Shoji, K.: "Drip Irrigation," Scientific American, 237,5, November 1977.

Chapter 43
Oil-Field Water Technology

THEORY OF OIL FORMATION

The organic theory, the most generally accepted hypothesis on the origin of oil, presumes that microscopic plant and animal life from the sea and tidal areas provided oil's raw materials, hydrogen and carbon.

Through millions of years, rivers transported great volumes of mud, sand and products of surface erosion to the sea floor, to be spread by tides and currents. Under the increasing weight of this accumulating debris, the ocean floors slowly sank and were compressed to form the sedimentary rocks which contain petroleum—sandstone, shale, porous limestone, and dolomite, a mixture of calcium and magnesium carbonates.

The organic components of trapped microscopic organisms were changed over millions of years to petroleum, through chemical, physical and biological influences (Figure 43.1).

Naturally occurring petroleum is complex and variable in chemical composition. Its color ranges from light greenish brown to black. It may be fluid or so viscous as to be nearly solid. The petroleum refiners classify crudes according to their base as follows:

1. Paraffin-base—high in wax and lube oil fractions, containing small amounts of naphthenes or asphalt; low in sulfur, nitrogen and oxygen compounds.

2. Asphalt base—high in pitch, asphalt and heavy fuel oil.

3. Mixed-base—characteristics midway between paraffin and asphalt bases.

4. Aromatic-base—high in low molecular weight aromatic compounds and naphthene, with smaller portions of asphalt and lube oils.

Crudes are commonly identified by API gravity, a figure which is inversely related to specific gravity (S.G.).

$$\text{API gravity} = \frac{141.5}{\text{S.G.}} - 131.5°$$

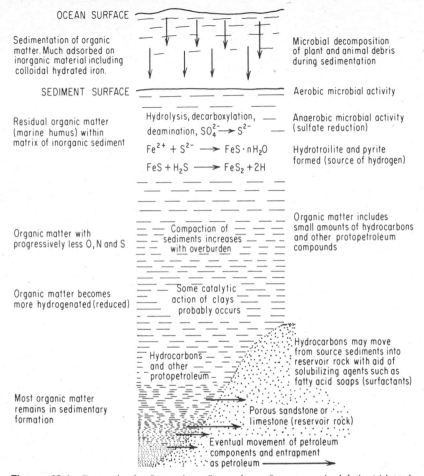

Figure 43.1 Events in the formation of petroleum from organic debris. *(Adapted from Petroleum Microbiology, Davis, J. B., Elsevier Publishing Company, Amsterdam, 1967.)*

API gravity can be confusing to those unfamiliar with petroleum terminology. In the oil industry, a "high gravity crude" is rich in volatile materials and has a low specific gravity (0.75–0.85), so the API gravity is in the range 35–55°. Some "heavy crudes" have a specific gravity close to that of water, and the API gravity may be as low as 15° at the standard temperature of 60°F (16°C).

THE OIL-BEARING RESERVOIR

Petroleum, found only in porous sedimentary rock, migrates laterally and upward reaching some local structure or trap having a caprock seal which contains the oil, creating the reservoir.

Many different shapes, sizes and types of geological structures form reservoirs. These include: (1) domes and anticlines, (2) fault traps, (3) unconformities, (4) dome and plug traps, (5) lens-type traps, and (6) combination traps. An anticlinal type of folded structure is shown in Figure 43.2, and a trap resulting from faulting is shown in Figure 43.3.

Figure 43.2 The separation of water and oil in an anticline, a folded structure topped by an impervious hood. *(Courtesy of American Petroleum Institute, from "Primer of Oil and Gas Production.")*

The length and width of a reservoir can vary from one to several miles, and the depth from a few feet to several hundred. A one acre (0.405 ha) reservoir with a depth of 10 feet (3.05 m) would contain 10 acre-feet, a common unit of measure. To estimate its petroleum content, the total pore volume (porosity) and percentage oil saturation (10–99%) must also be known. The remaining fluid is interstitial (or connate) water. The U.S. standard of measurement of volume in the petroleum industry is the barrel (42 gallons, 5.62 ft³, 0.16 m³).

A 10 acre-foot reservoir contains 435,600 ft³ (12,327 m³). With a porosity of 20% and an oil saturation of 80% this would contain:

$$435{,}600 \times 0.2 \times 0.8 = 69{,}696 \text{ ft}^3 \text{ of oil (1972 m}^3)$$
$$= 12{,}424 \text{ barrels}$$

PETROLEUM PRODUCTION

When the drill penetrates the reservoir, oil and gas are forced to the surface by natural reservoir pressure. The period of time during which oil is produced by natural reservoir pressure is referred to as primary production, a period of a few months or several years.

The flowing well is constructed of "strings" of concentric vertical pipes called casings and a smaller pipe, usually 2–3 inches (5–7.5 cm) in diameter, called tubing, through which produced fluid flows. The largest diameter casing (the surface string) extends to a depth of 200 to 1,500 feet (61–460 m); the intermediate string may reach a depth of up to 5,000 feet (1530 m); a third casing (the oil string) may reach the producing zone. Some producing zones are at depths of 20,000 feet (6100 m) or more. The tubing into the producing formation is secured by a packer which seals the space between the tubing and the final casing (Figure 43.4).

Occasionally intermediate level strings are perforated, allowing production to flow simultaneously from shallower producing zones.

A series of valves and flanges at the wellhead (called a Christmas tree) includes a small orifice plate (called a choke) (Figure 43.5) to control flow.

Figure 43.3 The separation of water and oil in sections of a fault, the displacement of layers along a slip plane. *(Courtesy of American Petroleum Institute, from "Primer of Oil and Gas Production.")*

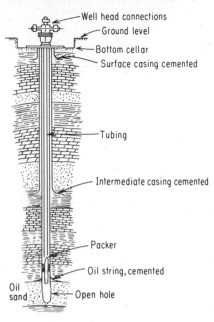

Well head connections
Ground level
Bottom cellar
Surface casing cemented

Tubing

Intermediate casing cemented

Packer

Oil string, cemented

Oil sand

Open hole

Figure 43.4 The typical arrangement of casing, string and tubing in an oil well. *(Courtesy of American Petroleum Institute, from "Primer of Oil and Gas Production.")*

When the natural reservoir energy subsides, some method of pumping is employed to maintain production (Figure 43.6).

Oil Dehydration

Oil leaving the producing well is a mixture of liquid petroleum, natural gas and formation water (Figure 43.7). During early primary production, water may be insignificant. Most production, however, contains sizable proportions of produced water (up to 90%). This must be separated from the oil, since pipeline specifications stipulate maximum water content—as low as 1%, but up to 3–4% in some localities.

The initial separation vessel in a modern treating plant is called a free-water-knockout (FWKO) (Figure 43.8). Free-water, defined as that which separates within five minutes, is drawn off to a holding tank, to be clarified prior to reinjection or discharge. Natural gas is also withdrawn from the FWKO and piped to storage. The remaining oil usually contains emulsified water and must be further processed to break the emulsion, usually assisted by heat, electrical energy, or both.

Heater treaters (Figure 43.9) are vertical or horizontal vessels in which the water-in-oil emulsion is resolved, invariably with the assistance of emulsion breaking chemicals. The electrostatic treater employs heat, but also uses high voltage alternating current to charge the water droplets, accelerating the process of coalescing smaller droplets into larger drops. The demulsified crude oil flows to a stock tank for pipeline shipment to a refinery.

Enhanced Recovery

Enhanced recovery describes any additional production after primary production that results from the introduction of artificial energy into the reservoir. This includes waterflooding, gas injection, and other processing involving fluid or energy injection whether for secondary or tertiary oil recovery.

Figure 43.5 This large "Christmas tree" is made up of 4-inch valves and fittings designed for 10,000 psi working pressure. *(Courtesy of McEvoy Oilfield Equipment Company.)*

Figure 43.6 This oil well pump is a walking beam unit. Submersible centrifugal units are also commonly used.

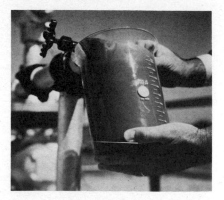

Figure 43.7 Oil is almost always produced as an emulsion, very different in appearance from finished oil products.

Secondary recovery is any enhanced recovery first undertaken in the reservoir. Usually, it follows primary production, but may be conducted concurrently with it. Waterflooding is the most common method of secondary recovery.

Tertiary recovery is enhanced recovery undertaken following secondary operations designed for total recovery of the remaining petroleum. As much as 50% of the original oil may remain in place after primary and secondary processes are terminated.

Secondary Recovery by Waterflooding

Waterflooding is injection of water as a uniform barrier through the producing formation from a series of injection wells toward the producing well. Such injection wells can either be converted producing wells or new wells drilled specifically for injection of a flooding water.

Proper spacing of the injection wells is important. Most reservoirs are flooded through wells distributed uniformly throughout the reservoir. Others may be flooded by peripheral injectors.

A typical arrangement, called a "five-spot pattern" is shown in Figure 43.10. The density of well spacing (the area enclosed by the perimeter of the five-spot pattern) may be 3-acre, 5-acre or whatever density is determined to be most efficient by the reservoir engineer.

The permeability of the reservoir rock has a great bearing on its suitability for

Figure 43.8 Free water and gas are separated from the produced fluid in this gravity separation vessel, simplifying emulsion breaking. (*Courtesy of American Petroleum Institute; from "Treating Oil Field Emulsions."*)

Figure 43.9 This heater-treater uses the heat of combustion of gas or oil to heat the emulsion from the free water knockout drum, assisting chemical treatment to yield an oil of minimum water content. *(Courtesy of American Petroleum Institute, from "Treating Oil Field Emulsions.")*

waterflooding. Rock is considered permeable if a significant fluid flow will pass through it in a short time; it is impermeable if the rate of passage is negligible.

The unit of permeability is the darcy, standardized by the American Petroleum Institute, as follows: "A porous medium has a permeability of one darcy when a single phase fluid of one centipoise viscosity that completely fills the voids (or pores) of the medium will flow through it at a rate of one centimeter per second per square centimeter of cross-sectional area under a pressure or equivalent hydraulic gradient of one atmosphere (760 mm of Hg) per centimeter."

The permeabilities of formation cores are generally in the range of 5–1000 millidarcies (md) (1 md = 0.001 d). A rough practical example of one darcy would be 1 cu ft (0.0283 m³) of sandstone passing approximately one barrel of oil (0.16 m³) per day with a pressure drop of 1 psi (0.068 bars, 0.0703 kg/cm²).

Permeability and porosity vary greatly both laterally and vertically in the typical reservoir rock. A rock whose permeability is 5 md or less is called a "tight sand" or a "dense limestone" according to its composition. The following are rough permeability ratings:

1–10 md	Fair permeability
10–100 md	Good permeability
100–1000 md	Very good permeability

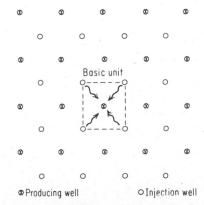

Figure 43.10 Typical 5-spot well arrangement.

⊗ Producing well   ○ Injection well

Figure 43.11 Field test unit for evaluating permeability and plugging tendency of a core subjected to a specific flood water. *(From McCune, C. C., "On Site Testing to Define Injection Water Quality Requirements," Society of Petroleum Engineers Publication 5865.)*

It is imperative for efficient flooding that the water be totally compatible with the reservoir formation. A desirable water for this purpose is that produced from the formation, after separation from the oil and gas. However, the amount of water required for flooding far exceeds the volume produced, so supplemental water is needed.

Produced water and supplemental surface waters must be clarified to remove residual oil accumulations, sand or dirt washed from the producing formation, oxidized inorganic or organic suspended solids, or corrosion products. Quality required for waterflooding is dictated by the permeability restriction of the reservoir. Currently, the most popular equipment for clarification is the flotation cell employing gas diffusion to produce clear effluent.

Where injection water must include surface or well water of lower salinity than the original formation water, chemical incompatibility with the formation rock may result. This may cause swelling of clay in the reservoir rock. Historically, the suitability of injection water has been determined through analyses of the waters in question, a membrane filtration, or laboratory work with formation cores. All of these procedures have the disadvantage that the waters have been removed from the actual reservoir environment and may have changed.

A field unit has been developed for defining injection water quality standards (Figure 43.11). The injection water does not undergo any change during sampling, handling or shipment, and storage. Formation rock is used in the study of the effect of chemical additions and filtration conditions.

Most injection waters are passed through some type of filter, the media and design depending on the reservoir permeability. Types of filters include mixed media beds, individual well cartridges, or septum filters using diatomaceous earth as a filter aid (Figure 43.12). In some cases more sophisticated treatment, such as clarification or lime softening, may be needed. Deaeration may be required to reduce corrosion or to prevent iron oxidation (Figure 43.13).

THE NATURE OF OIL FIELD WATERS

After establishing injection water quality, steps must be taken to eliminate or control scaling, corrosion, and fouling of surface equipment, tanks and lines to prevent interruption of water injection or a decrease in oil production.

It is necessary to conduct several types of analyses to identify and evaluate these potential problems. Analyses must be run at points throughout the water system, because changes through the system provide data for proper control. The job of injection system control starts at the producing well for it is here that water begins to change. As water enters the production tubing, a pressure drop occurs that in itself could cause precipitation either in the tubing string or in the formation. As the produced fluid approaches the surface, further pressure drop causes loss of gases and a reduction in temperature.

Substances in oil field waters are classified as: (1) dissolved ionic solids, (2) suspended solids, (3) dissolved gases, (4) problem-causing bacteria, and (5) residual oil.

Total Dissolved Solids (TDS)

In oil field brines, TDS ranges from less than 10,000 mg/l to over 350,000 mg/l, of which (NaCl) constitutes 80% or more. Troublesome cations found in oil field waters are calcium (Ca); magnesium (Mg); barium (Ba); strontium (Sr);

Figure 43.12 In this waterflooding operation, both sand filters and septum-type filters are used to prevent underground plugging. (*Courtesy L*A Water Conditioning Company.*)

Figure 43.13 Vacuum degasifiers remove dissolved oxygen from water used for secondary oil recovery on this offshore rig. *(Courtesy of Infilco Degremont Inc.)*

and ferrous iron (Fe). Commonly encountered anions are chloride (Cl), sulfate (SO_4); bicarbonate (HCO_3); and sulfide (S).

Potassium (K), lithium (Li), boron (B), zinc (Zn) and copper (Cu) are also frequently measured. A few typical brine combinations are shown in Table 43.1. The "as calcium carbonate" designation, valuable to engineers working with surface waters, is virtually unknown in oil field water work. The standardized API report (Figure 43.14) includes both tabular and graphical forms.

Suspended Solids

Various inorganic and organic solids are found in petroleum waters. These may be particles of metal oxides from well casings, or oxidized iron or manganese originally in the water. Other suspended solids may be silt, sand, clay or bacterial bodies. These particulates are collected on a 0.45 micron membrane filter for identification. The filtered solids are analyzed separately (Figure 43.15). A high concentration of Freon-soluble extractables usually indicates the need for better demulsification or clarification of the water to be injected. Hydrochloric acid soluble materials include carbonates of calcium, magnesium and iron, as well as oxides and sulfides of iron. Residue remaining after treatment could include silica, barium sulfate, calcium sulfate or heavy hydrocarbons such as asphaltenes, which are insoluble in most solvents. The residue could also include bacteria.

TABLE 43.1* Analyses of Several Formation Waters

State	County	Formation	Constituents, mg/l						
			Na	Ca	Mg	Cl	SO$_4$	HCO$_3$	TDS
Oklahoma	Kingfisher	Oswego	56,250	8,300	260	98,300	180	50	166,652
Kansas	Ellis	Arbuckle	16,800	2,630	690	30,500	2,880	315	54,072
New Mexico	Lea	San Andreas	9,150	1,500	500	17,800	2,000	1,000	32,329
Texas	Hopkins	Paluxy	5,640	630	40	8,350	120	500	15,417

* The form for water analysis reporting recommended by the American Petroleum Institute is shown in Figure 43.14.

Company			Sample No.	Date Sampled
Field	Legal Description		County or Parish	State
Lease or Unit	Well	Depth	Formation	Water, B/D
Type of Water (Produced, Supply, etc.)		Sampling Point		Sampled By

DISSOLVED SOLIDS

CATIONS   mg/l   me/l

Sodium, Na (calc.)
Calcium, Ca
Magnesium, Mg
Barium, Ba

ANIONS

Chloride, Cl
Sulfate, SO_4
Carbonate, CO_3
Bicarbonate, HCO_3

Total Dissolved Solids (calc.)

Iron, Fe (total)
Sulfide, as H_2S

OTHER PROPERTIES

pH
Specific Gravity, 60/60 F.
Resistivity (ohm-meters)____F.

WATER PATTERNS — *me/l*

STANDARD

LOGARITHMIC

Figure 43.14 API water analysis report form. (*Courtesy of American Petroleum Institute, from API RP 45, "API Recommended Practice for Analysis of Oil-Field Waters."*)

Dissolved Gases

The gases of greatest concern are hydrogen sulfide (H_2S), carbon dioxide (CO_2), and oxygen (O_2).

Hydrogen sulfide—Produced waters containing H_2S are called sour waters. Oil reservoirs can become sour through the activity of sulfate reducing bacteria in the producing formation. H_2S concentrations can reach several hundred mg/l. In many areas of the country elaborate mechanical systems are used to remove this gas from the produced water before reinjection.

As H_2S is extremely poisonous, all sour oil field operators post conspicuous signs at tanks or vessels cautioning against inspection without the use of breathing equipment.

H_2S in contact with iron produces iron sulfide, which can accelerate corrosion or act as a serious plugging agent. The sulfides of most metals are insoluble in water.

H_2S can also be produced in the water handling system by sulfate reducing bacteria. Any increase in H_2S concentration through the water system not caused by blending is considered an indication of bacterial activity.

H_2S in contact with dissolved oxygen can produce elemental sulfur, also a serious plugging agent.

$$H_2S + \tfrac{1}{2}O_2 \rightarrow = H_2O + S° \tag{1}$$

Carbon dioxide (CO_2) is an ionizable gas, forming weak carbonic acid when dissolved in water. It is one of the greatest contributors to production well and waterflood system corrosion. Production well concentrations of CO_2 can exceed 200 mg/l, much of which is lost to atmosphere when the produced fluids leave the well. Carbon dioxide is also responsible for dissolving limestone reservoir rock, increasing hardness and alkalinity.

Dissolved oxygen (DO) is rarely present in produced fluids coming from the reservoir, unless entrained through leakage, but it is perhaps the most serious corrodent participating in oil field water corrosion mechanisms.

It is also responsible for creating plugging agents through oxidation of ferrous iron and hydrogen sulfide. It is important to try to exclude oxygen from all vessels, casings and surface supply lines.

Problem-Causing Bacteria

Of several types of bacteria responsible for corrosion or production of plugging type solids, the most serious offender is the anaerobic sulfate-reducing bacterium, desulfovibrio desulfricans. Historically these bacteria have been identified through the serial dilution or "extinction" dilution technique. The

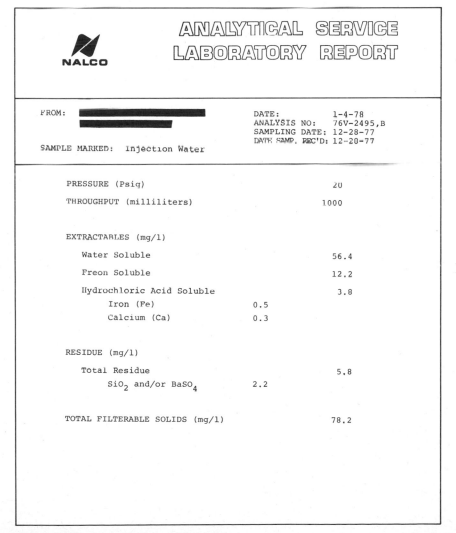

ANALYTICAL SERVICE LABORATORY REPORT

NALCO

FROM: ▓▓▓▓▓▓▓▓▓▓▓▓▓

SAMPLE MARKED: Injection Water

DATE: 1-4-78
ANALYSIS NO: 76V-2495,B
SAMPLING DATE: 12-28-77
DATE SAMP. REC'D: 12-20-77

PRESSURE (Psig)		20
THROUGHPUT (milliliters)		1000
EXTRACTABLES (mg/l)		
Water Soluble		56.4
Freon Soluble		12.2
Hydrochloric Acid Soluble		3.8
Iron (Fe)	0.5	
Calcium (Ca)	0.3	
RESIDUE (mg/l)		
Total Residue		5.8
SiO_2 and/or $BaSO_4$	2.2	
TOTAL FILTERABLE SOLIDS (mg/l)		78.2

Figure 43.15 Analysis of suspended solids.

disadvantage of this technique is that a time lapse of 7–30 days might result before positive determination is made.

Using a new technique, bacteria filtered onto a pad from a water sample (0.45 micron filter) are immediately immersed in boiling water containing a buffer solution that destroys the enzymes which would normally consume ATP (adenosine triphosphate) upon cessation of life. The preserved ATP is reacted with luciferin and luciferase enzymes in a photometric cell, and the photons of light produced indicate total bacteria population within minutes after sampling.

Residual Oil

For a qualitative determination of residual oil, freon extraction followed by weighing is recommended. This procedure requires time, limiting its use for monitoring.

A field procedure involving extraction of crude with chloroform gives good information concerning changes in oil concentration throughout the water system. In many cases, qualitative correlation with laboratory extraction methods is quite close. The chloroform extracted hydrocarbon is compared to prepared standards in a simple photometer. This method is restricted to use with crudes having a definite color.

MINERAL SCALES

The mineral scales of greatest concern to oil producers are calcium carbonate, calcium sulfate, and barium sulfate. Strontium sulfate, a less common scale, can also cause problems. Several iron compounds are also of concern, related to corrosion or to oxidation of ferrous iron as a consequence of oxygen intrusion. Table 43.2 lists common scales with system variables that affect their occurrence.

Mineral scales can form in many areas; supersaturation can occur in the formation face as the produced fluids enter the production tubing; scale can form throughout the length of the production tubing and on sucker rods and in downhole pumps; it can form in surface vessels and on the heating surfaces in the heater treater.

In the water handling system, scale can form in injection water pumps, surface lines leading to injection wells and rock surfaces in the injection formation.

Some scales can be removed by chemical treatment, an expensive, time con-

TABLE 43.2   Most Common Scales

Name	Chemical formula	Primary variables
Calcium carbonate (calcite)	$CaCO_3$	Partial pressure of CO_2, temperature, total dissolved salts

Calcium sulfate
  Gypsum (most common)
  Anhydrite $CaSO_4$
	$CaSO_4 \cdot 2H_2O$	Temperature, total dissolved salts, pressure

Barium sulfate Strontium sulfate	$BaSO_4$ $SrSO_4$	Temperature, total dissolved salts

Iron compounds
  Ferrous carbonate
  Ferrous sulfide
  Ferrous hydroxide
  Ferric hydroxide
  Ferric oxide
	
	$FeCO_3$
	FeS
	$Fe(OH)_2$
	$Fe(OH)_3$
	Fe_2O_3
		
		Corrosion, dissolved gases, pH

suming process. Scales such as barium sulfate, which cannot be removed chemically, may require replacement of surface lines or abandonment of the well.

Calcium Carbonate

Calcium carbonate equilibria are frequently upset in oil field waters, due to changes in temperature, pressure, and pH.

Because calcium carbonate solubility decreases with increasing temperature, injection from the surface to a warm formation increases the chance of calcium carbonate deposition. Its solubility increases as the total dissolved solids content increases. For instance, the addition of 200,000 mg/l NaCl increases $CaCO_3$ solubility by over 100%. Prediction of calcium carbonate scale potential has been the subject of much research. The Langelier saturation index attempted to relate calcium and alkalinity concentrations to pH, temperature and total dissolved solids. But this had limited value in oil field brines.

The Stiff-Davis index is now widely accepted for predicting calcium carbonate deposition in oil field systems. To be useful, the analytical data must be determined on freshly drawn samples; analyses determined in a laboratory are not reliable since the character of the water may change substantially. The Stiff-Davis index ranges from -2.0 to $+2.0$. Positive numbers indicate a progressively severe supersaturation; negative numbers indicate an undersaturated solution. The validity of the index depends on the accuracy of the analysis.

Calcium Sulfate

Most calcium sulfate deposits found in the oil field are gypsum ($CaSO_4 \cdot 2H_2O$), the predominant form at temperatures below 100°F (38°C); above this temperature anhydrite ($CaSO_4$) may be found. Gypsum solubility increases with temperature up to about 100°F, and then decreases with increasing temperature. Sodium chloride increases the solubility of anhydrite, as it does for calcium carbonate, up to a salt concentration of approximately 150,000 mg/l. Higher salt concentrations decrease calcium sulfate solubility. The addition of 150,000 mg/l NaCl to distilled water triples the solubility of gypsum.

One of the more recent predictive indexes for gypsum is that developed by Skillman, McDonald and Stiff. Calcium sulfate precipitation usually results from the mixing of two waters, one of which has a high calcium or sulfate concentration. A solubility graph relating calcium and sulfate concentration to total brine concentration is shown in Figure 43.16.

Barium Sulfate

Barium sulfate solubility is the lowest of the usual scales, approximately 2.3 mg/l in distilled water. The solubility of barium sulfate is also increased by increasing salt concentration. The addition of 100,000 mg/l NaCl to distilled water increases the solubility of barium sulfate from 2.3 mg/l to approximately 30 mg/l at 77°F (25°C).

The solubility of barium sulfate increases with temperature so that the combined effect of temperature and sodium chloride concentration can increase solubility to approximately 65 mg/l at 203°F (95°C).

Barium sulfate deposition usually results from the mixing of a barium-rich water with a sulfate-rich water. Such a combination should be avoided, but where mixing is unavoidable, chemical inhibitors may control deposits.

Scale Prevention

The first scale inhibitors were the inorganic polyphosphates, but their limitations were quickly discovered: above 140°F (60°C) they revert to orthophosphate, as they do at acidic pH or over a long residence time. The orthophosphate form

Instructions for using the graph:

1. Determine concentrations of Ca (as CaCO₃), SO₄ (as Na₂ SO₄) and Cl (as NaCl).

2. Plot the intersecting point of Ca and SO₄ concentrations on the graph.

3. If point lies above the diagonal line for NaCl level, the water will tend to precipitate CaSO₄. If point falls below the NaCl diagonal, the water is undersaturated and should not precipitate CaSO₄.

Figure 43.16   Calcium sulfate solubility graph at various brine levels.

does not inhibit scale. Present day oil field scale inhibitors are of three types: (1) esters of polyphosphoric acid, (2) phosphonates, and (3) organic polymers, such as polymers or co-polymers of acrylic or methacrylic acid.

The phosphate ester formulations are versatile for most oil field water applications. Phosphonates and polymer products have definite advantages where water temperatures exceed 200°F (90°C). Dosages vary with temperature and the concentration of suspended solids, since solids adsorb the inhibitor, requiring high concentrations for effective inhibition. Dosage is also directly proportional to the degree of supersaturation.

When applying scale inhibitors to producing wells the "squeeze" technique is frequently used. This involves injection of a scale inhibitor into the producing formation through the production tubing string under pressure. The scale inhibitor molecules adsorb to the formation, to be gradually released with the produced fluids. Scale inhibitor squeeze applications can last for periods up to six months. The need for renewed treatment is determined through tests for inhibitor residual in the produced fluids.

CORROSION

The primary corrodents in oil field water systems are carbon dioxide (CO_2), hydrogen sulfide (H_2S), and oxygen (O_2).

One reason oxygen is corrosive, even at low concentrations, is its participation in creating differential cells beneath deposits on metal surfaces, which become anodic to adjacent deposit-free areas. Control of oxygen corrosion in oil field water systems requires a conscientious effort to exclude air from all surface tanks and vessels and from the casings of producing wells. Field gas is used to maintain a positive gas blanket in these areas whenever possible.

After establishing control over oxygen exposure, it is then practical to use an oxygen scavenger to react with trace quantities of remaining oxygen. Several types of sulfite are used, including sodium bisulfite ($NaHSO_3$), ammonium bisulfate (NH_4HSO_3), sodium sulfite (NA_2SO_3), and sulfur dioxide (SO_2).

The chemistry is the same with all of these: the sulfite reacts with oxygen to form a sulfate ion.

$$SO_3^{-2} + \tfrac{1}{2}O_2 \rightarrow SO_4 \qquad (2)$$

The sulfite-oxygen reaction is influenced by temperature and pH. Optimum pH for quick reaction is above 7. Most oil field waters will range in pH from 6.0 to 7.5.

Catalysis of the reaction is necessary. Sometimes naturally occurring metal ions in the produced water will do the job, but usually the catalyst is provided in the sulfite formulation.

In high-oxygen fresh water systems, passivating inhibitors such as chromate supplemented by zinc and phosphate may provide an alternative to oxygen scavenging. However, the presence of H_2S or certain easily oxidized hydrocarbons in injection systems reduces chromate and precipitates zinc, so these alternatives are seldom applicable in waterfloods.

Hydrogen sulfide is corrosive because it ionizes to form a weak acid:

$$H_2S \rightarrow H^+ + HS^- \qquad (3)$$

Whenever H_2S is present, iron sulfide deposits. These deposits are cathodic to base metal, so it usually follows that severe pitting occurs beneath iron sulfide deposits, all as a consequence of the H_2S. Where O_2 intrudes into a sulfide system, the rate of corrosion can become uncontrollable. Carbon dioxide mixed with H_2S is also much more aggressive than either of the gases alone. Where H_2S is present, an efficient film forming inhibitor must be used to prevent severe, localized corrosion.

Invariably, corrosion inhibitors used in oil field water work are organic film formers. The molecules adsorb onto metal surfaces to shield the metal from the corrodents. Since the film forming corrosion inhibitors must be added to a wide range of brine concentrations and in many cases to a mixture of water and hydrocarbon, inhibitors with a wide range of solubilities must be available. In the producing well where a mixture of crude oil and brine must be treated, an inhibitor that is oil soluble and only slightly water dispersible is often required. This will film metal from the oil phase, providing long term persistency to the metal surface; that is, the film will be maintained even when the inhibitor feed is discontinued. This allows batch treatment of producing wells in many instances. One of the most common methods of treating producing wells is using a treating truck to pump inhibitor down the tubing or into the annulus, followed by an overflush of produced water. The application is repeated periodically at intervals depending on the aggressiveness of the corrodents.

In injection water systems where water is the predominant phase, inhibitors must be either totally water soluble or highly water dispersible to carry through the surface line and tubing system. These inhibitors are not persistent, and it is necessary to feed continuously, always maintaining a residual in the system. Loss of inhibitor residuals result in desorption of inhibitor film and loss of protection.

In monitoring the chemical program, inhibitor residuals are determined through field extraction tests for close control.

Corrosion monitoring is usually accomplished through a combination of metal weight-loss specimens, corrosion meters, pipe spools or nipples (which have the advantage of duplicating flow conditions), and "iron counts." Residual iron concentrations are valid in systems without hydrogen sulfide. Where H_2S is present, iron is deposited as iron sulfide.

BACTERIA CONTROL

Control of bacteria is important in oil field water operations because they can cause plugging of the injection water formation or serious corrosion.

The most troublesome of these organisms is the anaerobic sulfate-reducing bacteria, desulfovibrio desulfricans. Present in many oil bearing formations, it is involved in the chemical changes which occur during the formation of petroleum. It reduces inorganic sulfate (SO_4^{-2}) to sulfide (S^{-2}), which leads to iron sulfide precipitates.

Clostridia, another anaerobic sulfate reducing organism, is not as prevalent as desulfovibrio. This organism is reported to be thermophilic, preferring a temperature range of 55–70°C.

Several species of aerobic bacteria are also important, most of which are found in surface waters used to supplement produced water in a water flood. Some of the more important organisms are pseudomonas, flavobacterium, aerobacter, escherichia, and bacillus. These form slime masses, which can cause plugging or which shield the anaerobic desulfovibrio.

Iron bacteria are occasionally found in some water floods, the two major species being sphaerotilus and gallionella. These oxidize the ferrous ion (Fe^{+2}) to ferric ion (Fe^{+3}). Iron bacteria are identifiable through a microscopic analysis following staining.

Beggiatoa oxidize sulfide to sulfate. Beggiatoa usually grow in open produced water systems where a gathering line dumps into an open pit. They are often responsible for filter plugging.

Microbes are controlled by chemical application. The concentration of chemical and the period of contact varies among systems. Normally, chemical is fed at a selected dosage, such as 50–100 mg/l, for a period of 4–8 hours. Following application, samples are withdrawn from the system and microbial population is determined. The frequency of biocide application is dictated by such control tests.

In many situations, physical system clean-up is necessary to gain proper microbial control. Low spots in lines or tanks with bottom accumulations of sediment or debris protect bacteria from chemical contact. In these cases, the chemical program must be supplemented by a thorough "house cleaning."

SUGGESTED READING

Books

Reservoir Engineering Manual, Frank W. Cole; Gulf Publishing Co.
Geochemistry of Oilfield Waters, A. Gene Collins, Elsevier Scientific Publishing Co.
Geology of Petroleum, A. I. Levorsen, W. H. Freeman and Co.
Petroleum Production Engineering, L. C. Uren, McGraw-Hill, Inc.

API Publications

Primer of Oil and Gas Production.
Treating Oil Field Emulsions, Third Edition.

Glossary

Absorption: Assimilation of molecules or other substances into the physical structure of a liquid or solid without chemical reaction.

Activated sludge: An aerobic biological process for conversion of soluble organic matter to solid biomass, removable by gravity or filtration.

Adsorption: Physical adhesion of molecules or colloids to the surfaces of solids without chemical reaction.

Aerobic organism: An organism that requires oxygen for its respiration.

Aerosol: A colloidal system involving liquid or solid particulates dispersed in air.

Agglomerate: To gather fine particulates together into a larger mass.

Algae: Simple plants containing chlorophyll. Many are microscopic, but under conditions favorable for their growth they grow in colonies and produce mats and similar nuisance masses.

Alkalinity: By definition, total alkalinity (also called "M" alkalinity) is that which will react with acid as the pH of the sample is reduced to the methyl orange endpoint—about pH 4.2. Another significant expression is "P" alkalinity, which exists above pH 8.2 and is that which reacts with acid as the pH of the sample is reduced to 8.2.

Amphoteric: Capable of reacting in water either as a weak acid or as a weak base. For example, aluminum salts hydrolyze in water to produce a compound that may be considered a weak base, $Al(OH)_3$, or a weak acid, H_3AlO_3. A property of certain oxides makes them reactive both with acids and bases. Al_2O_3 is an example:

1. $Al_2O_3 + 3H_2SO_4 \rightarrow Al_2(SO_4)_3 + 3H_2O$
2. $Al_2O_3 + 2NaOH \rightarrow Na_2Al_2O_4 + H_2O$

Anaerobic organism: An organism that can thrive in the absence of oxygen.

Anion: A negatively charged ion resulting from dissociation of salts, acids, or alkalies in aqueous solution.

Anodizing: The treatment of a metal surface whereby the metal is made anodic.

API gravity: An index of specific gravity defined by the American Petroleum Institute.

API separator: A simple gravity separator meeting the design standards of the American Petroleum Institute for separation of oil and solids from wastewater.

Avogadro's number: The number of molecules in a gram-molecular weight of any substance, 6.02×10^{23}.

Bacteria: Microscopic single-cell plants which reproduce by fission or by spores, identified by their shapes: coccus, spherical; bacillus, rod-shaped; and spirillum, curved.

Base: An alkaline substance.

Biocide: A chemical used to control the population of troublesome microbes.

Biota: All living organisms of a region or system.

Black liquor: Kraft cooking liquor recovered from brown stock washers in the pulp mill.

Blast furnace: A furnace producing iron from ore by reduction with coke.

Blowdown: The withdrawal of water from an evaporating water system to maintain a solids balance within specified limits of concentration of those solids.

Blowpit: The vessel receiving cooked wood pulp from the digester.

BOD: Biochemical oxygen demand of a water, being the oxygen required by bacteria for oxidation of the soluble organic matter under controlled test conditions.

Broke: Trim or excess sheet from paper manufacture returned to a pulping device for recovery.

BS&W (bottom sediment and water): A measure of oil quality based on the volume percent of sediment and water that can be centrifuged from a sample.

Buffer: A substance in solution which accepts hydrogen ions or hydroxyl ions added to the solution as acids or alkalies, minimizing a change in pH.

Bulking: Production of a light, fluffy biomass, usually due to the presence of filamentous organisms.

Cake: A term applied to a dewatered residue from a filter, centrifuge, or other dewatering device.

Carbonate hardness: That hardness in a water caused by bicarbonates and carbonates of calcium and magnesium. If alkalinity exceeds total hardness, all hardness is carbonate hardness; if hardness exceeds alkalinity, the carbonate hardness equals the alkalinity.

Carryover: The presence of boiler water in steam caused by foaming or entrainment.

Catalysis: Addition of a material (catalyst) that does not take a direct part in a chemical reaction to increase the rate of the reaction.

Cation: A positively charged ion resulting from dissociation of molecules in solution.

Caustic soda: A common water treatment chemical, sodium hydroxide (lye).

Centrate: The liquid remaining after removal of solids as a cake in a centrifuge.

Chelating agents: Organic compounds having the ability to withdraw ions from their water solutions into soluble complexes.

Coagulation: The neutralization of the charges of colloidal matter (sometimes also considered to be flocculation).

COD: Chemical oxygen demand, a measure of organic matter and other reducing substances in water.

Coliform bacteria: Bacteria found in the intestinal tract of warm-blooded animals and used as indicators of pollution if found in water.

Colloids: Matter of very fine particle size, usually in the range of 10^{-5} to 10^{-7} cm in diameter.

Coalescence: The gathering together of coagulated colloidal liquid particles into a single continuous phase.

Concentration: The process of increasing the dissolved solids per unit volume of solution, usually by evaporation of the liquid; also, the amount of material dissolved in a unit volume of solution.

Concentration cell: The connection of two solutions of the same composition but different concentrations by a metal conductor to produce current flow through the circuit.

Concentration ratio: In an evaporating water system, the ratio of the concentration of a specific substance in the makeup to its concentration in the evaporated water, usually measured in the blowdown.

Condensate: Water obtained by evaporation and subsequent condensation.

Conduction: The transfer of heat through a body by molecular motion.

Conductivity: The ability of a substance to conduct heat or electricity. Electrical conductivity is usually expressed in micromhos/cm.

Connate water: Water produced with oil.

Consistency: In the pulp/paper industry, a term for the density in percent by weight dry matter, of a slurry of pulp.

Contaminant: Any foreign component present in another substance; e.g., anything in water that is not H_2O is a contaminant.

Convection: The transfer of heat through a fluid by circulating currents.

Coordinated phosphate: A boiler treatment scheme using phosphate buffers to avoid the presence of hydroxyl alkalinity.

Cracking: An oil-refining process that breaks large molecules into smaller ones.

Critical pressure: The pressure at the critical temperature above which the fluid no longer has the properties of a liquid, regardless of further increase in pressure.

Cupola: A furnace for melting scrap or pig iron with coke.

Cycles of concentration: Concentration ratio.

Dealkalization: Any process for reducing the alkalinity of water.

Decantation: An elutriation process, where the supernatant liquor contains recoverable leaching chemical.

Deinking: The process of removing ink from secondary fibers.

Demineralization: Any process used to remove minerals from water; however, commonly the term is restricted to ion exchange processes.

Desalination: The removal of inorganic dissolved solids from water.

Desalting: The removal of salt from crude oil.

Dialysis: A separation process depending on differences in diffusion rates of solutes across a permeable membrane.

Diatoms: Organisms related to algae, having a brown pigmentation and a siliceous skeleton.

Disinfection: Application of energy or chemicals to kill pathogenic organisms.

Dispersant: A chemical which causes particulates in a water system to remain in suspension.

Donnan effect: The rejection of diffusion of external ions by a semipermeable membrane because of a high internal concentration of ions of the same charge.

Drift: Entrained water in the stack discharge of a cooling tower.

Economizer: A heat exchanger in a furnace stack that transfers heat from the stack gas to the boiler feedwater.

EDTA: Ethylenediaminetetraacetic acid. The sodium salt is the usual form of this chelating material.

Electrolyte: A substance that dissociates into two or more ions when it dissolves in water.

Elution: The process of extracting one solid from another. Often used incorrectly to describe the regeneration of an ion exchanger.

Elutriation: The washing of a sludge with water to free it of its mother liquor.

Emulsion: A colloidal dispersion of one liquid in another.

Endothermic: Absorbing heat.

Enthalpy: The total heat content of a body.

Entrainment: The transport of water into a gas stream. In a boiler, this is carryover; in a cooling tower, drift.

Entropy: A mathematical expression applying to the limits to the availability of energy; a measure of the random motion of matter.

Enzyme: A chemical produced by living cells having the ability to reduce large organic molecules to units small enough to diffuse through the cell membrane.

EPA: Environmental Protection Agency.

Equalization: Minimization of variations in flow and composition by means of a storage reservoir.

Equivalent weight: The weight in grams of a substance which combines with or displaces one gram of hydrogen; usually obtained by dividing the formula weight by the valence.

Eutrophication: Enrichment of water, causing excessive growth of aquatic plants and an eventual choking and deoxygenation of the water body.

Exothermic: Evolving heat.

Facultative organisms: Microbes capable of adapting to either aerobic or anaerobic environments.

FDA: Food and Drug Administration.

Fermentation: The conversion of organic matter to CO_2, CH_4, and similar low-molecular-weight compounds by anaerobic bacteria.

Filler: Clay, calcium carbonate, or other minerals added to cellulose fiber in the production of certain grades of paper or board.

Filtrate: The liquid remaining after removal of solids as a cake in a filter.

Filtration: The process of separating solids from a liquid by means of a porous substance through which only the liquid passes.

Fission: In biology, the process of reproduction by cell splitting.

Flash: The portion of a superheated fluid converted to vapor when its pressure is reduced.

Flocculation: The process of agglomerating coagulated particles into settleable flocs, usually of a gelatinous nature.

Flotation: A process for separating solids from water by developing a froth in a vessel in such fashion that the solids attach to air particles and float to the surface for collection.

Flume: A raceway or channel constructed to carry water or to permit measuring its flow.

Fouling index: A measure of the tendency of a water to foul a reverse osmosis membrane, based on timed flow through a membrane filter at constant pressure.

Fourdrinier: A design of paper machine using a continuous wire for forming the sheet.

Freundlich isotherm: The plot of test data related to the removal of colloidal matter from water showing the process to be adsorption.

Fumes: An aerosol with solids as the dispersed colloids.

Fungi: As applied to water, simple, one-celled organisms without chlorophyll, often filamentous. Molds and yeasts are included in this category.

Galvanic couple: The connection of two dissimilar metals in an electrolyte that results in current flow through the circuit.

Gangue: The earthy material remaining from ore beneficiation.

Grains per gallon: A unit of concentration. 1 gpg = 17.1 mg/l.

Green liquor: The liquor resulting from dissolving molten smelt from the kraft recovery furnace in water.

Hardness: The concentration of calcium and magnesium salts in water. Hardness is a term originally referring to the soap-consuming power of water; as such it is sometimes also taken to include iron and manganese. "Permanent hardness" is the excess of hardness over alkalinity. "Temporary hardness" is hardness equal to or less than the alkalinity. These are also referred to as "non-carbonate" or "carbonate" hardness, respectively.

Heat rate: An expression of heat conversion to power, given in Btu/kWh. Theoretical conversion is 3413 Btu/kWh.

Henry's law: An expression for calculating the solubility of a gas in a fluid based on temperature and partial pressure.

Humidification: The addition of water vapor to air.

Hydrophilic: Having an affinity for water. Its opposite, non-water wettable, is hydrophobic.

Infiltration: Inleakage of groundwater into sewage piping.

Inhibitor: A chemical that interferes with a chemical reaction, such as corrosion or precipitation.

Ion: An atom or radical in solution carrying an integral electrical charge either positive (cation) or negative (anion).

Ion exchange: A process by which certain undesired ions of given charge are absorbed from solution within an ion-permeable absorbent, being replaced in the solution by desirable ions of similar charge from the absorbent.

Ionic strength: A measure of the strength of a solution based on both the concentrations and valences of the ions present.

Kraft: An alkaline chemical pulping process, using salt cake as makeup.

Langelier Index: A means of expressing the degree of saturation of a water as related to calcium carbonate solubility.

Leakage: The presence in the effluent of a species of ions in the feed to an ion exchanger.

Lignin: The major non-cellulose constituent of wood.

Lime: A common water treatment chemical. Limestone, $CaCO_3$, is burned to produce quicklime, CaO, which is mixed with water to produce slaked, or hydrated, lime, $Ca(OH)_2$.

Lipophilic: Having an affinity for oil. The opposite of hydrophilic; (i.e., hydrophobic).

Membrane: A barrier, usually thin, that permits the passage only of particles up to a certain size or of special nature.

Metabolize: To convert food, such as soluble organic matter, to cellular matter and gaseous by-products by a biological process.

Microorganism: Organisms (microbes) observable only through a microscope; larger, visible types are called *macroorganisms.*

Mineral: Any inorganic or fossilized organic material having a definite chemical composition and structure found in a natural state.

Mist: An aerosol with liquids as the dispersed colloids.

Mole: A unit weight or volume of a chemical corresponding to its molecular weight. A mole of water weighs 18 g, and its vapor occupies 22.4 liters at standard temperature and pressure.

Monomer: A molecule, usually an organic compound, having the ability to join with a number of identical molecules to form a polymer.

Noncarbonate hardness: Hardness in water caused by chlorides, sulfates, and nitrates of calcium and magnesium.

Noncondensibles: Gaseous material not liquefied when associated water vapor is condensed in the same environment.

NPDES permit: The National Pollution Discharge Elimination System permit required by and issued by EPA.

NSSC: The neutral sulfite, semichemical pulping process.

NTA: Nitrilotriacetic acid, a chelant with the sodium salt being the usual form.

Occlusion: An absorption process by which one solid material adheres strongly to another, sometimes occurring by co-precipitation.

Opacity: The percentage of light transmission through a plume.

Ore: A mineral containing useful substances which can be extracted.

Orifice: An opening through which a fluid can pass; a restriction placed in a pipe to provide a means of measuring flow.

Osmosis: The passage of water through a permeable membrane separating two solutions of different concentrations; the water passes into the more concentrated solution.

Oxidation: A chemical reaction in which an element or ion is increased in positive valence, losing electrons to an oxidizing agent.

Packing: The fill in a confined space in a stripping vessel, ranging from simply shaped units such as rocks or slats to complex shapes providing large surface area per unit volume.

Pasteurization: A process for killing pathogenic organisms by heat applied for a critical period of time.

Pathogens: Disease-producing microbes.

Periodic chart: An arrangement of the elements in order of increasing atomic numbers that illustrates the repetition (or periodicity) of key characteristics.

Permeability: The ability of a body to pass a fluid under pressure.

pH: A means of expressing hydrogen ion concentration in terms of the powers of 10; the negative logarithm of the hydrogen ion concentration.

Photosynthesis: The process of converting carbon dioxide and water to carbohydrates, activated by sunlight in the presence of chlorophyll, liberating oxygen.

Pickle liquor: Acid used in treating steel for removal of oxide scale.

Plankton: Small organisms with limited powers of locomotion, carried by water currents from place to place.

Polarize: In corrosion, to develop a barrier on the anodic or cathodic surface, disrupting the corrosion process.

Pollutant: A contaminant at a concentration high enough to endanger the aquatic environment or the public health.

Polyelectrolyte: A polymeric material having ion exchange sites on its skeleton.

Polymer: A chain of organic molecules produced by the joining of primary units called *monomers.*

Polyphosphate: Molecularly dehydrated orthophosphate.

Precipitate: An insoluble reaction product; in an aqueous chemical reaction, usually a crystalline compound that grows in size to become settleable.

Protozoa: Large, microscopic single-cell organisms higher on the food chain than bacteria, which they consume.

Pulp: Fibrous matter.

Radiation: In a furnace, the transfer of heat by energy waves, much like other forms of electromagnetic waves (e.g., light and radio waves).

Rag: Debris that accumulates at an oil-water interface.

Rankine cycle: The successive changes in heat content and temperature as water is converted to steam, expands through a prime mover, condenses, and returns to the boiler.

Recovery furnace: A furnace which burns black liquor from the kraft pulping process, to recover the cooking chemicals as smelt.

Red mud: The gangue from bauxite processing.

Redox potential: Reduction-oxidation potential measured against a standard electrode.

Reduction: A chemical reaction in which an element or compound gains electrons, being reduced in positive valence.

Regenerative heating: In utility stations, a scheme for reducing heat losses to the main condenser in the cycle by using steam extracted from the turbine to heat feedwater. In engineering designs, the use of a heat exchanger to preheat the feed to a process by extracting heat from the product.

Reheater: A heat exchanger located in a furnace to increase the temperature of steam extracted from a turbine for reinjection.

Resolution: The breaking of an emulsion into its individual components.

Ringlemann test: A method of comparing the opacity of a stack plume to an arbitrary set of standard disks of increasing degrees of discoloration.

Reverse osmosis: A process that reverses (by the application of pressure) the flow of water in the natural process of osmosis so that it passes from the more concentrated to the more dilute solution.

Reversion: The return of molecularly dehydrated phosphate (polyphosphate) to its hydrated origin (orthophosphate).

Salinity: The presence of soluble minerals in water.

Salt-splitting: The ability of an anion exchanger to convert a salt solution to caustic; the ability of a cation exchanger to convert a salt solution to acid.

Saturation index: The relation of calcium carbonate to the pH, alkalinity, and hardness of a water to determine its scale-forming tendency.

Saveall: A general term for several designs of devices used to recover fiber from white water and clarify the water for reuse.

Scale: The precipitate that forms on surfaces in contact with water as the result of a physical or chemical change.

Scale pit: A collection chamber alongside a rolling mill that receives roll cooling water containing metallic scale.

Scouring: The removal of surface debris from raw textile fibers.

Secondary fibers: In the paper industry, fibers reclaimed from waste paper.

Sedimentation: Gravitational settling of solid particles in a liquid system.

Seed: A particle or particles, usually crystalline, added to a supersaturated solution to induce precipitation.

Selectivity: The order of preference of an ion exchange material for each of the ions in the surrounding aqueous environment.

Sensible heat: Heat measurable by temperature alone.

Sequester: To form a stable, water-soluble complex.

Sewage: Waste fluid in a sewer.

Sinter: A clinker-like material produced in a special furnace from a mixture of coal and recovered iron-bearing materials, such as scale pit solids, used as charge for a blast furnace.

Sizing: A surface finish, such as starch, applied to paper and textile fibers.

Slag: In metallurgical processing, the impurities separated from molten metal during refining; in boiler furnaces, the noncombustible ash which has reached fusion temperatures.

Slop oil: A general term in oil refining applying to tramp oil discharge to the oily sewer during shutdown and startup or through abnormal operation.

Sludge volume index: An inverse measure of sluge density.

Slurry: A water containing a high concentration of suspended solids, usually over 5000 mg/l.

Smelt: Molten slag; in the pulp industry, the cooking chemicals tapped from the recovery boiler as molten material and dissolved in the smelt tank as green liquor.

Soda ash: A common water-treating chemical, sodium carbonate.

Sodium absorption ration (SAR): In irrigation water, a relationship between sodium and hardness used to predict acceptability for both the plant and soil being irrigated.

Softening: The removal of hardness (calcium and magnesium) from water.

Sour water: Waste waters containing malodorous materials, usually sulfur compounds.

Spore: A reproductive cell, or seed, of algae, fungi, or protozoa.

Stability index: An empirical modification of the saturation index used to predict scaling or corrosive tendencies in water systerms.

Stickwater: The distillate produced in the cooking of meat or in the rendering of fat and scraps.

Stiff-Davis index: An index used to predict the stability of brackish waters, such as those used in waterflooding.

Stoichiometric: The ratio of chemical substances reacting in water that corresponds to their combining weights in the theoretical chemical reaction.

Stokes' law: An expression for calculating the rate of fall of particles through a fluid based on densities, viscosity, and particle size.

Superheater: A heat exchanger located in a furnace to increase the temperature of steam leaving the boiler drum.

Supernate: The liquid overlying the sludge layer in a sedimentation vessel.

Surfactant: A surface active agent; usually an organic compound whose molecules contain a hydrophilic group at one end and a lipophilic group at the other.

Synergism: The combined action of several chemicals which produces an effect greater than the additive effects of each.

Tailings: The residue from separation of useful values from an ore.

Thermocline: The layer in a lake dividing the upper, current-mixed zone, from the cool lower stagnant zone.

Threshold treatment: The control of scale or deposits by application of sub-stoichiometric dosage of treatment chemical.

Transpiration: Respiration of plants.

Tuberculation: A corrosion process that produces hard mounds of corrosion products on the metal surface, increasing friction and reducing flow in a water distribution system.

Turbidity: A suspension of fine particles that obscures light rays but requires many days for sedimentation because of the small particle size.

Turnover: The mixing of lower and upper layers in a lake in spring and fall caused by temperature and density equalization.

USDA: United States Department of Agriculture.

USGS: United States Geological Survey, Department of the Interior.

Venturi: A device for measuring fluid flow, including a short converging cone succeeded on the same axis by a long diverging cone. This device is also used in gas scrubbing.

Waterflooding: A process of displacing oil from underground formations with water and returning it to the surface for recovery.

Weir: A spillover device used to measure or control water flow.

White liquor: Cooking liquor from the kraft pulping process produced by recausticizing green liquor with lime.

White water: The filtrate from a paper- or board-forming machine, usually recycled for density control.

Yield: The rate of production of cake from a dewatering device.

Zeta potential: The difference in voltage between the surface of the diffuse layer surrounding a colloidal particle and the bulk liquid beyond.

Appendix

SIGN CONVENTIONS IN ELECTROCHEMISTRY

In representing electrochemical processes, all half-cell reactions (those reactions that occur at each electrode) are written as reduction reactions, thus:

$$Na^+ + e \rightarrow Na \qquad E = -2.71 \text{ volts}$$

$$Fe^{+2} + 2e \rightarrow Fe \qquad E = -0.44 \text{ volts}$$

The addition of electrons to the system should be shown on the left side of the reaction. By definition these are cathodic reactions: reduction always occurs at the cathode and oxidation at the anode.

In the electrolytic cell, the anode may be shown with a minus charge, and the cathode with a positive charge. When the half-cells are coupled, electrons flow from the anode through the conductor to the cathode.

In electrolysis, an external source of electron flow (a battery, rectifier, or direct-current generator) is connected to the half-cells. The half-cell receiving electrons is the cathode, because that is where cations are reduced. The cathode may be shown with a positive sign, but this is unnecessary and may be confusing. Where a battery is used as the direct-current source, the negative pole of the battery is connected to the cathode, which may lead to a common and erroneous impression that the cathode of the electrolytic cell is negatively charged. In fact, the battery is itself an electrolytic cell, and its negative pole is the anode of that cell and is supplying electrons to the cathode of the cell being electrolyzed.

Confusion is avoided by noting the half-cell reactions being studied and identifying the cathode as that surface where reduction is occurring, with the anode being that surface where oxidation is occurring.

TABLE A.1   English/Metric Conversions

English unit	Multiplied by	Equals	Metric unit
Acres (43,560 ft²)	0.405		Hectares (ha)
(640 acres/sq mi)			
Acre-feet (acre-ft)	1234		Cubic meters (m³)
(325,851 gal/acre-ft)			
Barrel (bbl) liquid	0.16		m³
(42 gal/bbl)			
British thermal units (Btu)	0.252		Kilocalories (kcal)
Btu/lb	0.556		kcal/kg (cal/g)
Btu/hr/sq ft	2.69		kcal/hr/m²
Cubic feet (ft³)	28.32		Liters (l)
(1 cu ft H₂O = 62.4 lbs)			(1 l = 1000 ml = 1000 cm³)
(1 cu ft = 7.48 gal)	0.0283		Cubic meters (m³)
Cubic feet per second (cfs)	1.7		m³/min
(1 cfs = 449 gpm)	2.45 × 10³		m³/day
Fahrenheit degrees (F°)	0.556		Celsius degrees (C°)*
(absolute zero = − 460°F			(absolute zero = − 273°C
or 0° Rankine)			or 0° Kelvin)
Feet (ft)	30.48		Centimeters (cm)
(1 ft H₂O = 0.434 psi)	0.305		Meters (m)
Feet per second (ft/sec)	0.305		m/sec
Gallons (gal)	3.785		liters (l)
(1 gal H₂O = 8.345 lb)	0.00379		m³
(7.48 gal/cu ft)	3.785 × 10⁻³		m³
Gallons per minute (gpm)	5.45		m³/day
(695 gpm—1 mgd)			
gpm/sq ft	40.6		l/min/m²
(1 gpm/sq ft = 1.6 in./min)	4.06		cm/min
	0.0406		m³/min/m²
	0.0406		m/min
Grains per gallon (gpg)	17.1		Milligrams per liter (mg/l)
(1 gpg = 17.1 mg/l)			
Horsepower (hp)	0.746		Kilowatts (kw)
Inches (in.)	2.54		Centimeters (cm)
Mils (0.001 in.)	25.4		Microns (10⁻⁶ m)
Miles	1.61		Kilometers (km)
Million gallons daily (mgd)	3785		m³/day
(695 gpm = 1 mgd)	2.62		m³/min
Ounces (oz)	28.4		g
Ounces (fluid)	29.6		Milliliters (ml)
Pounds (lb)	0.454		Kilograms (kg)
	453.6		Grams (g)
Pounds per cubic foot (lb/ft³)	0.016		g/cm³
	16.02		kg/m³

TABLE A.1   English/Metric Conversions   (Continued)

English unit	Multiplied by	Equals	Metric unit
Pounds per square inch (psi)	0.068		Atmospheres (atm) or Bars
(1 psi = 2.31 ft H_2O)	703		kg/m^2
	0.0703		kg/cm^2
	51.7		mm/Hg
Square feet (ft^2)	0.093		m^2
Square inches (in^2)	6.452		cm^2
Square miles (sq mi)	260		ha (hectares)
Tons, long (t, long)	1016		kg
Tons, short (t, short)	0.907		Tons (t)
Tons of Refrigeration	3024		kcal/hr
(12,000 Btu/hr)			
Yards	0.9144		m

* For temperature conversions: (°F − 32) × 0.555 = °C.

TABLE A.2   Metric Prefixes

mega (M)	10^6	milli (m)	10^{-3}
kilo (k)	10^3	micro (μ)	10^{-6}
deci (d)	10^{-1}	nano (n)	10^{-9}
centi (c)	$10^{-?}$	pico (p)	10^{-12}

TABLE A.3 Common Chemicals Used to Treat Water

Chemical	Common name	Typical specs	Equiv. weight	Bulk density, lb/cu ft or lb/gal	Approx. pH 1% solution	Solubility
Aluminum sulfate [$Al_2(SO_4)_3 \cdot 14H_2O$]	Alum	Lump—17% Al_2O_3 Liquid—8.5% Al_2O_3	100*	60 11	3.4	4.2 lb/gal at 60°F
Bentonitic clay	Bentonite			60	—	Insoluble
Calcium carbonate ($CaCO_3$)	Limestone	96% $CaCO_3$	50	80	9	Insoluble
Calcium hydroxide [$Ca(OH)_2$]	Hydrated lime, slaked lime	96% $Ca(OH)_2$	40*	40	12	Insoluble
Calcium hypochlorite [$CA(OCl)_2 \cdot 4H_2O$]	HTH	70% Cl_2	103	55	6–8	3% at 60°F
Calcium oxide (CaO)	Burned lime, quicklime	96% CaO	30*	60	12	Slake at 10–20%
Calcium sulfate ($CaSO_4 \cdot 2H_2O$)	Gypsum	98% Gypsum	86*	55	5–6	Insoluble
Chlorine (Cl_2)	Chlorine	Gas—99.8% Cl_2	35.5	gas	—	0.07 lb/gal at 60°F
Copper sulfate ($CuSO_4 \cdot 5H_2O$)	Blue Vitriol	98% Pure	121*	75	5–6	2 lb/gal at 60°F
Dolomitic lime [$Ca(OH)_2 \cdot MgO$]	Dolomitic lime	36–40% MgO	67†	40	12.4	Insoluble
Ferric chloride ($FeCl_3 \cdot 6H_2O$)	Iron chloride	Lump—20% Fe Liquid—20% Fe	91*	70 13	3–4	45% at 60°F
Ferric sulfate [$Fe_2(SO_4)_3 \cdot 3H_2O$]	Iron sulfate	18.5% Fe	51.5*	70	3–4	30% at 60°F
Ferrous sulfate ($FeSO_4 \cdot 7H_2O$)	Copperas	20% Fe	139*	70	3–4	1 lb/gal at 60°F
Hydrochloric acid (HCl)	Muriatic acid	30% HCl 20° Baumé	120*	9.6	1–2	35% at 60°F
Sodium aluminate ($NaAlO_2$)	Aluminate	Flake—46% Al_2O_3 Liquid—26% Al_2O_3	100*	50 13	11–12	40% at 60°F
Sodium chloride (NaCl)	Rock salt, salt	98% Pure	58.5	60	6–8	2.6 lb/gal at 60°F
Sodium carbonate ($NaCO_3$)	Soda ash	98% Pure 58% Na_2O	53	60	11	1.5 lb/gal at 60°F
Sodium hydroxide (NaOH)	Caustic, Lye	Flake—99% NaOH Liquid—50–70%	40	60 12	12.8	70% at 60°F
Sodium phosphate (Na_2HPO_4)	Disodium phosphate	49% P_2O_5	47.3	55	9	20% at 60°F
Sodium metaphosphate ($NaPO_3$)	Hexametaphosphate	66% P_2O_5	34	47	5–6	1 lb/gal at 60°F
Sulfuric acid (H_2SO_4)	Oil of vitriol	94–96% 66° Baumé	50*	15	1–2	Infinite

* Effective equivalent weight of commercial product.
† Effective equivalent weight based on $Ca(OH)_2$ content.

TABLE A-4a Selecting Pipe Size for Water Systems

Range of flow, gal/min	Pipe size (std. wt.), in.	Velocity range, ft/s	Head loss, ft
1–2	½	1–2	2–10
2–5	¾	1–3	2–10
4–9	1	1.5–3.5	2–10
8–19	1¼	1.7–4.0	2–10
12–30	1½	1.9–4.7	2–10
23–55	2	2.4–5.3	2–10
38–85	2½	2.5–5.7	2–10
65–150	3	2.9–6.5	2–10
130–310	4	3.3–7.8	2–10
240–570	5	3.9–9.3	2–10
390–920	6	4.3–10.4	2–10
800–1300	8	5.1–8.3	2–5
1400–2400	10	5.7–9.8	2–5
2300–3700	12	6.5–10.0	2–5

* Based on coefficient of 100.

NOTE: Head loss is given in feet of water/100 ft. of pipe. To convert to psi: ft of water/2.3 = psi.

TABLE A-4b Useful Formulas for Estimating Capacity of Water Distribution Systems

1. Velocity (ft/s) through steel pipe:

$$V = 0.41 \times \text{gpm/pipe diam}^2 \ (d, \text{in inches}) = 0.41 \times \frac{\text{gpm}}{d^2}$$

2. Friction losses (in feet of water) through steel pipe:
    (a) Friction length (L) = pipe length (ft) + extra for fittings.

    Extra length for fittings:
gate valve	=	$0.3 \times$ pipe size (d)
elbow	=	$2.7 \times$ pipe size
side outlet tee	=	2 elbows
globe valve	=	5 elbows

    EXAMPLE: Estimate friction length (L) of a distribution system having 350 ft of 4″ pipe with 5 gate valves and 10 elbows
    L = length of pipe = 350 ft pipe
    + 5 × 0.3 × 4 =   6
    + 10 × 2.7 × 4 = <u>108</u>
                     664 ft total

    (b) Approximate head loss due to friction (H):
        $H = 0.1 \ (\text{gpm})^2/(d)^5 \times (L/100)$

        EXAMPLE: Estimate the head loss through the system above at 250 gpm:
        H = 0.1 (250)²/(4)⁵ × (664/100)
        = 0.1 (62,500/1024) × 6.64
        = 0.1 × 61 × 6.64 = 41 ft.
        41/2.3 = 17.7 psi

3. Horsepower for pumping (HP):

    $$HP = \frac{(\text{gpm}) \times \text{head loss}}{3960 \times \text{efficiency}}$$

    EXAMPLE: Estimate the horsepower required by the above system using a pump having an efficiency of 85%.

    $$HP = \frac{250 \times 41}{3960 \times 0.85} = 3.05$$

    Use a 5-hp motor to drive this pump

Index